SOURCES IN MEDIEVAL CULTURE AND HISTORY

KAY B. SLOCUM

Capital University

Prentice Hall

Boston   Columbus   Indianapolis   New York   San Francisco   Upper Saddle River
Amsterdam   Cape Town   Dubai   London   Madrid   Milan   Munich   Paris
Montréal   Toronto   Delhi   Mexico City   São Paulo   Sydney
Hong Kong   Seoul   Singapore   Taipei   Tokyo

Editorial Director: Craig Campanella
Executive Editor: Jeff Lasser
Editorial Assistant: Amanda Dykstra
Editorial Project Manager: Rob DeGeorge
Director of Marketing: Brandy Dawson
Senior Marketing Manager: Maureen E. Prado Roberts
Marketing Assistant: Marissa O'Brien
Senior Managing Editor: Ann Marie McCarthy
Project Manager: Debra Wechsler
Operations Specialist: Christina Amato
Creative Director, Central Design: Jayne Conte
Cover Designer: Margaret Kenselaar
Manager, Visual Research: Beth Brenzel
Manager, Rights and Permissions: Zina Arabia

Photo Researcher: Francelle Carapetyan
Image Permission Coordinator: Nancy Seise
Manager, Cover Visual Research & Permissions: Karen Sanatar
Cover Photo: French tapestry of peasant life. Ranald MacKechnie © Dorling Kindersley, courtesy of the Musee des Thermes et de l'Hotel de Cluny, Paris/Dorling Kindersley Media Library.
Full-Service Project Management: Sowmyaa Narayani
Composition: S4Carlisle
Printer/Binder: R. R. Donnelley/Harrisonburg
Cover Printer: R. R. Donnelley/Harrisonburg
Text Font: Garamond 3

Credits and acknowledgments borrowed from other sources and reproduced, with permission, in this textbook appear on appropriate page within text.

Library of Congress Cataloging-in-Publication Data
Sources in medieval culture and history / [edited by] Kay B. Slocum.
p. cm.
Includes bibliographical references and index.
ISBN-13: 978-0-13-615726-7 (alk. paper)
ISBN-10: 0-13-615726-2
1. Civilization, Medieval—Sources. 2. Middle Ages—Sources. I. Slocum,
Kay Brainerd.
CB351.S59 2010
909.07—dc22

2009053948

10 9 8 7 6 5 4 3 2 1

Prentice Hall
is an imprint

www.pearsonhighered.com

ISBN 13: 978-0-13-615726-7
ISBN 10:   0-13-615726-2

Contents

Chapter 2   *The Heirs of Rome: Germanic Kingdoms and the Byzantine Empire*   33

Chapter 3   *The Rise of Islam*   65

Chapter 5   *The Development of Vassalage and Agricultural Change*   *120*

Chapter 6   *The Centralization of Political Control from the Tenth to the Twelfth Century*   *150*

Chapter 7 *Monastic Reform, Pilgrimage, and Crusade*   185

Chapter 13 *Intellectual and Artistic Development in the High Middle Ages*   367

Chapter 14 The Fourteenth Century: Disorder and Vitality   396

Topical Contents

The Topical Contents will facilitate organization for those who wish to study the Middle Ages thematically, rather than chronologically. The material has been divided into sixteen categories as follows: (1) The Germanic Tribal Tradition, (2) Government, Politics, and the Law, (3) Islam, (4) Byzantium, (5) Daily Life, (6) Women, (7) Technology, (8) Medieval Warfare and the Crusades, (9) Religious History, (10) Papal–Imperial Relations, (11) Monasticism, (12) Pilgrimage, (13) Art and Architecture, (14) Literature, (15) Intellectual History and Philosophy, (16) Interpreting the Evidence

Preface

This anthology contains a variety of sources pertaining to the history and culture of the Middle Ages. The documents and images represent a broad spectrum of topics dealing with medieval civilization and illustrate social, intellectual, literary, and artistic history, as well as the political developments of the era. The book has been designed either to be used alone or to accompany the standard textbooks on medieval history, medieval literature, art history, and humanities. It consists of fourteen chapters arranged in chronological order, in which selections from primary sources are carefully coordinated to furnish an overview of the political and cultural life of the medieval period. In order to coordinate basic themes, the introductory material and the questions at the end of the selections provide cross-references among the chapters where appropriate.

The book contains many documents traditionally included in medieval history source readers, and it enhances this traditional content with selections that offer greater variety and style. In addition to literary excerpts, each chapter contains sections identified as "Interpreting the Evidence," in which images are specifically coordinated with documents, offering an opportunity to compare various ways of viewing an individual or a topic.

The materials in this book trace the development of medieval civilization from the era of the Roman Emperor Diocletian to the late fourteenth century. The events of these years are viewed from various perspectives, including selections from legal documents, annals, letters, contemporaneous biographies, theological and philosophical treatises, historical writings, and literary extracts. The sources have been chosen to integrate social and cultural history with more traditional material; hence, selections that inform the student about women and marginal groups in the medieval world are included alongside works that treat topics that are more common in the field, such as the *Rule* of Saint Benedict or *Magna Carta*. In addition, the inclusion of material from Muslim and Byzantine areas shows the multifaceted nature of medieval civilization. Some chapters deal with aspects of cultural history and include writings concerning art and architecture, as well as selections from literature and philosophical works.

Scholars do not agree on the exact timeframe of the Middle Ages. I have chosen to begin this collection with the division of the Roman Empire during the reign of the emperor Diocletion (284–305) because this event was a determining factor in the future development of civilization in both the East and the West. During the medieval era there were two distinct entities—the empire in the West, eventually known as the "Holy Roman Empire," and the Byzantine Empire in the East, which endured until the fifteenth century. The documents in this collection demonstrate various aspects of life in both geographical areas and trace interactions between the two empires.

The organization of the material moves chronologically from Late Antiquity to the Early Middle Ages, as the Roman world was transformed by the influences of the Germanic people and the Christian religion (Chapter 1). Several of the Germanic leaders established kingdoms in the subsequent centuries; the Visigoths conquered the Iberian Peninsula, the Franks assumed leadership in France, and the Ostrogoths settled in Italy, where Theodoric attempted to continue Roman traditions, as will be seen in Chapter 2. One of the most important events of the sixth century was the birth of Mohammad and the subsequent emergence of Islam (Chapter 3). The Muslims were a significant factor in the history of the Middle Ages, as the documents in this collection attest. For reasons of accessibility, diacritical markings have not been included in Arabic names and phrases.

The fusion of Germanic and Christian traditions was exemplified in the person and empire of Charlemagne, who, in addition to building a vast empire, patronized scholarship and the arts. The Carolingian contribution to medieval civilization was immense and created a bridge between antiquity and the High Middle Ages through its intellectual contributions (Chapter 4).

Following the reign of Charlemagne, the empire was destroyed due to many factors. In addition to warfare among the emperor's descendants, the Europeans were invaded from the south by the Muslims, from the east by the Magyars, and from the north by the Vikings. The civilization that emerged from this onslaught had a very different character. Instead of centralized government, the political system was based upon control by various powerful lords who established bonds of loyalty among themselves. They offered protection to the peasants, who were obligated to support their masters through agricultural labor. The documents contained in Chapter 5 demonstrate various aspects of the lives of aristocratic men and women as well as the lives of serfs, as the people bound to the manor were known.

During the tenth and eleventh centuries monarchs were able to consolidate their power in areas of Europe—a trend that continued in the High Middle Ages. Various documents, including historical accounts, letters, and legal codes, as well as visual and literary evidence, allow the reader to experience the stress and struggle of building kingdoms in England, France, Germany (known as the Holy Roman Empire for much of the period), Hungary, and the Iberian Peninsula (Chapters 6, 9, and Chapter 11).

Another broad theme of this book deals with the religious experience of medieval people. Chapter 7 discusses two aspects of spiritual fervor that characterized the eleventh and twelfth centuries—monasticism and the Crusades. Chapter 12 offers evidence of lay spirituality as well as the creation of new monastic orders.

Chapters 8, 10, and 13 deal with the artistic, literary, and philosophical aspects of medieval life during the eras often called Romanesque (the eleventh and twelfth centuries) and Gothic (the thirteenth century), though the chronological divide between the two styles is fluid. In particular, the "Interpreting the Evidence" sections offer an opportunity to analyze aspects of political and artistic history in tandem.

The book closes with a view of the fourteenth century, which was a time of creativity as well as crisis. The people of Europe and the Middle East dealt with famine, plague, war, peasant rebellion, and a crisis in the Church; however, as the documents demonstrate, it was also a time of spiritual regeneration and artistic as well as literary innovation.

Although the book is organized chronologically, the Contents at the beginning of the book is presented in two different ways in order to accommodate professors and students who choose to view the history of the era either topically or thematically. The approach on pages iii–xii presents the material as it is actually organized in the chapters themselves. The second version on pages xiii–xx offers a breakdown based on the following themes: (1) The Germanic Tribal Tradition, (2) Government, Politics, and the Law, (3) Islam, (4) Byzantium, (5) Daily Life, (6) Women, (7) Technology, (8) Medieval Warfare and the Crusades, (9) Religious History, (10) Papal–Imperial Relations, (11) Monasticism, (12) Pilgrimage, (13) Art and Architecture, (14) Literature, (15) Intellectual History and Philosophy, and (16) Interpreting the Evidence. The Topical Contents section can be used to facilitate an alternative method of teaching the era and provides ready access to the material for classes in humanities, art history, and medieval literature, in addition to standard history courses.

Acknowledgments

I would like to express my gratitude and appreciation to several scholars and colleagues whose comments and suggestions eased and enriched the process of writing this book. Among others, Denvy Bowman, Leslie Ross, Nigel Hiscock, John Cherry, and John V. Fleming offered vital advice and encouragement. The following reviewers provided helpful criticism that significantly improved the contents of the book: Eric Fournier, West Chester University of Pennsylvania; A. Daniel Frankforter; Penn State Erie–The Behrend College; Candace Gregory-Abbott, California State University, Sacramento; William V. Hudon, Bloomsburg University; Michael Markowski, Westminster College; Andrew G. Miller, DePaul University; Donald Prudlo, Jacksonville State University; Kevin Roddy, University of California, Davis; Leslie Ross, Dominican University of California; Brian Rutishauser; Fresno City College; and Elizabeth Todd, Case Western Reserve University.

Through the auspices of the sabbatical program at Capital University and the support of the Gerhold endowed chair in Humanities, I was able to complete the research and writing of this book. In particular, I would like to thank the Gerhold family for their generosity in establishing the endowment.

At Prentice Hall, Charles Cavaliere, Rob DeGeorge, and Debra Wechsler provided efficient direction and guidance. Most of all, I thank my husband, Dieter Droste, who offered constant encouragement as well as technological expertise. The creation of the book would not have been possible without him.

Introduction to the Student

This book is a collection of various kinds of historical documents, including edicts, letters, biographical and autobiographical writings, poetry, literature, philosophy, and statistical surveys. In addition, there are a number of visual sources, which can also be viewed as "historical documents," including manuscript illuminations, ivory carvings, mosaics, frescoes, sculpture, and photos of buildings. Where these appear, they are presented in conjunction with the written documents and are coordinated for comparative analysis in features titled "Interpreting the Evidence" that appear in every chapter.

As you study each of these sources, there are specific questions you should contemplate. First of all, what is the nature of the document? Is it an edict issued by a monarch, or a segment of a biography, or a statistical analysis, or a work of poetry or fiction? The answer to this question will determine the framework for your analysis.

Second, who was the author of the source and what was his or her relationship to the event being described? You should also observe when and where the document was written. For example, is it an eyewitness account, or an historical analysis written after the event? Is it a poem that reflects the aesthetic atmosphere of the time period? It is important to place this information in context, and to examine the document with this in mind. The introductory material for each document will help you to answer these questions, and your ideas about the material should take these facts into account.

As you read the source, analyze the reasons why it was created and what the potential audience may have been. Consider whether the account is reliable, or whether the author may have presented the material from a nonobjective point of view. For example, would a biographer working at the court of a king be likely to present an unfavorable portrayal of the monarch?

Questions for Discussion follow each of the documents. These are designed to stimulate conversation about the source, and to suggest paths of analysis; however, they are only a beginning for your research, and further questions should arise from your encounters with the material. As you will soon realize, the documents in this collection present a variety of interpretive challenges and offer many opportunities to experience the fascination of historical research and analysis.

Chapter 1

◦━◦⟨⟪✦⟫⟩◦━◦

The Threads of Medieval Civilization: The Late Roman Empire, Christianity, and the Germanic Migrations

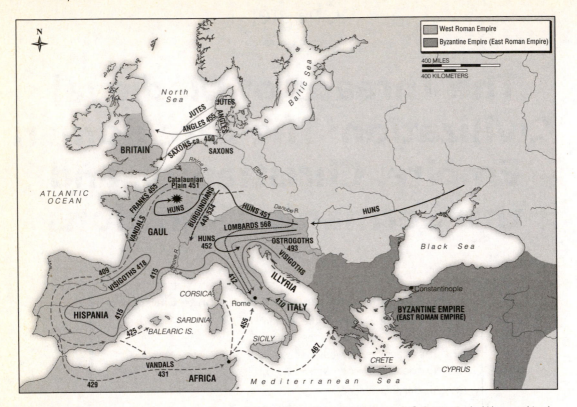

Divisions of the Roman Empire and the Germanic Migrations. *(From Kishalsnky et al., Civilization in the West, combined vol., 7th ed., p. 181.)*

Medieval civilization is an enormously complex and fascinating topic, and it is impossible to study all of its aspects in detail. It is feasible, however, to examine the primary influences that combined to create the vibrant culture of the Middle Ages. There were three prominent strands in this synthesis: the Greco-Roman tradition, Christianity, and Germanic tribal custom. Chapter 1 includes primary source readings that offer evidence of each of these features.

The first two documents recount the division of the Roman Empire by the emperor Diocletian, an act that had far-reaching consequences. The separation of east and west created, in effect, two empires. One of them, the eastern half, endured as the Byzantine Empire until 1453 A.D. The empire in the west, by contrast, was gradually transformed,

officially ending in 476 A.D. when the last Roman emperor was deposed. Recent scholars have recognized that this date has limited meaning, and believe that the western half gradually assimilated the influences of the Germanic tribes over several centuries, taking on new characteristics, but maintaining some Roman traditions. As we shall see, the Germanic tribal peoples settled in various areas of the west and eventually created their own successor kingdoms.

In addition to dividing the vast empire in an attempt to provide smooth succession to the throne and to increase effective imperial management, Diocletian made various attempts to solve the economic and social problems of the third century. His Edict on Maximum Prices was an effort to establish strict price and wage guidelines in order to stabilize the economy.

Diocletian's plan for establishing a peaceful transition between rulers failed after his retirement, and there was once again a struggle among the contenders for imperial power. The man who ultimately emerged as emperor was Constantine. His biographer, Eusebius, claimed that his victory was a result of his conversion to the Christian religion, as will be shown in a selection from his work. The imperial edicts and actions during Constantine's reign further authenticate the emperor's belief in Christianity, although some scholars have suggested that his motivation was political. Constantine legalized the practice of Christianity in the "Edict of Milan," and convened a church council at Nicaea, which established the "Nicene Creed." He was also the donor of St. Peter's Basilica, as may be seen in the "Interpreting the Evidence" comparison.

This chapter also includes sources concerning the first centuries of Christianity, beginning with the Roman persecutions of early believers. The dramatic account of the martyrdoms of Perpetua and Felicity indicates the severity of these attacks on Christians.

Two of the Church Fathers, Augustine and Jerome, are represented in this chapter. Both of these men struggled inwardly in the search for religious truth. Augustine recorded his conversion to Christianity in his work, Confessions, *which dramatically describes his experiences. Jerome fought his attraction to secular literature—the works of the great Greek and Roman writers; the letters presented here reveal his solution to this tension. The works of both men were vital in preserving the classical tradition and in creating the synthesis of Christianity and the Greco-Roman tradition, as will be seen in Chapters 2 and 4, which contain materials emphasizing this aspect of medieval culture.*

One of the most important developments of early Christianity was the growth of ecclesiastical organization. The first Christian groups were informal associations of believers, and although first-century writings refer to bishops, elders, and deacons, these positions may have been informal leadership roles. By the beginning of the second century, however, there was an obvious distinction between the clergy and laity—priests and laypeople. As congregations multiplied in a town, a bishop would be elected to coordinate their activities. Each priest was responsible to the bishop of his diocese (a geographical area), and by the time of the Edict of Milan, there were numerous bishops in the Roman Empire. They corresponded with one another, and occasionally convened councils to decide important issues. Inevitably, the bishops of the larger towns came to dominate

the others, and an administrative hierarchy began to develop. By the fifth century, one of the most important, the Bishop of Rome (eventually called pope, or "papa"), began to assert his right to jurisdiction over the Church and the other bishops. One of the first popes to claim this supremacy was Leo I (440–61). An excerpt from one of his sermons defines his argument for authority, a doctrine known in history as the "Petrine Theory."

An important issue in the organization of the Church was the method of appointing bishops. As early as the fourth century, church councils promulgated legislation that would confine the right to choose bishops to the clergy; according to canon (ecclesiastical) law, laymen were not permitted to appoint bishops, priests, or deacons. A document from the Eighth Synod of Constantinople (869) reaffirmed this legislation.

As the new religion took hold in society and gradually developed a bureaucracy, there were individuals who believed that true Christian belief could only be realized in isolation; withdrawal from worldly activity would allow them to follow the precepts of Christ, and to achieve spiritual fulfillment. The experience and practices of "eremitic" monasticism are evident in the description of St. Anthony as a "desert saint," who retreated from the secular world in order to seek a closer relationship with God. His actions are described in an excerpt from the Life of Saint Antony *by Athanasius.*

A more moderate style of monastic living was begun in the fourth century by Pachomius, and the practice was codified in the sixth century by Saint Benedict. His Rule, which became the foundation document for the Benedictine monastic order, codified the practice of group monasticism, known as "cenobitic" monasticism. Excerpts from the Rule, *correlated with the groundplan of the monastery at Saint Gall, demonstrate the contrast between the experience of St. Anthony and that of monks living in a community.*

The last of the three influential traditions in the development of medieval culture and civilization is that of the Germanic tribes. Although Germanic peoples had been living beyond the boundaries of the Roman Empire for centuries, it was not until the latter part of the reign of Marcus Aurelius (late second century) that they began to infiltrate the Empire. As the documents demonstrate, their presence transformed the Roman world in late antiquity. This chapter contains selections by two historians, Tacitus and Ammianus Marcellinus, which describe the Germanic people in detail; they discuss practices that may also be found in the medieval system often referred to as "vassalage," discussed in Chapter 5.

The late antique world was characterized by warfare between the Romans and the various tribes. This chapter closes with documents that describe some of this conflict. The first is a treaty made in 251 C.E. with the tribe of the Vandals, which shows the accommodations made by both sides. Finally, there is an account of a significant battle between the Romans and the Goths at Adrianople (378).

Imperial Administration and the Conversion to Christianity

Diocletian and the Division of the Roman Empire

1.1   Aurelius Victor, *Lives of the Emperors*

During the third century the Roman Empire faced a variety of challenges. In addition to economic and social distress of various kinds, there was no clear pattern for succession to the throne. This led to civil strife as, again and again, military leaders vied to become emperor. When Diocletian came to the throne in 284 he sought to remedy this problem by means of a fourfold division of the mammoth empire and a design for predictable succession. The ensuing rule by four men was known as a Tetrarchy. Two of the rulers were titled Augustus; they were the senior members of the foursome. The other two were known as caesars. Diocletian planned that after a twenty-year reign, the augusti would retire, and the caesars would take their positions; new men would then be chosen as caesars.

The empire was stabilized to some degree during Diocletian's reign, and he and his co-augustus did retire at the end of the twenty-year period, as stipulated. However, the succession was not a smooth as Diocletian intended. (See Document 1.3 in this chapter.) The following excerpt is from Lives of the Emperors, *a work by Aurelius Victor (320–c. 390), who was a Roman politician and historian.*

(From *Roman Civilization, Selected Readings, vol. II: The Empire*, ed. by Naphtali Lewis and Meyer Reinhold. Copyright © 1955 Columbia University Press. Reprinted with permission of the publisher.

As the burden of war . . . became heavier, a division of the Empire was made: all the countries beyond the Gallic Alps were entrusted to Constantius;[1] Herculius [Maxmianus][2] had Africa and Italy; Galerius,[3] ruled Illyria as far as the Black Sea; and Diocletian[4] retained all the rest. After this, part of Italy was subjected to the heavy burden of paying tribute . . . [when] a new law for regular tax payments was introduced. At that time it was still endurable, because not excessive, but it has grown in our age [the middle of the fourth century] into a scourge . . .

With no less zeal [than in their military exploits] the emperors took up the administration of civil affairs, establishing laws that were eminently just. They suppressed the *frumentarii*,[5] a group that was a veritable scourge and whom our *agentes in rebus* closely resemble. These men, who appear to have been established to investigate and report possible seditious movements that might exist in the provinces, trumped up false accusations, and under the universal terror they inspired, especially in persons in very remote areas, they practiced shameful rapine everywhere.

---

[1]Constantius lived from c. 250–306 and reigned as Caesar from 293–305.

[2]Herculius [Maximianus] lived from 249–310 and reigned as Augustus from 285–305.

[3]Galerius lived from c. 250 to 311 and reigned as Caesar from 293–305 and Augustus from 306–311.

[4]Diocletian lived from 236/7 to 316 and reigned as Augustus from 284–305.

[5]*Frumentarii* were imperial secret service agents established toward the end of the first century. They used their positions for personal advantage, thus gaining an evil reputation. By 319 C.E., or perhaps as early as Diocletian's reign, they were replaced by the *agentes in rebus*, an organization of spies with even wider powers; they ultimately became as notorious as their predecessors.

The emperors showed no less concern and solicitude for the provisioning of the city and the welfare of those who paid tribute. . . . The ancient cults were maintained in all their purity. Rome and other cities, especially Carthage, Milan, and Nicomedia, were extraordinarily embellished with new structures of great splendor. . . .

Diocletian kept his eyes on threatening dangers, and when he saw that the Roman state, in the course of destiny, was going to become a prey to civil wars and was approaching its breakup, so to speak, he celebrated the twentieth anniversary of his reign and abdicated the government of the state, although he was in good health. Herculius [Maximianus], who had held power one year less, he induced to follow his example, though he did so with great reluctance. Although a variety of explanations exist [for Diocletian's abdication], and the truth has been perverted, it is my view that it was out of the excellence of his character that, scorning ambition for power, he descended to the life of an ordinary citizen.

Questions for Discussion:

1. What does this source tell you about the condition of the Roman Empire in the late third century?
2. What were some specific problems faced by the government? By the citizens?
3. Discuss the ways in which Diocletian attempted to meet these challenges.

1.2   Lactantius, *De Mortibus Persecutorum*

A very different, and less positive, view of Diocletian was presented by Lactantius, an early Christian writer (c.250–c.325) whose opinion of the emperor was colored by the persecutions of Christians during Diocletian's reign. The following excerpt is from his work, De Mortibus Persecutorum *(On the Deaths of the Persecutors).*

(From Lactantius, *De Mortibus Persecutorum*, translated by J. L. Creed. Oxford: Clarendon Press, 1984, pp. 11–13. Reprinted by permission of Oxford University Press.)

Diocletian was an author of crimes and a deviser of evils; he ruined everything and could not even keep his hands from God. In his greed and anxiety he turned the world upside down. He appointed three men to share his rule, dividing the world into four parts and multiplying the armies, since each of the four strove to have a far larger number of troops than previous emperors had had when they were governing the state alone. The number of recipients began to exceed the number of contributors by so much that, with farmers' resources exhausted by the enormous size of the requisitions, fields became deserted and cultivated land was turned into forest. To ensure that terror was universal, provinces too were cut into fragments; many governors and even more officials were imposed on individual regions, almost on individual cities, and to these were added numerous accountants, controllers, and prefects' deputies. The activities of all these people were very rarely civil; they engaged only in repeated condemnations and confiscations, and in exacting endless resources—and the exactions were not just frequent, they were incessant, and involved insupportable injustices. And how could the arrangements for raising soldiers be endured?

This same Diocletian with his insatiable greed was never willing that his treasuries should be depleted; he was always amassing surplus wealth and funds for largess so that he could keep what he was storing, complete and inviolate. Since too by his various misdeeds he was causing an immense rise in prices, he tried to fix by law the prices of goods put up for sale. Much blood was then shed over small and cheap items, in the general alarm nothing appeared for sale, and the rise in prices got much worse until, after many had met their deaths, sheer necessity led to the repeal of the law.

Questions for Discussion:

1. Compare the accounts of Diocletian's reform measures according to Aurelius Victor and Lactantius. How and why do they differ?
2. Do you think either of the two sources presents an unbiased opinion? What reasons can you give for your analysis?

1.3   Diocletian's *Edict on Maximum Prices*

As Lactantius reported in the previous source, in addition to problems of governance, the Roman Empire faced severe economic collapse in the late third and early fourth centuries. Just as Diocletian had attempted to solve the problems of succession to the throne and the administration of such a vast area, he and his co-rulers moved to stabilize the economy. Citing various problems such as greed and profiteering, the emperor enacted the following Edict on Maximum Prices, *which established the prices of goods and commodities, as well as wages.*

(From *Roman Civilization, Selected Readings, vol. II: The Empire,* ed. by Naphtali Lewis and Meyer Reinhold. Copyright © 1955 Columbia University Press. Reprinted with permission of the publisher.

The Emperor Diocletian, the Emperor Maximian, and Constantius, most noble Caesar, and Galerius Valerius Maximian, most noble Caesar, declare:

. . . Therefore we, who by the gracious favor of the gods previously stemmed the tide of the ravages of barbarian nations by destroying them, must surround the peace which we established for eternity with the necessary defenses of justice.

If the excesses perpetrated by persons of unlimited and frenzied avarice could be checked by some self-restraint—this avarice which rushes for gain and profit with no thought for mankind . . . ; or if the general welfare could endure without harm this riotous license by which, in its unfortunate state, it is being very seriously injured every day, the situation could perhaps be faced with dissembling and silence, with the hope that human forbearance might alleviate the cruel and pitiable situation. But the only desire of these uncontrolled madmen is to have no thought for the common need. Among the unscrupulous, the immoderate, and the avaricious it is considered almost a creed . . . to desist from plundering the wealth of all only when necessity compels them. Through their extreme need, moreover, some persons have become acutely aware of their most unfortunate situation, and can no longer close their eyes to it. Therefore we, who are the protectors of the human race, are agreed, as we view the situation, that decisive legislation is necessary, so that the long-hoped-for solutions which mankind itself could not provide may, by the remedies provided by our foresight, be vouchsafed for the general betterment of all. . . .

We hasten, therefore, to apply the remedies long demanded by the situation, satisfied that no one can complain that our intervention with regulations is untimely or unnecessary, trivial or unimportant. These measures are directed against the unscrupulous, who have perceived in our silence of so many years a lesson in restraint but have been unwilling to imitate it. For who is so insensitive and so devoid of human feeling that he can be unaware or has not perceived that uncontrolled prices are widespread in the sales taking place in the markets and in the daily life of the cities? Nor is the uncurbed passion for profiteering lessened either by abundant supplies or by fruitful years. . . .

But now we must set forth in detail the causes which have pressed and driven us to cease our long-enduring forbearance and to take steps. . . . Who does not know that wherever the common safety requires our armies to be sent, the profiteers insolently and covertly attack the public welfare, not only in villages and towns, but on every road? They charge extortionate prices for merchandise, not just fourfold or eightfold, but on such a scale that human speech cannot find words to characterize their profit and their practices. Indeed, sometimes in a single retail sale a soldier is stripped of his donative (daily maintenance) and pay. Moreover, the contributions of the whole world for the support of the armies fall as profits into the hands of these plunderers, and our soldiers appear to bestow with their own hands the rewards of their military service and their veterans' bonuses upon the profiteers. The result is that the pillagers of the state itself seize day by day more than they know how to hold.

Aroused justly and rightfully by all the facts set forth above, and in response to the needs of mankind itself, which appears to be praying for release, we have decided that maximum prices of articles for sale must be established. We have not set down fixed prices, for we do not deem it just to do this, since many provinces occasionally enjoy the good fortune of welcome low prices and the privilege, as it were, of prosperity. Thus, when the pressure of high prices appears anywhere—may the gods avert such a calamity!—avarice . . . will be checked by the limits fixed in our statute and by the restraining curbs of the law.

It is our pleasure, therefore, that the prices listed in the subjoined schedule be held in observance in the whole of our Empire. And every person shall take note that the liberty to exceed them at will has been ended, but that the blessing of low prices has in no way been impaired in those places where supplies actually abound. . . . Moreover, this universal edict will serve as a necessary check upon buyers and sellers whose practice it is to visit ports and other provinces. . . .

It is agreed that even in the time of our ancestors it was the practice in passing laws to restrain offenses by prescribing a penalty. For rarely is a situation beneficial to humanity accepted spontaneously; experience teaches that fear is the most effective regulator and guide for the performance of duty. Therefore it is our pleasure that anyone who resists the measures of this statute shall be subject to a capital penalty for daring to do so. And let no one consider the statute harsh, since there is at hand a ready protection from danger in the observance of moderation. . . . We therefore exhort the loyalty of all, so that a regulation instituted for the public good may be observed with willing obedience and due scruple, especially as it is seen that by a statute of this kind provision has been made, not for single municipalities and peoples and provinces but for the whole world. . . .

The prices for the sale of individual items which no one may exceed are listed below.

The following list is a small sample of the prices and wages established:

I.	Wheat	1 army modius[6]	100 denarii[7]
	Barley	1 army modius	60 denarii
	Rye	1 army modius	60 denarii
	Beans, crushed	1 army modius	100 denarii
II.	Likewise for wines:		
	Aged wine first quality	1 Italian sextarius[8]	24 denarii
	Aged wine, second quality	1 Italian sextarius	16 denarii
	Ordinary	1 Italian sextarius	8 denarii
	Beer, Gallic or Pannonian[9]	1 Italian sextarius	4 denarii
	Beer, Egyptian	1 Italian sextarius	2 denarii
VII.	For wages:		
	Farm laborer, with maintenance	daily	25 denarii
	Carpenter, as above	daily	50 denarii
	Wall painter, as above	daily	75 denarii
	Picture painter, as above	daily	150 denarii
	Camel driver or ass and hinny driver, with maintenance	daily	25 denarii
	Shepherd, with maintenance	daily	20 denarii
	Muleteer, with maintenance	daily	25 denarii
	Veterinary, for clipping and preparing hoofs	per animal	6 denarii
	Veterinary, for bleeding and cleaning the head	per animal	20 denarii

---

[6] A *modius* was a term used for dry measure, equivalent to about 2 gallons.

[7] A *denarius* was a coin that varied in value during the Roman Empire. According to some scholars, it represented a day's wages for a common laborer. Others equate it with a day's wages for a soldier. It is not possible to compare the denarius accurately to today's currency, although in 2005 scholars suggested that it was probably worth about $21. By the time of Diocletian the denarius was subject to severe inflation, and Diocletian eventually replaced it with a new coinage, the nummus.

[8] A *sextarius* was a unit of liquid measure, equivalent to approximately 567 milliliters.

[9] Pannonia is present-day Hungary.

Barber	per man	2 denarii
Sewer cleaner, working a full day with maintenance	daily	25 denarii
Scribe, for the best writing	100 lines	25 denarii
Scribe, for second-quality writing	100 lines	20 denarii
Elementary teacher, per boy	monthly	50 denarii
Teacher of arithmetic, per boy	monthly	75 denarii
Teacher of shorthand, per boy	monthly	75 denarii
Teacher of Greek or Latin language and literature, and teacher of geometry, per pupil	monthly	200 denarii
Teacher of rhetoric or public speaking, per pupil	monthly	250 denarii
Advocate[10] or jurist, fee for a complaint		250 denarii
Advocate or jurist, fee for pleading		1000 denarii
Teacher of architecture, per boy	monthly	100 denarii
Check room attendant, per bather		2 denarii

Questions for Discussion:

1. What reasons did Diocletian give for establishing maximum prices and wages? Do you find any similarities between his analysis of the Roman economic situation and the circumstances faced by the United States in 2009?

2. Compare the different wages established for various jobs and professions. What seem to be the determining factors in setting the amounts? Do the differences seem reasonable to you?

3. Discuss Diocletian's objectives in issuing this edict.

The Emperor Constantine

1.4   The Conversion of Constantine

Following the retirement of Diocletian in 305 (see Document 1.1), there was a struggle for power among the successors. The caesars, Constantius in the west and Galerius in the east, were named augusti, but soon thereafter Constantius became ill and sent for his son, Constantine, to join him in York, England, where he was then residing. Constantius died within months, and his army acclaimed Constantine as augustus. Before long there was another contender, when Maxentius, Maximian's son, declared himself augustus. Galerius died in 311, and Constantine moved against Maxentius to defend his claim to the throne. The armies of the two men met north of Rome, at the Milvian Bridge, which crossed the Tiber River. Before the battle, Constantine experienced a vision that was recounted in detail by the early Christian writer Eusebius (c. 260– c. 340). Although the account is emotionally dramatic, it is important to remember that Eusebius was writing some decades following the battle, and he may have exaggerated Constantine's experience, as well as the use of Christian symbolism by his troops.

(From Eusebius, *Life of Constantine the Great, A Select Library of Nicene and Post-Nicene Fathers*, second series, vol. i [New York: The Christian Literature Co., 1890], pp. 489–491. Translation modernized.)

From *The Life of Constantine the Great* by Eusebius, Chapters 27–31.

    Being convinced that he needed some more powerful aid than his military forces could afford him . . . [Constantine] sought divine assistance, deeming the possession of arms and numerous soldiers of secondary importance, but believing the cooperating power of

---

[10]A lawyer.

Deity invincible and not to be shaken. He considered, therefore, on what God he might rely for protection and assistance. While engaged in this enquiry, the thought occurred to him, that, of the many emperors who had preceded him, those who had rested their hopes in a multitude of gods . . . at last had met with an unhappy end . . . ; while one alone who had pursued an entirely opposite course, who had condemned their error, and honored the one Supreme God during his whole life, had found him to be Savior and Protector of his empire, and the Giver of every good thing. Reflecting on this, . . . he felt it incumbent on him to honor his father's God alone.

Accordingly he called on him with earnest prayer and supplications that he would reveal to him who he was, and stretch forth his right hand to help him in his present difficulties. And while he was thus praying with fervent entreaty, a most marvelous sign appeared to him from heaven . . . [Constantine related] that about noon . . . he saw with his own eyes the trophy of a cross of light in the heavens, above the sun, bearing the inscription, CONQUER BY THIS. He was struck with amazement by this sight, and so was his whole army, which also witnessed the miracle. [Constantine] said that he doubted within himself what the import of this apparition could be. And while he continued to ponder and reason on its meaning, night suddenly came on; then in his sleep Christ appeared to him with the same sign which he had seen in the heavens, and commanded him to make a likeness of that sign, and to use it as a safeguard in all engagements with his enemies.

At dawn he arose, and communicated the marvel to his friends; and then, calling together the workers in gold and precious stones, he sat in the midst of them, and described to them the figure of the sign he had seen, bidding them represent it in gold and precious stones.

It was made in the following manner. A long spear, overlaid with gold, formed the figure of the cross by means of a transverse bar laid over it. On the top of the whole was fixed a wreath of gold and precious stones; and within this, the symbol of the Savior's name, two letters indicating the name of Christ by means of its initial characters, the letter P being intersected by X in its center; and these letters the emperor was in the habit of wearing on his helmet at a later period. From the cross-bar of the spear was suspended a cloth, a royal piece, covered with a profuse embroidery of most brilliant precious stones; and which, being also richly interlaced with gold, presented an indescribable degree of beauty to the beholder. This banner was of a square form, and the upright staff, whose lower section was of great length, bore a golden half-length portrait of the pious emperor and his children on its upper part, beneath the trophy of the cross, and immediately above the embroidered banner.

The emperor constantly made use of this sign of salvation as a safeguard against every adverse and hostile power, and commanded that others similar to it should be carried at the head of all his armies.

These things were done shortly afterwards. But at the time above specified, being struck with amazement at the extraordinary vision, and resolving to worship no other God save Him who had appeared to him, he sent for those who were acquainted with the mysteries of His doctrines, and inquired who that God was, and what was intended by the sign of the vision he had seen.

They affirmed that He was God, the only begotten Son of the one and only God; that the sign which had appeared was the symbol of immortality, and the trophy over death which He had gained in time past when sojourning on earth. They taught him also the causes of His advent, and explained to him the true account of His incarnation. Thus he was instructed in these matters, and was impressed with wonder at the divine manifestation which had been presented to his sight. Comparing, therefore, the heavenly vision with the interpretation given, he found his judgment confirmed; and, in the persuasion that the knowledge of these things had been imparted to him by Divine teaching, he determined thenceforth to devote himself to the reading of the inspired writings.

Moreover, he made the priests of God his counselors, and deemed it incumbent on him to honor the God who had appeared to him with all devotion. And after this, being fortified by well-grounded hopes in Him, he hastened to quench the threatening fire of tyranny.

Assuming therefore the Supreme God as his patron, and invoking His Christ to be his preserver and aid, and setting the victorious trophy, the salutary symbol, in front of his soldiers and body-guard, he marched with his whole forces, trying to obtain again for the Romans the freedom they had inherited from their ancestors.

The Battle at the Milvian Bridge

. . . So at this time Maxentius, and the soldiers and guards with him, "went down into the depths like stone," when, in his flight before the divinely-aided forces of Constantine, he decided to cross the river which lay in his way, over which, making a strong bridge of boats, he had framed an engine of destruction, really against himself, but in the hope of ensnaring him who was beloved by God. For his God stood by the one to protect him, while the other, godless, proved to be the miserable contriver of these secret devices to his own ruin . . . Thus, under divine direction, the machine erected on the bridge, with the ambuscade concealed therein, giving way unexpectedly before the appointed time, the bridge began to sink, and the boats with the men in them went bodily to the bottom. And first the wretch himself, then his armed attendants and guards, even as the sacred oracles had before described, "sank as lead in the mighty waters."

1.5   The *Edict of Milan*

Constantine and his co-emperor in the east, Licinius (d. 324), issued a proclamation in 313 that legalized the practice of all religions, including Christianity, and stated that all property confiscated from Christians must be returned. This edict, known historically as the "Edict of Milan," dramatically altered the circumstances of the Christian religion, and allowed it to grow exponentially. It became the state religion during the reign of the Emperor Theodosius (c. 346–395).

(From *Church and State through the Centuries*, translated by Sidney Z. Ehler and John B. Morall. London: Burns & Oates, 1954, pp. 5–6. By kind permission of Continuum International Publishing Group.)

From Lactantius, *De mortibus persecutorum.*

We, Constantinus and Licinius the Emperors, having met in concord at Milan and having set in order

Having sung praises to God, the Ruler of all and the Author of victory, . . . Constantine entered the imperial city in triumph. And here the whole body of the senate, and others of rank and distinction in the city, . . . along with all the people of Rome, . . . received him with acclamations and abounding joy; men, women, and children, with countless multitudes of servants, greeting him as deliverer, preserver, and benefactor, with incessant shouts. But he, being possessed of inward piety toward God, was neither rendered arrogant by these plaudits, nor uplifted by the praises he heard; but, knowing that he had received help from God, he immediately rendered a thanksgiving to him as the Author of his victory.

Questions for Discussion:

1. Many scholars have asserted that Constantine's conversion was based upon political motivations rather than religious belief. What reasons might be given for this view? Do you agree or disagree with this interpretation?
2. Does Constantine's vision seem plausible to you? Why or why not?
3. According to Eusebius, how did Constantine proclaim his new allegiance to the Christian God?

everything which pertains to the common good and public security, are of the opinion that among the various things which we perceived would profit men, or which should be set in order first, was to be found the cultivation of religion; we should therefore give both to Christians and to all others free facility to follow the religion which each may desire, so that by this means whatever divinity is enthroned in heaven may be gracious and favorable to us and to all who have been placed under our authority. Therefore we are of the opinion that the following decision is in accordance with sound and true reasoning: that no one who has given his mental assent to the Christian persuasion or to any other which he feels to be suitable to him should be compelled to deny his conviction, so that the Supreme Godhead ("Summa Divinitas") whose worship we freely observe, can assist us in all things with his accustomed favor and benevolence. Wherefore it is necessary for your xcellency to know that it is our pleasure that all restrictions which were previously put forward in official pronouncements concerning the sect of the Christians should be removed, and that each one of them who freely and sincerely carries out the purpose of observing the Christian religion may endeavor to practice its precepts without any fear or danger. We believed that these points should be fully brought to your attention, so that you might know that we have given free and absolute permission to practice their religion to the Christians. Now that you perceive what we have granted to them, your Exellency must also learn that for the sake of peace in our time a similar public and free right to practice their religion or cult is granted to others, so that every man may have free opportunity to worship according to his own wish. This has been done by us to avoid any appearance of disfavor to any one religion. We have decided furthermore to decree the following in respect of the Christians: if those places at which they were accustomed in former times to hold their meetings . . . have been at any previous time acquired from our treasury or from any other person, let the persons concerned be willing and swift to restore them to the Christians without financial recompense and without trying to ask a price. Let those who have received such property as a gift restore whatever they have acquired to the Christians in similar manner. If those who have bought such property or received it as a gift, seek some recompense from our benevolence, let them apply to the Vicar, by whom their cases will be referred to our clemency. You are to consider it your duty that all these things shall be handed over to the Christian body immediately and without delay by your intervention. And since the aforesaid Christians are known to have possessed not only those places at which they are accustomed to assemble, but others also pertaining to the law of their body, that is of the churches, not of private individuals, you are to order in accordance with the law which we have described above the return of all those possessions to the aforesaid Christians, that is to their bodies and assemblies without any further hesitation or argument. Our previous statement is to be borne in mind that those who restore this property without price may, as we have said, expect some compensation from our benevolence.

You ought to bring into play your very effective intervention in all these matters concerning the aforesaid Christian body so that there may be a swift fulfillment of our Edict, in which the interests of public quiet have been consulted by our clemency. Let all this be done, so that as we stated above, the divine favor, of which we have experienced so many instances, may continue with us to bless our successors through all time with public wellbeing. In order that the character of this our perpetual benevolence can reach the knowledge of all, it will be well for you to circulate everywhere, and to bring to the awareness of all, these points which have been written to you as above, so that the enactment of this our benevolence may not be hidden.

Questions for Discussion:

1. In what ways might this edict have contributed to the growth of the Christian religion?
2. In addition to extending freedom of worship to the Christians, what other benefits derived from the edict?
3. To what degree might the edict have been politically motivated?

1.6   The Council of Nicaea

In 325 C.E. Constantine was faced with a doctrinal division in the Christian Church. The essence of the conflict concerned the nature of Christ. One faction, led by Bishop Alexander of Alexandria, believed that Jesus was made by *God, but was of divine substance and co-essential with the Father, a concept known as homoousios. The opposing group, led by Arius, a high-ranking presbyter (priest) from Alexandria, saw Christ as a creature made in time, who did not possess the divine nature of the Father. In order to resolve this quarrel, which was growing in intensity and geographical extension, Constantine called a council of the Church, which met in the city of Nicaea. As Eusebius reported in his biography of Constantine, the council was composed of church prelates from throughout the Roman world. This meeting, called the Council of Nicaea, was the first of many "universal" councils to be held through the centuries, and it is important to remember that it was convened by the emperor, rather than an ecclesiastical dignitary; this fact, as we shall see in subsequent chapters, had significant ramifications in the struggle between the Church and medieval rulers. In addition, several other councils will be discussed in later chapters. (See Chapter 12, which contains information about the Council called Lateran IV). The most recent universal church council was Vatican II, which met during the 1960s.*

(From *Roman Civilization, Selected Readings, vol. II: The Empire*, ed. by Naphtali Lewis and Meyer Reinhold. Copyright © 1955 Columbia University Press. Reprinted with permission of the publisher.

The Council of Nicaea (325), from Eusebius, *Life of Constantine*.

Constantine summoned a general synod, inviting the bishops in all parts with honorary letters to be present as soon as possible. . . . At that time there were to be seen congregated in one place persons widely different from one another not only in spirit but also in physical appearance, and in the regions, places, and provinces from which they came. . . . From all the churches which had filled all Europe, Africa, and Asia, those who held the chief place among the servants of God assembled at the same time; and one sacred hall, extended as it were by the will of God, embraced in its compass Cilicians, Phoenicians, Arabs, Palestinians, Egyptians, Thebans,

Libyans, and some coming from Mesopotamia. A bishop from Persia also participated in the synod, nor was Scythia absent from this body. Pontus, likewise Galatia, Pamphylia, and Cappadocia, Asia, too, and Phrygia provided their most carefully chosen persons. Thracians also, Macedonians, Achaeans, and Epirotes, and those who are situated at a very long distance beyond these were nonetheless present. . . . Present among the body were more than 250 bishops. . . .

But on the day fixed for the council which was to put an end to the controversies, when the various persons who composed the synod were at hand, in the very middle of the hall of the palace which seemed to surpass all the rest in size, there were many seats arranged in rows on both sides; and all who had been summoned entered and each sat down in his place. After the entire synod had seated itself with seeming modesty, all at first fell silent, awaiting the coming of the emperor. Soon one of those closest to the emperor, then a second and a third entered. Others, too, preceded—not, as customary, from among the soldiers and bodyguard, but only those of his advisers who professed the faith of Christ. And when the signal was given which announced the entry of the emperor, all rose, and finally he himself approached proceeding down the center . . . dazzling the eyes of all with the splendor of his purple robe and sparkling with fiery rays, as it were, adorned for the occasion as he was with an extraordinary splendor of gold and jewels. . . . As for his soul, it was sufficiently apparent that he was adorned with the fear of God and religion.

Question for Discussion:

1. What reasons might have motivated Constantine to summon the Council of Nicaea?

1.7   The *Nicene Creed*

The Council of Nicaea formulated a statement of faith that remains the creed for many churches, both Catholic and Protestant. Its basic tenets followed the position of Bishop Alexander, affirming the divine nature of Christ. Alexander's deacon, Athanasius, who accompanied the bishop to Nicaea, soon became the leading spokesman for

Nicene Christianity. As you will see in the next chapter, not all of the converts to Christianity followed the dictates of the council. The Ostrogoths, for example, were Arian Christians, as were several of the other Germanic tribes. As you read the excerpts about the Ostrogoths, the Visigoths, and the Anglo-Saxons, in the following chapter, keep in mind the tenets of the creed and the ways in which they influenced the history of the early medieval era.

(From *The Seven Ecumenical Councils*, trans. by A. C. McGiffert and E. C. Richarson. The Library of Nicene and Post-Nicene Fathers, 2nd series, vol. XIV [New York: Charles Scribner's, 1900], p. 3.)

We believe in one God, the Father Almighty, maker of all things visible and invisible; and in one Lord Jesus Christ, the Son of God, the only-begotten of his Father, of the substance of the Father, God of God, Light of Light, very God of very God, begotten not made, being of one substance with the Father. By whom all things were made, both which be in heaven and in earth. Who for us men and for our salvation came down [from heaven] and was incarnate and was made man. He suffered and the third day he rose again, and ascended into heaven. And he shall come again to judge both the quick and the dead. And [we

believe] in the Holy Ghost. And whosoever shall say that there was time when the Son of God was not, or that before he was begotten he was not, or that he was made of things that were not, or that he is of a different substance or essence [from the Father] or that he is a creature, or subject to change or conversion—all that so say, the Catholic and Apostolic Church anathematizes [excommunicates] them.

Questions for Discussion:

1. The *Nicene Creed* continues to be an obligatory part of the liturgies of many churches. Why?
2. Why does the version of the *Creed* adopted by the Western, or Latin, Church differ from that of the Eastern Orthodox (Greek) Church?
3. How has the *Nicene Creed* changed over time?

INTERPRETING THE EVIDENCE

1.8 St. Peter's Basilica and Constantine's Gift

The Roman church commissioned by Constantine was built over the shrine long venerated by Christians as the burial place of St. Peter, which was one of the most important pilgrimage goals in the western world. In addition to its religious implications, the site developed political significance in the sixth and seventh centuries when the successors of Peter as Bishops of Rome, known as popes from the late 300s, established their authority over other bishops and asserted the supremacy of the Roman pontiff as the leader of Christendom (see Document 1.12). It was essential that the new building be grand and splendid in order to reinforce the claim of primacy by the Roman see, and to honor the apostle who was chosen by Christ for this role.

So that the church could accommodate a large congregation, the builders created a sizeable atrium, or

entry space, separated from the five-aisled basilica by a narthex—a porch or vestibule. The nave, or central part of the church, was separated from the side aisles by columns. The clerestory was the upper part of the nave, whose walls contained spaces for light. These openings were filled with beautiful stained glass in the later Middle Ages. You may turn to Documents 13.12 and 13.13 to see this development. Also note the "ambulatory," which was a walkway for passing in the church without going through the nave; this became an important feature in the pilgrimage churches as well as in Gothic cathedrals (see Documents 8.2, 10.3, and 13.10). As we shall see, in the later buildings the ambulatory was extended from the side aisles to surround the apse. This development allowed pilgrims and worshipers to have convenient access to the areas known as apsidal chapels, which provided repositories for sacred relics.

(continued)

The composite length of old St. Peter's was about 653 feet, with the interior of the basilica measuring 208 feet by 355 feet. In many ways the building was a typical rectangular Roman basilica; however, perhaps because of the significance of the church, the architects added a new component—the transept. The nave and transept together provided space for clergy, congregation, and a large crowd of pilgrims. It is important to note that the elements of the new design formed a tau cross, a pattern that came to be known as cruciform; this layout provided the basic model for church architecture throughout the Middle Ages and beyond. You will see this in Chapters 8, 10, and 13 as you study the groundplans of the church St. Madeleine in Vezelay, the abbey church of St. Denis, and Chartres Cathedral.

(Document from *The Book of the Popes*, translated by L. R. Loomis, *Records of Civilization*, no. 3 [New York: Columbia University Press, 1916], pp. 53–57.)

Document

At the same time Constantine Augustus built by request of Sylvester, the bishop (Pope Sylvester I, 314–335), the basilica of blessed Peter, the apostle, in the shrine of Apollo, and laid there the coffin with the body of the holy Peter; the coffin itself he enclosed on all sides with bronze, which is unchangeable: at the head 5 feet, at the feet 5 feet, at the right side 5 feet, at the left side 5 feet, underneath 5 feet and overhead 5 feet: thus he enclosed the body of

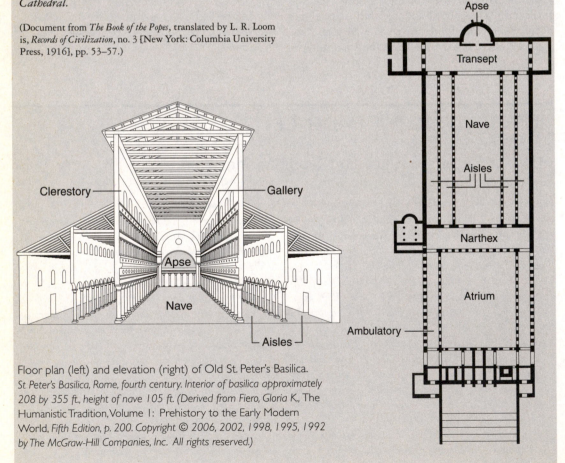

Floor plan (left) and elevation (right) of Old St. Peter's Basilica.
St Peter's Basilica, Rome, fourth century. Interior of basilica approximately 208 by 355 ft., height of nave 105 ft. (Derived from Fiero, Gloria K., The Humanistic Tradition, Volume 1: Prehistory to the Early Modern World, Fifth Edition, p. 200. Copyright © 2006, 2002, 1998, 1995, 1992 by The McGraw-Hill Companies, Inc. All rights reserved.)

blessed Peter, the apostle, and laid it away. And above he set porphyry columns for adornment and other spiral columns which he brought from Greece.[11]

He also made a vaulted roof in the basilica, gleaming with polished gold, and over the body of the blessed Peter, above the bronze which enclosed it, he set a cross of purest gold, weighing 150 lbs., in place of a measure, and upon it were inscribed these words: "CONSTANTINE AUGUSTUS AND HELEN AUGUSTA THIS HOUSE SHINING WITH SIMILAR ROYAL SPLENDOR A COURT SURROUNDS,"[12] inscribed in clear, enameled letters upon the cross.

He gave also 4 brass candlesticks, 10 feet in height, overlaid with silver, with figures in silver of the acts of the apostles, weighing each 300 lbs; 3 golden chalices, set with 45 prases [jade] and jacinths [orange zircons], weighing each 12 lbs.; 2 silver jars, weighing 200 lbs.; 20 silver chalices, weighing each 10 lbs.; 2 golden pitchers, weighing each 10 lbs.; 5 silver pitchers, weighing each 20 lbs.; a golden paten with a turret of purest gold and a dove, adorned with prases, jacinths and pearls, white stones, 215 in number, weighing 30 lbs.; 5 silver patens, weighing each 15 lbs.; a golden crown before the body, that is a chandelier, with 50 dolphins, which weighs 35 lbs.; 32 silver lamps in the body of the basilica, with dolphins, weighing each 10 lbs.; for the right of the basilica 30 silver lamps, weighing

each 8 lbs.; the altar itself of silver overlaid with gold, adorned on every side with gems, 400 in number, prases, jacinths and pearls, weighing 350 lbs.; a censer of purest gold adorned on every side with jewels, 60 in number, weighing 15 lbs.[13]

Constantine also gave properties which would yield money to support the basilica.

Likewise for revenue, the gift which Constantine Augustus offered to blessed Peter, the apostle, in the diocese of the East: in the city of Anthiocia: the house of Datianus, yielding 240 solidi.; the little house in Caene, yielding 20 and one third solidi; the barns in Afrodisia, yielding 20 solidi; the bath in Ceratheae, yielding 42 solidi, the mill in the same place, yielding 23 solidi; the cook shop in the same place, yielding 10 solidi; the garden of Maro, yielding 10 solidi; the garden in the same place, yielding 11 solidi; near the city of Anthiocia: the property Sybilles, a gift to Augustus, yielding 322 solidi, 150 decades[14] of papyrus, 200 lbs. of spices, 200 lbs. of oil of nard [a costly oil derived from an Asian plant call the spikenard], 35 lbs. of balsam.

Constantine donated additional properties in Egypt and Syria which provided further income for the support of the basilica. Since these areas came into the emperor's possession after 324, the foundation of the St. Peter's may be dated to the second half of Constantine's reign, when he was residing in Constantinople.

---

[11]The porphyry columns evidently supported the ciborium above the altar, and the spiral columns probably formed a colonnade that separated the confession from the nave. These columns were especially venerated because medieval people believed that they had once stood in the temple in Jerusalem. Several of them may be seen in the present-day St. Peter's.

[12]This inscription is incomplete. It has been suggested that the addition of four words and a minor rearrangement would result in the following sentence: "Constantine Augustus and Helena Augusta beautify with gold this royal house which a court, shining with similar splendor, surrounds."

---

[13]According to the historian and Christian apologist Orosius (c. 380–c. 418), the precious vessels of St. Peter's were hidden at the home of an aged virgin during Alaric's sack of Rome in 410. They were found by the barbarians, but when Alaric learned that they were the property of the basilica, he returned them.

[14]A *decade* was apparently a package containing ten sheets of papyrus.

(continued)

Questions for Discussion:

1. How does this source demonstrate the synthesis of ancient Roman and Christian religions?
2. Discuss the variety of properties given by Constantine for the support of St. Peter's basilica. What were his motivations for these gifts, and for donating the riches described in this source?
3. St. Peter's remains one of the most important religious sites in the Western world. Discuss the possible reasons for its fame and prosperity.

Early Christianity

1.9   The Martyrdom of Perpetua and Felicity

During the early centuries of the Christian religion, believers were sporadically persecuted and singled out as scapegoats. Since Christians were monotheistic, they refused to conform to the demands of the Romans that they worship the traditional panoply of gods. This dissent constituted treason against the state, and Christians were thus regarded as a threat to the empire. Some of the most severe persecutions took place during the reigns of Septimus Severus (r. 193–211) and Decius (r. 249–251), although the massacre of Christians under Diocletian and Galerius (beginning in 303) was even greater. A famous example of early Christian martyrdom is the case of a twenty-two- year-old woman from Roman North Africa, Vibia Perpetua, who, along with her servant Felicitas, refused to renounce her Christian belief. As a result, they were condemned to die in the arena. The following account was written by a witness of their martyrdom, which occurred in the persecution by Septimus Severus in 203.

(From *The Acts of the Christian Martyrs*, translated by Herbert Musurillo [Oxford: Clarendon Press, 1972], pp. 125–131. Reprinted by permission of Oxford University Press.)

The day of their victory dawned, and they marched from the prison to the amphitheater joyfully as though they were going to heaven, with calm faces, trembling, if at all, with joy rather than fear. Perpetua went along with shining countenance and calm step, as the beloved of God, as a wife of Christ, putting down everyone's stare by her own intense gaze. With them also was Felicitas, glad that she had safely given birth so that now she could fight the beasts, going from one blood bath to another, from a midwife to the gladiator, ready to wash after childbirth in a second baptism.

They were then led up to the gates and the men were forced to put on the robes of priests of Saturn, the women the dress of the priestesses of Ceres. But the noble Perpetua strenuously resisted this to the end.

"We came to this of our own free will, that our freedom should not be violated. We agreed to pledge our lives provided that we would do no such thing. You agreed with us to do this."

Even injustice recognized justice. The military tribune agreed. They were to be brought into the arena just as they were. Perpetua then began to sing a psalm: she was already treading on the head of the Egyptian. Revocatus, Saturninus, and Saturus began to warn the onlooking mob. Then when they came within sight of Hilarianus, they suggested by their motions and gestures: "You have condemned us, but God will condemn you" was what they were saying.

At this the crowds became enraged and demanded that they be scourged before a line of gladiators. And they rejoiced at this that they had obtained a share in the Lord's sufferings. But he who said, "Ask and you shall receive," [John 16:24] answered their prayer by giving each one the death he had asked for. For whenever they would discuss among themselves their desire for martyrdom, Saturninus indeed insisted that he wanted to be exposed to all the different beasts, that his crown might be all the more glorious. And so at the outset of the contest he and Revocatus were matched with a leopard, and then while in the stocks they were attacked by a bear, and he counted on being killed by one bite of a leopard. Then he was matched with a wild boar; but the gladiator who had tied him to the animal was gored by the boar and died a few days after the contest, whereas Saturus was only dragged along. Then when he was bound in the stocks awaiting the bear, the animal refused to come out of the cages, so that Saturus was called back once more unhurt.

For the young women, however, the Devil had prepared a mad heifer. This was an unusual animal, but it was chosen that their sex might be matched with that of the beast. So they were stripped naked, placed in nets and thus brought out into the arena. Even the crowd was horrified when they saw that one was a delicate young girl and the other was a woman fresh from childbirth with the milk still dripping from her breasts. And so they were brought back again and dressed in unbelted tunics.

First the heifer tossed Perpetua and she fell on her back. Then sitting up she pulled down the tunic that was ripped along the side so that it covered her thighs, thinking more of her modesty than of her pain. Next she asked for a pin to fasten her untidy hair for it was not right that a martyr should die with her hair in disorder, lest she might seem to be mourning in her hour of triumph.

Then she got up. And seeing that Felicitas had been crushed to the ground, she went over to her, gave her her hand, and lifted her up. Then the two stood side by side. But the cruelty of the mob was by now appeased, and so they were called back through the Gate of Life.

There Perpetua was held up by a man named Rusticus who was at the time a catechumen and kept close to her. She awoke from a kind of sleep (so absorbed had she been in ecstasy in the Spirit) and she began to look about her. Then to the amazement of all she said: "When are we going to be thrown to that heifer or whatever it is?"

When told that this had already happened, she refused to believe it until she noticed the marks of her rough experience on her person and her dress. Then she called for her brother and spoke to him together with the catechumens and said: "You must all 'stand fast in the faith' [I Corinthians 16:13] and love one another, and do not be weakened by what we have gone through." At another gate Saturus was earnestly addressing the soldier Pudens. "It is exactly," he said, "as I foretold and predicted. So far not one animal has touched me. So now you may believe me with all your heart: I am going in there and I shall be finished off with one bite of the leopard." And immediately as the contest was coming to a close a leopard was let loose, and after one bite Saturus was so drenched with blood that as he came away the mob roared in witness to his second baptism: "Well washed! Well washed!" For well washed indeed was one who had been bathed in this manner.

Then he said to the soldier Pudens: "Good-bye. Remember me, and remember the faith. These things should not disturb you but rather strengthen you."

And with this he asked Pudens for a ring from his finger, and dipping it into his wound he gave it back to him again as a pledge and as a record of his bloodshed.

Shortly after he was thrown unconscious with the rest in the usual spot to have his throat cut. But the mob asked that their bodies be brought out into the open that their eyes might be the guilty witnesses of the sword that pierced their flesh. And so the martyrs got up and went to the spot of their own accord as the people wanted them to, and kissing one another they sealed their martyrdom with the ritual kiss of peace. The others took the sword in silence and without moving, especially Saturus, who being the first to climb the stairway was the first to die. For once again he was waiting for Perpetua. Perpetua, however, had yet to taste more pain. She screamed as she was struck on the bone; then she took the trembling hand of the young gladiator and guided it to her throat. It was as though so great a woman, feared as she was by the unclean spirit, could not be dispatched unless she herself were willing.

Ah, most valiant and blessed martyrs! Truly are you called and chosen for the glory of Christ Jesus our Lord! And any man who exalts, honors, and worships his glory should read for the consolation of the Church these new deeds of heroism which are no less significant than the tales of old. For these new manifestations of virtue will bear witness to one and the same Spirit who still operates, and to God the Father almighty, to his Son Jesus Christ our Lord, to whom is splendor and immeasurable power for all the ages. Amen.

Questions for Discussion:

1. In what ways does Perpetua's behavior reflect her belief and dedication to her religion?
2. The account tells of male martyrs who accompany Perpetua and Felicity. In studying the source, what traditional gender roles do you find portrayed in the descriptions?
3. The phrase "The blood of the martyrs is the seed of the church" is attributed to the early Christian writer Tertullian (c. 160–c. 220). Do you agree with his premise? How does this source substantiate your view?

1.10   The *Confessions* of St. Augustine

Saint Augustine (354–430) was one of the most important men in the history of early Christianity. He was born in northern Africa approximately forty years after Constantine's vision and the subsequent Edict of Milan. *(See Documents 1.4 and 1.5). He became bishop of Hippo, where he witnessed the invasion of the Vandals, who swept through northern Africa in the early fifth century. Augustine's voluminous writings formed perhaps the most significant source for Christian thought during the Middle Ages and beyond. In addition, the monks, who became the educators of the new Europe, took their curriculum from Augustine's* De Doctrina Christiana, *which advocated a path rich in the classical Greco-Roman tradition (see Document 2.3).*

In the Confessions, *Augustine described in intimate detail his struggle to overcome the passions of the body in order to further his search for spiritual truth. His quest for God led him to explore various philosophies and religions, leading ultimately to the Christian faith. The following selection recounts his conversion experience.*

(From *The Confessions of St. Augustine*, translated by John K. Ryan [New York: Doubleday & Co., 1960], pp. 200–203.)

Augustine is sitting in a garden with his friend, Alypius, thinking deeply about his past and his search for religious truth. He recalls his lovers, and his sinful behavior:

Thus I was sick and tormented, and I upbraided myself much more bitterly than ever before . . . Within the hidden depths of my soul, O Lord, you urged me on. . . . This debate within my heart was solely of myself against myself. But Alypius, standing close by my side, silently awaited the outcome of my strange emotion. . . .

But when deep reflection had dredged out of the secret recesses of my soul all my misery and heaped it up in full view of my heart, there arose a mighty storm, bringing with it a mighty downpour of tears. That I might pour it all forth with its own proper sounds, I arose from Alypius's side—to be alone seemed more proper to this ordeal of weeping—and went farther apart, so that not even his presence would be a hindrance to me. Such was I at that moment, and he sensed it, for I suppose that I had said something in which the sound of my voice already appeared to be choked with weeping. So I had arisen, while he, in deep wonder, remained there where we were sitting. I flung myself down, how I do not know, under a certain fig tree, and gave free rein to my tears. The floods burst from my eyes, an acceptable sacrifice t-o you. Not indeed in these very words but to this effect I spoke many things to you: "And you, O Lord, how long? How long, O Lord, will you be angry forever? Remember not our past iniquities." For I felt that I was held by them, and I gasped forth these mournful words, "How long, how long? Tomorrow and tomorrow? Why not now? Why not in this very hour an end to my uncleanness?"

Such words I spoke, and with most bitter contrition I wept within my heart. And lo, I heard from a nearby house, a voice like that of a boy or a girl, I know not which, chanting and repeating over and over, "Take up and read. Take up and read." Instantly, with altered countenance, I began to think most intently whether children made use of any such chant in some kind of game, but I could not recall hearing it anywhere. I checked the flow of my tears and got up, for I interpreted this solely as a command given to me by God to open the book and read the first chapter I should come upon. For I had heard how Anthony had been admonished by a reading from the Gospel at which he chanced to be present, as if the words read were addressed to him: "Go, sell what you have, and give to the poor, and you shall have treasure in heaven, and come, follow me," and that by such a portent he was immediately converted to you.

So I hurried back to the spot where Alypius was sitting, for I had put there the volume of the apostle when I got up and left him. I snatched it up, opened it, and read in silence the chapter on which my eyes first fell: "Not in rioting and drunkenness, not in chambering and impurities, not in strife and envying; but put you on the Lord Jesus Christ, and make not provision for the flesh in its concupiscences." No further wished I to read, nor was there need to do so. Instantly, in truth, at the end of this sentence, as if before a peaceful light streaming into my heart, all the dark shadows of doubt fled away.

Then, having inserted my finger, or with some other mark, I closed the book, and, with a countenance now calm, I told it all to Alypius. What had taken place in him, which I did not know about, he then made known to me. He asked to see what I had read: I showed it to him, and he looked also at what came after what I had read for I did not know what followed. It was this that followed: "Now him that is weak in the faith take unto you," which he applied to himself and disclosed to me. By this admonition he was strengthened, and by a good resolution and purpose, which were entirely in keeping with his character, wherein both for a long time and for the better he had greatly differed from me, he joined me without any painful hesitation.

Thereupon we went in to my mother; we told her the story, and she rejoiced. We related just how it happened. She was filled with exultation and triumph, and she blessed you, "who are able to do above that which we ask or think." She saw that through me you had given her far more than she had long begged for by her piteous tears and groans. For you had converted me to yourself, so that I would seek neither wife nor ambition in this world, for I would stand on that rule of faith where, so many years before, you had showed me to her. You turned her mourning into a joy far richer than that she had desired, far dearer and purer than that she had sought in grandchildren born of my flesh.

Questions for Discussion:

1. Compare and contrast the accounts of the conversions of Constantine and Augustine. How are they different? Are there any similarities between the two?
2. Augustine mentions Saint Anthony in this section of his work. How was he influenced by the behavior of his predecessor? (See Document 1.14.)

1.11   Saint Jerome: *Letters*

Saint Jerome (345–420) and Augustine, among others, are known as Fathers of the Church. Jerome's influence permeated medieval life and culture, since his major work, the translation of the Bible from Greek and Hebrew into Latin, known as the Vulgate Bible, was the version of the scriptures used throughout the Middle Ages. His Letters were also an important contribution to the medieval literary tradition, since they provided models for the art of writing letters and furnished a source for ideas concerning monastic asceticism. The following selections from two of Jerome's letters demonstrate the tension between his commitment to the Christian life and his deep appreciation for classical literature, especially the works of the Roman orator Cicero (106–43 B.C.E.).

It is possible to see in Jerome's love of the classics and in the writings and rhetoric of Augustine and Athanasius aspects of the fusion that would take place between the Greek and Roman educational tradition and the Christian religion (Documents 1.10 and 1.14). This synthesis was carried forward throughout the Middle Ages. Analyze, for example, the selections concerning the Carolingian Renaissance (Chapter 4), and the documents that illustrate the medieval university curriculum (Chapter 13).

(From Jerome, *Letters*, translated by W. H. Freemantle, *Library of Nicene and Post-Nicene Fathers*, 2nd series, vol. vi [New York: Christian Literature Co., 1893], pp. 35–36; 149. Translation modernized.)

Letter to Eustochium (Letter 22)

Many years ago, when for the sake of the kingdom of heaven I had cut myself off from home, parents, sister, relations, and—harder still—from the dainty food to which I had been accustomed, I still could not bring myself to forego the library which I had formed for myself at Rome with great care and effort. And so, miserable man that I was, I would fast only that I might afterwards read Cicero. After many nights spent in vigil, after floods of tears called from my inmost heart, after the recollection of my past sins, I would once more take up [the Roman playwright] Plautus. And when at times I returned to my right mind, and began to read the prophets, their style seemed rude and repellent. I failed to see the light with my blinded eyes; but I attributed the fault not to them, but to the sun. While the old serpent was thus making me his plaything, about the middle of Lent a deep-seated fever fell upon my weakened body, and while it destroyed my rest completely—the story seems hardly credible—it so wasted my unhappy frame that scarcely anything was left of me but skin and bone. Meantime preparations for my funeral went on; my body grew gradually colder, and the warmth of life lingered only in my throbbing breast. Suddenly I was caught up in the spirit and dragged before the judgment seat of the Judge; and here the light was so bright, and those who stood around were so radiant, that I cast myself upon the ground and did not dare to look up. Asked who and what I was I replied: "I am a Christian." But He who presided said: "You are lying, you are a follower of Cicero and

not of Christ. For 'where thy treasure is, there will thy heart be also.'" Instantly I became dumb, and amid the strokes of the lash—for He had ordered me to be beaten—I was tortured more severely still by the fire of conscience, thinking about that verse, "In the grave who shall give thee thanks?" Soon I began to cry, saying: "Have mercy upon me, O Lord: have mercy upon me." Amid the sound of the whips this cry still made itself heard. At last the bystanders, falling down in front of Him who presided, prayed that He would give me space to repent my error. He might still, they urged, inflict torture on me, should I ever again read the works of the non-Christians. Under the stress of that awful moment I should have been ready to make even still larger promises than these. Accordingly I gave an oath and called upon His name, saying: "Lord, if ever again I possess worldly books, or if ever again I read such, I have denied You." Dismissed, then, after taking this oath, I returned to the upper world, and, to the surprise of all, my eyes were so drenched with tears that my distress served to convince even the incredulous. And to demonstrate that this was no idle dream . . . I call to witness the tribunal before which I lay, and the terrible judgment which I feared. May it never, hereafter, be my lot to fall under such an inquisition! I profess that my shoulders were black and blue, that I felt the bruises long after I awoke from my sleep, and that afterwards I read the books of God with a zeal greater than I had previously given to the books of men.

Jerome eventually found an answer to his dilemma. As he explained in the following letter, it was possible to purify the classical pagan writings; they could then be read and studied with enjoyment and impunity.

Letter to Magnus (Letter 52)

You ask me at the close of your letter why it is that sometimes in my writings I quote examples from secular literature and thus defile the whiteness of the church with the foulness of heathenism. I will now briefly answer your question.

[The Apostle Paul] had read in Deuteronomy the command given by the voice of the Lord that when a captive woman had had her head shaved, her eyebrows and all her hair cut off, and her nails pared, she might then be taken as a wife. Is it surprising that I too, admiring the fairness of her form and the grace of her eloquence, desire to make that secular wisdom which is my captive and my handmaid, a matron of the true Israel? Or that shaving off and cutting away all in her that is dead whether this be idolatry, pleasure, error, or lust, I take her to myself clean and pure and beget by her servants for the Lord of Sabaoth? My efforts promote the advantage of Christ's family, my so-called defilement

with an alien increases the number of my fellow-servants.

Questions for Discussion:

1. Why did Jerome find his love of Cicero's writings and those of Plautus and other Roman authors so terrifying?
2. How does Jerome employ a metaphor to explain his use of secular literature?

1.12 Pope Leo I and the Petrine Theory

The growth of power held by the Bishop of Rome (the Pope) was gradual. In the early centuries of Christianity, the Roman pontiff exercised authority primarily in his own bishopric. By the eleventh century, however, the organization of the Church was highly developed, and the supremacy of the Bishop of Rome over ecclesiastical matters was firmly established. Furthermore, as we shall see in Chapter 6, popes such as Gregory VII claimed preeminence in secular as well as religious matters.

One of the first popes to assert this doctrine of supremacy was Leo I (440–61). In order to confirm his power and establish the authority of his successors, he frequently referred to the "Petrine Theory" in his sermons and writings. This thesis proclaims the primacy of the Bishop of Rome (the Pope), declaring that Peter, the first Bishop of Rome, was superior to the other apostles. He was chosen by Christ as the leader of the Church; hence, his actions and words held more substance than those of his fellow disciples. Furthermore, Peter's successors (to the present day) inherited this authority, and hold the same primacy over the Church and all other bishops as Peter held over the other apostles. The following document, taken from one of Leo's sermons, states the main precepts of the doctrine.

(From *A Select Library of Nicene and Post-Nicene Fathers*, 2nd series, vol. xii, edited by Philip Schaff and Henry Wace [New York: The Christian Literature Co., 1895], p. 117. Translation - modernized.)

From Christ and through Saint Peter the priesthood is handed on in perpetuity.

For the solidity of that faith which was praised in the chief of the Apostles [Peter] is perpetual: and as that remains which Peter believed in Christ, so that remains which Christ instituted in Peter. For when, as has been read in the Gospel lesson, the Lord had asked the disciples whom they believed Him to be amid the various opinions that were held, and the blessed Peter had replied saying, "You are the Christ, the Son of the living God," the Lord says, "Blessed are you, Simon Barjona [Peter] because flesh and flood has not revealed it to you, but my Father, which is in heaven. And I say to you, that you are Peter, and upon this rock will I build my church, and the gates of Hades shall not prevail against it. And I will give to you the keys of the kingdom of heaven. And whatever you shall bind on earth, shall be bound in heaven; and whatever you shall loose on earth, shall be loosed also in heaven." (Matthew xvi, 16–19)

Saint Peter's work is still carried out by his successors.

The dispensation of Truth therefore abides, and the blessed Peter persevering in the strength of the Rock, which he has received, has not abandoned the helm of the Church, which he undertook. For he was ordained before the rest in such a way that from his being called the Rock, from his being pronounced the Foundation, from his being constituted the Doorkeeper of the kingdom of heaven, from his being set as the Umpire to bind and to loose, whose judgments shall retain their validity in heaven, from all these mystical titles we might know the nature of his association with Christ. And still today he more fully and effectually performs what is entrusted to him, and carries out every part of his duty and charge in Him and with Him, through Whom he has been glorified. And so if anything is won from the mercy of God by our daily supplications [prayers], it is of his work and merits whose power lives and whose authority prevails in his See [the bishopric of Rome]. For this, dearly beloved, was gained by that confession, which inspired in the Apostle's heart by God the Father, transcended all the uncertainty of human opinions, and was empowered with the firmness of a rock, which no assaults could shake. For throughout the Church Peter daily says, "You are the Christ, the Son of the living God," and every tongue which confesses the Lord, accepts the instruction his voice conveys.

This Faith conquers the devil, and breaks the bonds of his prisoners. It uproots us from this earth and plants us in heaven, and the gates of Hades cannot prevail against it. For with such solidity is it endowed by God that the depravity of heretics cannot mar it nor the unbelief of the heathen overcome it.

Questions for Discussion:

1. What are the specific images drawn from the words of Christ that Leo I cites in this sermon to establish his argument for the supremacy of the Bishop of Rome?
2. Leo employs the words "Rock," "Foundation," "Doorkeeper," and "Umpire" to describe Peter and his successors as Pope (Bishop of Rome). What are the religious and political implications of these images?

1.13   The Election of Bishops

As early as the fourth century, church councils established ecclesiastical legislation governing the choice of bishops. The Council of Laodicaea, for example, decreed that laymen did not have the right to choose those who are to be made bishops. At the Second Council of Nicaea, held in 787, a provision was passed that nullified the election of a bishop, priest, or deacon made by the nobility. The following document, taken from the statements promulgated in 869 at the Eighth Synod of Constantinople, refined and extended the stipulations concerning appointments to bishoprics.

(From *A Source Book for Mediaeval History*, edited by Oliver J. Thatcher and Edgar H. McNeal [New York: Charles Scribner's Sons, 1905], pp. 83–84.)

No layman, whether emperor or noble, shall interfere with the election or promotion of a patriarch, metropolitan (archbishop), or bishop, lest there should arise some unseemly disturbance or contention; especially since it is not fitting that any layman or person in secular authority should have any authority in such matters . . . If any emperor or nobleman, or layman of any other rank, opposes the canonical election of any member of the clergy, let him be anathema (excommunicated) until he yields and accepts the clear will of the church in the election and ordination of the bishop.

Questions for Discussion:

1. What does this ecclesiastical legislation demonstrate about the situation of the early Church with regard to secular powers? Why did the synod believe such stipulations were necessary?
2. As shown in the document, what methods did the ecclesiastical dignitaries use to assert their power? Discuss the reasons why their threats might have been effective.

1.14   The *Life of Saint Antony* by Athanasius

During the first century after the birth of Christ, Christians worshiped in small communities. As the religion developed, however, it began to acquire a hierarchical administration, with priests, bishops, and ultimately a pope—a system that some Christians saw as a degradation of the original values espoused by Christ and his apostles. These dissenters found it impossible to practice their religion within society, and withdrew to isolated areas, often to the desert, in order to live an ascetic lifestyle and to commune more directly with God. Many scholars point out that the motivations of these hermits contained a powerful spiritual component, as the hermits sought to imitate Christ's actions and to embody His words. They may have viewed their withdrawal from society as an alternative to martyrdom—a way of giving up one's life for Christ.

One of the most famous of these "desert saints" was Saint Anthony (251–356), whose life in the wilderness was described in a work attributed to the fourth-century bishop Athanasius of Alexandria (c. 296–373), the same man mentioned in the material concerning the Council of Nicaea (see Document 1.6 in this chapter), who became a leader of Nicene Christianity. Although there is some disagreement as to the attribution, the Life *provides a view of the origins of solitary monasticism, a tradition known as "eremitic" monasticism.*

(From *St. Athanasius: Select Works and Letters, A Select Library of Nicene and Post-Nicene Fathers*, 2nd series, vol. iv [New York: The Christian Literature Co., 1892], pp. 200, 209, 210.)

So he [Anthony] was alone in the inner mountain, spending his time in prayer and discipline. And the brethren who served him asked that they might come every month and bring him olives, pulse and oil, for by now he was an old man. There then he passed his life, and endured such great wrestlings, 'Not against flesh and blood' as it is written, but against opposing demons, as we learned from those who visited him. For there they heard tumults, many voices, and, as it were, the clash of arms. At night they saw the mountain become full of wild beasts, and him also fighting as though against visible beings, and praying against them. And those who came to him he encouraged, while kneeling he contended and prayed to the Lord. Surely it was a marvelous thing that a man, alone in such a desert, feared neither the demons who rose up against him, nor the fierceness of the four-footed beasts and creeping things, for all they were so many. But in truth, as it is written, 'He trusted in the Lord as Mount Sion,' with a mind unshaken and undisturbed; so that the demons rather fled from him, and the wild beasts, as it is written, 'kept peace with him.' . . .

Anthony . . . again withdrew to his cell, and was there daily a martyr to his conscience, and contending in the conflicts of faith. And his discipline was much severer, for he was ever fasting, and he had a garment of hair on the inside, while the outside was skin, which he kept until his end. And he neither bathed his body with water to free himself from filth, nor did he ever wash his feet, nor even endure so much as to put them into water, unless compelled by necessity. Nor did any one even see him unclothed, nor his body naked at all, except after his death, when he was buried. . . .

And so for nearly twenty years he continued training himself in solitude, never going forth and but seldom seen by any. After this, when many were eager and wishful to imitate his discipline, and his acquaintances came and began to cast down and wrench off the door by force, Anthony, as from a shrine, came forth initiated in the mysteries and filled with the Spirit of God. Then for the first time he was seen outside the fort by those who came to see him. And they, when they saw him, wondered at the sight, for he had the same habit of body as before, and was neither fat, like a man without exercise, nor lean from fasting and striving with the demons, but he was just the same as they had known him before his retirement. And again his soul was free from blemish, for it was neither contracted as if by grief, nor relaxed by pleasure, nor possessed by laughter or dejection, for he was not troubled when he beheld the crowd, nor overjoyed at being saluted by so many. But he was altogether even as being guided by reason, and abiding in a natural state. Through him the Lord healed the bodily ailments of many present, and cleansed others from evil spirits. And He gave grace to Anthony in speaking, so that he consoled many that were sorrowful, and set those at variance at one, exhorting all to prefer the love of Christ before all that is in the world. And while he exhorted and advised them to remember the good things to come, and the loving-kindness of God towards us, 'Who spared not His own Son, but delivered Him up for us all,' he persuaded many to embrace the solitary life. And thus it happened in the end that cells arose even in the mountains, and the desert was colonised by monks, who came forth from their own people, and enrolled themselves for the citizenship in the heavens.

Questions for Discussion:

1. What do you view as the most difficult aspect of Anthony's chosen lifestyle?
2. What does Athanasius report to be the results of Anthony's rejection of the world and his extreme discipline?
3. Anthony is a prototype of "eremitic monasticism," characterized by the choice of a solitary life. How did he inspire others to follow his example?

INTERPRETING THE EVIDENCE

1.15   The *Rule* of Saint Benedict and the Groundplan of St. Gall

In the fourth century a different kind of monastic commitment was begun by Pachomius (d. 346), which focused on group living—a mode of religious life known as "cenobitic" monasticism. In the sixth century, as group monastic practice became more prevalent, Saint Benedict of Nursia (c. 480–547), founder of the Benedictine order, was inspired to create a "rule" for the cenobitic life; it set forth clearly the monastic precepts of poverty, chastity, obedience, and stability of place. Realizing the difficulty of the monastic commitment, he was determined that his guidelines should be reasonable; thus, as he wrote in the Prologue, his instructions ordained "nothing severe and nothing burdensome." The following excerpts from the Rule, *written about 530, provide a window into the daily lives of the men and women who devoted themselves to the monastic life. Although the accompanying groundplan (page 25) of the monastery at St. Gall, Switzerland, refers to a monastery from the ninth century, some three hundred years after Benedict's death, it offers a fine example of the way a monastic establishment was designed in order to make a self-contained and stable existence possible.*

(Document from "The *Rule* of St. Benedict," in *Select Historical Documents of the Middle Ages*, trans. and ed. by Ernest F. Henderson [London: G. Bell and Sons, Ltd., 1925], pp. 284–285; 289; 292–293; 297–298; 301–302. Translation modernized.)

Document

From the *Rule* of St. Benedict

A monastery . . . ought so to be arranged that everything necessary, that is, water, a mill, a garden, a bakery, may be made use of, and different arts [crafts] be carried on within the monastery, so that there shall be no need for the monks to wander about outside. For this is not at all good for their souls. We wish, moreover, that this Rule be read very often in the congregation, lest any of the brothers excuse himself on account of ignorance.

Concerning the daily manual labor. Idleness is the enemy of the soul. And therefore, at fixed times, the brothers ought to be occupied in manual labor; and again, at fixed times, in sacred reading. Therefore we believe that, according to this disposition, both seasons ought to be arranged; so that, from Easter until the Kalends [1st] of October, going out early, from the first until the fourth hour they shall do what labor may be necessary. Moreover, from the fourth hour until about the sixth, they shall be free for reading. After the meal of the sixth hour, rising from

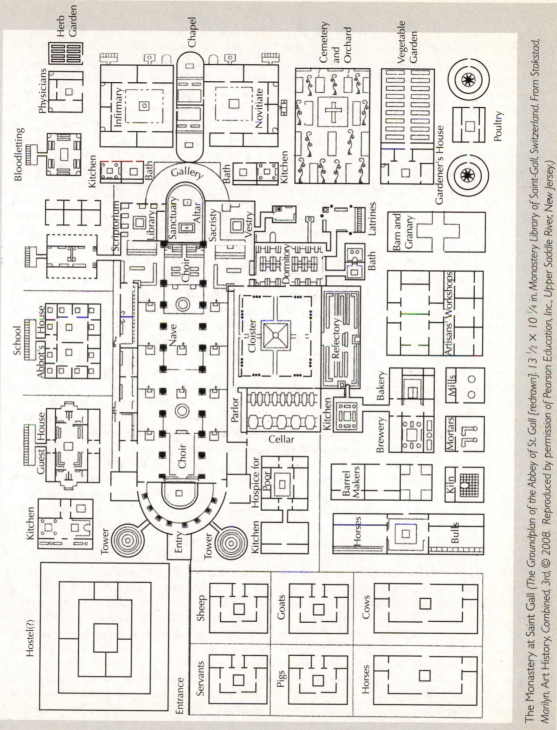

The Monastery at Saint Gall (*The Groundplan of the Abbey of St. Gall [redrawn]*. 13 ½ × 10 ¼ in. Monastery Library of Saint-Gall, Switzerland. From Stokstad, Marilyn, *Art History, Combined*, 3rd, © 2008. Reproduced by permission of Pearson Education, Inc., Upper Saddle River, New Jersey.)

(continued)

table, they shall rest silently in their beds; however, he that wishes to read may read to himself so that he will not disturb another. And the nona (the second meal) shall be eaten with more moderation about the middle of the eighth hour; and again they shall work at what is to be done until Vespers. But, if the circumstances or poverty of the place demand that they be occupied by themselves in picking fruits, they shall not be dismayed, for they are truly monks if they live by the labors of their hands, as did also our fathers and the apostles. Let all things be done with moderation, however, on account of the fainthearted. From the Kalends of October, moreover, until the beginning of Lent they shall be free for reading until the second full hour. At the second hour the tertia (morning service) shall be held, and all shall labor at the task with is enjoined upon them until the ninth. . . .

On the first day of Lent the brothers shall all receive separate books from the library, which they shall read entirely through in order. There shall be appointed one or two elders, who shall go round the monastery at the hours in which the brothers are engaged in reading, and see to it that no troublesome brother can be found who is open to idleness and trifling, and is not intent on his reading, being not only of no use to himself, but also stirring up others. If such a one—may it not happen— be found, he shall be admonished once and a second time. If he does not change, he shall be subject under the Rule to such punishment that the others may have fear. Nor shall brother join brother at unsuitable hours. Moreover, on Sunday all shall engage in reading, except those who are assigned to various duties. But if anyone is so negligent and lazy that he will not or can not read, some task shall be imposed upon him which he can do, so that he will not be idle. In the case of feeble or delicate brothers, a special labor or art is to be imposed, so that they shall neither be idle, nor so oppressed by the violence of labor as to be driven to run away. Their weakness is to be taken into consideration by the abbot.

How the monks shall sleep. They shall sleep separately in separate beds. They shall receive positions for their beds, after the manner of their characters, according to the dispensation of their abbot. If it can be done, they shall all sleep in one place. If, however, their number does not permit it, they shall rest by tens or twenties, with elders who will watch over them. A candle shall always be burning in that cell until early in the morning. They shall sleep clothed, their gowns tied with belts or with ropes; and they shall not have their knives at their sides while they sleep, lest perchance in a dream they should wound the sleepers. Furthermore, let the monks be always on the alert; and, when the signal is given, rising without delay, let them hasten to mutually prepare themselves for the service of God—with all gravity and modesty. The younger brothers shall not have beds by themselves, but interspersed among those of the older ones. And when they rise for the service of God, they shall encourage each other mutually with moderation, on account of the excuses that those who are sleepy are inclined to make.

Whether the monks should have anything of their own. More than anything else is this special vice to be cut off root and branch from the monastery, lest one should presume to give or receive anything without the order of the abbot, or should have anything of his own. He should have absolutely nothing—neither a book, nor tablets, nor a pen— nothing at all. For indeed it is not allowed to the monks to have their own bodies or wills in their own power. But everything that is necessary they must expect from the Father of the monastery (the abbot); nor is it allowable to have anything which the abbot did not give or permit. All things shall be common to all, as it is written:" Let not any man presume or call anything his own. "But if anyone shall have been discovered delighting in this most evil vice, being warned once and again, if he does not change, let him be punished.

[*Concerning meals*]. We believe that for the daily meals of the sixth as well as the ninth hour, two cooked dishes . . . are enough for all tables, so that whoever cannot eat one may partake of the other. Therefore, let two cooked dishes suffice for all the brothers, and, if it is possible to obtain apples or growing vegetables, a third may be added. One full pound of bread shall suffice for a day, whether there be one meal, or a breakfast and a supper . . . If the monks work harder than usual, it shall be in the will and power of the abbot, if it is possible, to increase the amount of food. However, surfeiting, above all things, must be guarded against, so that indigestion may never seize a monk; for nothing is so contrary to every Christian as surfeiting, as our Lord says:" Take heed to yourselves, lest your hearts be overcharged with surfeiting. "To younger boys the same quantity shall not be served, but less than that given to the older ones, moderation being observed in all things. Moreover, the eating of the flesh of quadrupeds shall be abstained from altogether by every one, except the weak and the sick.

Concerning the amount of drink. Each one has his own gift from God, the one in this way, the other in that. Therefore, it is with some hesitation that the amount of daily sustenance for others is fixed by us. Nevertheless, a hemina [almost half a liter] of wine a day is enough for each one. Those to whom God gives the ability of bearing abstinence shall know that they will have their own reward. But the prior shall judge if either the needs of the place, or labor or the heat of summer, requires more, considering in all things lest satiety or dunkenness creep in. Indeed we read that wine is not suitable for monks at all. But because, in our day, it is not possible to persuade the monks of this, let us agree at least as to the fact that we should not drink till we are sated, but sparingly. For wine can make even the wise to go astray.

[*Concerning clothing*]. Vestments shall be given to the brothers according to the quality of the places where they dwell, or the temperature of the air. For in cold regions more is required, but in warm, less. This, however, is a matter for the abbot to decide. We nevertheless think that for ordinary places there suffices for the monks a cowl and gown apiece—the cowl, in winter hairy, in summer plain or old, and a working garment, on account of their labors. As clothing for the feet, shoes and boots. Concerning the color and size of these things the monks shall not talk; but they shall be such as can be found in the province where they can be bought the most cheaply. The abbot, moreover, shall provide that the vestments are not too short for those using them, but of suitable length. And, when new ones are received, they shall always straightway return the old ones, to be kept in the vestiary on account of the poor. It is enough, moreover, for a monk to have two gowns and two cowls, on account of the nights, and on account of washing the things themselves. Everything, then, that is over this is superfluous, and ought to be removed. . . .

Trappings for the beds shall consist of a mat, a woollen covering, a woolen cloth under the pillow, and the pillow. And these beds are frequently to be searched by the abbot on account of private property, lest he find some. And, if anything is found belonging to any one which he did not receive from the abbot, he shall be subjected to the most severe discipline. And, in order that this special vice may be cut off at the roots, there shall be given by the abbot all things which are necessary, that is, a cowl, a gown, shoes, boots, a binder for the loins, a knife, a pen, a needle, a handkerchief, tablets, so that all excuse of necessity shall be removed.

Questions for Discussion:

1. Compare the *Rule* of St. Benedict with the description of the eremitic monasticism of St. Anthony (Document 1.14). What are the major differences? Are there any similarities?
2. What would you find to be the most difficult aspect of accepting this form of monasticism?
3. How did Benedict foster the education of his monks?
4. Why do you think the monks were not allowed to own anything?

The Germanic Tribal Tradition

Roman Views of the Germanic Tribes: Tacitus and Ammianus Marcellinus

Germanic people had been living beyond the boundaries of the Roman Empire for several centuries prior to the second century C.E. However, during the reign of Marcus Aurelius (121–180), Germanic tribes began to cross the Danube River, which marked the eastern border. Around this time, the barbarians, as the Romans called them, abandoned their formerly peaceful agricultural existence and began to migrate into the rich territories within the imperial boundaries. As we shall see, these incursions gradually transformed the Roman world. The next documents in this chapter offer views of the Germanic tribes by two Roman authors.

1.16   Tacitus, *Germania*

Cornelius Tacitus (c. 55–117 C.E.) was a famous Roman historian. During his childhood he lived close to the German border, and later in life probably added to his youthful impressions of the Germanic tribespeople through conversations with Roman soldiers, travelers, and merchants. His treatise, Germania, *provides, along with the works of Julius Caesar (100–44 B.C.E.), the most important early account of the Germanic tribes. His portrait of the character and habits of the Germans was not objective; it presented an idealized view of a simple and moral way of life through which Tacitus implicitly condemned the corruption and dissipation of Roman society during the first and second centuries A.D. Nonetheless, the analysis of Tacitus gives much valuable information concerning Germanic social organization. Section 13 in the document demonstrates practices such as the coming-of-age ceremony and the bonds between warriors, which some scholars have viewed as contributing to the development of the medieval system often called vassalage, discussed in Chapter 5.*

The role of women in Germanic tribal culture is also described by Tacitus; note their supportive attitudes during battle as well as their devotion to the marital bond.

(From *The Works of Tacitus*, vol. ii [New York: Harper & Brothers, 1883], pp. 295–296; 303–305; 308–310. Translation modernized.)

7. In the election of kings [the Germans] have regard to birth; in that of generals, to valor. Their kings do not have absolute or unlimited power; and their generals command less through the force of authority than of example. If they are daring, adventurous, and conspicuous in action, they procure obedience as a result of the admiration they inspire. None, however, but the priests are permitted to judge offenders, to inflict bonds or flogging, so that chastisement appears not as an act of military discipline, but as the instigation of the god whom they assume to be present with warriors. They also carry with them to battle certain images and standards taken from the sacred groves. It is a principal incentive to their courage that their squadrons and battalions are not formed by men casually collected, but by the assembling of families and clans. Their pledges also are near at hand; they have within hearing the yells of their women, and the cries of their children. These, too, are the most revered witnesses of each man's conduct, these his most liberal applauders. To their mothers and their wives they bring their wounds for relief, nor do these dread to count or to search out the gashes. The women also administer food and encouragement to those who are fighting.

8. Tradition relates, that armies beginning to give way have been rallied by the females, through the earnestness of their supplications, the interposition of their bodies, and the pictures they have drawn of impending slavery, a calamity which these people bear with more fear for their women than themselves; so that those states which have been obliged to give among their hostages the daughters of noble families, are the most effectually bound to fidelity. They even think that sanctity and prescience are inherent in the female sex; and therefore neither despise their counsels, nor disregard their responses.

13. The Germans transact no business, public or private, without being armed; but it is not customary for any person to assume arms till the state has approved his ability to use them. Then, in the

midst of the assembly, either one of the chiefs, or the father, or a relation, equips the youth with a shield and spear. This corresponds with the manly gown [the Roman toga]; this is the first honor conferred on youth. Before this they are considered as part of a household, afterward, as a member of the state. The role of chieftain is given to mere lads, whose descent is eminently illustrious, or whose fathers have performed signal services to the public; they are associated, however, with those of mature strength, who have already been declared capable of service; nor do they blush to be seen in the rank of companions. For the state of companionship itself has its several degrees, determined by the judgment of him whom they follow; and there is a great rivalry among the companions, as to which shall possess the highest place in the favor of their chief; and among the chiefs, which shall excel in the number and valor of his companions. It is their dignity, their strength, to be always surrounded with a large body of select youth, an ornament in peace, a bulwark in war. And not in his own country alone, but among the neighboring states, the fame and glory of each chief consists in being distinguished for the number and bravery of his companions. Such chiefs are courted by embassies, distinguished by presents, and often by their reputation alone decide a war.

14. In the field of battle, it is disgraceful for the chief to be surpassed in valor; it is disgraceful for the companions not to equal their chief; but it is reproach and infamy during the rest of life to retreat from the field surviving him. To aid, to protect him, and to place their own gallant actions to the account of his glory, is their first and most sacred engagement. The chiefs fight for victory; the companions for their chief. If their native country is long sunk in peace and inaction, many of the young nobles repair to some other state then engaged in war. For, besides that repose is unwelcome to their race, and toils and perils afford them a better opportunity of distinguishing themselves, they are unable, without war and violence, to maintain a large train of followers. The companion requires from the liberality of his chief, the warlike steed, the bloody and conquering spear; and in place of pay he expects to be supplied with a table, homely indeed, but plentiful. The funds for this munificence must be found in war and rapine; nor are they so easily persuaded to cultivate the earth, and await the produce of the seasons, as to challenge the foe, and expose themselves to wounds; nay, they even think it base and spiritless to earn by sweat what they might purchase with blood.

18. The matrimonial bond is, nevertheless, strict and severe among them; nor is there any thing in their manners more commendable than this. Almost singly among the barbarians, they content themselves with one wife; a very few of them excepted, who, not through incontinence, but because their alliance is solicited on account of their rank, practice polygamy. The wife does not bring a dowry to her husband, but receives one from him. The parents and relations assemble, and pass their approbation on the presents—presents not adapted to please a female taste, or decorate the bride, but oxen, a caparisoned steed, a shield, spear, and sword. By virtue of these, the wife is espoused; and she in her turn makes a present of some arms to her husband. This they consider as the firmest bond of union; these, the sacred mysteries, the conjugal deities. That the woman may not think herself excused from exertions of fortitude, or exempt from the casualties of war, she is admonished by the very ceremonial of her marriage, that she comes to her husband as a partner in toils and dangers; to suffer and to dare equally with him, in peace and in war: this is indicated by the yoked oxen, the harnessed steed, the offered arms. Thus she is to live; thus to die. She receives what she is to return inviolate and honored to her children; what her daughters-in-law are to receive, and again transmit to her grandchildren.

19. They live, therefore, fenced around with chastity, corrupted by no seductive spectacles, no convivial incitements. Men and women are alike unacquainted with clandestine correspondence. Adultery is extremely rare among so numerous a people. Its punishment is instant, and at the pleasure of the husband. He cuts off the hair of the offender, strips her, and in presence of her relations expels her from his house, and pursues her with stripes through the whole village. Nor is any indulgence shown to a prostitute. Neither beauty, youth, nor riches can procure her a husband, for none there looks on vice with a smile, or calls mutual seduction the way of the world. Still more exemplary is the practice of those states in which none but virgins marry, and the

expectations and wishes of a wife are at once brought to a period. Thus, they take one husband as one body and one life; that no thought, no desire, may extend beyond him; and he may he loved not only as their husband, but as their marriage. To limit the increase of children, or put to death any of the later progeny, is accounted infamous, and good habits have there more influence than good laws elsewhere.

20. In every house the children grow up, thinly and meanly clad, to that bulk of body and limb which we behold with wonder. Every mother suckles her own children, and does not deliver them into the hands of servants and nurses. No indulgence distinguishes the young master from the slave. They lie together amidst the same cattle, upon the same ground, till age separates, and valor marks out, the freeborn. The youths partake late of the pleasures of love, and hence pass the age of puberty unexhausted; nor are the virgins hurried into marriage; the same maturity, the same full growth, is required; the sexes unite equally matched, and robust; and the children inherit the vigor of their parents. Children are regarded with equal affection by their maternal uncles as by their fathers: some even consider this as the more sacred bond of consanguinity, and prefer it in the requisition of hostages, as if it held the mind by a firmer tie, and the family by a more extensive obligation. A person's own children, however, are his heirs and successors, and no wills are made. If there be no children, the next in order of inheritance are brothers, paternal and maternal uncles. The more numerous are a man's relations and kinsmen, the more comfortable is his old age; nor is it here any advantage to be childless.

Questions for Discussion:

1. What customs and practices characterize the Germanic warriors in contrast to the Romans?
2. Some scholars believe the descriptions of Tacitus may be read as a condemnation of Roman society. Assume this point of view and discuss the various aspects of Roman life he is criticizing.
3. What specific qualities does Tacitus praise when discussing Germanic women? What do his remarks imply about Roman matrons?

1.17   Ammianus Marcellinus, *History of the Roman Empire*

Ammianus Marcellinus (c. 330–395) was a Roman historian whose History of the Roman Empire *began with the accession of the emperor Nerva in 96, the point at which the* Annals *of Tacitus ends. Only the final eighteen books of his work survive; these deal with the history of Rome from 353 to 378, and cover events that took place during the author's lifetime. Ammianus, in addition to presenting facts about historical occurrences, included discussions of many geographical and ethnographical topics. One of these digressions describes the character and physical appearance of the Gauls—Celtic people living in a broad area that included present-day France, Germany west of the Rhine River, Belgium, the Netherlands, and northern Italy.*

(From *The Later Roman Empire* by Ammianus Marcellinus, selected and translated by Walter Hamilton, introduction and notes by Andrew Wallace-Hadrill (Penguin Classics, 1986). Translation copyright © Walter Hamilton, 1986. Introduction and Notes copyright © Andrew Wallace-Hadrill, 1986.)

Almost all Gauls are tall and fair-skinned, with reddish hair. Their savage eyes make them fearful objects; they are eager to quarrel and excessively truculent. When in the course of a dispute any of them calls in his wife, a creature with gleaming eyes much stronger than her husband, they are more than a match for a whole group of foreigners; especially when the woman, with swollen neck and gnashing teeth, swings her great white arms and begins to deliver a rain of punches mixed with kicks, like missiles launched by the twisted strings of a catapult. The voices of most sound alarming and menacing, whether they are angry or the reverse, but all alike are clean and neat, and throughout the whole region, and especially in Aquitaine, you will hardly find a man or woman, however poor, who is dirty and in rags, as you would elsewhere. They are fit for service in war at any age; old men embark upon a campaign with as much spirit as those in their prime; their limbs are hardened by the cold and by incessant toil, and there is no danger that they are not ready to defy. No one here ever cuts off his thumb to escape military service, as happens in Italy, where they have a special name for such malingerers *(murci)*. As a race they are given to drink, and are fond of a number of liquors that resemble wine; some of the baser sort wander about aimlessly in a fuddled state of perpetual intoxication, a condition which Cato[15] described as a kind of self-induced madness. There seems then to be some truth in what Cicero[16] said in his defence of Fonteius, that 'henceforth the Gauls will take their drink with water, a practice which they used to think equivalent to taking poison'.

Questions for Discussion:

1. Compare the views of Tacitus and Ammianus Marcellinus concerning Germanic women. How do they differ? Are there any similarities?
2. Is there an implied criticism of the Romans in the selection by Ammianus Marcellinus?

1.18   Treaty with the Vandals (271)

As mentioned earlier, the Germanic tribes had been living on the edges of the Roman Empire for centuries, and occasionally they made threatening incursions. This document, and the two that follow, discuss the military interactions between the Romans and the Germanic tribes during the third, fourth, and fifth centuries.

In 271, early in the reign of Aurelian (270–275), the Vandals crossed the Danube River, and were defeated by the Roman army. A treaty was made with the tribe, which promised two thousand Vandal cavalrymen to serve with the Romans; the remaining warriors would return to their homeland. The fact that the Romans were willing to sign such a pact with the tribe indicates that they were beginning to think of the Germans as a "state" that could be dealt with through a treaty, rather than regarding them simply as "barbarians." The circumstances were described by the third-century Greek historian, Dexippus.

(From *Roman Civilization, Selected Readings, vol II: The Empire,* 3rd Edition, ed. by Naphtali Lewis and Meyer Reinhold. Copyright © 1955 Columbia University Press. Reprinted with permission of the publisher.)

. . . the Vandals, after suffering a smashing defeat at the hands of the Romans, sent an embassy to the Romans to negotiate an armistice and a treaty. . . . The Roman soldiers were . . . assembled, and were asked by the king what they thought the better course in the existing circumstances. Deciding wisely . . . to preserve their present good fortune, they all voted for an end to the war, indicating their desire with a shout. . . .

The kings and chieftains of the barbarians came and, as they had been ordered, gave hostages not inferior to themselves in rank or station (their kings each give their sons as hostages without hesitation) . . . Thus they came to an agreement, and the treaty was drawn up. Thereafter two thousand Vandal cavalrymen would serve with the Romans, part of them drafted from the ranks and enrolled in this allied force, the rest volunteers undertaking military service of their own accord. The rest of the Vandal horde would return home, and the Roman governor would provide them with a market hard by the Danube.

Questions for Discussion:

1. What advantages did the Romans gain through this treaty?
2. Did the Vandals obtain any privileges?

[15]Cato "the Younger" (95–46 B.C.E.) was a Roman statesman noted for his self-discipline and moral integrity.
[16]Cicero (c. 106–43 B.C.E.) was a Roman senator and the most famous orator in Roman history. Ammianus Marcellinus frequently quoted his words or referred to his orations in his *History.*

1.19   The Battle of Adrianople (378)

During the reign of the emperor Valens (r. 364–378), the Roman army suffered a stunning defeat at the Battle of Adrianople (see the map on page 34). Scholars debate the reasons for the Gothic victory, which may have been the result of bad leadership, lack of strong morale on the part of the Roman forces, or simply the numerical superiority of the Goths. Valens was killed in the fray, losing to an army of Goths led by Fritegern, who had obtained permission from the emperor two years earlier to settle in Roman territory. The battle scene is described in the following selection by Ammianus Marcellinus.

(From *The Later Roman Empire* by Ammianus Marcellinus, selected and translated by Walter Hamilton, introduction and notes by Andrew Wallace-Hadrill (Penguin Classics, 1986). Translation copyright © Walter Hamilton, 1986. Introduction and Notes copyright © Andrew Wallace-Hadrill, 1986.)

Amid the clashing of arms and weapons on every side . . . our retreating troops rallied with shouts of mutual encouragement. But, as fighting spread like fire and numbers of them were transfixed by arrows and whirling javelins, they lost heart. Then the opposing lines came into collision like ships of war and pushed each other to and fro, heaving under the reciprocal motion like the waves of the sea. Our left wing penetrated as far as the very wagons, and would have gone further if it had received any support, but it was abandoned by the rest of the cavalry, and under pressure of numbers gave way and collapsed like a broken dyke. This left the infantry unprotected and so closely huddled together that a man could hardly wield his sword or draw back his arm once he had stretched it out. Dust rose in such clouds as to hide the sky, which rang with frightful shouts. In consequence it was impossible to see the enemy's missiles in flight and dodge them; all found their mark and dealt death on every side. The barbarians poured on in huge columns, trampling down horse and man and crushing our ranks so as to make an orderly retreat impossible. Our men were too close-packed to have any hope of escape; so they resolved to die like heroes, faced the enemy's swords, and struck back at their assailants. On both sides helmets and breast-plates were split in pieces by blows from the battle-axe. You might see a lion-hearted savage, who had been hamstring or had lost his right hand or been wounded in the side, grinding his clenched teeth and casting defiant glances around in the very throes of death. In this mutual slaughter so many were laid low that the field was covered with the bodies of the slain, while the groans of the dying and severely wounded filled all who heard them with abject fear.

In this scene of total confusion the infantry, worn out by toil and danger, had no strength or sense left to form a plan. Most had had their spears shattered in the constant collisions, so they made do with their drawn swords and plunged into the dense masses of the foe, regardless of their lives and aware that there was no hope of escape. The ground was so drenched with blood that they slipped and fell, but they strained every nerve to sell their lives dearly, and faced their opponents with such resolution that some perished at the hands of their own comrades. In the end, when the whole field was one dark pool of blood and they could see nothing but heaps of slain wherever they turned their eyes, they trampled without scruple on the lifeless corpses. . . .

At last a moonless night brought an end to these irreparable losses, which cost Rome so dear.

Questions for Discussion:

1. Discuss the historical writing style of Ammianus Marcellinus. Does his mode of expression differ from that of the other historians we have been studying? In what ways?
2. What do you think the attitudes of the Romans and the Germans would have been following the battle?

Chapter 2

✦

The Heirs of Rome: Germanic Kingdoms and the Byzantine Empire

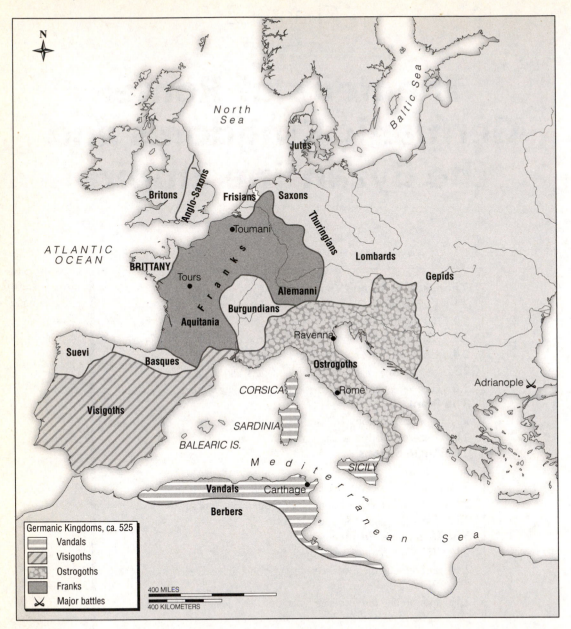

N

North Sea

Jutes

ATLANTIC OCEAN

Baltic Sea

Britons   Anglo-Saxons   Frisians   Saxons

Thuringians

Toumani

F r a n k s

Lombards

BRITTANY   Tours

Alemanni

Gepids

Burgundians

Aquitania

Ravenna

Suevi

Basques

Ostrogoths

Adrianople ✂

CORSICA

Rome

Visigoths

SARDINIA

BALEARIC IS.

M e d i t e r r a n e a n   S e a

SICILY

Vandals   Carthage

Berbers

Germanic Kingdoms, ca. 525

	Vandals
	Visigoths
	Ostrogoths
	Franks
✂	Major battles

400 MILES

400 KILOMETERS

Map of Europe, Showing Successor Kingdoms, East and West. (From Levack et al., *The West*, combined vol., 2nd ed., p. 193.)

During the fifth century the Roman Empire in the west was replaced by kingdoms created by Germanic tribes, most importantly the Ostrogoths in Italy, the Visigoths in Spain, the Franks in present-day France and Germany, and the Anglo-Saxons in the British Isles. All four were influenced by Roman traditions to one degree or another, although the Ostrogoths made the most significant effort to retain Roman customs and governance.

This is evident in the document taken from The Origin and Deeds of the Goths, *by Jordanes, and in the letters written by Cassiodorus on behalf of the Ostrogothic king, Theodoric. (Documents 2.1 and 2.2) The Greco-Roman intellectual heritage was prized by Theodoric, who patronized several influential scholars, including Boethius as well as Cassiodorus. Their writings are represented by Documents 2.3 and 2.4. These men were devoted to Greek philosophy and the Roman educational system, as their works attest. They are responsible, in many ways, for the continuation of the Roman Trivium (grammar, rhetoric, and logic) and the Quadrivium (music, arithmetic, geometry, and astronomy), which formed the curriculum of monastic schools (see Chapter 4), and provided the liberal arts program in the universities of the High Middle Ages, which will be discussed in Chapter 13.*

The Visigoths, who settled in the Iberian peninsula, were less interested in the preservation of Roman tradition than some of the other tribes. However, the works of several sixth-century scholars, including Isidore of Seville's The History of the Goths, *bear witness to a continuing tradition of scholarship and devotion to the preservation of history.*

Visigothic kings of the mid-seventh century felt a need to write down a code of laws that had been passed down by oral tradition before that time. Building upon many provisions of Roman law, the Forum Judicum, *or Visigothic Code, provided a legal framework for many aspects of society. The selections included here provide a small sample of legal measures regarding the treatment of women.*

The tribe known as the Franks established a kingdom that survived longer than the other Germanic successor states. Their first important king was Clovis, who became a Christian in the late fifth century. His conversion experience is described in The History of the Franks *by Gregory of Tours. Clovis also enacted a law code, sections of which appear in Document 2.8, that dealt primarily with personal, rather than public, law. It is interesting to note the provisions that pertain to the treatment of women in the Germanic tribes.*

The warrior society is described in dramatic detail by the author of the famous epic poem Beowulf. *In this anonymous source it is possible to see the importance of personal loyalty between the warriors and their leader, which is a characteristic of the fully developed system of vassalage, a quality emphasized in the Salic Laws presented in the previous document.*

Beginning in the fifth century, the Anglo-Saxons migrated to the British Isles from Scandinavia, where they eventually founded kingdoms. Originally devoted to pagan gods, several of their kings were converted to Christianity as a result of missionary activity during the late sixth and early seventh centuries; some scholars also attribute their conversions to the influence of the queens, such as Ethelburga. This period of Christianization was discussed by Bede, known as "the Venerable," in the History of the English Church and People. *The letter from Pope Boniface to Queen Ethelburga included in this chapter is taken from this work (Document 2.11).*

Anglo-Saxon England was not the only area of the British Isles to experience conversion by monks. The monastic movement in Ireland was also important, not only in the Christianization of their own country, but also in the conversion of Europe. One of the most important of the Irish monks was St. Columban (543–615), who traveled to Gaul and later to Italy; he founded several monasteries in both areas. Document 2.12, taken from the seventh-century Life of St. Columban *by the monk Jonas, describes his experiences in establishing religious practice and monasticism on the Continent.*

The eastern half of the Roman Empire, which resulted from the division of Diocletian described in Document 1.1, was known as the Byzantine Empire. Because of a vibrant economy, strong leadership, and a geographical location that was somewhat protected from the Germanic tribal migrations, this part of the empire continued to thrive. The most important Byzantine emperor of the late-antique world was Justinian, who made several significant contributions to medieval culture. The most far-reaching of these was the Corpus Iuris Civilis, *or Body of Civil Law, a compilation and restructuring of Roman law combined with his own legal edicts. Justinian, like Constantine, was a donor to the Church, and one of the most magnificent buildings in the world, Hagia Sophia, is a result of his patronage. The first "Interpreting the Evidence" feature (Document 2.14) contains a photograph of the church and a description by Justinian's historian, Procopius.*

Justinian was married to a fascinating woman, Theodora, whose character, and that of the emperor, may be viewed in two pairs of sources—visual and biographical. The visual sources are two marvelous mosaics from the church of San Vitale in Ravenna, which was Justinian's capital in northern Italy. These present the emperor and empress formally, with their couriers and dignitaries, while documents such as the Secret History *by Procopius offer a salacious portrait of their personalities.*

In this chapter it is possible to see various aspects of life in the late-antique world, and to observe the intertwining of influences that would form medieval civilization—the Greco-Roman tradition, Germanic tribal customs, and Christianity.

The Ostrogoths and Visigoths

2.1   Jordanes, *The Origins and Deeds of the Goths*

Jordanes was a sixth-century Christian historian of Germanic origin, who may have been a bishop. He wrote The Origin and Deeds of the Goths *(the* Getica*) in Constantinople in 551 or 552, during the reign of Justinian, to be discussed later in this chapter. His work is a shorter version of the* Gothic History *by Theodoric's courtier and secretary Cassiodorus, which is now lost. The following excerpt discusses the rise to power of the Ostrogoth Theodoric, often known as "Theodoric the Great," and his defeat of Odoacer (c. 434–493), who was the first Germanic ruler of the western empire. The selection also demonstrates the breadth of Germanic tribal activity in the world of late antiquity.*

(From Jordanes, *The Origin and Deeds of the Goths*, trans. Charles C. Mierow [Princeton, 1908], pp. 89–90, 92–95.)

After a certain time, when the wintry cold was at hand, the river Danube was frozen over as usual. For a river like this freezes so hard that it will support like a solid rock an army of foot-soldiers and wagons and carts and whatever vehicles there may be, nor is there need of skiffs and boats. So when Thiudimer [c.413–c.474], king of the Goths, saw that it was frozen, he led his army across the Danube and appeared unexpectedly to the Suavi from the rear . . . With the Suavi[1] there were the Alamanni,[2] then their confederates, who also ruled the Alpine heights, from which several streams flow into the Danube, pouring in with a great rushing sound. Into a place thus fortified King Thiudimer led his army in the wintertime and conquered, plundered and almost subdued the race of the Suavi as well as the Alamanni, who were mutually banded together. From there he returned as victor to his own home in Pannonia [today the southwestern part of Hungary] and joyfully received his son Theodoric [c. 454–526], once given as hostage to Constantinople and now sent back by the Emperor Leo [401–474] with great gifts. Now Theodoric had reached man's estate, for he was eighteen years of age and his boyhood was ended. So he summoned certain of his father's adherents and took to himself from the people his friends and retainers, almost six thousand men. With these he crossed the Danube, without his father's knowledge, and marched against Babai, king of the Sarmatians[3] [?–472], who had just won a victory over Camundus, a general of the Romans, and was ruling with insolent pride. Theodoric came upon him and killed him, and taking as booty his slaves and treasure, returned victorious to his father. Next he invaded the city of Singidunum, which the Sarmatians themselves had seized, and did not return it to the Romans, but reduced it to his own sway . . .

Shortly before Thiudimer died, he called the Goths together, and appointed his son Theodoric as heir of his kingdom.

When the Emperor Zeno [r. 474–491] heard that Theodoric had been appointed king over his own people, he received the news with pleasure and invited him to come and visit him in the city, appointing an escort of honor. Receiving Theodoric with all due respect, he placed him among the princes of his palace. After some time Zeno increased his dignity by adopting him as his son-at-arms and gave him a triumph in the city at his expense. Also, Theodoric was made Consul Ordinary, which is well known to be the supreme good and highest honor in the world. Nor was this all, for Zeno set up before the royal palace an equestrian statue to the glory of this great man.

Now while Theodoric was in alliance by treaty with the Empire of Zeno and was himself enjoying every comfort in the city, he heard that his tribe, dwelling as we have said in Illyricum [present-day Dalmatia], was not altogether satisfied or content. So he chose rather to seek a living by his own exertions, after the manner customary to his race, rather than to enjoy the advantages of the Roman Empire in luxurious ease while his tribe lived in want. After pondering

---

[1] Suavi were Germanic people living between the Elbe and Oder Rivers.
[2] Alamanni were Germanic people living around the Main River, and later in Alsace and northern Switzerland.

[3] Sarmatians were people of ancient Iranian origin who lived in the area of the Ural Mountains.

these matters, he said to the Emperor: "Though I lack nothing in serving your Empire, yet if Your Piety thinks it worthy, be pleased to hear the desire of my heart." And when as usual he had been granted permission to speak freely, he said: "The western country, long ago governed by the rule of your ancestors and predecessors, and that city which was the head and mistress of the world,—why is it now shaken by the tyranny of the Torcilingi[4] and the Rugi[5]? Send me there with my race. Thus if you but say the word, you may be freed from the burden of expense here, and, if by the Lord's help I shall conquer, the fame of Your Piety shall be glorious there. For it is better that I, your servant and your son, should rule that kingdom, receiving it as a gift from you if I conquer, than that one whom you do not recognize should oppress your Senate with his tyrannical yoke and a part of the republic with slavery. For if I prevail, I shall retain it as your grant and gift; if I am conquered, Your Piety will lose nothing—no, as I have said, it will save the expense I now entail." Although the Emperor was grieved that he should go, when he heard this he granted what Theodoric asked, for he was unwilling to cause him sorrow. He sent him forth enriched by great gifts and commended to his charge the Senate and the Roman People.

Theodoric departed from the royal city and returned to his own people. In company with the whole tribe of the Goths, who gave him their unanimous consent, he set out for Hesperia [Italy]. He went in straight march through Sirmium [present-day Serbia] to the places bordering on Pannonia [present-day Hungary] and, advancing into the territory of Venetia [northeastern Italy and western Slovenia] as far as the bridge of the Sontius [present-day Isonzo] River, encamped there. When he had halted there for some time to rest the bodies of his men and pack-animals, Odoacer [King of Italy] [c. 433–493] sent an armed force against him, which he met on the plains of Verona and destroyed with great slaughter. Then he broke camp and advanced

through Italy with greater boldness. Crossing the river Po, he pitched camp near the royal city of Ravenna, about the third milestone from the city in the place called Pineta. When Odoacer saw this, he fortified himself within the city. He frequently harassed the army of the Goths at night, sallying forth stealthily with his men, and this not once or twice, but often; and thus he struggled for almost three whole years. But he labored in vain, for all Italy at last called Theodoric its lord and the Empire obeyed his nod. But Odoacer, with his few adherents and the Romans who were present, suffered daily from war and famine in Ravenna. Since he accomplished nothing, he sent an embassy and begged for mercy. Theodoric first granted it and afterwards deprived him of his life.

It was in the third year after his entrance into Italy, as we have said, that Theodoric, by advice of the Emperor Zeno, laid aside the garb of a private citizen and the dress of his race and assumed a costume with a royal mantle, since he had now become the ruler over both Goths and Romans. He sent an embassy to Lodoin, king of the Franks, and asked for his daughter Audefleda [d. 526] in marriage. Lodoin freely and gladly gave her, and also his sons Celdebert and Heldebert and Thiudebert, believing that by this alliance a league would be formed and they would be associated with the race of the Goths. But that union was of no avail for peace and harmony, for they fought fiercely with each other again and again for the lands of the Goths; but never did the Goths yield to the Franks while Theodoric lived.

Questions for Discussion:

1. Theodoric the Ostrogoth was devoted to the preservation of Rome. Does this selection by Jordanes provide any clues as to why this became a central concern of his monarchy?

2. What methods did Theodoric use to consolidate his kingdom and establish his control?

3. How did Theodoric use "marriage diplomacy" to unite the tribes he conquered? Do you think this would have been an effective tool? Why or why not?

---

[4]Torcilingi were Germanic people living first in Gaul and later in Italy. Their leader was Odovacar.
[5]Rugi were Germanic people living around Pomerania and the Oder River.

2.2   Cassiodorus, *Letters*

After becoming king, Theodoric was determined to estab-
lish a stable and civilized government that would preserve
many aspects of Roman rule and culture, while encouraging
peaceful cohabitation between the Goths and the Roman
people. It is important to note that Theodoric was a believer
in the Arian form of Christianity (see Document 1.6),
although he fostered congenial relationships with the
Nicene Christians in a further attempt to preserve peace in
his kingdom. He also extended toleration to the Jews, al-
lowing them to rebuild their synagogue, and established
protection for their places of worship. These intentions are
evident in the many letters written to various dignitaries
by his councilor Cassiodorus (c. 485–c. 580). The first
letter included here concerns programs for the beautification
and preservation of the city of Rome. The second is a
proclamation to the Goths encouraging valor as they pre-
pare for war against the Gauls, and the third selection,
written to the Senate of Rome, encourages and praises the
peaceful relationship between the Romans and the Goths.
The final letter demonstrates that Theodoric was also
dedicated to preserving the rights of the Jews to worship
according to their beliefs.

(From *The Letters of Cassiodorus,* trans. Thomas Hodgkin [London:
Henry Frowde, 1886], pp. 156–158, 179–180, 185–186, 286.)

A. King Theodoric to Maximilian, *vir illustris*[6] and Andreas, *vir spectabilis*[7]

If the people of Rome will beautify their city we will
help them. Institute a strict audit (of which no one
need be ashamed) of the money given by us to the
different workmen for the beautification of the city.
See that we are receiving money's worth for the
money spent. If there is embezzlement anywhere,
cause the funds so embezzled to be disgorged. We
expect the Romans to help from their own resources
in this patriotic work, and certainly not to intercept
our contributions for the purpose. The wandering
birds love their own nests; the beasts hasten to their
own lodgings in the brake; the voluptuous fish,
roaming the fields of ocean, returns to its own well-
known cavern. How much more should Rome be
loved by her children!

B. King Theodoric to all the Goths

To the Goths a hint of war rather than persuasion to
strife is needed, since a warlike race such as ours delights in proving its courage. In truth, he shuns no
labor who hungers for the renown of valor. Therefore
with the help of God, whose blessing alone brings
prosperity, we plan to send our army to the Gauls[8]
for the common benefit of all, that you may have an
opportunity of promotion, and we the power of testing your merits; for in time of peace the courage
which we admire lies hidden, and when men have no
chance of showing what is in them, their relative
merits are concealed. We have therefore given our
Sajo[9] Nandius, instructions to warn you that, on the
eighth day before the kalends [first] of next July, you
move forward to the campaign in the name of God,
sufficiently equipped, according to your old custom,
with horses, arms, and every requisite for war. Thus
will you show at the same time that the old valor of
your fathers still dwells in your hearts, and also successfully perform your King's command. Bring forth
your young men for the discipline of Mars. Let them
see you do deeds which they may love to tell of to
their children. For an art not learned in youth is an
art missing in our riper years. The very hawk, whose
food is plunder, thrusts her still weak and tender
young ones out of the nest, that they may not become accustomed to soft repose. She strikes the lin-
gerers with her wings; she forces her callow young to
fly, that they may prove to be such in the future as
her maternal fondness can be proud of. Do you therefore, lofty by nature, and stimulated yet more by the
love of fame, endeavor to leave such sons behind you
as your fathers have left in leaving you.

---

[6]*Vir illustris* was a term for the man who held the highest rank in
the Senate.
[7]*Vir spectabilis* was a man holding a slightly lower rank than *vir
illustris*.

[8]Gauls were continental Celtic people living in the area of France,
Belgium, Switzerland, and northern Italy.
[9]A *sajo* was a Gothic officer whose duty was to see that the king's
mandates were carried out.

C. King Theodoric to the Senate of the City of Rome

. . . We especially like to remember how in the assignment of the [Gothic] Thirds he [Liberius, the Praetorian Prefect] joined both the possessions and the hearts of Goths and Romans alike. For whereas men often come into collision on account of their being neighbors, with these men the common holding of their farms proved in practice a reason for concord. Thus it has happened that while the two nations have been living in common they have concurred in the same desires. Lo! a new fact, and one wholly laudable. The friendship of the lords has been joined with the division of the soil; amity has grown out of the loss of the Provincials, and by the land a defender has been gained whose occupation of part guarantees the quiet enjoyment of the whole. One law includes them; one equal administration rules them, for it is necessary that sweet affection should grow between those who always keep the boundaries which have been allotted them.

D. King Theodoric to the Jews of Milan

"For the preservation of *civilitas* the benefits of justice are not to be denied even to those who are recognized as wandering from the right way in matters of faith. You complain that you are often wantonly attacked, and that the rights pertaining to your synagogue are disregarded. We therefore give you the needed protection of our Mildness, and ordain that no ecclesiastic shall trench on the privileges of your synagogue, nor mix himself up in your affairs. But let the two communities keep apart, as their faiths are different: you on your part not attempting to do anything *incivile* against the rights of the said Church. The law of thirty years' prescription, which is a world-wide custom, shall continue for your benefit also."

"But why, oh Jew, dost thou petition for peace and quietness on earth when thou canst not find that rest which is eternal?"

Questions for Discussion:

1. Discuss the various measures Theodoric employed to preserve the beauty and infrastructure of Rome.
2. How did Theodoric appeal to his people in order to rouse them against the tribe of the Gauls?
3. Why do you think Theodoric was willing to extend toleration to the Jews?

2.3   Cassiodorus, *An Introduction to Divine and Human Readings*

The lasting influence of Cassiodorus extends far beyond his role as minister and councilor in Theodoric's government. As a young man he had dreamed of founding a school that would combine Christian teachings with the classical pagan curriculum. His role at court was marginalized in the final years of Theodoric's reign, and after the king's death he retired from political life. He then established the famous monastery of Vivarium on his family estates in southern Italy, recognizing that the contemplative leisure of monastic existence was ideal for serious study. His work, An Introduction to Divine and Human Readings, *offers a curriculum that combines Holy Scripture with secular knowledge. This framework for scholarly education became* the standard educational plan for the medieval period, as will be seen in Chapters 4 and 13, and his program of preserving and transmitting the writings of the ancient world was widely adopted in the monastic schools of Europe. Cassiodorus, along with Boethius (see Document 2.4), was responsible for the preservation of the Roman curriculum: the Trivium (grammar, logic, and rhetoric) and the Quadrivium (astronomy, music, arithmetic, and geometry). The excerpts printed here demonstrate his commitment to the synthesis of classical and Christian scholarship.*

(From Cassiodorus, *An Introduction to Divine and Human Readings*, trans. by Leslie Webber Jones [New York: Octagon Books, Inc., 1966], pp. 127–129.)

On Figures of Speech and the Liberal Arts

1. We have decided that you ought to be cautioned about this matter too: since we can understand much in sacred literature as well as in the most learned interpreters through figures of speech, much through definitions, much through the art of grammar, much through the art of rhetoric, much through dialectics, much through the science of arithmetic, much through music, much through the science of geometry, much through astronomy, it is not unprofitable in the book which follows to touch briefly upon the elements of instruction laid down by secular teachers, that is, upon the arts and the sciences, together with their divisions, in order that those who have acquired knowledge of this sort may have a brief review and those who perhaps have been unable to read widely may learn something from the compendious discussion. Beyond any doubt knowledge of these matters, as it seemed to our Fathers, is useful and not to be avoided, since one finds this knowledge diffused everywhere in sacred literature, as it were in the origin of universal and perfect wisdom. When these matters have been restored to sacred literature and taught in connection with it, our capacity for understanding will be helped in every way.

2. May the task of the ancients be our task, in order that we may unfold very briefly in our second book, as has already been stated, what they set forth at great length in many codices; and may we with laudable devotion recall to the service of truth what they diverted for the practice of subtlety, in order that the learning which was thereby secretly removed may be honorably restored to the service of upright understanding. Surely in my opinion it is a necessary task, but in view of the difficulty an exceedingly arduous one, to try to describe the very copious sources of divine and human letters in two books; and I must quote those well-known lines of Sedulius [lived c. 470 A.D.] on this subject:

I ask great gifts, but thou know'st how to give them;
The less one hopes to get, the more thou'rt grieved.

What is Read by Those who Cannot Enter upon Philosophical Writings

1. But if certain simple-minded brothers cannot understand the excerpts which have been gathered in the following book, since practically all conciseness brings obscurity, let it be enough for them to examine briefly the divisions, usefulness, and excellence of these studies, in order that they may be seized with an eager striving of their minds to acquire a knowledge of the divine law. Through the various holy Fathers they will discover the source from which they can satisfy their ardent longing to the fullest extent. Let there be merely a genuine inclination to read and a sober wish to understand, and then may a suitable assiduity bring learning to those who were frightened at the start by the profundity of the text.

2. We know, however, that intelligence is not placed in letters alone, but that God gives perfect wisdom "to everyone according as he will." For if knowledge of good things were present in letters alone, surely unlettered men would not possess suitable wisdom. Since, however, many illiterate persons attain true understanding and feel an upright faith instilled from heaven, there is no doubt that God grants to pure and devout feelings that which He considers is advantageous to them. For it is written, "Blessed is the man whom thou shalt instruct, O Lord: and shalt teach him out of thy law." With good deeds, therefore, and with constant prayer we must seek to attain in the company of the Lord the true faith and the very holy works in which our everlasting life lies. For one reads: "Except the Lord build the house, they labor in vain that build it."

3. Nevertheless, the very holy Fathers have not decreed that the study of secular letters should be scorned, for these letters are not the least important means of instructing our minds in the understanding of the Sacred Scriptures; they have decreed, on the other hand, that, if knowledge of these matters is sought soberly and reasonably with the support of the divine grace, we should not hope to be advanced spiritually by reading them, but in the course of our reading

we should desire to have profitable and advantageous wisdom granted us by "the Father of lights." How many philosophers through eager reading of secular letters alone have failed to arrive at the fount of wisdom and, deprived of the true light, have been plunged into the blindness of ignorance! For, as someone has expressed it, that can never be fully discovered which is not sought in the proper manner.

4. Again, many of our Fathers, trained in letters of this sort and living by the law of the Lord, have attained true wisdom, as the blessed Augustine [354–430 A.D.] relates in his work, *On Christian Learning,* saying: "We see, do we not, with how much gold and silver and clothing Cyprian, a most agreeable teacher and a most blessed martyr, was enriched when he went out from Egypt? With how much Lactantius, and Victorinus, and Optatus, and Hilary were enriched?" We add Ambrose, and the aforesaid Augustine, and Jerome, and the many others included in the words "countless Greeks." Likewise enriched "was that most faithful servant of God, Moses himself, concerning whom it is written that he 'was learned in all the wisdom of the Egyptians.'" And imitating them carefully, but unhesitatingly, let us hasten to read both bodies of doctrine, if we can (for who would venture to doubt after the many examples of men of this sort?), with clear knowledge, as it has often been said before now, that the Lord can grant true and genuine wisdom, as the Book of Wisdom says: "Wisdom is 'from the Lord God, and hath been always with him, and abideth for all time.'"

Questions for Discussion:

1. How does the educational design of Cassiodorus continue the tradition established by the Roman system?
2. Does the work of Cassiodorus reflect the monastic program given in the *Rule* of Saint Benedict presented in Document 1.15? How?
3. In what ways does Cassiodorus continue and reinforce the attitude toward the study of secular literature offered in the *Letter from Jerome to Eustochium* (Document 1.11)?

2.4   Boethius, *The Consolation of Philosophy*

Boethius (c. 480–524) was another scholar employed and patronized by Theodoric the Ostrogoth. His literary aspiration was to translate the entire works of the ancient philosophers Plato and Aristotle from Greek into Latin, but he died before he could accomplish this goal. He also wrote "textbooks" concerning the Seven Liberal Arts (the Trivium and the Quadrivium), of which the volumes on arithmetic and music survive. His work on music, De musica, *formed the basis for the study of musical theory throughout the Middle Ages and into the fifteenth century.*

Tragically, he was implicated in a plot against Theodoric, and was imprisoned and ultimately executed by the order of the king in 524. While in prison, he wrote his most famous work, The Consolation of Philosophy, *which was widely read and translated during the Middle Ages and the Renaissance. The work consists of a long dialogue between the author and Lady Philosophy (the personification of philosophy), concerning many far-reaching issues. In the following selection Boethius reveals his version of the circumstances surrounding the charges against him.*

(From *The Consolation of Philosophy* by Boethius, trans. by S. J. Tester [Cambridge, MA: Harvard University Press, 1918], pp. 145–153.)

Bk. I, IV. "Now," she [Lady Philosophy] said, "have you understood what I have been saying? Has it penetrated your stricken mind? Or are you like an ass hearing the sound of a lyre? Why do you go on weeping, dissolving in tears? As Homer says, 'Speak out, don't hide it in your heart.' If you are looking for a healer's cure, you must lay bare the wounds." So I gathered my strength of mind and said: "Do you really still need to ask? Is my harsh treatment at fortune's hands not obvious enough? Are you not affected by the very appearance of this room? Do you not recognize the library, which you once chose for yourself as a secure dwelling-place in my house—the very room in which you used often to sit with me discoursing on the knowledge of all things human and divine? Was this how I looked, was this my expression, when I used to seek out with you the secrets of Nature? When with your rod you drew for me the paths of the stars? When you shaped my character and the whole manner of my life according to celestial models? Are these our rewards for obedient service to you? It was you who established through the words of Plato the principle that those states would be happy where philosophers were kings or their governors were philosophers. You, through that same Plato, told us that this was why philosophers must involve themselves in political affairs, lest the rule of nations be left to the base and wicked, bringing ruin and destruction on the good. It was in accordance with that teaching that I chose to apply in the practice of public administration what I learned from you in the seclusion of my private leisure. You and God, who has set you in the minds of philosophers, know me well, and that I undertook office with no other motives than the common purposes of all good men. That is why there arose serious and irreconcilable disagreements with wicked men, and, as consequence of keeping my conscience free, I have always maintained what is right and lawful in spite of the fact that I offended those more powerful than myself . . .

"No-one has ever turned me aside from the right, to commit injustice. That the fortunes of provincial families were ruined both by robbery by individuals and by taxation by the state grieved me no less than it did those who suffered so. When in a time of grievous famine it seemed there was to be by order a terrible and quite indefensible compulsory purchase of supplies which would have reduced the province of Campania to destitution, I took up the fight with the Praetorian Prefect for the sake of the common good, I fought against the enforcement of the purchase before the king, and I won. The wealth of Paulinus, a man of consular rank, which had already in their ambitious hope been all but devoured by those dogs of the court, I snatched even from their gaping jaws. To prevent Albinus,

another man of consular rank, being punished for a crime of which he was found guilty before being tried, I made an enemy of his accuser Cyprian. Ought I not to have been satisfied with the amount of strong feeling I stirred up against myself? But surely I ought to have been that much the more safe with the others, since in my regard for justice I kept no favors among the courtiers to ensure my own safety. Who are the accusers, then, by whom I have been brought down? One of them, Basil, once in the king's service but dismissed, was forced to denounce me because of his burden of debts. Two others were Opilio and Gaudentius: on account of their many different frauds they were condemned to exile by the king's judgement, but they refused to obey and took sanctuary in a temple. When the king learned of this he ordered that unless they left Ravenna by a certain date they should be branded on the forehead and driven out. Could they possibly have been more severely treated? And yet on that very date the accusation against me was lodged, with their names on it! I ask you! Was that the reward my exercise of office had earned? Did their previous conviction make them just accusers? Was fortune not the least bit ashamed, if not that innocence was thus accused, at least that the accusers were so base?

"Do you want to know what, in a word, was the charge against me? That I wanted to preserve the Senate. And how did I do that? I am charged with preventing those accusers from bringing forward proofs whereby the Senate might have been convicted of treason. What then do you think, Lady? Shall I deny the charge, so as not to cause you to be ashamed of me? But I did want the Senate to be preserved, nor shall I ever cease to want it so. Shall I then confess to the charge? But the chance of hindering their accuser has now passed. Shall I call it wrong to have wanted the preservation of the Senatorial order? That order had itself made it wrong, by its decrees against me. But self-deceiving ignorance cannot change the true worth of anything, nor do I think it would have been right for me, following Socrates' counsel, to conceal the truth or admit to falsehood. But what the truth of the matter is, I leave to your judgement and to that of philosophers; though so that the true details of this affair cannot lie concealed from later generations, I have written it down to be remembered."

Questions for Discussion:

1. Upon what principles does Boethius defend himself against the charges? Do his arguments reinforce what you have learned about Theodoric?

2. Compare the situation of Boethius with similar political circumstances in the contemporary world. How are they alike? How different?

3. Boethius was devoted, along with Cassiodorus, to the preservation of classical literature and philosophy. What specific evidence do you find for this statement in the *Consolation of Philosophy?*

2.5　Isidore of Seville, *History of the Goths, Vandals, and Suevi*

Originally both the Ostrogoths and Visigoths were part of the same Scandinavian tribe, the Goths (see Document 1.19 concerning the Battle of Adrianople). They split into two parts, and were then known as the Ostrogoths, or East Goths, and the Visigoths, or West Goths. As we have seen, the Ostrogoths, under Theodoric, established control over Italy. During the latter part of the fifth century, the Visigoths created a kingdom on the Iberian peninsula, exerting their hegemony over the native Hispano-Roman population by 497. Like the Ostrogoths, they originally practiced the Arian form of Christianity, but by 589 they had converted to Nicene Christianity. Their kingdom endured for a longer period than that of the Ostrogoths in Italy, lasting until the invasion of the Muslims in 711. Although they did not attempt to preserve Roman traditions to the same degree as the Ostrogoths, their intellectual culture produced several important scholars. One of these was Isidore, Bishop of Seville (c. 560–636). His major contribution was a vast encyclopedia known as the Etymologiae *(Etymologies). This was an historical study of every aspect of human endeavor, based upon an explanation of the derivation of Latin words. Another of Isidore's important contributions was the* History of the Goths, Vandals, and Suevi. *In the following excerpt from that work he discusses the conquering of the Iberian peninsula by the Visigoths under their leader, Leovigild (d. 586), who was the last of the Arian kings.*

(From *Isidore of Seville's History of the Goths, Vandals, and Suevi*, trans. by Guido Donini and Gordon B. Ford. Leiden: E.J. Brill, 1970, pp. 23–27. Reprinted by permission of Guido Donini and the Estate of Gordon B. Ford.)

In the era 606 (568), the third year of Justin II's [Byzantine Emperor, r. 565–578] rule, Leovigild became the ruler of Spain and Gaul and decided to enlarge his kingdom by war and to increase his power.

Indeed, with the eagerness of his army and the good fortune of his victories he acquired much with distinction. For he obtained Cantabria[10] and took Aregia[11], and all of Sabaria[12] was conquered by him. Very many rebellious cities of Spain also yielded to his arms; he also routed the Roman soldiers in various battles and recovered by fighting certain forts occupied by them. He then besieged his son Hermenegild, who was acting as a tyrant in his empire, and overcame him. Finally, he waged war against the Suevi and with amazing speed transferred their kingdom to the authority of his nation, gaining the mastery of most of Spain. For previously the nation of the Goths was limited within narrow boundaries. But the error of impiety obscured in him the glory of such virtue.

Indeed, filled with the madness of the Arian heresy, he stirred up persecution against Catholics and sent very many of the bishops into exile. He removed the revenues and privileges of the churches and by his acts of terror also compelled many to accept the Arian plague and deceived many people without persecution by alluring them with gold and gifts. And among the other infections of his heresy he even dared to rebaptize Catholics [Nicene Christians], and not only of the common people but also of the rank of the priestly class, such as Vincentius of Saragossa, who from a bishop became an apostate and, as it were, was hurled from heaven into hell.

---

[10]Cantabria was a Spanish province east of the Basque country in the area of the Pyrenees Mountains.
[11]Aregia was a Spanish city.
[12]Sabaria was a city in western Hungary.

But he was also baneful to some of his associates: for whatever men he saw who were most noble and powerful he either beheaded or proscribed and drove into exile. He was also the first to enrich the fisc[13] and the first to increase the treasury by robbery of the citizens and plunder of the enemy. He also founded a city in Celtiberia[14] which he named Recopolis after his son. In the laws, too, he corrected those things which had been set up inadequately by Euric[15], adding very many laws that had been omitted and removing some superfluous ones. He reigned for eighteen years and died of a natural death at Toledo.

In the era 624 (586), the third year of [Emperor] Mauricius' rule, after the death of Leovigild, his son Reccared was crowned with kingship; he was endowed with reverence for religion and was greatly different from his father in character. For the latter was irreligious and very much disposed to war, while he was devout in his faith and renowned for his love of peace; his father by the skills of war expanded the rule of his nation, while he with greater glory elevated the same nation by the victory of faith. For at the very beginning of his reign he embraced the Catholic faith and after removing the sin of their deep-rooted error he brought back the people of the whole Gothic nation to reverence for the true faith.

He then called together a synod of bishops from the various provinces of Spain and Gaul for the condemnation of the Arian heresy; this very religious ruler was present at this assembly and supported its proceedings by his presence and signature; together with all his subjects he renounced the falsehood which the nation of the Goths had up to now learned from the teaching of Arius, and proclaimed the unity of the three persons in God, saying that the Son was born from the Father consubstantially, that the Holy Spirit proceeds inseparably from the Father and the Son and is one Spirit of both, whence they are one.

He also waged war gloriously against hostile peoples with the aid of the faith which he had accepted. As the Franks were overrunning Gaul with about sixty thousand soldiers, he sent his general Claudius against them and triumphed with a glorious success. No greater or similar victory of the Goths in war ever took place in Spain. For many thousands of the enemy were killed and captured, and the remaining part of the army was put to flight contrary to its expectations and, with the Goths following closely behind, it was cut down up to the boundaries of its kingdom. He also frequently sent forces in opposition to the arrogant deeds of the Romans and the incursions of the Vascones,[16] in such a way that he seems not so much to have waged wars as rather to have trained his people, as it were, in the sport of wrestling for the sake of utility.

But he preserved with peace, set in order with justice, and ruled with temperance the provinces which his father had gained by battle. He was peaceful, gentle, of surpassing goodness, and had such charm in his countenance and bore such kindness in his heart that he would influence the minds of all and would draw even evil men to the disposition of love of him. He was so liberal that he restored to their proper jurisdiction the property of private citizens and the churches' estates which his father's disgrace had joined to the treasury; he was so clement that he often alleviated the people's tributes by the bestowal of leniency.

He also enriched many with gifts, elevated very many to public honors, set aside his property for the wretched and his treasures for the poor, knowing that kingship had been conferred on him for this purpose, that he should enjoy it beneficially and achieve a good end after good beginnings. For he increased his true and glorious faith, which he had accepted at the beginning of his reign, by a public confession of repentance at the end of his life. He passed away with a peaceful death at Toledo after reigning for fifteen years.

In the era 639 (601), the seventeenth year of Mauricius' rule, after King Reccared his son Livva became king, and his reign lasted two years; he was indeed born of a low-ranked mother, but was distinguished for the native quality of his virtues. After seizing despotic power Witteric drove him away from kingship in the first flower of his youth,

---

[13]*Fisc* denoted the value of royal holdings.

[14]Celtiberia were Celtic-speaking people of the north-central Iberian Peninsula.

[15]Euric (c. 415–484) was king of the Visigoths following the assassination of his brother, Theodoric II.

---

[16]The Vascones were people who lived in Navarra and northwest Aragon.

although he had done no harm, and after cutting off his right hand killed him in the twentieth year of his age, the second of his reign.

In the era 641 (603), the twentieth year of Mauricius' rule, after the death of Livva, Witteric assumed kingly power, which he had seized while his predecessor was alive, and held it for seven years; he was indeed a man vigorous in the art of war, but nevertheless without victories. For although he frequently fought battles against the Roman soldiers, he did not win any adequate glory except for capturing some soldiers at Sagunto with the help of his generals. In his life he did many unlawful things, and as for his death, he perished by the sword because he had worked with the sword. Indeed the death of an innocent man was not unavenged on

him: while he was eating a meal he was killed by some conspirators. His corpse was carried out with disgrace and buried.

Questions for Discussion:

1. Do you think that Isidore's account of the reigns of the Visigothic kings is biased? What are the reasons for your view?
2. Compare and contrast the reign of Theodoric with those of the Visigothic kings. What similarities do you see? What differences?
3. What do you learn from this source about the succession of the kings to the throne of the Visigoths?

2.6   The *Visigothic Code*: Provisions Concerning Women

In the middle of the seventh century, during the reigns of the kings Chintasvintus and Recenvintus (649–652), a body of legislation known as the Visigothic Code, *or* Forum Judicum, *was developed, building upon Roman law, but rarely adopting the clauses verbatim. The* Code *included "Ancient Laws" as well as those enacted during the reigns of the kings mentioned earlier. The code was divided into twelve books, and dealt with contracts, wills and inheritances, marital agreements, business transactions, crimes and torture, property rights, and heresy, among other matters. The selections here give only a hint of the comprehensive nature of the* Code; *they deal with provisions concerning women.*

(From *The Visigothic Code,* translated by S. P. Scott [Boston: The Boston Book Co., 1910], pp. 88–91.)

Ancient Law

I. Where a Freeman carries off a Free-woman by Force, he shall not be permitted to Marry her, if she was a Virgin.

If any freeman should carry off a virgin or widow by violence, and she should be rescued before she has lost her chastity, he who carried her off shall lose half of his property, which shall be given to her. But should such not be the case, and the crime should

have been fully committed, under no circumstances shall a marriage contract be entered into with him; but he shall be surrendered, with all his possessions, to the injured party; and shall, in addition, receive two hundred lashes in public; and, after having been deprived of his liberty, he shall be delivered up to the parents of her whom he violated, or to the virgin or widow herself, to forever serve as a slave, to the end that there may be no possibility of a future marriage between them. And if it should be proved that she has received anything from the property of the ravisher, on account of her injury, she shall lose it, and it shall be given to her parents, by whose agency this matter should be prosecuted. But if a man who has legitimate children by a former wife should be convicted of this crime, he alone shall be given up into the power of her whom he carried off; and his children shall have the right to inherit his property.

Flavius Recesvintus, King

II. Where Parents remove their Daughter from the Power of a Ravisher.

If the parents of the woman or girl who has been carried off should rescue her, the ravisher shall be given up to them, and, under no condition whatever, shall she be permitted to marry him; and should they presume to marry, both shall be put to death. If, however, they should take refuge with the bishop, or should claim the privilege of sanctuary, their lives shall be granted them; but they shall be separated and delivered over as slaves to the parents of the woman.

III. Where the Parents of a Girl, who has been Betrothed, consent that she should be Carried Away by Another.

If parents should connive at their daughter being carried away, after she has been betrothed to another, they shall be compelled to pay the latter four times the amount of the dowry agreed upon; and the ravisher shall be delivered up as a slave, absolutely, under the law, to the man who was betrothed to the girl.

Ancient Law

IV. Where Brothers, either during the Life of their Father, or after his Death, consent that anyone should Carry Away their Sister by Force.

If, during the life of their father, any brothers should consent to, or connive at, the carrying off of their sister, they shall receive the penalty to which ravishers are liable, excepting that of death. But it, after the death of their father, they should give up their sister to a ravisher, or permit her to be carried off by him; for the reason that they have disposed of her in marriage to a person of vile character, or against her own will, when they should have protected her honor, they shall lose the half of their property, which shall be given to their sister, and, in addition, they shall each

receive fifty lashes in public: so that others, admonished by this, may take warning. All accessories, who were present, shall receive the punishment prescribed by another law. And the ravisher, inexcusable by a former law, shall lose both his property and his rank.

Ancient Law

V. Where anyone Carries away by Violence a Woman who was Betrothed to Another.

If anyone should carry off a woman betrothed to another, we hereby decree that half of the property of the ravisher shall be given to the girl, and the other half to her betrothed. But if he should have little or no property, he shall be given up, with all his possessions, to those above mentioned; so that the ravisher having been sold as a slave, they may have an equal share in the price paid for him. The ravisher himself, if the crime shall have been consummated, shall be punished.

Ancient Law

VI. Where a Ravisher is Killed.

If any ravisher should be killed, it shall not be considered criminal homicide, because the act was committed in the defense of chastity.

Questions for Discussion:

1. What do these laws indicate about Visigothic society?
2. In your opinion, is enslavement a proper punishment for rape or abduction?
3. What were the reasons for the creation of the Visigothic Code?

The Franks

2.7   The Conversion of Clovis: Gregory of Tours, *History of the Franks*

The Franks comprised a number of Germanic tribes who, during the fifth century, expanded their territory from the area of the Rhine River in present-day Germany into Gaul. They were able to establish a kingdom that lasted

much longer than those of the Ostrogoths, Visigoths, and Vandals. Their success was due to a number of factors, not the least of which was continued leadership by able warriors. The first important king of the Franks was Clovis (r. 485–511), who spent two decades waging war against other tribes, eventually unifying the kingdom; the dynasty he founded is known as Merovingian in honor of a distant ancestor, Merovech. In 496, during a campaign against the Alemanni, Clovis experienced a conversion to Christianity, not unlike that of Constantine (see Document 1.4). The details were recorded some years later by the historian Gregory of Tours (c. 538–c. 594).

It is important to note that Clovis converted to the Nicene form of Christianity, which had been established as the orthodox theological doctrine by the Council of Nicaea (see Documents 1.6 and 1.7). This set him apart from other tribal leaders such as Theodoric the Ostrogoth (see Document 2.2), most of whom practiced Arian Christianity if they were no longer polytheistic. By adopting Nicene Christianity, Clovis established a close relationship between the Franks and the papacy that would endure for several centuries (see Chapter 4). Furthermore, his conversion meant that the Frankish people, who followed their leader in converting to Nicene Christianity, embraced the same religion as the indigenous Roman population.

(From *The History of the Franks* by Gregory of Tours, trans. by Ernest Brehaut [New York: Columbia University Press, 1916], pp. 39–41.)

The queen did not cease to urge him [Clovis] to recognize the true God and cease worshiping idols. But he could not be influenced in any way to this belief, until at last a war arose with the Alamanni, in which he was driven by necessity to confess what before he had of his free will denied. It came about that as the two armies were fighting fiercely, there was much slaughter, and Clovis's army began to be in danger of destruction. He saw it and raised his eyes to heaven, and with remorse in his heart he burst into tears and cried: "Jesus Christ, whom Clotilda asserts to be the son of the living God, who art said to give aid to those in distress, and to bestow victory on those who believe in you, I beseech the glory of your aid, with the vow that if you will grant me victory over these enemies, and I shall know that power which she says that people dedicated in your name have had from you, I will believe in you and be baptized in your name. For I have invoked my own gods, but, as I find, they have withdrawn from aiding me; and therefore I believe that they possess no power, since they do not help those who obey them. I now call upon you, I desire to believe in you, only let me be rescued from my adversaries." And when he said this, the Alamanni turned their backs, and began to disperse in flight. And when they saw that their king was killed, they submitted to the dominion of Clovis, saying: "Let not the people perish further, we pray; we are yours now." And he stopped the fighting, and after encouraging his men, retired in peace and told the queen how he had had merit to win the victory by calling on the name of Christ. This happened in the fifteenth year of his reign.

Then the queen asked saint Remi, bishop of Rheims, to summon Clovis secretly, urging him to introduce the king to the word of salvation. And the bishop sent for him secretly and began to urge him to believe in the true God, maker of heaven and earth, and to cease worshiping idols, which could help neither themselves nor anyone else. But the king said: "I gladly hear you, most holy father; but there remains one thing: the people who follow me cannot endure abandoning their gods; but I shall go and speak to them according to your words." He met with his followers, but before he could speak the power of God anticipated him, and all the people cried out together: "O pious king, we reject our mortal gods, and we are ready to follow the immortal God whom Remi preaches." This was reported to the bishop, who was greatly rejoiced, and told them to get the baptismal font ready. The squares were shaded with tapestried canopies, the churches adorned with white curtains, the baptistery set in order, the aroma of incense spread, candles of fragrant odor burned brightly, and the whole shrine of the baptistery was filled with a divine fragrance: and the Lord gave such grace to those who stood by that they thought they were placed amid the odors of paradise. And the king was the first to ask to be baptized by the bishop. Another Constantine advanced to the baptismal font, to terminate the disease of ancient leprosy and wash away with fresh water the foul spots that had long been borne. And when he entered to be baptized, the saint of God began with ready speech: "Gently bend your neck,

Sigamber; worship what you burned; burn what you worshiped." The holy bishop Remi was a man of excellent wisdom and especially trained in rhetorical studies, and of such surpassing holiness that he equaled the miracles of Silvester. For there is extant a book of his life which tells that he raised a dead man. And so the king confessed all-powerful God in the Trinity, and was baptized in the name of the Father, Son and Holy Spirit, and was anointed with the holy ointment with the sign of the cross of Christ. And of his army more than 3000 were baptized.

Questions for Discussion:

1. Compare the conversion story of Clovis with that of Constantine (Document 1.4). What similarities do you see? What differences?
2. Isidore of Seville (Document 2.5) describes the conversion of the Visigoths to Nicene Christianity. How does his account differ from that of Gregory of Tours?
3. Do you find the discussion of the influence of Clothilde to be convincing? What may have been the motivation of Gregory of Tours to include the queen in the conversion story?

2.8   Excerpts from the Salic Law

Clovis recognized the need for a formal law code, perhaps as a result of contact with the Roman legal system. Hence, around 500 C.E., a code of written legal provisions known as the Salic Law was instituted. The code consisted of sixty-five chapters, or "titles," which dealt with the process of government and with private issues. The first provision printed here stipulates procedures regarding the conduct of the judicial system, and others concern such issues as wounds, insults, assault and robbery, false accusation, and theft. Especially interesting are the sections concerning women, which demonstrate a great deal about the position of females in Merovingian society.

(From *Select Historical Documents of the Middle Ages*, ed. and trans. Ernest F. Henderson [London: G. Bell and Sons, Ltd., 1921], pp. 176–183.

Title 1. Concerning Summonses

1. If anyone be summoned before the" Thing"[17] (General Assembly) by the king's law, and do not come, he shall be sentenced to 600 denars, which make 15 shillings (solidi).
2. But he who summons another, and does not come himself, shall, if a lawful impediment have not delayed him, be sentenced to 15 shillings, to he paid to him whom he summoned.

3. And he who summons another shall walk with witnesses to the home of that man, and, if he be not at home, shall bid the wife or any one of the family to make known to him that he has been summoned to court.
4. But if he be occupied ill the king's service he can not summon him.
5. But if he shall be inside the hundred seeing about his own affairs, he can summon him in the manner explained above.

Title XIII. Concerning Rape committed by Freemen.

1. If three men carry off a free born girl, they shall be compelled to pay 30 shillings.
2. If there are more than three, each one shall pay 5 shillings.
3. Those who shall have been present with boats shall be sentenced to three shillings.
4. But those who commit rape shall be compelled to pay 2500 denars, which make 63 shillings.
5. But if they have carried off that girl from behind lock and key, or from the spinning room, they shall be sentenced to the above price and penalty.
6. But if the girl who is carried off be under the king's protection, then the "frith" (peace-money) shall be 2500 denars, which make 63 shillings.

---

[17]"The Thing" was the governing assembly of Germanic societies.

7. But if a bondsman of the king, or a leet, should carry off a free woman, he shall be sentenced to death.

8. But if a free woman have followed a slave of her own will, she shall lose her freedom.

9. If a freeborn man shall have taken an alien bonds-woman, he shall suffer similarly.

10. If anybody take an alien spouse and join her to himself in matrimony, he shall be sentenced to 2500 denars, which make 63 shillings.

Title XVII. Concerning Wounds.

1. If any one have wished to kill another person, and the blow have missed, he on whom it was proved shall be sentenced to 2500 denars, which makes 63 shillings.

2. If any person have wished to strike another with a poisoned arrow, and the arrow have glanced aside, and it shall be proved on him: he shall be sentenced to 2500 denars, which make 63 shillings.

3. If any person strike another on the head so that the brain appears, and the three bones which lie above the brain shall project, he shall be sentenced to 1200 denars, which makes 30 shillings.

4. But if it shall have been between the ribs or in the stomach, so that the wound appears and reaches to the entrails, he shall he sentenced to 1200 denars—which make 30 shillings—besides five shillings for the physician's pay.

5. If any one shall have struck a man so that blood falls to the floor, and it be proved on him, he shall he sentenced to 600 denars, which make 15 shillings.

6. But if a freeman strike a freeman with his fist so that blood does not flow, he shall be sentenced for each blow—up to 3 blows—to 120 denars, which make 3 shillings.

Title XVIII. Concerning him who, before the King, accuses an innocent Man.

1. If anyone, before the king, accuse an innocent man who is absent, he shall be sentenced to 2500 denars, which make 63 shillings.

Title XIX. Concerning Magicians.

1. If any one have given herbs to another so that he die, he shall be sentenced to 200 shillings (or shall surely be given over to fire).

2. If any person have bewitched another, and he who was thus treated shall escape, the author of the crime, who is proved to have committed it, shall he sentenced to 2500 denars, which make 63 shillings.

Title XXIV. Concerning the killing of little children and women.

1. If any one, have slain a boy under 10 years—up to the end of the tenth—and it shall have been proved on him, he shall be sentenced to 24000 denars, which make 600 shillings.

3. If anyone have hit a free woman who is pregnant, and she dies, he shall he sentenced to 28000 denars, which make 700 shillings.

6. If any one have killed a free woman after she has begun bearing children, he shall be sentenced to 24000 denars, which make 600 shillings.

7. After she can have no more children, he who kills her shall he sentenced to 8000 denars, which make 200 shillings.

Title XXX. Concerning Insults.

3. If any one, man or woman, shall have called a woman harlot, and shall not have been able to prove it, he shall be sentenced to 1800 denars, which make 45 shillings.

4. If any person shall have called another "fox," he shall be sentenced to 3 shillings.

5. If any man shall have called another "hare," he shall be sentenced to 3 shillings.

6. If any man shall have brought it up against another that he have thrown away his shield, and shall not have been able to prove it, he shall be sentenced to 120 denars, which make 3 shillings.

7. If any man shall have called another "spy" or "perjurer," and shall not have been able to prove it, he shall be sentenced to 600 denars, which make 15 shillings.

Title XLV. Concerning Migrators.

1. If anyone wish to migrate to another village and if one or more who live in that village do not wish to receive him, if there be only one who objects, he shall not have leave to move there.

2. But if he shall have presumed to settle in that village in spite of his rejection by one or two men, then some one shall give him warning. And if he be unwilling to go away, he who gives him warning shall give him warning, with witnesses, as follows: I warn you that you may remain here this next night as the Salic law demands, and I warn you that within 10 nights you shall go forth from this village. After another 10 nights he shall again come to him and warn him again within 10 nights to go away. If he still refuses to go, again 10 nights shall be added to the command, that the number of 30 nights, may be full. If he will not go away even then, then he shall summon him to the "Thing" (General Assembly) and present his witnesses as to the separate commands to leave. If he who has been warned will not then move away, and no valid reason detains him, and all the above warnings which we have mentioned have been given according to law, then he who gave him warning shall take the matter into his own hands and request the "comes" (count) to go to that place and expel him. And because he would not listen to the law, that man shall relinquish all that he has earned there, and, besides, shall be sentenced to 1200 denars, which make 30 shillings.

3. But if anyone have moved there, and within 12 months no one have given him warning, he shall remain as secure as the other neighbors.

Questions for Discussion:

1. How do you account for the differences in the fines stipulated in Title XXIV?
2. What are the differences in the penalties stipulated by the *Visigothic Code* (Document 2.6) and the *Salic Law* regarding rape?
3. The *Salic Law* predates the *Visigothic Code* by approximately 150 years. Do you see any advances in legal practice in the later set of laws?

The Anglo-Saxons

2.9   *Beowulf*

Beowulf *is probably the oldest of the Anglo-Saxon epic poems. Many scholars think that it was composed in the first half of the eighth century, probably by a poet in West Mercia (today the West Midlands of England), although recent research places the date closer to the year 1000, and there is no definitive historical consensus. The original language of the poem was Old English, which was spoken in the British Isles between the fifth and eleventh centuries. The epic was originally presented orally by a traveling actor/musician, probably for entertainment at court. The plot concerns the Germanic tribe of the Geats, who lived in southern Sweden, and the Danes, who inhabited the Danish island of Zealand. The action occurs in the time before the Anglo-Saxon migration to England was completed. The Anglo-Saxons who heard the poem may have regarded Beowulf, the hero of the Geats, as a distant ancestor.*

The plot contains three major episodes: Beowulf's encounter with the monster Grendel, his destruction of Grendel's vicious mother, and, many years later, his attempt to kill the fire-breathing dragon that threatens his people. The excerpt reprinted here, a translation in prose rather than poetic form, is taken from the third section.

The poem extols the values of the warrior society, in which the most important human relationships were between the warrior, or thane, *and his lord. A good king, such as Beowulf, was a valiant hero and protector of his men. These expectations reflect an incipient form of vassalage, to be discussed in Chapter 5.*

[Beowulf Attacks The Dragon]

Beowulf spoke, for the last time spoke words in boast: "In my youth I engaged in many wars. Old guardian of the people, I shall still seek battle, perform a deed of fame, if the evil-doer will come to me out of the earth-hall."

Then he saluted each of the warriors, the bold helmet-bearers, for the last time—his own dear companions. "I would not bear sword, weapon, to the worm, if I knew how else according to my boast I might grapple with the monster, as I did of old with Grendel. But I expect here hot battle-fire, steam and poison. Therefore I have on me shield and mail-shirt. I will not flee a foot-step from the barrow-ward, but it shall be with us at the wall as fate allots, the ruler of every man. I am confident in heart, so I forgo help against the war-flier. Wait on the barrow, safe in your mail-shirts, men in armor—which of us two may better bear wounds after our bloody meeting. This is not your venture, nor is it right for any man except me alone that he should spend his strength against the monster, do this man's deed. By my courage I shall get gold, or war will take your king, dire life-evil."

Then the brave warrior arose by his shield; hardy under helmet he went in his mail-shirt beneath the stone-cliffs, had trust in his strength—that of one man: such is not the way of the cowardly. Then he saw by the wall—he who had come through many wars, good in his great-heartedness, many clashes in battle when troops meet together—a stone arch standing, through it a stream bursting out of the barrow: there was welling of a current hot with killing fires, and he might not endure any while unburnt by the dragon's flame the hollow near the hoard. Then the man of the Weather-Geats, enraged as he was, let a word break from his breast. Stout-hearted he shouted; his voice went roaring, clear in battle, in under the gray stone. Hate was stirred up, the hoard's guard knew the voice of a man. No more time was there to ask for peace. First the monster's breath came out of the stone, the hot war-steam. The earth resounded. The man below the barrow, the lord of the Geats, swung his shield against the dreadful visitor. Then the heart of the coiled thing was aroused to seek combat. The good war-king had drawn his sword, the old heirloom, not blunt of edge. To each of them as they threatened destruction there was terror of the other. Firm-hearted he stood with his shield high, the lord of friends, while quickly the worm coiled itself; he waited in his armor. Then, coiling in flames, he came gliding on, hastening to his fate. The good shield protected the life and body of the famous prince, but for a shorter while than his wish was. There for the first time, the first day in his life, he might not prevail, since fate did not assign him such glory in battle. The lord of the Geats raised his hand, struck the shining horror so with his forged blade that the edge failed, bright on the bone, bit less surely than its folk-king had need, hard-pressed in perils. Then because of the battle-stroke the barrow-ward's heart was savage, he exhaled death-fire—the warflames sprang wide. The gold-friend of the Geats boasted of no great victories: the war blade had failed, naked at need, as it ought not to have done, iron good from old times. That was no pleasant journey, not one on which the famous son of Ecgtheow would wish to leave his land; against his will he must take up a dwelling-place elsewhere—as every man must give up the days that are lent him.

It was not long until they came together again, dreadful foes. The hoard-guard took heart, once more his breast swelled with his breathing. Encircled with flames, he who before had ruled a folk felt harsh pain. Nor did his companions, sons of nobles, take up their stand in a troop about him with the courage of fighting men, but they crept to the wood, protected their lives. In only one of them the heart surged with sorrows: nothing can ever set aside kinship in him who means well.

Questions for Discussion:

1. *Beowulf* is an Anglo-Saxon poem, as noted in the introduction to this reading. However, it concerns a Germanic warrior society that is typical of tribes other than the Scandinavian groups mentioned in the epic. What similarities do you see between the warriors of the poem and those described by Tacitus and Ammianus Marcellinus (Documents 1.16 and 1.17), and Jordanes (Document 2.1), Isidore of Seville (Document 2.5), and Gregory of Tours (Document 2.7)? Are there noticeable differences?

2. Describe and discuss the "ties of kinship" evident in the text. What were the expectations of tribal groups in this regard? Were they met?

3. According to the poem, what would you cite as the most important values of these warrior societies?

2.10   Bede, *A History of the English Church and People*

The Anglo-Saxons, like the Ostrogoths, the Visigoths, and the Franks, gradually established kingdoms in the British Isles and were eventually converted to Christianity. These developments were described by the "Venerable" Bede (c. 672–735), the most important writer of eighth-century England. His famous work, A History of the English Church and People, *describes the consolidation of the monarchy in southern England and the growth of Christianity in that country. According to Bede, there were several factors involved in the conversion of England, especially missionary activity. The following excerpt provides information about the program of Christianization begun by the monk Augustine of Canterbury (not the Augustine who wrote the* Confessions*), who was sent as an emissary by Pope Gregory I in the year 597.*

(From *A History of the English Church and People* by Bede, translated with an introduction by Leo Sherley-Price, revised by R. E. Latham (Penguin Classics 1955, Revised edition 1968). Copyright © Leo Sherley-Price, 1955, 1968.)

Reassured by the encouragement of the blessed father Gregory [Pope 590–604], Augustine and his fellow-servants of Christ resumed their work in the word of God, and arrived in Britain. At this time the most powerful king there was Ethelbert [c. 552–616], who reigned in Kent [southern England] and whose domains extended northwards to the river Humber, which forms the boundary between the north and south Angles. To the east of Kent lies the large island of Thanet. . . . It was here that God's servant Augustine landed with companions, who are said to have been forty in number. At the direction of blessed Pope Gregory, they had brought interpreters from among the Franks, and they sent these to Ethelbert, saying that they came from Rome bearing very glad news, which infallibly assured all who would receive it of eternal joy in heaven and an everlasting kingdom with the living and true God. On receiving this message, the king ordered them to remain in the island where they had landed, and gave directions that they were to be provided with all necessaries until he should decide what action to take. For he had already heard of the Christian religion, having a Christian wife of the Frankish royal house named Bertha, whom he had received from her parents on condition that she should have freedom to hold and practice her faith unhindered with Bishop Liudhard, whom they had sent as her helper in the faith.

After some days, the king came to the island and, sitting down in the open air, summoned Augustine and his companions to an audience. But he took precautions that they should not approach him in a house; for he held an ancient superstition that, if they were practicers of magical arts, they might have opportunity to deceive and master him. But the monks were endowed with power from God, not from the Devil, and approached the king carrying a silver cross as their standard and the likeness of our Lord and Savior painted on a board. First of all they offered prayer to God, singing a litany for the eternal salvation both of themselves and of those to whom and for whose sake they had come. And when, at the king's command, they had sat down and preached the word of life to the king and his court, the king said: 'Your words and promises are fair indeed; but they are new and uncertain, and I cannot accept them and abandon the age-old beliefs that I have held together with the whole English nation. But since you have traveled far, and I can see that you are sincere in your desire to impart to us what you believe to be true and excellent, we will not harm you. We will receive you hospitably and take care to supply you with all that you need; nor will we forbid you to preach and win any people you can to your religion.' The king then granted them a dwelling in the city of Canterbury, which was the chief city of all his realm, and in accordance with his promise he allowed them provisions and did not withdraw their freedom to preach. Tradition says that as they approached the city, bearing the holy cross and the likeness of our great King and Lord Jesus Christ as was their custom, they sang in unison this litany: 'We pray Thee, O Lord, in all Thy mercy, that Thy wrath and anger may be turned away from this city and from Thy holy house, for we are sinners. Alleluia.'

Augustine establishes his episcopal see at Canterbury.

As soon as they had occupied the house given to them they began to emulate the life of the apostles and the primitive Church. They were constantly at prayer; they fasted and kept vigils; they preached the word of life to whomsoever they could. They regarded worldly things as of little importance, and accepted only the necessities of life from those they taught. They practiced what they preached, and were willing to endure any hardship, and even to die for the truth which they proclaimed. Before long a number of heathen, admiring the simplicity of their holy lives and the comfort of their heavenly message, believed and were baptized. On the east side of the city stood an old church, built in honor of Saint Martin during the Roman occupation of Britain, where the Christian queen of whom I have spoken went to pray. Here they first assembled to sing the psalms, to pray, to say Mass, to preach, and to baptize, until the king's own conversion to the Faith gave them greater freedom to preach and to build and restore churches everywhere.

At length the king himself, among others, edified by the pure lives of these holy men and their gladdening promises, the truth of which they confirmed by many miracles, believed and was baptized. Thenceforward great numbers gathered each day to hear the word of God, forsaking their heathen rites and entering the unity of Christ's holy Church as believers. While the king was pleased at their faith and conversion, it is said that he would not compel anyone to accept Christianity; for he had learned from his instructors and guides to salvation that the service of Christ must be accepted freely and not under compulsion. Nevertheless, he showed greater favor to believers, because they were fellow-citizens the kingdom of heaven. And it was not long before he granted his teachers in his capital of Canterbury a place of residence appropriate to their station, and gave them possessions of various kinds to supply their wants.

Questions for Discussion:

1. King Ethelbert was concerned that the missionaries might be practitioners of "magic arts." Compare Bede's description with the code of Salian Law, (Document 2.8) provision XIX. How do you explain this fear, and in the case of the Franks, the legal stipulations?
2. This selection gives further evidence of the practice of "marriage diplomacy." How did this advance the cause of Christianity, in addition to providing an alliance between the Frankish house and Ethelbert?
3. Bede gives clear reasons for the spread of Christianity in Anglo-Saxon England. What were some of these?

2.11   Letter from Pope Boniface to Queen Ethelburga

The influence of aristocratic women was a significant factor in the conversion of several areas of Anglo-Saxon England. Just as the Frankish Queen Clothilda had entreated her husband, Clovis, to accept the Christian god (see Document 2.7), and Ethelbert's queen, Bertha, practiced Christianity (see Document 2.10), Queen Ethelburga urged her husband, Edwin, King of Northumbria (584–633), to become a Christian. As may be seen in the following letter, Pope Boniface (r. 619–625) viewed her as an ally in his quest to convert the English people; he encouraged her to pray for the king's enlightenment, pointing out that Edwin's conversion would bring his subjects into the Christian fold.

(From *A History of the English Church and People* by Bede, translated with an introduction by Leo Sherley-Price, revised by R. E. Latham (Penguin Classics 1955, Revised edition 1968). Copyright © Leo Sherley-Price, 1955, 1968.)

To his illustrious daughter, Queen Ethelberga, from Bishop Boniface, servant of the servants of God:

In His great providence, our loving Redeemer has offered a saving remedy to the human race, which He has saved from the Devil's enslaving tyranny by the shedding of His own precious Blood. Christ has made His Name known to the nations in various ways, so that they may acknowledge their Creator by accepting the mysteries of the Christian Faith. God in His mercy has revealed this truth to Your Majesty's own mind in your own mystical cleansing and regeneration. We have been greatly encouraged by God's goodness in granting you, through your own profession of faith, an opportunity to kindle a spark of the true religion in your husband; for in this way He will more swiftly inspire not only the mind of your illustrious Consort to love of Him, but the minds of your subjects as well.

We have been informed by those who came to report the laudable conversion of our glorious son King Eadbald [r. 616–640] that Your Majesty, who has also received the wonderful sacrament of the Christian Faith, shows a shining example of good works, pleasing to God. We also know that you carefully shun idol-worship and the allurements of temples and divinations; and that, having given your allegiance to Christ, you are unshakeably devoted to the love of our Redeemer and labor constantly to propagate the Christian Faith. Out of pastoral affection, we particularly enquired about your illustrious husband and learned that he still serves abominable idols and is slow to listen to the teaching of the preachers. It has caused us deep grief to hear that your partner remains a stranger to the knowledge of the most high and undivided Trinity. Our paternal responsibility moves us to urge Your Christian Majesty, imbued with the force of divine inspiration, not to avoid the duty imposed on us in season and out of season, in order that, with the assistance and strength of our Lord and Savior Jesus Christ, the King also may be added to the Christian fold. Only in this way will you enjoy the full privileges of marriage in perfect union; for the Scripture says, *"The two shall become one flesh."* But how can it be called a true union between you, so long as he remains alienated from the daylight of your Faith by the barrier of dark and lamentable error?

Let it therefore be your constant prayer that God of His mercy will bless and enlighten the King, so that you, who are united in one flesh by the ties of bodily affection, may after this fleeting life remain united for ever in the bond of faith. My illustrious daughter, persevere in using every effort to soften his heart by teaching him the commandments of God. Help him to understand the excellence of the mystery that you have accepted by believing and the marvelous worth of the reward that you have been accounted worthy to receive in this new birth. Melt the coldness of his heart by teaching him about the Holy Spirit, so that the warmth of divine faith may set his mind on fire through your constant encouragement and remove the numbing and deadening errors of paganism. If you do this, the witness of the Holy Spirit will most certainly be fulfilled in you, that *"the unbelieving husband shall be saved through the believing wife."* For this is why you have received our Lord's merciful goodness, in order that you may restore to your Redeemer with increase the fruits of faith and of the boundless blessings entrusted to you. We shall not cease from constant prayer that God will assist and guide you to accomplish this.

Having mentioned this matter, as fatherly duty and affection demands, we beg you to inform us, as soon as a suitable messenger is available, what measure of success God's goodness grants you in the conversion of your husband and the people over whom you reign. Good news will greatly relieve our mind, which anxiously awaits the longed-for salvation of you and yours. And when we see the glory of the divine atonement spreading ever more widely among you, we shall give glad and heartfelt thanks to God, the Giver of all good things, and to blessed Peter, Prince of the Apostles.

We impart to you the blessing of your protector, blessed Peter, Prince of the Apostles. With it we send you a silver mirror, together with a gold and ivory comb, asking Your Majesty to accept these gifts with the same goodwill as that with which we send them.

Questions for Discussion:

1. Pope Boniface advances various arguments to the queen in order to enlist her support in the conversion of England. What are some of these?
2. Why was the conversion of the king such an important goal?
3. Do you think "the Venerable" Bede was an unbiased historian? Why or why not?

2.12   Jonas, *The Life of St. Columban*

Anglo-Saxon England was not the only area of the British Isles to experience conversion by monks. Monasticism was also a potent force in Ireland, although the Irish monks, because of their relative isolation, had developed traditions that were somewhat different from those of their English counterparts. The Irish monastic movement proved to be a vital influence, not only in the conversion of their home country, but in the Christianization of Europe as well. One of the most important of the Irish monks was St. Columban (543–615), who traveled to Gaul, where he was influential in guiding the religious life of the Merovingian nobility. He founded several monasteries in Gaul, and later in Italy; the most famous of these is at Bobbio. The following account taken from the seventh-century Life of St. Colmban *by the monk Jonas describes his experiences in establishing religious practice and monasticism on the Continent. The biographer Jonas obtained his information from companions of Columban who worked with him as missionaries.*

(From *Readings in European History*, ed. by Leon Bernard and Theodore B. Hodges. New York: The MacMillan Co., 1958, pp. 70–72. Translation modified.)

Having collected a band of brethren, St. Columban . . . started out [from a monastery in Ireland] in the twentieth year of his life, and under the guidance of Christ went to the seashore with twelve companions. . . . They embarked, and began the dangerous journey across the channel and sailed quickly with a smooth sea and favorable wind to the coast of Brittany. . . . They decided to enter the land of Gaul. . . .

. . . At that time, either because of the numerous enemies from without, or on account of the carelessness of the bishops, the Christian faith had almost departed from that country. The creed alone remained. But the saving grace of penance and the longing to root out the lusts of the flesh were to be found only in a few. Everywhere that he went the noble man preached the Gospel. And it pleased the people, because his teaching was adorned by eloquence and enforced by examples of virtue.

. . . He found a place formerly strongly fortified . . . which had . . . been called Luxovium. . . . A great number of stone idols, which in the old heathen times had been worshiped with horrible rites, stood in the forest near at hand. Here then the excellent man began to build a monastery [Luxeuil]. At the news of this people streamed in from all directions in order to consecrate themselves to the practice of religion, so that the large number of monks scarcely had sufficient room. The children of the nobles from all directions strove to come there; despising the spurned trappings of the world and the pomp of present wealth, they sought eternal rewards.

Columban perceived that the people were rushing in from all directions to the remedy of penance, and that the walls of one monastery could with difficulty hold so great a throng of converts. Although they were of one purpose and heart, yet one monastery was insufficient for the abode of so great a number. Accordingly he sought out another spot especially remarkable for its bountiful supply of water and founded a second convent to which he gave the name of *Fontaines.* In this he placed men whose piety could not be doubted. After he had settled the bands of monks in these places, he stayed alternately at the two convents, and full of the Holy Ghost, he established the rule which they were to follow . . .

The fame of Columban had already penetrated into all parts of Gaul and Germany, and everyone was praising the venerable man. King Theuderic[18] (r. 511–533), too, came often to him and humbly begged his prayers . . . As he very often visited Columban, the holy man began to reprove him because he sinned with concubines . . . After this reproof from Columban, the king promised to abstain from such sinful conduct. But the old serpent came to his grandmother Brunhilda, who was a second Jezebel, and aroused her pride against the holy man, because she saw that Theuderic was obedient to him. For she feared that her power and honor would be lessened if, after the expulsion of the concubines, a queen should rule the court.

St. Columban happened one day to go to Brunhilda . . . As she saw him enter the court, she led to him the illegitimate sons of Theuderic. When St. Columban saw her, he asked what she wanted of him. Brunhilda answered, "These are the king's sons; give them your blessing." He replied, "Know that these boys will never bear the royal scepter, for they were born in sin." Enraged, she told the boys to go. When after this Columban left the court, a loud cracking noise was heard, the whole house trembled and everyone shook with

fear. But that did not succeed in checking the wrath of the wretched woman.

From that time she began to persecute the neighboring monasteries. She issued an order that none of the monks should be allowed to leave the lands of the monasteries, no one should receive them into other houses or give them any aid . . .

. . . Brunhilda began again to incite the king against Columban in every way; she urged all the nobles and others at court to do the same, and influenced the bishops to attack Columban's faith and to abolish his monastic rule. She succeeded so fully that the holy man was obliged to . . . leave the country . . .

[After many years of labor among the Alamans, Columban went to northern Italy—to "a lonely spot in the Apennines."] . . . The place had many advantages, it was unusually fertile, the water was full of fishes; it had long been called *Bobbio*, from the brook that flowed by it. There was another river in the neighborhood, by which Hannibal had once passed a winter and suffered the loss of a very great number of men, horses and elephants. Columban now went there, and with all diligence restored to its old beauty the church which was already half in ruins.

. . . After a single year in his monastery of Bobbio, Columban, the man of God, ended his devout life on the eleventh day before the Kalends of December [615] . . . His remains are buried there, where they have proved their virtues, by the aid of Christ. . . .

Questions for Discussion:

1. Why did Columban choose to build his monastery at Luxovium?
2. This selection mentions the social class of the "throngs" of converts. How do you account for the fact that the progeny of noblemen chose the monastic life? It is important to note that this association of the nobility with monasteries will be an important feature in our study of the Middle Ages.
3. Not all aristocratic women were instrumental in the adoption of Christianity. What reasons does the author give for the attitude and actions of Brunhilda?

---

[18]Theuderic was one of the sons of Clovis. According to the practice of the Merovingians, the kingdom was divided among the successors; Theuderic received the lands that became Austrasia.

The Byzantine Empire

2.13   The *Corpus Iuris Civilis* of Justinian

Justinian (r. 527–565) was the most important Byzantine emperor of late antiquity. His obsessive aim was to re-establish the Roman Empire as it had been during the reign of Augustus, and he began the "reconquest" of the western part of the empire by attacking the Ostrogoths in Italy. After a conflict that lasted some twenty-five years, he managed to establish feeble control. After Justinian's death, however, the Lombards conquered the resident forces of the Italian peninsula, ending the emperor's idealistic, but unrealistic ambition.

Although Justinian failed in his attempt to re-create the Roman Empire, he did make several enduring contributions. One of these was the compilation of laws known as the Corpus Iuris Civilis, *which is perhaps the most influential work of legal scholarship in the history of Western civilization. Justinian recognized the complexity of the maze of laws that had been enacted during the Roman Republic and Empire, and he instructed his legal and financial officials to sort out the tangle and produce an ordered legal system. The* Corpus *was divided into three sections: the* Codex, *which was a summary of previous Roman law; the* Digesta, *a compilation of legal opinion; and the* Institutiones, *a legal textbook. A compilation of new laws, the* Novellae Leges, *was added later. An excerpt from one portion of the* Digesta *demonstrates the motivating concept and design of the work.*

(From *The Digest of Justinian*, trans. Charles Henry Monro, v. 1 [Cambridge: Cambridge University Press, 1904], pp. xiii–xiv, xvi–xvii. Translation modified.)

On The Plan of The Digest

The Emperor Caesar Flavius Justinianus, pious happy renowned conqueror and triumpher, ever Augustus, greets Tribonianus his quaestor.[19]

1. In all things there is nothing so worthy of respect as the authority of enacted law, which explains things both divine and human and expels all

---

[19]A *quaestor* was a financial official.

iniquity; yet we find the whole course of our statutes, having come down from the foundation of the city of Rome and from the days of Romulus, to be in a state of such confusion that they reach to an infinite length and surpass the bounds of all human capacity. It was therefore our first desire to begin with the most sacred Emperors of old times, to amend their statutes, and to put them in a clear order, so that they might be collected together in one book, and, being divested of all superfluous repetition and most inequitable disagreement, might afford to all mankind the ready resource of their unalloyed character.

2. This work was accomplished and put together in one volume under our own brilliant name. We have endeavored to lift ourselves above scanty and somewhat unimportant matters and to arrive at the full and supreme amendment of the law, so as to amend and rearrange the entire Roman jurisprudence and to present in one volume the scattered books of a number of authors, a thing which no one ever dared to hope or to desire. The task appeared to us to be one of great difficulty, indeed it seemed impossible. However, we lifted our hands to Heaven, and, praying for the Eternal aid, we embraced this enterprise in our minds, trusting to God, who is able in the magnitude of His goodness to grant and complete achievements almost desperate. . . .

4. You, therefore, have our order to read and to work up the books dealing with Roman law left by the learned of old time to whom the most sacred Emperor allowed the privilege of writing and interpreting rules of law. The whole substance should be taken from them, all repetition and all discrepancy being as far as possible got rid of, so that a single and sufficient result might be presented in the place of the scattered materials of the past. Whereas, on the other hand, if other authors have written books dealing with

law, but their writings have not been received or used by any later authorities, we ourselves are not concerned to let their works affect our resolution. . . .

11. We therefore order that everything should be governed by those two books, one consisting of Imperial enactments, the other of the law consolidated and amended *(ius enucleatum)* and put together with a view to a book to be made; adding anything else that may come to be published by us to serve the use of an educational work *(institutiones),* in order that the immature mind of the student, being supplied with simple principles, may be the more easily brought to the comprehension of the higher learning.

12. Our complete work, such as it will be composed by you with God's assistance, shall bear the name of Digest or Pandects. No person learned in the law shall at any time venture to add any commentary thereto, lest he upset by his own language the concise method of this book, as was done in old time, when, by the contradictory opinions of expositors, the whole law was almost thrown into confusion: let it be enough to make some few corrections of it by

notes and an ingenious use of titles, avoiding any complaints that might arise from the habit of interpreting. . . .

14. All these things your Wisdom must, with the favor of God, endeavor to accomplish, together with other most able men, and bring it to a well-conceived and most speedy close, so that the complete book, digested into fifty heads, may be put before us in strong and eternal memory of the matter in hand. This will provide proof of the providence of Almighty God, to the glory of our rule and of your service. Given on the eighteenth day before the Kalends of January at Constantinople; in the consulship of the most honorable Lampadius and Orestes.

Questions for Discussion:

1. What do you think Justinian intended to accomplish by ordering the compilation of the Corpus Iuris Civilis?
2. What reasons can you give for the enduring importance of this work?
3. What specific actions does this order caution against? Why?

INTERPRETING THE EVIDENCE

2.14 Hagia Sophia and a Description of the Building by Procopius

In addition to his other projects, Justinian undertook an extensive construction program in his capital, Constantinople. The most famous of the buildings is the magnificent Hagia Sophia (Holy Wisdom), which symbolized the power of both emperor and Church. Begun in 532 and dedicated on Christmas Day (some scholars believe it was December 27), 537, Hagia Sophia was built on the site of an earlier basilica that was constructed during the reign of the emperor Theodosius. As may be seen in the groundplan (page 59), the structure combines the longitudinal axis of the Latin-cross plan (as seen in the *groundplan of St. Peter's, Document 1.8) with the square axis of the Greek-cross plan. The view of the interior substantiates the description by Justinian's historian Procopius (late fifth century–c. 562) appended here. Following the Turkish conquest of Constantinople in 1453, Hagia Sophia was dedicated as a mosque—hence the minarets evident in the groundplan and the arabic medallions seen in the interior photograph.*

(From Procopius, *"The Buildings of Justinian,"* in *The Library of the Palestine Pilgrims' Text Society*, vol. II. [London, 1897], pp. 5–11.)

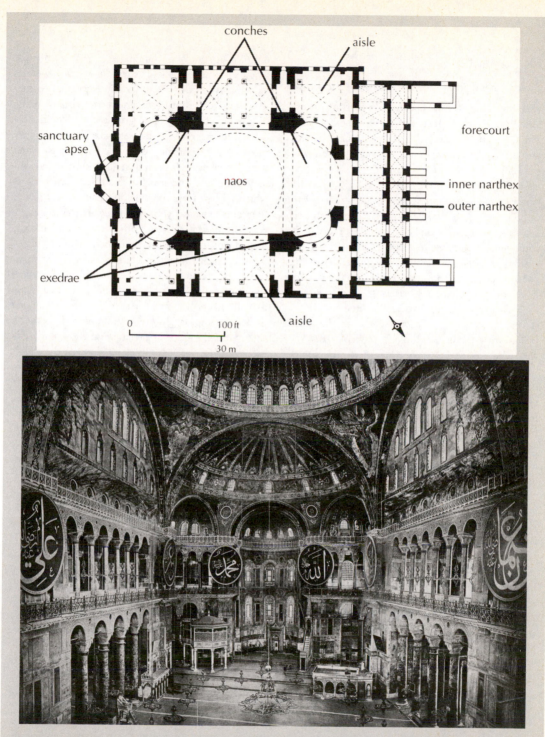

(top) Hagia Sophia, Constantinople. 532–537. Dome height 184 ft., diameter 112 ft. (© 1996 Harry N. Abrams, Inc.)

(bottom) Hagia Sophia, Constantinople. (From the Turkish Embassy Tourism Counselor's Office.)

(continued)

Document

From Procopius, *The Buildings of Justinian*

The lowest dregs of the people in Byzantium once assailed the Emperor Justinian in the rebellion called Nika, which I have clearly described in my 'History of the Wars.' To prove that it was not merely against the Emperor, but no less against God that they took up arms, they ventured to burn the church of the Christians. (This church the people of Byzantium call Sophia, *i.e., Wisdom.*) God permitted them to effect this crime, knowing how great the beauty of this church would be when restored. Thus the church was entirely reduced to ashes; but the Emperor Justinian not long afterwards adorned it in such a fashion, that if anyone had asked the Christians in former times if they wished their church to be destroyed and thus restored, showing them the appearance of the church which we now see, I think it probable that they would have prayed that they might as soon as possible behold their church destroyed, in order that it might be turned into its present form. The Emperor, regardless of expense of all kinds, pressed on its restoration, and collected together all the workmen from every land. Anthemius of Tralles, by far the most celebrated architect, not only of his own, but of all former times, carried out the King's zealous intentions, organized the labors of the workmen, and prepared models of the future construction. Associated with him was another architect named Isidorus, a Milesian by birth, a man of intelligence, and worthy to carry out the plans of the Emperor Justinian. It is, indeed, a proof of the esteem with which God regarded the Emperor, that He furnished him with men who would be so useful in effecting his designs, and we are compelled to admire the intelligence of the Emperor, in being able to choose the most suitable of mankind to carry out the noblest of his works.

The church consequently presented a most glorious spectacle, extraordinary to those who beheld it, and altogether incredible to those who are told of it. In height it rises to the very heavens, and overtops the neighboring buildings like a ship anchored among them: it rises above the rest of the city, which it adorns, while it forms a part of it, and it is one of its beauties that being a part of the city, and growing out of it, it stands so high above it, that from it the whole city can be beheld as from a watch-tower. Its length and breadth are so judiciously arranged that it appears to be both long and wide without being disproportioned. It is distinguished by indescribable beauty, for it excels both in its size and in the harmony of its proportion, having no part excessive and none deficient, being more magnificent than ordinary buildings, and much more elegant than those which are out of proportion. It is singularly full of light and sunshine; you would declare that the place is not lighted by the sun from without, but that the rays are produced within itself, such an abundance of light is poured into this church and [it] has small openings left on purpose, so that the places where these intervals in the construction occur may serve for conductors of light . . . As the arches are arranged in a quadrangular figure, the stonework between them takes the shape of a triangle; the lower angle of each triangle, being compressed between the shoulders of the arches, is slender, while the upper part becomes wider as it rises in the space between them, and ends against the circle which rises from thence, forming there its remaining angles. A spherical-shaped dome standing upon this circle makes it exceedingly beautiful; from the lightness of the building it does not appear to rest upon a solid foundation, but to cover the place beneath as though it were suspended from heaven by the fabled golden chain. All these parts surprisingly joined to one another in the air, suspended one from another, and resting only on that which is next to them, form the work into one admirably harmonious whole . . .

Let us now proceed to describe the remaining parts of the church. The entire ceiling is covered with pure gold, which adds glory to its beauty, though the rays of light reflected upon the gold from the marble surpass it in beauty; there are two porticos on each side, which do not in any way dwarf the size of the church, but add to its width. In length they reach quite to the ends, but in height they fall short of it; these also have a domed ceiling and are adorned with gold. Of these two porticos, the one is set apart for male, and the other for female worshipers; there is no variety in them, nor do they differ in any respect from one another, but their very equality and similarity add to the beauty of the church. Who could describe the galleries of the portion set apart for women, or the numerous porticos and cloistered courts with which the church is surrounded? Who could tell of the beauty of the columns and marbles with which the church is adorned? One would think that one had come upon a meadow full of flowers in bloom: who would not admire the purple tints of some and the green of others, the glowing red and glittering white, and those, too, which nature, like a painter, has marked with the strongest contrasts of color? Whoever enters there to worship perceives at once that it is not by any human strength or skill, but by the favor of God that this work has been perfected; his mind rises sublime to commune with God, feeling that He cannot be far off, but must especially love to dwell in the place which He has chosen; and this takes place not only when a man sees it for the first time, but it always makes the same impression upon him, as though he had never beheld it before. No one ever became weary of this spectacle, but those who are in the Church delight in what they see, and, when

they leave it, magnify it in their talk about it; moreover, it is impossible accurately to describe the treasure of gold and silver plate and gems, which the Emperor Justinian has presented to it; but by the description of one of them, I leave the rest to be inferred. That part of the church which is especially sacred, and where the priests alone are allowed to enter, which is called the Sanctuary, contains forty thousand pounds weight of silver.

Questions for Discussion:

1. Compare the groundplan and photograph of Hagia Sophia with the groundplan and drawing of old St. Peter's (see Document 1.8). What differences do you see? What similarities?
2. Analyze Constantine's gift of St. Peter's and Justinian's endowment of Hagia Sophia. Do you think the emperors shared a motivation in their patronage?
3. How, according to Procopius, did the emperor participate in the building of Hagia Sophia?

INTERPRETING THE EVIDENCE

2.15 Theodora and Justinian: The Mosaics at Ravenna and the *Secret History* by Procopius

The splendid mosaics (created between 525–47) in the Church of St. Vitale, Ravenna, Italy, include, among other images, portraits of Justinian and his wife, Theodora. Each is surrounded by a retinue; Justinian is accompanied by courtiers, soldiers, and ecclesiastical dignitaries, and the empress by guards, ladies of the court, and priests. The emperor and empress bear gifts for the Church—Justinian holds a Eucharistic plate and Theodora a chalice. The theme of offering donations is further reinforced by the images of the three wise men on Theodora's skirt.

The mosaics present a formal, majestic image of the monarchs. Another, quite different, impression may be
derived from reading the Secret History *of Procopius, which offers a "behind the scenes" view of the emperor and empress. Theodora was reputed to have been a "circus performer" (perhaps a prostitute) before her marriage to Justinian, and Procopius recounts this in his history. It is important to note that he evidently despised the empress; his writing sensationalizes her background and sexual adventures, in addition to providing a most unflattering account of her character.*

(From *The Secret History of Procopius*, trans. Richard Atwater [New York: Covici Friede, 1927], pp. 92–97; 161–164.)

(continued)

Justinian and His Court *(Court of Emperor Justinian, ca. 547 C.E. Early Christian mosaic, 264 by 365 cm. San Vatale, Ravenna, Italy. Scala/Art Resource, NY.)*

Document

From Procopius, *The Secret History*

I think this is as good a time as any to describe the personal appearance of the man [Justinian]. Now in physique he was neither tall nor short, but of average height; not thin, but moderately plump; his face was round, and not bad looking, for he had good color, even when he fasted for two days. . . .

Now such was Justinian in appearance; but his character was something I could not fully describe. For he was at once villainous and amenable; as people say colloquially, a moron. He was never truthful with anyone, but always guileful in what he said and did, yet easily hoodwinked by any who wanted to deceive him. His nature was an unnatural mixture of folly and wickedness. What in ancient times a peripatetic philosopher said was also true of him, that opposite qualities combine in a man as in the mixing of colors. I will try to portray him, however, insofar as I can fathom his complexity.

This Emperor, then, was deceitful, devious, false, hypocritical, two-faced, cruel, skilled in dissembling his thought, never moved to tears by either joy or pain, though he could summon them artfully at will when the occasion demanded, a liar always, not only offhand, but in writing, and when he swore sacred oaths to his subjects in their very hearing. Then he would immediately break his agreements and pledges, like the vilest of slaves, whom indeed only the fear of torture drives to confess their perjury. A faithless friend, he was a treacherous enemy, insane for murder and plunder, quarrelsome and revolutionary, easily led to anything evil, but never willing to listen to good counsel, quick to plan mischief and carry it out, but finding even the hearing of anything good distasteful to his ears.

How could anyone put Justinian's ways into words? These and many even worse vices were disclosed in him as in no other mortal: nature seemed to have taken the wickedness of all other men combined and planted it in this man's soul. And besides this, he was too prone to listen to accusations; and too quick to punish. For he decided such cases without full examination, naming the punishment when he had heard only the accuser's side of the matter. Without hesitation he wrote decrees for the plundering of countries, sacking of cities, and slavery of whole nations, for no cause whatever. So that if one wished to take all the calamities which had befallen the Romans before this time and weigh them against his crimes, I think it would be found that more men had been murdered by this single man than in all previous history.

He had no scruples about appropriating other people's property, and did not even think any excuse necessary, legal or illegal, for confiscating what did not belong to him. And when it was his, he was more than ready to squander it in insane display, or give it as an unnecessary bribe to the barbarians. In short, he neither held on to any money himself nor let anyone else keep any: as if his reason were not avarice, but jealousy of those who had riches. Driving all wealth from the country of the Romans in this manner, he became the cause of universal poverty.

Now this was the character of Justinian, so far as I can portray it.

Procopius's description of Theodora's actions (see photo below) is even more damning:

Theodora was overtaken with suspicion of one of her servants named Areobindus, a barbarian by birth, but a handsome young man, whom she had made her steward. Instead of accusing him directly, she decided to have him cruelly whipped in her presence (though they say she was madly in love

Theodora and Her Court *(The Mosaics at Ravenna, c. 547. San Vitale, Ravenna. Scala, Art Resource, NY.)*

(continued)

with the fellow) without explaining her reason for the punishment. What became of the man after that we do not know, nor has any one ever seen him since. For if the Queen wanted to keep any of her actions concealed, it remained secret and unmentioned; and neither was any who knew of the matter allowed to tell it to his closest friend, nor could any who tried to learn what had happened ever find out, no matter how much of a busybody he was.

No other tyrant since mankind began ever inspired such fear, since not a word could be spoken against her without her hearing of it: her multitude of spies brought her the news of whatever was said and done in public or in private. And when she decided the time had come to take vengeance on any offender, she did as follows. Summoning the man, if he happened to be notable, she would privately hand him over to one of her confidential attendants, and order that he be escorted to the farthest boundary of the Roman realm. And her agent, in the dead of night, covering the victim's face with a hood and binding him, would put him on board a ship and accompany him to the place selected by Theodora. There he would secretly leave the unfortunate in charge of another qualified for this work, charging him to keep the prisoner under guard and tell no one of the matter until the Empress should take pity on the wretch or, as time went on, he should languish under his bondage and succumb to death . . .

Then there was Basanius, one of the Green faction, a prominent young man, who incurred her anger by making some uncomplimentary remark. Basanius, warned of her displeasure, fled to the Church of Michael the Archangel. She immediately sent the Prefect after him, charging Basanius, however, not with slander, but pederasty. And the Prefect, dragging the man from the church, had him flogged intolerably while all the populace, when they saw a Roman citizen of good standing so shamefully mistreated, straightway sympathized with him, and cried so loud to let him go that Heaven must have heard their reproaches. Whereupon the Empress punished him further, and had him castrated so that he bled to death, and his estate was confiscated, although his case had never been tried. Thus, when this female was enraged, no church offered sanctuary, no law gave protection, no intercession of the people brought mercy to her victim; nor could anything else in the world stop her.

Questions for Discussion:

1. Look carefully at the mosaic images of the emperor and empress. What messages do these portraits send about power and religiosity? Provide specific examples.

2. Does the description by Procopius in his *Secret History* convince you of his claims about Justinian and Theodora? What reasons may have motivated him to write this extraordinarily negative work?

3. You have read about other queens in this chapter (Clothilde, Bertha, and Ethelburga). Does the mosaic image of Theodora compare in any way with what you know of these women?

Chapter 3

The Rise of Islam

During the seventh century, as the Franks were consolidating their power in western Europe, Islam, the world's third great monotheistic religion, arose in the Arabian peninsula. The new belief spread rapidly throughout northern Africa and the Near East, reaching as far east as India and as far west as the Iberian Peninsula within a century, as may be seen in the accompanying map. The teachings of Islam were founded upon a series of revelations given to the prophet Muhammad, who thought of himself as the latest in a series of

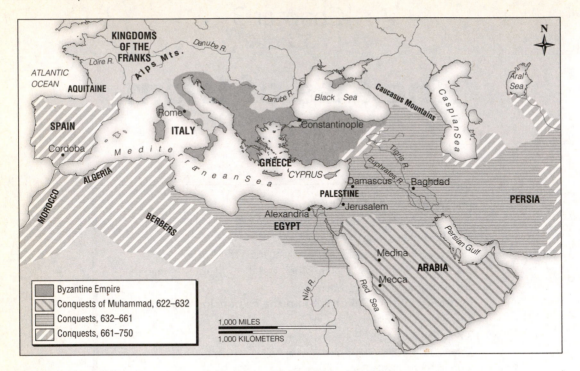

The Expansion of Islam. *(From Kagan et al., The Western Heritage, 10th ed., p. 182)*

prophets beginning with Abraham and extending through Jesus; hence, for Muslims, the religion of Islam is a continuation of the Judeo-Christian tradition. Muhammad's early religious experiences are described in this chapter in an excerpt from the biography by Ibn Ishaq, along with a discussion of the initial acceptance of the new religion.

The texts of the revelations received by Muhammad form the Islamic book of Holy Scripture, known as the Qu'ran, which was compiled after the death of the prophet. An account of the circumstances leading to this codification by his followers reveals their anxiety about the potential loss of the sacred teachings, and their desire to preserve them for posterity.

Passages from the Qu'ran established the "Five Pillars of Faith" to be practiced by all Muslims, as the followers of Islam are known. As the selections in this chapter demonstrate, the holy scriptures provide the instruction for

participating in Islamic religious life, including the confession of faith, participation in the daily rituals of prayer, the giving of alms, fasting during Ramadan, and the expectation of pilgrimage to Mecca.

A significant aspect of Islamic belief is that of jihad, or Holy War. The attitudes and teachings concerning jihad may be found both in the Qu'ran and in the teachings of Muhammad. Together they form a succinct view of the Islamic doctrine of war against the "infidel." The documents in this chapter demonstrate the conflicting ideas of inner personal struggle and aggressive warfare.

The role of women in Islamic society was also defined by stipulations in the Qu'ran. As Document 3.5 demonstrates, Muslim expectations for female behavior differ in significant ways from Western practices.

Following the death of Muhammad, the leaders of the religious community were faced with providing organization for the Islamic state and direction for the continuing mission to introduce the faith to the people of the expanding geographical areas. A new leader was required, and the circumstances of his election were to have far-reaching consequences; indeed, the contemporary conflict between the sunni and shia parties of the Islamic world has its roots in this choice. The account by the ninth-century scholar al-Tabari describes the establishment of the Islamic government following Muhammad's death and demonstrates the struggle between his potential successors and the resolution of the conflict.

The extraordinary expansion of Islamic domination during the seventh and eighth centuries included the conquest of al-Andalus—the southern portion of the Iberian Peninsula. As recounted by the chronicler Ibn Abd al-Hakam, the Muslim soldiers were able to assert control over the entire area in a relatively brief time.

The Muslim rulers in al-Andalus and elsewhere were faced with establishing rules and laws that would enable the Muslims to live with authority, as well as peace, in a diverse society that included Christians and Jews. Examples of this legal accommodation may be seen in the "Pact of Umar" and the "Treaty of Tudmir," which establish the rights of the "dhimmi" (non-Muslim people living under Muslim rule).

Muslim places of worship are known as mosques. This chapter's first "Interpreting the Evidence" feature contains a description of the first mosque built in Cairo, and includes documents that demonstrate the kinds of support donated for the continuation of the establishment.

One of the Five Pillars of Islam is prayer, which is practiced five times each day when Muslims respond to the call of the muezzins, or criers. The believers pray toward Mecca. In a mosque the proper direction is marked by a qibla wall, with a niche known as a mihrab. A photograph of a particularly beautiful example is included in this chapter's second "Interpreting the Evidence" feature. The image is accompanied by "Umar in Jerusalem," a document that describes the origins of the qibla.

The cultural legacy of Islam is extraordinary, as will be observed in detail in subsequent chapters. Included in Chapter 3 is an excerpt from the works of the ninth-century scholar Ibn Qutayba concerning the importance of poetry, and two examples of lyrics by Muslim and Jewish poets (Documents 3.15 and 3.16) that would have a strong influence on the verses of the troubadours (see Chapter 10). This chapter ends with one of Scheherazade's magical tales from The Thousand and One Nights. These literary selections provide brief examples of the seminal nature of the Islamic intellectual and cultural contributions to the medieval world.

Muhammad and the *Qu'ran*

3.1   The Night of Destiny: Ibn Ishaq, *The Life of Muhammad*

Muhammad, who was born in Mecca c. 570, viewed himself as the final messenger in a series of prophets extending from Abraham through Moses and Jesus. He was the human prophet of his god (Allah), whose teachings about Islam, meaning "submission to God's will," revealed the final truth to Jews and Christians—the "People of the Book." His work thus fulfilled the Judeo-Christian prophecy of deliverance. According to Islamic tradition, Muhammad began to receive communications from Allah in about 610, when he was approximately forty years old. On the night of the first revelation, which Muslims call the "Night of Power and Excellence," he had gone from the city of Mecca to the nearby mountain of Hira for a period of meditation. Here he was approached by a heavenly visitor, traditionally identified as the angel Gabriel. The following excerpt from the biography of Muhammad by Ibn Ishaq describes the circumstances.

The biographer lived about a century after Muhammad. No copy of his original work survives, but it was edited by Ibn Hisham (d. 834) about fifty years after Ibn Ishaq's death. This version borrowed heavily from the original, and is considered to be a faithful reflection of the earliest biography of the prophet.

(From *The Life of Muhammad* by Ibn Ishaq, trans. by A. Guillaume. Oxford: Oxford University Press, 1955, pp. 111–113. Copyright © 1955 Oxford University Press. Reprinted by permission.)

The Beginning of the Sending Down of the *Qu'ran*

The apostle began to receive revelations in the month of Ramadan. In the words of God, "The month of Ramadan in which the *Qu'ran* was brought down as a guidance to men, and proofs of guidance and a decisive criterion." And again, "Verily we have sent it down on the night of destiny, and what has shown you what the night of destiny is? The night of destiny is better than a thousand months. In it the angels and the spirit descend by their Lord's permission with every matter. It is peace until the rise of dawn. Again . . . by the perspicuous book, verily we have sent it down in a blessed night. Verily, we were warning. In it every wise matter is decided as a command from us. Verily we sent it down."

Then revelation came fully to the apostle while he was believing in Him and in the truth of His message. He received it willingly, and took upon himself what it entailed, whether of man's goodwill or anger. Prophecy is a troublesome burden-only strong, resolute messengers can bear it by God's help and grace, because of the opposition which they meet from men in conveying God's message. The apostle carried out God's orders in spite of the opposition and ill treatment which he met with.

Muhammad's wife, Khadija, was the first to accept the new religion.

Khadija believed in him and accepted as true what he brought from God, and helped him in his work. She was the first to believe in God and His apostle, and in the truth of his message. By her, God lightened the burden of His prophet. He never met with contradiction and charges of falsehood, which saddened him, but God comforted him by her when he went home. She strengthened him, lightened his burden, proclaimed his truth, and belittled men's opposition. May God Almighty have mercy upon her!

Then revelations stopped for a time so that the apostle of God was distressed and grieved. Then Gabriel brought him the Sura[1] of the Morning, in which his Lord, who had so honored him, swore that

He had not forsaken him, and did not hate him. God said, 'By the morning and the night when it is still, thy Lord hath not forsaken nor hated thee, meaning that He has not left you and forsaken you, nor hated you after having loved you. "And verily, the latter end is better for you than the beginning," i.e. What I have for you when you return to Me is better than the honor which I have given you in the world. "And your Lord will give you and will satisfy you," i.e. of victory in this world and reward in the next. "Did he not find you an orphan and give you refuge, going astray and guided you, found you poor and made you rich?" God thus told him of how He had begun to honor him in his earthly life, and of His kindness to him as an orphan poor and wandering astray, and of His delivering him from all that by His compassion.

"Do not oppress the orphan and do not repel the beggar." That is, do not be a tyrant or proud or harsh or mean towards the weakest of God's creatures.

"Speak of the kindness of thy Lord," i.e. tell about the kindness of God in giving you prophecy, mention it and call men to it.

So the apostle began to mention secretly God's kindness to him and to his servants in the matter of prophecy to everyone among his people whom he could trust.

During one of the revelations the angel Gabriel demonstrated the ritual of prayer, which would be practiced by all believers in Islam.

The apostle was ordered to pray and so he prayed. . . . A learned person told me that when prayer was laid on the apostle Gabriel came to him while he was on the heights of Mecca and dug a hole for him with his heel in the side of the valley from which a fountain gushed forth, and Gabriel performed the ritual ablution as the apostle watched him. This was in order to show him how to purify himself before prayer. Then the apostle performed the ritual ablution as he had seen Gabriel do it. Then Gabriel said a prayer with him while the apostle prayed with his prayer. Then Gabriel left him. The apostle came to Khadija and performed the ritual for her as Gabriel had done for him, and she copied him. Then he prayed with her as Gabriel had prayed with him, and she prayed his prayer.

---

[1]The term "sura" refers to a chapter in the *Qur'an* (pl. suwar). These are composed of verses, or ayat (sing. aya).

Questions for Discussion:

1. Why does Ibn Ishaq characterize prophecy as a "troublesome burden"? Do you agree?

2. Describe the portrayal of Muhammad's wife Khadija. How might her actions have become a model for Muslim women?
3. What is the ritual ablution? How did Muhammad receive directions for this action?

3.2   How the *Qu'ran* Was Assembled

The authorized Islamic book of Holy Scripture, known as the Qu'ran *("The Recitation"), was compiled in the mid-seventh century, several decades after the death of Muhammad. It consists of the 114 revelations received by the Prophet, which Muslims believe to be the transcript of a tablet preserved in heaven. Rather than being organized chronologically, the* Qu'ran *was arranged according to length. Hence, the earliest revelations, which were the shortest, appear toward the end of the text. The verses are known as* ayat *(sing.* aya*) and are organized into chapters, or* suwar *(sing.* sura*).*

Although Muslims maintain that the Qu'ran *was the literal word of God, of nearly equal importance are the deeds and words, or* sunna*, of Muhammad, which were recorded in narratives known as* hadiths*. These actions and sayings of the Prophet were regarded as demonstrating a clear manifestation of God's will; among other things, they provided guidance on matters not mentioned in the* Qu'ran*, and their practice became the pattern for community life. Over time the* hadiths *proliferated, and disagreement developed as to the authenticity of the individual accounts. The proper evaluation of the traditions rested with scholars, those individuals "learned in religion," who examined the reliability of the chain of narrators. They also analyzed the subject matter of the narratives in relation to the* Qu'ran *and verified tradition. During the ninth and tenth centuries, scholars in the Muslim world devoted themselves to sifting the enormous collections of anecdotes, and they authenticated and compiled those traditions worthy of being accepted and followed by the Muslim community. Six collections in particular were accepted as authoritative, including that of the scholar al-Bukarhi (810–870). The following document is from his collection known as* al-Sahih*, meaning "The Genuine"; the passage explains how and why the* Qu'ran *was compiled.*

(From *Islam: Volume II: From the Prophet Muhammad to the Capture of Constantinople*, by Bernard Lewis. (1987): pp. 1-2. Copyright © 1974 by Bernard Lewis. Reprinted by permission of Oxford University Press.)

Zayd ibn Thabit said: Abu Bakr [Muhammad's successor and the first *caliph—see page 75*] sent for me at the time of the battle of al-Yamama, and 'Umar ibn al-Khattab was with him. Abu Bakr said: 'Umar has come to me and said, "Death raged at the battle of al-Yamama and took many of the reciters of the *Qu'ran*. I fear lest death in battle overtake the reciters of the *Qu'ran* in the provinces and a large part of the *Qu'ran* be lost. I think you should give orders to collect the *Qu'ran*."

"What?" I asked 'Umar, "Will you do something which the Prophet of God himself did not do?"

"By God," replied 'Umar, "it would be a good deed."

'Umar did not cease to urge me until God opened my heart to this and I thought as 'Umar did.

Zayd continued: Abu Bakr said to me, "You are a young man, intelligent, and we see no fault in you, and you have already written down the revelation for the Prophet of God, may God bless and save him. Therefore go and seek the *Qu'ran* and assemble it."

By God, if he had ordered me to move a mountain it would not have been harder for me than his order to collect the *Qu'ran*. "What?" I asked, "Will you do something which the Prophet of God himself, may God bless and save him, did not do?"

"By God," replied Abu Bakr, "it would be a good deed."

And he did not cease to urge me until God opened my heart to this as he had opened the hearts of Abu Bakr and 'Umar.

Then I sought out and collected the parts of the *Qu'ran*, whether written on palm leaves or flat stones or in the hearts of men. Thus I found the end of the Sura of Repentance, which I had been unable to find anywhere else, with Abu'l-Khuzayma al-Ansari. These were the verses: "There came to you a Prophet from among yourselves. It grieves him that you sin. . . ." to the end [Sura ix, 129–130].

The leaves were with Abu Bakr until his death, then with 'Umar as long as he lived, and then with Hafsa, the daughter of 'Umar.

Anas ibn Malik said: Hudhayfa ibn al-Yaman went with 'Uthman when he was preparing the army of Syria to conquer Armenia and Adharbayjan, together with the army of Iraq. Hudhayfa was shocked by the differences in their reading of the *Qu'ran*, and said to 'Uthman, "O Commander of the Faithful, catch this community before they differ about their book as do the Jews and Christians."

'Uthman sent to Hafsa to say, "Send us the leaves. We shall copy them in codices and return them to you."

Hafsa sent them to 'Uthman, who ordered Zayd ibn Thabit, 'Abdallah ibn al-Zubayr, Sa'id ibn al-'As, and 'Abd al-Rahman ibn al-Harith ibn Hisham to copy them into codices. 'Uthman said to

the three of them who were of the tribe of Quraysh, "If you differ from Zayd ibn Thabit on anything in the *Qu'ran*, write it according to the language of Quraysh, for it is in their language that the *Qu'ran* was revealed."

They did this, and when they had copied the leaves into codices, 'Uthman returned the leaves to Hafsa. He sent copies of the codex which they made in all direction and gave orders to burn every leaf or codex which differed from it.

Questions for Discussion:

1. According to al-Bukhari, what was the original reason for beginning to compile the *Qu'ran*?
2. What sources were available for the compilation?
3. What difficulties were encountered in establishing an authentic version? How were these problems solved?

3.3   The Five Pillars of Islam: Passages from the *Qu'ran*

Muslims believe that the Qu'ran *is the literal, eternal Book of God, revealed to Muhammad to serve as a guide for human beings. Contained within its verses are directions that established the "Five Pillars of Islam"—five requirements for practicing the Islamic religious life. These consist of (1) the confession of faith, (2) recitation of prayers five times a day, (3) charitable contributions, or the giving of alms, (4) fasting from dawn to sunset during the month of Ramadan, and (5) pilgrimage to the holy city of Mecca and to the Ka'ba (the most holy sacred shrine). In addition, the* Qu'ran *speaks of many other aspects of Islamic life, such as* jihad, *or Holy War, and the proper position of women in Muslim society.*

(From *The Koran*, translated with notes by N.J. Dawood (Penguin Classics 1956, Fifth revised edition 1990). Copyright © N. J. Dawood, 1956, 1959, 1966, 1968, 1974, 1990, 1993, 1997, 1999, 2003.)

The Confession of Faith (*shahada*): "There is no god but Allah and Muhammad is His Prophet."

This testimony is given five times a day when the muezzin (crier) sounds the call to prayer. The monotheism expressed

by the statement reflects the core belief of Islam, which is expressed in the various passages of the Qu'ran, *including the following excerpt.*

Believers, have faith in God and His apostle, in the Book He has revealed to His apostle, and in the Scriptures He formerly revealed. He that denies God, His angels, His Scriptures, His apostles, and the Last Day has strayed far. (Sura 4: 136)

Prayer (*salat*)

This Book is not to be doubted. It is a guide for the righteous, who believe in the unseen and are steadfast in prayer; who give in alms from what we gave them; who believe in what has been revealed to you and what was revealed before you, and have absolute faith in the life to come. These are rightly guided by their Lord; these shall surely triumph. (Sura 2:1)

When your prayers are ended, remember God standing, sitting, and lying down. Attend regularly to your prayers so long as you are safe: for prayer is a duty incumbent on the faithful, to be conducted at appointed hours. (Sura 4: 103)

Almsgiving (*zakat*)

Have you thought of him that denies the Last Judgment? It is he who turns away the orphan and has no urge to feed the destitute.

Woe betide those who pray but are heedless in their prayer; who make a show of piety and forbid almsgiving. (Sura 107: 1–7)

Ramadan

Believers, fasting is decreed for you as it was decreed for those before you; perchance you will guard yourselves against evil. Fast a certain number of days, but if anyone among you is ill or on a journey, let him fast a similar number of days later; and for those that cannot endure it there is a penance ordained: the feeding of a poor man. He that does good of his own accord shall be well rewarded; but to fast is better for you, if you but knew it.

In the month of Ramadan the Koran was revealed, a book of guidance for mankind with proofs of guidance distinguishing right from wrong. Therefore whoever of you is present in that month let him fast. But he who is ill or on a journey shall fast a similar number of days later on. (Sura 2: 183)

Pilgrimage (the *hajj*)

Exhort all men to make the pilgrimage. They will come to you on foot and on the backs of swift camels from every distant quarter; they will come to avail themselves of many a benefit, and to pronounce on the appointed days the name of God over the cattle which He has given them for food. Eat of their flesh, and feed the poor and the unfortunate. (Sura 22: 26)

Then let the pilgrims tidy themselves, make their vows, and circle the Ancient House. Such is God's commandment. He that reveres the sacred rites of God shall fare better in the sight of his Lord. (Sura 22: 27)

Make the pilgrimage and visit the Sacred House for His sake. If you cannot, send such offerings as you can afford and do not shave your heads until the offerings have reached their destination. But if any of you is ill or suffers from an ailment of the head, he must do penance either by fasting or by almsgiving or by offering a sacrifice. (Sura 2: 196)

Make the pilgrimage in the appointed months. He that intends to perform it in those months must abstain from sexual intercourse, obscene language, and acrimonious disputes while on pilgrimage. God is aware of whatever good you do. Provide well for yourselves: the best provision is piety. Fear Me, then, you that are endowed with understanding. (Sura 2: 197)

Questions for Discussion:

1. Specific guidelines are prescribed by the *Qu'ran* for pilgrims. Identify these and discuss the various aspects of the directions.
2. What are the expectations for Ramadan?
3. Do you think all of the precepts presented here are equally important? Why or why not?

3.4   *Jihad*: Passages from the *Qu'ran* and the *Sayings* of Muhammad

An important concept in the Qu'ran *is that of Holy War, which is an obligation of the entire Islamic community. Jihad means literally "The Struggle," and refers to the inner, personal battle to follow the will of Allah and to live an unimpeachable Islamic life. The term also means aggressive warfare, undertaken against the nonbeliever. The first selection is from the* Qu'ran, *and the second consists of sayings of Muhammad regarding* jihad, *taken from a famous* hadith *collection,* Kanz al-Ummal, *by the sixteenth-century scholar al-Muttaqi.*

(From *The Koran*, translated with notes by N.J. Dawood (Penguin Classics 1956, Fifth revised edition 1990). Copyright © N. J. Dawood, 1956, 1959, 1966, 1968, 1974, 1990, 1993, 1997, 1999, 2003.)

(From *Islam: Volume II: From the Prophet Muhammad to the Capture of Constantinople*, by Bernard Lewis. (1987): pp. 209–211. Copyright © 1974 by Bernard Lewis. Reprinted by permission of Oxford University Press.)

From the *Qu'ran*

Let those who would exchange the life of this world for the hereafter, fight for the cause of God; whoever fights for the cause of God, whether he dies or triumphs, on him We shall bestow a rich recompense.

And how should you not fight for the cause of God, and for the helpless old men, women, and children who say: 'Deliver us, Lord, from this city of wrongdoers; send forth to us a guardian from Your presence; send to us from Your presence one that will help us'?

The true believers fight for the cause of God, but the infidels fight for the devil. Fight then against the friends of Satan. Satan's cunning is weak indeed. (Sura 4: 75)

Therefore fight for the cause of God. You are accountable for none but yourself. Rouse the faithful: perchance God will overthrow the might of the unbelievers. Mightier is God and more terrible is His punishment. (Sura 4: 82)

Fight for the sake of God those that fight against you, but do not attack them first. God does not love aggressors.

Slay them wherever you find them. Drive them out of the places from which they drove you. Idolatry is more grievous than bloodshed. But do not fight them within the precincts of the Holy Mosque unless they attack you there; if they attack you put them to the sword. Thus shall the unbelievers be rewarded: but if they mend their ways, know that God is forgiving and merciful.

Fight against them until idolatry is no more and God's religion reigns supreme. But if they desist, fight none except the evil-doers.

A sacred month for a sacred month: sacred things too are subject to retaliation. If anyone attacks you, attack him as he attacked you. Have fear of God, and know that God is with the righteous. (Sura 2: 190–194)

Sayings Ascribed to the Prophet (From al-Muttaqi, *Kanz*)

Jihad is incumbent upon you with every amir, whether he be godly or wicked and even if he commit major sins. Prayer is incumbent upon you behind every Muslim, be he godly or wicked and even if he commit major sins. Prayer is incumbent upon you for every Muslim who dies, be he godly or wicked and even if he commit major sins.

Paradise is under the shadow of swords.

Where the believer's heart shakes on the path of God, his sins fall away from him as the fruit falls off a date palm.

If anyone shoots an arrow at the enemy on the path of God and his arrow reaches his enemy, whether it hits him or misses, it is accounted equal in merit to liberating a slave.

He who draws his sword in the path of God has sworn allegiance to God.

He who fights so that the word of God may prevail is on the path of God.

He who dies fighting on the frontier in the path of God, God protects him from the testing of the tomb.

The unbeliever and the one who kills him will never meet in Hell.

God sent me as a mercy and a portent; He did not send me as a trader or as a cultivator. The worst of the community on the Day of Resurrection are the traders and the cultivators, except for those who are niggardly with their religion.

A day and a night of fighting on the frontier is better than a month of fasting and prayer.

The best thing a Muslim can earn is an arrow in the path of God.

He who equips a warrior in the Holy War for God has the same reward as he, while the warrior's reward is not diminished.

He who when he dies has never campaigned or even intended to campaign dies in a kind of hypocrisy.

Fight against the polytheists with your property, your persons, and your tongues.

Swords are the keys of Paradise.

A sword is sufficient witness.

God wonders at people who are led to Heaven in chains.

Every prophet has his monasticism, and the monasticism of this community is the Holy War in the path of God.

In Islam there are three dwellings, the lower, the upper, and the uppermost. The lower is the Islam of the generality of Muslims. If you ask anyone of them he will answer, "I am a Muslim." In the upper their merits differ, some of the Muslims being better than others. The uppermost is the *jihad* in the cause of God, which only the best of them attain.

Questions for Discussion:

1. The term *jihad* has two meanings, as discussed in the introductory material. How do you interpret the readings as a "struggle" to be a good Muslim?

2. What justification did Muhammad provide for aggressive warfare?
3. What did "monasticism" mean to Muhammad? How does his concept differ from the monasticism of the Christian community?

3.5   Women in Islamic Society

The Qu'ran *contains specific concepts about the position and role of women in Islamic society. These precepts, a source of tensions between the Islamic and Western traditions, remain in place today.*

(From *The Koran*, translated with notes by N. J. Dawood (Penguin Classics 1956, Fifth revised edition 1990). Copyright © N. J. Dawood, 1956, 1959, 1966, 1968, 1974, 1990, 1993, 1997, 1999, 2003.)

Men have authority over women because God has made the one superior to the other, and because they spend their wealth to maintain them. Good women are obedient. They guard their unseen parts because God has guarded them. As for those from whom you fear disobedience, admonish them, forsake them in beds apart, and beat them. Then if they obey you, take no further action against them. Surely God is high, supreme. (Sura 4: 34)

Enjoin believing men to turn their eyes away from temptation and to restrain their carnal desires. This will make their lives purer. God has knowledge of all their actions.

Enjoin believing women to turn their eyes away from temptation and to preserve their chastity; not to display their adornments (except such as are normally revealed); to draw their veils over their bosoms and not to display their finery except to their husbands, their fathers, their husbands' fathers, their sons, their step-sons, their brothers, their brothers' sons, their sisters' sons, their women-servants, and their slave-girls, male attendants lacking in natural vigor, and children who have no carnal knowledge of women. And let them not stamp their feet when walking so as to reveal their hidden trinkets. (Sura 24: 30)

Questions for Discussion:

1. What precepts in the *Qu'ran* explain the attitudes toward women in Islamic societies?
2. Compare the role of women in Frankish society as described by Tacitus and Ammianus Marcellinus (Chapter 1). Aside from Islamic doctrine, can you offer reasons for the differences?

The Founding of the Caliphate and the Expansion of Islam

3.6   The Founding of the Caliphate

After the death of Muhammad in 632, a new leader had to be chosen. It was essential for the community to continue its mission to defend the faith and law of Islam and to introduce the religion to the people of a wider geographical area; without strong direction the faith might be lost. There was no clear line of succession, and a group of Muhammad's closest associates chose Abu Bakr as khalifa *("caliph"), a term that combined the*

ideas of successor and deputy of the Prophet. His area of jurisdiction was known as the caliphate. *The following document is from the works of the historian al-Tabari (839–923).*

(From *Islam: From the Prophet Muhammad to the Capture of Constantinople*, vol. i, ed. and trans. by Bernard Lewis. New York: Oxford University Press, 1987, pp. 2–6. Copyright © 1987 Oxford University Press. Reprinted by permission.)

Hisham ibn Muhammad told me on the authority of Abu Mikhnaf, who said: 'Abdallah ibn 'Abd al-Rahman ibn Abi 'Umra, the Helper,[2] told me:

When the Prophet of God, may God bless and save him, died, the Helpers assembled in the porch of the Banu Sa'ida and said, "Let us confer this authority, after Muhammad, upon him be peace, on Sa'd ibn 'Ubada." Sa'd, who was ill, was brought to them, and when they assembled Sa'd said to his son or to one of his nephews, "I cannot, because of my sickness, speak so that all the people can hear my words. Therefore, hear what I say and then repeat it to them so that they may hear it." Then he spoke and the man memorized his words and raised his voice so that the others could hear.

He said, after praising God and lauding Him, "O company of the Helpers! You have precedence in religion and merit in Islam which no other Arab tribe has. Muhammad, upon him be peace, stayed for more than ten years amid his people, summoning them to worship the Merciful One and to abandon false gods and idols. But among his own people only a few men believed in him, and they were not able to protect the Prophet of God or to glorify his religion nor to defend themselves against the injustice which beset them. God therefore conferred merit on you and brought honor to you and singled you out for grace and vouchsafed to you faith in Him and in His Prophet and protection for Him and His companions and glorification to Him and His religion and holy war against His enemies. It was you who fought hardest against His enemy and weighed more heavily on His enemy than any other, until the Arabs obeyed the command of God willynilly and the distant ones gave obedience, humbly and meekly; until Almighty God, through you, made the world submit to His Prophet, and through your swords the Arabs drew near to him. And when God caused him to die, he was content with you and delighted with you. Therefore, keep this authority for yourselves alone, for it is yours against all others."

They all replied to him, "Your judgment is sound and your words are true. We shall not depart from what you say and we shall confer this authority on you. You satisfy us and you will satisfy the right believer."

Then they discussed it among themselves and some of them said, "What if the Emigrants[3] of Quraysh refuse, and say: 'We are the Emigrants and the first Companions of the Prophet of God; we are his clan and his friends. Why therefore do you dispute the succession to his authority with us?'" Some of them said, "If so, we would reply to them, 'An amir from us and an amir from you! And we shall never be content with less than that.'" Sa'd ibn 'Ubada, when he heard this, said, "This is the beginning of weakness."

News of this reached 'Umar, and he went to the house of the Prophet, may God bless and save him. He sent to Abu Bakr, who was in the Prophet's house with 'Ali ibn Abi Talib, upon him be peace, preparing the body of the Prophet, may God bless and save him, for burial. He sent asking Abu Bakr to come to him, and Abu Bakr sent a message in reply saying that he was busy. Then 'Umar sent saying that something had happened which made his presence necessary, and he went to him and said, "Have you not heard that the Helpers have gathered in the porch of the Banu Sa'ida? They wish to confer this authority on Sa'd ibn 'Ubada, and the best they say is, 'an amir from among us and an amir from among Quraysh.'" They made haste toward them, and they met Abu 'Ubayda ibn al-Jarrah. The three of them went on together, and they met 'Asim ibn 'Adi and 'Uwaym ibn Sa'ida, who both said to them: "Go back, for what you want will not happen." They said, "We shall not go back," and they came to the meeting.

'Umar ibn al-Khattab said: We came to the meeting, and I had prepared a speech which I wished to make to them. We reached them, and I was about to begin my speech when Abu Bakr said to me, "Gently! Let me speak first, and then afterwards say whatever you wish." He spoke. 'Umar said, "He said all I wanted to say, and more."

---

[2]The Helpers were people in Medina who joined Muhammad during his migration from Mecca (the *hegira*).

[3]The Emigrants were the Qurayshi Muslims from Mecca who accompanied the Prophet on the *hegira*.

'Abdallah ibn 'Abd al-Rahman said: Abu Bakr began. He praised and lauded God and then he said, "God sent Muhammad as a Prophet to His creatures and as a witness to His community that they might worship God and God alone, at a time when they were worshiping various gods beside Him and believed that they were intercessors for them with God and could be of help to them, though they were only of hewn stone and carved wood. Then he recited to them, 'And they worship apart from God those who could neither harm them nor help them, and they say these are our intercessors with God' [*Qu'ran* x, 19/18]. And they said, 'We worship them only so that they may bring us very near to God' [*Qu'ran* xxxix, 4/3]. It was a tremendous thing for the Arabs to abandon the religion of their fathers. God distinguished the first Emigrants of his people by allowing them to recognize the truth and believe in him and console him and suffer with him from the harsh persecution of his people when they gave them the lie and all were against them and reviled them. Yet they were not affrighted because their numbers were few and the people stared at them and their tribe was joined against them. They were the first in the land who worshiped God and who believed in God and the Prophet. They are his friends and his clan and the best entitled of all men to this authority after him. Only a wrongdoer would dispute this with them. And as for you, O company of the Helpers, no one can deny your merit in the faith or your great precedence in Islam. God was pleased to make you Helpers to His religion and His Prophet and caused him to migrate to you, and the honor of sheltering his wives and his Companions is still yours, and after

the first Emigrants there is no one we hold of equal standing with you. We are the amirs and you are the viziers. We shall not act contrary to your advice and we shall not decide things without you.". . .

Abu Bakr said, "Here is 'Umar and here is Abu 'Ubayda. Swear allegiance to whichever of them you choose." The two of them said, "No, by God, we shall not accept this authority above you, for you are the worthiest of the Emigrants and the second of the two who were in the cave and the deputy [*khalifa*] of the Prophet of God in prayer, and prayer is the noblest part of the religion of the Muslims. Who then would be fit to take precedence of you or to accept this authority above you? Stretch out your hand so that we may swear allegiance to you."

And when they went forward to swear allegiance to him, Bashir ibn Sa'd went ahead of them and swore allegiance to him . . . and when the tribe of Aws saw what Bashir ibn Sa'd had done . . . they came to him and swore allegiance to him. . . .

Hisham said on the authority of Abu Mikhnaf: 'Abdallah ihn 'Abd al-Rahman said: People came from every side to swear allegiance to Abu Bakr.

Questions for Discussion:

1. What were the difficulties faced by the followers of Muhammad in determining a successor?
2. How was the decision made to accept Abu Bakr as caliph?
3. The seeds of the present-day division between *sunni* and *shia* Muslims may be found in this document. Discuss.

3.7   The Accession Speech of Abu Bakr (632)

The historian Ibn Hisham (d. 834), whose biography of Muhammad was described in the introduction to Document 3.1, recounted Abu Bakr's response and acceptance speech following his choice as calif.

(From *Islam: From the Prophet Muhammad to the Capture of Constantinople*, voll. i, ed. and trans. by Bernard Lewis. New York: Oxford University Press, 1987, pp. 2–6. Copyright © 1987 Oxford University Press. Reprinted by permission.)

Then Abu Bakr spoke and praised and lauded God as is fitting, and then he said: O people, I have been appointed to rule over you, though I am not the best among you. If I do well, help me, and if I do ill, correct me. Truth is loyalty and falsehood is treachery; the weak among you is strong in in my eyes until I get justice for him, please God, and the strong among you is weak in my eyes until I exact justice from him, please God. If any people holds back from fighting the holy war for God, God strikes them with degradation. If weakness spreads among a people, God brings disaster upon all of them. Obey me as long as I obey God and His Prophet. And if I disobey God and His Prophet, you do not owe me obedience. Come to prayer, and may God have mercy on you.

Question for Discussion:

1. Analyze the concepts presented by Abu Bakr in his accession speech. What are the main themes?

3.8   Abu Bakr on the Rules of War (632)

As caliph, Abu Bakr was the leader of the community, but was not a messenger of Allah, and could not claim to receive continuing revelations. Nonetheless, an aura of holiness and divine choice surrounded him, and he did possess a kind of religious authority. He also had to establish political control, and undertook military action to affirm his leadership (the so-called Wars of the Ridda). The following proclamation, recounted by the historian al-Tabari, urged his followers to abide by specific rules of war.

(From *Islam: From the Prophet Muhammad to the Capture of Constantinople*, vol. i, ed. and trans. by Bernard Lewis. New York: Oxford University Press, 1987, pp. 2–6. Copyright © 1987 Oxford University Press. Reprinted by permission.)

O people I charge you with ten rules; learn them well!

Do not betray, or misappropriate any part of the booty; do not practice treachery or mutilation. Do not kill a young child, an old man, or a woman. Do not uproot or burn palms or cut down fruitful trees. Do not slaughter a sheep or a cow or a camel, except for food. You will meet people who have set themselves apart in hermitages; leave them to

accomplish the purpose for which they have done this. You will come upon people who will bring you dishes with various kinds of foods. If you partake of them, pronounce God's name over what you eat. You will meet people who have shaved the crown of their heads, leaving a band of hair around it. Strike them with the sword.

Go, in God's name, and may God protect you from sword and pestilence.

Questions for Discussion:

1. Are there any differences between the proclamation of Abu Bakr concerning war and the precepts set forth in the *Qu'ran* and the sayings of Muhammad?
2. Why do you think Abu Bakr decreed that people in hermitages should be spared?
3. What is the basic principle behind the proclamations concerning vegetation, livestock, and the sparing of certain citizens?

3.9   The Muslims Conquer Iberia

The Islamic conquest of the Iberian Peninsula began in 711 and was completed by 716. It was accomplished by a relatively small Muslim army, perhaps as few as 25,000. The reigning Visigothic monarchy (see Document 2.6) had been weakened by internal dissension, and was unable to halt the Muslim incursion. The earliest account of the conquest was contained in a collection of stories and legends by

the Arab scholar Ibn Abd al-Hakam (d. 871), a member of a prominent family of religious and legal scholars from Egypt. His work, the Futuh Misr *("Conquest of Egypt") was typical of the style of the Islamic culture of his time, which transmitted knowledge in the form of anecdotes or narratives. As the tradition developed, a short introduction (called an* isnad*) was often included as part of the narrative.*

This material provided a factual context for the anecdote, authenticating the source for the material. The following excerpt from the work of al-Hakam contains an introductory isnad, *beginning "He said." The "he" of this and similar phrases refers to the author, and reflects the circumstances of the prevailing oral tradition.*

According to al-Hakam, the Muslim commander Tariq was invited into Spain by a rival claimant to the throne. Within a brief period of time the Muslim soldiers were able to conquer all of the Iberian Peninsula except for the mountainous northern areas. The following excerpt from al-Hakam's chronicle demonstrates some of the tactics used by the Muslims during the initial phase of their invasion. Although modern historians doubt the truth of al-Hakam's account of the conquest, which they view as more myth than history, his work is valuable as a reflection of Muslim attitudes regarding the expansion of their religious and geographical control.

(From *Islam: From the Prophet Muhammad to the Capture of Constantinople*, vol. i, ed. and trans. by Bernard Lewis. New York: Oxford University Press, 1987, pp. 2–6. Copyright © 1987 Oxford University Press. Reprinted by permission.)

He said: Musa ibn Nusayr sent his son Marwan ibn Musa toward Tangier to garrison the coast. He and his companions found themselves overtaxed, and he therefore left, placing Tariq ibn Amr in command of his army. They numbered 1.700 men. According to another version, Tariq had 12,000 Berbers and only 16 Arabs, but this is not authentic. . . .

The straits between him and Spain were commanded by a foreigner called Julian, the lord of Ceuta and of a town in Spain, called al-Khadra' [Algeciras], on the Spanish side of the straits facing Tangier. Julian was subject to Rodrigo, the ruler of Spain, who lived in Toledo. Tariq corresponded with Julian and by blandishment brought him to the point of exchanging gifts.

Now Julian had sent one of his daughters to Rodrigo, the ruler of Spain, for him to educate and instruct her, but Rodrigo made her pregnant. When Julian heard of this, he said, "I can see no punishment and no retribution other than to send the Arabs against him." He therefore wrote to Tariq saying, "It is I who will bring you into Spain." Tariq was then at Tlemcen [a town in Algeria], and Musa ibn Nusayr was at Qayrawan [a town in Tunisia]. Tariq replied, "I cannot trust you unless, you send me hostages." Julian then sent him two daughters, as he had no other children. Tariq installed them in Tlemcen, and having made sure of them, he went to meet Julian, who was then at Ceuta [in Morocco] on the straits. Julian was delighted when he came and said to him, "It is I who will bring you into Spain."

In the straits between Ceuta and Spain there is a rock which is today called Jabal Tariq [the Mountain of Tariq]. At nightfall Julian brought ships and took him across the straits. They hid during the day, and at nightfall he sent the ships back to bring the rest of his men. They ferried them across until none remained, while the Spaniards noticed nothing. They thought that all this was the usual movement of ships about their business. Tariq himself sailed with the last party and joined his men. Julian and the merchants who were with him stayed behind at al-Khadra to please his companions and his countrymen. The Spaniards had by now heard of Tariq and his men and of their position.

Tariq set out on his way. With his men, he crossed a bridge which led from the mountain to a village called Qartajanna [Carteya—in the Spanish province of Cordova]. Then, advancing towards Cordova, he passed near an island in the sea, where he left his slave-girl, Umm Hakim, with a few of his men. From that day onward the island was called Jazirat Umm Hakim [the Island of Umm Hakim]. When the Muslims landed on this island, they found some wine growers and no one else. They made them prisoners. Then they picked on one of the wine growers, killed him, cut him to pieces, and cooked him while his surviving companions watched. Now the Muslims had already prepared meat in other pots. When this meat was ready, they threw away the cooked human flesh unbeknown to the Spaniards, and substituted and ate the meat which they had previously cooked. The surviving wine growers saw this and had no doubt but that they were eating the flesh of their friend. Then they released them, and they told the Spaniards that they ate human flesh and told them what had happened to the wine grower.

According to what my father 'Abdallah ibn 'Abd al-Hakam and Hisham ibn Ishaq told me, there was in Spain a house closed with many locks, to which every king on his accession added another lock of his own. This continued until the time of the king who was invaded by the Muslims. When he succeeded, they asked him to add a lock as all the kings before him had done. He refused and said, "I shall add nothing until I know what is inside." He gave orders to open it, and inside there were pictures of the Arabs, with this inscription, "When this door is opened, these people will enter this country."

When Tariq had crossed the straits, the army of Cordova came to meet him and were emboldened when they saw how few were his men. They joined battle and after fierce fighting were put to flight. Tariq pursued them and killed them all the way to Cordova. Rodrigo heard of this defeat and marched against them from Toledo. They met at a place called Shadhuna, by a river which is today called Wadi Umm Hakim. They fought fiercely, and Almighty

God caused Rodrigo and his men to perish. Mughith al-Rumi, a *ghulam* in the service of al-Walid ibn 'Abd al-Malik who commanded Tariq's cavalry, advanced on Cordova, and Tariq proceeded to Toledo, which he entered. His only concern was to ask about the table which had belonged to Solomon the son of David, according to what the People of the Book[4] claim.

Questions for Discussion:

1. What appeal might al-Hakam's narrative harve held for the Muslims of the ninth century? Why?
2. Do you see any similarities between this account of military victory by a ninth-century Arab scholar and the anonymous Anglo-Saxon epic *Beowulf?*
3. Does the account seem believable in any of its narrative? Which parts?

3.10   The *Treaty of Tudmir*

Following the rapid expansion of Islam during the seventh century, it was necessary for the Muslim leaders to develop policies that dealt with the non-Muslims living in the areas under their control, who were often in the majority. These people were granted the status of "dhimmi," or protected people. As long as they conformed to restrictions such as those set out in the "Treaty of Tudmir," and paid an annual tax, they were guaranteed personal safety and allowed to worship as they chose. This document is a peace treaty between Abd al-Aziz and Theodemir (Tudmir in Arabic), the ruler of Murcia.[5] Dating from 713, it provides a significant contrast to the violence of the account of the Muslim invasion of al-Andalus by al-Hakam. This treaty indicates that there were other measures than military aggression in establishing Muslim dominance in the southern Iberian Peninsula.

In the name of God, the merciful and the compassionate.

This is a document [granted] by Abd al-Aziz ibn Musa ibn Nusair to Tudmir, son of Ghabdush, establishing a treaty of peace and the promise and protection of God and his Prophet (may God bless him and grant him peace). We [Abd al-Aziz] will not set special conditions for him or for any among his men, nor harass him, nor remove him from power. His followers will not be killed or taken prisoner, nor will they be separated from their women and children. They will not be coerced in matters of religion, their churches will not be burned, nor will sacred objects be taken from the realm, [so long as] he [Tudmir] re-

(From *Medieval Iberia: Readings from Christian,* Muslim, *and Jewish Sources,* edited by Olivia Remie Constable. Philadelphia: University of Pennsylvania Press, 1997, pp. 37–38. Reprinted with permission of the University of Pennsylvania Press.)

[4]People of the Book were non-Muslim people who had received scriptures revealed by God before the time of Muhammad, primarily Jews and Christians.
[5]Murcia is a coastal area in Spain.

mains sincere and fulfills the [following] conditions that we have set for him. He had reached a settlement concerning seven towns: Orihuela, Valentilla, Alicante, Mula, Bigastro, Ello, and Lorca. He will not give shelter to fugitives, nor to our enemies, nor encourage any protected person to fear us, nor conceal news of our enemies. He and [each of] his men shall

[also] pay one dinar every year, together with four measures of wheat, four measures of barley, four liquid measures of concentrated fruit juice, four liquid measures of vinegar, four of honey, and four of olive oil. Slaves must each pay half of this amount. [*Names of four witnesses follow*]

The discussion questions for this document follow 3.11.

3.11   The *Pact of Umar*

The "Pact of Umar" is generally recognized as an agreement offered by Caliph Umar (r. 717–720) to the non-Muslim people living in Syria. Agreements such as this, known as "dhimma," provided a pattern for similar pacts in other areas, and influenced future relations between the groups. As may be seen, the regulations were not terribly burdensome, and, for the most part, allowed the Christians, Jews, and Muslims to live together peaceably; indeed, many non-Muslims made significant contributions to Islamic culture.

(From *Islam: From the Prophet Muhammad to the Capture of Constantinople*, vol. ii, ed. and trans. by Bernard Lewis. New York: Oxford University Press, 1987, pp. 217–219. Copyright © 1987 Oxford University Press. Reprinted by permission.)

We heard from 'Abd al-Rahman ibn Ghanam [d. 697] as follows: When 'Umar ibn al-Khattab, may God be pleased with him, accorded a peace to the Christians of Syria, we wrote to him as follows:

In the name of God, the Merciful and Compassionate.

This is a letter to the servant of God 'Umar [ibn, al-Khattab], Commander of the Faithful, from the Christians of such-and-such a city. When you came against us, we asked you for safe-conduct (*aman*) for ourselves, our descendants, our property, and the people of our community, and we undertook the following obligations toward you:

We shall not build, in our cities or in their neighborhood, new monasteries, churches, convents, or monks' cells, nor shall we repair, by day or by night, such of them as fall in ruins or are situated in the quarters of the Muslims.

We shall keep our gates wide open for passersby and travelers. We shall give board and lodging to all Muslims who pass our way for three days.

We shall not give shelter in our churches or in our dwellings to any spy, nor hide him from the Muslims.

We shall not teach the *Qu'ran* to our children.

We shall not manifest our religion publicly nor convert anyone to it. We shall not prevent any of our kin from entering Islam if they wish it.

We shall show respect toward the Muslims, and we shall rise from our seats when they wish to sit. We shall not seek to resemble the Muslims by imitating any of their garments, the *qalansuwa*,[6] the turban, footwear, or the parting of the hair. We shall not speak as they do, nor shall we adopt their *kunyas*.[7]

We shall not mount on saddles, nor shall we gird swords nor bear any kind of arms nor carry them on our persons.

We shall not engrave Arabic inscriptions on our seals.

We shall not sell fermented drinks.

We shall clip the fronts of our heads.

We shall always dress in the same way wherever we may be, and we shall bind the *zunnar*[8] round our waists.

We shall not display our crosses or our books in the roads or markets of the Muslims. We shall only use clappers in our churches very softly. We shall not raise our voices in our church services or in the presence of Muslims, nor shall we raise our voices, when following our dead. We shall not show lights on any

---

[6]The *qalansuwa* is a tall, often conical cap worn by men, either under a turban or by itself.
[7]*Kunya* is part of the Arab personal name. It was an appellation that consisted of *Abu* (father of) or *Umm* (mother of), which was then followed by a name, generally that of the eldest son.
[8]The *zunnar* was a belt, in particular the distinctive belt or sash that non-Muslims were required to wear in medieval Islam.

of the roads of the Muslims or in their markets. We shall not bury our dead near the Muslims.

We shall not take slaves who have been allotted to the Muslims.

We shall not build houses overtopping the houses of the Muslims.

(When I brought the letter to 'Umar, may God be pleased with him, he added, "We shall not strike any Muslim.")

We accept these conditions for ourselves and for the people of our community, and in return we receive safe-conduct.

If we in any way violate these undertakings for which we ourselves stand surety, we forfeit our covenant {dhimma}, and we become liable to the penalties for contumacy and sedition.

'Umar ibn al-Khattab replied: Sign what they ask, but add two clauses and impose them in addition to those which they have undertaken. They are: "They shall not buy anyone made prisoner by the Muslims," and "Whoever strikes a Muslim with deliberate intent shall forfeit the protection of this pact."

Questions for Discussion:

1. What do you see as the most significant obligations in the "Treaty" and the "Pact?" Why?
2. The "Pact" contains many restrictions concerning dress. What were the Muslims attempting to prevent by these stipulations?
3. Do you think that these agreements would have been successful in most of the Muslim world? Why or why not?

Muslim Art and Culture

INTERPRETING THE EVIDENCE

3.12 Al-Azhar Mosque and Documents of Support

The mosque is the official place of worship for Muslims. All mosques are oriented toward Mecca, and contain a qibla wall with a mihrab, indicating the direction for prayer. Although the origins of the traditional ground plan of a mosque are unclear, most scholars believe that the pattern was provided by Muhammad's house in Medina; his residence seems to have inspired the development of Muslim houses of worship. The first building designed as a mosque was in Medina; it is known as the "Quba Mosque." The following example illustrates the famous Egyptian mosque al-Azhar, which was begun in 970 C.E. In 988 the caliph gave salaries to a number of jurists who built houses nearby and came to the mosque on Fridays where they lectured. As noted in the document, the mosque was supported by various sorts of benefactions.

(Document from *Islam: From the Prophet Muhammad to the Capture of Constantinople*, vol. ii, ed. and trans. by Bernard Lewis. New York: Oxford University Press, 1987, pp. 3–8. Copyright © 1987 Oxford University Press. Reprinted by permission.)

Document

The Mosque of Al-Azhar

This was the first mosque founded in Cairo. The man who built it was the qa'id Jawhar, the scribe, the Sicilian, the freedman of the Imam Abu Tamim Ma'add, the Caliph, the Commander of the Faithful, al-Mu'izz li-Din Allah, when he laid out the plan of Cairo. The building of this mosque began on Saturday, 24 Jumada I 359 [April 4, 970] and was completed on 9 Ramadan 361 [June 24, 972].

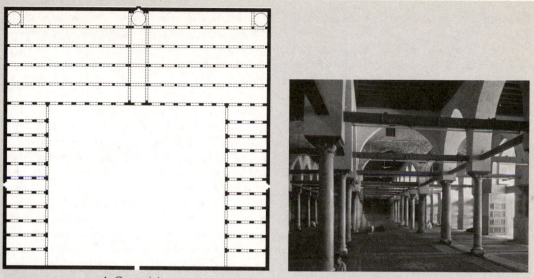

A. Groundplan

B. *Mihrab* aisle

The Mosque of al-Azhar (970–1415).
(Derived from John D. Hoag, History of World Architecture: Islamic Architecture, *p. 69. © 1973 by Electa, Milano Elemend Editori Associati. All Rights Reserved. Photo: The Qibla Liwan of the Mosque of al-Azhar, 970 AD (photo) by Islamic School (10th century) Cairo, Egypt/ Giraudon/ The Bridgeman Art Library.)*

The communal prayer was held in it. All around the dome in the first hall *{riwaq},* to the right of the prayer niche [*qibla*] and the pulpit, the following text was written:

> *In the name of God, the Merciful and the Compassionate. This is one of the buildings the construction of which was ordered by the servant and the favored of God Abu Tamim Ma'add, the Imam, al-Mu'izz li-Din Allah, Commander of the Faithful, may God bless him, his ancestors, and his noble descendants, by the hand of his slave Jawhar, the scribe, the Sicilian, in the year 360 {according to the Muslim calendar}.*

The first Friday that the communal prayer was performed there was on 7 Ramadan 361 [June 22, 972]. Later, al-'Aziz billah Abu Mansur Nizar, the son of al-Mu'izz li-Din Allah added something to it. Then, in the year 378 [988], the vizier Abu'l-Faraj Ya'qub ibn Killis asked the Caliph al-'Aziz billah to assign stipends to a number of jurists. He granted to each one of them a sufficient salary in money and ordered them to buy a house and reconstruct it. It was established next to the Azhar mosque, and every Friday they came to the mosque and formed circles to whom they lectured after the communal prayer and until the afternoon prayer. They also received a gift from the vizier[9] every year. They were thirty-five of them. On the day of the breaking of the fast al-'Aziz granted them robes of honor and gave them mules to ride.

It is said that in this mosque there is a talisman such that no sparrow or other bird, pigeon, wood pigeon, or the like, will nest or hatch there. It consists of the likenesses of three birds; each likeness is on the top of a column. Two of them are in the forepart of the mosque, in the fifth hall: one is on a column in the western part; the other is on one of the two columns on the left when one faces the pulpit of the muezzins. The third likeness is in

---

[9]A *vizier* was a court councilor or high administrator.

(continued)

the courtyard, on the southern columns toward the east.

Then al-Hakim bi-Amr Allah had further work done there. He constituted tenement houses in old Cairo as *waqf*[10] in favor of the Azhar mosque, the mosque in al-Maqs, the al-Hakim mosque, and the House of Wisdom in Cairo and incorporated this in a document, as follows:

This is a document, the provisions and details of which the chief *qadi*[11] Malik ibn Sa'id ibn Malik al Fariqi caused to be attested by the legal witnesses present at a judicial hearing held by him in Fustat of Egypt in the month of Ramadan of the year 400 [April–May 1010]. He called upon them to attest it, in his capacity as qadi of the servant and the favored of God, al-Mansur Abu 'Ali, the Imam al-Hakim bi-Amr Allah, Commander of the Faithful, the son of al-'Aziz billah, may God bless them both, with authority over Cairo, Fustat, Alexandria, the two holy places, may God preserve them, the provinces {*jund*} of Syria, Raqqa, and Rahba, the regions of the Maghrib, and their dependencies, and all that which God has enabled and will enable the Commander of the Faithful to conquer, of the lands of the East and of the West. This was in the presence of a man who stated that he had certain knowledge both of the places owned in their entirety and those jointly owned in shares, all of which shall be named and delimited in this document, and of the fact that they were the property {*mulk*} of al-Hakim until he constituted them as *waqf* in favor of the Azhar mosque in Cairo, the God-guarded, of the mosque in Rashida, and of the mosque in al-Maqs, which were both established and founded by his order, and of the House of Wisdom in Cairo, the God-guarded, which he had already constituted as a *waqf*, with all the books which it contains, prior to the date of the present document. Some of these buildings are assigned jointly and without division to the Azhar mosque, the Rashida mosque, and the House of Wisdom in

Cairo, the God-guarded; some are assigned to the Maqs mosque, in accordance with conditions which will be stated below.

The benefaction in favor of the Azhar mosque in Cairo, the God-guarded, the Rashida mosque, and the House of Wisdom in Cairo, the God-guarded, consists of the whole of the building known as the mint {*Dar al-Darb*}, the whole of the commercial building {*qaysariyya*} known as the wool *qaysariyya*, and the whole of the building known as the new pottery building, all situated in Fustat of Egypt.

The benefaction in favor of the Maqs mosque consists of the whole of four shops with living quarters above them and two storehouses, all situated in Fustat of Egypt in the district of the Banner {*al-Raya*}, to the west of the house formerly known as the pottery building. These two buildings, known by the name of the pottery building, are situated in the place known as the Rat Bath {*Hammam al-Farr*}. This includes all the jointly held shares of the four adjoining shops situated in Fustat of Egypt, also in the Banner district in the place known as the Rat Bath, these shops being known as "the shares of al-Qaysi."

These sites, within their limits, are constituted *waqf* in their entirety, including their land, buildings, ground floors, upper floors, rooms, latrines, shops, courtyards, approaches, passages, water conduits, and all rights pertaining thereto, both inside and outside.

He has made of all this a charitable foundation and an inviolable *waqf*, consecrated absolutely and in perpetuity, which it is unlawful to sell or give or make into private property {*tamlik*} and which shall remain subject to the conditions laid down and in accordance with the rules prescribed in this document. The passing of the years shall not weaken these rules, nor the vicissitudes of events transform them. They shall not be subject to exception or to reinterpretation, nor shall there be any need to seek a judicial ruling {*fatwa*} to renew their consecration. The stipulations shall remain valid through all changes in circumstances, until God shall inherit the earth and the heavens [*Qu'ran*, xix, 41].

---

[10]*Waqf* was an endowment of land or other income-producing property whose proceeds were designated by the founder for a specific purpose, such as the support of a mosque, school, or charity. The grant was permanent and irrevocable.

[11]A *qadi* was a judge who administered the Holy Law of Islam.

Whoever is responsible for the management and control of the *waqf* in every period shall make lettings in a God-fearing way so as to ensure the best advantage by making the offer known among those desirous of renting such premises. He shall, in the first instance, use the income for the upkeep of the properties as required and the maintenance of the assets in good repair, but without prejudice to the beneficiaries for which the *waqf* was established.

The surplus shall be divided into sixty parts.

The document continues with specific amounts to be used to pay for the maintenance of the mosque and salaries for clergy, criers (muezzins), and workmen.

Questions for Discussion:

1. Compare and contrast the groundplan of al-Azhar mosque with that of old St. Peter's (Document 1.8). Are there any similarities? How do the two buildings reflect the worship practices of their respective religions?
2. How do the provisions for the support of the mosque compare with Constantine's donations for St. Peter's?
3. The mosque functions as a place of worship, but there are several other uses mentioned in the description of al-Azhar mosque. What are these?

3.13   Qibla, "Umar in Jerusalem" and the *Qu'ran*

As one of the Five Pillars of Islam, prayer is an essential aspect of the religion. Five times each day Muslims respond to the call to prayer of muezzins *(criers). At first the believers were instructed to face Jerusalem, and afterward toward Mecca. Wherever Muslims are and whatever they are doing, they cease their activities and kneel to pray toward the holy city and the Ka'ba at the appointed hours. As specified by the* Qu'ran *". . . wherever you be, turn your faces towards it." All Muslim houses of worship, known as mosques, are oriented toward Mecca, and that direction is marked by a* qibla *wall with a niche known as a* mihrab.

The beautiful mihrab pictured here provides a fine example of the use of calligraphy, which was a prominent aspect of Islamic artistic expression. Equally important are motifs based on geometric designs and floral imagery. All three of these styles of ornamentation may be seen in this mihrab. The calligraphic inscriptions in this prayer niche are from the Qu'ran, and, as in other examples of Islamic art, they take on a sacramental character.

As may be seen in this image, the motifs are repeated again and again as an expression of variety within unity. The undulating imagery is bound only by the borders of the frame, reflecting this universal principle, which is fundamental to Islamic aesthetics. A similar use of intertwining patterns was also a prominent feature in Germanic art, and this tradition may be seen in the Carolingian book cover pictured in Chapter 4.

The origin of the qibla was included in the history of the ninth-century historian al-Tabari. In the following document, he describes how Umar created the niche for prayer in the early part of the seventh century. Some scholars believe that the idea of qibla orientation was derived from the Jewish practice of indicating the direction of Jerusalem in synagogues.

The Qu'ran also contains descriptions and stipulations about using the qibla, as noted in the following passages (Section B), which advise worshipers to face the qibla, and hence the Holy Mosque in Mecca.

Document A. (From *Islam: From the Prophet Muhammad to the Capture of Constantinople*, vol. ii, ed. and trans. by Bernard Lewis. New York: Oxford University Press, 1987, p. 3. Copyright © 1987 Oxford University Press. Reprinted by permission.)

Document B. (Document from *The Koran*, translated with notes by N. J. Dawood (Penguin Classics 1956, Fifth revised edition 1990). Copyright © N. J. Dawood, 1956, 1959, 1966, 1968, 1974, 1990, 1993, 1997, 1999, 2003.)

(continued)

(continued)

Mihrab.
("Mihrab" (mosaic). From Madrasa Imami, Isffahan. Persia (Iran). Founded 1354. Glazed and cut tiles. 11'3" × 7'16" (3.43 × 2.29 m). The Metropolitan Museum of Art. Harris Brisbane Dick Fund (39.20). Photograph © 1982 The Metropolitan Museum of Art/Art Resource, NY.)

Documents

A. Umar in Jerusalem (636)

On the authority of Raja ibn Hiwa, on the authority of an eyewitness: When 'Umar came from al-Jabiya to Aelia [Jerusalem] . . . he said, "Bring me Ka'b!"[12] and he was brought to him, and 'Umar asked him, "Where do you think we should put the place of prayer?"

"By the rock,"[13] answered Ka'b.

"By God, Ka'b," said 'Umar, "you are following after Judaism. I saw you take off your sandals."

"I wanted to feel the touch of it with my bare feet." said Ka'b.

"I saw you," said 'Umar. "But no. We shall make the forepart the *qibla,* as the Prophet of God, may God bless and save him, made the forepart of our mosques their *qibla.* Go along! We were not commanded concerning the rock, but we were commanded concerning the Ka'ba!"

So 'Umar made the forepart the *qibla.* Then 'Umar went up from the place where he had prayed to the heap of garbage in which the Romans had hidden the temple in the time of the children of Israel. And when this place came into their hands, they uncovered part of it and left the remainder.

'Umar said, "O people, do as I do." And he knelt by the heap and knelt on a fold of his cloak.

B. The *Qu'ran*

According to the Qu'ran*, worshippers must face the direction of the Holy Mosque:*

The foolish will ask: 'What has made them turn away from their *qibla?*'

Say: 'The East and the West are God's. He guides whom He will to the right path.'

We have made you a just community, so that you may testify against mankind and that your own Apostle may testify against you. We decreed your former *qibla* only in order that We might know the Apostle's true adherents and those who were to disown him. It was indeed a hard test, but not to those whom God has guided. God's aim was not to make your faith fruitless. He is compassionate and merciful to men.

Many a time have We seen you turn your face towards the sky. We will make you turn towards a *qibla* that will please you. Turn your face towards the Holy Mosque; wherever you be, turn your faces towards it.

Those to whom the Scriptures were given know this to be the truth from their Lord. God is never heedless of what they do. But even if you gave them every proof they would not accept your *qibla,* nor would you accept theirs; nor would any of them accept the *qibla* of the other. If, after all the knowledge you have been given, you yield to their desires, then you will surely become an evil-doer.

Those to whom We gave the Scriptures know Our apostle as they know their own sons. But some of them deliberately conceal the truth. This is the truth from your Lord: therefore never doubt it.

Each one has a goal towards which he turns. But wherever you are, emulate one another in good works. God will bring you all before Him. God has power over all things.

Whichever way you depart, face towards the Holy Mosque. This is surely the truth from your Lord. God is never heedless of what you do.

Whichever way you depart, face towards the Holy Mosque: and wherever you are, face towards it, so that men will have no cause to reproach you, except the evil-doers among them. Have no fear of them; fear Me, so that I may perfect My favor to you and that you may be rightly guided. (Sura 2: 142–150)

Questions for Discussion:

1. What meaning do you attribute to the directive that all Muslims must pray toward Mecca and the Ka'ba? Is the purpose solely a religious one?
2. Describe and discuss the styles of ornamentation that decorate the image of the *qibla*.

---

[12] Ka'b was a converted Jew who is thought to have introduced an number of Jewish beliefs and practices into Islam.
[13] The temple rock.

Poetic Voices from Islam

3.14   An Arabic Definition of Poetry by Ibn Qutayba

Poetry was more treasured than prose in the Islamic cultural tradition. It was intimately entwined with music, and began as a popular oral verse tradition practiced by traveling minstrels. The themes of the early, pre-Islamic, verses were similar to those of western European poetry—tribal culture, warfare, nomadic life, and romantic love. Later verses continued to focus on these topics, especially that of love, both heterosexual and homosexual. The following discussion of the importance of poetry by Ibn Qutayba, a ninth-century scholar, affirms the lasting value of verse as an essential way of preserving tales of brave deeds and acts of glory.

(From *Islam: From the Prophet Muhammad to the Capture of Constantinople*, vol. ii, ed. and trans. by Bernard Lewis. New York: Oxford University Press, 1987, p. 3. Copyright © 1987 Oxford University Press. Reprinted by permission.)

Poetry is the mine of knowledge of the Arabs, the book of their wisdom, the muster roll of their history, the repository of their great days, the rampart protecting their heritage, the trench defending their glories, the truthful witness on the day of dispute, the final proof at the time of argument. Whoever among them can bring no verse to confirm his own nobility and the generous qualities and honored deeds which he claims for his forebears, his endeavors are lost though they be famous, effaced by the passage of time though they be mighty. But he who binds them with rhymed verses, knots them with scansion, and makes them famous through a rare line, a phrase grown proverbial, a well-turned thought, has made them eternal against time, preserved them from negation, averted the plot of the enemy, and lowered the eye of the envious.

Question for Discussion:

1. Do you think that the Arab definition of poetry presented by Ibn Qutayba could be applied to poetry of all traditions? Discuss.

3.15   A Lyric from the *Kitab al-Aghani* ("The Book of Songs") by Abu l-Faraj al-Isfahani (c. 897–967)

The Kitab al-Aghani is a comprehensive collection of songs and poems from the beginning of Arab civilization through the ninth century. Numbering twenty-four volumes in the modern edition, the work is one of the most famous literary compilations of the Muslim world. In the poetry of the Kitab al-Aghani *it is possible to see many themes, such as nature, love, and longing for an absent lover, which would influence the development of troubadour lyrics (see Chapter 10) as well as the late-medieval works of Petrarch and Dante (see Chapter 14). Many of the poems in the* Kitab al-Aghani *originally had musical notation, but only the directions for performance remain. The collection as a whole provides a comprehensive picture of Muslim culture and society. In the introduction to the following poem (an* isnad—*see the introduction to Document 3.9), intellectual and social attitudes are clearly demonstrated.*

(From *Making the Great Book of Songs: Compilation and the Author's Craft in Abu l-Farj al-Isbahani's Kitab al-aghani*, by Hilary Kilpatrick. London: Routledge Curzon, 2003, p. 37. Reprinted by permission of Taylor & Francis Books UK.)

I was with Abu Dulaf al-Qasim when Muhammad ibn Wuhayb the poet came to visit him. Abu Dulaf treated the poet with great respect, and after he had left, Abu Dulaf's brother Ma'qil said to him, "Brother, you have treated this man in a way he does not deserve. He does not belong to a noble family, nor is he extremely cultivated, nor does he occupy and important position." "Oh, yes, brother, he certainly deserves such treatment. How could it be otherwise when he is the author of these lines:

Song

Asked to give evidence, my tears speak
And testify that I am in love.
And my mistress whom I serve

Recognizes that I adore her.
If I aspire to meet her,
Some hurdle blocks my path,
And fate, with its vicissitudes, engages me in
conflict
Over her, as if fate itself were her lover."

Question for Discussion:

1. What cultural values are demonstrated in the introduction to the poem (*isnad*) from the *Kitab al-Aghani?*

3.16   A Jewish Voice in al-Andalus: Samuel the Nagid

Samuel the Nagid (993–1055 or 1056) was the vizier (prime minister) of the ruler of Granada, one of the most important cities in al-Andalus. In addition to his duties at court, he was active in the administration of the Jewish community and found time for a wide variety of literary pursuits. The following poem expresses the anguish and pain of a broken heart.

(Reprinted from *Wine, Women, & Death: Medieval Hebrew Poems on the Good Life,* © 1986, by Raymond P. Scheindlin, published by The Jewish Publication Society, with the permission of the publisher.)

Burnt by passion's flame—
How can I refrain?
   Love has ruined me,
   Lain in wait for me,
   Ambushed, then gone free
Followed me amain,
Split my heart in twain.

   On my cheek the tear
   Made my secret clear.
   This please tell my dear:
Tears all men disdain.
How can I explain?

   Speak to him for me,
   Tell him of my plea.
   Do not silent be!

Broken love restrain
From a heart in pain.

Solace to me bring;
Ease for me the sting.
Ah, such suffering!
Sleepless have I lain,
Love my slumber's bane.

Lovers in distress
Cry for a caress.
My heart they oppress.
Come my darling swain,
Cling and kiss again.

   This my love song rings
   [   ]
"May true lovers twain
Never part again!"

Question for Discussion:

1. Do you see any themes in this poem that might also be observed in contemporary society?

3.17   Scheherazade: A Tale from *The Thousand and One Nights*

The multifaceted diversity of Islamic culture is colorfully demonstrated by a collection of stories known as The Thousand and One Nights, *often referred to as the* Arabian Nights. *Based upon the oral traditions of Persia and India as well as the Arabian peninsula, it was collected between the eighth and tenth centuries. The framework for the tales was based upon an Indian story that tells of Shahrasad (Scheherazade in English), the daughter of a palace official. She was a lovely woman who married a king so intent upon preventing infidelity by his wives that he had each one murdered on the morning after the wedding night. Scheherazade was able to avoid the fate of her predecessors through her clever storytelling, in which she wove fantasies featuring exotic characters such as Ali Baba, Sinbad, and Aladdin. As may be seen in the following tale, she designed each story so that it would reach a climax just before dawn, leaving the king eager to find out the conclusion. Each story is skillfully linked to the next, so that the new tale would engage the king's imagination and he would not send his wife to meet the fate of his earlier spouses.*

(From *Arabian Nights*, ed. by Hildegarde Hawthorne. Philadelphia: The Penn Publishing Co., 1928], pp. 26–34. Translation modernized.)

Scheherazade

Before Scheherazade went to the palace, she called her favorite slave girl Dinarzade, aside, and said, "As soon as I shall have presented myself before the sultan, I will beg him to allow you to sleep in the bridal chamber, so that I may enjoy your company for the last time. If I obtain this favor, as I expect, remember to awaken me tomorrow morning an hour before daybreak, and say, 'If you are not asleep, my mistress, I beg of you, until the morning appears, tell me one of those delightful stories you know.' I will immediately begin to tell one; and I flatter myself that by these means I shall free the kingdom from this terror." Dinarzade promised to do what was required.

Within a short time Scheherazade was taken to the palace by her father, and was admitted to the presence of the sultan. They were no sooner alone than the sultan ordered her to take off her veil. He was charmed with her beauty; but seeing that she was weeping, he demanded the cause. "Sire," answered Scheherazade, "I have a slave girl whom I love—I earnestly wish that she might be permitted to spend the night in this apartment, so that we may see each other again, and once more say a tender farewell. Will you allow me the consolation of giving her this last proof of my affection?" Schahriar agreed to it, and they sent for Dinarzade, who came right

away. The sultan passed the night with Scheherazade on an elevated couch, as was the custom among the eastern monarchs, and Dinarzade slept at the foot of it on a mattress, prepared for the purpose. Dinarzade, having awakened about an hour before daybreak, did what her mistress had ordered her. "My dear lady," she said, "if you are not asleep, I entreat you, as it will soon be light, to relate to me one of those delightful tales you know. It will, alas, be the last time I shall hear one."

Instead of answering her slave, Scheherazade addressed these words to the sultan: "Will your majesty permit me to indulge my slave in her request?" "Freely," replied he. Scheherazade began as follows:

The Story of the Merchant and the Genie

THERE was formerly a merchant, who was possessed of great wealth, in land, merchandise, and ready money. Having one day an affair of great importance to settle at a considerable distance from home, he mounted his horse, and with only a sort of cloak-bag behind him, in which he had put a few biscuits and dates, he began his journey. He arrived without any accident at the place of his destination; and having finished his business, set out on his return.

On the fourth day of his journey, he felt himself so incapacitated by the heat of the sun that he turned out of his road, in order to rest under some trees, by which there was a fountain. He alighted, and tying his horse to a branch of the tree, sat down on the bank of the pool to eat some biscuits and dates from his little store. When he had satisfied his hunger, he amused himself with throwing about the stones of the fruit with considerable force. Finally he washed his hands, his face, and his feet, and repeated a prayer, like a good Muslim.

He was still on his knees, when he saw a genie, white with age, and of enormous stature, advancing toward him with a scimitar in his hand. As soon as he was close he cried in a terrible voice: "Get up, that I may kill you with this scimitar, as you have caused the death of my son." He accompanied these words with a dreadful yell. The merchant, alarmed by the horrible figure of this genie, as well as the words he heard, replied in trembling accents: "How can I have slain him? I do not know him, nor have I ever seen him." "Didn't you," replied the genie, "on your arrival here, sit down, and take some dates from your wallet; and after eating them, did you not throw the stones around on all sides?" "This is all true," replied the merchant; "I do not deny it." "Well, then," said the other, "I tell you, you have killed my son; for while you were throwing the stones around, my son passed by invisibly. One of them struck him in the eye, causing his death and thus you have slain my son." "Ah, sire, forgive me," cried the merchant. "I have neither forgiveness nor mercy," added the genie, "and is it not just that he who has inflicted death should suffer it?" "I grant that; but I have done so innocently, and therefore I entreat you to pardon me, and allow me to live." "No, no," cried the genie, "I must destroy you, as you have done my son." At these words, he took the merchant in his arms, and having thrown him with his face on the ground, he lifted up his scimitar, in order to strike off his head.

Scheherazade, at this instant, perceiving it was day, broke off. "What a wonderful story," said Dinarzade. "The conclusion," answered Scheherazade, "is still more surprising, as you would agree if the Sultan would allow me to live another day, and in the morning permit me to continue telling it." Schah-riar, who had listened with interest to the narration, told her he would wait until tomorrow to order her execution, so that she might finish her story. He arose, and having prayed, went to the council.

The grand vizier [Scheherazade's father], in the meantime, was in a state of cruel suspense. Unable to sleep, he passed the night in lamenting the approaching fate of his daughter, whose executioner he was compelled to be. Dreading to meet the sultan, he was greatly surprised to see him enter the council chamber without giving him the horrible order he expected!

The sultan spent the day, as usual, in regulating the affairs of his kingdom, and on the approach of night, retired with Scheherazade to his apartment, Dinarzade again sleeping at the foot of the couch.

The next morning, the sultan did not wait for Scheherazade to ask permission to continue her story, but said, "Finish the tale of the genie and the merchant: I am curious to hear the end of it."

Question for Discussion:

1. In this entertaining tale there are obvious instances of Islamic religious practice. Identify these.

Chapter 4

Charlemagne and the Carolingian Renaissance

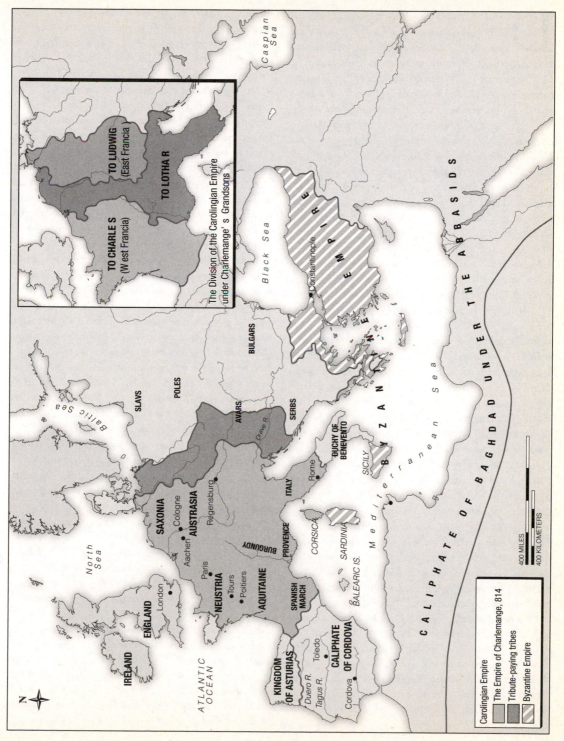

The Carolingian Empire *(From Levack et al., The West, Combined Volume, 2nd ed., p. 248)*

During the eighth and ninth centuries, a new dynasty emerged in western Europe. It was built upon the foundations established by Clovis and his successors during the Merovingian era (see Chapter 2). Due, in part, to the Merovingian practice of dividing the patrimony upon the death of the king, the rulers lost power over time. Furthermore, it was often necessary for the kings to travel around their realm in order to quell potential disturbances by the nobility. As a result of their frequent absences, a series of court officials known as "Mayors of the Palace" became increasingly influential, eventually making their office hereditary. The first powerful mayor was Charles Martel (c. 688–741), who is best known as the victor in a battle against the Muslims that halted their advance beyond the Pyrenees (for information about the Muslim presence in the Iberian Peninsula, see Chapter 3). Scholars do not agree about the date or exact place of the battle, but most believe that it took place in 733 or 734, either at Tours or Poitiers in southern France.

Upon Charles Martel's death, the office of mayor passed to his sons, Pepin the Short (714–768) and Carloman. Eventually Pepin was able to assert his authority after his brother retired to a monastery in 747. The new leader was unhappy with the fact that actual authority rested in his hands, while a Merovingian king remained on the throne. In order to clarify this situation, Pepin sent an emissary to the pope, asking who should bear the title of king. Pope Zachary (r. 741–752), seeing an advantage in supporting Pepin, declared that the man with the real power should be king. Following this decision Pepin was elected king by the Franks, according to tradition. Pope Zachary then sent his representative, Boniface, to anoint Pepin as ruler. This action further cemented the relationship between the pope and the Frankish rulers that had been initiated by Clovis (see Chapter 2). The resulting Frankish-papal alliance led to the establishment of a cultural entity with its political center of gravity north of the Alps and its religious capital in Rome. The new dynasty that had begun with Charles Martel became known as the Carolingian Dynasty because of the number of family members named Charles (Carolus).

When Pepin died in 768 his kingdom was divided, as was customary, between his two sons, Charles and Carloman. Carloman died within three years and Charles, later known as Charlemagne, or "Charles the Great," became the sole ruler. During the course of his reign he created an empire that many scholars have identified as the "First Europe"; he was crowned emperor by the pope on Christmas Day, 800.

The accomplishments of Charlemagne were vast, including the creation of the largest empire since the time of the Romans; furthermore, his patronage of art, religion, and scholarship was so significant that the cultural life of the era is known as the Carolingian Renaissance. An analysis of his reign offers a fine example of the blending of the "threads" identified and discussed in Chapter 1: the Greco-Roman tradition, Christianity, and Germanic culture. As the documents in this chapter will demonstrate, Charlemagne viewed himself as a Christian emperor, whose mission was to bring the faith to people he regarded as pagan. He was also dedicated to the pursuit and preservation of knowledge, which focused on the classical traditions of Greece and Rome. And since he was the heir to a kingdom established by Frankish warriors, his personality and his rulership were grounded in the customs of the Germanic tribes.

As might be expected, there were biographers who devoted much time and effort to describing the personality and actions of the emperor. One of these was Einhard (c. 770–840), a member of the imperial court who wrote the most famous account of Charlemagne's life. His Life of Charlemagne recounts the circumstances of the king's coronation as emperor (Document 4.1). There are several sources available for comparison with Einhard's account, including descriptions found in the biography of Pope Leo III (Document 4.2) and the Annals of Lorsch (Document 4.3). A Byzantine view of the ceremony contained in the Chronographia by Theophanes (Document 4.4), offers yet another perspective.

Einhard's biography also provides information about Charlemagne's military exploits in his quest to expand the empire. The emperor waged numerous wars over many decades; several of these, most notably those against the Saxons, are discussed in Document 4.5.

The Christianization of Germany was under way prior to the reign of Charlemagne, partly as a result of the efforts of Anglo-Saxon missionaries such as the monk Boniface. However, as may be seen in a letter from Boniface to the pope (Document 4.6), new dioceses were needed, and stronger clerical discipline was necessary for the conversion process to proceed effectively.

Charlemagne viewed himself as a Christian emperor, and he was determined to convert the pagan people he subjugated. Among other methods of establishing his authority, both civil and religious, he issued capitularies (legislative or administrative acts) for the new areas he conquered; a selection from these laws for Saxony demonstrates the strength of his control (Document 4.7).

In order to maintain his jurisdiction Charlemagne sent messengers throughout his empire, known as "missi dominici" (messengers of the lord).[1] These men, who reported to the emperor, were given strict rules for their tours of inspection; these directives were also stipulated in capitularies. Document 4.8 specifies the composition of the teams of messengers and outlines their areas of legal control.

Charlemagne also required detailed knowledge of his land holdings within the empire. The capitulary in Document 4.9 provides instructions for reporting the inventory, and stipulates what aspects of the estates should be reported, including animals, produce, and household effects. Of particular interest are the portions that pertain to the activities of women on his estates.

As part of his patronage of the arts, Charlemagne undertook an extensive building program. The most famous of his edifices was the palace church at Aachen, which remains in use as a place of worship to this day. As may be seen in the writings of his biographers, the emperor was intent upon creating a church "which should be finer than the ancient buildings of Rome." The "Interpreting the Evidence" feature in this chapter offers an opportunity to analyze the results of the emperor's vision.

As shown in Documents 4.11 and 4.12, Charlemagne was also intent upon providing the finest possible education for his children and the progeny of his noblemen. To this end he summoned famous scholars from various areas of Europe to establish a school at his palace. It is important to note that opportunities for education were also extended to talented boys of the lower classes, beginning a tradition that ultimately resulted in public education as we know it today. A letter, probably written by the scholar Alcuin but bearing the name of the emperor, stipulates that education should be available "to all who can learn" (Document 4. 13).

Charlemagne also patronized artists and craftsmen, who worked at Aachen and throughout the empire; they created beautiful and luxurious objects in a variety of media, including manuscript illumination, gold and silver metalwork, and ivory carving. Both gold and ivory were used to create elaborate covers for the precious hand-copied gospel books and psalters. A particularly fine example of ivory carving is presented in the "Interpreting the Evidence" feature, which includes a description of the technique of ivory carving by Theophilus.

There are very few extant writings by Carolingian women. One of the most important is the Handbook for William by the noblewoman Dhuoda (Document 4.15). In an excerpt from this book of instruction for her son, she emphasized the virtue of loyalty to one's lord as the most important personal quality. Her work provides a view of aristocratic behavioral expectations in the ninth century.

The Carolingian Empire endured as long as Charlemagne lived to enforce his laws and policies. In the decades following his death in 814 the empire was destroyed by a variety of calamities, including civil war between Charlemagne's grandsons. A division of the empire was finally stipulated in the Treaty of Verdun (843). In addition, western Europe was subject to invasions by the Vikings from the north, the Muslims from the south, and the Magyars from the east. These incursions were described in a variety of Annals, or yearly reports, usually written by monastic scribes (Documents 4.17–4.19), and a document by Liudprand of Cremona (Document 4.20). Although some scholars believe that the accounts may have exaggerated the violence of these assaults, selections from these records illustrate the peril of the attacks.

Thus, within fifty years after the death of Charlemagne, Europe was terrorized and divided. The dire circumstances led to the emergence of a new political system that was not based upon strong monarchical authority; instead it was characterized by the dominance of various noble magnates. An early example of this development, which also illustrates political accommodation with the Vikings, is given in the final selection of this chapter. In the account, Rollo, a Viking chieftain, is given control over an area of Normandy by King Charles III, "the Simple" (879–922). Chapter 5 will analyze this new political pattern in detail.

---

[1]In this context, "lord" means the emperor.

The Coronation of Charlemagne

4.1   Einhard: The Coronation

Most historians agree that the coronation of Charlemagne was one of the important events of the Middle Ages. However, there has never been agreement as to the true nature and motivation for the ceremony. Basic questions remain: Who was responsible, and what did that person or group of persons hope to achieve? The earliest sources, presented in the following documents, demonstrate the division of opinion concerning what happened in Rome.

In his biography of the emperor, Einhard describes the circumstances leading to Charlemagne's trip to Rome. He reports that Pope Leo III had a number of enemies who had attempted to deprive him of the papacy, and in April of 799 he was violently attacked by armed men who attempted to tear out his tongue and eyes. He was left bleeding in the street, and managed to crawl to a nearby monastery, where he miraculously recovered the full capacity of sight and speech. The pope then made his way to Germany, where he sought the aid of Charlemagne, remaining several months.

At the end of the year, the king traveled to Rome in order to support the pope, and to "restore the church." A council was convened to explore the accusations against Leo, and the pope took a solemn oath that he was not guilty of the charges.

In the following document Einhard describes the coronation ceremony, claiming that Charlemagne did not seek the title or the position of emperor; indeed, he would not have entered St. Peter's Cathedral if he had known of the pope's intention.

(From *Two Lives of Charlemagne* by Einhard and Notker the Stammerer, translated with an introduction by Professor Lewis Thorpe [Penguin Classics, 1969]. Copyright © Professor Lewis Thorpe, 1969.)

These were not the sole reasons for Charlemagne's last visit to Rome. The truth is that the inhabitants of Rome had violently attacked Pope Leo, putting out his eyes and cutting off his tongue, and had forced him to flee to the King for help. Charlemagne really came to Rome to restore the Church, which was in a very bad state indeed, but in the end he spent the whole winter there. It was on this occasion that he received the title of Emperor and Augustus. At first he was far from wanting this. He made it clear that he would not have entered the cathedral that day at all, although it was the greatest of all the festivals of the Church, if he had known in advance what the Pope was planning to do. Once he had accepted the title, he endured with great patience the jealousy of the so-called Roman Emperors,[2] who were most indignant at what had happened. He overcame their hostility only by the sheer strength of his personality, which was much more powerful than theirs. He was forever sending messengers to them, and in his dispatches he called them his brothers.

Question for Discussion:

1. Is Einhard's account of the coronation objective? What reasons might he have had to deny Charlemagne's involvement in the planning of the ceremony?

4.2   The *Biography of Pope Leo III* (d. 816)

Leo III had been elected to the papacy in 795. Shortly thereafter he dispatched a letter to Charlemagne, notifying him of the unanimous choice; he also sent the keys of the confession of St. Peter and the standard of the city of Rome. His action was probably intended to remind the king that he was the protector of the Holy See. Charlemagne responded with a letter of congratulation and a generous donation, which greatly enriched the papal treasury. Read the following document within this context.

(From *The Coronation of Charlemagne: What Did It Signify?*, ed. by Richard E. Sullivan. Boston: D.C. Heath and Co., 1959, p. 2. Reprinted by permission of Mary Newell as Executor of the Estate of Richard E. Sullivan.)

After these things, the day of the birth of our Lord Jesus Christ having come, all were again gathered in

---

[2] The emperors at Constantinople considered themselves to be the sole heirs of the Roman emperors. At the time of Charlemagne's coronation, Empress Irene was ruling the Byzantine Empire.

the aforesaid basilica of the blessed Peter the Apostle. And then the gracious and venerable pontiff with his own hands crowned him [Charles] with a very precious crown. Then all the faithful people of Rome, seeing the defense that he gave and the love that he bore for the holy Roman Church and her Vicar, by the will of God and of the blessed Peter, the keeper of the keys of the kingdom of heaven, cried with one accord in a loud voice: "To Charles, the most pious Augustus, crowned by God, the great and peace-giving Emperor, life and victory." While he was invoking diverse saints before the holy confession of the blessed Peter the Apostle, it was proclaimed three times and he was constituted by all to be Emperor of the Romans. Then the most holy pontiff anointed Charles with holy oil, and likewise anointed his most excellent son to be king, upon the very day of the birth of our Lord Jesus Christ; and when the Mass was finished, then the most serene lord Emperor offered gifts.

Question for Discussion:

1. Some scholars believe that the coronation was engineered by the papacy. Does this source reflect that possibility? Discuss.

4.3   The *Annals* of Lorsch

The Annals *(yearly records) of the abbey at Lorsch (Germany) add yet another dimension to the discussion.*

(From *The Coronation of Charlemagne: What Did It Signify?*, ed. by Richard E. Sullivan. Boston: D.C. Heath and Co., 1959, p. 2. Reprinted by permission of Mary Newell as Executor of the Estate of Richard E. Sullivan.)

And because the name of emperor had now ceased to exist in the land of the Greeks and because they had a woman as emperor, it was seen both by the apostolic Leo himself and all the holy fathers who were present in that council [i.e., the council held to decide the fate of Leo III and before which he took his purification oath] and the rest of the people, that they ought to name as emperor Charles himself, king of the Franks, who now held Rome itself, where the Caesars were always accustomed to have their residence, and the rest of the places which they held in Italy, Gaul, and Germany. For Almighty God conceded all these places into his hands, and therefore it seemed to them to be just, that he—with the aid of God and with all the Christian people asking—should not be lacking that title. King Charles did not wish to deny their request, and with all humility, subjecting himself to God and to the petition of the priests and all the Christian people, he received the title of emperor through the coronation of the lord pope Leo on the day of the birth of the Lord. And the first thing he did was to recall the holy Roman Church from that discord which existed there to peace and order.

Questions for Discussion:

1. What reasons did the chronicler provide to justify the coronation?
2. What gender issues are present in this document?

4.4   A View from Byzantium: The *Chronicle* of Theophanes

In the eyes of the west, the imperial authority had been transferred to the Franks as a result of Charlemagne's coronation; however, the Byzantines found such claims to be ridiculous. They believed the emperor in Constantinople to be the legitimate Roman sovereign; hence, the actions of the pope and Charlemagne were regarded as insubordination.

The following document, taken from the Chronographia *by the chronicler Theophanes (c. 758–817), describes the events of Christmas Day, 800. His work ignores the political ramifications of the ceremony, and focuses instead on the anointing of Charlemagne, a western practice that was not followed in the Byzantine Empire until after 1204.*

(From *Byzantium: Church, Society, and Civilization Seen through Contemporary Eyes*, by Deno John Geanakoplos. © 1984 by The University of Chicago Press. All rights reserved.)

In this same year there was an uprising of the relatives of the blessed Pope Hadrian in Rome, who incited the people to rise against Leo the Pope. And after seizing him they blinded him. . . Leo fled to Charles, king of the Franks, who took sharp revenge on his enemies and reestablished him again on his own throne. And from this time onward Rome was under the authority of the Franks. The pope recompensed him [Charlemagne] by crowning him emperor of the Romans in the church of the Holy Apostle Peter, anointing him with oil from head to foot and clothing him in the imperial garb and crown, in the month of December, the 25th, the ninth indiction.

In another passage Theophanes describes events surrounding the coronation:

In this year on December 25, in the ninth indiction, Charles, king [*rex*] of the Franks, was crowned by Leo the Pope. And although he wanted to attack Sicily he delayed preparing a fleet, instead preferring to marry Irene [the Byzantine Empress], and he sent for this purpose envoys the following year [801], in the tenth indiction. . . . And these envoys from Charles and from Pope Leo arrived at [the court of] the most pious Irene, seeking to secure a marriage between Charles and her, and to unite East and West. This would have happened had it not been prevented by the frequent objections [speeches] of Aetius [one of her eunuch advisers].

Questions for Discussion:

1. What implications are there in this document concerning the actions of the pope and Charlemagne?
2. According to Theophanes, Charlemagne preferred to marry Irene rather than attacking Sicily. What are the ramifications of this statement?

The Creation and Governance of the Empire

4.5   Einhard: Charlemagne's Wars against the Saxons

In his Life of Charlemagne, *Einhard summarized the territorial boundaries of Charlemagne's empire. According to his biographer, the emperor expanded his inheritance to include Aquitaine and Gascony, the Iberian Peninsula as far as the Ebro River, all of Italy, Saxony, Pannonia (present-day Hungary), Dacia (present-day Croatia), and much of Dalmatia (present-day Yugoslavia). (See the map on page 91.)*

Among the most difficult campaigns were those undertaken by Charlemagne against the surrounding Germanic tribes, including groups in Aquitaine (southern France) and the Longobards (Lombards) of northern Italy. These campaigns lasted for much of his reign, since many of the areas erupted in rebellion again and again. As Einhard

recounted in his Life of Charlemagne, *his most difficult opponents were the Saxons, who lived in eastern Germany.*

(From *Two Lives of Charlemagne* by Einhard and Notker the Stammerer, translated with an introduction by Professor Lewis Thorpe [Penguin Classics, 1969]. Copyright © Professor Lewis Thorpe, 1969.)

Now that the war in Italy was over, the one against the Saxons, which had been interrupted for the time being, was taken up once more. No war ever undertaken by the Frankish people was more prolonged, more full of atrocities or more demanding of effort. The Saxons, like almost all the peoples living in Germany, are ferocious by nature. They are much given to devil worship and they are hostile to our religion. They think it no dishonor to violate and transgress the laws of God and man. Hardly a day passed without some incident or other which was well calculated to break the peace. Our borders and theirs were contiguous and nearly everywhere in flat, open country, except, indeed, for a few places where great forests or mountain ranges interposed to separate the territories of the two peoples by a clear demarcation line. Murder, robbery and arson were a constant occurrence on both sides. In the end, the Franks were so irritated by these incidents that they decided that the time had come to abandon retaliatory measures and to undertake a full-scale war against these Saxons.

War was duly declared against them. It was waged for thirty-three long years and with immense hatred on both sides, but the losses of the Saxons were greater than those of the Franks. This war could have been brought to a more rapid conclusion, had it not been for the faithlessness of the Saxons. It is hard to say just how many times they were beaten and surrendered as suppliants to Charlemagne, promising to do all that was exacted from them, giving the hostages who were demanded, and this without delay, and receiving the ambassadors who were sent to them. Sometimes they were so cowed and reduced that they even promised to abandon their devil worship and submit willingly to the Christian faith; but, however ready they might seem from time to time to do all this, they were always prepared to break the promises they had made. I cannot really judge which of these two courses can be said to have come the more easily to the Saxons, for, since the very beginning of the war against them, hardly a year passed in which they did not vacillate between surrender and defiance.

However, the King's mettlesome spirit and his imperturbability, which remained as constant in adversity as in prosperity, were not to be quelled by their ever-changing tactics, or, indeed, to be wearied by a task which he had once undertaken. Not once did he allow anyone who had offended in this way to go unpunished. He took vengeance on them for their perfidy and meted out suitable punishment, either by means of an army which he led himself or by dispatching a force against them under the command of his counts. In the end, when all those who had been offering resistance had been utterly defeated and subjected to his power, he transported some ten thousand men, taken from among those who lived both on this side of the Elbe and across the river, and dispersed them in small groups, with their wives and children, in various parts of Gaul (France) and Germany. At long last this war, which had dragged on for so many years, came to an end on conditions imposed by the King and accepted by the Saxons. These last were to give up their devil worship and the malpractices inherited from their forefathers; and then, once they had adopted the sacraments of the Christian faith and religion, they were to be united with the Franks and become one people with them.

Questions for Discussion:

1. What reasons does Einhard give for the continuing difficulties Charlemagne faced with the Saxons?
2. How did the emperor finally resolve the issues?

4.6 Missionary Activity in the Empire: Letter of Boniface to Pope Zacharias (742)

The most important ecclesiastical leader in the conversion of the German realm was an Anglo-Saxon monk, Boniface, often known as the "Apostle of Germany." Traveling from England, he and his fellow monks worked primarily in the eastern part of the kingdom (Bavaria, Thuringia, Hesse, and Friesland). As may be seen in this letter to the pope written during the joint reign of Charlemagne's father Pepin and *his brother Carloman, Boniface created new dioceses and wished to ordain bishops to communicate his religious message effectively. Christianity was not unknown in the region, according to Boniface, but there was evidently a serious crisis concerning clerical discipline that he hoped to correct.*

(From *Readings in European History*, ed. by Leon Bernard and Theodore Hodges [New York: The MacMillan Co., 1958], pp. 72–74.)

We have . . . to inform Your Paternity that by the grace of God we have appointed three bishops over those peoples in Germany who have been to a certain extent won over and converted and we have divided the province into three dioceses. The bishoprics of these three towns or cities where they were ordained we beg you to confirm and establish by your authority in writing. We have appointed one episcopal see in the fortress called Würzburg, another in the town of Buraburg, and a third in a place called Erfurt, which was formerly a city of heathen rustics. The choice of these three places we earnestly pray you to strengthen and confirm by your own charter and by authority of your apostolic office, so that, God willing, there may be in Germany three episcopal sees founded and established by apostolic order and under the authority and direction of St. Peter. And may neither the present nor any future generation presume to break up these dioceses or to defy the orders of the Apostolic See.

Be it known also to Your Paternity that Karlmann [Carloman, Pepin's brother], duke of the Franks, summoned me to him and requested me to bring together a council in the part of the Frankish kingdom which is under his rule. He promised that he would do something toward reforming and reestablishing the ecclesiastical discipline, which for a long time, not less than sixty or seventy years, has been despoiled and trampled upon. If, therefore, he is really willing, under divine inspiration, to carry out this purpose, I should have the advice and direction of your authority—that is, the authority of the Apostolic See. The Franks, according to their elders, have not held a council for more than eighty years, nor have they had an archbishop or established or restored anywhere the canon law of the Church. For the most part the episcopal sees in cities are in the hands of greedy laymen or are exploited by adulterous and vicious clergymen and publicans for secular uses. If, then, I am to undertake this business by your orders and at the instance of the aforesaid duke, I desire to have at once the command and the suggestions of the Apostolic See, together with the Church canons.

If I find among these men certain so-called deacons who have spent their lives since boyhood in debauchery, adultery, and every kind of filthiness, who entered the diaconate with this reputation, and who now, while they have four or five concubines . . . still read the Gospel and are not ashamed or afraid to call themselves deacons—nay rather, entering upon the priesthood, they continue in the same vices, add sin to sin, declare that they have a right to make intercession for the people in the priestly office and to celebrate Mass, and, still worse, with such reputations advancing from step to step to nomination and appointment as bishops—may I have the formal prescription of your authority as to your procedure in such cases so that they may be convicted by an apostolic judgment and dealt with as sinners? And certain bishops are to be found among them who, although they deny that they are fornicators or adulterers, are drunkards and shiftless men, given to hunting and to fighting in the army like soldiers and by their own hands shedding blood, whether of heathens or Christians. Since I am the recognized servant and legate of the Apostolic See, my word here and your word there ought to agree, in case I should send messengers, as I have done in the past, to learn the decision of your authority. . . .

Some of the ignorant common people, Alemanians, Bavarians, and Franks, hearing that many of the offenses prohibited by us are practiced by the city of Rome imagine that they are allowed by the priests there and reproach us for causing them to incur blame in their own lives. They say that on the first day of January year after year, in the city of Rome and in the neighborhood of St. Peter's church by day or night, they have seen bands of singers parading the streets in pagan fashion, shouting and chanting sacrilegious songs and loading tables with food day and night, while no one in his own house is willing to lend his neighbor fire or tools or any other convenience. They say also that they have seen there women with amulets and bracelets of heathen fashion on their arms and legs, offering them for sale to willing buyers. All these things, seen by evil-minded and ignorant people, are a cause of reproach to us and a hindrance to our preaching and teaching. . . .

Some bishops and priests of the Frankish nation who were adulterers and fornicators of the worst kind, whose children born during their episcopate or priesthood bear witness against them, now declare, on returning from the Apostolic See, that the Roman Pontiff has given them permission to carry on their episcopal service in the Church. Against this we maintain that we have never heard that the Apostolic See had ever given a decision contrary to canonical decrees.

All these things, beloved master, we make known to you that we may give an answer to these people upon your authority and that under guidance of your instruction the sheep of the Church may not be led astray and that the ravening wolves may be overcome and destroyed.

We are sending you some trifling gifts, not as being worthy of Your Paternity, but as a token of our affection and our devoted obedience, a warm rug and a little silver and gold.

Questions for Discussion:

1. What was Boniface requesting of the pope in this letter? What did he hope to achieve?
2. Describe and discuss the variety of corrupt activities mentioned in the letter. Do you think the descriptions were purposeful and effective? Why or why not?

4.7   *Capitulary* for Saxony (775–790)

Once Charlemagne had conquered an area such as Saxony, he needed to maintain his control over religious observance as well as political activity; thus, he issued laws in the form of capitularies that defined proper and improper ritual and behavior. The following selections from the Capitulary Concerning the Areas of Saxony *demonstrate the emperor's protection of churches and clergy, and stipulate penalties and punishments (including death) for refusing to conform to the tenets and practices of Christianity.*

(From *Translations and Reprints*, ed. by D. C. Munro, vol 6.5: *Laws of Charles the Great* [Philadelphia: University of Pennsylvania Press, 1899], pp. 2–5.)

1. First, it was pleasing to all that the churches of Christ, which are now being built in Saxony and consecrated to God, should not have less, but greater and more illustrious honor, than the fanes [sacred places] of the idols had.
2. If anyone shall have fled to a church for refuge, let no one presume to expel him from the church by violence, but he shall be left in peace until he shall be brought to the judicial assemblage; and on account of the honor due to God and the saints, and the reverence due to the church itself, let his life and all his members be granted to him. Moreover, let him plead his

cause as best he can and he shall be judged; and so let him be led to the presence of the lord king, and the latter shall send him where it shall have seemed fitting to his clemency.
3. If anyone shall have entered a church by violence and shall have carried off anything in it by force or theft, or shall have burned the church itself, let him be punished by death.
4. If anyone, out of contempt for Christianity, shall have despised the holy Lenten fast and shall have eaten flesh, let him be punished by death. But, nevertheless, let it be taken into consideration by a priest, lest anyone from necessity has been led to eat flesh.
5. If anyone shall have killed a bishop or priest or deacon, let him likewise be punished capitally.
6. If anyone deceived by the devil shall have believed, after the manner of the pagans, that any man or woman is a witch and eats men, and on this account shall have burned the person, shall have given the person's flesh to others to eat, or shall eaten it himself, let him be punished by a capital sentence.
7. If anyone, in accordance with pagan rites, shall have the body of a dead man to be burned and shall have reduced bones to ashes, let him be punished capitally.

8. If anyone of the race of the Saxons hereafter concealed among them shall have wished to hide himself unbaptized, and shall have scorned to come to baptism and shall have wished to remain a pagan, let him be punished by death.

9. If anyone shall have sacrificed a man to the devil, and after the manner of the pagans shall have presented him as a victim to the demons, let him be punished by death.

10. If anyone shall have formed a conspiracy with the pagans against the Christians, or shall have wished to join with them in opposition to the Christians, let him be punished by death; and whosoever shall have consented to this same fraudulently against the king and the Christian people, let him be punished by death.

11. If anyone shall have shown himself unfaithful to the lord king, let him be punished with a capital sentence.

12. If anyone shall have ravished the daughter of his lord, let him be punished by death.

13. If anyone shall have killed his lord or lady, let him be punished in a like manner.

14. If, indeed, for these mortal crimes secretly committed any one shall have fled of his own accord to a priest, and after confession shall have wished to do penance, let him be freed from death by the testimony of the priest.

15. Concerning the lesser chapters all have consented. To each church let the parishioners present a house and two *mansi*[3] of land, and for each one hundred and twenty men, noble and free, and likewise *liti*,[4] let them give to the same church a man-servant and a maid-servant.

16. And this has been pleasing, Christ being propitious, that whenever any receipts shall have come into the treasury, either for a breach of the peace or for any penalty of any kind, and in all income pertaining to the king, a tithe shall be rendered to the churches and priests.

17. Likewise, in accordance with the mandate of God, we command that all shall give a tithe of their property and labor to the churches and priests; let

the nobles as well as the freemen, and likewise the *liti,* according to that which God shall have given to each Christian, return a part to God.

18. That on the Lord's day no meetings and public judicial assemblages shall be held, unless in a case of great necessity or when war compels it, but all shall go to the church to hear the word of God, and shall be free for prayers or good works. Likewise, also, on the special festivals they shall devote themselves to God and to the services of the church, and shall refrain from secular assemblies.

19. Likewise, it has been pleasing to insert in these decrees that all infants shall be baptized within a year; and we have decreed this, that if anyone shall have despised to bring his infant to baptism within the course of a year, without the advice or permission of the priest, if he is a noble he shall pay 120 *solidi*[5] to the treasury, if a freeman 60, if a *litus* 30.

20. If anyone shall have made a prohibited or illegal marriage, if a noble 60 *solidi,* if a freeman 30, if a *litus* 15.

21. If anyone shall have made a vow at springs or trees or groves, or shall have made any offering after the manner of the heathen and shall have partaken of a repast in honor of the demons, if he shall be a noble 60 *solidi,* if a freeman 30, if a *litus* 15. If, indeed, they have not the means of paying at once, they shall be given into the service of the church until the *solidi* are paid.

22. We command that the bodies of Saxon Christians shall be carried to the church cemeteries and not to the mounds of the pagans.

. . .

34. We have forbidden that all the Saxons shall hold public assemblies in general, unless perchance our *missus* [official messenger] shall have caused them to come together in accordance with our command; but each count shall hold judicial assemblies and administer justice his jurisdiction. And this shall be cared for by the priests, lest it be done otherwise.

---

[3] Arable land surrounding the house.
[4] A class of person between a freeman and a serf.

[5] A *solidus* was a gold coin, weighing about 4.54 grams. It had been introduced by the Romans, and its weight and value remained virtually unaltered until the tenth century.

Questions for Discussion:

1. Compare Charlemagne's *Capitulary* with the Salic Law (Document 2.8) and the Visigothic Code (Document 2.6). What similarities do you see?
2. Why does the capitulary forbid public assemblies by the Saxons?
3. Discuss the measures stipulated in this capitulary that were specifically designed to establish religious conformity.

4. After analyzing Document 4.5, which concerns the Saxon Wars, do you think the harsh penalties stipulated in the *Capitulary* were reasonable? Were they justified?
5. Which of Charlemagne's capitularies specifically require the loyalty of his subjects? How does this reflect Germanic tradition? Roman tradition? What are the differences between the two?

4.8 *General Capitulary* for the *Missi Dominici* (802)

In order to maintain religious and civil authority over the people of his vast empire, Charlemagne established teams of men, known as missi dominici *(messengers of the lord). These emissaries were directed to travel through the country in order to make certain that the people were obeying the emperor's laws, and to report their findings to the emperor. Each team of messengers consisted of two individuals, one from the clergy and the other from the noble class. The men were rotated frequently, ensuring that nobody would be able to establish a base of power that might threaten the authority of the emperor. The following capitulary stipulates the expectations of Charlemagne, and extends the process of justice to his representatives.*

(From *Translations and Reprints*, ed. by D. C. Munro, vol 6.5: *Laws of Charles the Great* [Philadelphia: University of Pennsylvania Press, 1899], pp. 16–18, 27.)

First chapter. Concerning the embassy sent out by the lord emperor. Therefore, the most serene and most Christian lord emperor Charles has chosen from his nobles the wisest and most prudent men, both archbishops and some of the other bishops also, and venerable abbots and pious laymen, and has sent them throughout his whole kingdom, and through them by all the following chapters has allowed men to live in accordance with the correct law. Moreover, where anything which is not right and just has been enacted in the law, he has ordered them to inquire into this most diligently and to inform him of it; he desires, God granting, to reform it. And let no one, through his cleverness or astuteness, dare to oppose or thwart the written law, as many might do, or the judicial sentence passed upon him, or to do injury to the churches of God or the poor or the widows or the wards or any Christian. But all shall live entirely in accordance with God's precept, justly and under a just rule, and each one shall be admonished to live in harmony with his fellows in his business or profession; the canonical clergy ought to observe in every respect a canonical life without heeding base gain, nuns ought to keep diligent watch over their lives, laymen and the secular clergy ought rightly to observe their laws without malicious fraud, and all ought to live in mutual charity and perfect peace. And let the *missi* themselves make a diligent investigation whenever any man claims that an injustice has been done to him by anyone, just as they desire to deserve the grace of omnipotent God and to keep their fidelity promised to Him, so that entirely in all cases everywhere, in accordance with the will and fear of God, they shall administer the law fully and justly in the case of the holy churches of God and of the poor, of wards and widows and of the whole people. And if there shall be anything of such a nature that they, together with the provincial counts, are not able of themselves to correct it and to do justice concerning it, they shall, without any ambiguity, refer this, together with their reports, to the judgment of the emperor; and the straight path of justice shall not be impeded by anyone on account of flattery or gifts from anyone, or on account of any relationship, or from fear of the powerful.

2. Concerning the fidelity to be promised to the lord emperor. And he commanded that every man in

his whole kingdom, whether ecclesiastic or layman, and each one according to his vow and occupation, should now promise to him as emperor the fidelity which he had previously promised to him as king; and all of those who had not yet made that promise should do likewise, down to those who were twelve years old. And that it shall be announced to all in public, so that each one might know, how great and how many things are comprehended in that oath; not merely, as many have thought hitherto, fidelity to the lord emperor as regards his life, and not introducing any enemy into his kingdom out of enmity, and not consenting to or concealing another's faithlessness to him; but that all may know that this oath contains in itself this meaning:

3. First, that each one voluntarily shall strive, in accordance with his knowledge and ability, to live wholly in the holy service of God in accordance with the precept of God and in accordance with his own promise, because the lord emperor is unable to give to all individually the necessary care and discipline.

4. Secondly, that no man, either through perjury or any other wile or fraud, on account of the flattery or gift of anyone, shall refuse to give back or dare to abstract or conceal a serf of the lord emperor or a district or land or anything that belongs to him; and that no one shall presume, through perjury or other wile, to conceal or abstract his fugitive fiscaline serfs who unjustly and fraudulently say that they are free.

5. That no one shall presume to rob or do any injury fraudulently to the churches of God or widows or orphans or pilgrims; for the lord emperor himself, after God and His saints, has constituted himself their protector and defender.

6. That no one shall dare to lay waste a benefice of the lord emperor, or to make it his own property.

7. That no one shall presume to neglect a summons to the lord emperor; and that no one of the counts shall be so sumptuous as to dare to dismiss thence anyone of those who military service, either on account of relationship or flattery gifts from anyone.

8. That no one shall presume to impede at all in any way a ban or command of the lord emperor, or to dally with his work or impede or to lessen or in any way to act contrary to his will or commands. And that no one shall dare to neglect to pay dues or tax.

9. That no one, for any reason, shall make a practice in court of defending another unjustly, either from any desire of gain when the cause is weak, or by impeding a just judgment by his skill in reasoning, or by a desire of oppressing when the cause is weak. But each one shall answer for his own cause or tax or debt unless anyone is infirm or ignorant of pleading; for these the *missi* or the chiefs who are in the court or the judge who knows the case in question shall plead before the court; or if it is necessary, such a person may be allowed as is acceptable to all and knows the case well; but this shall be done wholly according to the convenience of the chiefs or *missi* who are present. But in every case it shall be done in accordance with justice and the law; and that no one shall have the power to impede justice by a gift, reward, or any kind of evil flattery or from any hindrance of relationship. And that no one shall unjustly consent to another in anything, but that with all zeal and goodwill all shall be prepared to carry out justice.

For all the above mentioned ought to be observed by the imperial oath.

. . .

40. Lastly, therefore, we desire all our decrees to be known in our whole kingdom through our *missi* now sent out, either among the men of the church, bishops, abbots, priests, deacons, canons, all monks or nuns, so that each one in his ministry or profession may keep our ban or decree, or where it may be fitting to thank the citizens for their good will, or to furnish aid, or where there may be need still of correcting anything. Likewise also to the laymen and in all places everywhere, whether they concern the guardianship of the holy churches or of widows and orphans and the weaker; or the robbing of them; or the arrangements for the assembling of the army; or any other matters; how they are to be obedient to our precept and will, or how they observe our ban, or how each one strives in all things to keep himself in the holy service of God; so that all these good things may be well done to the praise of omnipotent God, and we may return thanks where it is fitting. But where we believe there is anything unpunished, we shall so strive to correct it with all our zeal and will that with God's aid we may bring it to correction, both for our own eternal glory and that of all our faithful. Likewise we desire all the above to be fruitfully known by our counts or *centenarii*, our ministerials.

Questions for Discussion:

1. What qualities were expected of men chosen to be *missi*?
2. The *missi* were expected to report on specific activities they observed among the people. What were some of these?
3. What provisions in the capitulary established loyalty to the emperor?

Royal Estates

4.9 The Capitulary *De Villis*

Another of Charlemagne's capitularies, De Villis ("Concerning Country Estates"), provided instructions for the officials who were assigned to survey the emperor's holdings in order to collect statistics concerning the royal domain. The capitulary is explicit about the information to be included, specifying such items as the use of livestock on the manor, directions for the production of food products, and expectations for "women's work" as well as the production of such workers as blacksmiths, shoemakers, fishermen, and carpenters.

In this document it is possible to see the domestic and agricultural conditions of a typical Carolingian manor, which would be expected to provide hospitality to the emperor and his officials on a temporary basis. Such manors were essential features of economic life in the Middle Ages, as the discussion in Chapter 5 will demonstrate.

(From *Translations and Reprints*, ed. by D. C. Munro, vol 3.2 [Philadelphia: University of Pennsylvania Press, 1899], pp. 2–4.)

Each steward shall make an annual statement of all our income: an account of our lands cultivated by the oxen which our ploughmen drive and of our lands which the tenants of farms ought to plough; an account of the pigs, of the rents; of the obligations and fines; of the game taken in our forests without our permission; of the various compositions; of the mills, of the forest, of the fields, of the bridges, and ships: of the free-men and the hundreds who are under obligations to our treasury; of markets, vineyards, and those who owe wine to us; of the hay, fire-wood, torches, planks, and other kinds of lumber; of the waste-lands; of the vegetables, millet, panic;[6] of the wool, flax, and hemp; of the fruits of the trees, of the nut trees, larger and smaller; of the grafted trees of all kinds; of the gardens; of the turnips; of the fish-ponds; of the hides, skins, and horns; of the honey, wax; of the fat, tallow and soap; of the mulberry wine, cooked wine, mead, vinegar, beer, wine new and old; of the new grain and the old; of the hens and eggs; of the geese; the number of fishermen, smiths [workers in metal], sword-makers, and shoe-makers of the bins and boxes; of the turners and saddlers; of the forges and mines, that is iron and other mines; of the lead mines; of the tributaries; of the colts and fillies; they shall make all these known to us, set forth separately and in order, at Christmas, in order that we may know what and how much of each thing we have.

. . .

22. In each of our estates our stewards are to have as many cow-houses, piggeries, sheep-folds, stables for goats, as possible, and they ought never to be without these. And let them have in addition cows furnished by our serfs for performing their service, so that the cow-houses and plows shall be in no way weakened by the service on our demense. And when they have to provide meat, let them have steers lame, but healthy, and cows and horses which are not mangy, or other beasts which are not diseased and, as we have said, our cow-houses and plows are not to be weakened for this.

. . .

34. They must provide with the greatest care, that whatever is prepared or made with the hands, that is, lard, smoked meat, salt meat, partially salted meat, wine, vinegar, mulberry wine, cooked wine,

---

[6]Panic is a grass with edible grains.

garns (fermented liquer), mustard, cheese, butter, malt, beer, mead, honey, wax, flour, all should be prepared and made with the greatest cleanliness.

. . .

40. That each steward on each of our domains shall always have, for the sake of ornament, swans, peacocks, pheasants, ducks, pigeons, partridges, turtle-doves.

. . .

42. In each of our estates, the chambers shall be provided with counterpanes, cushions, pillows, bed-clothes, coverings for the tables and benches; vessels of brass, lead, iron and wood; andirons, chains, pot-hooks, adzes,[7] axes, augers, cutlasses and all other kinds of tools, so that it shall never be necessary to go elsewhere for them, or to borrow them. And the weapons, which are carried against the enemy, shall be well cared for, so as to keep them in good condition; and when they are brought back they shall be placed in the chamber.

43. For our women's work they are to give at the proper time, as has been ordered, the materials, that is the linen, wool, woad,[8] vermillion,[9] madder,[10] wool-combs, teasels,[11] soap, grease, vessels and the other objects which are necessary.

_____

[7]An adze was a tool used to cut and shape wood.
[8]Woad was a blue dye.
[9]Vermillion was a vivid red dye.
[10]Madder was a red dye of medium color.
[11]Teasel was an herb with spiny protrusions, probably used for combing the wool.

44. Of the food-products other than meat, two-thirds shall be sent each year for our own use, that is of the vegetables, fish, cheese, butter, honey, mustard, vinegar, millet, panic, dried and green herbs, radishes, and in addition of the wax, soap and other small products; and they tell us how much is left by a statement, as we have said above; and they shall not neglect this as in the past; because from those two-thirds, we wish to know how much remains.

45. Each steward shall have in his district good workmen, namely, blacksmiths, gold-smith, silver-smith, shoe-makers, turners, carpenters, sword-makers, fishermen, foilers, soap-makers, men who know how to make beer, cider, berry, and all the other kinds of beverages, bakers to make pastry for our table, net-makers who know how to make nets for hunting, fishing and fowling, and the other who are too numerous to be designated.

Questions for Discussion:

1. Describe and discuss the typical Carolingian estate. What were the responsibilities of the people living on the royal lands?
2. What commodities were produced on the estate?
3. Various supplies were stipulated in the inventory for "women's work." What were the women producing?
4. What were the various occupations of the workmen on this estate?

The Carolingian Renaissance and the Preservation of Classical Learning

INTERPRETING THE EVIDENCE

4.10 The Palatine Chapel at Aachen and Descriptions by Einhard and Notker

After Charlemagne decided that Aachen (today in western Germany) would be his capital, he determined that he would build a "sacred place"—a chapel designed so that it would reflect the glory of ancient Rome. It was constructed between 790 and 805, and has often been compared to the church of San Vitale at Ravenna. The chapel at Aachen, called the

Palatine Chapel at Aachen, 792–805.
(German Information Center.)

(continued)

Palatine Chapel, was built with stone from Roman ruins, and marble brought from Ravenna by permission of Pope Hadrian, probably in 786 or 787. Today the chapel forms the central component of the Aachen cathedral.

Both Einhard and another of his biographers, Notker "the Stammerer," discussed Charlemagne's motives in patronizing this splendid building. According to Einhard, the construction of the chapel was a result of the emperor's Christian piety.

(From *Two Lives of Charlemagne* by Einhard and Notker the Stammerer, translated with an introduction by Professor Lewis Thorpe [Penguin Classics, 1969]. Copyright © Professor Lewis Thorpe, 1969.)

Document

Charlemagne practiced the Christian religion with great devotion and piety, for he had been brought up in this faith since earliest childhood. This explains why he built a cathedral of such great beauty at Aachen, decorating it with gold and silver, with lamps, and with lattices and doors of solid bronze. He was unable to find marble columns for his construction anywhere else, and so he had them brought from Rome and Ravenna.

Notker "the Stammerer" (840–912), a monk from the monastery at St. Gall in Switzerland,[12] was another of Charlemagne's biographers. In his work De Carolo Magno *("Concerning Charles the Great"), Notker described the zeal with which the emperor pursued his goal, and recounted the problems that resulted from his placing a corrupt prelate in charge of the construction.*

Document

Whenever Charlemagne, who was the most energetic of Emperors, had the opportunity of resting a while, he preferred to labor in the service of God rather than relax at his ease. He conceived the idea of constructing on his native soil and according to his own plan a cathedral which should be finer than the ancient buildings of the Romans. Soon he was able to congratulate himself on having accomplished his wish. To help him in this building he summoned from all the lands beyond the seas architects and workmen skilled in every relevant art. He placed in charge of them all a certain abbot who was most experienced in this sort of work, but of whose fraudulent habits Charlemagne was completely unaware. As soon as the Emperor's back was turned, this man began to accept bribes and to let any man return home who wished to do so. Those who were unable to buy themselves out, or whom their masters refused to release, he burdened with immense tasks, just as the Egyptians once exacted inhuman labor from God's own people. He collected a vast store of gold, silver and silken cloth by this fraudulent behavior. In his room he displayed only the least precious articles, and the more valuable things he hid in boxes and chests. One day people suddenly reported to him that his house was on fire. He came running over and forced his way through the mass of flames into the room where the chests of gold were kept. He was not satisfied to rescue one box: he loaded a treasure-chest on to the shoulders of each of his servants, and only then turned to make his escape. As he emerged, a huge beam which had been dislodged by the fire fell on top of him. His body was consumed by earthly flames at the very moment when his soul was journeying off to the everlasting bonfire. In this way the Judgment of God kept watch for the devout Emperor Charlemagne, when his own attention was turned elsewhere by the affairs of his kingdom.

Questions for Discussion:

1. Study the photograph of the Palatine Chapel at Aachen. What features do you see that indicate the continuing tradition of Greco-Roman architecture?

2. Compare Charlemagne's chapel with the drawing of the elevation of Old St. Peter's (Document 1.8). What similarities do you observe?

3. How do Einhard and Notker explain Charlemagne's motivation in building the chapel? Might there have been other reasons not mentioned by his biographers?

---

[12]A groundplan and discussion of the monastery at St. Gall may be found in Chapter 1.

Charlemagne's Educational Programs: A Link to the Future

4.11   Einhard: The Emperor's Devotion to the Liberal Arts

In addition to building and administering his vast empire, Charlemagne was an avid patron of scholarship and the arts; indeed, his interest in culture fostered an era known to scholars as the Carolingian Renaissance. Partly because of the need for educated bureaucrats and literate clergymen, Charlemagne was devoted to improving the intellectual standards in his realm. In order to provide the best education for his children and the progeny of his noblemen, he invited prominent scholars to come to his palace at Aachen to establish a school. In addition to his biographers Einhard and Notker "the Stammerer," these included Alcuin of York, Peter of Pisa, and Paul the Deacon. Charlemagne established schools in monasteries and cathedrals throughout the empire, and encouraged the copying of scriptural and liturgical texts. As may be seen in the following excerpt from Einhard's biography, the emperor was also determined to improve his own educational level, and spent a great deal of time studying and learning from his tutors Alcuin and Peter of Pisa.

(From *Two Lives of Charlemagne* by Einhard and Notker the Stammerer, translated with an introduction by Professor Lewis Thorpe [Penguin Classics, 1969]. Copyright © Professor Lewis Thorpe, 1969.)

He paid the greatest attention to the liberal arts; and he had great respect for men who taught them, bestowing high honors upon them. When he was learning the rules of grammar he received tuition [instruction] from Peter the Deacon of Pisa, who by then was an old man, but for all other subjects he was taught by Alcuin, surnamed Albinus, another Deacon, a man of the Saxon race who came from Britain and was the most learned man anywhere to be found. Under him the Emperor spent much time and effort in studying rhetoric, dialectic and especially astrology. He applied himself to mathematics and traced the course of the stars with great attention and care. He also tried to learn to write. With this object in view he used to keep writing-tablets and notebooks under the pillows on his bed, so that he could try his hand at forming letters during his leisure moments; but, although he tried very hard, he had begun too late in life and he made little progress.

Question for Discussion:

1. What intellectual tasks did the emperor set for himself? Do you see these as a reflection of a common cultural objective? Why?

4.12   Notker "the Stammerer"

Another of Charlemagne's biographers, Notker "the Stammerer" makes clear in his writings that the emperor offered education to boys from poor homes as well as to sons of the nobility. The origins of modern concepts of education for all may be seen in these policies. Furthermore, Charlemagne's patronage provided an educational and cultural link between the classical Greek and Roman traditions and the late Middle Ages. The Carolingian curriculum, taken from the monasteries of late antiquity, would form the foundation for the study of the liberal arts in the medieval universities (see Chapter 13), and ultimately in early modern and contemporary institutions. The excerpt from the work of Notker shows that Charlemagne personally supervised the progress of the students; as may be observed,
he had little patience for students who wasted their educational opportunities.

(From *Two Lives of Charlemagne* by Einhard and Notker the Stammerer, translated with an introduction by Professor Lewis Thorpe [Penguin Classics, 1969]. Copyright © Professor Lewis Thorpe, 1969.).

When, after a long absence, Charlemagne returned to Gaul, with a long series of victories to his credit, he ordered the boys whom he had entrusted to Clement's care to visit to him and present to him their prose writings and their poems. Those of middle-class parentage and from very poor homes brought excellent compositions, adorned more than he could even have hoped with all the subtle refinements of knowledge; but the children of noble parents presented work which was poor and full of stupidity. Then Charlemagne, imitating in his great wisdom the justice of the eternal Judge, placed those who had worked well on his right hand and said to them: "My children, I am grateful to you, for you have tried your very hardest to carry out my commands and to learn everything which will be of use to you. Continue to study hard and to strive for perfection; and I will give you bishoprics and fine monasteries, and you will always be honored in my sight." Then he turned with great severity to those on his left, with a frown and a fiery glance which seemed to pierce their consciences, and scornfully thundered out these frightening words: "But you young nobles, you, the pleasure-loving and dandified sons of my leaders, who trust in your high birth and your wealth, and care not a straw for my command or for your own advancement, you have

neglected the pursuit of learning and have indulged yourselves in time-wasting follies and in the childish sport of fine living and idleness." When he had said this, he turned his august head and raised his unconquered right hand towards the heavens, and thundered forth an oath against them: "By the King of Heaven, I think nothing of your nobility and your fine looks! Others can admire you for these things if they wish! Know this for certain, unless you immediately make up for your previous idleness by diligent study, you will never receive anything worth having from Charlemagne!"

Question for Discussion:

1. What advantages does Charlemagne promise to those diligent students who make significant progress in their studies? How did this support the emperor's political and religious goals?

4.13   De Litteris Colendis ("On the Study of Letters")

Charlemagne's dedication to educating his people extended beyond the palace walls. This letter to Abbot Baugulf of Fulda (779–802), which was probably written by the emperor's tutor and adviser Alcuin (c. 735–804) about 800, demonstrates that the emperor expected the bishops and monks to make education available to all and to conscientiously teach anyone "able to learn." He advised the abbot to send copies of the letter to all of his fellow bishops, and to all of the monasteries within his jurisdiction.

(From *Translations and Reprints*, ed. by D. C. Munro, vol 6.5 [Philadelphia: University of Pennsylvania Press, 1899], pp. 12–14.)

Charles, by the grace of God, King of the Franks and Lombards and Patrician of the Romans, to Abbot Baugulf and to all the congregation, also to the faithful committed to you, we have directed a loving greeting by our ambassadors in the name of omnipotent God.

Be it known, therefore, to your devotion pleasing to God, that we, together with our faithful, have considered it to be useful that the bishoprics and

monasteries entrusted by the favor of Christ to our control, in addition to the order of monastic life and the intercourse of holy religion, in the culture of letters also ought to be zealous in teaching those who by the gift of God are able to learn, according to the capacity of each individual, so that just as observance of the rule imparts order and grace to honesty of morals, so also zeal in teaching and learning may do the same for sentences, so that those who desire to please God by living rightly should not neglect to please him also by speaking correctly. For it is written: "Either from thy words thou shalt be justified or from thy words thou shalt be condemned." For although correct conduct may be better than knowledge, nevertheless knowledge precedes conduct. Therefore, each one ought to study what he desires to accomplish, so that so much the more fully the mind may know what ought to be done, as the tongue hastens in the praises of omnipotent God without the hindrances of errors. For since errors should be shunned by all men, so much the more ought they to be avoided as far as possible by those who are chosen for this very purpose alone, so that they ought to be the special servants of truth. For when in the years just passed letters were often written to us from several monasteries in which it was stated that the brethren who lived there offered up in our behalf sacred and pious prayers, we have recognized in most of these letters both correct thoughts and uncouth expressions; because what pious devotion dictated faithfully to the mind, the tongue, uneducated on account of the neglect of study, was not able to express in the letter without error. From this it happened that we began to fear lest perchance, as the skill in writing was less, so also the wisdom for understanding the Holy Scriptures might be much less than it rightly ought to be. And we all know well that, although errors of speech are dangerous, far more dangerous are errors of the understanding. Therefore, we exhort you not only not to neglect the study of letters, but also with most humble mind, pleasing to God, to study earnestly in order that you may be able more easily and more correctly to penetrate the mysteries of the divine Scriptures. Since, moreover, images, tropes and similar figures are found in the sacred pages, no one doubts that each one in reading these will understand the spiritual sense more quickly if previously he shall have been fully instructed in the mastery of letters. Such men truly are to be chosen for this work as have both the will and the ability to learn and a desire to instruct others. And may this be done with a zeal as great as the earnestness with which we command it. For we desire you to be, as it is fitting that soldiers of the church should be, devout in mind, learned in discourse, chaste in conduct and eloquent in speech, so that whosoever shall seek to see you out of reverence for God, or on account of your reputation for holy conduct, just as he is edified by your appearance, may also be instructed by your wisdom, which he has learned from your reading or singing, and may go away joyfully giving thanks to omnipotent God. Do not neglect, therefore, if you wish to have our favor, to send copies of this letter to all your suffragans[13] and fellow-bishops and to all the monasteries. Farewell.

Questions for Discussion:

1. Compare Charlemagne's letter to Baugulf with Notker's remarks in Document 4.12. What common themes are evident?
2. What are the educational goals specified in this letter? How would these benefit Carolingian society?
3. What implications did Charlemagne's educational policies hold for the future? How did they benefit the culture of the succeeding centuries? Discuss.

---

[13]A suffragan is a bishop appointed to assist an archbishop or another bishop; he generally has administrative responsibilities.

INTERPRETING THE EVIDENCE

4.14 Ivory Book Cover and *De Diversis Artibus* by Theophilus

The artists and craftsmen who worked at Aachen created beautiful and luxurious items in a variety of media, including manuscript illumination, gold and silver metalwork, and ivory carving. Both gold and ivory were used to create elaborate covers for the precious hand-copied gospel books and psalters. The subject matter of these extraordinary objects consisted, as might be expected, of images of the lives of Christ, Mary, or the saints. The designs also included references to classical motifs, as may be seen in this example, which dates from c. 810, and Germanic or Celtic interlocking design.

(continued)

The so-called "Harrach-Diptych" is divided into two panels, creating the "diptych," or double panel. At the top of each side the evangelists are writing the gospels; their symbols appear in arched niches above their heads. Luke, symbolized by the winged Ox, and John, represented by the Eagle, are seated on the left side. Matthew, whose symbol is a winged man, and Mark, with his winged Lion, are on the right. Scenes from the life of Christ are in the second rank: the Nativity on the left and the Annunciation on the right. In the left panel at the bottom we see the angel appearing to the Marys at Christ's tomb, and on the right, the Crucifixion.

There are many references to Greco-Roman iconography in this dyptich. For example, each scene is framed by classical columns with Corinthian capitals, and classical rosettes decorate the areas between several of the arches. The figures are typical of early medieval style, with large heads attached to rounded shoulders.

There is a limited amount of documentation concerning the techniques of medieval ivory carvers. It is interesting to note that ivory became a popular luxury material following the death of the elephant given to Charlemagne by the Caliph Harun al-Rashid. One of the sources for information is the treatise De diversis artibus (c. 1110–1140) by the monk Theophilus, also known as Roger of Helmarshausen. Although the work was written in the twelfth century, it reflects methods in use for creating book covers, mirror backs, croziers, and knife handles from a previous era. In discussing the techniques, Theophilus used words for "ivory" and "bone" interchangeably.

(From *Theophilus: The Various Arts {De Diversis Artibus}*, trans. by C. R. Dodwell. Oxford: Clarendon Press, 1986, pp. 166–167. Reprinted by permission of Oxford University Press.)

Document

XCIII. Carving Bone

When carving bone, first trim a piece of it to the size that you want, and then spread chalk over it. Draw the figures with lead according to your wishes, and score the outlines with a sharp tracer so that they are quite clear. Then, with various chisels, cut the grounds as deeply as you wish and according to your ability and skill carve the figures or anything else you want. If you want to decorate your work with gold leaf, spread underneath it the glue of the bladder of the fish known as the sturgeon, cut the leaf into small pieces and apply them as you wish.

Also fashion round or ribbed handles of ivory, making a hole down the centre along its length. Then, with various files appropriate for this work, increase the size of the hole, so that the handle is the same shape inside as out. The handle should be fairly and consistently slender throughout. All around, delicately portray small flowers or animals, or birds, or dragons linked together by their necks and tails, and with fine tools pierce the grounds through. Then carve as finely and carefully as you can. When this has been done, fill up the hole inside with oak wood, which you cover with thin gilt copper so that the gold can be seen through the grounds. Then you fill up the hole at the top and bottom by marrying in two pieces of the same ivory, and these you secure with ivory pins so subtly that no one can detect how the gold was put in. After this, make a slit in the upper piece; in this the blade is inserted. The tang of the latter, when heated, can easily be pushed in since the inside is of wood and it will fit firmly.

Questions for Discussion:

1. Although Theophilus is describing the creation of a knife handle, the techniques he mentions may also be applied to the making of an ivory book cover such as the one pictured. What features are common to both?

2. How would book covers such as this, or similar ones made of gold, reflect the tripartite tradition of Greco-Roman, Christian, and Germanic influence?

Ivory Book Cover. (Harrach-Diptychon), Aachen, c. 810, 12.6 in. × 8.3 in. *(Schnüttgen Museum, Cologne.)*

4.15   A Carolingian Mother's Advice to Her Son: *Handbook for William* by Dhuoda

Dhuoda of Septimania (c. 806–after 843) was a noble-woman who married Bernard, Duke of Septimania, in 824 in the palace chapel at Aachen. Two years later she gave birth to a son, William. Duke Bernard was an important military leader who served briefly as the chancellor of Charlemagne's son, Louis the Pious, and was the godfather of Louis's son, who became Charles ("the Bald"). In 841, during the struggle for supremacy between Charles and his brother Louis ("the German"), Bernard was late in sending troops to an important battle. Charles was infuriated, and, in recompense, Bernard sent his son William, now fifteen years old, to Charles's court to serve as hostage for his father's future loyalty.

At this time Dhuoda was living in southern France supervising Bernard's land holdings. She wrote the Handbook *as an instruction manual for William's use in understanding the intricacies in the court of Charles and guiding his behavior. In the following passage, Dhuoda counsels her son to be unswervingly loyal to his lord. This was a quality deeply prized by Germanic tribespeople, as we observed in the* Germania *of* Tacitus *(Document 1.16) and the epic poem* Beowulf *(Document 2.9). It is also a fundamental characteristic of the political system of vassalage, to be explored in Chapter 5.*

Direction on your comportment toward your lord.

You have Charles as your lord; you have him as lord because, as I believe, God and your father, Bernard, have chosen him for you to serve at the beginning of your career, in the flower of your youth. Remember that he comes from a great and noble lineage on both sides of his family. Serve him not only so that you please him in obvious ways, but also as one clearheaded in matters of both body and soul. Be steadfastly and completely loyal to him in all things.

Think on that excellent servant of the patriarch Abraham. He traveled a great distance to bring back a wife for his master's son. Because of the confidence of him who gave the command and the wise trustworthiness of him who followed it, the task was fulfilled. The wife found great blessing and great riches in her many descendants. What shall I say of the attitude of Joab, of Abner, and of many others toward the king David? Facing dangers on their king's behalf in many places, they desired with all their might to please their lord more than themselves. And what of those many others in holy Scripture who faithfully obeyed their lords' commands? Because of their watchful strength they were found worthy to flourish in this world. For we know that, as Scripture tells, all honor and authority are given by God. Therefore we should serve our lords faithfully, without ill will, without reluctance, and without sluggishness. As we read, *there is no power but from God: and he . . . that resisteth the power, resisteth the ordinance of God.*

That is why, my son, I urge you to keep this loyalty as long as you live, in your body and in your mind. For the advancement that it brings you will be of great value both to you and to those who in turn serve you. May the madness of treachery never, not once, make you offer an angry insult. May it never give rise in your heart to the idea of being disloyal to your lord. There is harsh and shameful talk about men who act in this fashion. I do not think that such will befall you or those who fight alongside you because such an attitude has never shown itself among your ancestors. It has not been seen among them, it is not seen now, and it will not be seen in the future.

Be truthful to your lord, my son William, child of their lineage. Be vigilant, energetic, and offer him ready assistance as I have said here. In every matter of importance to royal power take care to show yourself a man of good judgment—in your own thoughts and in public—to the extent that God gives you strength. Read the sayings and the lives of the holy Fathers who have gone before us. You will there discover how you may serve your lord and be faithful to him in all things. When you understand this, devote yourself to the faithful execution of your lord's commands. Look around as well and observe those who fight for him loyally and constantly. Learn from them how you may serve him. Then, informed by their example, with the help and support of God, you will easily reach the celestial goal I have mentioned above. And may your heavenly Lord God be generous and benevolent toward you. May he keep you safe, be your kind leader and your protector. May he deign to assist you in all your actions and be your constant defender. *As it shall be the will* of God *in heaven so be it done. Amen.*

Questions for Discussion:

1. In Document 1.16, the Roman historian Tacitus described the bonds of loyalty between chiefs and their warriors. How does Dhuoda's advice to her son William incorporate some of these values?

2. Discuss the ways that Dhuoda's counsel reflects the Christian mission described by documents in this chapter.

A World Destroyed: The Disintegration of the Empire

4.16   The Treaty of Verdun (843)

The dissolution of the Carolingian Empire was caused by several factors that created widespread political instability, including wars between the successors of Charlemagne. The emperor's son, Louis the Pious, ruled under difficult political circumstances until his death in 840. War between Lothair, one of the grandsons of Charlemagne, and his brothers Louis "the German" and Charles "the Bald" broke out shortly thereafter. In 843, following several decades of conflict, the Treaty of Verdun established a tripartite division of the empire between the grandsons of the emperor: Charles "the Bald" received the western section, Louis "the German" ruled the eastern part, and Lothair was given the central area and northern Italy as well as the title of Holy Roman Emperor. The Annals of St. Bertin provide details of the division.

(From *The Annals of St-Bertin*, translated by Janet L. Nelson. Manchester, UK: Manchester University Press, 1991, p. 56. Reprinted by permission.)

(843) Charles went as arranged to meet his brothers, and joined them at Verdun. There the shares were allocated: Louis got everything east of the Rhine and on this side of it he got the *civitates* (cities) and districts of Speyer, Worms and Mainz; Lothar got the lands between the Rhine and the Scheldt where it runs into the sea, and inland by was of Cambrai, Hainaut, the regions of Loome and of Mezieres and the counties which lie next to each other on the western side of the Meuse down as far as where the Saone runs into the Rhone, and down the Rhone, and down the Rhone to where it flows into the sea, likewise with the counties situated on both sides of it. Beyond these limits, though, all he got was Arras, and that was through the generosity of his brother Charles. Charles himself was given everything else as far as Spain. Solemn oaths were sworn, and finally everyone departed to their various destinations.

Questions for Discussion:

1. Discuss the divisions of the Carolingian Empire described in Document 4.16 and shown in the map on page 91. Do these seem fair and reasonable to you? Why or why not?

2. Did one of the brothers have a geographical or political advantage?

Viking, Muslim, and Magyar Invasions

4.17   The *Annals* of St. Bertin

In addition to the trauma and dislocation caused by the wars between the son and grandsons of Charlemagne, western Europe was beset by incursions from a variety of non-Christian groups that surrounded the perimeter. These included the Muslims, attacking from the south, the Magyars, besieging from the east, and Scandinavian tribes, invading from the north. The most lasting effects were the result of these incursions by "the Northmen," as they were called by contemporaries. The effects of their destruction are recorded in the Annals[14] of various monastic establishments, which also give details concerning the reactions of Charles the Bald, Lothair, and Louis the German to the assaults. Several examples of these records follow. The dates indicate that the incursions continued throughout the second half of the ninth century.

(From *The Annals of St. Bertin*, translated by Janet L. Nelson. Manchester, UK: Manchester University Press, 1991, pp. 55–56. Reprinted by permission.)

(843) Lothar and Louis behaved peacefully, keeping themselves within the boundaries of their own realms; Charles travelled about in Aquitaine. While he was still based there, the Breton Nominoe

and Lambert, who had recently defected from their allegiance to Charles, slew Rainald duke of Nantes, and took large numbers of prisoners. So many and such great disasters followed, while brigands ravaged everything everywhere, that people in many areas throughout Gaul were reduced to eating earth mixed with a little bit of flour and made into a sort of bread. It was a crying shame—no, worse, a most execrable crime—that there was plenty of fodder for the horses of those brigands while human beings were short of even tiny crusts of earth-and-flour mixture.

Northmen pirates attacked Nantes, slew the bishop and many clergy and lay people of both sexes, and plundered the city. Then they attacked the western parts of Aquitaine to devastate them too. Finally they landed on a certain island [probably Noirmoutier], brought their households over from the mainland and decided to winter there in something like a permanent settlement.

---

[14]Annals consisted of chronological records of the events of the year. They were generally produced at monasteries.

4.18   The *Annals* of Xanten

(From *Readings in European History*, vol. i, ed. by James Harvey Robinson [Boston: Ginn & Co., 1904], pp. 158–160.)

(845) Twice in the canton of Worms there was an earthquake; the first in the night following Palm Sunday, the second in the holy night of Christ's Resurrection. In the same year the heathen broke in upon the Christians at many points, but more than twelve thousand of them were killed by the Frisians.[15] Another party of invaders devastated Gaul; of these more than six hundred men perished. Yet owing to his indolence Charles agreed to give them many thousand pounds of gold and silver if they would leave Gaul, and this they did. Nevertheless the cloisters of most of the saints were destroyed and many of the Christians were led away captive.

After this had taken place King Louis once more led a force against the Wends.[16] When the heathen had learned this they sent ambassadors, as well as gifts and hostages, to Saxony, and asked for peace. Louis then granted peace and returned home from Saxony. Thereafter the robbers were afflicted by a terrible pestilence, during which the chief sinner among them, by the name of Reginheri, who had plundered the Christians and the holy places, was struck down by the hand of God. They then took counsel and threw lots to determine from which of their gods they should seek safety; but the lots did not fall out happily, and on the advice of one of their Christian prisoners that they should cast their lot before the God of the Christians, they did so, and the lot fell happily. Then their king, by the name of Rorik, together with all the heathen people, refrained from meat and drink for fourteen days, when the plague ceased, and they sent back all their Christian prisoners to their country.

(846) According to their custom the Northmen plundered Eastern and Western Frisia and burned the town of Dordrecht, with two other villages, before the eyes of Lothaire, who was then in the

---

[15]The Frisians were people living in the coastal parts of the Netherlands and Germany.
[16]The Wends were people living in central Europe, west of the Oder river.

castle of Nimwegen, but could not punish the crime. The Northmen, with their boats filled with immense booty, including both men and goods, returned to their own country.

In the same year Louis sent an expedition from Saxony against the Wends across the Elbe. He personally, however, went with his army against the Bohemians, whom we call Beu-winitha, but with great risk. . . . Charles advanced against the Britons, but accomplished nothing.

At this same time, as no one can mention or hear without great sadness, the mother of all churches, the basilica of the apostle Peter, was taken and plundered by the Moors, or Saracens, (Muslims) who had already occupied the region of Beneventum. The Saracens, moreover, slaughtered all the Christians whom they found outside the walls of Rome, either within or without this church. They also carried men and women away prisoners. They tore down, among many others, the altar of the blessed Peter, and their crimes from day to day bring sorrow to Christians. Pope Sergius departed life this year.

Questions for Discussion follow Document 4.19.

4.19   The *Annals* of St. Vaast

(From *Readings in European History*, vol. i, ed. by James Harvey Robinson [Boston: Ginn & Co., 1904], pp. 163–166.)

(882) The Northmen in the month of October entrenched themselves at Condé, and horribly devastated the kingdom of Carloman, while King Charles with his army took his stand on the Somme [River] at Barleux. The Northmen ceased not from rapine and drove all the inhabitants who were left beyond the Somme. . . . [King Carloman gave them battle] and the Franks were victorious and killed almost a thousand of the Northmen. Yet they were in no wise discomfited by this battle. . . . They went from Condé back to their ships, and thence laid waste the whole kingdom with fire and sword as far as the Oise [River]. They destroyed houses, and razed monasteries and churches to the ground, and brought to their death the servants of our holy religion by famine and sword, or sold them beyond the sea. They killed the dwellers in the land and none could resist them.

Abbot Hugo, when he heard of these calamities, gathered an army and came to aid the king. When the Northmen came back from a plundering expedition . . . he, in company with the king, gave them chase. They, however, betook themselves to a wood, and scattered hither and yon, and finally returned to their ships with little loss. In this year died Hinckmar, archbishop of Rheims, a man justly esteemed by all.

(883) In the spring the Northmen left Condé and sought the country along the sea. Here they dwelt through the summer; they forced the Flemings to flee from their lands, and raged everywhere, laying waste the country with fire and sword. As autumn approached, Carloman, the king, took his station with his army in the canton of Vithman at Mianai, opposite Lavier, in order to protect the kingdom. The Northmen at the end of October came to Lavier with cavalry, foot soldiers, and all their baggage. Ships, too, came from the sea up the Somme and forced the king and his whole army to flee and drove them across the river Oise. The invaders went into winter quarters in the city of Amiens and devastated all the land to the Seine and on both sides of the Oise, and no man opposed them; and they burned with fire the monasteries and churches of Christ.

(885) On the twenty-fifth of July the whole host of the Northmen forced their way to Rheims. Their ships had not yet come, so they crossed the Seine in boats they found there, and quickly fortified themselves. The Franks followed them. All those who dwelt in Neustria and Burgundy gathered to make war upon the Northmen. But when they gave battle it happened that Ragnold, duke of Maine, was killed, with a few others. Therefore all the Franks retreated in great sorrow and accomplished nothing.

Thereupon the rage of the Northmen was let loose upon the land. They thirsted for fire and slaughter; they killed Christian people and took them captive and destroyed churches; and no man could resist them.

Again the Franks made ready to oppose them, not in battle, but by building fortifications to prevent the passage of their ships. They built a castle on the river Oise at the place which is now called Pontoise, and appointed Aletramnus to guard it. Bishop Gauzelin fortified the city of Paris.

In the month of November the Northmen entered the Oise, and besieged the castle the Franks had built. They cut off the water supply from the castle's garrison, for it depended on the river for water and had no other. Soon they who were shut up in the castle began to suffer for lack of water. What more need be said? They surrendered on condition that they be allowed to go forth unharmed. After hostages had been exchanged, Aletramnus and his men went to Beauvais. The Northmen burned the castle and carried off all that had been left by the garrison, who had been permitted to depart only on condition that they would leave everything behind except their horses and arms.

Elated with victory, the Northmen appeared before Paris, and at once attacked a tower, confident that they could take it quickly because it was not yet fully fortified. But the Christians defended it manfully and the battle raged from morning till evening. The night gave a truce to fighting and the Northmen returned to their ships. Bishop Gauzelin and Count Odo worked with their men all night long to strengthen the tower against assaults. The next day the Northmen returned and tried to storm the tower, and they fought fiercely till sunset. The Northmen had lost many of their men and they returned to their ships. They pitched a camp before the city and laid siege to it and bent all their energies to capture it. But the Christians fought bravely and stood their ground.

Questions for Discussion:

1. Describe the extent, both geographical and personal, of the damage inflicted by the Northmen, according to the *Annals*.
2. Why were the people of western Europe unable to defend themselves against the onslaught?

4.20   The Magyars: An Account by Liudprand of Cremona

In the ninth century a new threat appeared on the eastern borders, as the Magyars (Hungarians) attacked. The invaders launched innumerable raids throughout the empire, as may be seen in the following document. The battle described by Liutprand took place in 910 on the banks of the River Lech. Royal forces were defeated in this conflict, and the Magyars continued to ravage the eastern areas of the old Holy Roman Empire. In 955 they were vanquished by the armies of Otto I at a famous battle in the same area, known as the Battle of Lechfeld (see Document 6.5).

The following excerpt is from the works of Liudprand of Cremona (c. 920–972). He was a bishop and courtier during the reigns of the Lombard king Berengar and Emperor Otto I, and was sent on diplomatic missions by both of the monarchs. His account of the blood-thirsty invasions by the Hungarians is from a work titled Antapodosis *("Retribution").*

After the life-blood of King Arnulf (850–899), deserting his limbs, left his body lifeless, his son Louis (893–911)[17] was ordained king by all the people. But the death of so great a man could not escape the notice of the Hungarians, just as it could not escape anyone in the whole world; and so the day of his death was to them merrier and all holidays, more pleasing than all treasures. But why?

In the first year after his death and his offspring's ordination, having assembled a very big army, the Hungarians claimed for themselves the nation of the Moravians, which King Arnul had subdued with the aid of their might; they even occupied territories of the Bavarians, destroyed castles, burned churches, massacred communities, and drank the blood of their victims so that they would be feared more and more.

(From *The Complete Works of Liudprand of Cremona*, translated by Paolo Squatriti. Washington, D.C.: Catholic University Press, 2007}, pp. 75–77, 83–85. Reprinted by permission of the Catholic University Press.)

---

[17]Louis was crowned in 900, at the age of seven. The "boy king" was technically the head of government, but real control was in the hands of Archbishop Hatto I of Mainz.

Therefore King Louis, perceiving their cruelty and the decimation of his people, so aroused the spirits of all his men with fear that, if anyone considered being absent from the war which he was about to launch against the Hungarians, he would without doubt end his life in a noose. That numberless horde of the worst of peoples hastened to encounter his greatest of armies. Nor would you see a soul thirsting for a cold draught more avidly than that cruel nation longs for the day of battle; for nothing pleases them except to fight. Indeed, as I learned from the book written about their origin, their mothers cut their boys' faces with very sharp blades as soon as they come into the world so that, before they may receive the nourishment of milk, they may learn to endure wounds. The wounds that are inflicted on the bodies of the living in place of grief for dead relatives lend some credence to this story; truly they cry with blood, instead of tears as would "the godless and the impious in place of tears." Having gathered an army, hardly had King Louis come to Augsburg, which is a city on the border between the Swabians, Bavarians, and eastern Franks, when an unexpected and, even more, an unfortunate approach of this people was announced. On the following day both lines of battle assembled on the meadows along the river Lech, places suited to martial deeds by virtue of their ample space.

Before Aurora left the saffron couch of Tithon,[18] the nation of the Hungarians, thirsting for slaughter, avid for war, attack those yawning, that is, the Christians; for arrows, rather than noises, awoke several, and other, pierced in their cots, neither the clamor nor their wounds aroused, as life departed from them more quickly than sleep. Then there broke out heavy fighting all around, and the Turks,[19] turning their backs as if in flight, laid many low with their arrow shots . . . [*Louis's forces were winning when the Hungarians laid an ambush*]

. . . the Turks, since they were crafty, feigned flight, having laid ambushes. And when the people of the king, unaware of the deceit, chased them with a might thrust, the ambushers, falsely vanquished,

fell on them from all sides and annihilated the supposed victors. The king himself marveled that after being the victor he was now vanquished, and it was all the more burdensome for him because unexpected. There you could see the meadow and the fields completely littered with corpses, and rivers and banks turned red by the blood that mixed in; then the neighing of horses and the clamor of trumpets terrified those fleeing more and more, and emboldened their pursuers more and more.

Moreover, the Hungarians, having carried out their scheme, unable to satisfy their evil cravings with so great a massacre of Christians, instead ravaged and totally burned the kingdoms of the Bavarians, Franks, Swabians, and Saxons so as to satiate their lust for perfidy. Nor was there anyone who could withstand their advance except with great strain or in places strongly fortified by nature; and the people were made tributary to them for several years. . . .

At length, with the Christians killed and scattered, the Hungarians traversed all the places of the kingdom, ravaging them; nor was there anyone who resisted their presence except by chance in heavily fortified places. Clearly their strength prevailed, since a certain part of them depopulated Bavaria, Swabia, Francia, and Saxony; while another part did the same to Italy. But actually it was not their strength that earned this success, but God's true words, more lasting than the earth and heaven, could not be changed, as when through the prophet Jeremiah every nation, personified by the house of Israel, was threatened, saying: "Behold, I will bring upon you a people from afar, a strong people, an ancient people, a people whose language you shall not know, nor understand what they say. Their quiver is like an open sepulcher; they are all valiant; and they shall eat up your grain and your bread, they shall devour your sons and your daughters, they sall eat up your flock and your herds, they shall eat your vineyards and your figs; and with swords they shall destroy your strong cities, wherein you trust. Nevertheless, in those days, says the Lord God, I will not bring you to utter destruction."[20]

---

[18]Liudprand's works contain many references to classical works, such as those of the Roman poet Vergil, providing evidence of the continuation of the classical tradition into the tenth century.
[19]Liudprand uses the designation *Turks,* meaning Hungarians, several times in his work.

---

[20]Jeremiah 5.15–18.

Questions for Discussion:

1. Why were the Hungarians eager to invade at this particular time?
2. What justification does Liudprand give for the victories of the Hungarians?
3. Liudprand viewed the Hungarians as "others." Describe his view of their character and practices. Do you think his concepts were widely shared in the Middle Ages? Are these also typical attitudes toward those we see as "others" in the contemporary world? Discuss.

4.21   Normans in France: The Baptism of Rollo

As noted in Document 4.19, the Norsemen eventually began to settle along the coast of France in order to create permanent establishments. Among these were the people of Rollo the Viking. In 911 Rollo's forces were defeated by the army of king Charles "the Simple" (879–929), but after the battle, the king realized that he could no longer continue to turn back the invasions of the Vikings. Rather than pay Rollo to leave, as was customary, the king decided to give Rollo the coastal lands occupied by his people with the understanding that he would defend the area against other Viking raids. As part of his agreement with King Charles, Rollo pledged his loyalty to the king, and converted to Christianity. In return, King Charles granted Rollo the area of Normandy and the title Duke of Normandy. In the following account of the homage ceremony, when he was required to kiss the foot of King Charles, he refused, thinking it was too humiliating. Thus, he ordered one of his warriors to act as a proxy. What follows is an amusing account from the Chronicle of Saint Denis *that describes an otherwise serious commitment to a relationship often called "vassalage." The various aspects of this system based on bonds of loyalty will be explored in Chapter 5.*

(From *A Source Book of Mediaeval History*, edited by Frederic Austin Ogg [New York: American Book Company, 1907], pp. 171–173. Translation modernized.)

The king had at first wished to give to Rollo the province of Flanders, but the Norman rejected it as being too marshy. Rollo refused to kiss the foot of Charles when he received from him the duchy of Normandy. "He who receives such a gift," said the bishops to him, "ought to kiss the foot of the king." "Never," replied he, "will I bend the knee to anyone, or kiss anybody's foot." Nevertheless, impelled by the entreaties of the Franks, he ordered one of his warriors to perform the act in his place. This man seized the foot of the king and lifted it to his lips, kissing it without bending and so causing the king to tumble over backwards. At that there was a loud burst of laughter and a great commotion in the crowd of onlookers. King Charles, Robert, Duke of the Franks, the counts and magnates, and the bishops and abbots, bound themselves by the oath of the Catholic faith to Rollo, swearing by their lives and their bodies and by the honor of all the kingdom, that he might hold the land and transmit it to his heirs from generation to generation throughout all time to come. When these things had been satisfactorily performed, the king returned in good spirits into his domain, and Rollo with Duke Robert set out for Rouen.

In the year of our Lord 912 Rollo was baptized in holy water in the name of the sacred Trinity by Franco, archbishop of Rouen. Duke Robert, who was his godfather, gave to him his name. Rollo devotedly honored God and the Holy Church with his gifts. . . . The pagans, seeing that their chieftain had become a Christian, abandoned their idols, received the name of Christ, and with one accord desired to be baptized. Meanwhile the Norman duke made ready for a splendid wedding and married the daughter of the king [Gisela] according to Christian rites.

Rollo gave assurance of security to all those who wished to dwell in his country. The land he divided among his followers, and, as it had not been used for a long time, he improved it by the construction of new buildings. It was settled by the Norman warriors and by immigrants from outside regions. The duke established for his subjects certain inviolable rights and laws, confirmed and published by the will of the leading men, and he compelled all his people to live peaceably together. He rebuilt the churches, which had been entirely ruined; he restored the temples, which had been destroyed by the ravages of the pagans; he repaired and added to the walls and fortifications of the cities; he subdued the Britons who rebelled against him; and with the provisions obtained from them he supplied all the country that had been granted to him.

Questions for Discussion:

1. What measures were taken by Rollo to establish his authority in Normandy?

2. In addition to pledging his loyalty to the king, how did Rollo integrate himself and his people into the resident population?

3. Assuming that the account is true, compare this example of "marriage diplomacy" with those we studied in the first three chapters. How is Rollo's marriage similar to these? Do you see any differences in the objectives of such unions?

Chapter 5

The Development of Vassalage and Agricultural Change

Following the disintegration of the Carolingian Empire in the ninth century, the authority of centralized government lessened significantly. The embryonic kingdoms continued to have monarchs, but they were often less powerful than the nobles. The situation in which King Charles "the Simple" had to make accommodation with Rollo "the Viking" was not atypical (see Document 4.21). In order to establish a modicum of peace and civil order, a system developed that became the dominant form of political organization; it was based upon bonds of loyalty between men of the noble class, known as lords and vassals, who had specific responsibilities to one another. The practice was known by contemporaries as vassalage, whereas some modern scholars have used the term feudalism to define it. There is a great deal of current debate as to whether this is useful terminology, since there was much variety in the practice throughout Europe, and the concept has become overly formulaic. Nonetheless, it is important to recognize aspects of vassalage in the literature and art of the Middle Ages, and as several of the following chapters will demonstrate, an understanding of this tradition is essential to the appreciation of medieval culture.

The bonds of loyalty established between the noblemen were confirmed by formalized rituals. Again, these varied between eras and from place to place, but the selections contained in this chapter provide typical examples of the commitment ceremonies. These include a document illustrating the homage ceremony (Document 5.1) in addition to a description of one aspect of the ceremony known as immixtio manuum. (Document 5.2). Difficult circumstances arose when vassals pledged their loyalty to more than one lord, and Document 5.3 stipulates rules for dealing with multiple homage. There were also clear expectations of the responsibilities of the vassal to his lord, including, but not limited to, military service, as shown in Documents 5.4 and 5.5.

Men who became knights participated in elaborate rituals that established their position. These ceremonies are described in an excerpt from The Book of Chivalry *by Geoffroi de Charny (Document 5.6).*

Warfare was a constant threat, especially in the tenth and eleventh centuries. The nobles spent their lives fighting, and often settled quarrels through violent means. The code of chivalry that characterized the later Middle Ages provided a civilizing influence, but even more crucial were the actions of the ecclesiastical dignitaries in attempting to provide civil order. These edicts, designed to limit feudal warfare, were known as the "Peace of God" and "Truce of God." Gradually, these measures became more and more effective in establishing a peaceful atmosphere. Documents in this chapter are proclamations from the Synod of Charroux in 989 and the Archbishop of Arles, 1035–41.

The medieval castle was one obvious manifestation of military conflict. Originally built as a defensive fortification, it began to fulfill several purposes in the later Middle Ages. Although the structure did not abandon its military origins, it became a composite building that provided a relatively comfortable home for the noblemen and his family, while remaining a place of protection and defense. The discussion in Documents 5.9 and 5.10 includes images of a fortification from the Bayeux Tapestry (late eleventh century), and Bodiam Castle, built in the fourteenth century. These examples offer an excellent opportunity to examine the development of castle architecture.

The feudal system, or vassalage, was supported by an economic base often called manorialism, a pattern that continued to exist well into the fourteenth century in most areas of western Europe, and until the late nineteenth century in Russia. As part of the agreement between the nobles, the vassal received a grant of land from his lord, known as a fief, which contained one or more agricultural settlements known as manors. The function of the system depended upon the labor of men and women who were tied to the land, known as serfs. These people had specific duties to their manor lord and to the church, as will be seen in Documents 5.11 through 5.13, including fees to be paid when a daughter married. It was possible, under certain circumstances, for a serf to obtain his freedom, as illustrated in Document 5.14.

Women had specific duties on the manor, often providing help to their husbands in sowing and harvesting the crops, and assuming the responsibilities of caring for sheep, goats, and cows; their activities are recorded in The Book of the Office of the Seneschal and another anonymous treatise. They also worked as servants for the lord and his family, as shown in Document 5.18. Visual evidence from the Luttrell Psalter depicting women's activities on the manor is offered in Document 5.19.

The eleventh century was a time of great significance for the future development of medieval civilization. As a result of a somewhat more benign political atmosphere, climatic change, and technological innovation, the population of Europe experienced dramatic growth. The climate had been growing warmer since the ninth century, allowing for a higher agricultural yield, and the daily diet of medieval people was enriched by the introduction of legumes, which provided a source of protein. Food sources were expanded by the three-field agricultural system, which made increased crop harvest possible. In addition, as the documents from Walter of Henley's Husbandry included in this chapter will demonstrate, technological innovation such as development of the moulboard plow, the rigid horse collar, and the horseshoe led to better agricultural techniques (Document 5.20). Even more important were the evolution of the watermill and the development of windmills, which enabled more efficient food production. These machines are represented in documents from the Domesday Book, the Chronicle of Jocelin of Brakelond, and illustrations from the Luttrell Psalter.

By the end of the century, the political situation in most areas of western and central Europe was relatively peaceful. The more stable circumstances, coupled with population growth and technological development, had established an atmosphere poised for the emergence of cities, the resurgence of trade, and the growth of economic power, which we will study in the following chapters.

Aristocratic Life: The Experience of the Knight

Rituals of Homage and Fealty

5.1   The Homage Ceremony

As mentioned, the dominant political system of the Middle Ages was based upon bonds of loyalty between men of the noble class. These ties were formalized in a public ceremony in which the vassal would do homage and swear fealty to his lord. Ceremonies such as the one in which Rollo swore fealty to King Charles (see Document 4.21) developed over time into rituals with common features. There were three distinct parts to these ceremonies: first, the declaration "volo" ("I am willing to be your man"), then a kiss and the immixtio manum (the mixing of hands) along with the swearing of fealty, and finally an oath taken with the hand on relics of a saint or on the Holy Scriptures, which formalized the arrangement.

As part of the agreement, the vassal received a fief from his lord. This was a grant of land that enabled the vassal to support himself and his family, and provided enough income for the vassal to afford the horses and armor that were required for the heavy armed combat of the Middle Ages. The grant of Normandy to Rollo by King Charles is an early example of this practice. Often the lord presented his new vassal with a symbol of the fief during the homage ceremony, which might be a stalk of grain or a clod of earth. Once accepted, the vows endured for the lifetimes of the men involved, and the agreements were inherited by their oldest sons, and sometimes daughters. The following documents describe the ceremonies involved in the pledge between lord and vassal.

(From *Readings in European History*, ed. by James Harvey Robinson [Boston: Ginn and Company, 1904], pp. 179–180.)

First they did their homage thus. The count asked the vassal if he were willing to become completely his man, and the other replied, "I am willing" (*volo*); and with hands clasped, placed between the hands of the count, they were bound together by a kiss. Secondly, he who had done homage gave his fealty to the representative of the count in these words, "I promise on my faith that I will in future be faithful to Count William, and will observe my homage to him completely against all persons, in good faith and without deceit." And, thirdly, he took his oath to this upon the relics of the saints. Afterward the count, with a little rod which he held in his hand, gave investitures to all who by this agreement had given their security and accompanying oath.

5.2   *Immixtio Manuum*

(From *A Source Book for Medieval History*, by Oliver J. Thatcher and Edgar H. McNeal [New York: Charles Scribner's Sons, 1905], p. 363.)

The man should put his hands together as a sign of humility, and place them between the two hands of his lord as a token that he vows everything to him and promises faith to him; and the lord should receive him and promise to keep faith with him. Then the man should say: "Sir, I enter your homage and faith and become your man by mouth and hands [i.e., by taking the oath and placing his hands between those of the lord], and I swear and promise to keep faith and loyalty to you against all others, and to guard your rights with all my strength."

Questions for Discussion:

1. Does the homage ceremony remind you of a similar celebration in the contemporary world? Define the comparisons.
2. Compare the meaning of the homage ceremony with the bonds established in the Salic Law (Document 2.8). What common themes do you see?

5.3   Homage to Several Lords

It was possible for a man to pledge himself to more than one lord, which sometimes led to a case of conflicting loyalties if two of the lords fought each other. There were provisions to establish loyalty in this case, as may be seen in the following excerpt.

(From *A Source Book for Medieval History*, by Oliver J. Thatcher and Edgar H. McNeal [New York: Charles Scribner's Sons, 1905], pp. 364–365.)

I, John of Toul, make known that I am the liege man [vassal] of the lady Beatrice, countess of Troyes, and of her son, Theobald, count of Champagne, against every creature, living or dead, saving my allegiance to lord Enjorand of Coucy, lord John of Arcis, and the count of Grandpré. If it should happen that the count of Grandpré should be at war with the countess and count of Champagne on his own quarrel, I will aid the count of Grandpré in my own person, and will send to the count and the countess of Champagne the knights whose service I owe to them for the fief which I hold of them. But if the count of Grandpré shall make war on the countess and the count of Champagne on behalf of his friends and not in his own quarrel, I will aid in my own person the countess and count of Champagne, and will send one knight to the count of Grandpré for the service which I owe him for the fief which I hold of him, but I will not go myself into the territory of the count of Grandpré to make war on him.

Question for Discussion:

1. Document 5.3 defines an act of homage in which the vassal pledges assistance to two different lords. How was this resolved in the case of conflicting loyalties?

Obligations of Vassals

5.4   Feudal Aids

The vassal was committed to joining the armed force of his lord, or, as seen in the previous selection, he could send an armed knight in his place if a conflict of interest arose. This was his primary responsibility. He also pledged to honor the person of his lord and his lord's wife and daughters; that is, he could not harm his lord physically or attempt to seduce the lord's women. In addition, the vassal was obligated to provide "feudal aids," which were occasional expenses. These included accompanying his lord on a crusade, contributing to a ransom if his lord were captured, providing hospitality to his lord and the lord's retinue, and giving money to support the festivities at the knighting of the lord's eldest son and the marriage of his eldest daughter.

(From *A Source Book for Medieval History*, by Oliver Thatcher and Edgar McNeal [New York: Charles Scribner's Sons, 1905], p. 367.)

In the chatelainerie [territory dependent on a castle] of Poitou and that region, according to the custom of the land, those who hold fiefs pay five aids to the lord: for the knighting of the lord's son, for the marriage of the lord's oldest daughter, for the rachat[1] of the lord's fief, for the crusade, and for the ransom of the lord from the hands of the Saracens (Muslims).

---

[1]Rachat was the repurchase or surrender of the fief.

5.5   Inheritance Provisions

By the thirteenth century the customs of inheritance were clearly and firmly established, as may be seen in the famous document Magna Carta, formulated during the reign of King John of England (1189–1223). (Other provisions will be discussed in Chapter 11, Document 11. 5.) The following clauses deal with situations in which the heir is under age or a widow. The document also establishes fair expectations concerning contributions to ransom, knighting, and marriage.

(From *A Source Book for Medieval History*, by Oliver Thatcher and Edgar McNeal [New York: Charles Scribner's Sons, 1905], pp. 367–368.)

If one of our knights or barons or other tenants-in-chief [i.e., direct vassals] who hold by military service shall die and shall leave an heir who is of age, the heir shall receive his father's fiefs by paying only the ancient relief [a form of inheritance tax]; namely, the heir or heirs of an earl shall pay 100 pounds for the whole earldom; the heir or heirs of a knight shall pay 100 solidi for the whole fief of the knight; and those who inherit smaller holdings shall pay smaller reliefs according to the ancient custom.

But if the heir of any of our tenants-in-chief is under age and is under our wardship, he shall have his fiefs when he comes of age without relief or fine.

No widow shall be forced to marry unless she wishes to; but she must give security that she will not marry without our consent, if she holds of us [i.e., if she is the king's vassal], or without the consent of her lord, if she holds of another.

No scutage[2] or aid shall be exacted in our kingdom, unless by the common consent of the realm, except for the ransom of our body, the knighting of our oldest son, and the marriage of our oldest daughter, and these shall be levied at reasonable rates.

---

[2]Scutage was a money payment made to the king in lieu of personal military service.

Questions for Discussion:

1. What was the primary purpose of the system of vassalage? Do you think it was effective?
2. How did the inheritance provisions protect the heirs?
3. What options were available to the widows who inherited the fiefs? Why were clauses such as this included in *Magna Carta*?

The Rituals of Knighting from the *Book of Chivalry* by Geoffroi De Charny

5.6   The Knighting Ceremony

The process of becoming a knight was long and arduous. In order to avoid the "softening" influence of their mothers, aristocratic boys were taken from their families at about the age of seven and sent to be trained at the castle of another knight, often the lord of the father. As squires the boys were trained in military warfare, horsemanship, weaponry, and other matters necessary to the obligation of knighthood. There was a strong emphasis on the principles of chivalry, especially in the later Middle Ages. When the young squire was ready to become a knight, he took part in an elaborate ritual, which is described in the following excerpt from the Book of Chivalry *by Geoffroi de Charny, one of the most famous knights of the fourteenth century. He was a man whose superior military skills and actions exemplified the chivalric ideals of the Middle Ages. Indeed, according to Froissart, he was "the most worthy and valiant of them all." His death on the battlefield of Poitiers in 1356, clutching the sacred banner of the kings of France in his hands, was an appropriately heroic end to his career.*

De Charny was the author of three works on chivalry and its practices. The following selection from Livre de chevalerie *("Book of Chivalry")* describes the rituals involved in the knighting of a young man. Although it was written in the fourteenth century, the ceremonies it discusses began to develop as early as the eleventh century.*

(From *The Book of Chivalry of Geoffroi de Charny*, ed. and trans. by Richard W. Kaeuper and Elspeth Kennedy. Philadelphia: University of Pennsylvania Press, 1996, pp. 167–171. Reprinted with permission of the University of Pennsylvania Press.)

And in order that it should be better understood why and for what good reasons the rite of entry into the order of chivalry was established, it is best to describe how it is performed and thus give a greater knowledge of it. You should know that when a new knight is to be made, first of all he must confess, repent of all his sins, and make sure that he is in a fit state to receive the body of Our Lord [the Host]. On the eve of the ceremony, all those who are to be knighted the next day should enter a bath and stay there for a long time, reflecting on the need to cleanse their bodies henceforth from all impurities of sin and dishonorable ways of life; they should leave all such impurities in the water. Then they should come out of the water in the bath with a clear conscience and should go and lie in a new bed in clean white sheets; there they should rest as those who have emerged from a great struggle against sin and from the great peril of the devils' torment. The bed signifies repose, stemming from virtue, from a clear conscience, from making one's peace with God with regard to all past actions that might have angered Him. Then the knights should come to the beds to dress those to be knighted; the stuff in which they dress them, the linen and all that goes with it should be new: this signifies that just as the body of each one should be cleansed of all the impurities of sin, so should it be clothed in new, white, and clean material, signifying that they should all from henceforth keep themselves pure and free from sin. Then the knights should robe them in red tunics, signifying that they are pledged to shed their blood to defend and maintain the faith of Our Lord and the rights of the Holy Church and all the other just rights set out above which it is the knight's duty to protect. Then the knights bring black hose and put them on those to be knighted; this signifies that they should remember that from the earth they have come and to the earth they must return for the death which awaits them, they know not at what hour; therefore they should put all pride beneath their feet. Then the knights bring them white belts with which they gird them, signifying that they should surround their bodies with chastity and purity of the flesh. After that the knights bring them red cloaks and place them on their shoulders as a sign of great humility, for cloaks in this form were made in ancient times in all humility. Then the knights bring them joyfully into the church, and in the church they must remain and keep vigil all night until dawn, praying very devoutly to Our Lord that it may please Him to forgive the unworthy sleeping and watching of which they have been guilty in the past and that He grant them to keep vigil henceforth in His grace and in His service. The next day, the knights bring them to mass, to hear it devoutly, praying to Our Lord that He may grant them grace to enter and maintain this order in His service and His grace. When mass has been sung, the knights lead them to the person or persons destined to confer the order. For each one to be knighted he gives two gilded spurs, one to each of two knights; these two knights each fasten one to a foot, signifying that gold is the most coveted of all metals and is placed on their feet as a sign that they should remove from their hearts all unworthy covetousness of riches. Then the knight who is to confer the order of knighthood takes a sword; as the sword cuts on both sides of the blade, so should they defend and maintain right, reason, and justice on all sides without being false to the Christian faith or to the rights of the Holy Church for anyone. Then the knights who confer the order on them should kiss them as a sign of confirmation of the order conferred on them and received by them, and that peace, love, and loyalty may be in them; thus should they strive on behalf of and uphold the order with all their hearts wherever they can. Then these knights should give them the *collee* [a light tap, probably here with sword] as a sign that they should for ever more remember this order of knighthood which they have received and carry out all the activities that may

pertain to this order. And thus are these things done and so should they be done. Those are blessed by fortune who conduct themselves in such a manner as the estate requires. If anyone does the contrary, it would have been better for him never to have been made a knight. It can be held that there are three different ways of entering the order of knighthood. Some may choose to enter it when young, so that they can strive longer without fear and without sparing their bodies or possessions in all the services and conditions which pertain, can and should pertain to knighthood. Others want to have the order of knighthood so that people will say that they are knights and so that they will receive greater attention and honor than they did before; but they do not want to fulfill the true conditions and services of knighthood. For that reason it might be said of these men that they may well have the order of knighthood but not the reputation of being a knight, for men may have the order who are not real knights. There are also some ancient men of worth who want to spend their old age and end their days in the order of knighthood; they want to enter at this advanced age and they can indeed do so in keeping with the estate of knighthood, for they should have more sense and judgment than the young, and all the qualities of maturity and of virtuous living ought to be in them. Thus they can give help and comfort in many good and needful ways through their good sense, and the good young knights can do their part with their swords, maintaining and protecting the faith, reason, and justice. Good knights can and should live loyally and honorably.

Questions for Discussion:

1. Describe and discuss the form and purpose of the knighting rituals.
2. The author stipulates that there are three ways or stages when a man might enter knighthood. What are these? How does de Charny justify the differences?
3. Symbolism was an important mode of thought and theory during the Middle Ages. What symbolic aspects are present in the knighting ritual?

Medieval Warfare and the Peace and Truce of God

Private warfare was endemic in the Middle Ages, since feudal nobles insisted on settling their quarrels without recourse to law. This continuous strife meant that the weaker members of society were subjected to violence and oppression. As early as the tenth century, peasants banded together to demand that the constant fighting be controlled. These protests, though unorganized, proclaimed that the continuous violence was an offense against God. Their gatherings, which became known as "Peace of God" rallies, were an attempt to halt or ameliorate the warfare.

The codes of conduct associated with chivalry offered one hope of lessening the continuing strife. Perhaps in response to the actions of the peasant mobs, a more direct effort was made by the Church, which proclaimed periods of time designated as the "Peace of God" in an attempt to control the constant battling. As early as the time of Charlemagne, measures had been taken to safeguard churches and the clergy (review the Capitulary for Saxony, *Document 4.7), but these needed reinforcement. In the tenth century the "Peace of God" was proclaimed by the Church in order to protect the disadvantaged, as well as clergymen who were committed to a life of nonviolence. The "Truce of God" established particular times of the week and year when fighting should not occur. These measures became formalized as universal precepts when they were proclaimed by Pope Urban II at the Council of Clermont in 1095, where the pope also called for a crusade to the Holy Land. His proclamations will be explored more fully in Chapter 7.*

5.7   Peace of God, Proclaimed in the Synod of Charroux (989)

(From *A Source Book for Medieval History*, by Oliver Thatcher and Edgar McNeal [New York: Charles Scribner's Sons, 1905], p. 412.)

Following the example of my predecessors, I, Gunbald, archbishop of Bordeaux, called together the bishops of my diocese in a synod at Charroux, . . . and we, assembled there in the name of God, made the following decrees:

1. Anathema[3] against those who break into churches. If anyone breaks into or robs a church, he shall be anathema unless he makes satisfaction.
2. Anathema against those who rob the poor. If anyone robs a peasant or any other poor person of a sheep, ox, ass, cow, goat, or pig, he shall be anathema unless he makes satisfaction.
3. Anathema against those who injure clergymen. If anyone attacks, seizes, or beats a priest, deacon, or any other clergyman, who is not bearing arms (shield, sword, coat of mail, or helmet), but is going along peacefully or staying in the house, the sacrilegious person shall be excommunicated and cut off from the church, unless he makes satisfaction, or unless the bishop discovers that the clergyman brought it upon himself by his own fault.

Questions for Discussion:

1. Compare this document with the *Capitulary for Saxony* (Document 4.7). What similarities do you find? What differences?
2. Why was "anathema" considered to be a severe penalty?
3. What specific segments of society were protected by the Peace of God?

---

[3]*Anathema* in this document means a formal ecclesiastical curse accompanied by excommunication.

5.8   Truce of God, Proclaimed by the Archbishop of Arles (1035–41)

(From *A Source Book for Medieval History*, by Oliver Thatcher and Edgar McNeal [New York: Charles Scribner's Sons, 1905], pp. 414–416.)

In the name of God, the omnipotent Father, Son, and Holy Spirit. Reginald, archbishop of Arles, with Benedict, bishop of Avignon, Nithard, bishop of Nice, the venerable abbot Odilo [of Cluny], and all the bishops, abbots, and other clergy of Gaul, to all the archbishops, bishops, and clergy of Italy, grace and peace from God, the omnipotent Father, who is, was, and shall be.

1. For the salvation of your souls, we beseech all you who fear God and believe in him and have been redeemed by his blood, to follow the footsteps of God, and to keep peace one with another, that you may obtain eternal peace and quiet with Him.

2. This is the peace or truce of God which we have received from heaven through the inspiration of God, and we beseech you to accept it and observe it even as we have done; namely, that all Christians, friends and enemies, neighbors and strangers, should keep true and lasting peace one with another from vespers on Wednesday to sunrise on Monday, so that during these four days and five nights, all persons may have peace, and, trusting in this peace, may go about their business without fear of their enemies.

3. All who keep the peace and truce of God shall be absolved of their sins by God, the omnipotent Father, and His Son Jesus Christ, and the Holy Spirit, and by St. Mary with the choir of virgins, and St. Michael with the choir of angels, and St. Peter with all the saints and all the faithful, now and forever.

4. Those who have promised to observe the truce and have willfully violated it, shall be excommunicated by God the omnipotent Father, and His Son Jesus Christ, and the Holy Spirit, from the communion of all the saints of God, shall be accursed and despised here and in the future world, shall be damned with Dathan and Abiram and with Judas who betrayed his Lord, and shall be overwhelmed in the depths of hell, as was Pharaoh in the midst of the sea, unless they make such satisfaction as is described in the following:

5. If anyone has killed another on the days of the truce of God, he shall be exiled and driven from the land and shall make a pilgrimage to Jerusalem, spending his exile there. If anyone has violated the truce of God in any other way, he shall suffer the penalty prescribed by the secular laws and shall do double the penance prescribed by the canons (ecclesiastical laws).

6. We believe it is just that we should suffer both secular and spiritual punishment if we break the promise which we have made to keep the peace. For we believe that this peace was given to us from heaven by God; for before God gave it to his people, there was nothing good done among us. The Lord's Day was not kept, but all kinds of labor were performed on it.

7. We have vowed and dedicated these four days to God: Thursday, because it is the day of his ascension; Friday, because it is the day of his passion; Saturday, because it is the day in which he was in the tomb; and Sunday, because it is the day of his resurrection; on that day no labor shall be done and no one shall be in fear of his enemy.

8. By the power given to us by God through the apostles, we bless and absolve all who keep the peace and truce of God; we excommunicate, curse, anathematize, and exclude from the holy mother church all who violate it.

9. If anyone shall punish violators of this decree and of the truce of God, he shall not be held guilty of a crime, but shall go and come freely with the blessing of all Christians, as a defender of the cause of God. But if anything has been stolen on other days, and the owner finds it on one of the days of the truce, he shall not be restrained from recovering it, lest thereby an advantage should be given to the thief.

10. In addition, brothers, we request that you observe the day on which the peace and truce was established by us, keeping it in the name of the holy Trinity. Drive all thieves out of your country, and curse and excommunicate them in the name of all the saints.

11. Offer your tithes and the first fruits of your labors to God, and bring offerings from your goods to the churches for the souls of the living and the dead, that God may free you from all evils in this world, and after this life bring you to the kingdom of heaven, through Him who lives and reigns with God the Father and the Holy Spirit, forever and ever. Amen.

Questions for Discussion:

1. What constitutes the "Truce of God" according to this document?
2. Discuss the various penalties for violating the Truce of God. Do you think they are reasonable?
3. What do you view as the purpose of these decrees? What do you think they accomplished?

INTERPRETING THE EVIDENCE
The Medieval Castle

The medieval castle had many functions. It began as a structure built primarily for defense, but over time its function expanded to become, in addition, a residence for the lord and his family. The earliest castles were built of wood, and consisted of a palisade, or keep, built on top of a hill that was often man-made, rather than natural. When dirt was taken to establish the mound, or "motte," a ditch was created that provided extra protection. This trench was often filled with water, creating the "moat." A drawbridge, which could be taken in when the castle was threatened, allowed access to the fortification.

The central area in front of the motte castle was called the "bailey." (See the accompanying illustration). Eventually the structures were replaced by stone buildings, as may be seen in the accompanying sketch.

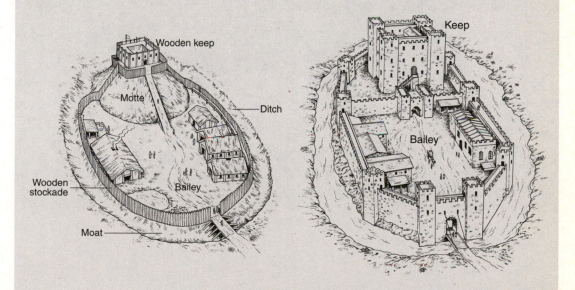

(Derived from Fiero, Gloria K., *The Humanistic Tradition, Volume 1: Prehistory to the Early Modern World*, Fifth Edition, p. 255. Copyright © 2006, 2002, 1998, 1995, 1992 by The McGraw-Hill Companies, Inc. All rights reserved.)

5.9   The Bayeux Tapestry

One of the earliest representations of a castle may be found in the eleventh century embroidery commonly known as the Bayeux Tapestry. The tapestry, which records the Norman view of the invasion of England in 1066, will be more fully discussed in the next chapter. It should be noted that the references to castles in the documents concerning William the Conqueror in that chapter refer to "motte and bailey" structures such as the one pictured in the embroidery. In this image, soldiers (or hired workmen) are scooping dirt to create the motte. The caption (partially cut off) refers to the "Castellum at Hesteng" ("the castle at Hastings"). The accuracy of the "stripes" on the motte has been borne out by recent research, which has found that extant eleventh-century fortifications used wooden supports as represented on the tapestry. As will be seen in Chapter 6, William the Conqueror built many such castles throughout England.

From the Bayeux Tapestry (Picture Desk, Inc./Kobal Collection.)

5.10 Bodiam Castle

By the fourteenth century, castles throughout Europe had become places of luxurious residence for wealthy aristocrats. A beautiful example is Bodiam Castle, in Sussex, England, which was built by Sir Edward Dalyngrigge between 1385 and 1389. Scholars do not agree as to the defensive nature of the fortifications at Bodiam; some historians believe that the primary purpose was to create a comfortable manor house that embodied a symbolic and idealistic vision of a medieval castle. However, Dalyngrigge did obtain permission from the king to place crenellations on the outer walls of his residence. (Calendar Patent Rolls 1385–9, 42, 123). Despite the controversy,

the ruins of Bodiam offer an impressive model of the strength and symmetry of a late medieval castle.

As may be seen in the following photograph and plan, the castle is surrounded by a water-filled moat that reflects the defensive arrangement of circular towers on all four corners. As the plan shows, the interior consisted of the basic components of an aristocratic household: great hall, apartments, a chapel, kitchen with pantry and buttery, and the retainers' hall.

(Published in *Bodiam Castle*, by David Thackry [Great Britain: The National Trust, 1991], p. 59.)

Bodiam Castle, England, 1385–1389. *(Angelo Homak/Alamy Images)*

(continued)

Document

The Licence to Crenellate[4] Bodiam Castle

The King to all men to whom etc. greeting. Know that of our special grace we have granted and given license on behalf of ourselves and our heirs, so far as in us lies, to our beloved and faithful Edward Dalyngrigge Knight, that he may strengthen with a wall of stone and lime, and crenellate and may construct and make into a Castle his manor house of Bodyham, near the sea, in the County of Sussex, for the defence of the adjacent country, and the resistance to our enemies, and may hold his aforesaid house so strengthened and crenellated and made into a Castle for himself and his heirs for ever, without let or hindrance of ourselves or our heirs, or of any of our agents whatsoever. In witness of which etc. The King at Westminster 20 October.

Questions for Discussion:

1. Why did Dalyngrigge need to obtain a license from the king to crenellate his castle?
2. Look carefully at the plan of Bodiam Castle. What are the various defensive features included in the structure? What aspects of the plan accommodate the daily life and religious requirements of the owner and his family?

---

[4]A crenellation is a battlement or rampart built around the top of a tower or castle wall. It has regular gaps for firing guns or arrows. Crenellations may be seen on the towers in the photograph of Bodiam Castle.

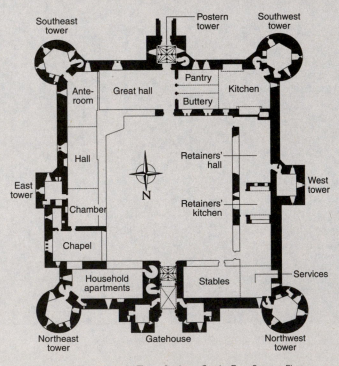

(Derived from The National Trust, *Bodiam Castle: East Sussex*. First published in Great Britain in 1991 by the National Trust. © 1991 The National Trust; reprinted 1995, 1999, 2001, 2004, 2007.)

Those Who Work

INTERPRETING THE EVIDENCE

Life on the Manor

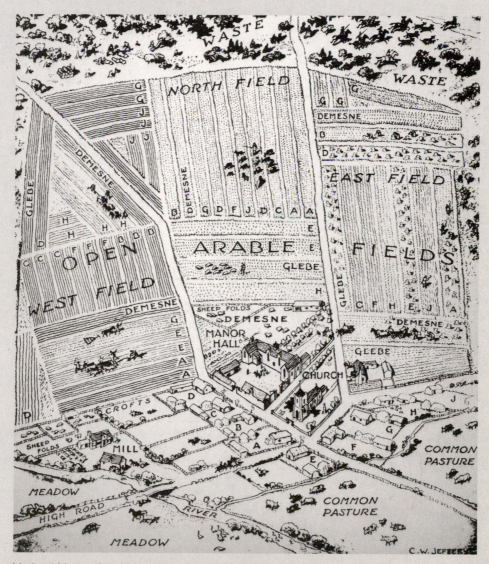

Medieval Manor. (The Granger Collection, New York.)

The fiefs, or grants of land, that the vassal received from his lord included organized agricultural settlements known as manors. These were worked by the serfs[5] according to a customary labor routine. A portion of the manor (known as the demesne*) was cultivated for the benefit of the lord, who also collected taxes and fines from the peasants and required them to repair roads, bridges, and fortifications.*

These duties were known as "boon work," which also included working extra hours at sowing and harvest time.

There were various services available on the manor, including a community mill, oven, and brewery. The serfs were required to use these facilities, and would pay by giving a portion of grain, a loaf of bread, or a keg of beer to the representative of the lord who managed these "banalaties."

There was also a church on the manor, and the serfs cultivated the land dedicated to the church, known as "glebe land." The church was, of course, the center of religious experience, but it also functioned as a social center for the manor.

[5]Serfs were unfree peasants. However, they were not owned by the lord; that is, they were not slaves. They were, nonetheless, "bound" to the land, and could not leave the manor.

5.11   The Village of Cominor from the *Domesday Book*

One of the best sources for understanding life on the manor may be found in the Domesday Book, *a survey of England ordered by William (the Conquerer) in 1086. (His invasion of England will be discussed in Chapter 6). He decreed that there be a survey of the whole of England that would include an account of all of the lands and people, "men both bound and free, both those who lived in cottages and those who had their homes and their share in the fields." In addition, the assessment reported the number of ploughs and animals. The* Domesday Book, *as the survey became known, gives evidence of different categories of people; these include freemen, socmen, villeins, bordars, and half-tenants. The freemen and socmen were usually bound to their lord by the payment of money rents, and were dependent on his jurisdiction. The villein was the typical unfree peasant; he was subject to labor service and some payments (in kind), but he did have his share in the open fields of the manor. The bordars and half-tenants usually possessed a small holding.* Domesday *also records slaves, but the term occurs infrequently. Although the* Domesday Book *refers specifically to England, it portrays serfdom in circumstances typical of all of western Europe and Russia. This part of the survey provides details concerning Cumnor, a village in Berkshire, four miles west of Oxford.*

(From the Printed Edition of *Domesday Book*, 1783, vol. i. p. 59, col. I.)

The Abbey of Abbendone holds Cominor. It has belonged to the Abbey T.RE., [during the reign of Edward "the Confessor" (c. 1003–1066)] and always it was assessed at fifty hides;[6] now at thirty hides. There is land for fifty ploughs.[7] On the demesne are nine ploughs; and there are sixty villeins and sixty-nine bordars with twenty-six ploughs. There are four serfs and two mills worth fifty shillings; and from the fisheries is yielded forty shillings; and there are two hundred acres of meadow. There is a church. T.RE. it was worth thirty pounds; and afterwards, as now, fifty pounds.

Questions for Discusssion:

1. Does it appear that the land has gained or lost value since the time of Edward the Confessor?

2. What sources of income other than land appear in the survey?

[6]A hide was a measure of land for tax assessment, approximately 120 acres in size.

[7]In the *Domesday Book* the word implies a plough team with its eight oxen and the plough itself.

5.12 A Manor Belonging to Peterborough Abbey (c. 1125)

The following excerpt from an early-twelfth-century survey describes a manor belonging to Peterborough Abbey, c. 1125. The document refers to specific categories of peasants as discussed in the introduction to this section, including full villeins, half-villeins, socmen, and half-tenants.

(From *Readings in European History*, vol. i, by James Harvey Robinson [Boston: Ginn & Co., 1904], p. 399.)

In Wermington are 7 hides at the taxation of the king. And of this land 20 full villeins and 29 half-villeins hold 34 virgates[8] and a half; and for these the full villeins work 3 days a week through the year; and the half-tenants as much as corresponds to their tenancies. And these men have in all 16 plows, and they plow 68 acres and a half and besides this they do 3 boon-works with their plows, and they ought to bring from the woods 34 wagonloads of wood. And all these men pay—£4 11S. 4d.; and at the love feast of St. Peter, 10 rams and 400 loaves and 40 platters and 34 hens and 260 eggs. And there are 8 socmen who have 6 plows. In the demesne of the court are 4 plows and 32 oxen and 9 cows and 5 calves and 1 riding horse and 129 sheep and 61 swine and 1 draught horse and 1 colt. And there is 1 mill with 1 virgate of land, and 6 acres which pays 60S. and 500 eels. And Ascelin, the clerk (clergyman), holds the church with 2 virgates of land, from the altar of St. Peter of Borough. Robert, son of Richard, has 2 virgates and a half. In this vill[9] 100 sheep can be placed.

---

[8]A virgate was a quarter of a hide.

[9]A vill was a village.

5.13 A Manor in Sussex (1307)

This fourteenth-century survey of a manor in the English county of Sussex describes the responsibilities of the inhabitants, including monetary rents, requirements for various sorts of labor, and fees such as heriot. *The document also stipulates the obligation of the lord to provide a certain amount of food and assesses its valuation in relation to the work accomplished.*

(From *Readings in European History* , vol. i, by James Harvey Robinson [Boston: Ginn & Co., 1904], pp. 400–404.)

Extent of the manor of Bernehorne, made on Wednesday following the feast of St. Gregory the pope, in the thirty-fifth year of the reign of King Edward. . . . [Edward III, r. 1327–1377)

Ralph of Leybourne holds a cottage and 1 acre of land in Pinden and owes 3S. at Easter and Michaelmas,[10] and attendance at the court in the manor every three weeks, also relief and heriot[11]. . . .

Alexander Hamound holds a little piece of land near Aldewisse and owes 1 goose of the value of 2d.

The sum of the whole rent of the free tenants, with the value of the goose, is 18S. 9d.

They say, moreover, that John of Cayworth holds a house and 30 acres of land, and owes yearly 2S. at Easter and Michaelmas; and he owes a cock and two hens at Christmas of the value of 4d.

And he ought to harrow [see Document 5.20 for an illustration of harrowing] for 2 days at the Lenten sowing with one man and his own horse and his own harrow, the value of the work being 4d.; and he is to receive from the lord on each day,

---

[10]Michaelmas is the Feast of St. Michael, held on September 29.

[11]*Heriot* was the right of the lord to take the serf's best horse or piece of clothing when he died.

(continued)

3 meals, of the value of 5d., and then lord will be at a loss of 1d. Thus his harrowing is of no value to the service of the lord.

And he ought to carry the manure of the lord for 2 days with one cart, with his own 2 oxen, the value of the work being 8d.; and he is to receive from the lord each day 3 meals at the value as above. And thus the service is worth 3d. clear.

And he ought to carry the hay of the lord for 1 day with a cart and 3 animals of his own, the price of the work being 6d. And he shall have from the lord 3 meals of the value 22 d. And thus the work is worth 3 2 d. clear.

And he ought to carry in autumn beans or oats for 2 days with a cart and 3 animals of his own, the value of the work being 12d. And he shall receive from the lord each day 3 meals of the value given above. And thus the work is worth 7d. clear.

And he ought to carry wood from the woods of the lord as far as the manor, for two days in summer, with a cart and 3 animals of his own, the value of the work being 9d. And he shall receive from the lord each day 3 meals of the price given above. And thus the work is worth 4d. clear.

And he ought to find 1 man for 2 days to cut heath,[12] the value of the work being 4d., and he shall have 3 meals each day of the value given above: and thus the lord will lose, if he receives the service, 3d. Thus that mowing is worth nothing to the service of the lord.

And he ought to carry to Battle, twice in the summer season, each time half a load of grain, the value of the service being 4d. And he shall receive in the manor each time 1 meal of the value of 2d. And thus the work is worth 2d. clear.

The totals of the rents, with the value of the hens, is 2S. 4d.

The total of the value of the works is 2S. 32d., owed from the said John yearly. . . .

John Lyllingwyst holds a house and 4 acres of land and owes at the two terms 2S., attendance at the manor court, relief, and *heriot*.

The same John holds 1 acre of land in the fields of Hoo and owes at the two periods 2S., attendance, relief, and *heriot*. . . .

And it is to be noted that none of the above-name villeins can give their daughters in marriage nor cause their sons to be tonsured,[13] nor can they cut down timber growing on the lands they hold, without license of the bailiff or sergeant of the lord, and then for building purposes and not otherwise. And after the death of anyone of the aforesaid villeins, the lord, shall have as a *heriot* his best animal, if he had any; if, however, he have no living beast, the lord shall have no *heriot*, as they say. The sons or daughters of the aforesaid villeins shall give, for entrance into the holding after the death of their predecessors, as much as they give of rent per year.

Note: Fines and penalties, with *heriots* and reliefs, are worth yearly 5S.

Questions for Discussion:

1. Study the description of manorial holdings and serfdom. What were the common duties of the villeins? What was their obligation for "boon work"?
2. Why would the lord expect a fee for the marriage of a peasant's daughter or the adopting of the monastic vocation by his son?
3. What was the *heriot* taken by the lord when a serf died? What accommodation was made if the heirs could not fulfill this requirement?

---

[12] Heath is a low-growing evergreen plant.

[13] When a man became a monk the hair of the crown of his head was shaved; this was called a tonsure. A fee was due to the lord if a peasant's son joined a monastic order.

5.14   Freedom for the Serf (1278)

There were several categories that differentiated the peasantry, as we have observed in the previous documents. It was, however, possible for a serf to gain his freedom, as illustrated by the provisions in the following excerpt, which dates from 1278.

(From *Readings in European History,* vol. 1, by James Harvey Robinson [Boston: Ginn & Co., 1904], pp. 405–406.)

To all the faithful of Christ to whom the present writing shall come, Richard, by the divine permission abbot of Peterborough and of the Convent of the same place, eternal greeting in the Lord:

Let all know that we have manumitted (freed) and liberated from all yoke of servitude William, the son of Richard of Wythington, whom previously we have held as our born bondman, with all his progeny (children) and all his chattels, so that neither we nor our successors shall be able to require or exact any right or claim in the said William, his progeny, or his chattels. But the same William, with his whole progeny and all his chattels, shall remain free and quit and without disturbance, exaction, or any claim on the part of us or our successors by reason of any servitude forever.

We will, moreover, and concede that he and his heirs shall hold the messuages (dwellings), land, rents, and meadows in Wythington which his ancestors held from us and our predecessors, by giving and performing the fine which is called *merchet*[14] for giving his daughter in marriage, and tallage[15] from year to year according to our will,—that he shall have and hold these for the future from us and our successors freely, quietly, peacefully, and hereditarily, by paying to us and our successors yearly 40S. sterling, at the four terms of the year, namely: at St. John the Baptist's day 10S., at Michaelmas 10S., at Christmas 10S., and at Easter 10S., for all service, exaction, custom, and secular demand; saving to us, nevertheless, attendance at our court of Castre every three weeks, wardship, and relief, and outside service of our lord the king, when they shall happen.

And if it shall happen that the said William or his heirs shall die at any time without an heir, the said messuage, land, rents, and meadows with their appurtenances shall return fully and completely to us and our successors. Nor will it be allowed to the said William or his heirs to give, sell, alienate, mortgage, or encumber in any way, the said messuage, land, rents, meadows, or any part of them, by which the said messuage, land, rents, and meadows should not return to us and our successors in the form declared above. And if this should occur later, their deed shall be declared null, and what is thus alienated shall come to us and our successors. . . .

Given at Borough, for the love of Lord Robert of good memory, once abbot, our predecessor and maternal uncle of the said William, and at the instance of the good man, Brother Hugh of Mutton, relative of the said abbot Robert, A.D. 1278, on the eve of Pentecost.

Questions for Discussion:

1. The document shows that William still retained various responsibilities to the lord. What were these?
2. Do you see this agreement as an improvement on serfdom? Why or why not?

---

[14]Merchet was a fee paid to the lord when a peasant's daughter was married.
[15]A land tax.

5.15 The Lord's Manor House (Mid-Thirteenth Century)

The peasants lived in modest dwellings, which they usu-
ally shared with their livestock.

By contrast, the manor house residence of the lord
was relatively spacious and comfortable, as may be seen in
the following description from the mid-thirteenth century.

(From *Readings in European History,* vol. 1, by James Harvey
Robinson [Boston: Ginn & Co., 1904]. Translation modernized.)

He [the vassal] received also a sufficient and handsome hall with a fine oak roof. On the western side
is a good bed, on the ground a stone chimney, a
wardrobe, and another small chamber; at the eastern end are a pantry and a buttery. Between the hall
and the chapel is a side room. There is a decent
chapel covered with tiles, a portable altar, and a
small cross. In the hall are four tables on trestles.
There is also a good kitchen well covered with
tiles, with a furnace and ovens, one large and the
other small, for cakes. There are two tables. Alongside the kitchen is a small house for baking. There
is also a new granary covered with oak shingles,
and a building for the dairy, although it is divided.
There is a chamber suited for clergymen and a necessary chamber. There is also a henhouse. These are
within the inner gate.

Outside of the gate is an old house for servants, and a good stable, long and divided. To the
east of the principal building, beyond the smaller
stable, is a solar[16] for the use of the servants. There
is also a building which holds a bed, and also two
barns, one for wheat and one for oats. These buildings are enclosed with a moat, a wall, and a hedge.
Beyond the middle gate is a good barn, and a stable for cows and another for oxen, but these are old
and ruined. Also beyond the outer gate is a pigsty.

Question for Discussion:

1. This document provides details concerning a
   fourteenth-century manor house. How does
   the description compare with the photograph and groundplan of Bodiam Castle
   (Document 5.10)? What similarities do you
   see? What differences?

---

[16]A solar was a room in a castle or manor house that offered privacy, usually for the ladies of the family. This solar evidently
provided an area to be used by the servants.

Women's Work

The women on a medieval manor had many tasks. They
helped their husbands with the work of weeding the fields
and harvesting, they baked bread and cooked food for
their families, and they wove cloth and made rough gar-
ments. The care of animals belonging to the family or the
serf community was frequently a duty of women, as
records from all over Europe demonstrate. They often
worked as shepherdesses or dairymaids. The following

excerpt, taken from The Book of the Office of
Seneschal, *an anonymous thirteenth-century record of*
inspections, describes the duties associated with a position
as dairymaid.

(From *The Book of the Office of Seneschal,* anonymous, in *Walter of
Henley's Husbandry,* trans. By Elizabeth Lamond, 1890,
pp. 117–119.)

5.16   The Office of Dairymaid from the *Book of the Office of Seneschal*

The dairymaid ought to be faithful and of good repute, and keep herself clean, and ought to know her business and all that belongs to it. She ought not to allow any underdairymaid or another to take or carry away milk, or butter, or cream, by which the cheese shall be less and the dairy impoverished. And she ought to know well how to make cheese and salt cheese, and she ought to save and keep the vessels of the dairy, that it need not be necessary to buy new ones every year. And she ought to know the day when she begins to make cheese and of what weight, and when she begins to make two cheeses a day, of how much and of what weight, and then the bailiff and the provost ought to inspect the dairy often and the cheeses, when they increase and decrease in weight, and that no harm be done in the dairy, nor any robbery by which the weight shall be lessened.

And they ought to know and prove and see when the cows make a stone [about 14 pounds] of cheese and butter, and when the ewes [female sheep] make a stone of the same, that they may be able the more surely to answer in the account. No cow shall be milked or suckled after Michaelmas [September 29th], and no ewe after the feast of our Lady, for the reason aforesaid.

The dairymaid ought to help to winnow the corn when she can be present, and she ought to take care of the geese and hens and answer for the returns and keep and cover the fire, that no harm arise from lack of guard.

Another anonymous treatise from approximately the thirteenth century gave additional advice about the proper responsibilities of a dairymaid.

5.17   The Yield from the Dairy

[and How the Dairymaid ought to answer for the small livestock of the court and for their issue]

You must have, in each place where there is a dairy, a man or woman to keep the small live stock there, as said before. If it is a man, he must do everything as a woman would, and he ought to take every sixteen weeks a quarter [of corn], because of the advantage he has from the milk, where other servants take it every twelve weeks. And she must winnow all the corn, and shall be paid for a half-day to pay the woman who helps her. And she ought to winnow four quarters of wheat or of rye and six quarters of barley and peas and beans . . . for a penny, and eight quarters of oats for a penny. . . . And the dairywoman must take care of all the small animals in the court, as sucking-pigs and peacocks and their issue, and geese and their issue, and capons and cocks and hens and chickens and eggs and their issue. . . . And if this is a manor where there is no dairy, it is always good to have a woman there, at a much less cost

than a man, to keep the small animals there and what there is within the court, and answer for all produce there as a dairywoman would—that is to say, when sows farrow (give birth) for their pigs, for peacocks and their chicks, if there are any, for geese and their goslings, for capons, cocks, hens, and their chickens and eggs—and she ought to answer for the half of the winnowing[17] of the corn also as the dairywoman.

Questions for Discussion:

1. These selections give information about various duties required of the dairywoman. What are some of these?
2. Why would a woman be paid "at much less cost than a man"? Discuss.

_____

[17] Winnowing is separating grain from chaff.

5.18   The Serving Maid

Women also worked as maidservants on the manor. The following description of some of their duties is by an English scholar, Alexander Neckham (1157–1227), who wrote about daily life in the twelfth century.

(From *Women's Lives in Medieval Europe: A Sourcebook*, edited by Emilie Amt [New York: Routledge, 1993], p. 181.)

There should be a serving maid who will place eggs under the sitting hens and will give maslin [mixed rye and wheat] to the geese, and who will feed the ailing lambs with milk from a ewe other than the mother, in her gentleness. She will keep the calves to be weaned, whose teeth are few, in an enclosure near the barn. On holidays her clothing should be a cast-off pellicle [cloak] and a wimple [head covering]. It is her practice to give the swineherd, plowmen, and other herdsmen whey [the watery part of milk that separates when it is made into cheese], but to the master and his friends, clabber [curdled milk] in cups, and to offer in the evening bran bread to the dogs in the pen.

INTERPRETING THE EVIDENCE: WOMEN'S WORK

5.19   Visual Evidence from the *Luttrell Psalter*

Much of our information about women's work in the Middle Ages comes from manuscript illuminations: Look at the following images from the Luttrell Psalter, a fourteenth-century manuscript now in the British Library (Additional MS 42130) to be discussed later, and compare them with the documentary sources we have studied. In addition to this chapter, review the document pertaining to Charlemagne's estate, Document 4.9.

Woman Spinning
(British Library, London, GB/HIP/Art Resource, New York.)

At harvest time all available workers on a manor were pressed into service, including the women. In this image from the Luttrell Psalter, *a team of three women are cutting the ripe grain with sickles. A man follows behind them, binding the cut stems with cords of twisted straw. The grain, probably barley in this illumination, will be used to* feed the livestock and for making ale. The facial expressions of the women indicate that the work is quite taxing.

The vignette below from the Luttrell Psalter *portrays a woman feeding her hens and chicks. The woman's bare feet and the distaff*[18] *under her arm indicate that this is a domestic scene—she has briefly stepped outside into the yard to accomplish her task. As she scatters grain for the chicks, one is perched on a water dish, taking a drink. Notice that the hen is tied by one foot to prevent her from wandering away. Poultry was a valuable asset, providing not only eggs and meat, but also feathers to be used in bedding, and occasionally for making writing utensils.*

The following highly detailed illumination contains a great deal of information about the care of sheep. The sheepfold encloses twenty animals. The two with

Women Harvesting Grain *(British Library, London/The Bridgeman Art Library Ltd.)*

---

[18]A distaff is a staff or rod on which wool or flax is wound before spinning.

Woman Feeding Hens and Chicks
(© British Library Board. [Add.42130, f. 166v])

Sheep Tending
(© British Library Board. [Add.42130, f.163v])

horns undoubtedly represent rams; one of these has a bell between his horns, which will help the shepherdess to locate the flock as it is grazing in the countryside. One of the ewes is being milked, implying that the jugs carried by the two women walking away from the sheepfold contain sheep's milk. The small purse dangling from the belt of one of the women is a reminder of the value of sheep in the medieval world. They provided milk, meat, and cheese as well as wool for spinning and weaving, skin for vellum manuscripts, horn for small utensils, and tallow for candles. In addition, they had the advantage of being sustained on very poor grazing land.

INTERPRETING THE EVIDENCE

Rural Life and Technological Development

Our sources for knowledge of daily peasant life in the medieval era are limited, and historians must seek information in legal documents, court records, chronicles of monasteries, and account roles such as those included in Documents 5.11 through 5.13. Additional details about rural life are also provided by pictorial information such as sculpture and manuscript illumination. One of the finest of these visual sources is the Luttrell Psalter, *a magnificent fourteenth-century manuscript now in the British Library. As its title indicates, it contains texts of the psalms and canticles, a calendar of church festivals and saints' days, and the Office of the Dead. The margins of the folios are embellished with representations of daily rural activities. The imagery in this manuscript offers a view into peasant life and medieval technology that may be compared effectively with the documentary sources already presented in this chapter, and with the treatise by Walter of Henley known as* Husbandry.

5.20 Walter of Henley's *Husbandry* and the *Luttrell Psalter*

Walter of Henley was a thirteenth-century English agricultural writer whose treatise, Husbandry, *describes many aspects of rural economy, including the sowing of land, the management of animals for plowing, and other matters pertaining to successful agricultural production. Although his treatise dates from the middle of the thirteenth century, the techniques he advocated were developing as early as the tenth or eleventh centuries. The following excerpts advise how oxen should be fed, how the land should be plowed and sown, and provide instruction concerning the control of flooding and excess moisture. The accompanying visual material includes images of a heavy moulboard plow and a harrow, pulled by a horse with a rigid collar—another eleventh-century innovation.*

(From *Walter of Henley's Husbandry*, trans. by Elizabeth Lamond [London: Longman's, Green & Co., 1890], pp. 11–17.)

Document

Of Overseeing Your Laborers.

At the beginning of fallowing and second fallowing and of sowing let the bailiff, and the master, or the provost, be all the time with the ploughmen, to see that they do their work well and thoroughly, and at the end of the day see how much they have done, and for so much shall they answer each day after unless they can show a sure hindrance. And because customary servants neglect their work it is necessary to guard against their fraud; further, it is necessary that they are overseen often; and besides the bailiff must oversee all, that they all work well, and if they do not well let them be reproved.

With a team of oxen with two horses you draw quicker than with a team all horses, if the ground is not so stony that oxen cannot help themselves with their feet. Why? I will tell you: the

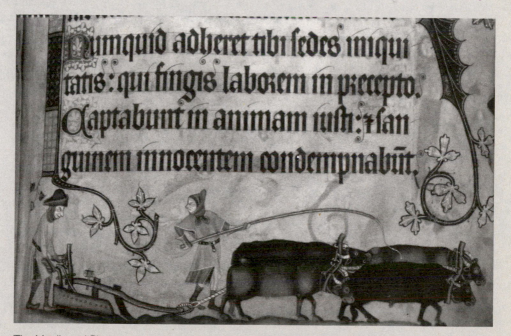

The Moulboard Plow
(The Art Archive/Picture Desk, Inc./Kobal Collection.)

(continued)

horse costs more than the ox. Besides a plough of oxen will go as far in the year as a plough of horses, because the malice of ploughmen will not allow the plough [of horses] to go beyond their pace, no more than the plough of oxen. Further, in very hard ground, where the plough of horses will stop, the plough of oxen will pass. And will you see how the horse costs more than the ox? I will tell you. It is usual and right that plough beasts should be in the stall between the feast of St. Luke [October 18th] and the feast of the Holy Cross in May, five-and-twenty weeks, and if the horse is to be in a condition to do his daily work, it is necessary that he should have every night at the least the sixth part of a bushel of oats, price one halfpenny, and at the least twelve pennyworth of grass in summer. And each week more or less a penny in shoeing, if he must be shod on all four feet. The sum is twelve shillings and fivepence in the year, without fodder and chaff.

The image above from the Luttrell Psalter *shows a team of oxen pulling a heavy moulboard plow, which produced a deep furrow and turned the earth over. The moulboard was the device that guided the plow and turned the soil. Its use was the first step in preparing the field to be sown. These plows were used primarily in heavy clay areas, and proved to be of great value in the northwestern part of Europe and England, where the soil was much more dense than that of the Mediterranean area.*

In this illumination the plough is shown in detail, including a mallet on the shaft that was presumably used to knock dirt clogs from the mechanism. The ploughman is obviously exerting force to maintain the direction of the plow and the depth of the furrow, while his assistant controls the team of oxen.

Document

How you Must Keep Your Oxen.

And if the ox is to be in a condition to do his work, then it is necessary that he should have at least three sheaves and a half of oats in the week, price one penny, and ten sheaves of oats should yield a bushel of oats in measure; and in summer twelve pennyworth of grass:

the sum three shillings, one penny, without fodder and chaff. And when the horse is old and worn out then there is nothing but the skin; and when the ox is old with ten pennyworth of grass he shall be fit for the larder, or will sell for as much as he cost. April is a good time for fallowing, if the earth breaks up after the plough; and for second fallowing after St. John's Day, when the dust rises behind the plough; and for ploughing for seed when the earth is firm and not too cracked. But he who has much to do cannot wait for all the good seasons. And when you fallow, if you find good earth deep down, then plough a square ridge, to let the good land rest, but do not cut off the bad land; and plough cleanly, so that none remains covered or uncovered. At second fallowing do not go too deep, but so that you can just destroy the thistles, for if the earth is ploughed too deep at second fallowing, and the earth is full of water, then when one must plough for sowing the plough shall reach no sure ground, but goes floundering, as in mud. And if the plough can go two finger-lengths deeper than at second fallowing, then the plough will find sure ground, and clear and free it from mud, and make fine and good ploughing.

Question for Discussion:

1. What reasons does Walter of Henley give for using oxen rather than horses for agricultural purposes?

Document

To Keep the Ridge.

At sowing do not plough large furrows, but little and well laid together, that the seed may fall evenly; if you plough a large furrow to be quick you will do harm. How? I will tell you. When the ground is sown, then the harrow will come and pull the corn into the hollow which is between the two ridges, and the large ridge shall be uncovered, that no corn can grow there. And will you see this? When the corn is above ground go to the end of the ridge, and you will see that I tell you truly. And if the land must be sown below the ridge see that it is ploughed with small furrows, and the earth raised as much as you are able. And see that the ridge which is between the two furrows is narrow.

And let the earth which lies like a crest in the furrow under the left foot after the plough be overturned, and then shall the furrow be narrow enough.

In the image below, the peasant is sowing the land from a specially designed wicker basket that is supported by a cord worn around his neck. He is dealing with interference from the crows, who are eating the freshly sown seeds and even invading the seed sack. His dog is attempting to aid in frightening away the birds.

Document

To Sow Your Lands.

Sow your lands in time, so that the ground may be settled and the corn rooted before great cold. If by chance it happens that a heavy rain comes or falls on the earth within eight days of the sowing, and then a sharp frost should come and last two or three days, if the earth is full of holes the frost will penetrate through the earth as deep as the water entered, and so the corn, which has sprouted and is very tender, will perish. There are two kinds of land for spring seed which you must sow early, clay land and stony land. Why? I will tell you. If the weather in March should be dry, then the ground will harden too much and the stony ground become more dry and open, so it is necessary that such ground be sown early, that the corn may be nourished by the winter moisture.

In the image above the horse pulls a harrow, which was a wooden frame with wooden or metal teeth. It was drawn over the sown seed to cover it with earth in order to prevent the birds from picking the field clean. The animal is wearing a rigid horsecollar, another innovation of the eleventh century. The improved harness did not restrict the animal's wind supply as did earlier versions; obviously, this facilitated more efficient animal power. A peasant goads the horse as another man slings pebbles at the menacing crows.

Document

To Free Lands from Too Much Water.

Chalky ground and sandy ground need not be sown so early; for these are two evils escaped to be overturned in great moisture, but at sowing let the

Sowing
(British Library, London/The Bridgeman Art Library Ltd.)

(continued)

Harrowing
(HIP/Art Resource, New York.)

ground be a little sprinkled. And when your lands are sown let the marshy ground and damp ground be well ridged, and the water made to run, so that the ground may be freed from water. Let your land be cleaned and weeded after St. John's Day; before that is not a good time. If you cut thistles fifteen days or eight before St. John's Day, for each one will come two or three. Let your corn be carefully cut and led into the grange.

Question for Discussion:

1. How have the agricultural techniques described by Walter of Henley changed in the past thousand years? Are there any precepts that have remained the same?

5.21 Watermills in the *Domesday Book* and the *Luttrell Psalter*

The population growth and expansion of the economy that occurred in western Europe after the year 1000 would not have been possible without significant technological development. Although the watermill was invented in the ancient world, it was improved during the Middle Ages. Perhaps the most important innovation was the windmill, developed in the twelfth century. The mills were used for grinding and crushing grain, grinding corn, fulling cloth, tanning leather, and a variety of other purposes. In this image from the Luttrell Psalter, *it is possible to see that the medieval watermill was a small timber-framed building with a thatched roof that housed the wheel and the grinding*

stones. The door is closed with a heavy lock, no doubt to prevent thievery. Notice that the water of the river contains woven fish traps with their wide mouths facing the current of the water; a fish and an eel have been caught inside.

(From *English Historical Documents: 1042–1189*, ed. by David C. Douglas and George W. Greenaway. Copyright © 1961 Eyre & Spottiswoode. Reprinted with permission of Cambridge University Press.)

The Domesday Book (see the discussion in Document 5.11) recorded over 6,000 watermills that were used for the heavy work of grinding the wheat, barley, oats, and other

Watermill
(British Library, London, GB/HIP/Art Resource, New York.)

grain crops. In the following example taken from the survey, it is possible to see that the use of this technology was widespread in eleventh-century England.

Document

From the *Domesday Book*

Hurstingstone hundred   A manor. In Hartford King Edward had 15 hides assessed to the geld. There is land for 17 ploughs. Rannulf the brother of Ilger keeps it now. There are 4 ploughs now on the demesne; and 30 villeins and 3 bordars have 8 ploughs. There is a priest; 2 churches; 2 mills rendering 4 pounds; and 40 acres of meadow. Woodland for pannage,[19] 1 league

---

[19]Pannage was the practice of allowing pigs to forage for food in wooded areas.

in length and half a league in breadth. *T.R.E.* it was worth 24 pounds; now 15 pounds.

Leightonstone hundred   A manor. In Keyston King Edward had 4 hides of land assessed to the geld. There is land for 12 ploughs. There are 2 ploughs now on the demesne; and 24 villeins and 8 bordars have 10 ploughs; 86 acres of meadow. Scattered woodland for pannage 5 furlongs in length and 1 1/2 furlongs in breadth. *T.R.E.* it was worth 10 pounds; now the same. Rannulf, the brother of Ilger, keeps it.

A manor. In Brampton King Edward had 15 hides assessed to the geld. There is land for 15 ploughs. There are 3 ploughs now on the demesne; and 36 villeins and 2 bordars have 14 ploughs. There is a church and a priest; 100 acres of meadow. Woodland for pannage half a league in length and

(continued)

2 furlongs in breadth. Two mills rendering 100 shillings. *T.R.E.* it was worth 20 pounds; now the same. Rannulf, the brother of Ilger, keeps it.

A manor. In Godmanchester King Edward had 14 hides assessed to the geld. There is land for 57 ploughs. There are 2 ploughs now on the king's demesne on 2 hides of this land; and 80 villeins and 16 bordars have 24 ploughs. There is a priest and a church; 3 mills rendering 100 shillings; 160 acres of meadow; and 50 acres of woodland for pannage. From the pasture come 20 shillings. From the meadows come 70 shillings. *T.R.E.* it was worth 40 pounds; now it is worth the same 'by tale'.

Question for Discussion:

1. Compare this selection with the earlier excerpt from the *Domesday Book* (Document 5.11). Do the holdings described here seem to have held their value since the time of King Edward? What reasons can you give for your analysis?

5.22 Windmills in the *Chronicle* of Jocelin of Brakelond and the *Luttrell Psalter*

The use of windmills was introduced in England toward the end of the twelfth century and became common throughout Europe in the thirteenth century. These machines were adapted from the mechanism of the watermill, but the waterwheels were replaced by wind-driven sails, and the mechanism was elevated on a post. As may be seen in the image, a wooden body containing the equipment of the mill was elevated on an upright post strengthened by side supports. The cloth sails were fitted in much the same way as the sails of a boat. These could be turned to catch the wind by a long beam, which comically provides a seat for the dog in this image. The use of windmills was a practical innovation, particularly in areas that experienced freezing conditions during the winter. Notice in the image that a woman is carrying a heavy burden of grain to the mill.

Windmill
(AKG-Images / The British Library.)

The economic value of mills may be seen in the Chronicle of Jocelin of Brakelonde (born c. 1155), which covers the period between 1173 and 1190. His work offers a view of life in a large medieval monastery, and deals with economic as well as religious matters. It is possible to see in Jocelyn's remarks that the mills provided significant monetary benefit to their owners, in this case, to the monastery. As may be seen in the document, Abbot Samson was determined to protect his interests and those of his abbey when a mill was built nearby.

(From *The Chronicle of Jocelin of Brakelond*, ed. By Ernest Clarke [London: John Murray, 1907], pp. 75–76. Translation modernized.)

Document

Herbert the dean erected a windmill upon Haberdon. When the abbot heard of this, his anger was so kindled that he would scarcely eat or utter a single word. On the next morning, after hearing mass, he commanded the sacrist,[20] that without delay he should send his carpenters there to overturn it completely, and carefully put the wooden materials in safe keeping.

The dean, hearing this, came to him, saying that it was legal for him to do this upon his own land, and that the benefit of the wind ought not to be denied to anyone. He further said that he only wanted to grind his own corn there, and no one else's, lest it should be imagined that he did this to the damage of the neighboring mills. The abbot, his anger not yet appeased, answered, "I give you as many thanks as if you had cut off both my feet. By the mouth of God I will not eat bread until that building be torn down. You are an old man, and you should have known that it is not lawful even for the King or his justiciar[21] to alter or appoint a single thing within the banlieue [outskirts], without the permission of the abbot and convent; and why have you presumed to do such a thing? Nor is this without prejudice to my mills, as you assert, because the burgesses [townsmen] will run to you and grind their corn at their pleasure, nor can I by law turn them away, because they are freemen. Nor would I endure that the mill of our cellarer,[22] lately set up, should stand, except that it was erected before I was abbot. "Begone," he said, "begone: before you have come to your house, you shall hear what has befallen your mill."

But the dean being afraid before the face of the abbot, by the counsel of his son, Master Stephen, forestalled the servants of the sacrist, and without delay caused that very mill which had been erected by his own servants to be destroyed. So that when the servants of the sacrist came there, they found nothing to be pulled down.

Question for Discussion:

1. Why was the abbot so angry about the dean's mill? What does his fury indicate about the value of this technological innovation?

---

[20]The sacrist was responsible for the care of the church and its furnishings.

[21]The justiciar was the head of the royal judicial system, and was the highest official of the court in the king's absence.
[22]The cellarer was the monastic official in charge of procuring food for the monastery.

Chapter 6

The Centralization of Political Control from the Tenth to the Twelfth Century

The era following the dissolution of the Carolingian Empire was one of political fragmentation. The eastern part of the realm, which eventually became Germany, stretched from the Rhine River in the west to the Elbe, the Saale, and the Danube rivers in the east. The western part, which comprised roughly the area of present-day France, reached from the Rhine River to the Atlantic Ocean and extended to the Mediterranean Sea in the south. A division had occurred in Lothair's "Middle Kingdom" (see Document 4.16), creating Burgundy, Provence, and Lotharingia, which became part of the German realm in 925. By the mid-eleventh century the northern part of the Italian peninsula contained the kingdom of Italy, the Papal States, and several independent Lombard principalities, while the south had been conquered by Normans. (See the accompanying map.)

As we have seen, a political system based upon bonds of loyalty had developed in the lands of the old Carolingian Empire (see Chapter 4). Powerful families in several of these areas established royal dynasties, although the king's power was severely limited in the eleventh and twelfth centuries by the practice of vassalage. In France, the election of Hugh Capet in 987 enabled the Capetians to establish the foundation for a dynasty that lasted for nearly five hundred years, but this was unusual.

England, which had been unified by the successors of Alfred the Great, was invaded in 1066 by the Normans, who were descendents of Duke Rollo (see Document 4.21).

They were led by William the Conqueror, who, by using various measures of intimidation, was able to assert his authority over the Anglo-Saxons, resulting in a strong, stable monarchy that lasted into the twelfth century. The documents in this chapter offer three views of the Norman Conquest: the first is a pictorial image from the Bayeux Tapestry, the second is a poem from the Anglo-Saxon Chronicle, and the third is an account from the Gesta Guillelmi by William of Poitiers. In order to stabilize his regime, William the Conqueror established various legal statutes, as may be seen in Document 6.5. The reaction of the native Anglo-Saxons to William's regime was recorded in the Anglo-Saxon Chronicle (Document 6.6).

The Muslims continued to dominate much of the Iberian Peninsula. However, the descendants of the Visigoths were able to establish Christian kingdoms in the northern area. They began an attempt to take back the Muslim holdings—an effort that would take several centuries. The actions on the part of one of the monarchs, Sancho, the king of Aragon (r. 905–925), are recounted in The Chronicle of San Juan de la Pena. The excerpt included here describes his fierce determination to regain Christian territory.

Carolingian power gradually declined in the eastern part of the old Holy Roman Empire, and when the last of the Carolingians, Louis "the Child," died in 911, the dukes elected their own king of the area they called eastern Francia. The first man elected king, Conrad of Franconia (911–919), was weak, but his successor, Henry "the

Europe in the Tenth and Eleventh Centuries (From Frankforter-Spellman, *The West*, 2nd ed., pp. 247, 2500.)

Fowler," Duke of Saxony, was the founder of what was later called the Saxon Dynasty. Henry's son, Otto I "the Great," was the most successful of the Saxon kings, ushering in an era of Ottonian rule that was considered to be a political and cultural renaissance. One of Otto's most important actions was to vanquish at last the invading Magyars at the Battle of Lechfeld in 955 (see the earlier attempts to stop the Magyars in Document 4.20). This *chapter includes an account of the battle taken from a work by one of Otto's courtiers, Liudprand of Cremona.*

The kings in Germany, who were often known as "Holy Roman Emperor," sought to exert control over northern Italy, and during the twelfth century they became embroiled in a struggle with the papacy, known variously in history as "The Investiture Controversy" or "The Investiture Struggle." This chapter provides documents that enable the analysis of this important conflict between the emperor and the pope, including a statement by Pope Gregory VII regarding papal prerogatives, with a response from King Henry IV. There is also an account of the dramatic meeting between pope and king at Canossa, in northern Italy (Document 6.16), where Henry appeared as a penitent seeking forgiveness from Gregory. Although there were several decrees against lay investiture during the decades following this confrontation (Document 6.17), it was not until the Concordat of Worms in 1122 that the "Investiture Controversy" was eventually settled (Document 6.18).

After their defeat at the Battle of Lechfeld in 955, the Magyars gradually established an organized government in their domain. They had been introduced to Christianity by missionaries in the ninth century, but the new religion did not become widely practiced until the last part of the tenth century. King Stephen (r. 997–1038) was baptized as a boy, and adopted the religion seriously. In 1000, his Christian rule was recognized by the pope, who also sent him a splendid crown (Document 6.19). In order for Christianity to flourish in his realm, the king enacted laws that are included in Document 6.20.

Rus, the medieval Russian state, was established by Scandinavian traders in the ninth century. The first historical rulers of the capital, Kiev, were Oleg (r. 882–913) and Igor (913–945); they were able to maintain and spread Kievan authority throughout the eastern Slavic lands. When Igor was killed in 945, his widow Olga was left in charge of the state, since their son Sviatoslav was still a minor. According to The Russian Primary Chronicle, she proved to be a dynamic ruler (Document 6.21). In the middle of the tenth century she adopted Christianity, and, like the conversions of earlier monarchs we have studied, this was an act that began the dissemination of the religion among her people. Olga attempted unsuccessfully to convert her son Sviatoslav, but her grandson Vladimir officially accepted the belief and declared Christianity the religion of the state.

Denmark was the first of the Viking kingdoms to adopt Christianity, during the reign of Harold (c. 940–c. 985). Although Harald's people were willing to accept Christ, the old folk religion survived tenaciously in Scandinavia for two centuries. As recounted in The Saga of Olaf Tryggvason, an epic tale written in the late twelfth century, the kings faced extreme opposition in attempting to Christianize their people. As the excerpt in Document 6.22 from the Saga recounts, Olaf, King of Norway (r. c. 995–c. 1000) used force to convert his unwilling subjects.

During the era when Europe was recovering from the onslaught of the Vikings, the Muslims, and the Magyars, Byzantium was experiencing a "Golden Age" of intellectual, artistic, and mercantile progress. The government was guided by Byzantine emperors who held a quasi-divine status, which they reinforced by an elaborate ceremonial system. The rituals became so complex that manuals were written for use by the courtiers who guided the protocol. One of the most important of these was On Ceremonies, written by the Emperor Constantine VII Porphyrogenitus in the tenth century. In the preface to this work the emperor stated the reasons for extensive courtly ritual; the ceremonies served to impress the imperial image on the minds of the people, and to foster respect for government.

This chapter emphasizes documents that illustrate the consolidation of power in western Europe during the tenth, eleventh, and twelfth centuries. Through these sources it is possible to explore the development of the western monarchies and to analyze their political and religious associations with Russia, Scandinavia, and the Byzantine Empire.

The Monarchies of France, England, and Christian Iberia

France

6.1   The Election of Hugh Capet as King of France (987)

According to the Treaty of Verdun (See Document 4.16), the western part of the Carolingian Empire was bestowed upon Charles the Bald, who ruled from 843 to 877. Many of his successors were weak and ineffectual, resulting in a struggle for power among the great nobles. In 888, when the remaining members of the Carolingian family were minors, the magnates elected Odo, son of Robert the Strong, as king. The tenth century was marked by a continuing struggle for control between the feudal lords; during that century three kings were elected from the descendants of Robert the Strong, and four from the Carolingian house. King Charles "the Simple" (r. 898–922), who ceded Normandy to Rollo the Viking, was one of the Carolingians (see Document 4.21). In 987, the Church, committed to the concept of peace, urged the nobles to elect a powerful king. The following excerpt from the Four Books of Histories, *written by the monk Richer, describes the procedure that resulted in the election of Hugh Capet. Although his reign lasted only nine years and he did not accomplish a great deal during that time, Hugh established a dynasty that endured on the throne until 1328.*

(From *Readings in European History,* vol. 1, by James Harvey Robinson [Boston: Ginn & Co., 1904], pp. 194–196.)

Meanwhile the nobles of Gaul who had taken the oath came together at the appointed time at Senlis; when they had all taken their places in the assembly, the duke made a sign to the archbishop of Rheims, who spoke as follows: "King Louis, of divine memory, left children; we must therefore take counsel as to the choice of a successor, in order that the country shall not come to ruin through neglect and the lack of a pilot. Our deliberations on this subject were recently postponed, by common consent, in order that each one might here voice the sentiments with which God might inspire him, and that from all these individual opinions a general and collective decision might be reached.

"Now that we are once more assembled together, let us endeavor, in all prudence and rectitude, not to sacrifice reason and truth to our personal likes or dislikes. We know that Charles has his partisans, who claim that the throne belongs to him by right of birth. Regarding the question from this point of view, we reply that the throne cannot be acquired by hereditary right. Nor should one be placed upon it who is not distinguished alike by nobility of body and wisdom of mind, and by his good faith and magnanimity. We see in the annals of history rulers of illustrious origin deposed on account of their unworthiness, and replaced by incumbents of equal, or even of inferior, birth.

"And what is there to recommend Charles of Lorraine? He is feeble and without honor, faith, or character; he has not blushed to become the servitor of a foreign king [the emperor], nor to take to wife a girl of only knightly rank. How could the great duke bear that a woman belonging to the lowest rank of his vassals should be queen and rule over him? How could he give precedence to a woman, when his equals and even his superiors in birth bend the knee before him and place their hands beneath his feet? If you consider this matter carefully, you will see that Charles' fall has been brought about through his own fault rather than that of others. Make a choice, therefore, that shall insure the welfare of the state instead of being its ruin. If you wish ill to your country, choose Charles; if you wish to see it prosperous, make Hugh, the glorious duke, king. Do not let yourselves be misled by your sympathy for Charles, nor blinded to the common good by hatred of the duke. For if you blame the good, how can you praise the bad? If you praise the bad, how despise the good? Remember the words of the Scripture: 'Woe unto them that call evil good, and good evil; that put darkness for light, and light for darkness.' Choose the duke, therefore; he is the most illustrious among us all by reason of his exploits, his nobility, and his military following. Not only the state, but every individual interest, will find in him a protector. His great-heartedness will render him a father to you all. Who has ever fled to him for aid and been disappointed? Who that has been left in the lurch by his friends has he ever failed to restore to his rights?"

This discourse was received with universal applause, and by unanimous consent the duke was raised to the throne. He was crowned at Noyon on the first of June, by the archbishop and the other bishops, as king of the Gauls, the Bretons, the Danes [Normans?], the Aquitanians, the Goths, the Spaniards, and the Gascons. Surrounded by the nobles of the kingdom, he issued decrees and made laws according to royal custom, judging and disposing of all matters with success.

Questions for Discussion:

1. What reasons did the archbishop give for disregarding the claim of Charles of Lorraine to the throne?
2. According to the source, the archbishop stated that the "glorious duke" Hugh was worthy of being king. Why? How would the country prosper under his leadership?
3. Why were the nobles willing to disregard the prevailing law of inheritance?

INTERPRETING THE EVIDENCE: Three Views of the Norman Conquest

6.2   The *Anglo-Saxon Chronicle* (1066)

The conquest of England by the Normans (descendants of Rollo, whom King Charles "the Simple" had named Duke of Normandy) took place in 1066. The establishment of the Norman dynasty was another example of disputed inheritance; although, as observed in this document, the circumstances were quite different from those in France.

There are at least three differing views of the events leading to the Norman invasion. The source of the dispute concerned the right of succession to the throne of England, held by Edward the Confessor (r. 1042–1066). According to the Anglo-Saxon Chronicle, *Edward, who did not have an heir, had indicateid that the next king should be Harold of Wessex, the son of a powerful noble. As may be seen in the following poem from the* Chronicle, *". . . the wise ruler entrusted the realm to a man of high rank, to Harold himself."*

(From *English Historical Documents: 1042–1189*, ed. by David C. Douglas and George W. Greenaway. Copyright © 1961 Eyre & Spottiswoode. Reprinted with permission of Cambridge University Press.)

Now royal Edward, England's ruler
To the Savior resigns his righteous soul

His sacred spirit to God's safe keeping
In the life of this world he lived awhile
In kingly splendor strong in counsel.
Four and twenty was his tale of winters
That ruler of heroes lavish of riches
In fortunate time he governed the Welshmen
Ethelred's son; ruled Britons and Scots
Angles and Saxons, his eager soldiers.
All that the cold sea waves encompass
Young and loyal yielded allegiance,
With all their heart to King Edward the noble.
Ever gay was the courage of the guiltless king
Though long ago, of his land bereft
He wandered in exile, over earth's far ways
After Cnut overcame Ethelred's kin
And Danes had rule of the noble realm
Of England for eight and twenty years
In succession distributing riches.
At length he came forth in lordly array
Noble in goodness, gracious and upright
Edward the glorious, guarding his homeland
Country and subjects—till on a sudden came

(continued)

Death in his bitterness, bearing so dear
A lord from the earth. And angels led
His righteous soul to heaven's radiance.
Yet the wise ruler entrusted the realm
To a man of high rank, to Harold himself
A noble earl who all the time
Had loyally followed his lord's commands
With words and deeds and neglected nothing
That met the need of the people's king.

And Earl Harold was now consecrated king and he met little quiet in it as long as he ruled the realm.

Questions for Discussion:

1. According to the poem, what was the extent of King Edward's realm?
2. What reasons did the poet give for Edward's bequeathing of the kingdom to Harold?

6.3   The Bayeux Tapestry

A very different interpretation of the right to the throne is offered in an embroidery panel known as the Bayeux Tapestry, which recounts the events of the invasion of England according to the Normans. The work is immense, measuring some 230 feet in length and 20 inches in width. It was commissioned by Odo, the Bishop of Bayeux, who was the brother of William the Conqueror. The circumstances of the production are unclear, but it is generally assumed that the needlework was done by women, probably working at Canterbury.

As may be seen in this segment from the eleventh-century embroidery, the Normans believed that Harold had sworn allegiance to William of Normandy—an act that precluded his claiming the throne of England because Edward the Confessor had, in fact, named William as his heir.

From the Bayeux Tapestry. *(Harold Swears an Oath that he will accept William as King of England, from The Bayeux Tapestry [embroidery on linen] [detail of 115615], French School [11th century] / With special authorization of the city of Bayeux, Musee de la Tapisserie, Bayeux, France / The Bridgeman Art Library Ltd.)*

6.4 *Gesta Guillelmi* by William of Poitiers (1071)

The circumstances of Harold's pledge, which are not mentioned in the Anglo-Saxon Chronicle, *are recounted in the following selection from the work* Gesta Guillelmi ("The Deeds of William") *by the Norman William of Poitiers, who was the chaplain of William "the Conqueror."*

(From *The Gesta Guillelmi of William of Poitiers*, trans. by R. H. C. Davis and Marjorie Chibnall. Oxford: Clarendon Press, 1998, pp. 69–71. Reprinted by permission of Oxford University Press.)

About the same time Edward [the Confessor], king of the English, protected the position of William (whom he loved as a brother or son and had already appointed his heir) with a stronger pledge than before. He wished to prepare in advance for the inevitable hour of death, which, as a man who strove for heaven through his holy life, he believed to be near at hand. To confirm the pledge with an oath, he sent Harold, the most distinguished of his subjects in wealth, honor and power, whose brother and nephew had been received as hostages for William's succession. And this was very prudently done, so that Harold's wealth and authority could check the resistance of the whole English people, if, with their accustomed fickleness and perfidy, they were tempted to revolt.

Harold, after escaping the dangers of the crossing as he sailed to undertake this mission, landed on the coast of Ponthieu, where he fell into the hands of Count Guy. He and his men were seized and taken into custody; a misfortune that a man as proud as he would gladly have exchanged for shipwreck. For certain Gallic peoples have been led through avarice to adopt a cunning practice, which is barbarous and utterly removed from Christian justice. They lay ambushes for the powerful and wealthy, thrust them into prison, and torture and humiliate them. When they have reduced them almost to the point of death they turn them out, usually ransomed at a very high price.

When Duke William heard of the fate of the man who had been sent to him, he immediately dispatched envoys, got Harold out of prison by a mixture of prayers and threats, and went to meet him and receive him honorably. Guy behaved well and, without being compelled by force, himself brought the man whom he could have tortured, killed, or sold at pleasure to the castle of Eu, and handed him over to William. William thanked him appropriately, giving him lands that were both extensive and rich, and adding very great gifts of money besides. He escorted Harold most honorably to Rouen, the chief city of his principality, where every kind of hospitality restored and cheered those who had suffered the trials of the journey. He congratulated himself warmly on having so great a guest, the envoy of the kinsman and friend who was especially dear to him, hoping to have in him a faithful mediator between himself and the English, to whom Harold was second only to the king.

In a council summoned to Bonneville, Harold swore fealty to him according to the holy rite of Christians. And, as the most truthful and distinguished men who were there as witnesses have told, at the crucial point in the oath he clearly and of his own free will pronounced these words that as long as he lived he would be the vicar [representative] of Duke William in the court of his lord King Edward; that he would strive to the utmost with his counsel and his wealth to ensure that the English monarchy should be pledged to him after Edward's death; that in the mean time the castle of Dover should be fortified by his care and at his expense for William's knights; likewise that he would furnish with provisions and garrisons other castles to be fortified in various places chosen by the duke. The duke, after he had received him as his vassal and before he took the oath, confirmed all his lands and powers to him at his request. For there was no hope that Edward, already sick, could live much longer.

Questions for Discussion:

1. According to the *Gesta*, King Edward sent Harold as an emissary to William. What were his motives for this action?

(continued)

2. What ceremony does the image from the Bayeux Tapestry portray? (See Documents 5.1 and 5.2). How would the meaning of this ritual enable William of Normandy to assert his claim to the throne of England?

3. Does the *Gesta* reinforce the meaning of the Bayeux Tapestry? How?

In 1066, following the death of Edward, Harold was crowned as King of England. He faced several threats. An invasion took place in northern England led by his brother, Svein Godwinsson, and another claimant to the throne, Harold Hardrada of Norway. Their forces were defeated by King Harold at the Battle of Stamford Bridge, and Harold Hardrada was killed. Soon thereafter,

William of Normandy landed on the southern coast; Harold marched southward, encountering William's army at Hastings. A fierce battle ensued, in which King Harold was killed and his soldiers were routed. Another panel from the Bayeux Tapestry contains an image of the death of Harold. The caption reads:

HAROLD REX INTERFECTUS EST (Harold the King was killed).

Question for Discussion:

1. Note the images in the border: what were the "spoils of war"?

From the Bayeux Tapestry. *(Erich Lessing/Art Resource, New York.)*

England and William the Conqueror

6.5   Statutes of William the Conqueror (c. 1070)

After the conquest of England by the Normans, the new king, William "the Conqueror," undertook various measures to secure his control over the restive and unhappy population. Soon after his victory he began to build motte-and-bailey castles (see the illustration in Document 5.9) throughout the country—a vast construction program that led to the creation of some 500 castles by the beginning of the twelfth century. To create an army, he maintained the fyrd—the Anglo-Saxon force that had originally been summoned to fight the Danes. Further, in order to ensure the loyalty of the aristocracy, William required all the nobles to swear direct personal allegiance to him as liege lord in the "Oath of Salisbury." He also instituted a system of laws that clarified the relationship of the new king to the Church, his own Norman knights, and the resident people of his new kingdom.

(From *Select Historical Documents of the Middle Ages*, trans. by Ernest F. Henderson [London: G. Bell and Sons, 1925], pp. 7–8.)

1. Firstly that, above all things, he wishes one God to be venerated throughout his whole kingdom, one faith of Christ always to be kept inviolate, peace and security to be observed between the English and the Normans.

2. We decree also that every free man shall affirm by a compact and an oath that, within and without England, he desires to be faithful to king William, to preserve with him his lands and his honor with all fidelity, and first to defend him against his enemies.

3. I will, moreover, that all the men whom I have brought with me, or who have come after me, shall be in my peace and quiet. And if one of them shall be slain, the lord of his murderer shall seize him within five days, if he can; but if not, he shall begin to pay to me forty-six marks of silver as long as his possessions shall hold out. But when the possessions of the lord of that man are at an end, the whole hundred [county] in which the slaying took place shall pay in common what remains.

4. And every Frenchman who, in the time of my relative king Edward, was a sharer in England

of the customs of the English, shall pay according to the law of the English what they themselves call "onhlote" and "anscote." This decree has been confirmed in the city of Gloucester.

5. We forbid also that any live cattle be sold or bought for money except within the cities, and this before three faithful witnesses; nor even anything old without a surety and warrant. But if he do otherwise he shall pay, and shall afterwards pay a fine.

6. It was also decreed there that if a Frenchman summon an Englishman for perjury or murder, theft, homicide, or "ran"—as the English call evident rape which can not be denied—the Englishman shall defend himself as he prefers, either through the ordeal of iron,[1] or through wager of battle. But if the Englishman be infirm he shall find another who will do it for him. If one of them shall be vanquished he shall pay a fine of forty shillings to the king. If an Englishman summon a Frenchman, and be unwilling to prove his charge by judgment or by wager of battle, I will, nevertheless, that the Frenchman purge himself by an informal oath.

7. This also I command and will, that all shall hold and keep the law of Edward the king with regard to their lands, and with regard to all their possessions, those provisions being added which I have made for the utility of the English people.

8. Even man who wishes to be considered a freeman shall have a surety, that his surety may hold him and hand him over to justice if he offend in any way. And if any such one escape, his sureties shall see to it that, without making difficulties, they pay what is charged against him, and that they clear themselves of having known of any fraud in the matter of his escape. The hundred and county shall be made to answer as our predecessors decreed. And

---

[1]In the ordeal of iron, the accused had to carry a heated weight of iron a certain distance; he was considered not guilty if after three days his hand had healed without infection.

those that ought of right to come, and are unwilling to appear, shall be summoned once; and if a second time they are unwilling to appear, one ox shall be taken from them and they shall be summoned a third time. And if they do not come the third time, another ox shall be taken: but if they do not come the fourth time there shall be forfeited from the goods of that man who was unwilling to come, the extent of the charge against him,—"ceapgeld" as it is called,—and besides this a fine to the king.

9. I forbid anyone to sell a man beyond the limits of the country, under penalty of a fine in full to me.

10. I forbid that anyone be killed or hung for any fault, but his eyes shall be torn out or his testicles cut off. And this command shall not be violated under penalty of a fine in full to me.

Questions for Discussion:

1. Compare the laws of William the Conqueror with the Salic Law (Document 2.8) and the *Capitularies* of Charlemagne (Documents 4.7 & 4.8). What provisions are common to all three?

2. How do laws 1, 3, and 6 attempt to establish peaceful coexistence between the natives of England and the Normans?

3. Discuss the implications of the second law with regard to the provisions of vassalage studied in Chapter 5. How did William's version differ from the norm?

6.6   The *Anglo Saxon Chronicle*

As may be seen from the following document, the native people of England were not convinced that the measures of the new king would benefit their country. He had promised to be a "faithful lord" to them, but his actions, at least from the point of view of the writer of the Chronicle, *did not coincide with his words.*

(From *The Anglo-Saxon Chronicle*, trans. by James Ingram [London: J.M. Dent & Sons, 1912], pp. 149–150. Translation modernized.)

. . . William returned to Hastings, and waited there to know whether the people would submit to him. But when he found that they would not come to him, he went up with all his force that was left and that came since to him from over sea, and ravaged all the country that he overran, until he came to Berkhampstead; where Archbishop Aldred came to meet him . . . with all the best men from London, who submitted then because they needed to, when the most harm was done. It was very ill-advised that they did not so before, seeing that God would not make things better because of our sins. And they gave him hostages and took oaths; and he promised them that he would be a faithful lord to them; though in the midst of this they plundered wherever they went. Then on midwinter's day Archbishop Aldred consecrated him king at Westminster, and gave him possession with the Scriptures, and also swore him, before he would set the crown on his head, that he would govern this nation as well as any king before him, if they would be faithful to him. Nevertheless he laid very heavy tribute on men, and in Lent went over to Normandy, taking with him Archbishop Stigand, and Abbot Aylnoth of Glastonbury, . . . and many other good men of England. Bishop Odo [William's brother] and Earl William lived here afterwards, and wrought castles widely through this country, and harassed the miserable people; and ever since has evil increased very much.

Questions for Discussion:

1. Although William promised that he would be a faithful lord to the people, the *Anglo-Saxon Chronicle* relates actions by the king that contradict this pledge. What were these?

2. Would the enforcement of the laws stipulated by William have provided a justification for his deeds?

Iberia

6.7   A Christian Monarch in Iberia: Sancho Abarca, King of Navarre

As a result of the seventh-century Muslim invasion of the Iberian Peninsula, the Visigothic inhabitants retreated into the mountainous northern areas, where they formed several kingdoms. (See Document 3.9.) By the tenth century these included Castille, Leon, Navarre, and Aragon. This account of the reign of King Sancho Abarca (r. 905–925) is taken from the fourteenth-century Chronicle of San Juan de la Pena, *which was commissioned by King Pedro IV of Aragon (r. 1336–1387). It was the first complete history of the kingdom, and was no doubt written to provide an historical justification for the authority of the Crown of Aragon. The work is a compilation of various chronicles, histories, and orally transmitted tales. The following excerpt, which tells of the monarch's miraculous birth and his ascent to the throne, is obviously influenced by heroic chansons de geste ("cantares de gesta" in Spanish) such as* Beowulf *(Document 2.9), the poem* El Cid *(Document 7.17), and the* Song of Roland, *to be studied in Chapter 8. Of particular pertinence in the tale of Sancho are the many references to warfare against the Muslims on the Spanish peninsula, which was a recurring theme throughout the* Chronicle.

(From *The Chronicle of San Juan de la Pena,* translated by Lynn H. Nelson. Philadelphia: University of Pennsylvania Press, 1991, pp. 10–12. Reprinted with permission of the University of Pennsylvania Press.)

When the king [Garcia Iniguez, r. 851–c. 880] was interred, his pregnant wife Onenga survived him. A tragic event occurred one day while she was passing through the valley of Aibar. A number of Saracens made a sudden attack upon the queen, killed all of her family, and pierced her through the stomach with a lance. She immediately died from this wound. A very short while afterward, a noble baron of the mountains of Aragon passed through the valley. Contemplating the terrible slaughter of Christians that had taken place there, he saw a baby's hand thrust out of the wound in the queen's stomach. He dismounted, cut open the queen's womb as carefully as he could, and drew forth a live male child, whom he carried away with him and had baptized. He gave him the name of Sancho Garces and had him reared in an honorable fashion.

For some years, the people of the land managed the government themselves, murmuring and complaining and not without cause because there was no surviving heir, being unaware of the child's survival. One day, the nobles, knights, and people of the loand were called together to elect some noble baron as king, and they determined to hold a general assembly to decide the matter. When the noble baron who had saved the child from death so that he might someday be brought to light learned of this, he had the child dressed in shepherd fashion, complete with peasant sandals. When his cousins, friends, and vassals had gathered, and he was fittingly attired, the baron went to the assembly at the appointed hour. Entering the palace where the meeting was being held, he was received with honor by all those who were participating in the discussion. Holding the child between his legs, he cried out in a loud voice, "Barons! Take this child, take off the clothes he wears, and take him as your king, for he is in truth your lord. You all know that his mother, the queen, was pregnant when she died on that unfortunate occasion. I am the one who passed through the valley where she lay slain and saw a baby's hand reaching out through the wound in its mother's belly. And God be praised! I drew the child out alive and without injury from her womb. My kinsmen and vassals who were then present, stand in witness thereof, and if anyone claims to the contrary, let him enter the field of battle, and I will come to do trial by combat with him."

When he had said these things, everyone rose up, shouting "Viva, viva! Because this and none other is our lord!" They immediately removed from the child the clothes in which he was dressed and with great joy clad him in royal garments. On that day, they held a solemn feast in his honor. Because he had come to them clad and shod as if he were a shepherd boy, they called him Sancho Abarca.[2]

---

[2] Abarcas are the traditional footwear of the peasants in the area of the western Pyrenees Mountains. The cover only part of the foot, and are tied to the calf of the leg with strings.

He was an extraordinary man and began to fight the Saracens [Muslims] vigorously. He conquered the territory from Cantabria to Najera, to the Montes de Oca and Tudela, all the plain of Pamplona, and even a large part of the mountains. When he had conquered all the mountains of Aragon, he had many castles and fortresses built there to hold back the Saracens. He had many battles with them, in all of which he emerged victorious.

Once, in the midst of the winter season, when he had stationed himself near the mountains, he learned that the Saracens were holding the city of Pamplona under a very strict siege. Confiding in the grace of Omnipotent God, he crossed the snow-covered mountains with men from Cantabria and others of his realms. Since his men were accustomed to being constantly out of doors, they were slowed neither by heat nor cold. Arriving at dawn and committing himself to God, he attacked the Saracens so fiercely that they were completely defeated, and none escaped to return to his own land. Having gained a great victory and offering praise to god and His saints, Sancho and his men gathered booty from the Saracen camp, and the city of Pamplona stood delivered from the great danger it had faced.

King Sancho Abarca had loyal vassals and sturdy warriors, all eager to battle against the Saracens. They were accustomed, even the knights, to carry short spears and travel on foot. The king and his vassals also sometimes traveled on foot and sometimes on horseback. None of them refused to undertake whatever task he might be assigned. Sancho Abarca always thought about how to obtain victory and honor from the enemies of the faith. He was greatly loved by his vassals for this, particularly since he marched with them like a comrade-in-arms and did not avoid exposing himself to the dangers of battle. When he marched with them shod in his peasant sandals, suffering weariness and fatigue, his men's love for him was great indeed.

He seized many places in Cantabria, among which one is today called Sancho Abarca.

He took Queen Toda as his wife, and fathered by her one son, named Garcia, and four daughters. One, named Urraca, married King Alfonso IV of Leon [r. 925–931]; another, called Maria, married King Ordono II of Leon [r. 950–956]; the third, named Sancha, married King Ramiro II of Leon [r. 931–950]; and the fourth, Blasuita, married Count Munoz of Vizcaya. He built many monasteries and churches in the county of Aragon and endowed the monastery of San Juan de la Pena with many goods.

King Sancho Abarca ruled twenty-eight years. He died in the Year of Our Lord, 905, and was buried with honor in the monastery of San Juan de la Pena. [Actually, King Sancho Abarca began his reign in 905 and died in 925].

Questions for Discussion:

1. In this account, how does Sancho Abarca embody the qualities of a medieval Christian king?
2. According to the *Chronicle*, the king was greatly beloved by his vassals and the people of his country, and the author cites specific reasons. What were some of these?

The Ottonian Empire and Germany

The Deeds of Otto the Great: The Battle of Lechfeld (955)

6.8   Liutprand of Cremona

Charlemagne's grandson, Louis the German, who was given the eastern section of the empire in the Treaty of Verdun, died in 877. The following half-century was chaotic, with ineffectual descendants of Louis attempting to maintain their positions while dealing with the invasions of the Magyars.

Since there was no strong central government, leadership was provided by powerful local families, and "stem duchies" were developed, based upon the old tribal frontiers.

The last member of the Carolingian dynasty was Louis the Child, who died in 911. The "stem dukes" then elected one of their weakest members, Conrad of Franconia, who reigned until 918. The next king was Henry, Duke of Saxony, one of the most powerful of the magnates. He proved to be an effective monarch, and left a strengthened kingdom to his son, Otto I (r. 936–973), who was one of the most important rulers of the Middle Ages. The era of his reign, and that of his son and grandson, was known as the "Ottonian" period. One of the most significant actions of Otto I was the defeat of the Magyars at the Battle of Lechfeld (955). The following selection contains an account by one of Otto's courtiers, Liutprand, Bishop of Cremona (c. 920–972).

(From *A Source Book for Mediaeval History*, by Oliver J. Thatcher and Edgar H. MacNeal [New York: Charles Scribner's Sons, 1905], pp. 75–77. Translation modernized.)

While Otto was in Saxony, ambassadors of the Hungarians came to him, under the pretext of the old alliance and friendship, but in reality, it was supposed, in order to discover the outcome of the civil war in which Otto had been engaged. After he had entertained them and sent them away with gifts, he received a message from his brother, the duke of Bavaria, saying: "The Hungarians are overrunning your land, and are preparing to make war upon you." As soon as the king heard this, he immediately marched against this enemy, taking with him only a few Saxons, since the rest were occupied at that time with a conflict against the Slavs. He pitched his camp in the territory of the city of Augsburg and was joined there by the army of the Franconians and Bavarians and by Duke Conrad with a large following of knights. Conrad's arrival so encouraged the warriors that they wished to attack the enemy immediately. Conrad was by nature very bold, and at the same time very wise in council, two things which are not usually found in the same man. He was irresistible in war, whether on foot or on horseback, and was dear to his friends in peace as well as in war. It now became apparent through the skirmishes of the advance posts that the two armies were not far apart. A fast was proclaimed in the camp, and all were commanded to be ready for battle on the next morning. They all arose at dawn, made peace with one another, and promised to aid first their own leaders and then each other. Then they marched out of the camp with standards raised, some eight legions in all. The army was led by a steep and

difficult way in order to avoid the darts of the enemy, which they use with great effect if they can find any bushes to hide behind. The first, second, and third lines were composed of Bavarians led by the officers of Duke Henry, who himself was lying sick some distance from the field of battle—a sickness from which he died not long after. The fourth legion was composed of Franconians, under the command of Duke Conrad. The king commanded the fifth line. This was called the royal legion and was made up of selected warriors, brave youths, who guarded the standard of the angel, the emblem of victory. The sixth and seventh lines were composed of Suabians, commanded by Duke Burchard, who had married the daughter of the brother of Otto [Hedwig, daughter of Henry]. The eighth was made up of a thousand chosen warriors of the Bohemians, whose equipment was better than their fortune; here was the baggage and the impedimenta, because the rear was thought to be the safest place. But it did not prove to be so in the outcome, for the Hungarians crossed the Lech [River] unexpectedly, and turned the flank of the army and fell upon the rear line, first with darts and then at close quarters. Many were slain or captured, the whole of the baggage seized, and the line put to rout. In like manner the Hungarians fell upon the seventh and sixth lines, slew a great many and put the rest to flight. But when the king perceived that there was a conflict going on in front and that the lines behind him were also being attacked, he sent Duke Conrad with the fourth line against those in the rear. Conrad freed the captives, recovered the booty, and drove off the enemy. Then he returned to the king, victorious, having defeated with youthful and untried warriors an enemy that had put to flight experienced and renowned soldiers.

. . . When the king saw that the whole brunt of the attack was now in front . . . he seized his shield and lance, and rode out against the enemy at the head of his followers. The braver warriors among the enemy withstood the attack at first, but when they saw that their companions had fled, they were overcome with dismay and were slain. Some of the enemy sought refuge in nearby villages, their horses being worn out; these were surrounded and burnt to death within the walls. Others swam the river, but were drowned by the caving in of the bank as they attempted to climb out on the other side. The strongholds were taken and the captives released on the day of the battle; during the next two days the remnants of the enemy were captured in the neighboring towns, so that scarcely any escaped. Never was so bloody a victory gained over so savage a people.

Question for Discussion:

1. Compare the actions of Otto and Sancho Abarca (Document 6.7). How are they similar: What differences do you see?

INTERPRETING THE EVIDENCE: Otto III

6.9   The *Chronicon* of Thietmar of Merseburg

Otto III (r. 983–1002), the grandson of Otto I "the Great," became emperor at the age of three, and was raised in the custody of his mother, the former Byzantine princess Theophano, who ruled for him until her death in 991. His grandmother Adelaide, widow of Otto I, then acted as regent until 996. As a young adult, Otto's hope was to reestablish Rome as the center of his Empire, and to emulate Charlemagne in his patronage of scholarship and the Church. The following selection, from the Chronicon *by Thietmar of Merseburg, reflects the wide dimension of Otto's hegemony, as he visits various areas in his empire and establishes an archbishopric at Gniezno (Poland).*

(From *Ottonian Germany: The Chronicon of Thietmar of Merseburg*, trans. by David A. Warner. Manchester, U.K.: Manchester University Press, 2001, pp. 183–186. Reprinted by permission.)

When he arrived at Zeitz [southern Germany], the emperor was received in a manner appropriate to an emperor by Hugh II, third pastor of that see [*c.*10 February]. Then he went by a direct route to Meissen [Germany] where he was honorably received by Eid, the venerable bishop of this church, and by Margrave Ekkehard whom he regarded highly. Then, having traversed the territories of the Milzeni, he was met as he arrived at the district of Diadesi by Boleslav whose name is interpreted as 'greater praise' not by merit but by old custom. With great rejoicing, Boleslav offered the emperor hospitality at a place called Eulau [Germany]. It would be impossible to believe or describe how the emperor was then received by him and conducted to Gniezno. Seeing the desired city from afar, he humbly approached

barefoot. After being received with veneration by Bishop Unger, he was led into the church where, weeping profusely, he was moved to ask the grace of Christ for himself through the intercession of Christ's martyr. Without delay, he established an archbishopric there, as I hope legitimately, but without the consent of the aforementioned bishop to whose diocese this whole region is subject. He committed the new foundation to Radim, the martyr's brother, and made subject to him Bishop Reinbern of Kolberg, Bishop Poppo of Krakow, and Bishop John of Wroclaw, but not Unger of Poznari. And with great solemnity, he also placed holy relics in an altar which had been established there.

Because the emperor wished to renew the ancient custom of the Romans, now mostly obliterated, he did many things which received a rather mixed reaction. He dined alone at a semicircular table which, moreover, was elevated above the others. As he had doubts regarding the location of the bones of Emperor Charles, he secretly had the pavement over their supposed resting place ripped up and excavations carried out until they were discovered, on the royal throne. After taking a gold cross which hung around the emperor's neck and part of his clothing, which remained uncorrupted, he replaced everything with great veneration. But how should I recall each of his comings and goings through all of his bishoprics and counties? With everything well disposed north of the Alps, Otto betook himself to the Roman Empire and, arriving at the Romulan citadel, was received with great honor by the pope and his fellow bishops [14 August].

6.10 The *Gospel Book of Otto III*

An illumination from the Gospel Book of Otto III *(produced between 997 and 1000) shows the emperor receiving homage from four parts of the empire, personified by female figures that represent Lavinia,*

Germania, Gallia, and Roma. In this elegant portrait it is evident that the Ottonian emperors wished to express their power and dignity by wearing elaborate robes and splendid jewels.

The *Gospel Book of Otto III*, 997–1000. 13 in. × 9 3/8 in. Staatsbibliothek, Munich. Clm. 4453, fol. 23v., 24r. *(Bayerische Staatsbibliothek.)*

6.11 The *Book of the Golden City of Rome*

The description of the emperor's robes in The Book of the Golden City of Rome, *probably written about 1030, coordinates quite clearly with the illumination.*

(From *Early Medieval Art 300–1150: Sources and Documents*, ed. by Caecilia Davis-Weyer. Englewood Cliffs, NJ: Prentice Hall Publishers, 1986, pp. 115–116. Reprinted by permission.)

We come now to the garments of the emperor and in the first place to the cloak. The cloak is a garment which is worn sideways and which is not sewn but held by golden clasps. The toga is round with its great fold bulging and, so to speak, overflowing.

Coming from the right it is slung over the left shoulder, as can be seen in pictures and statues, which we call togaed statues. The Emperor and the Romans wore the toga in times of peace but in times of war they wore the cloak. The proper measure of a toga is six ells.[3] The emperor's trabea is a kind of toga, purple and scarlet in color, which the emperors should wear during processions. Romulus first

_____

[3]An ell was a unit of measure, originally the length of the forearm. It was used in tailoring.

(continued)

invented it as a garment to distinguish kings. It is called trabea because it elevates the emperor and in past and future raises him to more lofty heights of honor and designates him as the sole ruler of all. The cloak of the emperor is a precious garment of scarlet, purple, and gold. It is a garment of war and it is because of future wars that the emperor wears it. The cloak resembles a "cyclas";[4] it is round and interwoven with purple.

The emperor should wear a shirt of very fine and white linen with a golden ornament. The golden border around its hem is one ell wide.

He should also have a scarlet tunic, adorned with gold, gems and precious pearls at the shoulders, around the neck, the hem and the wrists, with 72 little bells and as many pomegranates around the hem.

The belt or girdle of the emperor should be made from gold and precious stones, with 72 little bells, shaped like pomegranate flowers and a subcinctorium[5] made in the same fashion. And on each end of the girdle a golden circle adorned with precious stones and pearls, having around its rim the motto: "Rome the head of the universe holds the reins of the orb of the world." In the middle of the circle should be a representation of the three regions of the world: Asia, Africa, Europe.

The dalmatic[6] of the emperor is interwoven with gold, with golden eagles and pearls in front and back and with 365 little golden bells attached to it.

The emperor's epiloricum[7] should be made with eagles and pearls in front and back.

The golden mantle of the emperor should have a golden zodiac, made from pearls and precious stones. On its fringes should sit 365 little golden bells shaped like pomegranate flowers and as many pomegranates.

He should also have golden stockings with four eagles made from pearls. The straps of the stockings should be of gold and precious stones and pearls, having 24 little golden bells made in the shape of pomegranate flowers.

The emperor's shoes should be made of gold, pearls and precious stones, on which should be fashioned eagles and lions and dragons.

The pallium[8] and the mitre of the emperor. The emperor should have a pallium around his neck, and a mitre on his head, and also a golden necklace, armbands, bracelets and rings.

. . . The gloves of the sole ruler should be made from the brightest gold having Romulus and Scipio pictured with gold and gems and precious stones on one glove and Julius and Octavian on the other.

Questions for Discussion:

1. Why do you think the directions for imperial clothing are so specific? Give examples of the symbolism.
2. Compare the image of Otto III with the mosaic depiction of Justinian in Document 2.15. What similarities do you see in the clothing of the emperors? What differences do you observe?
3. Describe the portrayals of the dignitaries surrounding the emperors in both images. Do you think the earlier portrait may have influenced the artist who created this illumination?

---

[4]A cyclas was a state garment for women with a wide border around the hem. (See the image of Theodora in Document 2.15)
[5]A subcinctorium was an ornamental vestment. Today it is a term reserved for an item of clothing worn by the pope.
[6]A dalmatic is a long cloak with wide sleeves.
[7]The epiloricum was a garment worn above the armor.

[8]The pallium is a Y-shaped strip of cloth that encircles the shoulders and hangs down in front and back. It was generally worn by archbishops as an ecclesiastical symbol in the medieval era, and remains so today. The clergymen on Otto's left are wearing dalmatics.

INTERPRETING THE EVIDENCE: Monastic-Feudal Connections

6.12 Grant of Land to a Monastery

By the eleventh century vassalage and the holding of fiefs had become a feature of political and economic life throughout Europe (see Chapter 5). It was a system that pertained to members of the aristocracy, and the feudal relationships were not confined to laypersons. Both men and women of high rank in the clergy often entered into vassalage, holding fiefs from secular lords. They fulfilled their military responsibilities by sending substitutes or providing a monetary payment. The following document is a typical grant from a nobleman to a monastic establishment, for either men or women, demonstrating the economic features and rights of the fief and the responsibilities of the clergy.

(From *Readings in European History*, vol. 1, by James Harvey Robinson [Boston: Ginn & Co., 1904], pp. 362–364.)

Lord Luithold, the count, gave for the support of Christ's poor, the monks of this monastery of the holy Mother of God, half of the manor which is called Derendingen. This has excellent soil and is said to include twelve or more hides of arable land alone. He also gave meadows full good, and a half right to the exercise of all legal powers in the whole manor. He gave two groves, two mills, and a half right to the church on the same manor, and the sole right to the church of St. Blasius hard by the manor. To these two churches, that is to those portions of the churches which are under our jurisdiction, belongs one grove of five hides.

And he gave half of the manor which is called Undingen which includes twelve hides of fertile land and meadows and extends over an area of more than sixty hides of woods and of pastures for cattle. There is also an inn there.

And he also gave us the whole manor of Altenburg, with the sole right to the chapel, and a mill. The estate is believed to comprise almost fourteen hides of arable lands and meadows, without counting the woods and pastures.

He granted us, too, a half of the church at Oferdingen with four hides of fine arable land situated there, and at Neuhausen one mansus; likewise at Dusslingen one, and two at Immenweiler,—which afterwards we exchanged for two at Stubichahe. Also ten mansus at Scephbouch and four at Willsingen and three mills at Husin,—which were afterwards given in exchange to Rudolph of Reutlingen for Wimsheim. Also near the town of Chur a fourth part of the church in the manor called Maifeld. . . .

Describing with pride the foundation [1089] and history of his monastery of Zwifalt in Swabia, the monk Ortlieb gives the following account of "our family" [*nostra familia*]. Now this our monastery church possesses many persons who, because of the oppression of their former lords and of the burdens which weighed them down, have come under our jurisdiction in order to have peace. Some of these are tillers of the soil, some vinedressers; others are bakers, cobblers, artisans, merchants, and those who follow various trades and callings. Some of those who pay their dues to the monastery are on a different footing from others. Even among those who belong directly to the monastery some pay money yearly, while others contribute wax towards making a certain great candle. What all these pay in dues to the monastery is all handed over to the custodian of the church.

Some of those under our jurisdiction belong to the people's church across the river, some to St. Stephen's church at Tigerfeld, or to the church of St. Blasius at Derendingen, or to other churches under our control. While these pay their dues to the particular church to which they are known to belong, they are all, nevertheless, like the others, numbered among the members of our monastery family, and they should obey our decrees, no matter if they pay dues to some other church or monastery.

And it is to be noted that the people of Tigerfeld and those who pay their dues to that church are to be judged, at appointed times, by the advocate of that place in the presence of the provost of our monastery. If anyone should be convicted of any

(continued)

(continued)

rash act, or of failure to pay his dues, one part of the fine exacted shall go to the advocate and two parts to our community. . . .

Among our men some owe service of this kind, namely: when the lord abbot, prior, provost, or others among the brethren would travel anywhere, these men with their horses, do accompany the brethren and minister unto them obediently. And in order that this service may be rightfully required of them they are granted certain benefices. They assuredly rejoice to be honored by this distinction because they have the right to have under them men we call clients, or *ministeriales*. Yet in spite of this, no man of ours has ever become so perverse or haughty that he presumed to ride with us in military array,

or refused to carry the wallet of any of our monks upon his pack horse. The founders of our monastery did not intend to give us such men, and we have not consented to receive any one who might prove troublesome to us or to our successors.

Questions for Discussion:

1. Does the description of the fief granted to the monastery resemble those of the manors documented in Chapter 5? What are the similarities? Are there any differences?
2. Describe the variety of persons living on the manors belonging to the monastery. What are their responsibilities?

6.13   The Cross of Abbess Matilda of Essen

The relationship of vassalage involving clerical and laypersons was formalized through an homage ceremony, as may be seen in the illustration on page 169 of the enamel processional cross of Abbess Matilda of Essen (r. 973–1011). The image at the base of the cross (detail) shows Matilda's brother Otto, Duke of Swabia and Bavaria, handing her the abbatial cross, confirming his protection of her abbey.

Questions for Discussion:

1. Describe and discuss the symbolism of the image of Matilda and her brother Otto. How does this fulfill the ritual of a typical homage ceremony?
2. Crosses such as the one pictured here were carried in public processions on important feast days. What symbolic qualities would this particular example have conveyed to the people watching the pageantry?

The Cross of Abbess Matilda of Essen. ca. 1000, 17.5 in. × 11.6 in., Domschatzkammer Essen. Scanned from Kaus Gereon Beuckers, *Farbiges Gold: Die ottonischen Kreuze in der Domschatzkammer Essen und ihre Emails.* (© Dr. Ulrich Knapp.)

The Cross of Abbess Matilda of Essen. ca. 1000, 17.5 in. × 11.6 in., Domschatzkammer Essen. Scanned from Kaus Gereon Beuckers, *Farbiges Gold: Die ottonischen Kreuze in der Domschatzkammer Essen und ihre Emails.* (© Dr. Ulrich Knapp.)

The Investiture Controversy

During the eleventh century a struggle occurred between the Holy Roman Emperor Henry IV and Pope Gregory VII that resulted in lasting consequences. Prior to the reign of Henry (r. 1056–1106), the administration of Church government had been conducted under the watchful eye of royalty. Kings were free to appoint bishops, archbishops, and other members of the clergy who served not only as spiritual leaders, but as royal vassals with secular responsibilities. It was customary for the king and other powerful men to confer the offices of the clergy in a ceremony known as "lay investiture," in which they were "invested" or consecrated with the ring and crozier.[9] (In the previous document Abbess Matilda is being "invested" by her brother Otto, the Duke of Swabia and Bavaria). The investiture ceremony was an extension or adaptation of the ceremony of homage and fealty described in Documents 5.1, 5.2, and 5.3). It is important to remember that the ceremony symbolized a relationship of power; the lord, or magnate who gave the fief or the office, was the person in the relationship who held the authority. When these relationships involved lay rulers and bishops and other ecclesiastical dignitaries, problems began to emerge. Bishops, in particular, were important local representatives of royal power, and monarchs wanted loyal men who could be trusted in these positions. Although many kings had been scrupulous in appointing men who were spiritually worthy, there were many circumstances in which people were chosen who were morally unfit (see, for example the moral state of the clergy as described in the letter from Boniface to the Pope {742}, Document 4.6). The call for reform that began in the eighth century became increasingly strident in the eleventh century. Three issues were seen as vital: clerical celibacy, simony (the sale of ecclesiastical offices), and the custom of powerful laypeople appointing ecclesiastical officials.

Pope Gregory VII (r. 1073–1085), who was deeply influenced by the reform movement to be discussed more fully in the next chapter, sought to end the practice of lay investiture. His desire to abolish this practice led to a confrontation with the Holy Roman Emperor Henry IV.

---

[9]A crozier is a staff surmounted by a crook (resembling a shepherd's staff) or a cross. It is carried by bishops or abbots as a symbol of pastoral office. Matilda is holding a crozier in the previous selection.

6.14   The Pope's Prerogatives According to Gregory VII

In the following document, Gregory declared that the pope was the head of all society, and the Church was superior to the secular world. His concept of his office and papal power is outlined in the following excerpt from his "Dictatus Papae," a list of twenty-seven assertions included in his official register (1075). Although the list was never published, it is justly famous as a document that provides valuable evidence of the pope's view of his role in society just prior to his struggle with Henry IV.

(From Readings in European History, ed. by James Harvey Robinson [Boston: Ginn & Co., 1904], pp. 274–275.)

The Roman church was founded by God alone.

The Roman bishop [the Pope] alone is properly called universal.

He alone may depose bishops and reinstate them.

His legate, though of inferior grade, takes precedence, in a council, of all bishops and may render a decision of deposition against them.

He alone may use the insignia of empire.

The pope is the only person whose feet are kissed by all princes.

His title is unique in the world.

He may depose emperors.

No council may be regarded as a general one without his consent.

No book or chapter may be regarded as canonical without his authority.

A decree of his may be annulled by no one; he alone may annul the decrees of all.

He may be judged by no one.

No one shall dare to condemn one who appeals to the papal see.

The Roman church has never erred, nor ever, by the witness of Scripture, shall err to all eternity.

He may not be considered Catholic who does not agree with the Roman church.

The pope may absolve the subjects of the unjust from their allegiance [fealty].

Inasmuch as we have learned that, contrary to the ordinances of the holy fathers, the investiture with churches is, in many places, performed by lay persons, and that from this cause many disturbances arise in the Church by which the Christian religion is degraded, we decree that no one of the clergy shall receive the investiture with a bishopric, or abbey, or church, from the hand of an emperor, or king, or of any lay person, male or female. If he shall presume to do so, let him know that such investiture is void by apostolic authority, and that he himself shall lie under excommunication until fitting satisfaction shall have been made.

Following the ordinances of the holy fathers, as we decreed in our former councils held by the mercy of God concerning the regulation of ecclesiastical offices, so also now by apostolic authority we decree and confirm: that, if anyone shall henceforth receive a bishopric or abbey from the hands of any lay person, he shall by no means be reckoned among the bishops and abbots; nor shall any hearing be granted him as bishop or abbot. Moreover we further deny him the favor of St. Peter and entrance to the Church, until, coming to his senses, he shall surrender the position that he has appropriated through criminal ambition and disobedience—which is the sin of idolatry. We decree, moreover, that the same rule be observed in the case of inferior ecclesiastical positions.

Likewise if any emperor, king, duke, margrave, count, or any secular dignitary or person shall presume to bestow the investiture with bishoprics, or with any ecclesiastical office, let him know that he is bound by the bonds of the same condemnation. And, furthermore, unless he come to his senses and relinquish her prerogatives to the Church, let him feel, in this present life, the divine wrath both in body and estate, in order that at the Lord's coming his soul may be saved.

Questions for Discussion:

1. Describe and discuss the concept of papal power presented in Gregory's *Dictatus Papae*.
2. Which of the provisions constitute the most direct threats to imperial authority?

6.15   Letter from Henry IV

In 1075, Gregory issued an admonition to the king, writing that "... heaping wounds upon wounds, you have handed over the sees [bishoprics] of Fermo and Spoleto—if indeed a church may be given over by any human power—to persons entirely unknown to us . . ." Henry IV refused to recognize the provisions of the statement. The pope threatened to deprive the king of his office and excommunicate him, and in retaliation, Henry convened a synod of bishops. Claiming that Gregory was not worthy of the papacy because he had challenged royal authority, the council declared the pope to be a usurper. The king then issued a statement deposing the pope. There are two versions of this letter from Henry. The first was sent to Gregory with a copy of the renunciation passed by the synod. The second was a propaganda message that Henry circulated throughout Germany in order to gain support for his position.

(From *Imperial Lives and Letters of the Eleventh Century*, edited and translated by Theodor E. Mommsen & Karl F. Morrison, pp. 146–151. © 1962; reprinted 2000 Columbia University Press. Reprinted with the permission of the publisher.)

Version One:

(1) To the Pope:

Henry, King by the grace of God, to Hildebrand:[10]

Although hitherto I hoped for those things from you which are expected of a father and obeyed you in all respects to the great indignation of our vassals, I have obtained from you a requital (retaliation) suitable from one who was the most pernicious enemy of our life and kingly office. After you had first snatched away with arrogant boldness all the hereditary dignity owed me by that [Apostolic] See, going still further you tried with the most evil arts to alienate the kingdom of Italy. Not content with this, you have not feared to set your hand against the

---

[10]Hildebrand was Gregory's name before he became pope.

most reverend bishops, who are united to us like most cherished members and have harassed them with most arrogant affronts and the bitterest abuses against divine and human laws. While I let all these things go unnoticed through patience, you thought it not patience but cowardice and dared to rise up against the head itself, announcing, as you know, that (to use your own words) you would either die or deprive me of my life and kingly office.

Judging that this unheard of defiance had to be confuted not with words, but with action, I held a general assembly of all the foremost men of their kingdom, at their supplication. When they had made public through their true declaration (which you will hear from their own letter) those things they had previously kept silent through fear and reverence, they took public action to the end that you could no longer continue in the Apostolic See. Since their sentence seemed just and righteous before God and men, I also give my assent, revoking from you every prerogative of the papacy which you have seemed to hold, and ordering [you] to descend from the throne of the city whose patriciate is due me through the bestowal of God and the sworn assent of the Romans.

Version 2

Henry, King not by usurpation, but by the pious ordination of God, to Hildebrand, now not Pope, but false monk:

You have deserved such a salutation as this because of the confusion you have wrought; for you left untouched no order of the Church which you could make a sharer of confusion instead of honor, of malediction instead of benediction.

For to discuss a few outstanding points among many: Not only have you dared to touch the rectors of the holy Church—the archbishops, the bishops, and the priests, anointed of the Lord as they are— but you have trodden them under foot like slaves who know not what their lord may do. In crushing them you have gained for yourself acclaim from the mouth of the rabble. You have judged that all these know nothing, while you alone know everything. In any case, you have sedulously used this knowledge not for edification, but for destruction, so greatly

that we may believe Saint Gregory, whose name you have arrogated to yourself, rightly made this prophesy of you when he said: "From the abundance of his subjects, the mind of the prelate is often exalted, and he thinks that he has more knowledge than anyone else, since he sees that he has more power than anyone else."

And we, indeed, bore with all these abuses, since we were eager to preserve the honor of the Apostolic See. But you construed our humility as fear, and so you were emboldened to rise up even against the royal power itself, granted to us by God. You dared to threaten to take the kingship away from us—as though we had received the kingship from you, as though kingship and empire were in your hand and not in the hand of God.

Our Lord, Jesus Christ, has called us to kingship, but has not called you to the priesthood. For you have risen by these steps: namely, by cunning, which the monastic profession abhors, to money; by money to favor; by favor to the sword. By the sword you have come to the throne of peace, and from the throne of peace you have destroyed the peace. You have armed subjects against their prelates; you who have not been called by God have taught that our bishops who have been called by God are to be spurned; you have usurped for laymen the bishops' ministry over priests, with the result that these laymen depose and condemn the very men whom the laymen themselves received as teachers from the hand of God, through the imposition of the hands of bishops.

You have also touched me, one who, though unworthy, has been anointed to kingship among the anointed. This wrong you have done to me, although as the tradition of the holy Fathers has taught, I am to be judged by God alone and am not to be deposed for any crime unless—may it never happen—I should deviate from the Faith. For the prudence of the holy bishops entrusted the judgment and the deposition even of [the late Roman emperor] Julian the Apostate not to themselves, but to God alone. The true pope Saint Peter also exclaims, "Fear God, honor the king." You, however, since you do not fear God, dishonor me, ordained of Him.

Wherefore, when Saint Paul gave no quarter to an angel from heaven if the angel should preach heterodoxy, he did not except you who are now teaching heterodoxy throughout the earth. For he says, "If anyone, either I or an angel from heaven, preach any other gospel unto you than that which we have preached unto you, let him be accursed." Descend, therefore, condemned by this anathema and by the common judgment of all our bishops and of ourself. Relinquish the Apostolic See which you have arrogated. Let another mount the throne of Saint Peter, another who will not cloak violence with religion but who will teach the pure doctrine of Saint Peter.

I, Henry, King by the grace of God, together with all our bishops say to you: Descend! Descend!

Questions for Discussion:

1. Compare the two versions of Henry's letter. Are there significant differences, or is the variation merely rhetorical?
2. What are the specific issues Henry raises concerning the pope's attitude and behavior?

6.16　The Incident at Canossa

Gregory answered, inevitably, by declaring Henry to be excommunicated and deposed from his throne. The German princes, who were threatened by Henry's growing power, rebelled against their sovereign, and the king was forced to accede to the pope's demands. In 1077 he traveled to Canossa, in northern Italy, where the pope was staying. As the following document recounts, Henry appeared abjectly before Gregory, barefoot and as a humble penitent, begging forgiveness. The pope ultimately removed the sentence of excommunication, and "received him again into the bosom of Holy Mother Church."

(From *Power and the Holy in the Age of the Investiture Conflict,* by Maureen C. Miller. Boston: Bedford/St Martin's, 2005, pp. 97–98.)

Henry came, as he was ordered to, and since that castle had been enclosed by a triple wall, having been received within the space of the second wall, his band of retainers having been left outside, his regalia laid aside, displaying nothing pertaining to the kingship, showing no ceremony, with bare feet and fasting from morning until vespers, he waited for the decision of the Roman Pontiff. He did this a second day, and then a third. On the fourth day, finally having been admitted into the pope's presence, after many opinions were voiced on each side, he was finally absolved from the excommunication under these conditions: that on the day and at the place designated by the pope, he promptly call a general council of the German princes and respond to the accusations they had made, with this pope, if it seemed expedient, presiding as judge. By the council's ruling, it would

be decided according to ecclesiastical law whether Henry should retain the realm, if he cleared himself of the charges, or whether, with equanimity, he should be deprived of it, if by proven crimes he be held unworthy of the royal honor. . . . But if he, having cleared all obstructions, remained powerful and [even] much strengthened in the realm, nonetheless he would be subject to the Roman pontiff, always obedient to [the pope's] commands and admonishments, consenting to the correction of whatever customs had grown up against ecclesiastical laws in his realm and emerge as a joint-laborer [with the pope] to the best of is ability. Finally, if any of these provisions was not fulfilled, this absolution from the excommunication, now so fervently sought, would be void and he would be held a convicted and confessed [sinner], denied an audience for asserting his innocence, and the princes of the entire realm, all freed from their sworn bonds, might proceed to create another king whose election received their consent.

The king accepted the conditions gladly and promised with the most holy affirmations that he would keep them all. Nor did the promiser hold faith lightly.

Questions for Discussion:

1. What conditions did the pope place on the absolution of Henry from excommunication?
2. Describe and discuss how the pope's stipulations affected Henry's relationship with the German princes.

6.17   Decrees against Lay Investiture

Following the encounter at Canossa, the king proceeded to take measures to strengthen his royal authority. He moved to rally the support of the moderate princes, and proceeded to invest new bishops. In two instances he invalidated the elections of local candidates in order to appoint men who were loyal to the crown. These actions infuriated Gregory, whose motivation was to reform the German church and restrict lay influence; it seemed clear to the pope that this could not be effected as long as Henry controlled episcopal selection. In order to assert papal authority, decrees were passed against lay investiture at two synods, in 1078 and 1080.

(From *Select Historical Documents of the Middle Ages*, edited by E. F. Henderson [London: George Bell & Sons, 1892], pp. 365–66.)

Decree of November 19, 1078: Inasmuch as we have learned that, contrary to the establishments of the holy fathers, the investiture with churches is, in many places, performed by lay persons; and that from this cause many disturbances arise in the church by which the Christian religion is trodden under foot: we decree that no one of the clergy shall receive the investiture with a bishopric or abbey or church from the hand of an emperor or king or of any lay person, male or female. But if he shall presume to do so he shall clearly know that such investiture is bereft of apostolic authority, and that he himself shall lie under excommunication until fitting satisfaction shall have been rendered.

Decree of March 7, 1080: Following the statutes of the holy fathers, as, in the former councils which by the mercy of God we have held, we decreed concerning the ordering of ecclesiastical dignities, so also now we decree and confirm: that, if any one henceforth shall receive a bishopric or abbey from the hand of any lay person, he shall by no means be considered as among the number of the bishops or abbot. Moreover we further deny to him the favor of St. Peter and the entry of the church, until, coming to his senses, he shall desert the place that he has taken by the crime of ambition as well as by that of disobedience—which is the sin of idolatry. In like manner also we decree concerning the inferior ecclesiastical dignities.

Likewise if any emperor, king, duke, margrave, count, or any one at all of the secular powers or persons, shall presume to perform the investiture with bishoprics or with any ecclesiastical dignity,—he shall know that he is bound by the bonds of the same condemnation. And, moreover, unless he comes to his senses and relinquishes to the church her own prerogative, he shall feel, in this present life, the divine displeasure as well with regard to his body as to his other belongings: in order that, at the coming of the Lord, his soul may be saved.

Question for Discussion:

1. Do these two decrees simply reiterate the pope's position, or do they strengthen papal authority in a significant way? Discuss.

In the next installment of this saga, Henry, disregarding the pledge he made at Canossa, marched on Rome in 1084. The pope, taking refuge in the fortress of St. Angelo, appealed to his Norman ally, Robert Guiscard, Duke of Apulia and Calabria, for aid. The Norman armies moved to the capital, but looted the city and retreated to southern Italy, taking the pope along. He died a few months later, a bitter and disillusioned man. Henry spent the last few years of his reign attempting to curtail his rebellious nobility.

6.18   The Concordat of Worms (1122)

There were several more confrontations between popes and kings during the following decades, which served to clarify the issues and to propose ways of compromising. The Investiture Controversy was finally resolved in 1122, with the Agreements of Worms. The following documents record the promises of Pope Calixtus II (r. 1119–1124) and King Henry V (r. 1106–1125) regarding lay investiture.

The most important result of the lengthy struggle between popes and monarchs was an increase in the power of the papacy. Gregory's successors were able to make his concepts of papal authority a reality. They did this by establishing both theological and legal foundations for their hegemony, which they enforced through efficient institutions.

(From *A Source Book for Mediaeval History*, ed. by Oliver J. Thatcher and Edgar H. McNeal [New York: Charles Scribner's Sons, 1905], pp. 165–166.)

The Promise of Calixtus II

Calixtus, bishop, servant of the servants of God, to his beloved son, Henry, by the grace of God emperor of the Romans, Augustus.

We hereby grant that in Germany the elections of the bishops and abbots who hold directly from the crown shall be held in your presence, such elections to be conducted canonically and without simony or other illegality. In the case of disputed elections you shall have the right to decide between the parties, after consulting with the archbishop of the province and his fellow-bishops. You shall confer the regalia of the office upon the bishop or abbot elect by giving him the scepter, and this shall be done freely without exacting any payment from him; the bishop or abbot elect on his part shall perform all the duties that go with the holding of the regalia.

In other parts of the empire the bishops shall receive the regalia from you in the same manner within six months of their consecration, and shall in like manner perform all the duties that go with them. The undoubted rights of the Roman church, however, are not to be regarded as prejudiced by this concession. If at any time you shall have occasion to complain of the carrying out of these provisions, I will undertake to satisfy your grievances as far as shall be consistent with my office. Finally, I hereby make a true and lasting peace with you and with all of your followers, including those who supported you in the recent controversy.

The Promise of Henry V

In the name of the holy and undivided Trinity.

For the love of God and his holy church and of Pope Calixtus, and for the salvation of my soul, I, Henry, by the grace of God, emperor of the Romans, Augustus, hereby surrender to God and his apostles, Sts. Peter and Paul, and to the holy Catholic church, all investiture by ring and staff. I agree that elections and consecrations shall be conducted canonically and shall be free from all interference. I surrender also the possessions and regalia of St. Peter which have been seized by me during this quarrel, or by my father in his lifetime, and which are now in my possession, and I promise to aid the church to recover such as are held by any other persons. I restore also the possessions of all other churches and princes, clerical or secular, which have been taken away during the course of this quarrel, which I have, and promise to aid them to recover such as are held by any other persons.

Finally, I make true and lasting peace with pope Calixtus and with the holy Roman church and with all who are or have ever been of his party. I will aid the Roman church whenever my help is asked, and will do justice in all matters in regard to which the church may have occasion to make complaint.

All these things have been done with the consent and advice of the princes whose names are written below:

Adelbert, archbishop of Mainz; Frederick, archbishop of Cologne, etc.

Questions for Discussion:

1. What compromises were stipulated in the Agreements of Worms? Were there any unresolved issues?
2. Some scholars have viewed the "Investiture Controversy" as the beginning of a tradition that separated church and state. What provisions in the agreement can be cited in support of this theory?

Eastern Europe, Russia, and Scandinavia

Hungary

6.19 "Apostolic King": A Letter From Pope Sylvester II to King Stephen of Hungary

Since the time of Charlemagne, the Holy Roman Emperors had been dedicated to sponsoring the process of Christianization in eastern Europe and Russia. Saints Cyril (826–869) and Methodius (827–885) had brought the Christian message to the area in the ninth century, and as we have seen, Otto I established the bishopric of Magdeburg to serve as a center from which missionaries could be sent to convert the Slavic peoples. Following Otto's victory at the Battle of Lechfeld in 955 (Document 6.8), the Hungarians gradually established an organized government, and eventually officially adopted Christianity. Within three decades the Hungarian Prince Géza (r. 972–997) accepted missionaries from Germany, and his son Stephen (r. 997–1038) established the conversion of his country. In recognition of the new Christian monarchy, Pope Sylvester II sent a crown to Hungary, as well as the following letter.

(From *A Source Book for Medieval History*, by Oliver J. Thatcher and Edgar H. McNeal [New York: Charles Scribner's Sons, 1905], pp. 119–121.)

Sylvester, bishop, servant of the servants of God, to Stephen, king of the Hungarians, greeting and apostolic benediction. Your ambassadors, especially our dear brother, Astricus, bishop of Colocza, were received by us with the greater joy and accomplished their mission with the greater ease, because we had been divinely forewarned to expect an embassy from a nation still unknown to us. . . . Therefore we first give thanks to God the Father, and to our Lord Jesus Christ, because he has found in our time another David, and has again raised up a man after his own heart to feed his people Israel, that is, the chosen race of the Hungarians. Secondly, we praise you for your piety toward God and for your reverence for this apostolic see, over which, not by our own merits, but by the mercy of God, we now preside. Finally, we commend the liberality you have shown in offering to St. Peter yourself and your people and your

kingdom and possessions by the same ambassadors and letters. For by this deed you have clearly demonstrated that you already are what you have asked us to declare you [i.e., a king]. But enough of this; it is not necessary to commend him whom God himself has commended and whose deeds openly proclaim to be worthy of all commendation. Now therefore, glorious son, by the authority of omnipotent God and of St. Peter, the prince of apostles, we freely grant, concede, and bestow with our apostolic benediction all that you have sought from us and from the apostolic see; namely, the royal crown and name, the creation of the metropolitanate [archbishopric] of Gran, and of the other bishoprics. Moreover, we receive under the protection of the holy church the kingdom which you have surrendered to St. Peter, together with yourself and your people, the Hungarian nation; and we now give it back to you and to your heirs and successors to be held, possessed, ruled, and governed. And your heirs and successors, who shall have been legally elected by the nobles, shall duly offer obedience and reverence to us and to our successors in their own persons or by ambassadors, and shall confess themselves the subjects of the Roman church, who does not hold her subjects as slaves, but receives them all as children. They shall persevere in the catholic faith and the religion of our Lord and Savior Jesus Christ, and strive always to promote it. And because you have fulfilled the office of the apostles in preaching Christ and propagating his faith, and have tried to do in your realm the work of us and of our clergy, and because you have honored the same prince of apostles above all others, therefore by this privilege we grant you and your successors, who shall have been legally elected and approved by the apostolic see, the right to have the cross borne before you as a sign of apostleship, after you have been crowned with the crown which we send and according to the ceremony which we have committed to your ambassadors. And we likewise give you full power by our apostolic authority to control and manage all the churches of your realm, both present and future, as divine grace may guide you, as representing us and our successors. All these things are contained more fully and explicitly in that general letter which we have sent by our messenger to you and to your nobles and faithful subjects. And we pray that omnipotent God, who called you even from your mother's womb to the kingdom and crown, and who has commanded us to give you the crown which we had prepared for the duke of Poland, may increase continually the fruits of your good works, and sprinkle with the dew of his benediction this young plant of your kingdom, and preserve you and your realm and protect you from all enemies, visible and invisible, and, after the trials of the earthly kingship are past, crown you with an eternal crown in the kingdom of heaven. Given at Rome,

March 27, in the thirteenth indiction [the year 1000].

Questions for Discussion:

1. What reasons does the pope give for bestowing his apostolic benediction on King Stephen?
2. Who is the more powerful in the relationship between King Stephen and Pope Sylvester? What evidence can you draw from the letter to substantiate your opinion?

6.20 The Laws of King Stephen I of Hungary

The laws established by King Stephen I (1000–38) provided the legislative foundation for the Kingdom of Hungary. They were formulated to implement the teachings of Christianity, and to protect the religious institutions introduced by the king's father, Prince Géza (c. 972–97), which grew in number during the reign of Stephen. The provisions extended to both ecclesiastical and secular matters, providing legislation for the dioceses of the church as well as the royal counties.

The date of the compilation of the laws is uncertain, but scholars believe that the first book was issued during the early years of Stephen's reign, and the second in the last decade (c. 1030–38). The author is unknown, but historians speculate that the laws were written at the request of the king by a missionary from the west, perhaps a monk. It is evident that the legislation was influenced by papal canons and Frankish royal capitularies.

(From *The Laws of the Medieval Kingdom of Hungary*, vol. 1, trans. and ed. by János M. Bak, György Bónis, and James Ross Sweeney [Bakersfield, CA: Charles Schlacks, Jr.], pp. 1–3, 5–8. Reprinted by permission of the publisher.)

Preface to the royal law

The work of the royal office subject to the rule of divine mercy is by custom greater and more complete when nourished in the Catholic faith than any other office. Since every people use their own law, we, governing our monarchy by the will of God and emulating both ancient and modern caesars, and after reflecting upon the law, decree for our people too the way they should lead an upright and blameless life. Just as they are enriched by divine laws, so may they similarly be strengthened by secular ones, in order that as the good shall be made many by these divine laws so shall the criminals incur punishment. Thus we set out below in the following sentences what we have decreed.

1. The state of ecclesiastical things.

Should anyone, swollen with haughty pride, hold the house of God in contempt, or mistreat the possessions consecrated to God and placed for His service under protective royal immunity, or presume to injure them, let him be excommunicated as an invader and desecrator of the house of God. It is fitting that he should also feel the indignation of his lord, the king, whose good will be disparaged and whose good order subverted. Therefore the king commands that the immunity which he has granted be preserved unimpaired by everyone subject to him. He gives no assent nor should assent be given to foolish assertions that possessions ought not to be given to the church, that is, to the Lord of Lords. Rather they receive the protection of the king in the same way as his own inheritance. He gives even more attention to them, for, just as God is greater than man, the affairs of God take precedence over the possessions of mortals. Thus the man who glories more in his own than in the things of the Lord is badly deceived. The divinely ordained defender and keeper of the things of God ought not only to preserve them with diligent care, but also increase them, and those things which we have called the more important should be defended and increased even more than his own things. If anyone, therefore, should be so foolhardy as to try through the devices of his own wickedness to turn the king away from right purpose, and it should appear that no remedies can be effectively applied, even though he may be temporarily necessary, he should be cut off by the king and cast away just as according to the Gospel: If your foot, or your hand, or your eye offend you, cut it off, or pluck it out, and cast it from you.

. . .

8. The observance of the Lord's day.

If a priest or *ispan,* or any faithful person find anyone working on Sunday with oxen, the ox shall be confiscated and given to the men of the castle to be eaten; if a horse is used, however, it shall be confiscated, but the owner, if he wishes, may redeem it with an ox which should be eaten as has been said. If anyone uses other equipment, this tool and his clothing shall be taken, and he may redeem them, if he wishes, with a flogging.

9. More on the same.

Priests and *ispanok* shall enjoin village reeves to command everyone both great and small, men and women, with the exception of those who guard the fire, to gather on Sundays in the church. If someone remains at home through their negligence let them be beaten and shorn.

. . .

16. Drawing the sword.

In order that peace should remain firm and unsullied among the greater and the lesser of whatever station, we forbid anyone to draw the sword with the aim of injury. If anyone in his audacity should put this prohibition to the test, let him be killed by the same sword.

. . .

19. Gathering at church and those who mutter or chatter during mass.

If some persons, upon coming to church to hear the divine service mutter among themselves and disturb others by relating idle tales during the celebration of mass and by being inattentive to Holy Scripture with its ecclesiastical nourishment, they shall be expelled from the church in disgrace if they are older, and if they are younger and common folk they shall be bound in the narthex of the church in view of everyone and punished by whipping and by the shearing off of their hair.

. . .

27. The abduction of girls.

If any warrior debased by lewdness abducts a girl to be his wife without the consent of her parents, we decree that the girl should be returned to her parents, even if he raped her, and the abductor shall pay ten steers for the abduction, although he may afterwards have made peace with the girl's parents. If a poor man who is a commoner should attempt this, he shall compensate for the abduction with five steers.

28. Those who fornicate with bondwomen of another.

In order that freemen preserve their liberty undefiled, we wish to warn them. Any transgressor who fornicates with a bondwoman of another, should know that he has committed a crime, and he is to be whipped for the first offense. If he fornicates with her a second time, he should be whipped and shorn; but if he does it a third time he shall become a slave together with the woman, or he may redeem himself. If, however, the bondwoman should conceive by him and not be able to bear but dies in childbirth, he shall make compensation for her with another bondwoman.

The fornication of bondmen.

If a bondman of one master fornicates with the bondwoman of another, he should be whipped and shorn; and if the woman should conceive by him and dies in childbirth, the man shall be sold and half of his price shall be given to the master of the bond-woman, the other half shall be kept by the master of the bondman.

29. Those who desire bondwomen as wives.

In order that no one who is recognized to be a freeman should dare commit this offense, we set forth what has been decreed in this royal council as a source of terror and caution so that if any freeman should choose to marry a bondwoman of another with her master's consent, he shall lose the enjoy-ment of his liberty and become a slave forever.

30. Those who flee their wives by leaving the country.

In order that people of both sexes may remain and flourish under fixed law and free from injury, we establish in this royal decree that if anyone in his im-pudence should flee the country out of loathing for his wife, she shall possess everything which her hus-band rightfully possessed, so long as she is willing to wait for her husband, and no one shall force her into another marriage. If she voluntarily wishes to marry, she may take her own clothing leaving behind other goods, and marry again. If her husband, hearing this, should return, he is not allowed to replace her with anyone else, except with the permission of the bishop.

31. Theft committed by women.

Because it is terrible and loathsome to all to find men committing theft, and even more so for women, it is ordained by the royal council, that if a married woman commits theft, she shall be redeemed by her husband, and if she commits the same offense a sec-ond time, she shall be redeemed again; but if she does it a third time, she shall be sold.

...

33. On witches.

If a witch is found, she shall be led, in accor-dance with the law of judgment into the church and handed over to the priest for fasting and instruction in the faith. After the fast she may return home. If she is discovered in the same crime a second time, she shall fast and after the fast she shall be branded with the keys of the church in the form of a cross on her bosom, forehead, and between the shoulders. If she is discovered on a third occasion, she shall be handed over to the judge.

34. On sorcerers.

So that the creatures of God may remain far from all injury caused by evil ones and may not be exposed to any harm from them—unless it be by the will of God who may even increase it—we establish by decree of the council a most terrible warning to magicians and sorcerers that no person should dare to subvert the mind of any man or to kill him by means of sorcery and magic. Yet in the future if a man or a woman dare to do this he or she shall be handed over to the person hurt by sorcery or to his kindred, to be judged ac-cording to their will. If, however, they are found prac-ticing divination as they do in ashes or similar things, they shall be corrected with whips by the bishop.

Questions for Discussion:

1. Compare the laws of King Stephen with those we have studied before: (1) the Salic Law (Document 2.8), (2) the Capitularies of Charlemagne (Documents 4.7 and 4.8), and (3) the Statutes of William the Conqueror (Document 6.5). What similarities are there? Differences?
2. Were the monarchs (Clovis, Charlemagne, William the Conqueror, and Stephen) hoping to achieve similar objectives by enacting these codes? What were their goals?

Russia

6.21   Olga "the Beautiful": A Tenth-Century Russian Ruler

The first historical ruler of Kiev, the capital of Rus (the medieval Russian state), was the Varangian, Oleg, who ruled from 882 to 913. When he died he was succeeded by Prince Igor, who was able to maintain and spread Kievan authority throughout the eastern Slavic lands. Igor reigned until 945, when he was killed by the Drevelians[11] while collecting tribute from them. His sudden death left his widow Olga in charge of the state, since their son Sviatoslav was still a minor. As may be seen in this excerpt from The Russian Primary Chronicle, *she was a strong and forceful ruler who was able to maintain and strengthen Kievan authority. Olga was the first famous woman in Russian history. She converted to Christianity in 954 or 955, and eventually became a saint in the Russian Orthodox Church. Olga unsuccessfully attempted to convert her son, Sviatoslav, but her grandson Vladimir accepted the faith and declared Christianity to be the religion of the state.*

The Russian Primary Chronicle *is the most important historical work of early medieval Rus. Written about 1113, it was based upon Byzantine chronicles and oral sagas. Although the monk Nestor was long thought to be the author, modern scholars view the* Chronicle *as a composite work.*

(From *The Russian Primary Chronicle, Laurentian Text*, trans. by Samuel Hazzard Cross and Olgerd P. Sherbowitz-Wetzor. 3rd printing. Mediaeval Academy of America Publication 60. Cambridge, Mass.: The Mediaeval Academy of America, 1973, pp. 79–81. Reprinted by permission.)

Now Olga gave command that a large deep ditch should be dug in the castle with the hall, outside the city. Thus, on the morrow, Olga, as she sat in the hall, sent for the strangers, and her messengers approached them and said, "Olga summons you to great honor." But they replied, "We will not ride on horseback nor in wagons, nor go on foot; carry us in our boats." The people of Kiev then lamented, "Slavery is our lot. Our Prince is killed, and our Princess intends to marry their prince." So they carried the Derevlians in their boat. The latter sat on the cross-benches in great robes, puffed up with pride. They thus were borne into the court before Olga, and when the men had brought the Derevlians in, they dropped them into the trench along with the boat. Olga bent over and inquired whether they found the honor to their taste. They answered that it was worse than the death of Igor. She then commanded that they should be buried alive, and they were thus buried.

Olga then sent messages to the Derevlians to the effect that, if they really required her presence, they should send after her their distinguished men, so that she might go to their Prince with due honor, for otherwise her people in Kiev would not let her go. When the Derevlians heard this message, they gathered together the best men who governed the land of Dereva, and sent them to her. When the Derevlians arrived, Olga commanded that a bath should be made ready, and invited them to appear before her after they had bathed. The bathhouse was then heated, and the Derevlians entered in to bathe. Olga's men closed up the bathhouse behind them, and she gave orders to set it on fire from the doors, so that the Derevlians were all burned to death.

Olga then sent to the Derevlians the following message, "I am now coming to you, so prepare great quantities of mead in the city where you killed my husband, that I may weep over his grave and hold a funeral feast for him." When they heard these words, they gathered great quantities of honey and brewed mead. Taking a small escort, Olga made the journey with ease, and upon her arrival at Igor's tomb, she wept for her husband. She bade her followers pile up a great mound and when they had piled it up, she also gave command that a funeral feast should be held. Thereupon the Derevlians sat down to drink, and Olga bade her followers wait upon them. The Derevlians inquired of Olga where the retinue was which they had sent to meet her. She

---

[11]The Drevelians were an East Slavic tribe that had been defeated by Oleg during his territorial expansion.

replied that they were following with her husband's bodyguard. When the Derevlians were drunk, she bade her followers fall upon them, and went about herself egging on her retinue to the massacre of the Derevlians. So they cut down five thousand of them; but Olga returned to Kiev and prepared an army to attack the survivors.

Olga, together with her son Sviatoslav, gathered a large and valiant army, and proceeded to attack the land of the Derevlians. The latter came out to meet her troops, and when both forces were ready for combat, Sviatoslav cast his spear against the Derevlians. But the spear barely cleared the horse's ears, and struck against his leg, for the prince was but a child. Then Sveinald and Asmund said, "The prince has already begun battle; press on, vassals, after the prince." Thus they conquered the Derevlians, with the result that the latter fled, and shut themselves up in their cities.

Olga hastened with her son to the city of Iskorosten, for it was there that her husband had been slain, and they laid siege to the city. The Derevlians barricaded themselves within the city, and fought valiantly from it, for they realized that they had killed the prince, and to what fate they would in consequence surrender.

Olga remained there a year without being able to take the city, and then she thought out this plan. She sent into the town the following message: "Why do you persist in holding out? All your cities have surrendered to me and submitted to tribute, so that the inhabitants now cultivate their fields and their lands in peace. But you had rather die of hunger, without submitting to tribute." The Derevlians replied that they would be glad to submit to tribute, but that she was still bent on avenging her husband. Olga then answered, "Since I have already avenged the misfortune of my husband twice on the occasions when your messengers came to Kiev, and a third time when I held a funeral feast for him, I do not desire further revenge, but am anxious to receive a small tribute. After I have made peace with you, I shall return home again."

The Derevlians then inquired what she desired of them, and expressed their readiness to pay honey and furs. Olga retorted that at the moment they had neither honey nor furs, but that she had one small request to make. "Give me three pigeons," she said, "and three sparrows from each house. I do not desire to impose a heavy tribute, like my husband, but I require only this small gift from you, for you are impoverished by the siege." The Derevlians rejoiced, and collected from each house three pigeons and three sparrows, which they sent to Olga with their greetings. Olga then instructed them, in view of their submission, to return to their city, promising that on the morrow she would depart and return to her own capital. The Derevlians re-entered their city with gladness, and when they reported to the inhabitants, the people of the town rejoiced.

Now Olga gave to each soldier in her army a pigeon or a sparrow, and ordered them to attach by a thread to each pigeon and sparrow a piece of sulphur bound with small pieces of cloth. When night fell, Olga bade her soldiers release the pigeons and the sparrows. So the birds flew to their nests, the pigeons to the cotes, and the sparrows under the eaves. Thus the dove-cotes, the coops, the porches, and the haymows were set on fire. There was not a house that was not consumed, and it was impossible to extinguish the flames, because all the houses caught fire at once. The people fled from the city, and Olga ordered her soldiers to catch them. Thus she took the city and burned it, and captured the elders of the city. Some of the other captives she killed, while she gave others as slaves to her followers. The remnant she left to pay tribute.

She imposed upon them a heavy tribute, two parts of which went to Kiev, and the third to Olga in Vyshgorod; for Vyshgorod was Olga's city. She then passed through the land of Dereva, accompanied by her son and her retinue, establishing laws and tribute. Her trading posts and hunting-preserves are there still. Then she returned with her son to Kiev, her city, where she remained one year.

Questions for Discussion:

1. Discuss the unusual measures Olga took in guaranteeing control of her territory.
2. How does Olga compare with the Byzantine Empress Theodora (Document 2.15)? Do you see them as kindred spirits? Why or why not?

Scandinavia

6.22   The *Saga of Olaf Tryggvason*

Denmark was the first of the Viking kingdoms to adopt Christianity, during the reign of Harald (c. 940–c. 985). Although Harald's people were willing to accept Christ, they viewed him as less powerful than the ancient Norse gods. Recognizing that a unified religion provided a foundation for a stable country, Harald decreed that Christ alone would be worshiped in his kingdom. Nonetheless, the old folk religion survived tenaciously for two centuries. The Saga of Olaf Tryggvason, an epic tale written in the late twelfth century, tells of the struggle the Scandinavian kings faced in attempting to Christianize their people. As the following excerpt from the Saga recounts, Olaf, King of Norway (r. c. 995–c. 1000), used force to convert his unwilling subjects.

(From *The Sagas of Olaf Tryggvason and of Harald the Tyrant* [London: Williams and Norgate, 1911], pp. 66–70. Translation modernized.)

After the Danish King, Harald Gormson, had embraced the faith of Christ he made a proclamation throughout his dominions that all men must allow themselves to be baptized, and must turn to the true Faith. He himself enacted the order, making use of force and chastisement when nothing else could prevail. He sent two Earls who were called Urgutherjot and Brimiskiar to Norway with a great host, and their mission was that they should proclaim Christianity throughout the land; they should also do the same in Vik [in the region of Oslo], which had done direct homage unto Harald himself. They subjugated people readily enough, and many country folk were baptized there. However, it came to pass that after the death of Harald, his son Svein Two-beard soon went to war in Saxland, Frisland, and at last also in England, and then those in Norway who had received Christianity returned to sacrifices, as practiced in the old times in the north country. But after Olaf Tryggvason became King in Norway he lived for a long time in the summer at Vik, where he was made welcome with great show of affection; and to that place came also many of his kindred, and others who were allied to him, and many that had been good friends with his father. Then Olaf summoned

to him his uncle, and his step-father Lodin, and his step-brothers Thorgeirr and Hyrning, and laying the matter before them asked them most earnestly to join him with all their might, in supporting the spreading of the message of Christianity, for it was his wish to carry this message throughout the whole of his dominions. And he said that he would have it his way or die. "I will make all of you great and powerful men, for it is upon you that I chiefly rely because you are kin and brethren to me." So all were agreed to do what he asked them and to support him in that which he desired, and to have fellowship with all those who would follow their counsel. Then King Olaf proclaimed that he would invite all men in his realm to become Christians, and those who had agreed to this before did his bidding immediately, and as they were the most powerful of those present, all the others did according to their example. Thereafter all folk were baptized in the eastern part of Vik, and then the King went to the northern parts of the area and invited all men to receive Christianity; and those who said no he chastised severely, slaying some, and maiming some, and driving others away from the land. So it came to pass that all the people of that kingdom where his father King Tryggvi had ruled before, and likewise that which his kinsman Harald the Grenlander had possessed, received Christianity according to the bidding of King Olaf. Thus, in that summer and in the winter thereafter the people of the whole of Vik were made Christian.

Early in the spring-time King Olaf left Vik and went north-west to Agdir and summoned the peasants to a Thing, and told all men to let themselves be baptized. And because none of the peasantry dared to rise up against the King, the people were baptized wherever he went, and the men embraced Christianity.

There were many bold men in Hordaland who were related to Horda Kari. To him had been born four sons: firstly, Thorleif the Wise, secondly, Ogmund who was the father of Thorolf Skialg, the father of Erling of Soli; thirdly, Thord the father of Klyp the 'hersir' (he that slew Sigurd Sleva

Gunnhildson) and fourthly, Olmod the father of Ak-sel who was the father of Aslak Fitiar-skalli. This stock was the greatest and bravest in Hordaland.

Now when these kinsmen heard the disquieting tidings that the King was coming from the east along the coast, and with him a large host who forced all men to break the old laws of the old gods, and imposed penalties with sore chastisements on all those who disobeyed him, they agreed to meet together to make plans for they knew that the King would soon be upon them; it was therefore agreed among them that they would one and all be present at the Gula-Thing, and there they would meet Olaf Tryggvason.

As soon as he came to Rogaland Olaf summoned a Thing, and the peasantry came in great numbers, fully armed. And they made speeches and held consultations among themselves, and chose three men who were the most eloquent among them to answer the King at the Thing. Moreover, they spoke against him and made it known that they would not suffer their laws to be broken even if it were the King who ordained them. Now when the peasants were assembled at the Thing and the Thing was opened, King Olaf rose up and spoke, talking at the beginning smoothly and fairly, although it was obvious from his words that it was his will that they should accept Christianity. And after he had finished with fair words he vowed that those who spoke against him and would not do his bidding would bring upon themselves his wrath and chastisement. Now when the King had finished speaking one of

the yeomen who was the most eloquent stood up; he had been chosen as the first to answer King Olaf. But when he was about to speak was he taken with such a coughing and choking that he could not speak a word, and he sat down again. Even though it had gone badly for the first man, another man rose to his feet to take up the answer, but when he began to talk he stammered so much that he couldn't get a word out. Then all who were present fell to laughing, so that the yeoman sat down again. Then the third man stood up with the intent of speaking against King Olaf, but he was so hoarse and husky that no man could hear what he said, so he also sat down. Now none of the chosen yeomen was left to speak against the King, and no one else would answer him, so the resistance that had been planned came to nothing. In the end, therefore, all were agreed to do the King's bidding, and all the Thing folk were christened there and then before the King departed from them.

Questions for Discussion:

1. Do you see any similarities between the *Saga of Olaf Tryggvason* and the Anglo-Saxon epic *Beowulf* (Document 2.9)? Describe these.
2. How does the *Saga* continue the governance tradition of the Salic Law (Document 2.8)?
3. Compare the actions of Olaf in Christianizing his people with those of Charlemagne described in Document 4.5. What are the similarities? The differences?

The Byzantine Empire

6.23   Preface to *On Ceremonies* by Emperor Constantine VII

Ritualistic court behavior was an important feature of life in the Byzantine Empire, especially the elaborate ceremonies surrounding the emperor and his entourage. The sixth-century mosaic images of Justinian and Theodora (Document 2.15) offer early examples of the impressive

pageantry associated with the monarchy, and the rich tradition was expanded during the reigns of their successors. These activities did a great deal to impress the imperial image on the minds of the populace. The numerous ceremonies were so complex that lengthy handbooks were written for the courtiers who guided the protocol. One of the most important of these was On Ceremonies, *written by the Emperor Constantine VII Porphyrogenitus in the tenth century. In the preface, the emperor set forth the reasons for extensive courtly ritual; the ceremonies were significant symbolic actions that produced responses of admiration and awe, thereby impressing the imperial image on the minds of the people. Such reactions also served to engender respect for the government.*

(From *Byzantium: Church, Society, and Civilization Seen through Contemporary Eyes,* ed. by Deno John Geanakoplos. © 1984 by The University of Chicago Press. All rights reserved.)

Some, who do not much care for necessary matters, would perhaps view this present enterprise [the composition of this manual] as superfluous; for us, however, this work is very dear, for it appears worthy of all our care and more fitting, in fact, than all other cares, since, thanks to a praiseworthy ritual, the imperial power appears more majestic, grows in prestige, and at the same time evokes the admiration both of strangers and of our own subjects.

Many things, in fact, by nature tend to disappear with the passing of time, which has created and exhausted them. Of this number is the great and precious matter that is the expression and codification of imperial ceremonial. Because it was neglected and, so to speak, perishing, the empire was viewed truly as without adornment and without beauty. Moreover, just as one would call disorderly a body badly constituted, one in which the limbs are joined together pell-mell and without unity, so it is with the imperial government when it is not conducted and governed with order. When this is the case, the state differs in nothing from the conduct of an uneducated individual.

In order to escape that condition, [i.e. being swept along in disorder], and so that we do not appear to insult the imperial majesty, we have

believed it would be appropriate to gather together carefully, from the right and the left, whatever was established by the ancients and transmitted by their contemporaries or seen by ourselves and established for us and introduced in our time, to set it forth in the present work in a synthesis easily understood, and to pass on to our successors the tradition of ancestral customs [which had] fallen into disuse. They will be like flowers we gather from the meadows to embellish incomparably the imperial splendor. They will be like a mirror, radiant and of a perfect clarity. And we will place them in the center of the palace [and] will see there what is appropriate to the imperial power and what befits the senatorial organization.

And, in order that our text be clear and of easy understanding, we have employed a common and simple style, and we have used the current language for words and expressions applied a long time ago to each matter. Therefore, may the imperial power, being employed with measure and good order, reproduce the harmonious movement that the Creator gives to this entire universe, and may [the empire] appear to our subjects more majestic and, at the same time, more pleasing and admirable. We must therefore speak of each ceremony in order to say how and according to what rules it is necessary to carry it out and complete it.

Questions for Discussion:

1. What is the primary reason given by the emperor for compiling his manual?
2. How does the Byzantine concept of imperial majesty compare with the documents concerning Otto III (Interpreting the Evidence, Documents 6.9 through 6.11)? Are there any differences?
3. Discuss the emperor's concept of "good order."

Chapter 7

Monastic Reform, Pilgrimage, and Crusade

The economic growth and political development of Europe that began after the year 1000 continued to progress during the eleventh and twelfth centuries. This era also witnessed significant geographical expansion and spiritual regeneration, as the European people experienced renewed religious fervor. This religiosity was part of a huge religious revival among both clergy and laypeople that came to encompass, among other things, monastic reform, heresy, the Investiture Controversy, and new forms of religious art. One impetus for the renewal came from Carolingian monastic purification movements that began as early as the reign of Charlemagne. An additional call for change resulted from protests against the continuous violence caused by conflict between the feudal lords. The "Peace of God" and "Truce of God" movements

presented in Documents 5.7 And 5.8 represented early attempts by the Church to curb the violence of the feudal nobility.

Some members of the aristocracy sympathized with the plea for protection and freedom by the common people and the monks. One important example was William, Duke of Aquitaine, who founded a monastery at Cluny (in Burgundy, France) in 910. The charter promised protection of the monks from marauding magnates, and guaranteed that they would have free and independent rights to elect the abbot, without lay interference. William provided holdings for the monastery that would furnish support indefinitely, and stipulated that the monks would follow the Rule of Saint Benedict (see Document 1.15). The monastic establishment at Cluny

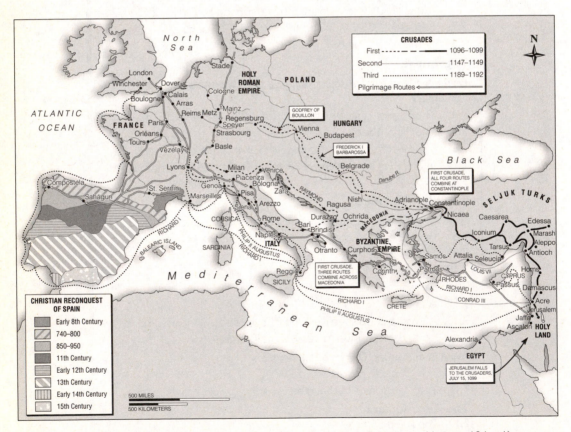

Pilgrimage and Crusade Routes in the Twelfth Century (From Kagan et al., *The Western Heritage*, 10th ed.)

differed from earlier foundations in that the monks devoted themselves to prayer and the performance of the liturgy, rather than accepting the obligation of manual labor. During the following two centuries, the monastery at Cluny became very wealthy, and the monks developed elaborate liturgical rites in which they used costly ecclesiastical ornaments. An account by Odilo of Cluny describes the services and processions in detail.

By the twelfth century some monastic critics saw the lifestyle and practices of the monks at Cluny as having departed from the obligations of poverty, chastity, and obedience stipulated by the Rule of Saint Benedict. *A particularly vocal critic was Saint Bernard of Clairvaux (1090–1153), who was an early member of a new order, the Cistercians, that emerged partly as a result of such criticism (Document 7.2). His objections to Cluniac luxury were vehemently expressed in his writing, as the excerpt in Document 7.3 demonstrates.*

Another example of the growing religious ardor of the European people was the practice of participating in pilgrimages. Although journeys to Jerusalem and Rome had been popular throughout late antiquity and the early Middle Ages, more and more people undertook these travels in the eleventh and twelfth centuries. Accounts by two pilgrims to Jerusalem demonstrate the motivations and circumstances of such journeys (Documents 7.4 and 7.5). Throughout Europe, men and women who could not make the long trip to the Holy Land went to local shrines to venerate the relics of saints. Two of the most popular of these sites were Santiago de Compostela and Canterbury, England. Some pilgrims recorded their experiences, and excerpts from their diaries and guidebooks appear in Documents 7.6 and 7.7.

One of the motives expressed by William of Aquitaine in the foundation document of Cluny was his quest for "the redemption of his soul." This search for personal salvation was also an important factor in the crusading movement, as European knights were exhorted to take back the sacred Christian areas that had fallen to the Muslims during the seventh and eighth centuries. The First Crusade was initiated by Pope Urban II (r. 1088–1099), whose words at the Council of Clermont in 1095 stirred the warriors of Europe to undertake this mission. Although there is no documentary record of his remarks, several eyewitnesses recorded their impressions of the speech in

later writings. A comparison of the reactions of the author of the Gesta Francorum *("Deeds of the Franks"), Fulcher of Chartres, Robert the Monk, and Balderic of Dol, offers a vision of the power of the pope's message. (Documents 7.8–7.11).*

The pope's speech also galvanized an unofficial crusade, enlisting people from the lower classes as well as some nobles; they journeyed forth in a movement often called the "Peasants' Crusade." As they traveled through Germany they perpetrated brutal massacres on the Jewish residents. An account of these disasters is contained in the Chronicle of Solomon bar Simson; *an excerpt is included in Document 7.12.*

A woman's perspective on the crusade and the character of the Frankish warriors was given by the historian Anna Comnena (1093–1153). The Alexiad, *her account of the reign of her father, Alexius I (1048–1118), includes commentary on the motivations and behavior of the crusaders (Document 7.13).*

Quite naturally, the Muslims experienced the events of the crusade from a different point of view. A vivid Muslim account was written by the historian Ibn al-Athir, whose words offer an interesting comparison with those of the Christian historians (Document 7.14).

A new monastic military order, the Templars, was established in the Holy Land after the success of the First Crusade in order to protect the pilgrimage and trade routes. These men combined the spiritual quest of the monk with the military zeal of the medieval knight, as we shall see in two accounts of the founding of the order (Documents 7.15 and 7.16).

The crusading fervor also inspired the "Reconquista," as the Christians of northern Iberia fought to reclaim the southern areas that had been controlled by Islam since the eighth century (see Document 3.9). The poem El Cid *recounts the adventures of a Spanish nobleman whose involvement is rhapsodized in the verses (Document 7.17). A prose account of the Conquest of Lisbon offers further evidence of the progress of the crusade against the Muslims on the Iberian Peninsula (Document 7.18).*

This chapter contains documents that reflect all of these developments, and demonstrate the variety and complexity of the spiritual and political experiences of this era.

The Monastic Reform Movement

INTERPRETING THE EVIDENCE

7.1   Foundation Charter of the Abbey of Cluny (910), Groundplan, and Description by Odilo of Cluny

The origins of the movement of regeneration began with Carolingian monastic renewal as advocated by Benedict of Aniane (c. 745–821) and other reformers, who hoped to return monasteries to the strict practice of the Rule of Saint Benedict *(Document 1.15). Another potent factor may be found in the popular protests against the endemic warfare of the ninth and tenth centuries as peasants cried out against the oppression of powerful and warlike lords, calling for protection by the Church. As we have seen, an early response by the ecclesiastical councils resulted in measures known as the "Peace of God" and "Truce of God" (Documents 5.7 and 5.8). These deterrents served to lessen the degree of conflict.*

The protests were often led by monks, who demanded protection from attacks on their monasteries. The first monastic establishment to be granted independence and protection was a donation by William, Duke of Aquitaine, who provided the foundation for a new Benedictine Abbey at Cluny in Burgundy. The charter contains a list of the properties given to the abbey by the duke, and makes clear the duke's expectations concerning the carrying out of monastic duties according to the Rule of Saint Benedict *(see Chapter 1), emphasizing the performance of the liturgy.*

The abbey at Cluny differed from earlier Benedictine monasteries in several ways, including its organizational structure, its regulations prohibiting landholding based on feudal responsibilities, and its focus on prayer and liturgy. Whereas earlier Benedictine monasteries had been only loosely associated with one another, the Cluniac order eventually created an extensive federation in which the subsidiary monasteries were known as priories, and the leaders, or priors, were responsible to the abbot of Cluny. They held meetings at

Cluny once a year to submit reports and to deal with matters of administration. The foundation charter indicates that the monks were free of feudal responsibilities, and, as noted in the excerpt, the devotion of the monks to the performance of the liturgy was the central focus of their monastic practice.

(From *Select Historical Documents of the Middle Ages*, trans. and ed. by Ernest F. Henderson [London: G. Bell & Sons, 1925], pp. 329–333.)

The Foundation Charter of the Order of Cluny. Sept. 11, 910 A.D.

To all right thinkers it is clear that the providence of God has so provided for certain rich men that, by means of their transitory possessions, if they use them well, they may be able to merit everlasting rewards. As to which thing, indeed, the divine word, showing it to be possible and altogether advising it, says: "The riches of a man are the redemption of his soul." (Prov. xiii.) I, William, count and duke by the grace of God, diligently pondering this, and desiring to provide for my own safety while I am still able, have considered it advisable—nay, most necessary, that from the temporal goods which have been conferred upon me I should give some little portion for the gain of my soul. I do this, indeed, in order that I who have thus increased in wealth may not, perchance, at the last be accused of having spent all in caring for my body, but rather may rejoice, when fate at last shall snatch all things away, in having reserved something for myself. Which end, indeed, seems attainable by no more suitable means than that, following the precept of Christ: "I will make his poor my friends" (Luke xvi. 9), and making the act not a temporary but a lasting one, I should support at my own expense a congregation of monks. And this is my trust, this my hope, indeed, that although I myself am unable to despise all things, nevertheless, by receiving despisers of the world, whom I believe to be righteous, I may receive the reward of the righteous. Therefore be it known to all who live in the unity of the faith and who await the mercy of Christ, and to those who shall succeed them and who shall continue to exist until the end of the world, that, for the love of God and of our Savior Jesus Christ, I hand over from my own rule to the holy apostles, Peter, namely, and Paul, the possessions over which I hold sway, the town of Cluny, namely, with the court and demesne manor, and the church in honor of St. Mary the mother of God and of St. Peter the prince of the apostles, together with all the things pertaining to it, the vills, indeed, the chapels, the serfs of both sexes, the vines, the fields, the meadows, the woods, the waters and their outlets, the mills, the incomes and revenues, what is cultivated and what is not, all in their entirety. Which things are situated in or about the country of Macon, each one surrounded by its own bounds. I give, moreover, all these things to the aforesaid apostles—I, William, and my wife Ingelberga—first for the love of God; then for the soul of my lord king Odo, of my father and my mother; for myself and my wife—for the salvation, namely, of our souls and bodies;—and not least for that of Ava who left me these things in her will; for the souls also of our brothers and sisters and nephews, and of all our relatives of both sexes; for our faithful ones who adhere to our service; for the advancement, also, and integrity of the catholic religion. Finally, since all of us Christians are held together by one bond of love and faith, let this donation be for all,—for the orthodox, namely, of past, present or future times. I give these things, moreover, with this understanding, that in Cluny a regular monastery shall be constructed in honor of the holy apostles Peter and Paul, and that there the monks shall congregate and live according to

the rule of St. Benedict, and that they shall possess, hold, have and order these same things unto all time. In such wise, however, that the venerable house of prayer which is there shall be faithfully frequented with vows and supplications, and that celestial converse shall be sought and striven after with all desire and with the deepest ardor; and also that there shall be sedulously directed to God prayers, beseechings and exhortations as well for me as for all, according to the order in which mention has been made of them above. And let the monks themselves, together with all the aforesaid possessions, be under the power and dominion of the abbot Berno, who, as long as he shall live, shall preside over them regularly according to his knowledge and ability. But after his death, those same monks shall have power and permission to elect anyone of their order whom they please as abbot and rector, following the will of God and the rule promulgated by St. Benedict,—in such a way that neither by the intervention of our own or of any other power may they be impeded from making a purely canonical election. Every five years, moreover, the aforesaid monks shall pay to the church of the apostles at Rome ten shillings to supply them with lights; and they shall have the protection of those same apostles and the defense of the Roman pontiff; and those monks may, with their whole heart and soul, according to their ability and knowledge, build up the aforesaid place. We will, further, that in our times and in those of our successors, according as the opportunities and possibilities of that place shall allow, there shall daily, with the greatest zeal be performed there works of mercy towards the poor, the needy, strangers and pilgrims. It has pleased us also to insert in this document that, from this day, those same monks there congregated shall be subject neither to our yoke, nor to that of our relatives, nor to the sway of the royal might, nor to that of any earthly power. And, through God and all his saints, and by the awful day of judgment, I warn and objure that no one of the secular princes, no count, no bishop whatever, not the pontiff of the aforesaid Roman see, shall invade the property of

(continued)

these servants of God, or alienate it, or diminish it, or exchange it, or give it as a benefice to anyone, or constitute any prelate over them against their will. And that such unhallowed act may be more strictly prohibited to all rash and wicked men, I subjoin the following, giving force to the warning. I adjure ye, O holy apostles and glorious princes of the world, Peter and Paul, and thee, O supreme pontiff of the apostolic see, that, through the canonical and apostolic authority which you have received from God, you do remove from participation in the holy church and in eternal life, the robbers and invaders and alienators of these possessions which I do give to you with joyful heart and ready will; and be protectors and defenders of the aforementioned place of Cluny and of the servants of God abiding there, and of all these possessions—on account of the clemency and mercy of the most holy Redeemer. If anyone—which Heaven forbid, and which, through the mercy of God and the protection of the apostles I do not think will happen,—whether he be a neighbor or a stranger, no matter what his condition or power, should, through any kind of wile, attempt to do any act of violence contrary to this deed of gift which we have ordered to be drawn up for love of almighty God and for reverence of the chief apostles Peter and Paul: first, indeed, let him incur the wrath of almighty God, and let God remove him from the land of the living and wipe out his name from the book of life, and let his portion be with those who said to the Lord God: Depart from us; and, with Dathan and Abiron whom the earth, opening its jaws, swallowed up, and hell absorbed while still alive, let him incur everlasting damnation. And being made a companion of Judas let him be kept thrust down there with eternal tortures, and, lest it seem to human eyes that he pass through the present world with impunity, let him experience in his own body, indeed, the torments of future damnation, sharing the double disaster with Heliodorus and Antiochus, of whom one being coerced with sharp blows scarcely escaped alive; and the other, struck down by the divine will, his members putrefying and swarming with vermin, perished most

miserably. And let him be a partaker with other sacrilegious persons who presume to plunder the treasure of the house of God; and let him, unless he come to his senses, have as enemy and as the one who will refuse him entrance into the blessed paradise, the key-bearer of the whole hierarchy of the church, and, joined with the latter, St. Paul; both of whom, if he had wished, he might have had as most holy mediators for him. But as far as the worldly law is concerned, he shall be required, the judicial power compelling him, to pay a hundred pounds of gold to those whom he has harmed; and his attempted attack, being frustrated, shall have no effect at all. But the validity of this deed of gift, endowed with all authority, shall always remain inviolate and unshaken, together with the stipulation subjoined. Done publicly in the city of Bourges. I, William, commanded this act to be made and drawn up, and confirmed it with my own hand.

Questions for Discussion:

1. What did William mean by the following phrase: "although I myself am unable to despise all things, nevertheless, by receiving despisers of the world, whom I believe to be righteous, I may receive the reward of the righteous"?
2. Analyze the bequest. Would this property provide the monastery with a great deal of wealth?
3. What did William hope to achieve through his endowment?
4. What provisions did the charter make to ensure that the monks would not be subject to secular involvement?

By the twelfth century, Cluny had become one of the wealthiest and most important monasteries in Europe. Under the fifth abbot Odilo (994–1048), the original wooden structures of the cloister were replaced by buildings of stone. The groundplan shows the areas of Odilo's rebuilding and the expansion of the monastery. Fortunately for historians, the abbot wrote a description of the church as it existed at the time of his predecessor, Abbot Majolus, and described his own plans for the monastery.

(From *Early Medieval Art 300–1150: Sources and Documents*, ed. by Caecilia Davis-Weyer. Englewood Cliffs, NJ: Prentice Hall Publishers, 1971, pp. 129–132. Reprinted by permission.)

A Description of the Monastery

The church is 140 feet long, and 43 feet high and has 160 glass windows. The chapter house is 45 feet long and 34 feet wide. It has 4 windows to the east, 3 to the north, 12 galleries to the west, each with 2 columns. The auditory is 30 feet long. The commissary is 90 feet long. The dormitory is 160 feet long and 34 feet wide. There are 97 glass windows, all the height of a man standing on tiptoe and 2 ½ feet wide. The walls are 23 feet high. The latrine is 70 feet long and 23 feet wide. 45 seats have been arranged in this place and above each seat is a little window in the wall, 2 feet high and ½ foot wide. And above the seats is a timber construction and above this construction of wood are 17 windows, 3 feet high and 1 ½ feet wide. The heated room is 25 feet wide and 25 feet long. It is 75 feet from the door of the latter to the entrance of the church. The refectory is 90 feet long, 25 feet wide, with walls 23 feet high, with 8 glass windows on each side, which are 5 feet high and 3 feet wide. The kitchen for the monks is 30 feet long and 25 feet wide and so is the kitchen for the laymen. The buttery is 70 feet long and 60 feet wide. The almonry is 10 feet wide and 60 feet long, its length corresponding to the width of the buttery. The galilee[1] is 65 feet long and 2 towers stand before it and beneath them is the atrium where the laymen stand so that they do not get in the way of processions. The distance from the south door to the north door is 280 feet. The sacristy together with the tower in front of it is 58 feet long. The oratory of the Virgin is 45 feet long and 20 feet wide with walls 23 feet high. The first room of the infirmary is 27 feet wide and 23 feet long with 8 beds, and as many latrines are outside in the portico along the wall of the same building, and the cloister of the same building is 12 feet wide. The second room and the third and the fourth are arranged in the same way. The fifth, where the sick come to have their feet washed on the Sabbath and where dead brethren are enshrouded, may be smaller. The sixth cell should be arranged as the place where the servants wash the platters and other utensils. Next to the galilee a palace should be constructed 135 feet long and 30 feet wide for the reception of all those guests who come to the monastery on horseback. On one side of this house 40 beds with as many covered pillows should be prepared where as many men may rest, with 40 latrines. And on the other side 30 little beds should be made where ladies and other respectable women may rest, with 30 latrines where they may satisfy their needs undisturbed. In the middle of the palace should be placed tables like those in the refectory, where both men and women may eat. For great feasts this house should be adorned with draperies and coverings and cloths spread over the benches. In front of it there should be another house, 45 feet long and 30 feet wide, for its length should extend to the sacristy and in it should sit all the tailors and cobblers to sew and stitch what the chamberlain orders them to make. And a table should be prepared for them there that is 30 feet long and another table should be placed by it so that the width of both is 7 feet. Between that structure and the sacristy, the church, and also the galilee there should be a cemetery where laymen may be buried. From the southern gate to the northern gate on the west side a house should be constructed, 280 feet long and 25 feet wide, and stables should be made there for horses, divided into stalls. Above the stables there should be an upper story where the servants eat and sleep, and a table 80 feet long and 4 feet wide should be provided for them. And those guests who cannot be fed in the guesthouse mentioned above should eat here. And at the entrance of this house there should be a suitable place where those men may go who arrive on foot, and they should receive free food and drink from the almoner according to their needs. At a distance of 60 feet from the

---

[1] A western ante-room of the church proper.

refectory, at the entrance of the latrine, 12 cellars should be made and as many bathtubs, where at set times baths may be prepared for the brethren. And behind that place the house for the novices should be constructed. It should be divided into 4 rooms, the first for meditation, the second for meals, the third for sleep, and a fourth, on one side, as a latrine. Close by should be another building where goldsmiths and jewellers and glaziers may come to practice their arts. Between the bath rooms and the dwellings of the novices and the goldsmiths there should be a building 125 feet long and 25 feet wide and its length should extend all the way to the bakery. The latter together with the tower at its entrance, is 70 feet long and 20 feet wide.

Questions for Discussion:

1. Compare the groundplan of Cluny with that of St. Gall in Chapter 1 (Document 1.15). Do you see any differences or "improvements"?
2. Odilo's description includes provisions for guests and for goldsmiths and jewelers. Comment.

Rather than engaging in physical labor themselves, the monks hired workers to tend to the agricultural necessities of the monastery; thus, they could devote themselves to prayer and the performance of the liturgy. Over time the ceremonies became more and more elaborate, and costly ecclesiastical objects were commissioned for the services. The records that contain Odilo's description of the monastery also provide details concerning the services and processions that took place at the abbey. As may be seen, the monks used exquisite decorations, sumptuous vestments, and precious liturgical objects in their worship services; this practice was a continuation and expansion of the ceremonial rites present since the early Christian centuries, and was a natural outgrowth of the Cluniac devotion to prayer and the liturgy. However, the Cluniac customs drew much criticism, most vehemently addressed by Saint Bernard of Clairvaux (see Documents 7.2 and 7.3), who called for a reform that would achieve the monastic ideal more closely.

The Procession on Palm Sunday

How the fathers should celebrate Palm Sunday. On the Saturday before Palm Sunday three coverings should be placed before vespers over the three altars behind the principal altar. The reliquaries[2] of the saints should be fitted onto wooden frames so that they can be properly carried. The banners and the palm branches with flowers should be prepared so that there will be no delay in the morning. And bench covers for the choir should also be prepared. After the mass of the day has been said, the main altar should be adorned with a cover that is interwoven with gold. Every bell should ring for Vespers. . . .

After coming back into the church they should celebrate Terce,[3] after which the priest should go before the altar and standing at its northern corner he should bless the branches of the palms and the other trees. He should not say "The Lord be with you" and "Let us pray" at that point. But as soon as the prayer over the palms and flowers begins, and after they have been blessed, he should sprinkle blessed water on them and accepting the golden thurible[4] he should cense the main altar first and then the palm branches. The sextons of the church should take the palms and give them one after the other to the Lord Abbot and to all the brethren standing in the choir. And while they begin to hand them out the librarian should intone the antiphon of the three youths. And the librarian should take the tunics and make those younger brothers whom he has selected to carry the gospel books put them on. Then the lay brothers should take four crosses, two gold thuribles, the holy water, four candlesticks, and one of the priests should take the arm of St. Maurus [a relic owned by the

---

[2]Reliquaries are containers, made of wood, silver, or gold, that store bones, teeth, locks of hair, or shreds of garments belonging to the saints. They are often carried in processions such as the one being described, and are venerated by the faithful. The arm of St. Maurus would have been encased in an arm-shaped container of silver or gold, perhaps with inlaid with precious gems.
[3]Terce was the third canonical hour—about 9 A.M.
[4]A thurible was an incense burner, suspended on chains, which the priest (or abbot) used to cense the altar.

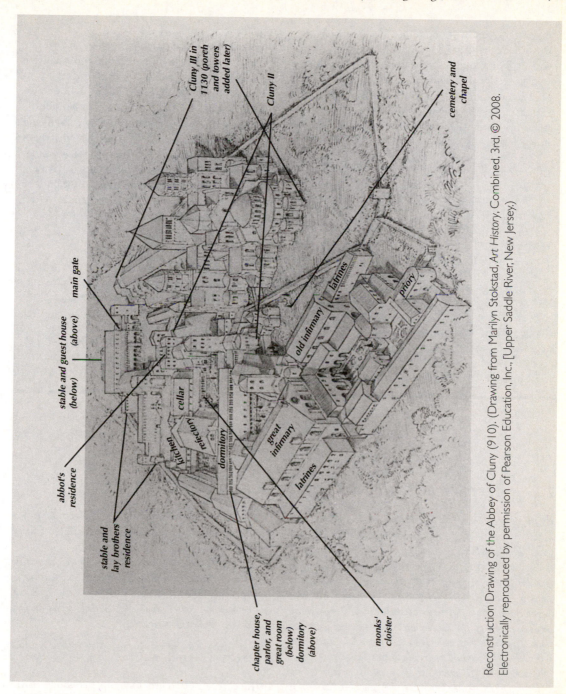

Reconstruction Drawing of the Abbey of Cluny (910). (Drawing from Marilyn Stokstad, *Art History*, Combined, 3rd, © 2008. Electronically reproduced by permission of Pearson Education, Inc., [Upper Saddle River, New Jersey].)

monastery] and three or eight priests should carry the other ornaments. Of sixteen other lay brothers two or four should carry the likeness of St. Peter with its relics and another two or four the body of St. Marcellus, the pope, and two or four others the casket of St. Gregory and two or four others the relics of many other holy fathers. They should go in the following order:

First about 30 servants with banners, walking two by two, banners,
the relics of many holy fathers, carried by four or two brothers,
the relics of Pope Gregory, carried by four or two brothers,
the relics of the holy Pope Marcellus, carried by four or two brothers,
St. Peter's likeness should be carried by four brothers . . .

The description of the processional order continues, mentioning crosses, holy water, a crucifix, two thuribles, two candlesticks, two scepters, the "apple" (probably a globe given to the abbey by King Henry II), and the reliquary with the arm of St. Maurus.

The icon [probably the likeness of Saint Peter owned by the abbey] may be omitted on that day and it is also permitted to omit the apple and the scepters on this day on account of the weather.

After these the children follow two by two with their teachers, and afterwards other adults, namely the Priors proceeding two by two during the antiphon, having gathered together with them those who are able and trained to sing. Last comes the Lord Abbot followed by all ranks of laymen. While they leave the church all the bells should be rung; the two largest bells should continue to ring until the procession returns to the Galilee.

Questions for Discussion:

1. In your experience, do elaborate processions such as these take place in the contemporary world? Describe the circumstances.
2. Do you see any contradictions between the religious practices at Cluny and the *Rule of Saint Benedict*? (See Document 1.15).

7.2   Bernard of Clairvaux and the Cistercian Order

By the twelfth century the Benedictine monks at abbeys such as Cluny had amassed a significant amount of wealth, and many had developed a somewhat lavish lifestyle. Their seeming attention to luxury was severely criticized by monks who believed in a return to the austere monastic ideals of poverty. One of the most important and vocal critics was Saint Bernard of Clairvaux (1090–1153), who was an early member of the Cistercian order—a new monastic foundation that reflected his values; it was dedicated to a renewal of the original precepts of Saint Benedict.

In 1115, Bernard and a small group of his fellow monks left the Cistercian monastery at Citeaux to establish another abbey at Clairvaux. His difficulties in establishing the settlement and his commitment to the new

foundation were described by William of Saint-Thierry, a friend and biographer of Bernard, in his Life of Saint Bernard.

Bernard eventually became one of the most important men of the first half of the twelfth century. He was deeply involved with the political and religious issues of the era, and his sermons, letters, and other writings represented the tradition of monastic spirituality.

(From *A Sourcebook of Mediaeval History*, ed. by Frederic Austin Ogg [New York: American Book Co., 1907], pp. 256–258.)

In June, 1115, Bernard took up his abode in the "Valley of Wormwood" as it was called, and began to look for means of shelter and sustenance against the approaching winter. The rude fabric which he and his monks raised with their own hands was long preserved by the pious veneration of the Cistercians. It consisted of a building covered by a single roof, under which chapel, dormitory, and refectory were all included. Neither stone nor wood hid the bare earth, which served for a floor. Windows scarcely wider than a man's head admitted a feeble light. In this room the monks took their frugal meals of herbs and water. Immediately above the refectory was the sleeping apartment. It was reached by a ladder, and was, in truth, a sort of loft. Here were the monks' beds, which were peculiar. They were made in the form of boxes, or bins, of wooden planks, long and wide enough for a man to lie down in. A small space, hewn out with an axe, allowed room for the sleeper to get in or out. The inside was strewn with chaff, or dried leaves, which, with the woodwork, seem to have been the only covering permitted. . . .

The monks had thus got a house over their heads; but they had very little else . . . their food during the summer had been a compound of leaves intermixed with coarse grain. Beechnuts and roots were to be their main support during the winter. And now to the privations of insufficient food was added the wearing out of their shoes and clothes. Their necessities grew with the severity of the season, until at last even salt failed them; and presently Bernard heard murmurs. He argued and exhorted; he spoke to them of the fear and love of God, and strove to rouse their drooping spirits by dwelling on the hopes of eternal life and Divine recompense. Their sufferings made them deaf and indifferent to their abbot's words. They would not remain in this valley of bitterness; they would return to Citeaux. Bernard, seeing they had lost their trust in God, reproved them no more; but himself sought in earnest prayer for release from their difficulties. Presently a voice from heaven said, "Arise, Bernard, your prayer is granted." Upon which the monks said, "What did you ask of the Lord?" "Wait, and you shall see, you of little faith," was the reply; and presently a stranger came who gave the abbot ten livres.

Questions for Discussion:

1. What reasons does William of Saint-Theirry give in this passage from the *Life of Bernard* for the saint's commitment to his new foundation at Clairvaux?
2. How does the description of the new foundation reflect the monastic vows of poverty, chastity, and obedience?

7.3   Bernard on Cluny

Bernard was dedicated to a renewal of the original spirit of monasticism as stipulated in the Rule *of Saint Benedict (Document 1.15), and in his foundation at Clairvaux he hoped to provide an atmosphere in which these values could flourish. It is no surprise that he spoke out against the Benedictine tradition as practiced at Cluny, as may be seen in the following document.*

(From *A Medieval Garner*, by G. C. Coulton [London: Constable & Co., 1910], pp. 68–69.)

Marvel how monks could grow accustomed to such intemperance in eating and drinking, clothing and bedding, riding abroad and building, that, wherever these things are practiced most busily and with most pleasure and expense, there religion is thought to be best kept. For behold! spare living is taken for covetousness, sobriety for austerity, silence for melancholy; while, on the other hand, men rebaptize laxity as "discretion," waste as "liberality," garrulousness as "affability," giggling as "jollity," effeminacy in clothing and bedding as "neatness." . . .

Who, in those first days when the monastic Order began, would have believed that monks would ever come to such sloth? . . . Dish after dish is set on the table; and instead of the mere flesh-meat from which men abstain, they receive twofold in mighty fishes. Though you have eaten your fill of the first course, yet when you come to the second you shall seem not even to have tasted the first; for all is dressed with such care and art in the kitchen that, though you have swallowed four or five dishes, the first are no hindrance to the last, nor does satiety lessen your appetite. . . . For (to say nothing of the rest) who may tell of the eggs alone, in how many ways they are tossed and vexed, how busily they are turned and turned again, beaten to froth or hard-boiled or minced, now fried and now baked, now stuffed and now mixed, or again brought up one by one? . . . What shall I say of water-drinking, when watered wine is on no account admitted? All of us, forsooth, in virtue of our monkish profession, have infirm stomachs, and are justified in not neglecting the Apostle's salutary advice as to "drinking wine"; yet (I know not why) we omit that word "little" with which he begins. . . . Men seek for their garments, not the most useful stuff they may find, but the most delicately woven. . . . "Yet, you say, "Religion is not in the dress, but in heart." Well said. But you, when you want to buy a frock, go from city to city, scouring the markets, searching the fairs from booth to booth, scanning the merchant's shops, turning over each man's store, unrolling vast bales of cloth, touching with your fingers, bringing close to your eyes, holding up to the sunlight, and rejecting whatever is seen to be too coarse or too slight; on the other hand, whatever pleases you with its purity and gloss, that you seek to buy at once at any price: I ask you, therefore, do you do this from your heart, or in mere simplicity? . . . Yet I marvel, since the Rule says that all faults of the Disciple concern the Master, and our Lord through His prophet threatened to require the blood of those who die in their sins at the hand of their Pastors—I marvel how our Abbots permit such things to be done; unless it be perchance (if I may risk the word) that no man confidently rebukes that wherein he does not trust himself to be without blame. . . . I lie, if I have not seen an Abbot with a train of sixty horses and more; on seeing such pass by, you would say that they are not fathers of monasteries but lords of castles, not rulers of souls but princes of provinces. . . .

Questions for Discussion:

1. According to Bernard, what particular aspects of the *Rule* of Saint Benedict were being disregarded at Cluny?
2. After reading the selections pertaining to the Benedictine Order at Cluny, do you think Saint Bernard's objections were justified?

Pilgrimage

Pilgrimage Journeys: Jerusalem, Santiago de Compostela, and Canterbury

People in the Middle Ages decided to undertake pilgrimages for many reasons, including the expiation of sinful behavior, spiritual reward, the promise of healing, and pure adventure. (Document 5.8 provides an example of pilgrimage to Jerusalem stipulated as a penance for killing someone during the days of the Truce of God). The tradition of pilgrimage began in the early years of Christianity, and the practice was one of the "Five Pillars of Islam" *(see the discussion in Chapter 3). The most holy site for pilgrimage in the Middle Ages continued to be Jerusalem, where individuals could "walk in the footsteps of the Lord." Another important destination was Rome, the place where Peter and Paul had been martyred. The journeys to these places were often long, arduous, and dangerous, but people saw the rewards as surmounting the difficulties.*

7.4   The Pilgrim Udalrich

The following excerpt recounts the experiences of a pilgrim named Udalrich, who had been advised to undertake a pilgrimage in order to make recompense for his sins.

(From *Readings in European History*, vol. 1, edited by James Harvey Robinson [Boston: Ginn & Co., 1904], p. 336.)

The holy Udalrich, having spent some time at home, began to be oppressed in soul lest the duties imposed upon him by his uncle were not sufficiently pleasing to God. Wishing therefore, to be free and entirely unhampered in order to make a pilgrimage for Christ's sake, he gave up his benefices[5] and started for Jerusalem. He took with him his servant who was at the same time his almoner,[6] and a single horse.

From the day he left Freising until he entered Jerusalem he never mounted his horse until he had repeated the Psalter from beginning to end, in the meantime ordering Martin, his servant, to ride, and meditating long by the way.

[5]A benefice, or fief, was a landholding granted by a lord. See the explanation in Chapter 5, Document 5.1.
[6]An almoner distributed charity (alms).

When at last this saintly man reached the holy places, it is not possible to relate with what emotion he greeted the memorials of the birth, passion, resurrection, and ascension of our Lord, with what genuflections he adored them, and with what floods of tears he watered them. The simple strength of his prayer and supplication exceeds the power of words. He literally fulfilled the utterances of the Psalmist: "I am weary with my groaning; all the night make I my bed to swim; I water my couch with my tears." His companions were filled with astonishment, and as for himself he lost his eyesight before his time, as will appear later.

God had given him outpourings from above and from below, that is, compunction due not only to his love of the celestial kingdom, but springing also from his apprehension of the torments of hell;—but perfect love casts out fear. At last, asked by one of his associates why he bemoaned himself so long every night and permitted no one about him to sleep, and why he did not spare his failing eyes, he replied that he was tired of the long pilgrimage in this world, that he longed to die and be with Christ, nor was he troubled over the failing light.

7.5   The Pilgrim Saewulf

The pilgrim Saewulf, who was probably from Britain, traveled to the Holy Land between 1101 and 1103. This excerpt from his account points to the dangers encountered during a pilgrimage.

So we climbed up from Joppa into the city of Jerusalem. The journey lasted two days and it was by a very hard mountain road. It was very dangerous too, because the Saracens,[7] who are continually

(From *Jerusalem Pilgrimage: 1099–1185*, ed. by John Wilkinson, Joyce Hill, and W. F. Ryan (Hakluyt Society). Copyright © 1988. Reprinted by permission of David Higham Associates Limited.)

[7]*Saracens* was a term used by people of the Middle Ages that meant Muslims.

plotting an ambush against Christians, were hiding in the caves of the hills and among rocky caverns. They were awake day and night, always keeping a look-out for someone to attack, whether because he had not enough people with him, or because he was fatigued enough to leave a space between himself and his party. Sometimes the Saracens could be seen everywhere in the neighborhood, and sometimes they disappeared.

Anyone who has taken that road can see how many human bodies there are in the road and next to the road, and there are countless corpses which have been torn up by wild beasts. It might be questioned why so many Christian corpses should lie there unburied, but it is in fact no surprise. There is little soil there, and the rocks are not easy to move. Even if the soil were there, who would be stupid enough to leave his brethren and be alone digging a grave! Anybody who did this would dig a grave not for his fellow Christian but for himself! So in that road not only poor and weak people have dangers to face, but also the rich and strong. Many are killed by the Saracens and many of heat and thirst—many through lack of drink and many from drinking too much. But we with all our company arrived at our goal unharmed, *Praise be to the Lord,*

who has not relinquished his ear from my prayer or his mercy from me. Amen.

Questions for Discussion:

1. Why did Udarich undertake the pilgrimage to Jerusalem?
2. According to Saewulf, what were the most dangerous aspects of the pilgrimage?
3. Is there an essential difference between the pilgrimage tradition of Islam and these accounts by medieval Christians? Discuss.

7.6   The *Pilgrim's Guide to Santiago de Compostela*

Santiago de Compostela was named after the apostle James, who, according to legend, preached the gospel in Spain during the first century C.E. He returned to Palestine, where he was beheaded by Herod Agrippa in 44 C.E. His followers stole his body and placed it in a small boat, which drifted to the coast of northern Spain, where it was buried in a secret place. In 813 his body was discovered by a hermit, who followed a star to "campus stellae" (field of the star). Hearing the story, Bishop Teodomiro investigated, and reported the discovery of the important relic. Alfonso II, King of Asturias (791–842) declared Saint James to be the patron saint of his kingdom, and in 830 had a chapel built over the remains of the saint, where many miracles had been reported. The chapel formed the nucleus of the cathedral at Santiago de Compostela, and the site became a popular pilgrimage destination.

The Pilgrim's Guide to Santiago de Compostela, probably written between 1139 and 1173, provided advice for pilgrims wishing to travel to the shrine. Most travelers to this site followed a route that began in Paris, continued into southern France, crossed the Pyrenees, and then traversed northern Spain almost to the Atlantic Ocean. As may be seen, it was an arduous route, along which the pilgrim might encounter unscrupulous people.

In this chapter of The Guide, *the author discusses the route and the topography of southern France and northern Spain, along with descriptions of the native populations of the areas. In the following selection we join the traveler as he leaves Gascony in southern France and heads toward the Pyrenees Mountains, which divide France and the Iberian Peninsula.*

(From *The Pilgrim's Guide to Santiago de Compostela*, ed. and trans. by William Melczer. New York: Italica Press, 1993. Copyright 1993 by William Melczer. Used by permission of Italica Press.)

On leaving that country [Gascony], to be sure on the road of St. James, there are two rivers that flow near the village of Saint-Jean-de-Sorde, one to the right and one to the left, and of which one is called brook and the other river. There is no way of crossing them without a raft. May their ferrymen be damned! Though each of the streams is indeed quite narrow, they have the habit of demanding one coin from each man, whether poor or rich, whom they ferry over, and for a horse they ignominiously extort by force four. Now, their boat is small, made of a single tree, hardly capable of holding horses. Also, when boarding it one must be most careful not to fall by chance into the water. You will do well in pulling your horse by the reins behind yourself in the water, outside the boat, and to embark but with few passengers, for if it is overloaded it will soon become endangered.

Also, many times the ferryman, having received his money, has such a large troop of pilgrims enter the boat that it capsizes and the pilgrims drown in the waves. Upon which the boatmen, having laid their hands upon the spoils of the dead, wickedly rejoice.

Then, already near the pass of Cize, one reaches the Basque country [the western Pyrenees], on the seashore of which, towards the north, lies the city of Bayonne. This land, whose language is barbarous, is wooded, mountainous, devoid of bread, wine, and all sorts of food for the body except that, in compensation, it abounds in apples, cider, and milk.

In this land, that is to say near Port-de-Cize in the town called Ostabat and in those of Saint-Jean and Saint-Michel-Pied-de-Port, there are evil toll-gatherers who will certainly be damned through and through. In point of fact, they actually advance towards the pilgrims with two or three sticks, extorting by force an unjust tribute. And if some traveler refuses to hand over the money at their request, they beat him with the sticks and snatch away the toll-money while cursing him and searching even through his breeches. These are ferocious people; and the land in which they dwell is savage, wooded and barbarous. The ferociousness of their faces and likewise of their barbarous speech scares the wits out of those who see them. Though according to the rules and regulations they should not demand a tribute from anybody but merchants, they unjustly cash in from pilgrims and all sorts of travelers. Whenever they ought to receive, according to the usage, four or six coins for a certain service, they cash in eight or twelve, that is to say, double.

Wherefore we admonish and entreat that these toll-gatherers as well as the king of Aragon and the other powers that be who receive from them the tribute money, as well as all those who are in agreement with them, that is to say, Raymond de Soule, Vivien d' Aigremont, and the viscount of Saint-Michel with all their future progeny, together with the said ferrymen as well as Arnaud de la Guigne with all his future progeny, no less than the other lords of the said streams who unjustly cash in from the ferrymen the toll-money for the crossing, and also the priests who, knowingly, confer upon them the penitence and the Eucharist and celebrate for them the divine office or admit them into the church—all these, until such a time that they expiate their sins through a long and public penance, and further introduce moderation in their tributes, [let them] be diligently excommunicated not merely in the episcopal sees of their lands but also in the basilica of St. James

in the presence of pilgrims. And if a prelate, no matter who, would wish, out of charity or interest, to pardon them, may he be stricken with the sword of anathema.

It ought to be known that these toll-gatherers should by no means collect tribute from pilgrims, and that the said ferrymen should demand for the crossing of two men, provided they are rich, but one *obolum*, and for a horse, according to the regulations, one coin only. But from the poor they should ask nothing at all. And furthermore, they must have large enough boats in which men and mounts can easily fit in.

In the Basque country there is on the road of St. James a very high mountain, which is called Port-de-Cize, either because that is the gate of Spain, or because it is by that mountain that the necessary goods are transported form one country to the other. Its ascent is eight miles long, and its descent, equally eight. In fact, its height is such that it seems to touch the sky: to him who climbs it, it seems as if he was able to touch the sky with his hand. From its summit one can see the sea of Bretagne and that of the west, as well as the boundaries of three regions, that is to say, Castilla [Castile], Aragon, and France. On the summit of this mountain there is a place called the Cross of Charles, because it was here that Charles [Charlemagne—see Chapter 4], setting out with his armies for Spain, opened up once a passageway with axes, hatchets, pickaxes and other implements, and that he first erected the sign of the cross of the Lord and, falling on his knees and turning towards Galicia [the northern area of Spain where Santiago de Compostela is located], addressed a prayer to God and St. James. Wherefore the pilgrims, falling on their knees and turning towards the land of St. James, use to offer there a prayer while each planted his own cross of the Lord like a standard. Indeed, one can find there up to a thousand crosses; and that is why that place is the first station of prayer of St. James.

On that mountain, before Christianity had spread out on Spanish lands, the impious Navarrese [the people of Navarre] and the Basques used not merely to rob the pilgrims going to St. James, but also to ride them as if they were asses and before long to slay them. Near this mountain, to be sure, towards the north, there is a valley called Valcarlos where Charles himself encamped together with his armies after his warriors had been slain at Roncesvalles. Many pilgrims proceeding to Santiago who do not want to climb the mountain go that way.

Afterwards, in descending from the summit, one finds the hospice[8] and the church with the rock that Roland, the formidable hero, split with his sword in the middle, from top to bottom, in a triple

---

[8]The hospice was a place where pilgrims were able to rest and receive food and drink.

stroke. Next, one comes to Roncesvalles, the site where, to be sure, once took place the big battle in which King Marsile, Roland, Olivier as well as forty thousand Christian and Saracen soldiers were slain. [This is the event described in the *Song of Roland*, to be discussed in Chapter 8].

Question for Discussion:

1. What are the most dangerous aspects of the journey to Santiago de Compostela? Compare these with the experiences of the Jerusalem pilgrims.

INTERPRETING THE EVIDENCE

7.7   Pilgrimage to Canterbury: Thomas Becket and a Stained-Glass Panel from Canterbury Cathedral

Another important pilgrimage destination, which developed later than those we have analyzed, was the city of Canterbury, in England, where pilgrims visited the tomb of Thomas Becket, the martyred archbishop of Canterbury (see Chapter 9 for a discussion of the issues involved in his murder). As the following excerpts from the works of Becket's contemporaries indicate, accounts of miracles performed by the martyr soon after his murder encouraged the popularity of his shrine among people from all walks of life. The Canterbury pilgrimage was also the destination of the pilgrims of Chaucer's Canterbury Tales, *to be discussed in Chapter 14.*

One of the extant accounts of the beginning of the cult of Becket was written in 1172–1173 by an unknown author who is known to posterity as the "Lambeth Anonymous."

(From the *Lambeth Anonymous*, trans. by Michael Staunton, in *The Lives of Thomas Becket,* Manchester, UK: Manchester University Press, 2001, p. 210. Reprinted by permission.)

Without question his glory came to be multiplied far beyond the injury inflicted. For, to be brief, the report of wonders not only reached the innermost and outermost corners of England, but also spread rapidly through many people of foreign races. It roused cities, towns, villages and even huts everywhere in England to such an extent that from the lowliest up to the greatest, few remained who did not come to see and honor the tomb of the famous martyr. Ordained and lay, poor and rich, commoners and nobles, fathers and mothers with children, lords with their households, all went there, drawn by the same spirit of devotion. The streets which led to Canterbury were so crowded with the throng of those working in stalls and shops and those coming and going, that almost everywhere it seemed as busy as a marketplace. Nights hardly less than days, winters hardly less than summers, slowed down the travelers' journey. For in a harsher time the more difficult it was, the sweeter it was considered to honor the promise to visit, because where the approach was more difficult the hope of reward was greater.

Equally a great concourse of pilgrims went there from remote regions overseas, so that they differed little in number from the natives, and—as great men worthy of belief who visited holy places throughout the world witness—neither the seat of the blessed Peter [Rome], nor the memorial of James the Greater [Santiago de Compostela] or any other saint, nor indeed that glorious sepulcher of Christ, were so continuously or more crowded with men, or in offering was veneration more clear to be seen.

Becket's associate, the distinguished scholar John of Salisbury (c. 1115–1180), depicted the beginning of the pilgrimage tradition at Canterbury in the following way:

(From *Thomas of Canterbury: His Death and Miracles*, 2 vols., by Edwin A. Abbott [London: Adam and Charles Black, 1898], I, p. 227.)

"... there [at the site of Becket's martyrdom and tomb] ... great miracles are wrought ... For in the place of his passion, and in the place where he lay before the great altar previous to burial, and in the place where he was at last buried, paralytics are cured, the blind see, the deaf hear, the dumb speak, the lame walk, lepers are cured ... and (a thing unheard of from the days of our fathers) the dead are raised."

In the early thirteenth century, Becket's remains were moved from the crypt of Canterbury Cathedral, where his body had been interred since soon after the murder, to a magnificent new chapel adjoining the choir of the cathedral. The area, known as Trinity Chapel, was surrounded by stunning stained-glass windows that pictured many of Becket's miracles. (See the discussion in Chapter 9). The illustration below shows pilgrims on the road to Becket's shrine.

Questions for Discussion:

1. Does the stained-glass image from Canterbury Cathedral authenticate the verbal descriptions of the pilgrimage to Canterbury? How?
2. What does the stained-glass window indicate about the reasons for the pilgrimage? What might the pilgrims be seeking from their journey?

Pilgrimage to Canterbury: Stained-Glass Panel from Canterbury Cathedral. *(Picture Desk, Inc./Kobal Collection.)*

The First Crusade

"God Wills It!": Pope Urban's Summons to the First Crusade

The crusades to the Holy Land, which began at the end of the eleventh century and continued during the twelfth and thirteenth centuries, were among the most important events of the Middle Ages. Virtually all of the people of Europe and the countries of the eastern Mediterranean area were profoundly affected by these wars. There is much scholarly debate concerning the motivations of the men who "took up the Cross" in order to regain control of Jerusalem and other sacred sites of Christianity from the Muslims. Some historians have written that economic gain and political influence were at least as important as religious fervor in prompting men to join the crusades, although current scholars give more credence to truly religious motivation. Certainly the most obvious mandate came from the papacy.

The First Crusade was publicly proclaimed by Pope Urban II (r. 1088–1099) at the Council of Clermont on November 27, 1095. Urban was an ardent reformer who had traveled widely in an effort to advance the ideas of the supremacy of the papacy articulated by Gregory VII (see Document 6.14) and to gain popular support. The crusades were tied to this effort, as the papacy advocated war to regain the Holy Land, which had been under Muslim rule since 639. Participation in this endeavor had a spiritual connotation that was encouraged by the Church. We do not have a record of Urban's exact words, but there are various accounts based on the testimony of eyewitnesses. The following sources, written during the euphoric period after the capture of Jerusalem in 1099, are taken from the anonymous Gesta Francorum *("The Deeds of the Franks"), the* Chronicle *of Fulcher of Chartres, and works by Robert the Monk and Balderic of Dol; these accounts provide a clear indication of the pope's strong exhortation.*

7.8   From the *Gesta Francorum* ("*Deeds of the Franks*")

The Gesta Francorum *("The Deeds of the Franks") was written by an unknown crusader. His work probably dates from about 1100. Much of the material he provided was used for other accounts, such as those of Robert the Monk (Document 7.10) and Balderic of Dol (Document 7.11).*

(From *The First Crusade: The Accounts of Eye-Witnesses and Participants*, translated by August Krey [Princeton: Princeton University Press, 1921], pp. 28–29.)

When that time was at hand which the Lord Jesus daily points out to His faithful, especially in the Gospel, saying, "If any man would come after me, let him deny himself and take up his cross and follow me," a mighty agitation was carried on throughout all the region of Gaul. [Its theme was] that if anyone desired to follow the Lord zealously, with a pure heart and mind, and wished faithfully to bear the cross after Him, he would no longer hesitate to take up the way to the Holy Sepulcher.

And so Urban, Pope of the Roman see, with his archbishops, bishops, abbots, and priests, set out as quickly as possible beyond the mountains and began to deliver sermons and to preach eloquently, saying: "Whoever wishes to save his soul should not hesitate humbly to take up the way of the Lord, and if he lacks sufficient money, divine mercy will give him enough." Then the apostolic lord continued, "Brethren, we ought to endure much suffering for the name of Christ—misery, poverty, nakedness, persecution, want, illness, hunger, thirst, and other [ills] of this kind, just as the Lord said to His disciples: 'Ye must suffer much in My name,' and 'Be not ashamed to confess Me before the faces of men; verily I will give you mouth and wisdom,' and finally, 'Great is your reward in Heaven.'" And when this speech had already begun to be noised abroad, little by little, through all the regions and countries of Gaul, the Franks, upon hearing such reports, had crosses sewn on their right shoulders, saying that they followed with one accord the footsteps of Christ, by which they had been redeemed from the hand of hell.

Question for Discussion:

1. What primary reason for the crusade is evident in this brief excerpt from the *Gesta Francorum?*

7.9   Fulcher of Chartres

Fulcher of Chartres (1059–1127) was present at the Council of Clermont when Pope Urban preached about the urgent necessity for a crusade. He joined the Frankish crusading armies, and remained in Jerusalem as chaplain to Baldwin after the kingdom was established. He probably began his Chronicle *in 1101. Because of his close association with the crusading princes and his presence during the events of the First Crusade, his account may be the most reliable.*

(From *The First Crusade: The Accounts of Eye-Witnesses and Participants,* translated by August Krey [Princeton: Princeton University Press, 1921], pp. 29–30.)

But the Pope added at once that another trouble, still more grievous than that already spoken of . . . was besetting Christianity from another part of the world. He said: "Since, O sons of God, you have promised the Lord to maintain peace more earnestly than you have until now, and faithfully to sustain the rights of Holy Church, there still remains for you, who are newly aroused by this divine correction, a very necessary work, by which you can show the strength of your good will by a certain further duty, God's concern and your own. For you must hasten to carry aid to your brethren dwelling in the East, who need your help, which they often have asked. For the Turks, a Persian people,[9] have attacked them, as many of you already know, and have advanced as far into the Roman territory as that part of the Mediterranean which is called the Arm of St. George; and, by seizing more and more of the lands of the Christians, they have already often conquered them in battle, have killed and captured many, have destroyed the churches, and have devastated

the kingdom of God. If you allow them to continue much longer, they will subjugate God's faithful yet more widely.

"Wherefore, I exhort with earnest prayer—not I, but God—that, as heralds of Christ, you urge men of all ranks, knights as well as foot-soldiers, rich as well as poor, to hasten to exterminate this vile race from the lands of your brethren, and to aid the Christians in time. I speak to those present; I proclaim it to the absent; moreover, Christ commands it. And if those who set out should lose their lives on the way by land, or in crossing the sea, or in fighting the pagans, their sins shall be remitted. This I grant to all who go, through the power vested in me by God. Oh, what a disgrace, if a race so despised, base, and the instrument of demons, should so overcome a people endowed with faith in the all-powerful God, and resplendent with the name of Christ! Oh, what reproaches will be charged against you by the Lord Himself if you have not helped those who are counted, like yourselves, of the Christian faith! Let those who have been accustomed to make private war against the faithful carry on to a successful issue a war against infidels, which ought to have been begun before now. Let these who for a long time have been robbers now become soldiers of Christ. Let those who once fought against brothers and relatives now fight against barbarians, as they ought. Let those who have been hirelings at low wages now labor for an eternal reward. Let those who have been wearing themselves out to the detriment of body and soul now labor for a double glory. On the one hand will be the sad and poor, on the other the joyous and wealthy; here the enemies of the Lord; there His friends. Let no obstacle stand in the way of those who

---

[9]Seljuk Turks who attacked countries both east and west throughout Persia.

are going, but, after their affairs are settled and expense money is collected, when the winter has ended and spring has come, let them zealously undertake the journey under the guidance of the Lord."

Questions for Discussion:

1. To which segments of society is the pope addressing his remarks?

2. It is evident in this speech that the pope hoped to end the private warfare so endemic of medieval society in the tenth and eleventh centuries. Discuss this aspect of his plea for the crusade.

3. Would the remission of sins by the pope have been a motivating factor? How does this compare with Muhammad's exhortation to fight a *jihad*? (See Document 3.4.)

7.10   Robert the Monk

Robert the Monk (generally identified as the monk who was chosen abbot of Saint-Remi of Rheims in 1094) wrote his account of Urban's speech in the first quarter of the twelfth century. Although he relied on information provided in the Gesta Francorum, *he may have been present to hear Urban at Clermont.*

(From *The First Crusade: The Accounts of Eye-Witnesses and Participants*, translated by August Krey [Princeton: Princeton University Press, 1921], pp. 30–33.)

"Oh, race of Franks, race from across the mountains, race chosen and beloved by God—as shines forth in very many of your works—set apart from all nations by the situation of your country, as well as by your Catholic faith and the honor of the holy church! To you our discourse is addressed, and for you our exhortation is intended. We wish you to know what a grievous cause has led us to your country, what peril, threatening you and all the faithful, has brought us.

"From the confines of Jerusalem and the city of Constantinople a horrible tale has gone forth and very frequently has been brought to our ears; namely, that a race from the kingdom of the Persians, an accursed race, a race utterly alienated from God, a generation, which has neither directed its heart nor entrusted its spirit to God, has invaded the lands of those Christians and has depopulated them by the sword, pillage, and fire; it has led away a part of the captives into its own country, and a part it has destroyed by cruel tortures; it has either entirely destroyed the churches of God or appropriated them for the rites of its own religion. They destroy the altars, after having defiled them with their uncleanness. They circumcise the Christians, and the blood of the circumcision they either spread upon the altars or pour into the vases of the baptismal font. When they wish to torture people by a base death, they perforate their navels, and, dragging forth the end of the intestines, bind it to a stake; then with flogging they lead the victim around until his viscera have gushed forth, and he falls prostrate upon the ground. Others they bind to a post and pierce with arrows. Others they compel to extend their necks, and then, attacking them with naked swords, they attempt to cut through the neck with a single blow. What shall I say of the abominable rape of the women? To speak of it is worse than to be silent. The kingdom of the Greeks is now dismembered by them and deprived of territory so vast in extent that it can not be traversed in a march of two months. On whom, therefore, is the task of avenging these wrongs and of recovering this territory incumbent, if not upon you? You, upon whom above other nations God has conferred remarkable glory in arms, great courage, bodily energy, and the strength to humble the hairy scalp of those who resist you.

"Let the deeds of your ancestors move you and incite your minds to manly achievements; likewise, the glory and greatness of King Charles the Great, and his son Louis, and of your other kings, who have destroyed the kingdoms of the pagans, and have extended in these lands the territory of the Holy Church. Let the Holy Sepulcher of the Lord, our Savior, which is possessed by unclean nations, especially move you, and likewise the holy places, which are now treated with ignominy and irreverently polluted with filthiness. Oh, most valiant soldiers and descendants of invincible ancestors, be not degenerate, but recall the valor of your forefathers!

"However, if you are hindered by love of children, parents, and wives, remember what the Lord says in the Gospel, 'He that loves father, or mother more than me, is not worthy of me. Every one that hath forsaken houses, or brethren, or sisters, or father, or mother, or wife, or children, or lands for my name's sake shall receive an hundred-fold and shall inherit everlasting life.' Let none of your possessions detain you, no solicitude for your family affairs, since this land which you inhabit, shut in on all sides by the sea and surrounded by mountain peaks, is too narrow for your large population; nor does it abound in wealth; and it furnishes scarcely food enough for its cultivators. Hence it is that you murder and devour one another, that you wage war, and that frequently you perish by mutual wounds. Let therefore hatred depart from among you, let your quarrels end, let wars cease, and let all dissensions and controversies slumber. Enter upon the road to the Holy Sepulcher; wrest that land from the wicked race, and subject it to yourselves. That land which, as the Scripture says, 'flows with milk and honey' was given by God into the possession of the children of Israel.

"Jerusalem is the navel of the world; the land is fruitful above others, like another paradise of delights. This the Redeemer of the human race has made illustrious by His advent, has beautified by His presence, has consecrated by suffering, has redeemed by death, has glorified by burial. This royal city, therefore, situated at the center of the world, is now held captive by His enemies, and is in subjection to those who do not know God, to the worship of the heathen. Therefore, she seeks and desires to be liberated and does not cease to implore you to come to her aid. From you, especially, she asks succor, because, as we have already said, God has conferred upon you, above all nations, great glory in arms. Accordingly, undertake this journey for the remission

of your sins, with the assurance of the imperishable glory of the kingdom of heaven."

When Pope Urban had said these and very many similar things in his urbane discourse, he so influenced to one purpose the desires of all who were present that they cried out, "God wills it! God wills it!" When the venerable Roman pontiff heard that, with eyes uplifted to heaven he gave thanks to God and, with his hand commanding silence, said:

"Most beloved brethren, to-day is manifest in you what the Lord says in the Gospel, 'Where two or three are gathered together in My name there am I in the midst of them.' Unless the Lord God had been present in your minds, all of you would not have uttered the same cry. For, although the cry issued from numerous mouths, yet the origin of the cry was one. Therefore I say to you that God, who implanted this in your breasts, has drawn it forth from you. Let this then be your battle-cry in combat, because this word is given to you by God. When an armed attack is made upon the enemy, let this one cry be raised by all the soldiers of God: 'God wills it! God wills it!'

"And we do not command or advise that the old, or the feeble, or those unfit for bearing arms, undertake this journey; nor ought women to set out at all without their husbands, or brothers, or legal guardians. For such are more of a hindrance than aid, more of a burden than an advantage. Let the rich aid the needy; and, according to their means, let them take with them experienced soldiers. The priests and clerks of any order are not to go without the consent of their bishops; for this journey would profit them nothing if they went without such permission. Also, it is not fitting that laymen should enter upon the pilgrimage without the blessing of their priests.

"Whoever, therefore, shall determine upon this holy pilgrimage and shall make his vow to God to that effect and shall offer himself to Him as a living sacrifice, holy, acceptable unto God, shall wear the sign of the cross of the Lord on his forehead, or on his breast. When, having truly fulfilled his vow, he wishes to return, let him place the cross on his back between his shoulders. Such, indeed, by two-fold action will fulfill the precept of the Lord, as He commands in the Gospel, 'He that does not take his cross and follow after me, is not worthy of me.'"

Questions for Discussion:

1. This account by Robert the Monk explains more fully the reasons that may or may not have been given by Pope Urban to undertake a crusade. What were these? Discuss the rhetorical techniques used in this document.

2. According to Robert, Urban called the crusade a "holy pilgrimage." Discuss how the two are similar. How are they different?

3. Does the medieval crusade reflect, in any way, the twenty-first-century experience in Iraq? What are the reasons for your opinion?

7.11   Balderic of Dol

Balderic of Dol (c. 1050–1130) was abbot of Bourgeuil and archbishop of Dol after 1107. His account also depends heavily on the Gesta Francorum. *This very brief excerpt from his work emphasizes the proper emblems to be sewn to the crusader's clothing.*

(From *The First Crusade: The Accounts of Eye-Witnesses and Participants*, trans. by August Krey [Princeton: Princeton University Press, 1921], pp. 28–33, 40.)

The most excellent man concluded his oration and by the power of the blessed Peter absolved all who vowed to go and confirmed those acts with apostolic blessing. He instituted a sign well suited to so honorable a profession by making the figure of the Cross the stigma of the Lord's Passion, the emblem of the soldiery, or rather, of what was to be the soldiery of God. This, made of any kind of cloth, he ordered to be sewed upon the shirts, cloak, and byrra[10] of those who were about

to go. He commanded that if anyone, after receiving this emblem, or after taking openly the vow, should shrink from his good intent through base change of heart, or any affection for his parents, he should be regarded an outlaw forever, unless he repented and again undertook whatever of his pledge he had omitted. Furthermore, the Pope condemned with a fearful anathema all those who dared to molest the wives, children, and possessions of these who were going on this journey for God. . . .

Questions for Discussion:

1. According to Balderic, what did the wearing of the cross signify? What were the implications of adopting this insignia?

2. Compare the accounts of the *Gesta Francorum*, Fulcher of Chartres, Robert the Monk, and Balderic of Dol. Which do you find to be the most convincing? Which is the most powerful in terms of rhetoric?

---

[10]A *byrra* was a short woolen cloak with a hood.

7.12   A Hebrew Chronicle: The Massacres of Jews

The proclamation of Pope Urban at Clermont inspired the lower classes of society as well as the knights. Although the peasants lacked training and supplies for warfare, as many as 50,000 set out very soon for Jerusalem, led

by a charismatic preacher known as Peter the Hermit and a poor knight called Walter Sansvoir. Many of the participants were no doubt pious, but the army included runaway serfs, adventurers, and criminals. This expedition, now known as the "Popular Crusade" or the "Peasants' Crusade," became extremely militant as adventurers joined them. As they passed through Germany they assaulted the Jews, primarily those living in the Rhineland, claiming that their attacks were justified because they were avenging the crucifixion of Christ. The following excerpt from the works of Solomon bar Simson, a Jewish historian writing in 1140, provide details of the dreadful massacres.

(From *The Jews and the Crusaders*, translated by Shlomo Eidelberg. © 1996 Ktav Publishing House, pp. 21–23, 68–71. Reprinted by permission of Ktav Publishing House.)

—this year turned . . . to sorrow and groaning, weeping and outcry. Inflicted upon the Jewish People were the many evils related in all the admonitions; those enumerated in Scripture as well as those unwritten were visited upon us.

At this time arrogant people, a people of strange speech, a nation bitter and impetuous, Frenchmen and Germans, set out for the Holy City, which had been desecrated by barbaric nations, there to seek their house of idolatry and banish the Ishmaelites [Muslims] and other denizens of the land and conquer the land for themselves. They decorated themselves prominently with their signs, placing a profane symbol—a horizontal line over a vertical one—on the vestments of every man and woman whose heart yearned to go on the stray path to the grave of their Messiah. Their ranks swelled until the number of men, women, and children exceeded a locust horde covering the earth; of them it was said: "The locusts have no king [yet go they forth all of them by bands]." Now it came to pass that as they passed through the towns where Jews dwelled, they said to one another: "Look now, we are going a long way to seek out the profane shrine and to avenge ourselves on the Ishmaelites, when here, in our very midst, are the Jews—they whose forefathers murdered and crucified him for no reason. Let us first avenge ourselves on them and exterminate them from among the nations so that the name of Israel will no longer be remembered, or let them adopt our faith and acknowledge the offspring of promiscuity."

When the Jewish communities became aware of their intentions, they resorted to the custom of our ancestors, repentance, prayer, and charity. The hands of the Holy Nation turned faint at this time, their hearts melted, and their strength flagged. They hid in their innermost rooms to escape the swirling sword. They subjected themselves to great endurance, abstaining from food and drink for three consecutive days and nights, and then fasting many days from sunrise to sunset, until their skin was shriveled and dry as wood upon their bones. And they cried out loudly and bitterly to God.

But their Father did not answer them. . . .

. . . on the Sabbath, the foe attacked the community of Speyer and murdered eleven holy souls who sanctified their Creator on the holy Sabbath and refused to defile themselves by adopting the faith of their foe. There was a distinguished, pious woman there who slaughtered herself in sanctification of God's Name. She was the first among all the communities of those who were slaughtered. The remainder were saved by the local bishop without defilement [i.e., baptism], as described above.

On the twenty-third of Iyar they attacked the community of Worms. The community was then divided into two groups; some remained in their homes and others fled to the local bishop seeking refuge. Those who remained in their homes were set upon by the steppe-wolves who pillaged men, women, and infants, children and old people. They pulled down the stairways and destroyed the houses, looting and plundering; and they took the Torah Scroll, trampled it in the mud, and tore and burned it. The enemy devoured the children of Israel with open maw. . . .

Question for Discussion:

1. How does Salomon bar Simson explain the massacres?

7.13   A Woman's Perspective: From *The Alexiad* by Anna Comnena

Anna Comnena (1093–1153) was the daughter of the Byzantine emperor Alexius I (1048–1118). The princess was one of the earliest known woman historians, and her account of her father's reign offers a vivid and exciting view of the era. Her reactions to the circumstances of the First Crusade and the character and motivations of the Frankish warriors give an interesting perspective by a woman raised and educated in the Byzantine court.

Book X

Before he [Emperor Alexius I] had enjoyed even a short rest, he heard a report of the approach of innumerable Frankish[11] armies. Now he dreaded their arrival for he knew their irresistible manner of attack, their unstable and mobile character and all the peculiar natural and concomitant characteristics which the Frank retains throughout; and he also knew that they were always agape for money, and seemed to disregard their truces readily for any reason that cropped up. For he had always heard this reported of them, and found it very true. However, he did not lose heart, but prepared himself in every way so that, when the occasion called, he would be ready for battle. And indeed the actual facts were far greater and more terrible than rumor made them. For the whole of the West and all the barbarian tribes which dwell between the further side of the Adriatic and the pillars of Heracles, had all migrated in a body and were marching into Asia through the intervening Europe, and were making the journey with all their household. The reason of this upheaval was more or less the following. A certain Frank, Peter by name, nicknamed Cucupeter, had gone to worship at the Holy Sepulcher and after suffering many things at the hands of the Turks and Saracens who were ravaging Asia, he got back

to his own country with difficulty. But he was angry at having failed in his object, and wanted to undertake the same journey again. However, he saw that he ought not to make the journey to the Holy Sepulcher alone again, lest worse things befall him, so he worked out a cunning plan. This was to preach in all the Latin countries that "the voice of God bids me announce to all the Counts in France that they should all leave their homes and set out to worship at the Holy Sepulcher, and to endeavor wholeheartedly with hand and mind to deliver Jerusalem from the hand of the Hagarenes." And he really succeeded. For after inspiring the souls of all with this quasi-divine command he contrived to assemble the Franks from all sides, one after the other, with arms, horses and all the other paraphernalia of war. And they were all so zealous and eager that every highroad was full of them. And those Frankish soldiers were accompanied by an unarmed host more numerous than the sand or the stars, carrying palms and crosses on their shoulders; women and children, too, came away from their countries. And the sight of them was like many rivers streaming from all sides, and they were advancing towards us through Dacia [present-day Romania] generally with all their hosts. Now the coming of these many peoples was preceded by a locust which did not touch the wheat, but made a terrible attack on the vines. This was really a presage as the diviners of the time interpreted it, and meant that this enormous Frankish army would, when it came, refrain from interference in Christian affairs, but fall very heavily upon the barbarian Ishmaelites who were slaves to drunkenness, wine, and Dionysus. For this race is under the sway of Dionysus and Eros, rushes headlong into all kind of sexual intercourse, and is not circumcised either in the flesh or in their passions. It is nothing but a slave, nay triply enslaved, to the ills wrought by Aphrodite. For this reason they worship and adore Astarte and Ashtaroth too and value above all the image of the moon, and the golden figure of Hobar

[11] All westerners were generally referred to as "Franks."

in their country. Now in these symbols Christianity was taken to be the corn because of its wineless and very nutritive qualities; in this manner the diviners interpreted the vines and the wheat. However let the matter of the prophecy rest.

The incidents of the barbarians' approach followed in the order I have described, and persons of intelligence could feel that they were witnessing a strange occurrence. The arrival of these multitudes did not take place at the same time nor by the same road (for how indeed could such masses starting from different places have crossed the straits of Lombardy all together?). Some first, some next, others after them and thus successively all accomplished the transit, and then marched through the Continent. Each army was preceded, as we said, by an unspeakable number of locusts; and all who saw this more than once recognized them as forerunners of the Frankish armies. When the first of them began crossing the straits of Lombardy sporadically the Emperor summoned certain leaders of the Roman forces, and sent them to the parts of Dyrrachium and Valona with instructions to offer a courteous welcome to the Franks who had crossed, and to collect abundant supplies from all the countries along their route; then to follow and watch them covertly all the time, and if they saw them making any foraging-excursions, they were to come out from under cover and check them by light skirmishing. These captains were accompanied by some men who knew the Latin tongue, so that they might settle any disputes that arose between them.

Let me, however, give an account of this subject more clearly, and in due order. According to universal rumor Godfrey, who had sold his country, was the first to start on the appointed road; this man was very rich and very proud of his bravery, courage and conspicuous lineage; for every Frank is anxious to outdo the others. And such an upheaval of both men and women took place then as had never occurred within human memory, the simpler-minded were urged on by the real desire of worshiping at our Lord's Sepulcher, and visiting the sacred places; but the more astute, especially men like Bohemund and those of like mind, had another secret reason, namely, the hope that while on their travels they might by some means be able to seize the capital itself, looking upon this as a kind of corollary. And

Bohemund disturbed the minds of many nobler men by thus cherishing his old grudge against the Emperor. Meanwhile Peter, after he had delivered his message, crossed the straits of Lombardy before anybody else with thousand men on foot, and one hundred thousand on back, and reached the capital by way of Hungary. For Frankish race, as one may conjecture, is always very hotheaded and eager, but when once it has espoused a cause, it is uncontrollable.

The Emperor, knowing what Peter had suffered before from the Turks, advised him to wait for the arrival of the other Counts, but Peter would not listen for he trusted to the multitude of his followers, so crossed and pitched his camp near a small town called Helenopolis. After him followed the Normans numbering ten thousand, who separated themselves from the rest of the army and devastated the country round Nicaea, and behaved most cruelly to all. For they dismembered some of the children and fixed others on wooden spits and roasted them at the fire, and on persons advanced in age they inflicted every kind of torture. But when the inhabitants of Nicaea became aware of these doings, they threw open their gates and marched out upon them, and after a violent conflict had taken place they had to dash back inside their citadel as the Normans fought so bravely. And thus the latter recovered all the booty and returned to Helenopolis. Then a dispute arose between them and the others who had not gone out with them, as is usual in such cases, for the minds of those who had stayed behind were aflame with envy, and thus caused a skirmish after which the headstrong Normans drew apart again, marched to Xerigordus and took it by assault. When the Sultan heard what had happened, he dispatched Elchanes against them with a substantial force. He came, and recaptured Xerigordus and sacrificed some of the Normans to the sword, and took others captive, at the same time laid plans to catch those who had remained behind with Cucupeter. He placed ambushes in suitable spots so that any coming from the camp in the direction of Nicaea would fall into them unexpectedly and be killed. Besides this, as he knew the Franks' love of money, he sent for two active-minded men and ordered them to go to Cucupeter's camp and proclaim there that the Normans had gained possession of Nicaea, and were now dividing everything in it. When this report was circulated among Peter's followers, it upset them terribly. As soon as they heard the words 'partition' and 'money' they started in a disorderly crowd along? the road to Nicaea, all but unmindful of their military experience and the discipline which is essential for those starting out to battle. For, as I remarked above, the Latin race is always very fond of money, but more especially when it is bent on raiding a country; it then loses its reason and gets beyond control. As they journeyed neither in ranks nor in squadrons, they fell foul of the Turkish ambuscades near the river Dracon and perished miserably. And such a large number of Franks and Normans were the victims of the Ishmaelite sword, that when they piled up the corpses of the slaughtered men which were lying on either side they formed, I say, not a very large hill or mound or a peak, but a high mountain as it were, of very considerable depth and breadth—so great was the pyramid of bones. And later men of the same tribe as the slaughtered barbarians built a wall and used the bones of the dead to fill the interstices as if they were pebbles, and thus made the city their tomb in a way. This fortified city is still standing to-day with its walls built of a mixture of stones and bones. When they had all in this way fallen a prey to the sword, Peter alone with a few others escaped and re-entered Helenopolis; and the Turks who wanted to capture him, set fresh ambushes for him. But when the Emperor received reliable information of all this, and the terrible massacre, he was very worried lest Peter should have been captured. He therefore summoned Constantine Catacalon Euphorbenus (who has already been mentioned many times in this history), and

gave him a large force which was embarked on ships of war and sent him across the straits to Peter's aid. As soon as the Turks saw him land they fled. Constantine, without the slightest delay, picked up Peter and his followers, who were but few, and brought them safe and sound to the Emperor. On the Emperor's reminding him of his original thoughtlessness and saying that it was due to his not having obeyed his, the Emperor's, advice that he had incurred such disasters, Peter, being a haughty Latin, would not admit that he himself was the cause of the trouble, but said it was the others who did not listen to him, but followed their own wills, and he denounced them as robbers and plunderers who, for that reason, were not allowed by the Savior to worship at His Holy Sepulcher. Others of the Latins, such as Bohemund and men of like mind, who had long cherished a desire for the Roman Empire, and wished to win it for themselves, found a pretext in Peter's preaching, as I have said, deceived the more single-minded, caused this great upheaval and were selling their own estates under the pretence that they were marching against the Turks to redeem the Holy Sepulcher.

Questions for Discussion:

1. How did Anna Comnena describe the character and motivations of the Franks?
2. How does Anna's account of the behavior of the Franks correlate with that of Solomon bar Simson? What are the similarities? What differences do you see?

7.14   Ibn al-Athir: A Muslim View of the Crusade

Ibn al-Athir (1160–1233) was the author of Kamil at-Tawarikh *("The Perfect History," or "The Collection of Histories"), an extensive history of the Muslim world from the era before Muhammad to 1231. His work is a very important source for the period of the Crusades, and his account of the fall of Jerusalem is thought to be the most complete and convincing version of*

those available to us. The excerpt here begins with a description of the Frankish assault on the city of Ma'arrat an-Nu'man.

(From *Arab Historians of the Crusades*, translated by Francesco Gabrieli, translated from the Italian by E. J. Costello. Copyright © University of California Press. Reproduced by permission of Taylor & Francis Group UK.)

The Franks Take Ma'arrat an-Nu'Man

After dealing this blow to the Muslims [at Antioch] the Franks marched on Ma'arrat an-Nu'man and besieged it. The inhabitants valiantly defended their city. When the Franks realized the fierce determination and devotion of the defenders they built a wooden tower as high as the city wall and fought from the top of it, but failed to do the Muslims any serious harm. One night a few Muslims were seized with panic and in their demoralized state thought that if they barricaded themselves into one of the town's largest buildings they would be in a better position to defend themselves, so they climbed down from the wall and abandoned the position they were defending. Others saw them and followed their example, leaving another stretch of wall undefended, and gradually, as one group followed another, the whole wall was left unprotected and the Franks scaled it with ladders. Their appearance in the city terrified the Muslims, who shut themselves up in their houses. For three days the slaughter never stopped; the Franks killed more than 100,000 men and took innumerable prisoners. After taking the town the Franks spent six weeks shut up there, then sent an expedition to 'Arqa, which they besieged for four months. Although they breached the wall in many places they failed to storm it. Munqidh, the ruler of Shaizar, made a treaty with them about 'Arqa and they left it to pass on to Hims. Here too the ruler Janah ad-Daula made a treaty with them, and they advanced to Acre by way of an-Nawaqir. However they did not succeed in taking Acre.

The Franks Conquer Jerusalem

Taj ad-Daula Tutush was the Lord of Jerusalem but had given it as a fief to the amir Suqman ibn Artuq the Turcoman. When the Franks defeated the Turks at Antioch the massacre demoralized them, and the Egyptians, who saw that the Turkish armies were being weakened by desertion, besieged Jerusalem under the command of al-Afdal ibn Badr al-Jamali. Inside the city were Artuq's sons, Suqman and Ilghazi, their cousin Sunij and their nephew Yaquti. The Egyptians brought more than forty siege engines to attack Jerusalem and broke down the walls at several points. The inhabitants put up a defence, and the siege and fighting went on for more than six weeks. In the end the Egyptians forced the city to capitulate, in sha'ban 489/August 1096. Suqman, Ilghazi and their friends were well treated by al-Afdal, who gave them large gifts of money and let them go free. They made for Damascus and then crossed the Euphrates. Suqman settled in Edessa and Ilghazi went on into Iraq. The Egyptian governor of Jerusalem was a certain Iftikhar ad-Daula, who was still there at the time of which we are speaking.

After their vain attempt to take Acre by siege, the Franks moved on to Jerusalem and besieged it for more than six weeks. They built two towers, one of which, near Sion, the Muslims burnt down, killing everyone inside it. It had scarcely ceased to burn before a messenger arrived to ask for help and to bring the news that the other side of the city had fallen. In fact Jerusalem was taken from the north on the morning of Friday 22 sha'ban 492/15 July 1099. The population was put to the sword by the Franks, who pillaged the area for a week. A band of Muslims barricaded themselves into the Oratory of David and fought on for several days. They were granted their lives in return for surrendering. The Franks honored their word, and the group left by night for Ascalon. In the Masjid al-Aqsa the Franks slaughtered more than 70,000 people, among them a large number of Imams and Muslim scholars, devout and ascetic men who had left their homelands to live lives of pious seclusion in the Holy Place. The Franks stripped the Dome of the Rock of more than forty silver candelabra, each of them weighing 3,600 drams, and a great silver lamp weighing fortyfour Syrian pounds, as well as a hundred and fifty smaller silver candelabra and more than twenty gold ones, and a great deal more booty. Refugees from Syria reached Baghdad in ramadan, among them the qadi Abu Sa'd al-Harawi. They told the Caliph's ministers a story that wrung their hearts and brought tears to their eyes. On Friday they went to the Cathedral Mosque and begged for help, weeping so that their hearers wept with them as they described the sufferings of the Muslims in that Holy City: the men killed, the women and children taken prisoner, the homes pillaged. Because of the terrible hardships they had suffered, they were allowed to break the fast.

Questions for Discussion:

1. Describe the battle tactics used by the Franks.

2. How does al-Athir's view of the Franks compare with that of Anna Comnena in the previous source?

Two Accounts of the Origins of the Templars

7.15   The *Chronicle* of William of Tyre

The First Crusade resulted in the foundation of small crusader kingdoms in the Holy Land. The political environment was not stable, and new monastic orders emerged whose primary function was to protect the travelers along pilgrim routes against Muslim attack. They were known as the Military Orders, and were formed by ascetic warrior monks who dedicated themselves to the monastic values of chastity, obedience, and poverty. The Knights of the Temple, or "Templars," were the first to create an explicitly military monastic order. Their name derived from the fact that the site of their headquarters was near to the Temple of Solomon. Their origin is described in the following accounts: the first is from the Chronicle of William of Tyre *(c. 1130–c. 1190) and the second from the* Chronicle of Michael the Syrian.*

(From *A Source Book for Mediaeval History*, ed. by Oliver J. Thatcher and Edgar H. McNeal [New York: Scribner's Sons, 1905], pp. 493–494.)

In the same year [1118–19] certain nobles of knightly rank, devout, religious, and God-fearing, devoting themselves to the service of Christ, made their vows to the patriarch [of Jerusalem] and declared that they wished to live forever in chastity, obedience, and poverty, according to the rule of regular canons. Chief of these were Hugo de Payens and Geoffrey of St. Orner. Since they had neither a church nor a house, the king of Jerusalem gave them a temporary residence in the palace which stands on the west side of the temple. The canons of the temple granted them, on certain conditions, the open space around the aforesaid palace for the erection of their necessary buildings, and the king, the nobles, the patriarch, and the bishops, each from his own possessions, gave them lands for their support. The patriarch and bishops ordered that for the forgiveness of their sins their first vow should be to protect the roads and especially the pilgrims against robbers and marauders. For the first nine years after their order was founded they wore the ordinary dress of a layman, making use of such clothing as the people, for the salvation of their souls, gave them. But in their ninth year a council was held at Troyes [1128] in France at which were present the archbishops of Rheims and Sens with their suffragans, the cardinal bishop of Albano, papal legate, and the abbots of Citeaux, Clairvaux, and Pontigny, and many others. At this council a rule was established for them, and, at the direction of the pope, Honorius III, and of the patriarch of Jerusalem, Stephen, white robes were appointed for their dress. Up to their ninth year they had only nine members, but then their number began to increase and their possessions to multiply. Afterward, in the time of Eugene III, in order that their appearance might be more striking, they all, knights as well as the other members of a lower grade, who were called serving men, began to sew crosses of red cloth on their robes. Their order grew with great rapidity, and now [about 1180] they have 300 knights in their house, clothed in white mantles, besides the serving men, whose number is almost infinite. They are said to have immense possessions both here [in Palestine] and beyond the sea [in Europe]. There is not a province in the whole Christian world which has not given property to this order, so that they may be said to have possessions equal to those of kings. Since they dwelt in a palace at the side of the temple they were called "Brothers of the army of the temple." For a long time they were steadfast in their purpose and were true to their vows, but then they forgot their humility, which is the guardian of all virtues, and rebelled against the patriarch of Jerusalem who had assisted in the establishment of their order and had given them their first lands, and refused him the obedience which their predecessors had shown him. They also made themselves very obnoxious to the churches by seizing their tithes and first-fruits and plundering their possessions.

Questions for Discussion follow Document 7.16.

7.16   The *Chronicle* of Michael the Syrian

Michael the Syrian (1126–1199) was the Jacobite Patriarch of Antioch. The Jacobites were Syrians who believed in the single nature of Christ, rather than embracing the doctrine of two complete natures following the incarnation as held by the Roman and Orthodox churches. They were allowed freedom of worship under Frankish rule. Michael's Chronicle *traced history from the era before the birth of Muhammad to 1194–1195.*

(From *The Templars*, translated by Malcolm Barber and Keith Bate. Manchester, UK: Manchester University Press, 2002, pp. 27–29. Reprinted by permission.)

At the beginning of the reign of Baldwin II a Frenchman came from Rome to Jerusalem to pray. He had made a vow not to return to his own country, but to become a monk after helping the king in the war for three years; he and the thirty knights who accompanied him would end their lives in Jerusalem. When the king and his barons saw that they had achieved remarkable things in the war and had been of use to the city during their three-year service, they advised the man to serve in the army with his thirty knights and defend the place against brigands rather than to become a monk in the hope of saving only his own soul.

Now this man, whose name was Hou(g) de Payn, accepted the advice, the thirty knights who accompanied him joined and united with him. The king gave them the House of Solomon to live in and some villages for their subsistence. At the same time the patriarch gave them some villages belonging to the Church.

They imposed upon themselves a monastic rule of life, not taking a wife, not bathing, having no personal possessions whatsoever, but having everything in common. This way of living began to make them famous: the spread of their reputation to all countries incited royal princes, kings, the great and the humble to come and join this spiritual fraternity; whoever became a brother gave all he possessed to the community, whether it was villages, towns or whatever. They increased in number, evolved and found themselves in possession of lands not only in the land of Palestine but particularly in those regions joined to Italy and Rome.

They have written customs and a rule. Whoever comes to be a brother is tested for one year. The rules are read to him seven times, and each time he is asked: 'Well, have you perhaps any misgivings? Perhaps you won't be able to assume these rules right to the end? (If so), praise God and return home.' At the end of the year, they say prayers and clothe in their habit he who accepts the yoke and promises to endure it. Afterwards, anyone who falls short of his promise is killed by the sword, without mercy or pity.

Their custom is as follows: nobody is permitted to have personal possessions, whether it be house, money or whatever; nor can he be absent without the permission of the master; nor to sleep other than in their houses; nor to eat bread at the table of a common manor; nor, when ordered to go somewhere to die there, to say, 'I will not go'. But one must, as promised, work with faith in this ministry until one dies.

When somebody dies, 40 masses are said for him; for 40 days 40 poor people are fed everyday in his name; he is remembered in perpetuity in the raising of the host in their churches; and if he is killed in battle he is considered a martyr. If someone is discovered to have kept something secret from the community or if at death he is found to be in possession of something he has not given to the community, he is not deemed worthy of burial.

Their clothing is a very simple white habit. Nothing else is permitted. When they sleep they are not allowed to undress or to ungird their loins.

Their food is as follows: Sundays, Tuesdays and Thursdays they eat meat; the other days milk, eggs and cheese. Only the priests who officiate in their churches drink wine each day, with the bread, as do the soldiers, that is to say the knights on exercise, and the footsoldiers in combat. Each worker keeps to his own trade, as do those who work in the fields; in each town or village in which they have a house there is a head and a steward who fix the tasks that each person who happens to be there has to do.

The master in chief of all lives in Jerusalem: he gives orders to everyone and is never permitted to do anything personal. Of all corn, wine, etc., that is harvested or garnered he distributes a tenth to the poor; each time that bread is baked in one of their houses, one in ten loaves is reserved for the needy. On days when the table is laid and the brothers eat the bread, what is left is given to the needy. Twice a week there is a special distribution of bread and wine for the needy.

Although their original establishment was created with the task of escorting along the roads the pilgrims who came to pray, afterwards they went with the kings to war against the Turks. Their numbers increased to 100,000. They owned fortresses and built strongholds themselves in all the lands under Christian domination. Their wealth in gold and other possessions increased, as it did in armor of all types, in flocks of sheep, oxen, pigs, camels, horses, until they had more than all the kings. And yet they were all poor and detached from everything. They are friendly and charitable to all who worship the Cross. In all their countries and particularly in Jerusalem they founded hospitals so that any stranger who falls ill will find a place; they serve and look after him until he is cured and then give him provision for the journey and send him off in peace. If, on the other hand, he dies, they take care of his burial.

Questions for Discussion:

1. Compare the *Rule* of Saint Benedict (Document 1.15) with the descriptions of the Templars by William of Tyre and Michael the Syrian. What requirements were common to both forms of monasticism? What are the differences between them?
2. What was the original mission of the Templars? Both authors describe the deviation from this purpose as the order grew, but they do not agree as to their moral standards. Discuss their differing opinions.

The Reconquista

7.17   The *Poem of the Cid*

The crusading ideal was not limited to the Holy Land. Historians have recognized warfare in other areas that focused on wrenching control from the Muslims. One of the most prominent of these movements took place in Iberia, and the effort was known as the Reconquista, or "recovery." The movement was from north to south, as territories were taken by Christian armies, and often lost and reconquered; the full "recovery" was not completed until 1492.

During the eleventh century two powerful kings from the north, Alfonson VI of Castile and Leon (r. 1065–1109) *and Sancho "the Great" of Aragon and Navarre, advanced against the Muslims. An important victory occurred in 1085 when Alfonso captured the city of Toledo, ending almost 400 years of Islamic rule.*

One of Alfonso's vassals was the Spanish hero Rodrigo Diaz de Vivar (c. 1043–99), usually known as "El Cid" ("the lord"). According to the plot of the poem, the Cid's relationship with the king was less than ideal. Alfonso is portrayed as a man of cruelty and poor judgment, and, at the beginning of the epic, the king's mind has been poisoned against the Cid by his jealous enemies. The result is a sentence of exile for the Cid, who is determined to win back his honor and reputation. Through heroic efforts as a military leader, he ultimately regains all that he has lost during his expulsion from Alfonso's kingdom.

Rodrigo's legendary personality and career became the subject of a famous epic, The Poem of the Cid, *probably first written down in the late twelfth or early thirteenth century. Like* Beowulf *(Document 2.9), the anonymous poem was originally sung or chanted by a professional musician to entertain a court audience. The following excerpt gives a laudatory portrait of the hero's military exploits as he fights against the count of Barcelona, and describes his generous nature.*

(From *Poem of the Cid*, trans. by Paul Blackburn [Norman, OK: University of Oklahoma Press, 1998], pp. 52–57. Reprinted by permission of the University of Oklahoma Press.)

The Cid Harangues his Men

"All right, knights, stow the loot,
    get your armor on and your weapons loose,
    and quickly!
Don Ramon is going to give us a great battle, he
has such a mob of Moors and Christians with him,
he won't let us off with anything less than a fight.
If we keep on going, they'll only cut us off, so
let the battle be here.

Tighten your cinches and keep your arms at ready.
    See?
They're coming down the mountainside all
    wearing britches,
their cinches are loose and the saddles are all
    low-cantled;
we'll ride better, our Galician saddles have high
    backs, and
we've leather shin guards over the britches.
With one hundred knights we ought to thin those
    crowded ranks.
If you meet them with lances before they reach the
    valley floor,
for every blow you strike you'll empty out three
    saddles.
Try to take my prizes from me, will he?
Ramon Berenguer will see today
who it is he has come seeking
in this pine grove of Tevar."

The Cid Wins the Battle, and Takes as Prize the Sword "Colada."

By the time the Cid had finished his speech, the
    men were ready.
Armed and in their saddles, they watched
the Catalan force descending the slope. When
they were almost to the bottom near the valley
    flats, the Cid
ordered the attack.
The men responded with a will, using
their pennoned lances so well that
while wounding some, they unhorsed still others.
The man born in a good hour has taken the
    battle, taken
Ramon Berenguer, count of Barcelona, and won
Colada, worth over one thousand marks.

The Count of Barcelona a Prisoner. He Prefers to Die of Hunger

Honor to his beard, he
won this battle,
took the count prisoner,
led him to his own tent,
and ordered his faithful men
to mount guard over him.
The Cid left the tent and gave a leap, his
troops were coming in from all directions,
booty was plentiful, and the Cid pleased.
A great meal was on the fires for mio Cid don
    Rodrigo,
but the count don Ramon ignores it all.
They bring him food, set it before him,
he mocks them all and will not touch it.
"I wouldn't touch a mouthful for everything
    in Spain.
I'd rather I lost my body first and my soul
next, for
having been beaten in a fight with such
ill-shod beggars."

The Cid Promises the Count his Freedom

You'll hear what Ruy Diaz said: "Count,
come on, eat, eat this bread, drink this wine.

If you do as I say, you'll go free, if not,
you'll never see the Christian world again."

The Count Refuses

"You eat, don Rodrigo, then relax and take it easy, I
choose to die. I want nothing to eat."
By the third day, they still cannot persuade him.
They are still occupied
dividing up the great spoils they'd taken, but
they cannot make him touch a piece of bread.

The Cid Reiterates his Promise to the Count. He Sets Him at Liberty and Says Farewell

"Eat something, Count," the Cid urged,
"you'll never see another Christian if you don't eat,
and if you do and satisfy me, I'll turn you loose,
Count, with two of your noblemen, free, understand?"
The count heard this and grew more cheerful.
"Cid, if you do as you say, I
shall marvel at your action all my life."
"Then eat, don Ramon,
and when you're satisfied,
I'll set you free and two men besides.
But what you have lost in the field
and what I have won,
you may be sure I won't give back a plugged dinar.
I need all of it for the men
who share my beggary with me.
We meet our needs by taking from you and from
    others,
and it shall continue as long
as it pleases our Father in heaven,
as I am a man living under the wrath of my king,
and in exile."
The count was happy and asked for water
that he might wash his hands.
They fetched it in and gave it to him at once.
He sat down to eat with the two knights
whom the Cid had freed
God, he ate with a will!
The man born in a good hour sat beside him, said:
"Eat up! and if your eating
does not give me pleasure, why,
we'll not budge from here, we
shall not part from each other!"

Then the count said, "Gladly eat very gladly!"
He and his knights fell to eating quickly.
It's a pleasure for mio Cid to sit there watching,
    closely,
because Ramon Berenguer moves his hands so
    quickly.
"Please, Cid, have our horses ready,
we're all set, and'll ride off at once.
I haven't eaten with such enthusiasm since
the day I was made a count.
The taste of this meal you've given me
will never be forgotten."
Three richly saddled palfreys they gave them,
and costly garments, cloaks of fur and mantles.
Count don Ramon took his place between the two
    knights, and
the Castillian rode out with them to say farewell
at the edge of camp:
"Now, be off with you, Count, frank and free.
You have my thanks for what you've left with me.
And should you have any idea that you want revenge,
should you ever come looking for me, just let me
    know.
Either you'll leave some of your goods with me,
or cart off some of mine."
"No danger of that, mio Cid, just forget it, I've
paid you enough to last me the whole year.
I've no intention of seeking you out again."

The Count Leaves Distrustfully. The Wealth of the Exiles

The count dug in his spurs, rode off in haste.
He kept turning his head and looking back, afraid
that the Cid might change his mind-one thing
that mighty man would never do for all the money
    in the world,
for never in his life
had he given a treacherous word.
The count is gone;
el Cid de Bivar turns back,
returns to his men.
He joins their celebration over the great and
    marvelous
swag that they've taken. His men
are all so rich, they hardly
know how much they have.

Questions for Discussion:

1. How does the Cid embody the qualities of the ideal Christian knight?

2. In the next chapter you will read *The Song of Roland.* As you study that poem, keep in mind a possible correlation with the Cid.

7.18   The Conquest of Lisbon

The Spanish Reconquista took place over several centuries, and was not completed until the reign of Ferdinand and Isabella in 1492. This "crusade" to take back the land the Muslims had conquered in the eighth century was incremental, with many small advances and setbacks. One example of the progress of the Christians is the conquest of Lisbon; the following description is from an anonymous account.

In 1147, at the beginning of the Second Crusade to the Holy Land, a group of crusaders from England stopped in Portugal on their way. King Alfonso VII of Leon and Castile enlisted their help in his campaign to take the city of Lisbon from the Muslims.

(From *The Crusades: A Reader*, edited by S. J. Allen and Emilie Amt. Peterborough, Canada: Broadview Press, 2003, pp. 304–307. Reprinted with permission of the publisher.)

[2.] The city of Lisbon at the time of our arrival consisted of sixty thousand families paying taxes. . . . The city was populous beyond belief, for, as we learned from its *alcayde,* or governor, after the capture of the city, it had one hundred fifty-four thousand men, not counting women and children. . . . The reason for such a dense population was that there was no established religion there. Each man was a law unto himself. As a result the basest element from every part of the world had gathered there, like the bilge water of a ship, a breeding ground for every kind of lust and impurity. . . .

[3. King Alfonso now asked the crusaders to delay going to Jerusalem and to help him capture Lisbon.] To frame a reply to this we all assembled in council . . . [where] William Viel, yet breathing out threatenings and piratical slaughter, and his brother Ralph and almost all the men of Southampton and Hastings, together with those who had come to besiege Lisbon five years before this, all with one voice declared that they took the king's promise [of rewards and plunder] to be nothing but treachery; and, bringing up many points against it which were either false or, if in any respect true, to be imputed to their own foolishness rather than the king's baseness, or things which were even more obvious, [they said] that they were unwilling to bear the expense of a long labor in the siege. Moreover, it would be more profitable if they should sail quickly past the coast of Spain and then extort much easy money from the merchant vessels of Africa and Spain. And, besides, they recalled that the wind at that season was very favorable for voyagers to Jerusalem. And they said that they would not wait for anyone, if only they should have eight or ten ships associated with them, and many other similar things which depend upon the turn of fate rather than upon virtue. But the greater part of our force, setting aside every objection, agreed to remain. . .

[4. After an unsuccessful attempt to persuade the Muslims to surrender the city, the crusaders besieged Lisbon.] The Moors, meanwhile, made frequent sorties against our men by day because they held three gates against us. With two of these gates on the side of the city and one on the sea, they had an easy way to get in and out. On the other hand, it was difficult for our men to organize themselves. The sorties caused casualties on both sides, but theirs were always greater than ours. While we kept watch, meanwhile, under their walls through the days and nights, they heaped derision and many insults upon us. . . . They also continuously attacked blessed Mary, the mother of God, with insults and with vile and abusive words, which infuriated us. They said that we venerated the son of a poor woman with a worship equal to that due to God, for we held that he was a God and the Son of God, when it is apparent that there is only one God who began all things that have begun and that he has no one

coeval with him and no partaker in his divinity. . . .
They attacked us with these and similar calumnies.
They showed to us, moreover, with much derision
the symbol of the cross. They spat upon it and
wiped the feces from their posteriors with it. At last
they urinated on it, as on some despicable thing, and
threw our cross at us. . . .

[5. Meanwhile,] the men of Cologne five times
began to dig mines for the purpose of overturning
the [city] wall and were as many times overwhelmed.
Hence our forces again had cause for deep discouragement, and, murmuring much among themselves,
they were making such complaints as that they
might have been better employed elsewhere, when,
after some days, there came to us by the determination of divine mercy no small consolation.

For in the evening ten Moors entered a skiff beneath the wall and rowed away in the direction of the
castle of Palmela. But our men pursued them so
closely that they abandoned the skiff in desperation,
and everything they were carrying in it. Letters were
found in it, directed to several parties and written in
the Arabic language. An example of one, as I got it
from an interpreter, is as follows:

"To Abu Muhammed, king of Evora, [from] the
unfortunate people of Lisbon: may he maintain his
kingdom in safety. What great and terrible and unexpected disasters have come upon us, the desolate
ruin of our city and the great effusion of noble
blood—memorials, alas, of our everlasting grief—
proclaim. Already the second moon has almost passed
since the fleet of the Franks, which has been born
hither to our borders with the aid of heaven and earth
and sea, has kept us shut within the circuit of this
close-drawn wall. And what is to be hoped for amid
this sum of woes is more than doubtful, except only
to look for succor by means of ransom. But with our
cooperation we doubt not that you will liberate the
city and the country from the barbarians. For they are
not so very numerous or warlike, as their tower and
engines which we have burned with force and arms
bear witness. Otherwise, let your prudence beware,
for the same outcome of events and evils awaits you."

And the other letters besought the same things
from parents and other relatives and friends, and
from debtors; and . . . also gave information concerning their supply of bread and other foodstuffs.

When our men learned of these things, their spirits
were greatly encouraged to continue the attack
against the enemy for some days longer. After a short
time the corpse of a man who had been drowned was
found beneath our ships; and on an arm a letter was
tied, of which the tenor was as follows:

"The king of Evora to the men of Lisbon. . . .
Having long since entered into a truce with the king
of the Portuguese, I cannot break faith and wage war
upon him and his people. For the rest, take heed in
good time. Buy safety with your money, lest that
prove a cause of your hurt which ought to be a cause
of your well-being. Farewell. Give something
worthwhile to this our messenger."

So, finally, as the Moors' last hope of relief was
destroyed, our men kept watch the more vigilantly
. . . [and the siege continued until the Moors agreed
to surrender].

[6.] When these matters had been agreed upon
by both sides, the arrangements which the Moors
had proposed on the previous day for the delivery of
the city, were accepted. It was decided among us
that one hundred and forty of our armed men and
one hundred and sixty of the Flemish and the
Cologne contingents should enter the city before
everyone else and peacefully take over the fortifications of the upper fortress so that the enemy might
bring all of their money and possessions there and
give a guarantee by swearing before our men. When
all these things had been collected, the city was then
to be searched by our men. If any further possessions
were found, the man in whose house they were discovered was to pay for it with his head. When everyone had thus been despoiled, they were to be let go
in peace outside of the city. When the gates had
been opened and those who were chosen were allowed to enter, the men of Cologne and the Flemings thought up a sly method of deceiving us: they
requested our men to allow them to enter first for
the sake of their honor. When they had received permission and got a chance to enter first, they slipped
in more than two hundred of their men, in addition
to those who had been selected. These were also in
addition to others who had already slipped through
the ruined places in the walls which lay open to
them, while none of our men, except those selected,
had presumed to enter.

The archbishop and the other bishops went in front of us with the Lord's cross and then our leaders entered together with the king and those who had been selected. How everyone rejoiced! What special glory for all! What great joy and what a great abundance there was of pious tears when, to the praise and honor of God and of the most Holy Virgin Mary the saving cross was placed atop the highest tower to be seen by all as a symbol of the city's subjection, while the Archbishop and bishops, together with the clergy and everyone, intoned with wonderful rejoicing the *Te Deum Laudamus* and the *Asperge me,* together with devout prayers.

Questions for Discussion:

1. How does the author account for the sizeable population of Lisbon?
2. Describe the ways in which the two sides perceived and reacted to the religion of the other.
3. What were the motivations and actions of the crusaders? Are these similar to the goals and behaviors of the men who participated in the First Crusade? (See Documents 7.8–7.14.)
4. Why were some of the men unwilling to help Alfonso VII?
5. How does the author explain the ultimate victory of the crusaders?

Chapter 8

Romanesque Culture

The term "Romanesque," or "Roman-like," was originally used by nineteenth-century historians and scholars to define an architectural style that they saw as similar to the development of the Romance languages from Latin. This definition was soon broadened to include not only architecture, but also the literature and visual arts of the eleventh and twelfth centuries. Current scholars have questioned the applicability of the term, since there is much overlap between Romanesque style and the subsequent "Gothic" tradition (see Chapter 13). Furthermore, although architects and artists were undoubtedly influenced by the Roman artifacts that remained, recent historians of architecture and art have recognized other influences, such as the Germanic artistic tradition (see Chapter 4), as well as Byzantine and Islamic structure and design.

The vast program of building during the eleventh century was described by Rodulphus Glaber

(985–1047), *who referred to the phenomenon as "a white mantle of churches" in his* Five Books of History. *His account (Document 8.1) demonstrates the motivations that inspired architects to create a vast number of new churches and cathedrals, and that introduced an innovative artistic style.*

One of these buildings was the church of Sainte Madeleine at Vézelay. Built on a groundplan similar to that of Old St. Peter's (see Chapter 1), this structure has prominent Romanesque features in the nave. Sainte Madeleine was one of the most popular of the churches built along the pilgrimage routes—an interest that may be attributed to the numerous miracles that occurred at that site. Many of these wondrous occurrences were described in The Vézelay Chronicle *(Document 8.2), which offers potent illustrations of twelfth-century spirituality.*

An excellent example of Romanesque sculpture is the western tympanum[1] of the cathedral of Saint Lazar in Autun (Burgundy, France). The imagery in this sculptural program portrays Christ on Judgment Day, with the people on his right side being led to heaven, and those doomed to spend eternity in hell on his left. The sculptures offered a reminder of the peril of a sinful life to all who entered, and the accompanying excerpt from The Book of Miracles *by Peter the Venerable serves the same didactic purpose (Document 8.3).*

The cult of the saints may be traced to the early centuries of Christianity, when accounts of the martyrdoms shaped the concept of sanctity. (See, for example the Martyrdom of Perpetua and Felicity, Document 1.9). The Christians believed that martyrs ascended directly to heaven, into the presence of God. Thus, they were ideally situated to intercede on behalf of living believers, and miracles were worked by God, through the saints. Many people focused on the tangible physical remains, or relics, of the saints—clothing or body parts that remained as a memorial. These were treasured for their holiness as well as their innate potential for healing. Often the sacred objects were enclosed in elaborate containers of gold, silver, or crystal, *where they became a focus of veneration. One fine example of the cult of relics may be found at Conques, a popular pilgrimage site in the mid-Pyrenees along the road to Compostela (see Document 7.6), where the church possessed the relics of Saint Foy. The excerpts in this chapter from the* Book of Saint Foy, *coupled with the image of Saint Foy's reliquary, offer fine examples of the cult of saints that was such a vital part of the medieval experience (Document 8.4). A further account, taken from the* Ecclesiastical History of the English People *by the Venerable Bede, offers a report of the miraculous powers of Saint Cuthbert, whose relics cured a severe infection of the eye (Document 8.5).*

Goldsmiths and silversmiths were highly skilled during this era, as the photograph of the chalice of Abbot Suger of Saint Denis (1081–1151) amply demonstrates. Directions for the creation of a chalice by Theophilus (Document 8.6) explain some of the intricacies involved in the production of such vessels. However, these vibrant new works of sculpture and gold did not exist without criticism, as may be seen in the excerpt from the letter by the Cistercian theologian, Bernard of Clairvaux (Document 8.7).

The literature of the Romanesque era continued the traditions of the past, to a degree. For example, The Song of Roland *is a great epic poem that is viewed by some as being in the style of* Beowulf *(see Document 2.9), though the motif of the Christian knight is a product of a later time. The excerpt in this chapter (Document 8.8) demonstrates in literary form the behavior and aspirations of vassalage (see Documents 5.1 and 5.6) when synthesized with the conventions of Christian chivalry.*

One of the first female playwrights in the Middle Ages was the German nun Roswitha of Gandersheim (c. 935–c. 1000). Her play, Abraham *(Document 8.9), tells the story of Mary, a woman who falls into prostitution but is redeemed by her return to the religious life. The script offers an interesting parallel to the secular literature by Marie de France and the trobairitz (female troubadours) to be studied in Chapter 10.*

All of these facets of Romanesque culture—architecture, art, and literature—will be explored in the following documents, which represent the vibrant artistic expression of the era.

---

[1]The tympanum is the semi-circular space above the door of a church or cathedral. It is often filled with sculpture.

Architecture, Sculpture, and Objects of Devotion

8.1   "A White Mantle of Churches": The *Five Books of History* by Rodulphus Glaber

In the following excerpt the eleventh-century monastic historian Rodulphus Glaber (985–1047) discusses the phenomenon of church and cathedral building that took place beginning in the eleventh century. As Glaber remarked, there was a virtual competition between communities to erect the highest and most beautiful structures. Many of these churches were constructed along pilgrimage routes to Santiago de Compostela (see Document 7.6), such as the church of Saint Madeline at Vézelay (Document 8.2), where pilgrims could enter to venerate the relics of saints.

(From *Rodulfus Glaber: The Five Books of the Histories*, ed. and trans. by John France. Oxford: Clarendon Press, 1989, p. 115–121. Reprinted by permission of Oxford University Press.)

Reconstruction of Churches Throughout the Whole World

Just before the third year after the millennium, throughout the whole world, but most especially in Italy and Gaul, men began to reconstruct churches, although for the most part the existing ones were properly built and not in the least unworthy. But it seemed as though each Christian community were aiming to surpass all others in the splendor of construction. It was as if the whole world were shaking itself free, shrugging off the burden of the past, and cladding itself everywhere in a white mantle of churches. Almost all the episcopal churches and those of monasteries dedicated to various saints, and little village chapels, were rebuilt better than before by the faithful.

Question for Discussion

1. What factors may have motivated the vast increase in the construction of churches during this era?

INTERPRETING THE EVIDENCE

8.2   *The Vézelay Chronicle* and the Church of Sainte Madeleine

As discussed in Document 7.6, one of the most popular pilgrimage routes to the shrine of Santiago de Compostela extended from Paris, through south-western France, and then across northern Spain. Along the path were churches that contained the relics of important saints.

Many of the churches exemplified a new style of building that later scholars identified as "Romanesque," or "Roman-like." These buildings generally exhibited a groundplan derived from the Roman basilica (see Chapter 1), and were constructed with thick walls necessary for the support of a high elevation, and small windows. The nave of the church of St. Madeline in the southern French town of Vézelay (constructed c. 1104–1132) is an excellent example of these pilgrimage churches.[2]

The people of the town witnessed a miracle in the church during a fire in 1120, when the body of Mary Magdalene resting in her shrine and other precious relics were not burned. The event was described in the following excerpt from the Vézelay Chronicle *by Hugh of Poitiers (d. 1167), a Benedictine monk at the abbey of Vézelay.*

(From *The Vézelay Chronicle*, trans. by John Scott and John O. Ward. Binghamton, NY: Medieval & Renaissance Texts & Studies, 1992, pp. 284–285. Copyright Arizona Board of Regents for Arizona State University. Reprinted with permission.)

---

[2]The apse and ambulatory of the cathedral, built after the nave, display features of Gothic style, to be discussed in Chapter 13.

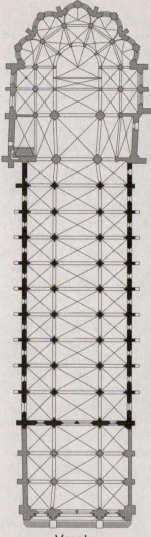

Vezelay

The Church of Sainte Madeleine at Vézelay, width 90 ft., 1104–32.

The Church of Sainte Madeleine at Vézelay. *(Dagli Orti/Picture Desk, Inc./Kobal Collection.)*

The Sepulchre of the Blessed Mary Magdalene Catches Fire.

Relics Are Found in a Statue of the Blessed Virgin.

. . . Now while Abbot William was visiting the houses subject to him in the neighborhood of Beauvais, he entered the district of Amiens and came to the monastery of Villeselve on the first Saturday of Advent. That night there came to him one of his servants, named Gerald, who told him of the woeful state of the church of Vézelay. For in the meantime a certain presage both of future calamity and of solace had occurred at that church. In the vault above the tomb of God's blessed lover Mary Magdalene such a blaze accidentally broke out that even the supports [*tirannos*] above it, which the French call beams [*trabes*], were burnt. But the wooden image of Mary, blessed mother of God, which stood on the floor of the vault, was not harmed by the fire at all, although it was a little

(continued)

blackened. The silken phylactery[3] which hung from the neck of the image of the infant Jesus did not smell of smoke, nor did its color change at all, not even slightly. Hence it was as clear as crystal that the image itself would not have been affected by smoke in the slightest, except by divine dispensation for the purpose of revealing, when it was repaired, the inestimable treasure hidden within it. For when this image was sent to the restorer, he declared that it had, so it seemed to him, a cunningly hidden little door between its shoulders. When he heard this, Prior Gilo ordered the image to be carried into the sacristy, and calling in with him Geoffrey, the subprior, Gervaise, the sacrist, Gerard, the constable, Maurice, the succentor, and Lambert, the restorer of the statue, he took a knife and scratched off the paint himself; but they could not discover any sign of a joint in the uncovered wood. Then he took a little iron hammer and tried to discover by ear what none could discern with his eyes, and hearing a sort of hollow sound, the bold man, armed with joyful hope, piously broke open the little door with his own hands. He found in it hairs of the chaste Virgin, the like of whom had not been seen before nor has been seen since, and part of the tunic of the same Mary, mother of God, and a bone of the blessed John the Baptist. He also found bones of the blessed apostles Peter, Paul, and Andrew in one bundle, and one joint of the thumb of the blessed James the Lord's brother, and two bundles of bones of the blessed apostle Bartholomew, and most of an arm of one of the Innocents, relics of St. Clement, and a portion of the hair of the queen St. Radegund; a piece of the vestments of the three boys Shadrack, Meshak, and Abednego, and a section from the purple robe in which our Lord Jesus Christ was clothed during his passion. With each of these items they found individual notes which distinguished one from another; and while all of the notes were so ancient that they could hardly be read, three others were found which were illegible; and of whom they spoke God only knows. Those which could be read they had

___
[3]The phylactery was a small bag carrying a relic.

transcribed, and tied the old notes to the new in testimony. After they had carefully inspected all these things they returned them to the place where they had been before, and placed the statue with these saints' relics over the high altar. Then everyone put on copes and, with all the larger and smaller bells ringing, praised the Creator of all, who had deigned to place in their custody, and for the protection of that place, so many and such illustrious relics.

Then all the people came flocking, both pilgrims and locals, and there was wonderfully great joy and exultation in the church, in the whole town, and in the neighboring countryside, with people hurrying to the joyful celebration from the fields and surrounding villages. Gilo, barely managing to curb everyone's clamor, gestured with his hand for silence and in a few well-chosen words declared the cause of praise and joy, while all wept for happiness. When later they tried to return the image to the vault over the tomb of God's lover, such a throng of people wished to kiss it or just touch it that they were barely able to replace it in its original position intact with all the people around. The monks did not permit the statue to be touched, lest they be accused of avarice. So the divine fire which broke forth was a portent of imminent tribulation, but the finding of the saints' relics indicated that there would be a good end to that tribulation. The monks of Vézelay wrote to their abbot, William, about this to comfort him on the pilgrimage he had undertaken.

Questions for Discussion:

1. Compare the groundplan of the church at Vézelay with that of Old St. Peter's (Document 1.8). What similarities do you see? What differences?
2. What were the various relics encapsulated in the wooden sculpture?
3. Why were the monks afraid they would be accused of avarice?

INTERPRETING THE EVIDENCE

8.3   The Western Tympanum at Autun and the "Besetting Demons"

Medieval people were imbued with the idea that the devil was an ever–present threat, and believed that demons and angels were constantly vying for human souls. The outcome of the struggle for each individual would be decided on Judgment Day, and this subject was often chosen for sculptural representation over the doors of churches and cathedrals in a semi-circular area known as a tympanum. In this prominent location the image presented a constant reminder of the reality of death and the day of reckoning to the people who entered.

The tympanum above the west portal of the twelfth-century cathedral[4] at Autun is a typical example of this theme. Christ is enthroned in the center, rendering justice at the final accounting. Heaven is on his right side, where angels are taking the souls of the faithful. On his left, grimacing devils grab those who have not been worthy of salvation. Notice on both sides the trumpeters who are sounding the call for Judgment Day.

[4]Autun was originally built as a pilgrimage church, rather than a cathedral.

The Western Tympanum at Autun, c. 1130–1135. (©Ancient Art & Architecture/DanitaDelimont.com)

(continued)

(continued)

The sculptures at Autun (probably carved between 1120 and 1135) were long attributed to "Gislebertus," whose signature ("Gislebertus hoc fecit"—"Gislebertus made this") was cited as an early example of an artist proclaiming his creative accomplishment. Recent art historians, however, have questioned this interpretation, advancing the theory that Ghislebertus was a patron, rather than a sculptor.

Not surprisingly, the writings of medieval theologians also emphasized the threats of lurking demons, and recounted miracles in which the devil was confronted and defeated. In the following document, Peter the Venerable (c. 1092–1156), Abbot of Cluny and general of the Cluniac order, described how demons preyed upon a pious monk.

(From *Perspectives on Western Art: Source Documents and Readings*, ed. by Linnea H. Wren and David J. Wren. Copyright © 1987 Linnea Wren. Reprinted by permission of Westview Press, a member of the Perseus Books Group.)

From Peter the Venerable, *The Book of Miracles:* The Besetting Demons

At another time another brother, who was a carpenter, lay by night in a place somewhat removed from the rest. The place was lighted with a lamp, as is customary in the dormitories of monks. While he lay on his bed, not yet asleep, he beheld a monstrous vulture, whose wings and feet were scarce able to bear the load of his vast body, laboring and panting towards him, until it stood over against his bed. While the brother beheld this in amazement, behold! two other demons in human form came and spoke with that vulture—or rather, that fiend—saying, "What are you doing here? Can you do any work in this place?" "No," said he; "for they all thrust me hence by the protection of the cross and by sprinkling of holy water and by muttering of psalms. I have labored hard all this night, consuming my strength in vain; because of this I have come here baffled and wearied. But do tell me where you have been and how you have prospered." To which the others made reply: "We are come from Chalons, where we made one of Geoffrey of Donzy's knights fall into adultery with his host's wife. Then again we passed by a certain monastery, where we made the master of the school fornicate with one of his boys. But you, sluggard, why don't you get up, and at least cut off the foot of this monk, which he has stretched in disorderly fashion beyond his bed-clothes?" Whereupon the other seized the monk's axe which lay under the bed, and heaved it up to strike with all his force. The monk, seeing the axe thus raised aloft, withdrew his foot in fear; so that the demon's stroke fell harmlessly upon the end of the bed; whereupon the evil spirits vanished immediately. The brother who had seen this vision related it all right away, next morning, to father Hugh, who sent to Chalons and to Tournus to assure himself of the truth of the tale. Here, searching narrowly into those things which the demons had asserted, he found that these ministers of lies had told the truth.

But some man will say: "Seeing that the evil spirits far surpass all human cunning in the subtlety of their malice (for their natural nimbleness is clogged by no bodily weight, and so they are rendered free in all their motions and are all the more sagacious by long experience), how is it that they betray their wicked designs or deeds to men's ears? Do they not understand how often men are saved from their most subtle snares by these revelations of their wiles, and the demons are thus frustrated of their purpose? Why, then, did they betray their evil deeds in the hearing of that brother, and confess themselves unable to work the wickedness that they desired?" To this we must answer that, great as are their powers for evil, and prompt as is their will to deceive us, yet by God's hidden disposition they are often so wondrously and incomprehensibly caught in their own false wiles, that they are sometimes compelled unwillingly to serve that human salvation which is always contrary to their desire.

Questions for Discussion:

1. Describe the various tortures being applied to the souls in the tympanum.
2. What were the various evil activities of the demons that terrorized the innocent monk? How were they thwarted in their designs?

INTERPRETING THE EVIDENCE

8.4   The Reliquary and Miracles of Saint Foy, Virgin Martyr

The cult of Saint Foy at Conques in southern France reached its high point as a pilgrimage goal during the eleventh century, although the site and reliquary continue to attract a great deal of attention in the contemporary world. The relics of the saint, a virgin who had been martyred in the third century, were taken to the monastery at Conques in the ninth century, when a piece of Foy's skull was enclosed in a three-dimensional reliquary statue (pictured here). This type of sculpture was relatively rare, partly because of the early Christian prohibition against idol worship. One section in the document excepted here is emblematic of this distrust of religious statuary.

Beginning in 900, a number of donations were given to the monastery at Conques by wealthy individuals of power and authority, in large part a result of the miracle-working reputation of Saint Foy. The Book of Miracles, *written about 1010 by Bernard of Angers, records many wondrous occurrences, such as the replacement of a man's eyeballs that had been ripped out a year earlier. Bernard had made three pilgrimages to Conques, and, although he was initially skeptical of the cult, he eventually acknowledged the power of the saint.*

(From *Readings in Medieval History*, 3rd ed., edited by Patrick J. Geary [Canada: Broadview Press, 2003], pp. 333–335. Copyright © 2003 by Patrick J. Geary. Reprinted by permission of University of Toronto Press Higher Education Division.)

The Miracles of Saint Foy

There are many and undeniable indications that divine justice exercises a terrible judgment upon those who speak against Saint Foy. We will tell about one most extraordinary event when we speak about the image of the holy martyr. It is an ancient custom in all of Auvergne, Rodez, Toulouse and the neighboring regions that the local saint has a statue of gold, silver, or some other metal according to their means. This statue serves as a reliquary for the head of the saint or for

The Reliquary of Saint Foy, Virgin Martyr, late tenth–early eleventh century. 33 ½ in. high. *(Courtesy Cathedral Treasury, Conques, France.)*

(continued)

a part of his body. The learned might see in this a superstition and a vestige of the cult of demons, and I myself who am but an ignoramus had the same impression the first time that I saw the statue of Saint Gerard enthroned on the altar resplendent with gold and stones, with an expression so human that the simple people sense that they are being watched by the gaze of an inquisitor and they pretend that it winks at pilgrims whose prayers it answers. I admit to my shame that turning to my friend Bernerius and laughing I whispered to him in Latin, "What do you think of the idol? Wouldn't Jupiter or Mars be happy with it?" And Bernerius was inspired to add rather ingenuous pleasantries and to revile the statue. We were not wrong: When one adores the true God, it is inappropriate and absurd to make images of plaster, wood or bronze except for the image of the Lord crucified that Christian piety makes with love to celebrate the memory of the passion of the Lord and which all of the holy Church has adopted. As for saints, it is sufficient that the truthful books or frescoes on walls recall their memory. For we do not tolerate statues of saints for any reason, unless as an ancient abuse and an eradicable and inborn custom of the ignorant. In certain regions these images take on such an importance that if, for example, I had the misfortune to express my reflections on the image of St. Gerard out loud, I would have had to pay dearly for my crime.

Three days later we arrived at Saint Foy. At the moment that we entered the monastery it happened by chance that the back of the sanctuary where the holy image is kept was open. We approached but the crowd was such that we could not prostrate ourselves like so many others already lying on the floor. Unhappy, I remained standing, fixing my view on the image and murmuring this prayer, "Saint Foy, you whose relics rest in this sham, come to my assistance on the day of judgment." And this time again I looked at my companion the scholastic Bernerius from out of the corner because I found it outrageous that all of these rational beings should be praying to a mute and inanimate object. My idle talk or little understanding nevertheless did not come from a clean conscience, because I should not have disrespectfully called a sacred image, which is not consulted for divination by means of sacrifices like an idol but is rather for revering the memory of a martyr in honor of the highest God, a sham like those of Venus or Diana. Later I greatly regretted to have acted so stupidly toward the saint of God. This was because among other miracles Don Adalgerius, at that time dean and later as I have heard, abbot (of Conques and Figeac), told me a remarkable account of a cleric named Oldaric. One day when the venerable image had to be taken to another place, because he thought himself smarter than the others, his heart was so twisted that he restrained the crowd from bringing offerings and he insulted and belittled the image of the saint with various insults. The next night, a lady of imposing severity appeared to him: "You," she said, "how dare you insult my image?" Having said this, she flogged her enemy with a staff which she was seen to carry in her right hand. He survived only long enough to tell the vision in the morning.

Thus there is no place left for arguing whether the effigy of Saint Foy ought to be venerated since it is clear that he who reproached the holy martyr nevertheless retracted his reproach, nor is it a spurious idol where nefarious rites of sacrifice or of divination are conducted, but rather a pious memorial of the holy virgin before which great numbers of faithful decently and eloquently implore her efficacious intercession for their sins. And what is more wisely to be recognized, the container of the relics of the saints was made as a votive offering of the craftsman in the form of that person and is by far a more precious treasure than the ark of the covenant was of old. In the statue of Saint Foy her whole head is preserved, which is surely one of the most noble pearls of the celestial Jerusalem. Out of consideration of her merits, the divine goodness effects such prodigies that I have never heard the like concerning any other saint in our time. Therefore the image of Saint Foy is not something which ought to be destroyed or vituperated, especially since it has never led anyone to fall back into the error of paganism nor has it lessened the virtues of the saints nor caused the slightest harm to religion.

Questions for Discussion:

1. What objections to the veneration of relics are raised by the author and Bernier in the conversation at the beginning of the excerpt?
2. In this account, which is typical of medieval hagiography (works about the lives and actions of saints), how did Saint Foy establish the validity of her powers?
3. Describe the reliquary. Does it represent your idea of a proper repository for saintly relics?

8.5   The Relics of Saint Cuthbert

Saint Cuthbert (635–687) was instrumental in the Christianizing of the British Isles. He was most closely associated with Lindesfarne, where he assisted in the acceptance of Roman Christianity. He died in 687, and his tomb became a site of numerous miracles. According to the Venerable Bede, when his tomb was opened eleven years after his death, his body was found in an almost lifelike state. As may be seen in the first excerpt from Bede's Ecclesiastical History of the English Nation, *Cuthbert's new shrine was the site of many miracles, and became a pilgrimage goal. The second passage describes a healing miracle that resulted from contact with Cuthbert's relics. It is evident from this account that medieval people believed that even the tiniest portion of a saintly body, such as a few hairs, or scraps of clothing worn by the saint, had miraculous properties.*

(From *The Ecclesiastical History of the English Nation Written by the Venerable Bede* [London: J.M. Dent and Co., 1893], pp. 294–298.)

In order to show with how much glory the man of God, Cuthbert, lived after death, his holy life having been indicated before his death by frequent miracles; when he had been buried eleven years, Divine Providence put it into the minds of the brethren to take up his bones, expecting, as is usual with dead bodies, to find all the flesh consumed and reduced to ashes, and the rest dried up, and intending to put the same into a new coffin, and to lay them in the same place, but above the pavement, for the honor due to him. They acquainted Bishop Edbert with their design, and he consented to it, and ordered that the same should be done on the anniversary of his burial. They did so, and opening the grave, found all the body whole, as if it had been alive, and the joints pliable, more like one asleep than a dead person; besides, all the vestments the body had on were not only found, but wonderful for their freshness and gloss. The brothers seeing this, with much amazement hastened to tell the bishop what they had found; he being then alone in a place remote from the church, and encompassed by the sea. There he always used to spend the time of Lent, and was accustomed to stay there with great devotion, forty days before the birth of our Lord, in abstinence, prayer, and tears. There also his venerable predecessor, Cuthbert, had some time served God in private, before he went to the isle of Farne [Lindesfarne].

They brought him also some part of the garments that had covered his holy body; which presents he thankfully accepted, and attentively listening to the miracles, he with wonderful affection kissed those garments, as if they had been still upon his father's body, and said, "Let the body be put into new garments in lieu of these you have brought, and so lay it into the coffin you have provided; for I am certain that the place will not long remain empty, having been sanctified with so many miracles of heavenly grace; and how happy is he to whom our Lord, the author and giver of all bliss, shall grant the privilege of lying in the same." The bishop having said this and much more, with many tears and great humility, the brothers did as he had commanded them, and when they had dressed the body in new garments, and laid it in a new coffin, they placed it on the pavement of the sanctuary. Soon after, God's beloved bishop, Edbert, fell grievously sick, and his distemper daily increasing, in a short time, that is, on the 6th of May, he also departed to our Lord; and they laid his body in the grave of the holy father Cuthbert, placing over it the coffin, with the uncorrupted remains of that father. The miracles sometimes wrought in that place testify the merits of them both; some of which we before preserved the memory of in the book of his life, and have thought fit to add some more in this *History,* which have lately come to our knowledge.

The following chapter from Bede's history describes how Saint Cuthbert's relics healed an infection of the eye.

Nor is that cure to be passed over in silence, which was performed by his relics three years ago; and was told me by the brother himself, on whom it was wrought. It happened in the monastery, which, being built near the river Dacore, has taken its name from the same, over which, at that time, the religious Suidbert presided as abbot. In that monastery was a youth whose eyelid had a great swelling on it, which growing daily, threatened the loss of the eye. The surgeons applied their medicines to ripen it, but in vain. Some said it ought to be cut off; others opposed it, for fear of worse consequences. The brother having long suffered with this malady, and seeing no human means likely to save his eye, but that, on the contrary, it grew daily worse, suddenly was cured, through the Divine Goodness, by the relics of the holy father, Cuthbert; for the brethren, finding his body uncorrupted, after having been many years buried, took some part of the hair, which they might, at the request of friends, give or show, in testimony of the miracle.

One of the priests of the monastery, named Thridred, who is now abbot there, had a small part of these relics by him at that time. One day in the church he opened the box of relics, to give some part to a friend that begged it, and it happened that the youth who had the distempered eye was then in the church; the priest, having given his friend as much as he thought fit, delivered the rest to the youth to put it into its place. Having received the hairs of the holy head, by some fortunate impulse, he clapped them to the sore eyelid, and endeavored for some time, by the application of them, to soften and abate the swelling. Having done this, he again laid the relics into the box, as he had been ordered, believing that his eye would soon be cured by the hairs of the man of God, which had touched it; nor did his faith disappoint him. It was then, as he is accustomed to relate it, about the second hour of the day; but he, being busy about other things that belonged to that day, about the sixth hour of the same, touching his eye suddenly, found it as sound with the lid, as if there never had been any swelling or deformity on it.

Question for Discussion:

1. Discuss your reactions to the premise that saintly relics have healing capabilities. Do you know of similar accounts in the contemporary world?

INTERPRETING THE EVIDENCE

8.6 Suger's Chalice and *On the Various Arts* by Theophilus

During the Middle Ages, architects and artists did not claim to have created their works. Instead, they were taught to view their creations as the products of talents, skills, and abilities that were gifts from God. Hence, God was the true creator. This concept was clearly shown by Roger of Helmarshausen, a twelfth-century German artist and philosopher whose treatise De diversis artibus *("Concerning the Various Arts") was written under his pseudonym Theophilus (see also Document 4.14). In the following excerpt, King David advises his son Solomon concerning the construction of a temple and the creation of various liturgical vessels. This passage also provides justification for the religious aesthetic of elaborate church decoration and beautiful ornamentation.*

(From *An Essay upon Various Arts*, by Theophilus, trans. by Robert Hendrie [London: John Murray, 1847], pp. 203–207.}

Preface to the Third Book

. . . [King David] had read in Exodus that God had given a command to Moses for the construction of the tabernacle, and had selected by name the masters of the works, and that he had filled them with the spirit of wisdom and intelligence and science, in every knowledge, for inventing and executing work in gold and silver, and brass, gems, wood, and in art of all kinds. He had discerned, by means of pious reflection, that God complacently beheld decoration of this kind, which He was appointing to be constructed under the teaching and authority of his Holy Spirit; and he believed that without His inspiration no one could mold any work of this kind. Therefore, [speaking to his son Solomon] most beloved son, you will not doubt, but believe with an entire faith, that the Spirit of God has filled your heart when you have adorned his temple with so much beauty, and with such variety of work; and that you may not chance to fear, I can prove, with clear reasoning, that whatever

you may be able to learn, understand, or invent in the arts, is ministered to you as a gift of the sevenfold Spirit.

Through the spirit of wisdom you know that all created things proceed from God, and that without him nothing exists. Through the spirit of intelligence you have acquired the faculty of genius, in whatever order, in what variety, in what proportion, you may choose to apply to your varied work. Through the spirit of counsel you do not hide the talent conceded to you by God, but by working and teaching openly, with humility, you faithfully expound to those who desire to learn. Through the spirit of perseverance you shake off all lethargy of sloth, and whatever with quick diligence you commence, you carry through with full vigor to the completion. Through the spirit of science accorded to you, you rule with genius from an abounding heart, and from that with which you entirely overflow you bestow with the confidence of a well-stored mind for the common good. Through the spirit of piety you regulate the nature, the destination, the time, the measure and the means of the work; and, through a pious consideration, the price of the fee, that the vice of avarice or covetousness may not steal in. Through the spirit of the fear of God you meditate that you can do nothing from yourself, but you consider that you possess, or will, nothing unconceded by God; but by believing, confiding and giving thanks, you ascribe to divine compassion whatever you have learned, or what you are, or what you may be.

Animated, dearest son, by these covenants with the virtues, you have confidently approached the house of God, have decorated with the utmost beauty ceilings or walls with various work, and, showing forth with different colors a likeness of the paradise of God, glowing with various flowers, and verdant with herbs and leaves, and cherishing the

(continued)

lives of the saints with crowns of various merit, you have, after a fashion, shown to beholders everything in creation praising God, its Creator, and have caused them to proclaim him admirable in all his works. Nor is the eye of man even able to decide upon which work it may first fix its glance; if it beholds the ceilings, they glow like draperies; if it regards the walls, there is the appearance of paradise; if it marks the abundance of light from the windows, it admires the inestimable beauty of the glass and the variety of the most costly work. But if by chance a faithful mind should behold a representation of our Lord's passion expressed in drawing, it is penetrated with compunction; if it beholds how many sufferings the saints have bodily supported, and how many rewards of eternal life they have received, it quickly induces the observance of a better life; if it regards how much rejoicing is in heaven, and how much suffering in the flames of hell, it is animated by hope for its good actions, and is struck with fear by the consideration of its sins.

Act therefore now, well-intentioned man, happy before God and men in this life, happier in a future, in whose labor and study so many sacrifices are offered up to God; henceforth warm yourself with a more ample invention, hasten to complete with all the study of thy mind those things which are still wanting among the utensils of the house of the Lord, without which the divine mysteries and the services of ceremonies cannot continue. These are the chalices, candelabra, incense burners, vials, pitchers, caskets of sacred relics, crosses, missals and other things which useful necessity requires for the use of the ecclesiastical order.

Question for Discussion:

1. In this excerpt, King David is ostensibly speaking to his son, Solomon. His program for successful artistic accomplishment offers a pattern to be emulated by artists and craftsmen. What does he advise?

Chapter 4 included a selection from the work of Theophilus that provided specific directions for carving

ivory. He also wrote about the techniques used for creating liturgical vessels, including precise directions for forming bejeweled chalices made of silver and gold. One of the most beautiful examples of the medieval goldsmith's art is the chalice used by Abbot Suger of Saint Denis, whose expansion of his abbey church has often been viewed as the birth of Gothic style. (See Chapter 10.) It is also typical of the objects that drew sharp criticism from Saint Bernard of Clairvaux.

(From *Theophilus: The Various Arts {De Diversis Artibus}*, trans. by C. R. Dodwell. Oxford: Clarendon Press, 1986, pp. 98–99; 100–101; 104–105.)

Suger's Chalice, 7 ¼ in. high, top diameter 11.6 in. Sardonyx cup Second/first century B.C.E., mounting 1137–1140. *(French Cup, Alexandrian. "Chalice of the Abbot Suger of Saint-Denis." Photograph © Board of Trustees, National Gallery of Art, Washington, D.C. Photo: Philip A. Charles.)*

Making a Gold Chalice

Whatever the kind of gold you have, if you want to make a chalice from it, and to ornament it with stones, enamels and pearls, you begin in this way.

First, test each piece of gold to see if it can be beaten with a hammer without breaking. Put on one side any that is not broken, and on the other any that is, for melting. Then take a piece of baked brick and, according to the amount of gold to be heated, cut a hollow in it to take the gold; if you have no brick, then make a hollow in a square sandstone with an iron tool. Put it on the fire and blow it, and, when it is red hot, put in the gold. Place coals over it and blow for a very long time. Then take out the gold and beat it with a hammer. If it is not broken it will do. If, in fact, it is broken, replace it again on another stone, and continue like this until it cannot be broken by hammering. But if it cracks a little, melt it with sulphur and, in this way, it can be put right.

When this is done, melt all the gold alike, reducing it to one mass, and divide it up by weight in the same way as you divided up the silver above, and, in the same way, beat it out to the shape that you prefer. The handles you will fashion as you please. If you want to make them with gemmed work, beat out two pieces of the gold, so thin that the mark of a finger-nail can be lightly impressed on it, and cut them out to the shape that you want the handles to have. Two of these pieces make up one handle. Then make the flux for soldering in this way. . . .

Soldering the Gold

When this [the flux] has been prepared, take the two pieces of gold from which you formed one of the handles, and place them in front of you. On these, place the gems that you want to apply, and the pearls, each one in position.

Then beat some gold out thin and long, and draw from it thick, medium and fine wires, and file them with the file mentioned above, so that beading appears on them. When these [wires] have been reheated, put the gems back in their places and fasten them separately. Then, with fine tweezers, fit a piece of the thicker wire on the surface of both the pieces of gold round the edge, and, with the shears, make very fine incisions all the way round; in these you fix the wires so that they do not slip until they are soldered.

Then take a flat piece of gold, beaten smooth with a wooden mallet, and on it successively attach several of the medium wires in such a way that they are not touching each other but have a space between. At their extremities, fine incisions are made in the thin gold in which they are held. Take the vessel containing the flux, shake it vigorously so that the powder is well mixed, and, with a fine feather, paint it carefully everywhere over this gold and over the wires. Put the gold on the fire, blow with your mouth and bellows until you see the flux flow all round like running water, immediately sprinkle with a little water, take the gold off and carefully wash it. Apply the flux again, and solder as before until all the wires hold firmly. After this, cut them into small pieces like strips, in such a way that each strip has a wire, and you then bend them round [the stones] and so make the settings. These are large or small, according to the size of each stone, and, in them, you enclose the stones and set them in position. . . .

Setting the Gems and Pearls

When this has been done, take a thin strip of gold and attach it to the upper rim of the bowl, taking it round from one handle to the other. The width of this strip is the same as the size of the stones which you want to set. Placing these in their order, you so arrange them that, first, there is a stone with four pearls set at its corners, then an enamel, next to it a stone with pearls, and then an enamel again. You arrange them like this, with the stones always standing next to the handles, and you prepare the settings and grounds of the stones, and the settings for the enamels, and solder them as above. You do the same on the other side of the bowl. If you want to place gems and pearls in the middle of the body, you proceed in the same way, and, when this is done, you affix them and solder them, like the handles.

(*continued*)

After this, you fit single pieces of thin gold in all the settings in which the enamels are to be placed. When they have been carefully adjusted, you take them out and, using a measure and rule, you cut a strip of gold which should be somewhat thicker. These strips you bend twice round the edge of each piece, in such a way that there is a small gap all round between the strips; this space is called the border of the enamel. Then, using the same measure and rule, you cut cloisons of extremely thin gold. You bend them round with fine tweezers, and form whatever designs you want to make in the enamels, either circles, or scrolls, or flowers, or birds, or animals, or figures. You adjust the cloisons with delicacy and care, each one in its place, and you stick them on with paste over the fire. When you have filled one piece, you solder it with the greatest care lest the delicate work and the thin gold come apart or melt. This you do two or three times, until each of the cloisons is firmly fixed.

Questions for Discussion:

1. This description of the method to be used for creating gold chalices was written in the twelfth century. Do you think that the techniques advocated here are still being practiced by workers in gold and silver? Do you recognize any that might be obsolete?
2. Study the photograph of Suger's chalice. What features do you recognize from the treatise of Theophilus? Are there areas of the object that are not described in the methodology?

8.7   "O Vanity of Vanities!": Bernard of Clairvaux on Religious Art

Bernard of Clairvaux (1090–1153) was dismayed by what he considered to be the ostentatious artistic display in churches and monasteries. In keeping with his views concerning simple liturgical practice, he was radically opposed to the elegant ornamentation of churches. To him, stained glass, golden chalices, elaborate sculpture, and complex liturgical music distracted the mind of the worshiper from the important focus on God and spiritual matters. Bernard reluctantly admitted that it might be acceptable to lead laypeople to a worshipful state of mind by means of colorful windows and rich objects, but, as he stated in the famous "Letter to William of St. Thierry," he was unalterably opposed to the use of intricate sculpture in the monastery. These were expressly forbidden, "because, when we busy ourselves with such things, the profit of good meditation is often neglected, or the discipline of religious gravity."

But these are small things; I will pass on to matters greater in themselves, yet seeming smaller because they are more usual. I say nothing of the vast height of your churches, their immoderate length, their superfluous breadth, the costly polishings, the curious carvings and paintings which attract the worshiper's gaze and hinder his attention, and seem to me in some sort a revival of the ancient Jewish rites. Let this pass, however: say that this is done for God's honor. But I, as a monk, ask of my brother monks as the pagan [poet Persius] asked of his fellow-pagans: "Tell me, O Pontiffs" (he said) "why is this gold in the sanctuary?" So say I, "Tell me, you poor men" (for I break the verse to keep the sense) "tell me, you poor (if, indeed, you are poor), why is this gold in your sanctuary?" And indeed the bishops have an excuse which monks have not; for we know that

(From *A Medieval Garner*, by G. C. Coulton [London: Constable & Co., 1910], pp. 70–73. Reprinted in *Early Medieval Art: 300–1500*, ed. by Caecilia Davis-Weyer [Toronto: University of Toronto Press, 1986]. Translation modified.)

they, being advisors both to the wise and the unwise, and unable to excite the devotion of carnal folk by spiritual things, do so by bodily adornments. But we [monks] who have now come forth from the people; we who have left all the precious and beautiful things of the world for Christ's sake; who, in order to win Christ, have counted but dung all things fair to see or soothing to hear, sweet to smell, delightful to taste, or pleasant to touch—in a word, all bodily delights—whose devotion, pray, do we monks intend to excite by these things? What profit, I say, do we expect from them? The admiration of fools, or the oblations of the simple? Or, since we are scattered among the nations, have we perhaps learned their works and do we now serve their graven images? To speak plainly, does the root of all this lie in covetousness, which is idolatry, and do we seek not profit, but a gift? If you ask, "How?" I say: "In a strange fashion." For money is so artfully scattered that it may multiply; it is expended that it may give increase, and prodigality gives birth to plenty: for at the very sight of these costly yet marvelous vanities men are more kindled to offer gifts than to pray. Thus wealth is drawn up by ropes of wealth, thus money brings money; for I know not how it is that, where ever more abundant wealth is seen, there do men offer more freely. Their eyes are feasted with relics cased in gold, and their purse-strings are loosened. They are shown a most comely image of some saint, whom they think all the more saintly if he is more gaudily painted. Men run to kiss him, and are invited to give; there is more admiration for his comeliness than veneration for his sanctity. Hence the church is adorned with gemmed crowns of light—nay, with lusters like cartwheels, encircled with lamps, but no less brilliant with the precious stones that stud them. Moreover we see candelabra standing like trees of massive bronze, fashioned with marvelous subtlety of art, and glistening no less brightly with gems than with the lights they carry. What do you think is the purpose of all this? The compunction of penitents, or the admiration of beholders? O vanity of vanities, yet no more vain than insane! The church is resplendent in her walls, beggarly in her poor; she clothes her stones in gold, and leaves her sons naked; the rich man's eye is fed at the expense of the indigent. The curious find their

delight here, yet the needy find no relief. Do we not revere at least the images of the Saints, which swarm even in the inlaid pavement whereon we tread? Men spit often in an Angel's face; often, again, the countenance of some Saint is ground under the heel of a passer-by. And if does not spare these sacred images, why not even the fair colors? Why do you make that so fair which will soon be made so foul? Why lavish bright hues upon that which will be trodden under foot? Why are these comely forms in places where they are defiled with customary dust? And, lastly, what are such things as these to you poor men, you monks, you spiritual folk? Unless perhaps here also you may answer the poet's question in the words of the Psalmist: "Lord, I have loved the habitation of Thy House, and the place where Thine honor dwells." I grant it, then, let us accept that this is to be done in the church; for, though it is harmful to vain and covetous folk, yet it is not to the simple and devout. But in the cloister, under the eyes of the brethren who read there, what profit is there in those ridiculous monsters, in that marvelous and deformed comeliness, that comely deformity? To what purpose are those unclean apes, those fierce lions, those monstrous centaurs, those half-men, those striped tigers, those fighting knights, those hunters winding their horns? Many bodies are there seen under one head, or again, many heads to a single body. Here is a four-footed beast with a serpent's tail; there, a fish with a beast's head. Here again the forepart of a horse trails half a goat behind it, or a horned beast bears the hind quarters of a horse. In short, so many and so marvelous are the varieties of diverse shapes on every hand, that we are more tempted to read in the marble than in our books, and to spend the whole day in wondering at these things rather than in meditating on the law of God. For God's sake, if men are not ashamed of these follies, why at least do they not shrink from the expense?

The abundance of my matter suggested much more for me to add; but from this I am distracted both by my own anxious business and by the too hasty departure of Brother Oger, [the bearer of this letter]. . . . This is my opinion of your Order [the Benedictines] and mine; nor can any man testify more truly than you, and those who know me as you do, that I am inclined to say these things not about you but to your faces. What in your Order is laudable, I praise and publish abroad; what is reprehensible, I hope to persuade you and other friends to amend. This is no detraction, but rather attraction: wherefore I wholly pray and beseech you to do the same by me. Farewell.

Questions for Discussion:

1. Discuss Bernard's diatribe against religious art, especially as it relates to the monastic life. How do you account for his negative views?
2. Analyze the reliquary of Saint Foy (Document 8.4) from Bernard's point of view.

Literature

8.8   "Noble Lord, Knight of Gentle Birth": From *The Song of Roland*

One of the most famous epic poems of the medieval era is The Song of Roland. *This anonymous work concerns a historical event that occurred during the reign of Charlemagne (see the reference to the location in Document 7.6), though the poem, based on oral tradition, was written down some 300 years later. In 778 Charlemagne marched into Spain to fight the Muslims. Soon, however, he faced a Saxon rebellion at home, and was forced to abandon his Spanish campaign. As he returned to his kingdom, his rear guard was ambushed by Basque soldiers, who slaughtered Charlemagne's men and disappeared.*

The plot of the poem promotes the idea that dying is the highest sign of a man's worth. The story concerns Roland, a trusted warrior, "the right hand of the emperor's body," who was caught in the ambush of the soldiers in the rear. Roland, always brave, refused to call for help as he was besieged in the pass until it was too late. He was the ideal Christian knight—loyal to God, his lord, and his companions.

(From *The Song of Roland*, trans. by Jessie Crosland [London: Chatto & Windus, 1924], pp. 72–84.)

CLIV

Count Roland was a noble warrior, Gautier del Hum a very good knight, and the archbishop a proven man of valor. Each of them is unwilling to desert the other; in the thick of the fight they strike down the heathen. A thousand Saracens [Muslims] are dismounted and on foot, and there are forty thousand on horseback. But, to my knowledge, they dare not approach; they hurl lances and spears, arrows and dart, winged bolts and shafts. . . . At the first onslaught they have killed Gautier; they have pierced the shield of Turpin [Archbishop] of Reims, broken his helmet and wounded him in the head, broken and torn his hauberk and wounded him with four lances through the body and killed his battle steed beneath him. Great is the grief when the archbishop falls.

CLV

When Turpin of Reims feels himself overthrown and struck through the body by four lances, quickly the baron leaps up again. He looks for Roland, he hastens towards him and says but one word: "I am not beaten! A good vassal will never cease to fight as long as he lives." He draws Almace, his sword of burnished steel; in the thickest part of the battle he strikes a thousand blows and more. Charles said afterwards that he had spared no one; he found four hundred heathen [Muslims] lying round about him—some wounded, some pierced right through, and many there were who had lost their heads. So says the chronicle, and he who was present at the battle; the baron Gilles, for whom God works miracles, wrote the account of it in the monastery of Laon. He who does not know these things understands little of this story.

CLVI

Count Roland is fighting nobly, but his body is burning hot and covered with sweat. He has a grievous pain in his head; his temple is broken from sounding the horn. But he wishes to know whether Charles [Charlemagne] will come, so he draws forth his horn and feebly sounds it. The emperor stood still and listened: "Lords," said he, "it goes very badly with us! Roland, my nephew, leaves us today. I hear by the sound of his horn that he is at the point of death. He who wishes to be with him over there must ride quickly; blow your trumpets—as many as there are in the army." Sixty thousand men blow so loudly that the hills and the valleys echo to the sound. The heathen hear it and they are not disposed to scorn it ; one says to the other: "Charles will soon be here."

CLVII

The heathen say: "The emperor is returning. Listen to the trumpets of the men of France. If Charles comes we shall suffer great loss. If Roland lives, he will renew this war and we shall have lost Spain, our native land." Four hundred helmeted men, of those who are considered best on the battle-field, band themselves together, and deliver a very terrible attack on Roland. Now the count has enough to do on his own account.

CLVIII

Count Roland, when he sees them approaching, shows himself strong and proud and ready for the conflict. He will not turn in flight as long as he lives. He is seated on his horse called Veillantif; he spurs it forward with his golden spurs and rushes into the thick of the fight to attack them. Archbishop Turpin is close beside him, and they say to one another: "Forward, friend! we have heard the horns of those of France; Charles, the mighty king, is on his way back."

CLIX

Count Roland never loved a coward, nor a proud man, nor an ill-conditioned man—nor even a knight if he were not courageous. He called to archbishop Turpin:

"Sire, you are on foot and I on horseback; out of love to you I will take my stand here and together we will suffer either good or ill. I will not abandon you for any mortal man. Even this attack of the heathen we will repulse, and the best blows given shall be those of Durendal." Said the archbishop: "Dishonored be he who does not strike hard! Charles is returning and he will avenge us well."

CLX

The heathen say: "To our misfortune were we born! What a dreadful day has dawned for us today. We have lost our lords and our peers and now Charles the warrior, is returning with his great army. We can hear the trumpets of the Frenchmen quite distinctly and loud is the noise of their battle-cry Montjoie. Count Roland's spirit is so fierce that he will never be vanquished by mortal man. Let us aim at him from a distance and leave him on the field of battle." And so they aimed at him with their darts and their arrows, their spears and lances and feathered shafts. They have broken and pierced Roland's shield and torn and dismailed his hauberk; but his body within they have not yet touched. But they have wounded Veillantif in thirty places and have struck him dead beneath the count. Then the heathen flee and leave him standing there. Count Roland remains there dismounted and on foot.

CLXI

The heathen flee in wrath and evil humor; they strive their utmost to make their way towards Spain. Count Roland has not the wherewithal to pursue them, for he has lost Veillantif, his warhorse and, . . . he has to remain on foot. He went to the assistance of archbishop Turpin; he unlaced the gilded helmet from his head, he took off his white, supple hauberk, he tore his jerkin to pieces and stuffed the strips into his gaping wounds. Then he lifted him, pressing him gently against his breast, and laid him down tenderly on the green grass. Then in a gentle voice he besought him: "Noble lord, give me your permission to go! All our comrades whom we loved so dearly are dead and we cannot leave them there. I must go and search for them and pick them out and gather them together here and range them before you." The archbishop replied: "Go and return hither! The field is yours, thank God, and mine."

CLXII

Roland departs and wanders over the field by himself. He searches the valleys and the hills. . . . There he found Gerin and his companion Gerier, and Berenger and Aton; there too he found Ansels and Samson, and the aged Girard de Roussillon. One by one the baron brought them and came with them to the archbishop and placed them in a row before his knees. The archbishop cannot refrain from weeping; he raises his hand and gives them his benediction. Then he says: "Ill-fated you have been, lords! May the God of glory receive your souls and place them in paradise among the holy flowers! And now my own death is causing me anguish; I shall never see the great emperor again."

CLXIII

Roland sets out again to search the field and this time he has found his comrade Oliver. He held him tightly in his arms against his breast and brought him to the archbishop as best he could and laid him on a shield beside the others. And the archbishop absolved him and made the sign of the cross upon him. Then the grief and the pity of it all increased. And Roland said: "Fair comrade Oliver, you were son of Duke Renier who held the region of Val de Runiers. You had no equal in any land for breaking a lance or shattering a shield, for vanquishing and laying low the proud, for helping and counseling the valiant, for. . . ."

CLXIV

Count Roland, when he sees all his peers dead, and Oliver too whom he loved so much, was overcome with tenderness and he began to weep. The color left his face and his grief was so great that he could not stand. Whether he will or no, he falls down in a swoon. The archbishop said: "You have had an evil fate, baron!"

CLXV

The archbishop, when he saw that Roland had fainted, was filled with such great grief that never has there been greater. He stretched out his hand and picked up the horn. There is some running water in Roncevaux; he tried to go to it that he might give some to Roland. He sets out tottering, with little steps and slow; he is so weak that he cannot go any further. He has lost so much blood that he has no strength. In shorter time than one would take to cross an acre of ground, his heart failed him and he fell to the ground. His death is causing him great anguish.

CLXVI

Count Roland recovers from his swoon; he gets up on his feet but his suffering is very great. He looks down the valley and up the slope; on the green grass, a little beyond his comrades, he sees the noble baron lying, the archbishop whom God placed here in his name. He is confessing his sins and looking upwards; with his hands clasped towards heaven, he prays God to grant him paradise. Turpin is dead, the warrior of Charles. Both by great battles and by very fine sermons he was always a champion against the heathen. May God grant him his holy benediction.

CLXVII

Count Roland sees the archbishop on the ground; he sees his bowels lying outside his body and his brains in a heap upon his forehead. Upon his breast, between the two shoulder blades, he has crossed his beautiful white hands. Deeply Roland makes lament according to the custom of his land: "Ah! noble lord, knight of gentle birth, today I commend thee to the glorious God of heaven. Never will there be a man who serves him more willingly. Since the days of the apostles never has there been such a prophet for upholding the faith and for attracting men to it. May your soul know no lack and may the door of paradise be open to it!"

CLXVIII

Roland feels that his own death is near; his brain is issuing forth out of his ears. Concerning his peers he prays God that he will call them to him, then on his own behalf he prays to the angel Gabriel. He takes the horn that he may have no reproach, and in the other hand he takes Durendal his sword. Somewhat further than a cross-bow can shoot an arrow he walks on the plough land in the direction of Spain; he mounts on a hillock and there under a fine tree there are four steps made of marble. He has fallen face downwards on the green grass and there he has lost consciousness for death is very near.

CLXIX

High are the hills and very high the trees, and there are four steps there of shining marble. Count Roland has swooned on the green grass. A Saracen [Muslim] who was feigning to be dead and lying amongst the others has been watching him all the time. He has besmeared his face and body with blood, and getting up on his feet he hastily runs towards him. He was big and strong and courageous, and his pride incites him to his fatal folly. He seized hold of Roland, both of his body and his arms and said one word: "The nephew of Charles is vanquished! I will take his sword to Arabia." As he drew it from him the count regained his senses a little.

CLXX

Roland feels that he is taking his sword. He opens his eyes and says a word to him: "I know that you are not one of ours!" He grips the horn from which he does not wish to be parted, and strikes the heathen on his helmet studded with gold. He smashes the steelwork and the head and the bones, he strikes both his eyes out of his head and overthrows him at his feet, dead. Then he said to him: "Heathen son of a slave, how were you so daring as to seize me, whether for right or for wrong? No one will hear of it but he will hold thee for a fool. Now my horn is split right in the wide part, and the crystal and the gold is all knocked off."

CLXXI

Roland feels that his sight is failing; he rises to his feet and exerts himself as much as he can, but all the color has fled from his face. There is a dark rock in front of him and he strikes ten blows on it in grief and anger. The steel grates but it does not break nor splinter. "Ah!" said the count, "Holy Mary, help me! Durendal, good sword, how ill-fated thou were! When I have left this life, I can care for thee no longer. Many are the battlefields on which I have been victorious through you, and many are the broad lands I have conquered for Charles the hoary-bearded. May you never belong to a man who would flee before anyone! A very good vassal has wielded you this longtime; never will there be another such in the free land of France."

CLXXII

Roland strikes his sword on the hard stone. . . . The steel grates, but it neither breaks nor splinters. When he sees that he cannot break it he begins to lament over it to himself: "Ah! Durendal, how beautiful thou art, how clear and bright! How dost thou shine and sparkle in the sunlight! Charles was in the valleys of Moriane when God sent word to him by an angel from heaven that he should give thee to a count and a leader. It was then that the great and noble king girded it on me. With it I conquered Anjou and Brittany, Poitou and the Maine. With it I conquered proud Normandy, and Provence and Aquitaine and Lombardy and the whole of Romania; with it I conquered Bavaria and all Flanders and Burgundy and the whole of Poland, and Constantinople which owed allegiance to him, and Saxony where he acts as he will. With it I conquered

Scotland . . . and England which he called his chamber; with it I have conquered many countries and lands which now belong to Charles whose beard is growing white. I have such grief and heaviness for this sword; I would much rather die than leave it in the hands of the heathen. Oh God, and Father, let not France suffer this shame."

CLXXIII

Roland struck upon the dark stone and shattered it in more pieces than I can tell you. The sword grates, but it does not splinter nor break; it rebounds upwards towards the sky. When the count perceives that he cannot break it, he laments over it very gently to himself: "Ah! Durendal, how beautiful and holy thou art! In thy gilded pommel are many relics: Saint Peter's tooth and some of St. Basil's blood, some of the hairs of my lord Saint Denis and a piece of the garment of holy Mary. It is not right that thou should be in the possession of the heathen; you should ever be in the guardianship of Christians. May no man who commits a cowardice possess you! By means of you I shall have vanquished many wide lands which are now in the possession of Charles the hoary-bearded. The emperor has become powerful and rich thereby."

CLXXIV

Roland feels that death holds him fast, for it has traveled down from his head to his heart. He has hastened to get beneath a pine-tree; there on the green grass he lays himself down on his face, and he places his sword and the horn beneath him. He has turned his head in the direction of the heathen folk, for he wishes intently that Charles and all his army may say: He has died like a conqueror, the noble count. In few words he confesses himself again and again, and holds forth his glove to God for his sins.

CLXXV

Roland feels that the end of his time has come. He lies on a rocky hillock looking towards Spain, and with one hand he beats his breast: "God, I am guilty before thee on account of the sins both great and small that I have committed, from the hour I was born to this day on which I am struck down!" He has stretched out his right glove towards God. The angels of heaven descend to him.

CLXXVI

Count Roland has laid himself down beneath a pine tree and has turned his face towards Spain. He began to call many things to mind: the many lands he had conquered, sweet France, and the men of his lineage, and Charlemagne, his lord, who nurtured him. He cannot restrain himself from weeping and sighing, but he is not forgetful of himself; he confesses himself and prays God for his mercy: "O true Father, who didst never lie, thou who didst raise St. Lazarus from the dead and save Daniel from the lions, save my soul from all the perils that beset it on account of the sins which I have committed in my life." He held out his right glove to God, and St. Gabriel took it from his hand. His head was resting on his arm and his hands were clasped, and thus he went to his end. God sent down his angel Cherubin and St. Michel du Peril; with them came St. Gabriel, and they carry the soul of the count to Paradise.

Questions for Discussion:

1. How does Roland embody the ideal Christian knight?
2. Discuss the portrayal of the Muslims in this poem. How did Christians view the "other"?
3. Stanza CLXXIII describes the relics carried by Roland, which he fears will fall into the hands of the Muslims. Compare these with other accounts of relics in this chapter.
4. In Stanza CLXXII, Roland reflects on all the areas where he has fought in Charlemagne's wars. How does this account compare with Einhard's description of Carolingian expansion? (Document 4.5).
5. Compare *The Song of Roland* with *Beowulf* (Document 2.9). Are any themes characteristic of both poems?

8.9   *Abraham*: A Play by Roswitha of Gandersheim

Roswitha of Gandersheim (c. 935–c. 1000) was a German nun at Gandersheim, a powerful and exclusive royal convent. Her origins are unknown, but since she entered the religious life as a child, it is assumed that she was of aristocratic background, since the oblation of children was a common practice of the nobility. She has long been recognized as the first German woman to have composed literary texts. Her works, written in Latin, were addressed to her convent sisters, and consisted of poetry, historical legends, and dramatic works.

The prologue to her plays, dedicated to her abbess Gerberg, indicates her motivation for literary composition, and expresses the difficulties associated with her chosen craft. The play entitled Abraham *is a typical didactic religious drama of the era.*

(From *The Plays of Roswitha*, trans. by Christopher St. John [London: Chatto & Windus, 1923], pp. xxxiv–xxxv; 71–91.)

To Gerberg

ILLUSTRIOUS Abbess, venerated no less for uprightness and honesty than for the high distinction of a royal and noble race, Roswitha of Gandersheim, the last of the least of those fighting under your ladyship's rule, desires to give you all that a servant owes her mistress.

O my Lady, bright with the varied jewels of spiritual wisdom, your maternal kindness will not let you hesitate to read what, as you know, was written at your command! It was you who gave me the task of chronicling in verse the deeds of the Emperor, and you know that it was impossible to collect them together from hearsay. You can imagine the difficulties which my ignorance put in my way while I was toiling over this work. There were things of which I could not find any written record, nor could I elicit information by word of mouth which seemed sufficiently reliable. I was like a person in a strange land wandering without a guide through a forest where the path is concealed by dense snow. In vain he tries to follow the directions of those who have shown the way. He wanders from the path, now by chance strikes it again, until at last, penetrating the thickness of the wood, he reaches a place where he may take a long desired rest, and sitting down there, does not proceed further until someone overtakes him, or he discovers the footprints of one who has gone before. Even so have I, obeying the command to undertake a complete chronicle of great deeds, gone on my way, trembling, hesitating, and vacillating, so great was the difficulty of finding a path in the forest of these royal achievements.

And now, worn out by the journey, I am holding my peace and resting in a suitable place. I do not propose to go further without better guidance. If I could be inspired by the eloquent words of learned folk (either already set down or to be set down in the future) I might perhaps find a means of glozing [minimizing] my uncouth workmanship. At present I am defenseless at every point, because I am not supported by any authority. I also fear I shall be accused of temerity in presuming to describe in my humble uncultured way matters which ought to be set forth with all the ceremony of great learning. Yet if my work is examined by those who know how to weigh things fairly, I shall be more easily pardoned on account of my sex and my inferior knowledge, especially as I did not undertake it of my own will but at your command. Why should I fear the judgment of others, since if there are mistakes I should fall only under your censure, and why should I not escape reproof seeing that I was anxious to keep silence? I should deserve blame if I sought to withhold my work. In any case I leave the decision to you and your friend, Archbishop William, to whom you have thought fit to show these unpolished lines.

Abraham

Characters:

ABRAHAM.
EPHREM.
MARY.
A FRIEND TO ABRAHAM.
AN INN-KEEPER.

Abraham

SCENE I

Abraham. Brother Ephrem, my dear comrade in the hermit life, may I speak to you now, or shall I wait until you have finished your divine praises?

EPHREM. And what can you have to say to me which is not praise of Him Who said: "Where two or three are gathered together in My Name, I am with them"?

ABRAHAM. I have not come to speak of anything which He would not like to hear.

EPHREM. I am sure of it. So speak at once.

ABRAHAM. It concerns a decision I have to make. I long for your approval.

EPHREM. We have one heart and one soul. We ought to agree.

ABRAHAM. I have a little niece of tender years. She has lost both her parents, and my affection for her has been deepened by compassion for her lonely state. I am in constant anxiety on her account.

EPHREM. Ought you who have triumphed over the world to be vexed by its cares!

ABRAHAM. My only care is her radiant beauty! What if it should one day be dimmed by sin.

EPHREM. No one can blame you for being anxious.

ABRAHAM. I hope not.

EPHREM. How old is she?

ABRAHAM. At the end of this year she will be eight.

EPHREM. She is very young.

ABRAHAM. That does not lessen my anxiety.

EPHREM. Where does she live?

ABRAHAM. At my hermitage now; for at the request of her other kinsfolk I have undertaken to bring her up. The fortune left her ought, I think, to be given to the poor.

EPHREM. A mind taught so early to despise temporal things should be fixed on heaven.

ABRAHAM. I desire with all my heart to see her the spouse of Christ and devoted entirely to His service.

EPHREM. A praiseworthy wish.

ABRAHAM. I was inspired by her name.

EPHREM. What is she called?

ABRAHAM. Mary.

EPHREM. Mary! Such a name ought to be adorned with the crown of virginity.

ABRAHAM. I have no fear that she will be unwilling, but we must be gentle.

EPHREM. Come, let us go, and impress on her that no life is so sweet and secure as the religious one.

SCENE II

ABRAHAM. Mary, my child by adoption, whom I love as my own soul! Listen to my advice as to a father's, and to Brother Ephrem's as that of a very wise man. Strive to imitate the chastity of the holy Virgin whose name you bear.

EPHREM. Child, would it not be a shame if you, who through the mystery of your name are called to mount to the stars where Mary the mother of God reigns, chose instead the low pleasures of the earth?

MARY. I know nothing about the mystery of my name, so how can I tell what you mean?

EPHREM. Mary, my child, means "star of the sea"—that star which rules the world and all the peoples in the world.

MARY. Why is it called the star of the sea?

EPHREM. Because it never sets, but shines always in the heavens to show mariners their right course.

MARY. And how can such a poor thing as I am—made out of slime, as my uncle says—shine like my name?

EPHREM. By keeping your body unspotted, and your mind pure and holy.

MARY. It would be too great an honor for any human being to become like the stars.

EPHREM. If you choose you can be as the angels of God, and when at last you cast off the burden of this mortal body they will be near you. With them you will pass through the air, and walk on the sky. With them you will sweep round the zodiac, and never slacken your steps until the Virgin's Son takes you in His arms in His mother's dazzling bridal room!

MARY. Who but an ass would think little of such happiness! So I choose to despise the things of earth, and deny myself now that I may enjoy it!

EPHREM. Out of the mouths of babes and sucklings! A childish heart, but a mature mind!

ABRAHAM. God be thanked for it!

EPHREM. Amen to that.

ABRAHAM. But though by God's grace she has been given the light, at her tender age she must be taught how to use it.

EPHREM. You are right.

ABRAHAM. I will build her a little cell with a narrow entrance near my hermitage. I can visit her there often, and through the window instruct her in the psalter and other pages of the divine law.

EPHREM. That is a good plan.

MARY. I put myself under your direction, Father Ephrem.

EPHREM. My daughter! May the Heavenly Bridegroom to Whom you have given yourself in the tender bud of your youth shield you from the wiles of the devil!

SCENE III

ABRAHAM. Brother Ephrem, Brother Ephrem! When anything happens, good or bad, it is to you I turn. It is your counsel I seek. Do not turn your face away, brother—do not be impatient, but help me.

EPHREM. Abraham, Abraham, what has come to you? What is the cause of this immoderate grief? Ought a hermit to weep and groan after the manner of the world?

ABRAHAM. Was any hermit ever so stricken? I cannot bear my sorrow.

EPHREM. Brother, no more of this. To the point; what has happened?

ABRAHAM. Mary! Mary! my adopted child! Mary, whom I cared for so lovingly and taught with all my skill for ten years! Mary—

EPHREM. Well, what is it?

ABRAHAM. Oh God! She is lost!

EPHREM. Lost? What do you mean?

ABRAHAM. Most miserably. Afterwards she ran away.

EPHREM. But by what wiles did the ancient enemy bring about her undoing?

ABRAHAM. By the wiles of false love. Dressed in a monk's habit, the hypocrite went to see her often. He succeeded in making the poor ignorant child love him. She leapt from the window of her cell for an evil deed.

EPHREM. I shudder as I listen to you.

ABRAHAM. When the unhappy girl knew that she was ruined, she beat her breast and dug her nails into her face. She tore her garments, pulled out her hair. Her despairing cries were terrible to hear.

EPHREM. I am not surprised. For such a fall a whole fountain of tears should rise.

ABRAHAM. She moaned out that she could never be the same—

EPHREM. Poor, miserable girl!

ABRAHAM. And reproached herself for having forgotten our warning.

EPHREM. She might well do so.

ABRAHAM. She cried that all her vigils, prayers, and fasts had been thrown away.

EPHREM. If she perseveres in this penitence she will be saved.

ABRAHAM. She has not persevered. She has added worse to her evil deed.

EPHREM. Oh, this moves me to the depths of my heart!

ABRAHAM. After all these tears and lamentations she was overcome by remorse, and fell headlong into the abyss of despair.

EPHREM. A bitter business!

ABRAHAM. She despaired of being able to win pardon, and resolved to go back to the world and its vanities.

EPHREM. I cannot remember when the devil could boast of such a triumph over the hermits.

ABRAHAM. Now we are at the mercy of the demons.

EPHREM. I marvel that she could have escaped without your knowledge.

ABRAHAM. If I had not been so blind! I ought to have paid more heed to that terrible vision. Yes, I see now that it was sent to warn me.

EPHREM. What vision?

ABRAHAM. I dreamed I was standing at the door of my cell, and that a huge dragon with a loathsome stench rushed violently towards me. I saw that the creature was attracted by a little white dove at my side. It pounced on the dove, devoured it, and vanished.

EPHREM. There is no doubt what this vision meant.

ABRAHAM. When I woke I turned over in my mind what I had seen, and took it as a sign of some persecution threatening the Church, through which many of the faithful would be drawn into error. I prostrated myself in prayer, and implored Him Who knows the future to enlighten me.

EPHREM. You did right.

ABRAHAM. On the third night after the vision, when for weariness I had fallen asleep, I saw the beast again, but now it was lying dead at my feet, and the dove was flying heavenwards safe and unhurt.

EPHREM. I am rejoiced to hear this, for to my thinking it means that some day Mary will return to you.

ABRAHAM. I was trying to get rid of the uneasiness with which the first vision had filled me by thinking of the second, when my little pupil in her cell came to my mind. I remembered, although at the time I was not alarmed, that for two days I had not heard her chanting the divine praises.

EPHREM. You were too tardy in noticing this.

ABRAHAM. I admit it. I went at once to her cell, and, knocking at the window, I called her again and again, "Mary! My child! Mary!"

EPHREM. You called in vain?

ABRAHAM. "Mary," I said. "Mary, my child, what is wrong? Why are you not saying your office?" It was only when I did not hear the faintest sound that I suspected.

EPHREM. What did you do then?

ABRAHAM. When I could no longer doubt that she had gone, I was struck with fear to my very bowels. I trembled in every limb.

EPHREM. I do not wonder, since I, hearing of it, find myself trembling all over.

ABRAHAM. Then I wept and cried out to the empty air, "What wolf has seized my lamb? What thief has stolen my little daughter?"

EPHREM. You had good cause to weep! To lose her whom you had cherished so tenderly!

ABRAHAM. At last some people came up who knew what had happened. From them I learned that she had gone back to the world.

EPHREM. Where is she now?

ABRAHAM. No one knows.

EPHREM. What is to be done?

ABRAHAM. I have a faithful friend, who is searching all the cities and towns in the country. He says he will never give up until he finds her.

EPHREM. And if he finds her—what then?

ABRAHAM. Then I shall change these clothes, and in the guise of a man of the world seek her out.

It may be that she will heed what I say, and even after this shipwreck turn again to the harbor of her innocence and peace.

EPHREM. And suppose that in the world they offer you flesh meat and wine?

ABRAHAM. If they do, I shall not refuse; otherwise I might be recognized.

EPHREM. No one will blame you, brother. It will be but praiseworthy discretion on your part to loosen the bridle of strict observance for the sake of bringing back a soul.

ABRAHAM. I am the more eager to try now I know you approve.

EPHREM. He Who knows the secret places of the heart can tell with what motive every action is done. That scrupulous and fair Judge will not condemn a man for relaxing our strict rule for a time and descending to the level of weaker mortals if by so doing he can make more sure of rescuing an errant soul.

ABRAHAM. Help me with your prayers. Pray that I may not be caught in the snares of the devil.

EPHREM. May He Who is supreme good itself, without Whom no good thing can be done, bless your enterprise and bring it to a happy end!

SCENE IV

ABRAHAM. Can that be my friend who two years ago went to search for Mary ? Yes, it is he!

FRIEND. Good-day, venerable father.

ABRAHAM. Good-day, dear friend. I have waited so long for you. Of late I had begun to despair.

FRIEND. Forgive me, father. I delayed my return because I did not wish to mock you with doubtful and unreliable news. As soon as I had discovered the truth I lost no time.

ABRAHAM. You have seen Mary?

FRIEND. I have seen her.

ABRAHAM. Where is she? Come, sir, speak! Tell me where.

FRIEND. It goes to my heart to tell you.

ABRAHAM. Speak—I implore you.

FRIEND. She lives in the house of a man who trades in the love of young girls like her. A profitable business, for every day he makes a large sum of money out of her lovers.

ABRAHAM. Her lovers? Mary's lovers?

FRIEND. Yes.

ABRAHAM. Who are they?

FRIEND. There are plenty of them.

ABRAHAM. Good Jesu, what is this monstrous thing I hear? Do they say that she, whom I brought up to be Thy bride, gives herself to strange lovers?

FRIEND. It comes naturally to harlots.

ABRAHAM. If you are my friend, get me a saddlehorse somewhere and a soldier's dress. I am going to get into that place as a lover.

FRIEND. Father, mine are at your service.

ABRAHAM. And I must borrow a felt hat to cover my tonsure.[5]

FRIEND. That is most necessary, if you do not want to be recognized.

ABRAHAM. I have one gold piece. Should I take it to give this man?

FRIEND. You should, for otherwise he will never let you see Mary.

SCENE V

ABRAHAM. Good-day, friend.

INN-KEEPER. Who's there? Good-day, Sir. Come in!

ABRAHAM. Have you a bed for a traveler who wants to spend a night here?

INN-KEEPER. Why certainly! I never turn anyone away.

ABRAHAM. I am glad of it.

INN-KEEPER. Come in then. and I will order supper for you.

ABRAHAM. I owe you thanks for this kind welcome, but I have a greater favor to ask.

INN-KEEPER. Ask what you like. I will do my best for you.

ABRAHAM. Accept this small present. May the beautiful girl who, I am told, lives here, have supper with me?

INN-KEEPER. Why should *you* wish to see her?

ABRAHAM. It would give me much pleasure. I have heard so much talk of her beauty.

INN-KEEPER. Whoever has spoken to you of her has told only the truth. It would be hard to find a finer wench.

ABRAHAM. I am in love with her already.

INN-KEEPER. It's queer that an old man like you should dangle after a young girl.

ABRAHAM. I swear I came here on purpose to feast my eyes on her.

SCENE VI

INN-KEEPER. Mary, come here! Come along now and show off your charms to this young innocent!

MARY: I am coming.

ABRAHAM. Oh, mind, be constant! Tears, do not fall! Must I look on her whom I brought up in the desert,[6] decked out with a harlot's face? Yes, I must hide what is in my heart. I must strive not to weep, and smile though my heart is breaking.

INN-KEEPER. Luck comes your way, Mary! Not only do young gallants of your own age flock to your arms, but even the wise and venerable!

MARY. It is all one to me. It is my business to love those who love me.

ABRAHAM. Come nearer, Mary, and give me a kiss.

MARY. I will give you more than a kiss. I will take your head in my arms and stroke your neck.

ABRAHAM. Yes, like that!

MARY. What does this mean? What is this lovely fragrance. So clean, so sweet. It reminds me of the time when I was good.

ABRAHAM. On with the mask! Chatter, make lewd jests like an idle boy! She must not recognize me, or for very shame she may fly from me.

MARY. Wretch that I am! To what have I fallen! In what pit am I sunk!

ABRAHAM. You forget where you are! Do men come here to see you cry!

INN-KEEPER. What's the matter, Lady Mary? Why are you in the dumps? You have lived here two years, and never before have I seen a tear, never heard a sigh or a word of complaint.

---

[5]Monks shave the crowns of their heads in memory of Christ's crown of thorns. This is called a tonsure.

[6]Abraham is referring to the monastic life. The term "desert" refers to withdrawal from the world. Refer to Document 1.14 for the origins of this tradition.

MARY. Oh, that I had died three years ago before I came to this!

ABRAHAM. I came here to make love to you, not to weep with you over your sins.

MARY. A little thing moved me, and I spoke foolishly. It is nothing. Come, let us eat and drink and be merry, for, as you say, this is not the place to think of one's sins.

ABRAHAM. I have eaten and drunk enough, thanks to your good table, Sir. Now by your leave I will go to bed. My tired limbs need a rest.

INN-KEEPER. As you please.

MARY. Get up my lord. I will take you to bed.

ABRAHAM. I hope so. I would not go at all unless you came with me.

SCENE VII

MARY. Look! How do you like this room? A handsome bed, isn't it? Those trappings cost a lot of money. Sit down and I will take off your shoes. You seem tired.

ABRAHAM. First bolt the door. Someone may come in.

MARY. Have no fear. I have seen to that.

ABRAHAM. The time has come for me to show my shaven head, and make myself known! Oh, my daughter! Oh, Mary, you who are part of my soul! Look at me. Do you not know me? Do you not know the old man who cherished you with a father's love, and wedded you to the Son of the King of Heaven?

MARY. God, what shall I do! It is my father and master Abraham!

ABRAHAM. What has come to you, daughter?

MARY. Oh, misery!

ABRAHAM. Who deceived you? Who led you astray?

MARY. Who deceived our first parents?

ABRAHAM. Have you forgotten that once you lived like an angel on earth!

MARY. All that is over.

ABRAHAM. What has become of your virginal modesty? Your beautiful purity?

MARY. Lost. Gone!

ABRAHAM. Oh, Mary, think what you have thrown away! Think what a reward you had earned by your fasting, and prayers, and vigils. What can

they avail you now! You have hurled yourself from heavenly heights into the depths of hell!

MARY. Oh God, I know it!

ABRAHAM. Could you not trust me? Why did you desert me? Why did you not tell me of your fall? Then dear brother Ephrem and I could have done a worthy penance.

MARY. Once I had committed that sin, and was defiled, how could I dare come near you who are so holy?

ABRAHAM. Oh, Mary, has anyone ever lived on earth without sin except the Virgin's Son?

MARY. No one, I know.

ABRAHAM. It is human to sin, but it is devilish to remain in sin. Who can be justly condemned? Not those who fall suddenly, but those who refuse to rise quickly.

MARY. Wretched, miserable creature that I am!

ABRAHAM. Why have you thrown yourself down there? Why do you lie on the ground without moving or speaking? Get up, Mary! Get up, my child, and listen to me!

MARY. No! no! I am afraid. I cannot bear your reproaches.

ABRAHAM. Remember how I love you, and you will not be afraid.

MARY. It is useless. I cannot.

ABRAHAM. What but love for you could have made me leave the desert and relax the strict observance of our rule? What but love could have made me, a true hermit, come into the city and mix with the lascivious crowd? It is for your sake that these lips have learned to utter light, foolish words, so that I might not be known! Oh, Mary, why do you turn away your face from me and gaze upon the ground? Why do you scorn to answer and tell me what is in your mind.

MARY. It is the thought of my sins which crushes me. I dare not look at you; I am not fit to speak to you.

ABRAHAM. My little one, have no fear. Oh, do not despair! Rise from this abyss of desperation and grapple God to your soul!

MARY. No, no! My sins are too great. They weigh me down.

ABRAHAM. The mercy of heaven is greater than I you or your sins. Let your sadness be dispersed by its glorious beams. Oh, Mary, do not let apathy prevent your seizing the moment for repentance. It matters not how wickedness has flourished. Divine grace can flourish still more abundantly!

MARY. If there were the smallest hope of forgiveness, surely I should not shrink from doing penance.

ABRAHAM. Have you no pity for me? I have sought you out with so much pain and weariness! Oh shake off this despair which we are taught is the most terrible of all sins. Despair of God's mercy—for that alone there is no forgiveness. Sin can no more embitter His sweet mercy than a spark from a flint can set the ocean on fire.

MARY. I know that God's mercy is great, but when I think how greatly I have sinned, I cannot believe any penance can make amends.

ABRAHAM. I will take your sins on me. Only come back and take up your life again as if you had never left it.

MARY. I do not want to oppose you. What you tell me to do I will do with all my heart.

ABRAHAM. My daughter lives again! I have found my lost lamb and she is dearer to me than ever.

MARY. I have a few possessions here—a little gold and some clothes. What ought I to do with them?

ABRAHAM. What came to you through sin, with sin must be left behind.

MARY. Could it not be given to the poor, or sold for an offering at the holy altar?

ABRAHAM. The price of sin is not an acceptable offering to God.

MARY. Then I will not trouble any more about my possessions.

ABRAHAM. Look! The dawn! It is growing light. Let us go.

MARY. You go first, dearest father, like the good shepherd leading the lost lamb that has been found. The lamb will follow in your steps.

ABRAHAM. Not so! I am going on foot, but you—you shall have a horse so that the stony road shall not hurt your delicate feet.

MARY. Oh, let me never forget this tenderness! Let me try all my life to thank you! I was not worth pity, yet you have shown me no harshness; you have led me to repent not by threats but by gentleness and love.

ABRAHAM. I ask only one thing, Mary. Be faithful to God for the rest of your life.

MARY. With all my strength I will persevere, and though my flesh may fail, my spirit never will.

ABRAHAM. You must serve God with as much energy as you have served the world.

MARY. If His will is made perfect in me it will be because of your merits.

ABRAHAM. Come, let us hasten on our way.

MARY. Yes, let us set out at once. I would not stay here another moment.

SCENE VIII

ABRAHAM. Courage, Mary! You see how swiftly we have made the difficult and toilsome journey.

MARY. Everything is easy when we put our hearts into it.

ABRAHAM. There is your deserted little cell.

MARY. God help me! It was the witness of my sin. I dare not go there.

ABRAHAM. It is natural you should dread the place where the enemy triumphed.

MARY. Where, then, am I to do penance?

ABRAHAM. Go into the inner cell. There you will be safe from the wiles of the serpent.

MARY. Most gladly as it is your wish.

ABRAHAM. Now I must go to my good friend Ephrem. He alone mourned with me when you were lost, and he must rejoice with me now that you have been found.

MARY. Of course.

SCENE IX

EPHREM. Well, brother! If I am not mistaken, you bring good news.

ABRAHAM. The best in the world.

EPHREM. You have found your lost lamb?

ABRAHAM. I have, and, rejoicing, have brought her back to the fold.

EPHREM. Truly this is the work of divine grace.

ABRAHAM. That is certain.

EPHREM. How is she spending her days? I should like to know how you have ordered her life. What does she do?

ABRAHAM. All that I tell her.

EPHREM. That is well.

ABRAHAM. Nothing is too difficult for her—nothing too hard. She is ready to endure anything.

EPHREM. That is better.

ABRAHAM. She wears a hair shirt, and subdues her flesh with continual vigils and fasts. She is making the poor frail body obey the spirit by the most rigorous discipline.

EPHREM. Only through such a severe penance can the stains left by the pleasures of the flesh be washed away.

ABRAHAM. Those who hear her sobs are cut to the heart, and the tale of her repentance has turned many from their sins.

EPHREM. It is often so.

ABRAHAM. She prays continually for the men who through her were tempted to sin, and begs that she who was their ruin may be their salvation.

EPHREM. It is right that she should do this.

ABRAHAM. She strives to make her life as beautiful as for a time it was hideous.

EPHREM. I rejoice at what you tell me. To the depths of my heart.

ABRAHAM. And with us rejoice phalanxes of angels, praising the Lord for the conversion of a sinner.

EPHREM. Over whom, we are told, there is more joy in heaven than over the just man who needs no penance.

ABRAHAM. The more glory to Him, because there seemed no hope on earth that she could be saved.

EPHREM. Let us sing a song of thanksgiving—let us glorify the only begotten Son of God, Who of His love and mercy will not let them perish whom He redeemed with His holy blood.

ABRAHAM. To Him be honor, glory, and praise through infinite ages. Amen.

Questions for Discussion:

1. In the preface, Roswitha says, ". . . . if my work is examined by those who know how to weigh things fairly, I shall be more easily pardoned on account of my sex and my inferior knowledge. . . .," and in Scene II Mary says she is "made out of slime." What do these passages indicate about the self-concept of medieval women? Might this self-denigration be a device of the author?

2. In Scene III Roswitha describes Mary's seduction by the devil. Compare this scene with the account of Peter the Venerable about the "besetting demons" (Document 8.3).

3. What is the message of Roswitha's play? How do you think it would have been received by medieval people?

Chapter 9

Religion and Politics in the Twelfth Century

In the twelfth century, many of the royal dynasties of Europe took measures to consolidate the power they had acquired in the previous hundred years. In France, another Capetian, Louis VI ("the Fat") became king in 1106. His power was limited by his wealthy and unruly vassals, but, as will be seen in Document 9.1, he was able, through various means, to strengthen the authority of the crown. When he died in 1137 he left a large domain to his son, Louis VII, although much of the land was lost when the marriage between Louis and Eleanor of Aquitaine, heiress to a large area in southern France, was dissolved. In 1180 the throne was inherited by Philip Augustus, Louis's son by his second wife, who proved to be one of the strongest kings of the High Middle Ages.

Europe in the Twelfth Century (From Levack et al., *The West*, Combined Volume, 2nd ed., p. 295.)

When William I ("the Conqueror"), King of England, died in 1087, the crown passed to his second son, William Rufus ("the Red"). He ruled until 1100, when he was killed in a hunting accident. His brother, Henry, then asserted his claim to the throne, proving to be a powerful king who strengthened royal authority in England. Unfortunately, his only sons were killed in a shipwreck in 1120, and Henry attempted to secure the throne for his daughter, Matilda, who was then married to Geoffrey of Anjou. (Matilda was the future mother of Henry II). The barons of England refused to support Matilda as queen when Henry I died, and the crown was given to Stephen of Blois, a grandson of William I. Stephen was not a strong monarch, and when he died in 1154 after a chaotic rule, Henry II ascended the throne.

Henry, through inheritance and his marriage to Eleanor of Aquitaine, was able to create a vast kingdom that included England and much of France, known as the Angevin Empire. His accomplishments are extolled in the first part of the excerpt from the Instruction of a Prince by Gerald of Wales (Document 9.2), although the second portion is considerably less than laudatory. Gerald also describes the conflict between Henry and Archbishop Thomas Becket, which led to the murder of the archbishop. During the struggle between the men, Henry's mother, Queen Matilda, wrote to Becket in an attempt to effect a compromise. Her letter (Document 9.3) did not have the desired result, and the quarrel ended with Becket's murder (Document 9.4). The archbishop was immediately recognized as a martyr who lost his life in defense of the Church. There were soon reports of numerous miracles at the site of the martyrdom in Canterbury Cathedral, and a shrine was eventually erected there to hold the martyr's remains. By the twelfth century, the shrine had become a major pilgrimage site (see Document 7.7) The "Interpreting the Evidence" feature (Document 9.5) relates a miracle of Becket in two forms: literary text and stained-glass.

In Germany, Lothair, duke of Saxony, was elected following the death of Henry V, the last of the Salian kings. He ruled from 1125 until his death in 1137, when Conrad III (r. 1137–1152), of the house of Hohenstaufen, was chosen. These kings were selected because of their lack of strength, and, predictably, they were not able to curtail the power of the nobility. The state of near chaos during Conrad's reign impelled the electors to make the next choice based upon power, and they elected Frederick I ("Barbarossa"), who ruled until his untimely death during the Third Crusade (1190). The selections included in this chapter make clear that the problems between the Holy Roman Emperor and the pope during the Investiture Controversy (see Documents 6.14 through 6.18) had not been entirely solved. Frederick faced his own struggle with Adrian IV, as Documents 9.6 through 9.10 will demonstrate.

Following the First Crusade, small "crusader" kingdoms were established in the Holy Land. The political and social relationship between the Frankish rulers and the Muslims was a complicated affair, as will be seen in the excerpts from the History of Fulcer of Chartres and the Memoirs of Usāmah ibn-Munquidh (Documents 9.11 and 9.12).

During the twelfth century, the kings and knights of western Europe undertook two more "Holy Wars" to the area of the eastern Mediterranean. Their ostensible motivation was, once more, to regain areas of the Holy Land from the Muslims. One of the most famous battles leading to the Third Crusade took place at the "Horns of Hattin," in which the crusaders were annihilated by Saladin's forces; the Muslim armies then moved on to recapture Jerusalem. Documents 9.13 and 9.14 offer two interpretations of the event, one by the Christian writer Otto of St. Blasien and the other from the Life of Saladin by Ibn Shaddad. As might be expected, the excerpts make clear that the Muslim version of the war was quite different from that of Christian historians.

In response to the disaster, Pope Clement III issued a papal proclamation that again furnished the impetus for the Third Crusade, undertaken to recover the most holy city (Document 9.15). The crusading armies were led by the charismatic rulers of France, England, and the Holy Roman Empire: Philip Augustus (r. 1180–1223), Richard the Lion Heart (r. 1189–1199), and Frederic Barbarossa (r. 1155–1190), who lost his life while on the crusade (Document 9.16).

An analysis of the documents in this chapter offers insight into the developement of power and authority by the kings of England and France, and provides evidence of a new stuggle between the papacy and the German monarch. The final section demonstrates the further expansion of European influence in the Mediterranean area, as the leaders of western Europe embarked upon the Third Crusade to the Holy Land.

Politics in France and England

9.1   Power and the Monarchy: *Deeds of Louis the Fat* by Suger

*By the twelfth century the consolidation of royal author-
ity in France was a political reality, although the land-
holdings of the king were small when compared to those of
his great vassals, such as William X of Aquitaine (the
father of Eleanor). The Capetian kings had the advantage of a succession of male heirs, but the power of the nobles remained a threat until the thirteenth and fourteenth
centuries. One of the important kings of the twelfth century, Louis VI ("the Fat"), was determined to maintain
his control. With the advice of Suger, the abbot of St. Denis, Louis began to build an efficient bureaucracy, in addition to undertaking military action against his unruly
noblemen. Suger, who was also the royal biographer,
praised the king's actions in the following excerpt from his*
Life of Louis VI.

(From *Readings in European History,* by James Harvey Robinson
[Boston: Ginn & Co., 1904], pp. 202–205.)

A king, when he takes the royal power, vows to put
down with his strong right arm insolent tyrants
whenever he sees them subject the state to endless
wars, rejoice in rapine, oppress the poor, destroy the
churches, give themselves over to lawlessness
which, had it not be checked, would flame out into
ever greater madness; for the evil spirits who insti-
gate them are accustomed to cruelly strike down
those whom they fear to lose, but give free rein to
those whom they hope to hold, while they add fuel
to the flames which are to devour their victims to all
eternity.

Such an utterly abandoned man was Thomas of
Marle. While King Louis [VI] was busy with many
wars, he laid waste the territories of Laon, Rheims,
and Amiens, devouring like a raging wolf. He spared
neither the clergy—fearing not the vengeance of the
Church—nor the people for humanity's sake. And
the devil aided him, for the success of the foolish
does ever lead them to perdition. Slaying all men,
spoiling all things, he seized two manors, exceedingly rich, from the abbey of the nuns of St. John of
Laon. He fortified the two exceeding strong castles,
Crecy and Nogent, with a marvelous wall and very

high towers, as if they had been his own; and made
them like to a den of dragons and a cave of robbers,
from which he laid waste almost the whole country
with fire and pillage; and he had no pity.

The Church of France could no longer bear this
great evil; therefore the clergy, who had met together in a general synod at Beauvais, proceeded to
pass a sentence of condemnation upon the enemy of
the Church's true spouse, Jesus Christ. The venerable Cono, bishop of Praeneste and legate of the holy
Roman Church, troubled past endurance by the
complaints of churches, of the orphans, of the poor,
did smite this ruthless tyrant with the sword of the
blessed Peter, which is general anathema. He did
also ungird the knightly sword belt from him,
though he was absent, and by the judgment of all declared him infamous, a scoundrel, unworthy of the
name of Christian.

And the king was moved by the pleas of this
great council and quickly led an army against him.
He had the clergy, to whom he was always humbly
devoted, in his company, and marched straight
against the castle of Crecy. It was well fortified; yet
he took it unprepared because his soldiers smote
with an exceedingly strong hand; or rather, because
the hand of the Lord fought for him. He stormed the
strongest tower as if it were the hut of a peasant, and
put to confusion the wicked men and piously destroyed the impious. Because they had no pity upon
other men, he cut them down without mercy. None
could behold the castle tower flaming like the fires
of hell and not exclaim, "The whole universe will
fight for him against these madmen."

After he had won this victory, the king, who
was ever swift to follow up his advantage, pushed
forward toward the other castle, called Nogent.
There came to him a man who said: "Oh, my lord
king, it should be known to thy Serenity that in that
wicked castle dwell exceeding wicked men who are
worthy to lie in hell, and there only. They are those
who, when you issued commands to destroy the
commune of Laon, burned with fire not only the city

of Laon, but the noble church of the Mother of God, and many others in addition. And almost all the noble men of the city suffered martyrdom because they were true to their faith and defended their lord the bishop. And these evil men were not afraid to raise their hands against thy venerable Bishop Gaudin, the anointed of the Lord, defender of the church, but killed him most cruelly, and exposed his naked body on the open road for beasts and birds of prey to feed upon; but first they cut off his finger with the pontifical ring. And they have agreed together, persuaded by the wicked Thomas, to attack and hold your tower."

The king was doubly animated by these words, and he attacked the wicked castle, broke open the abominable places of confinement, like prisons of hell, and set free the innocent; the guilty he punished with very heavy punishment. He alone avenged the injuries of many. Thirsty for justice, he ordained that whatsoever murderous wretches he came upon should be fastened to a gibbet, and left as common food for the greed of kites, crows, and vultures. And this they deserved who had not feared to raise their hand against the Lord's anointed.

When he had taken these two castles and given back to the monastery of St. John the domains that had been seized, he returned to the city of Amiens and laid siege to a tower of that city which was held by a certain Adam, a cruel tyrant who was laying waste the churches, and all the surrounding regions. He held the place under siege for almost two years, and at last forced those who defended it to give themselves up. When he had taken it he destroyed it utterly, and thus brought peace to the realm. He fulfilled most worthily the duty of a king who bears not the sword in vain, and he deprived the wicked Thomas and his heirs forever of the lordship over that city. . . .

It is known that kings have long arms; and to show that the king's strength was not confined within the narrow boundaries of certain places, a man, Alard de Guillebaut by name a clever man, with an oily tongue, came from the frontiers of Berri to the king. He laid the grievance of his stepson before his lord the king, and entreated him humbly that he would summon by his royal authority a certain noble baron, Aymon by name, surnamed

Vais-Vache, lord of Bourbon, who refused to do him justice. Moreover he asked that the king should restrain Aymon from despoiling, with presumptuous audacity, his nephew, the son of his older brother, Archambaut, and to fix according to French custom what portion of goods each of them ought to have.

Now the king loved justice and had compassion on the churches and the poor. And he feared that these wars would make wickedness flourish, and that the poor might be harassed and bear the punishment for the pride of others. So after vainly summoning Aymon, who would not trust himself to trial and refused to obey the summons, Louis gave way neither to pleasure nor to sloth, but marched with a great army toward the territory of Bourges. There he directed his forces against Aymon's castle of Germigni, which was well fortified, and battled to reduce it by a vigorous assault.

Then Aymon saw that he could not hold out, and he surrendered, hoping to save himself or his castle. He saw only this one way to safety—that he should throw himself at the king's feet. There he prostrated himself again and again, while all the crowd marveled, and prayed the king to have compassion upon him. He gave up his castle, and, as humble now as he had once been proud, submitted himself utterly to the king's justice. The king kept the castle and took Aymon to France to be judged there; and justly and piously, by the decision and arbitration of the French, he settled the dispute which had arisen between the uncle and nephew.

King Louis spent freely both of money and the sweat of his brow to relieve the sufferings and oppressions of many. He made many such expeditions throughout the country for the relief of churches and of the poor, but we must pass over these, as it would but weary the reader to narrate them. . . .

Question for Discussion:

1. This excerpt offers an excellent example of the feudal violence that was the focus of the "Peace of God" and "Truce of God" (see Documents 5.7 and 5.8). Discuss the measures, both military and legal, taken by King Louis VI to control his vassals in order to create a peaceful and protected environment.

9.2   Henry II and the Angevin Empire: The *Instruction of a Prince* by Gerald of Wales

When the English King Henry I died in 1135, the noblemen refused to honor the claim to the throne of Matilda, Henry's daughter; instead, they supported Stephen of Blois, who was a grandson of William the Conqueror. He ruled until 1154, proving to be an extremely weak king, as reported in contemporary sources, such as the Anglo-Saxon Chronicle. *It is evident that England was plunged into a state of chaos during his reign.*

After the period of turmoil during the first half of the twelfth century, Henry II inherited the throne of England. As may be seen in the following excerpt from The Instruction of a Prince, *written c. 1218 by the historian Gerald of Wales (c. 1146–1223), Henry was able—through his inheritances, his marriage to Eleanor of Aquitaine, and his conquests—to create the "Angevin Empire," which included England and much of France.*

(From *The Church Historians of England*, vol. V, pt. 1, trans. by Joseph Stevenson [London: Seeleys, 1858], pp. 137–144. Translation modified.)

The Creation of the Angevin Empire

. . . When Henry II was raised to the throne of the kingdom, at the very commencement of his reign, by a signal instance of good fortune, not only those who had detained the kingdom from him, but all the disturbers of peace in the realm, not only foreigners, but also those of his brother, as well as his own sons afterwards, were extinguished suddenly, and, as it were, almost by a miracle. Every obstacle to tranquillity and quiet was removed for this pacific king by the favor of a singular good fortune. Thus, therefore, by reigning prosperously, he not only, by God's grace, peacefully reduced his own hereditary dominions under his power, but also victoriously triumphed over remote and foreign kingdoms, which belonged to none of his predecessors from the coming of the Normans or even of the Angles. For he made for Ireland with his fleet; and, having passed over the deep sea, he splendidly reduced it under subjection; and he also subdued Scotland, having taken their king, William, prisoner: and, contrary to anything which had occurred before, adding so noble an increase to the Anglican crown, he gloriously extended the boundaries and limits of the kingdom from the southern ocean to the northern islands of the Orkneys, including, by his powerful hand, in one monarchy, the whole island of Britain as it is itself included by the ocean. We have no authentic account that anyone had ever done this before, from the time when the Picts and Scots first occupied the northern parts of the island since the days of Claudius Caesar, who not only added Scotland to the British kingdom, but the Orkney islands also to the Roman empire. . . .

Moreover, in the parts of Guienne, in France, beyond the sea, besides Anjou, Maine, and Tours, which fell to him by patrimonial right, and Poitou also, and the whole of Gascony, as far as the Pyrennean mountains of Spain, which he acquired by marriage, he reduced, by arms, under his own dominion, Auvergne, and Berry, and Gisors, together with the Vexin of Normandy, formerly taken away from Normandy. Nor, abusing the easy and simple nature of the holy man, king Louis, had he by his courage extended the sphere of his power to the empire of France only, but even also to that of Rome, invited as well by the whole of Italy, as more frequently by the city of Rome itself, by reason of the daily warfare, and the inexorable discord, which had arisen between the emperor Frederick and his subjects; having gained a way for himself, though not having effectually preserved it, for this purpose, through the valley of Maurienne and of the Alps. . . . as the fame of his name was celebrated through the whole world, it was, above all the kings and princes of the earth, a glory to the faithful, and a terror to the infidels. All the princes also of the earth, Christian as well as infidel, and as Frederick of Germany, so Manuel of Greece, and as Noradin in his own time, and after him Saladin (1138–1193), and as these of Asia, so also those of Europe and of Spain, as well those of the household of faith as infidels, were accustomed to honor and to visit him by valuable presents and by frequent ambassadors.

Although the previous passage speaks of Henry's virtues, in another section of the work, Gerald of Wales portrayed the king's character from quite another point of view. As may be seen in this document, the historian viewed Henry's marriage to Eleanor, his dealings with the nobility, and his relationship with Archbishop Thomas Becket in a negative light.

Concerning his Enormous Sins Afterwards

For, in the first place, as is sufficiently notorious, he unduly took away Eleanor, queen of France, from her husband and lord, Louis, king of France, and united her to himself in the bond of matrimony: by whom, under unhappy auspices, in process of time, he had the offspring already spoken of; through which, as we have said, on account of this and his other most grievous crimes, some of which we will subsequently enumerate, the Lord wished him to be humbled, and to be recalled to repentance, (for affliction will bring a man to his senses;) or, if he had been found obstinate, that the father should be punished by his own offspring, and the murderer tormented by his own flesh.

For he had been an oppressor of the nobility from the beginning, even to the end of his reign, considering things right or wrong according to his own convenience or advantage. He was a seller and secret accuser of justice, changeable and crafty in word; and not only was he an unscrupulous violator of his promises, but of his pledged faith and of his oath; an open adulterer, ungrateful and irreligious to God, a heavy oppressor of the church, and a son born to destruction; from whence he went on to such a height of wickedness and perfidy, that, as his father, in his time, cruelly raged against the blessed Gerard, bishop of Séez, so also this man, taking after his father in evil, and far more deeply staining his own times with his cruelty, presumed to rage against our glorious martyr Thomas, archbishop of Canterbury. But, for the honor of the martyr, we have thought it not useless also to add to this account what we have written in the "Prophetical History."

Questions for Discussion:

1. What does Gerald characterize as Henry's virtues in the first excerpt?
2. In the second document, Gerald vehemently criticizes the king. Are the two accounts diametrically opposed, or can they be viewed simply as different aspects of the monarch's character?

The Becket Controversy

9.3   A Mother's Plea: Letter from Empress Matilda to Thomas Becket

Henry II and Thomas Becket had been close friends, and Becket had served the king as Chancellor of England. When the Archbishop of Canterbury died, Henry appointed Becket to that post, expecting that Thomas would bend the policies of the Church to the will of the king. Becket, however, experienced a spiritual transformation, and was determined to protect the interest of the Church from the encroachments of secular authority.

The ensuing quarrel between Thomas Becket and King Henry was concerned primarily with the right of the royal courts to try and sentence clerics who had committed crimes. The archbishop maintained that the Church held the authority to deal with its own members.

In the letter, Henry's mother, Empress Matilda (1102–1167), urged Becket to reconsider his position, and to remember his earlier friendship with the king. The plea had no effect on the outcome of the dispute, as may be observed in the following account of Becket's murder from the Vita *("Life") by Becket's associate, Edward Grim (Document 9.4).*

(From *Letters of Royal and Illustrious Ladies of Great Britain*, vol. 1, ed. by Mary Anne Everett Wood [London: Henry Colburn, 1846], pp. 10–11.)

To Thomas archbishop of Canterbury, [from] Matilda the empress.

My lord pope sent to me, enjoining me, for the remission of my sins, to interfere to renew peace and concord between you and the king, my son, and to try to reconcile you to him. You, as you well know, have asked the same thing from me; wherefore, with the more good-will, for the honor of God and the Holy Church, I have begun and carefully treated of that affair. But it seems a very hard thing to the king, as well as to his barons and council, seeing he so loved and honored you, and appointed you lord of his whole kingdom and of all his lands, and raised you to the highest honors in the land, believing he might trust you rather than any other; and especially so, because he declares that you have, as far as you could, roused his whole kingdom against him; nor was it your fault that you did not disinherit him by main force. Therefore I send you my faithful servant, Archdeacon Laurence, that by him I may know your will in these affairs, and what sort of disposition you entertain towards my son, and how you intend to conduct yourself, if it should happen that he fully grants my petition and prayer on your behalf. One thing I plainly tell you, that you cannot recover the king's favor, except by great humility and most evident moderation. However, what you intend to do in this matter signify to me by my messenger and your letters.

Questions for Discussion:

1. What justification does Matilda give for Henry's anger against the archbishop?
2. According to Matilda, what measures should Becket take to effect a reconciliation?
3. Discuss the reasons why Matilda felt justified in writing to Becket on behalf of Henry II.

9.4   Becket's Martyrdom: From the *Vita* by Edward Grim

Although there is no direct proof that Henry II ordered the murder of Thomas Becket, he is known to have shouted to a group of his knights, "Who will rid me of this troublesome priest?" Four of his vassals took his words to heart, and traveled to Canterbury, where they accosted the archbishop in his cathedral as was preparing to offer the evening Vespers service. There were five eyewitness accounts of the martyrdom, and all substantially agree on the details. The following description of the events is from the biography of Becket by Edward Grim, who was wounded in the arm during the attack.

(From *The Lives of Thomas Becket*, trans. by Michael Staunton. Manchester, UK: Manchester University Press, 2001, pp. 202–203. Reprinted by permission.)

Therefore they rushed at him and laid their sacrilegious hands on him, roughly manhandling and dragging him, intending to kill him outside the church, or carry him away in chains, as they later admitted. But since he could not easily be moved from the pillar, one of them attached himself and applied himself particularly fiercely. . . . The invincible martyr seeing then that the hour was at hand when the miseries of mortal life would be ended, and that the crown of immortality prepared for him and promised to him by the Lord was now within reach, bent his head in the manner of prayer, joined his hands together and lifted them up, and commended his cause and that of the Church to God, St Mary and the blessed martyr Denis.

Hardly had he said the words than the evil knight, fearing that he would be snatched by the people and escape alive, suddenly leapt on him and wounded God's sacrificial lamb in the head, cutting off the top of the crown, which the oil of holy chrism had dedicated to God. The same blow almost cut off the arm of this witness who, as everyone fled, monks and clerks, steadfastly stood by the archbishop, and held him in his arms until his arm was struck. Behold the simplicity of the dove, behold the wisdom of the serpent, in this martyr, who offered his body to the persecutors, so that he preserve unharmed his head, that is his soul and the Church, nor did he devise a defense or trap against the killers of the flesh. O worthy shepherd who, lest the sheep be torn to pieces, so bravely presented himself to the jaws of the wolves! . . . Then he received another blow in the head but still remained immoveable. But at the third blow he bent his knees and elbows, offering himself as a living sacrifice, saying in a low voice,

"For the name of Jesus and the well-being of the Church I am prepared to embrace death." But as he lay prostrate the third knight inflicted a grave wound.... The fourth knight warded off those arriving on the scene so that the others could carry out their murder more freely and wantonly. But the fifth . . . put his foot on the neck of the holy priest and precious martyr, and, horrible to say, scattered the brains with the blood over the pavement. "Let us go, knights," he called out to the others, "this fellow will not get up again."

Questions for Discussion:

1. Compare the imagery in the description of Becket's martyrdom with that of Perpetua and Felicity (Document 1.9). What similarities are there?
2. Many centuries separate the martyrdom of Becket from those of the early Christians. How are the motivations of the martyrs portrayed in the accounts? Are they identical?

INTERPRETING THE EVIDENCE

9.5   A Miracle of Saint Thomas of Canterbury and a Stained-Glass Panel from Trinity Chapel, Canterbury Cathedral

Beginning shortly after the martyrdom in 1170, the site of Becket's murder became an important pilgrimage site, as noted earlier (see Document 7.7). People from all parts of England and the European continent traveled to Canterbury to visit his shrine in Canterbury Cathedral. Two of the monks, Benedict of Peterborough and William of Canterbury, soon began to record the many miracles that resulted from the saint's intervention. These included various sorts of healing, both physical and psychological. As found in Benedict's account, a particularly unusual miracle occurred in the case of Eilward of Westoning from the town of Bedfordshire.

(From *St. Thomas of Canterbury: His Death and Miracles*, 2 vols., by Edwin A. Abbott [London: Adam and Charles Black, 1898], I., pp. 80–102.)

There was one of the common folk, Eilward by name, in the king's town of Weston in the county of Bedford. One of his neighbors, Fulk, owed him a *denarius* as part of rent for cornland, and put off payment on the excuse of not having the money. One day, a holiday, when they were going to the alehouse together, as is the English custom, Eilward asked for his money, and Fulk denied the debt

on oath. Then Eilward asked him to pay half, as he was going to have some beer, and keep the other half for himself for beer. When Fulk still refused, the other said he would get even with him.

After they had both gotten drunk, Eilward, leaving the ale-house before the other, turned aside to Fulk's cottage, tore away the bar, burst into the house, and carried away a great grindstone and a pair of gloves, both scarcely of the value of a *nummus*. The boys, who were playing in the courtyard, cried out, and running to the tavern called their father out to reclaim his property. Fulk followed the thief, broke the man's head with the grindstone, wounded him in the arm with a knife, brought him back to the cottage, bound him, and called in Fulk, the beadle of the village, to know what he must do with his prisoner. "The charge," said the beadle, "is not heavy enough. If you tie a few more things round the prisoner and produce him thus, you can accuse him of breaking the law." The debtor agreed, and fastened round his prisoner's neck an awl, and some clothes, together with the grindstone and the gloves, and on the following day brought him thus before the king's officers.

(continued)

So having been taken to Bedford he was kept in the prison there for a month. He sent for a priest, in whose hearing (after confessing his sins) he vowed a pilgrimage to Jerusalem if he escaped, and he begged that he might be branded with a cross on the shoulder. The priest branded him accordingly, but also suggested that he should seek the protection of the Saints, and especially of St. Thomas, measuring his body for the length and thickness of a candle to be offered to the Martyr, and also giving him a bundle of rods that self-punishment might accompany his invocations. Then he left him, saying that the judges had forbidden any priest to have further access to the accused. However, the Priest still sent messages to his window to comfort and strengthen him in secret. Also the Prior of Bedford often supplied him with food, visited him and had him out for a breathing-space now and then, in the open air.

At the beginning of the fifth week he was called up for trial. On his asserting that he took what he took, as a pledge, and that he did not take the other articles at all, he was again remanded to prison. In the fifth week he was again tried on the charge of stealing simply the grindstone and the gloves. For the accuser, fearing to undergo the ordeal of battle demanded by the accused, condemned by silence all his previous charges, and—having on his side the viscount and the judges—managed to free himself from obligation to fight, and to secure that the accused should be tried by ordeal of water.

Now it was the Sabbath, and the examination was put off till the third day of the following week, Eilward being again kept in prison, and not allowed by the cruelty of his keeper to keep vigil in the church—a right conceded by the compassion of religion to all that are to purge themselves [by ordeal] from criminal charge. In prison, however, he devoutly kept the watch that he was not allowed to keep in the church.

When brought out to the water [ordeal], he was met by the village priest, who exhorted him to bear all patiently, looking to remission of sins, to entertain no anger in his heart, to forgive all his enemies heartily [all they had done to him], and not to despair of the compassion of God. He replied, "May the will of God and the Martyr Thomas be fulfilled in me."

When plunged into the water he was found guilty. The beadle, Fulk, now seized him, saying, "This way, rascal, this way!" "Thanks be to God," said the other, "and to the holy Martyr Thomas!" Dragged to the place of execution, he was deprived of his eyes, and also mutilated [castrated] according to law. As for his left eye, they at once extracted that, whole; as for the right, after being lacerated and chopped to pieces it was at last with difficulty gouged out. The members of which he had been deprived by mutilation they hid under the sod; and (in accordance with what is read about the man that "fell among robbers") they stripped him, and, after inflicting wounds on him as aforesaid, they "departed, leaving him half dead."

He was mutilated by his accuser Fulk, and the official of the same name (by whose suggestion and advice the man is believed to have been brought into this misery), and by two other executioners with them. When they asked pardon, for the love of God and St. Thomas the Martyr, he freely forgave them, crying aloud that he would go to the Martyr's memorial, blind though he was. He persisted in the cry with a wonderful faith—knowing that it was more glorious for the Martyr to restore eyes that had been taken away than to preserve them when not taken.

He was attended by none but his twelve-year-old daughter, who had also begged food for him when in prison. For, since all his goods were confiscated, all his friends spurned him, and there was no one, of all those dear to him, to take compassion on him. Such a stream of blood gushed from his wounds that, in fear of his death, those who were present sent for a priest. To him he confessed. By degrees, however, when the flow of blood was assuaged, led by the little girl, he returned to Bedford, where he threw himself down against the wall of a house; and all that day, till evening, no man showed him kindness. But at nightfall, one Eilbrict took compassion on him, and willingly welcomed him into his house from the cold and rain.

There, after many vigils and prayers, in the first watch of the tenth night, he [St. Thomas], whom he had invoked, appeared to Eilward in his sleep, clothed in snow-white garments, with his pastoral staff painting the sign of the cross on his forehead and on his eyeless sockets. A second time he appeared, before dawn, bidding him to persevere in watching and praying, and place his hope in God, and the blessed Virgin Mary, and St. Thomas who had come to visit him: "If, on the night of the morrow, you keep watch with a waxen light before the altar of the blessed Mary in her church close by, and devote yourself to prayer, in faith, and without doubting, you shall be gladdened by the restoration of your eyes." The maidservant also had a similar dream. When she told it to Eilward, he replied, "So it may be when it shall please God and His blessed Martyr, Thomas."

When it was growing toward evening and the sun was toward setting, the eyelids of his left eye began to itch. In order to scratch them, he removed a waxen poultice which had been applied, either for the purpose of drawing out the purulent matter of the empty orbs, or for the purpose of closing the eye-lids themselves. And, as by the wonderful power of God he opened his eyelids, he saw a shine on the house-wall in front of him which resembled the brightness of a lantern: for it was the red sunlight, since the sun was by this time about to set. But he, ignorant of the truth, and distrusting himself about the matter, called the master of the house, and showed him what he saw. "You are mad, Eilward, you are mad," replied his host: "be silent! You know not what you are saying." "Sir," he said, "I assure you I am not mad: but I think I see what I say with my left eye." Shaken in his mind, and anxious to ascertain the truth, his host spread out his hand before his eyes and said to him, "Do you see what I am doing?" He answered, "Your hand is moved before my eyes and drawn this way and that." Then he told Eilbricht, in order, all about his visions, and the precepts or promises he had received.

The thing was noised abroad. A multitude collected, and, among them, Osbern the dean— who had control, or rather service, of the above-mentioned church. He brought the good man before the altar, instructed and strengthened his faith, and then placed a light in his hand. As soon as this was done, Eilward declared he distinctly saw the altar cloth; then, the image of the blessed Virgin Mary; then, objects of smaller size.

The people marveled more and more. Presently, testing the source of his sight, they detected two very small pupils latent, deep in the head, scarcely as large as the pupils of the eye of a little bird. These were incessantly increasing, and prolonged by their slow augmentation the wonder of all that saw them. The shouts of the people went up to heaven; they gave God due praise; the bells were set ringing; crowds flocked in from their beds; keeping vigil with their brother who had received the gift of light, they sleeplessly awaited the light of the sun.

In the morning, the whole of the town gathered together, and then, examining the man more closely, they found that whereas, before, both his eyes were parti-colored, now he had one parti-colored, but the other quite black. Now came, among others, the priest of St. John's church, the same who had received Eilward's confession after mutilation. When he beheld the wonderful miracle of God, he said "Why do we wait for papal precept? No more delaying for me! This very moment will I begin, and conduct to the end, a solemn service, in the name of Thomas the glorious friend of God, since in truth he is a martyr beyond price. Who can hesitate to give the name of martyr to one who does such mighty and such merciful deeds?" So he ran to his church, set the bells ringing, and was as good as his word.

Now no longer bereft of light, just as he had been dragged with ignominy through the midst of the town to endure his punishment, so now through the very same street, amid the praise and applause of the people, he was led back to the church of St. Paul, where also he passed the eve of the Lord's day in vigil. Departing thence he hastened his journey to [the shrine of] St. Thomas, the author of his restoration. Whatever gifts folk gave him, he bestowed on the poor, for love of the Martyr. . . .

On his coming to London, he was received with congratulations by Hugh, Bishop of Durham, who would not let him go away until he had sent a messenger to Bedford and had been certified of the facts after diligent inquiry.

But even after we had received him in our house at Canterbury, although he had been preceded by the testimony of very many witnesses, we did not feel satisfied until we heard the substance of the above-written statements confirmed by the letter and testimony of the citizens of Bedford.

(continued)

For they directed to us a document of which the contents were as follows:

"The Burgesses of Bedford to the convent of Canterbury and to all the faithful in Christ, health! Be it known to the convent of Canterbury, and further to all catholics, that God hath wrought in Bedford a wonderful and illustrious miracle on account of the merits of the most holy Thomas, the Martyr. For it happened that a countryman of Westoning, Eilward, by name, for some theft, of the value of only one *nummus*, having been taken and brought before the viscount of Bedford, and before

A Miracle of Saint Thomas of Canterbury in a Stained-Glass Panel from Trinity Chapel, Canterbury Cathedral, England. Early thirteenth century. *(Sonia Halliday Photographs)*

the knights of the county, and having been by them publicly condemned, was deprived of his eyes and privy members, in the presence of clergy and laity, [men] and women. This is also testified by the chaplain of St. John in Bedford, to whom the aforesaid countryman confessed [after mutilation]. And this same is testified by his host, Eilbrict by name, in whose house he was afterwards received—namely that he was entirely without eyes and testicles when first he was received in his house. And afterwards, invoking oftentimes the merits of St. Thomas the Martyr, by an apparition of the aforesaid Martyr he was gloriously and wonderfully restored to health."

The miracle of Eilward of Westoning is pictured in one of the windows that surround Trinity Chapel in Canterbury Cathedral, where images such as this were used by the priests to relate miracle stories to an illiterate congregation. The brilliantly colored stained-glass panels created a potent religious atmosphere for the countless pilgrims who streamed into the chapel to worship at the shrine of Thomas Becket in the years between 1220 and the destruction of the memorial by Henry VIII in 1538.

In the left panel Eilward is tried before the magistrates; on the right he is blinded and castrated according to the decree. At the bottom Eilward points to his eyes, indicating his recovered eyesight, and at the top he rides away from Canterbury, having given thanks at the shrine.

Questions for Discussion:

1. Was Eilward's punishment legal, according to the customs and laws of England? (Document 6.5)
2. The visual program of the window is called "continuous narrative," meaning that the panels flow together to illustrate a story. Point out the various images that correlate directly with the account of the miracle.

Politics in Germany

9.6   Letter of Frederick I to Pope Eugene III

In 1152 the nobility of Germany, seeking a strong leader who could provide stability, elected as king Frederick I ("Barbarossa" or "Red Beard"), Duke of Swabia (r. 1152–1190). According to the historian Otto of Freising, he was "desired by all, and with the approval of all." Upon his election, Frederick wrote to the pope, announcing that he had been "raised to the throne," and that he would continue the "custom of the Roman emperors" in relationship to the papacy. In this document he promised to defend the rights and property of the Church.

(From A Source Book for Medieval History, ed. by Oliver J. Thatcher and Edgar H. McNeal [New York: Charles Scribner's Sons, 1905], pp. 178–179.)

To his most beloved father in Christ, Eugene, pope of the holy Roman church [r. 1145–1153], Frederick, by the grace of God king of the Romans, Augustus, [sends] filial love and reverence.

. . . Following the custom of the Roman emperors, we have sent to you as ambassadors, Eberhard, venerable bishop of Bamberg, Hillo, bishop elect of Trier, and Adam, abbot of Eberach, to notify you of our election and of the condition of the church and the realm.

After the death of Conrad, king of the Romans, all the princes of the kingdom came together at Frankfurt, and on the day of their assembling elected us king. The princes displayed complete harmony in this election and the people received it with the greatest approval and delight. Five days later, just after the middle of Lent, we were anointed at Aachen by your beloved sons, the archbishop of Cologne and other venerable bishops, and were raised to the throne with their solemn benediction. And now that we have been invested with the royal authority and dignity by the homage of the secular princes and the benediction of the bishops, we intend to assume the royal character, as set forth in our coronation oath; namely, to love and honor the pope, to defend the holy Roman church and all ecclesiastical persons, to maintain peace and order, and to protect the widows and the fatherless and all the people committed to our care. God has established two powers by which this world should be ruled, the papacy and the empire; therefore we are prepared to obey the priests of Christ, in order that, through our zeal, the word of God may prevail during our time, and that no one may disobey with impunity the laws of the holy

fathers or the decrees of the councils, and that the church may enjoy her ancient honor and dignity and the empire be restored to its former strength. We know that you were greatly distressed at the death of our uncle and predecessor Conrad, but we assure you, beloved father, that we have succeeded him not only in the kingdom, but also in the love which he bore you. We undertake his work of defending the holy Roman church, and we intend to carry on the plans which he made for the honor and liberty of the apostolic see. Your enemies shall be our enemies, and those that hate you shall suffer our displeasure.

Question for Discussion:

1. Discuss the promises Frederick made to the pope in his letter. How do his statements reflect the Concordat of Worms (1122)? (See Document 6.18.)

9.7   Pope Eugene's Reply

Throughout the Middle Ages there were various sources of tension between popes and monarchs, as we have seen. It had not been determined, for instance, how much authority was held by the pope in deciding the election of the German kings. In the previous document Frederick announced his election to Pope Eugene and outlined his future policies. In reply, Eugene sent a letter dated May 7, 1152, stating that he "approved" the election, but he did not use the strong word "confirm."

(From *A Source Book for Medieval History*, ed. by Oliver J. Thatcher and Edgar H. McNeal [New York: Charles Scribner's Sons, 1905], pp. 178–179.)

Eugene, bishop, servant of the servants of God, to his beloved son in Christ, Frederick, illustrious king of the Romans, greeting and apostolic benediction.

We have received the messengers and the letter which you sent to inform us of your election by the unanimous vote of the princes. . . . We give thanks unto God, from whom comes every good and perfect gift, for this good news, and We

heartily approve your election. We are confident that you intend to take upon yourself the fulfillment of the promise which your uncle and predecessor, Conrad, gave to us and to the holy Roman church. We, on our part, shall labor for your advancement and exaltation, as is the duty of our office. We have sent you an ambassador, who will disclose to you our purpose and intention. In the meantime, we admonish you to bear in mind your oath to defend the church and the clergy of God, to keep peace and order, and to protect the widows and the fatherless, and all your people, that those who obey you and trust in you may rejoice, and that you may win glory with men and eternal life with the king of kings.

Question for Discussion:

1. What expectations does the pope express concerning Frederick's responsibilities? What does he promise in return?

9.8   Treaty of Constance, 1153

Pope Eugene was in a precarious situation. He had been forced to leave Rome as a result of a rebellion by the citizens against him and his rule, and his lands to the south were being threatened by Roger, the king of Sicily. Furthermore, the Greek emperor was formulating plans to take over parts of Italy. In order to secure Frederick's allegiance, the pope insisted that he promise not to make alliances with his enemies without papal consent.

Frederick, who wished to have the pope's blessing in his quest for the imperial crown, was making plans to invade the territory of the Normans in southern Italy and Sicily because he considered this area to be part of his empire. He was afraid that the pope, who hoped to gain control of the Greek Church, might form an alliance with the Greek emperor and aid him in his efforts to conquer Italian land. Hence, the ambassadors of the two men formulated the following agreement.

(From *A Source Book for Medieval History*, ed. by Oliver J. Thatcher and Edgar H. McNeal [New York: Charles Scribner's Sons, 1905], pp. 178–179.)

In the name of the Lord, amen. This is a copy of the agreement and convention made between the pope, Eugene III, and Frederick, king of the Romans, by their representatives; on the part of the pope: cardinals Gregory of Santa Maria in Trastevere, Ubald of San Prassede, Bernard of San Clemente, Octavian of Santa Cecilia, Roland of San Marco, Gregory of Sant Angelo, Guido of Santa Maria in porticu, and Bruno, abbot of Chiaravalle; on the part of the king: Anselm, bishop of Havelberg; Hermann, bishop of Constance; Udalrich, count of Lenzburg; Guido; count of Guerra, and Guido, count of Bianderati.

The king will have one of his ministerials [ministers] to swear for him that he will not make a peace or a truce either with the Romans or with Roger of Sicily without the consent of the pope. The king will use all the power of his realm to reduce the Romans to subjection to the pope and the Roman church. He will protect the honor of the papacy and the regalia of St. Peter against all men to the best of his ability, and he will aid the church in recovering what she has lost. He will never grant any land in Italy to the king of the Greeks, and will use all his power in keeping him out. All these things the king promises to observe and to do in good faith.

The pope, on his part, promises on his apostolic faith, with the consent of the cardinals, that he will ever honor the king as the most dearly beloved son of St. Peter, and that he will give him the imperial crown whenever he shall come to Italy for it. He will aid the king in maintaining and increasing the honor of his realm, as his office demands. If anyone attacks the honor or the authority of the king, the pope at the request of the king will warn him to make satisfaction, and will excommunicate him if he refuses to heed the warning. The pope will not grant any land in Italy to the king of the Greeks, and will use all the resources of St. Peter to drive him out if he invades that land. All these things shall be observed in good faith by both parties, unless they are changed by mutual consent.

Question for Discussion:

1. What promises are made in this treaty by the emperor? By the pope? Which of the men is benefiting the most from this agreement— Frederick or Pope Eugene? Why?

9.9   The "Stirrup Episode"

During his reign, Frederick attempted to extend his authority into the kingdoms of Burgundy and Italy, hoping ultimately to create an empire that spread from the North Sea to the Mediterranean. He married Beatrice of Burgundy in 1156, using "marriage diplomacy" to establish his claim over her lands. Italy proved to be more of a problem. As Frederick moved to assert his control over the towns of northern Italy, he incurred the animosity of the next pope, Adrian IV (1154–1159). Their strained relationship is evident in the account of a confrontation between the two, known as the "Stirrup Episode" (1155).

(From *A Source Book for Medieval History*, ed. by Oliver J. Thatcher and Edgar H. McNeal [New York: Charles Scribner's Sons, 1905], pp. 176–181.)

The king [Frederick] advanced with his army to the neighborhood of Sutri and encamped in Campo Grasso. The pope, however, came to Nepi, and on the day after his arrival was met there by many of the German princes and a great concourse of clergy and laymen, and conducted with his bishops and cardinals to the tent of the king. But when the cardinals who came with the pope saw that the king did not come forward to act as the esquire of the pope [i.e., to hold his stirrup while he dismounted], they were greatly disturbed and terrified, and retreated to Civita Castellana, leaving the pope before the tent of the king. And the pope, distressed and uncertain what he should do, sadly dismounted and sat down on the seat which had been prepared for him. Then the king prostrated himself before the pope, kissing his feet and presenting himself for the kiss of peace. But the pope said: "You have refused to pay me the due and accustomed honor which your predecessors, the orthodox emperors, have always paid to my predecessors, the Roman popes, out of reverence for the apostles, Peter and Paul; therefore I will not give you the kiss of peace until you have made satisfaction." The king, however, replied that he was not under obligations to perform the service. The whole of the following day was spent in the discussion of this point, the army in the meantime remaining there. And after the testimony of the older princes had been taken, especially of those who had been present at the meeting of King Lothar and pope Innocent (II), and the ancient practice had been determined, the princes and the royal court decided that the king ought to act as the esquire of the pope and hold his stirrup, out of reverence for the apostles, Peter and Paul. On the next day the camp of the king was moved to the territory of Nepi, on the shores of lake Janula, and there King Frederick, in accordance with the decision of the princes, advanced to meet the pope, who was approaching by another way. And when the pope came within about a stone's throw from the emperor, the emperor dismounted and proceeded on foot to meet the pope, and there in the sight of his army he acted as the pope's esquire, holding his stirrup for him to dismount. Then the pope gave him the kiss of peace.

Questions for Discussion:

1. Why do you think the issue of the stirrup was so important to the pope? What did the action (or inaction) of the king symbolize?
2. How does this account reflect the obligations of homage and fealty required of vassals? (Refer to Document 5.1.)
3. Compare the "Stirrup Episode" with the earlier event when Duke Rollo refused to kiss the foot of the French king (Document 4.21).

9.10   The "Besançon Episode"

The "Besançon Episode" was another chapter in the long chain of conflicts between the papacy and the German monarchy. In 1156, Pope Adrian IV made a treaty with William of Sicily, bringing to a close the longstanding conflict between the papacy and the Norman kings of Sicily over control of the area. Although the document was, in many ways, favorable to the pope, there were some privileges ceded to William that were viewed as papal rights in other countries. The treaty offended Frederick Barbarossa, partly because the agreement had been made without consulting him. Furthermore, Frederick had his own claims to Sicily, and these were ignored. In the Treaty of Constance (Document 9.8), the emperor had promised not to support the Normans without the consent of the pope, and evidently he assumed that the papacy was bound by the same pledge. Frederick claimed that the pope had broken the Treaty of Constance by signing the treaty with William.

In order to show his displeasure, he did not punish perpetrators who captured the Archbishop of Lund in 1157, as may be seen in the following letter of complaint from the pope.

(From *A Source Book for Medieval History*, ed. by Oliver J. Thatcher and Edgar H. McNeal [New York: Charles Scribner's Sons, 1905], pp. 183–188.)

A Letter from Pope Adrian to Frederick, September 1157

Adrian, bishop, servant of the servants of God, to his beloved son Frederick, illustrious emperor of the Romans, greeting and apostolic benediction. We wrote to you a few days ago recalling to your mind that execrable crime which was recently committed in Germany and expressing our grief that you had allowed it to go unpunished. For our venerable brother, Eskil, archbishop of Lund, on his return from the apostolic seat, was seized and made captive in your land by certain impious and wicked persons, who even threatened him and his companions with drawn swords and subjected them to dishonor and indignity.

Not only are these facts well known to you, but the report of them has spread to the most distant regions. It was your duty to avenge this wicked deed and to draw against its perpetrators the sword entrusted to you by God for the punishing of evil-doers and the protection of good men. But it is reported that you have palliated this offence and allowed it to go unpunished, so that those who committed the sacrilege are unrepentant and believe that they have done this with impunity. We are entirely at a loss to understand this negligence of yours, for our conscience does not accuse us of having offended you in any way. Indeed we have always regarded you as our most beloved son and as a Christian prince established by the grace of God upon the rock of the apostolic confession. We have loved you with sincere affection and have always treated you with the greatest kindness. You should remember, most glorious son, how graciously your mother, the holy Roman church, received you last year, how kindly she treated you, and how gladly she conferred upon you the imperial crown, the highest mark of dignity and honor; how she has always fostered you on her kindly bosom, and has always striven to do only what would be pleasing and advantageous to you. We do not regret having granted the desires of your heart; nay, we would

be glad to confer even greater benefits (*beneficia*) upon you, if that were possible, because of the advantage and profit that you would be able to confer upon the church of God and upon us. But the fact that you have allowed this terrible deed, which is an offence against the church and the empire, to go unpunished has made us fear that you have been led by evil counselors to imagine that you have some grievance against your mother, the holy Roman church, and against us. In regard to this matter and other important affairs, we have sent you these legates, two of the best and dearest of those about us, namely, our beloved sons, Bernard, cardinal priest of Santa Clara, and Roland, chancellor and cardinal priest of San Marco, men conspicuous for their piety, wisdom, and honesty. We beseech you to receive them honorably and kindly, to treat them justly, and to give full credence to the proposals which they make, as if we were speaking in person.

The pope's letter generated an angry response from the emperor, who was enraged by the use of the term beneficium (fief).

Manifesto of Frederick, October 1157

God, from whom proceeds all authority in heaven and in earth, has entrusted the kingdom and the empire to us, his anointed, and has ordained that the peace of the church be preserved by the imperial arms. Therefore it is with great sorrow that we are forced to complain to you of the head of the church which Christ intended should reflect his character of charity and love of peace. For the actions of the pope threaten to produce such evils and dissensions as will corrupt the whole church and destroy its unity, and bring about strife between the empire and the papacy, unless God should intervene. These are the circumstances: We held a diet at Besançon for the purpose of considering certain matters which concerned the honor of the empire and the security of the church. At that diet legates of the pope arrived, saying that they came on a mission that would redound greatly to the honor and advantage of the empire. We gave them an honorable reception on the first day of their arrival, and on the second day, as is the custom, we called together all the princes to listen to their message. . . . Then they delivered their message in the form of a letter from the pope, of which the general tenor was as follows: the pope had conferred the imperial crown upon us and was willing to grant us even greater fiefs (*beneficia*). This was the message of fraternal love which was to further the union of the church and the empire, and bind them together in the bonds of peace, and to inspire the hearts of its hearers with love and fidelity for both rulers! Not only were we, as emperor, incensed by this false and lying statement, but all the princes who were present were so enraged that they would undoubtedly have condemned the two priests to death off-hand had they not been restrained by our presence. Moreover, we found in their possession many copies of that letter, and blank forms sealed by the pope to be filled out at their discretion, with which they were intending to spread this venom throughout the churches of Germany, as is their custom from of old, and to denude the altars, rob the houses of God, and despoil the crosses. Therefore, in order to prevent their further progress, we compelled them to return to Rome by the way they had come. We hold this kingdom and empire through the election of the princes from God alone, who by the passion of his Son placed this world under the rule of two swords; moreover, the apostle Peter says: "Fear God, honor the king" [1 Peter 2 :17]. Therefore, whoever says that we hold the imperial crown as a benefice from the pope resists the divine institution, contradicts the teaching of Peter, and is a liar. . . .

Adrian's response put forth a linguistic explanation for the use of the term "beneficium," obviously hoping to diffuse Frederick's anger.

Letter of Adrian IV to the Emperor, February, 1158

Ever since we were called by the will of God to the government of the universal church, we have tried to honor you in every way, in order that your love and reverence for the apostolic seat might daily increase. Therefore we were greatly astonished to learn that you were incensed at us and that you had treated with such scant respect the legates . . . whom we had sent to you for the purpose of learning your wishes. We are informed that you were enraged because we used the word *beneficium,* at which surely the mind of so great a person as yourself should not have been disturbed. For although with some that word has come to have a

meaning different from its original sense, yet it ought to be taken in the sense in which we have used it and which it has had from the beginning. For *beneficium* comes from *bonum* and *factum,* and we used it to mean not a *feudum* (fief), but a "good deed," in which sense it is used throughout the holy Scriptures; as when we are said to be guided and nourished by the *beneficium* of God, which means not the "fief," but the kindness of God. You surely admit that in placing the imperial crown upon your head we performed an act that would be regarded by all men as a "good deed." Moreover, if you misunderstood the phrase "we conferred the imperial crown upon you," and distorted it from its ordinary meaning, it could only be because you wished to misunderstand it or because you accepted the interpretation of persons who wished to disturb the peace existing between the church and the empire. For we meant by the words "we conferred" no more than "we placed," as we said above. In ordering the recall of the ecclesiastics whom we sent to make a visitation of the churches in Germany according to the right of the Roman church, you must surely recognize that you acted unwisely, for if you had any grievance you should have informed us, and we would have undertaken to satisfy your honor. Now by the advice of our beloved son Henry, duke of Bavaria and Saxony, we have sent you two legates, our brothers Henry, cardinal priest of San Nereo and Sant Achilleo, and Hyacinth, cardinal deacon of Santa Maria in Cosmedin, both wise and honorable men, and we urge you to receive them honorably and kindly, and to accept the message which they deliver as coming from the sincerity of our heart; so agreeing with them through the mediation of our son the duke, that no discord may remain between you and your holy mother, the Roman church.

Questions for Discussion:

1. Why was Frederic enraged by the use of the word *beneficium*? How does the pope justify the term in his letter?

2. Discuss the issues of power and control presented by these documents. When you compare this situation to the Investiture Controversy (Documents 6.14 through 6.18), do you see any progress in imperial–papal relations in the intervening century?

The Crusader Kingdoms and the Third Crusade

The Crusader Kingdoms

9.11   The *History* of Fulcher of Chartres (1059–1127)

As a result of the First Crusade, the victorious crusaders established small kingdoms in the Holy Land. Their establishment and development were described by the historian Fulcher of Chartres, who accompanied Stephen of Blois on the First Crusade; he then served as chaplain to Baldwin of Boulogne, who became the second king of Jerusalem in 1100. Fulcher probably continued in this post until 1115, when he became a canon of the Church of the Holy Sepulcher. He began his three–volume History *with an account of the speech of Pope Urban II at Clermont (Document 7.9), and continued his chronicle until 1127, when he apparently died of plague. His description of the kingdom of Jerusalem under Baldwin I offers an eyewitness account of the environment of the Holy Land following the First Crusade.*

(From *The Crusades: A Reader*, edited by S. J. Allen and Emilie Amt. Peterborough, Canada: Broadview Press, 2003, pp. 87–88. Reprinted with permission of the publisher.)

. . . In the beginning of his reign Baldwin [I, the king of Jerusalem] as yet possessed few cities [that is, only Jerusalem, Bethlehem, and Joppa] and people. Through that same winter he stoutly protected his kingdom from enemies on all sides. And because they found out that he was a very skillful fighter, although he had few men, they did not dare to attack him. If he had had a greater force he would have met the enemy gladly.

Up to that time the land route was completely blocked to our pilgrims. Meanwhile they, French as well as English, or Italians and Venetians, came by sea as far as Joppa. At first we had no other port. These pilgrims came very timidly in single ships, or in squadrons of three or four, through the midst of hostile pirates and past the ports of the Saracens, with the Lord showing the way. When we saw that they had come from our own countries in the West, we promptly and joyfully met them as if they were saints. From them each of us anxiously inquired concerning his homeland and his loved ones. The new

arrivals told us all that they knew. When we heard good news we rejoiced; when they told of misfortune we were saddened. They came on to Jerusalem; they visited the Holy of Holies, for which purpose they had come. Following that, some remained in the Holy Land, and others went back to their native countries. For this reason the land of Jerusalem remained depopulated. There were not enough people to defend it from the Saracens if only the latter dared attack us.

But why did they not dare? Why did so many people and so many kingdoms fear to attack our little kingdom and our humble people? Why did they not gather from Egypt, from Persia, from Mesopotamia, and from Syria at least a hundred times a hundred thousand fighters to advance courageously against us, their enemies? Why did they not, as innumerable locusts in a little field, so completely devour and destroy us that no further mention could be made of us in a land that had been ours from time immemorial? For we did not at that time have more than three hundred knights and as many footmen to defend Jerusalem, Joppa, Ramala, and also the stronghold of Haifa. We scarcely dared to assemble our knights when we wished to plan some feat against our enemies. We feared that in the meantime they would do some damage against our deserted fortifications.

Truly it is manifest to all that it was a wonderful miracle that we lived among so many thousands and as their conquerors made some of them our tributaries and ruined others by plundering them and making them captives. But whence came this virtue? Whence this power? Truly from him whose name is the Almighty, who, not unmindful of his people laboring in his name, in his mercy aids in their tribulations those who trust in him alone. Moreover God promises to reward with everlasting glory in the life to come those whom he sometimes makes happy with very little temporal reward.

Oh time so worthy to be remembered! Often indeed we were sad when we could get no aid from our friends across the sea. We feared lest our enemies, learning how few we were, would sometime rush down upon us from all sides in a sudden attack when none but God could help us. We were in need of nothing if only men and horses did not fail us. The men who came by sea to Jerusalem could not bring horses with them, and no one came to us by land. The people of Antioch were not able to help us, nor we them. . . .

Questions for Discussion:

1. How does Fulcher describe the circumstances of the Franks in the crusader kingdoms?
2. In Documents 7.4 and 7.5, pilgrimage to Jerusalem was described by two men who made the journey. Does Fulcher's discussion of pilgrims reflect the experience of Udalrich and Saewulf?

9.12   The *Memoirs* of Usāmah Ibn-Munquidh

As may be seen from the following excerpt from the memoirs of Usāmah ibn-Munquidh (1095–1188), the Frankish warriors who remained in the Holy Land were viewed with disdain by the Muslims who lived there. His remarks provide an interesting perspective on Frankish–Muslim relations in the generation following the establishment of the crusader states.

(From *An Arab-Syrian Gentleman and Warrior in the Period of the Crusades: Memoirs of Usāmah ibn-Munquidh*, translated by Philip K. Hitti. Copyright © 1929 Columbia University Press. Reprinted with permission of the publisher.)

An Appreciation of the Frankish Character

Their lack of sense:

Mysterious are the works of the Creator, the author of all things! When one comes to recount cases regarding the Franks, he cannot but glorify Allah (exalted is he!) and sanctify him, for he sees them as animals possessing the virtues of courage and fighting, but nothing else; just as animals have only the virtues of strength and carrying loads. I shall now give some instances of their doings and their curious mentality.

In the army of King Fulk [of Jerusalem] [r. 1131–1143], son of Fulk, was a Frankish reverend knight who had just arrived from their land in order to make the holy pilgrimage and then return home. He was of my intimate fellowship and kept such constant company with me that he began to call me "my brother." Between us were mutual bonds of amity and friendship. When he resolved to return by sea to his homeland, he said to me:

"My brother, I am leaving for my country and I want you to send with me your son (my son, who was then fourteen years old, was at that time in my company) to our country, where he can see the knights and learn wisdom and chivalry. When he returns, he will be like a wise man."

Thus there fell upon my ears words which would never come out of the head of a sensible man; for even if my son were to be taken captive, his captivity could not bring him a worse misfortune than carrying him into the lands of the Franks. However, I said to the man:

"By thy life, this has exactly been my idea. But the only thing that prevented me from carrying it out was the fact that his grandmother, my mother, is so fond of him and did not this time let him come out with me until she exacted an oath from me to the effect that I would return him to her."

Thereupon he asked, "Is your mother still alive?" "Yes," I replied. "Well," he said, "do not disobey her."

Newly arrived Franks are especially rough: One insists that Usāmah should pray eastward.

Everyone who is a fresh emigrant from the Frankish lands is ruder in character than those who have become acclimatized and have held long association with the Muslims. Here is an illustration of their rude character.

Whenever I visited Jerusalem I always entered the Aqṣa Mosque, beside which stood a small mosque which the Franks had converted into a church. When I used to enter the Aqṣa Mosque, which was occupied by the Templars, who were my friends, the Templars would evacuate the little adjoining mosque so that I might pray in it. One day I entered this mosque, repeated the first formula, "Allah is great," and stood up in the act of praying, upon which one of the Franks rushed on me, got hold of me and turned by face eastward saying, "This is the way you should pray!" The Templars again came in to him and expelled him. They apologized to me, saying, "This is a stranger who has only recently arrived from the land of the Franks

and he has never before seen anyone praying except eastward." Thereupon I said to myself, "I have had enough prayer." So I went out and have ever been surprised at the conduct of this devil of a man, at the change in the color of his face, his trembling and his sentiment at the sight of one praying towards the *qibla*.

Questions for Discussion:

1. How does Usāmah view the character of Frankish knights? According to this excerpt from his *Memoirs*, what qualities are valued in a Muslim knight?
2. Discuss the interactions of the Franks and the Muslims as described by Usāmah. What do his reflections tell you about the relationships between the two groups in the crusader kingdoms?

The Third Crusade

The "Horns of Hattin": Overture to the Third Crusade
9.13 The *Chronicle* of Otto of St. Blasien

The crusading fervor that began at the end of the eleventh century (see Chapter 7) became even more intense during the course of the twelfth century. There were two major crusades to the Holy Land, the Second (1147–1149) and Third (1189–1192). The Second Crusade was led by Louis VII of France and Conrad III of Germany. In the Third Crusade, the English were led by Richard the Lion Heart, the French by Philip Augustus, and the Germans by Frederick Barbarossa. These rulers were responding to renewed aggression by the Muslims under the leadership of Saladin (1138–1193), and in particular, the capture of Jerusalem.

One of the crucial battles leading to the crusade took place at Hattin[1] (near Tiberius in present-day Israel) on July 4, 1187. The outcome was disastrous for the crusaders, as Saladin's forces triumphed. The Christian forces

were annihilated, and the leaders, including Reinaldus, the governor of Kerak, were taken prisoner and beheaded. The Muslim forces then moved on to capture Jerusalem, an event that prompted the Third Crusade. The motivations for the conflict and justifications for the result were described very differently by the Christian writer Otto of St. Blasien (d. 1223) and Saladin's biographer, Ibn Shaddad (1144–1234).

(From *A Source Book for Mediaeval History*, by Oliver J. Thatcher and Edgar H. McNeal [New York: Charles Scribner's Sons, 1905], pp. 529–530.)

In the year 1187, Saladin, king of the Saracens, seeing the very base conduct of the Christians, and knowing that they were afflicted with discord, hatred, and avarice, thought the time was favorable and so planned to conquer all Syria and Palestine. He collected a very large army of Saracens from all over the

---

[1]The site is often called the "Horns of Hattin" because of twin peaks in the area.

orient and made war on the Christians. Attacking them everywhere in Palestine with fire and sword, he took many fortresses and cities and killed or took prisoner all their Christian inhabitants, and put Saracen colonists in their place. The king of Jerusalem and the noble prince, Reinaldus [of Chatillon, governor of Kerak], and other nobles collected a large army and went out to meet Saladin. The true cross was carried at the head of the army. But they were defeated [at the battle of the Horns of Hattin, July 4, 1187] and many thousands of Christians were slain. The true cross, alas! was captured by the Saracens, and the Christians were put to flight. The king and Reinaldus and many others were taken prisoner, and carried off to Damascus, where . . . Reinaldus was beheaded, confessing the true faith. The pagans were made bold by this victory and took all the cities of the Christians except Tyre, Sidon, Tripolis, and Antioch, and a few other cities and fortresses which were the best fortified and most difficult to take. After taking Acco, where there is a port which had been the sole refuge of the Christians, they besieged Jerusalem. They destroyed all the churches about the city, among them those in Bethlehem and on the Mount of Olives. Finally the Christians surrendered, Jerusalem was taken, and the holy places were profaned and inhabited by pagans [Oct. 2, 1187].

I think that I should relate that while Jerusalem was besieged by the pagans, one of the towers of the city was taken, many of the Christians defending it were slain, and the standard of Saladin was raised over it. This caused the people to despair and they gave up the defense of the walls. And on that day the city came very nearly being taken and destroyed. But a certain German knight, seeing this, and made bold by the desperate situation, urged some of his companions to join him in making a bold attack on the enemy. They retook the tower, killed the pagans in it, tore down the standard of Saladin and threw it to the ground. By this act, he restored courage to the Christians and persuaded them to return to the defense of the walls. After the city had surrendered, as has been said, the sepulcher of the Lord was held in veneration for the sake of gain. . . .

9.14   Ibn Shaddad: *The Life of Saladin*

Ibn Shaddad (Baha al-Din ibn Shaddad, 1145–1234) was a personal friend and adviser of Saladin. His most famous work was a biography of the sultan, which provides a vivid and colorful account of the events surrounding the Muslim leader. He was present during many of the battles of the Third Crusade; thus his chronicle represents the impressions of an eyewitness.

(From *The Life of Saladin*, by Beha Eddin [Ibn Shaddad] [London: Committee of the Palestine Exploration Fund, 1897], pp. 110–114.)

The Sultan [Saladin] believed that it was his duty, above all things, to devote his whole strength to fulfill the command we have received to war against the infidels, in recognition of God's mercy in establishing his dominion, in making him master of so many lands, and granting him the obedience and devotion of his people. Therefore he sent an order to all his troops to join him at Ashtara. When he had mustered and reviewed them, as we have narrated above, he made his dispositions, and marched full speed upon the enemy's territory—

may God confound their hopes!—on the 17th of the month Rabi'a II. [June 26, 1187]. He used always to attack the enemy on a Friday, at the hour of prayer, believing that the prayers that the preachers were offering from their pulpits at that time would bring him good luck, because their petitions that day were generally granted. At this hour, then, he began his march, holding his army in readiness to fight. He heard that the Franks, having received intelligence of his mustering of troops, had assembled in the plain of Seffuria, in the territory of Acre, and meant to come out and meet him and give him battle. He therefore took up a position close to the Sea of Tiberias, near a village called es-Sennabra. He next encamped on the top of the hill that lies to the west of Tiberias. There he remained ready for battle, thinking that the Franks would advance and attack him as soon as they had ascertained his movements; but they did not stir from their position. It was on Wednesday, the 21st of this same month [June 30, 1187], that the Sultan pitched his camp there. Seeing that the enemy were not moving, he left his infantry drawn up opposite the enemy and went down to Tiberias with a troop of light cavalry. He attacked that city and carried it by assault within an hour, devoting it to slaughter, burning, and sacking. All that were left of the inhabitants were taken prisoner. The castle alone held out. When the enemy heard the fate of Tiberias, they were forced to break through their policy of inaction, to satisfy this call upon their honor, and they set out for Tiberias forthwith to drive the invaders back. The scouts of the Muslim army discerned their movement, and sent people to inform the Sultan. When he received this message he detached a sufficient force to blockade the castle, and then rejoined the army with his force. The two armies met on the summit of the hill to the west of Tiberias. This was on the evening of Thursday, the 22nd of the same month. Darkness separated the combatants, who passed the night under arms in order of battle, until the following day, Friday, the 23rd [July 2, 1187]. Then the warriors of both armies mounted their steeds and charged their opponents; the soldiers in the vanguard discharged their arrows; and the infantry came into action and fought furiously. This took place in the territory belonging to a village called Lubiya. The Franks saw they must bite the dust, and came on as though driven to certain death; before them lay disaster and ruin, and they were convinced that the next day would find them numbered among the dead. The fight raged obstinately; every horseman hurled himself against his opponent until victory was secured, and destruction fell upon the infidels. Night with its blackness put an end to the battle. Terrible encounters took place that day; never in the history of past generations have such feats of arms been told. The night had been spent under arms, each side thinking every moment that they would be attacked. The Muslims, knowing that behind them lay the Jordan, and in front the territory of the enemy, felt that God alone was able to save them. God, having granted His aid to the Muslims, gave them success, and sent them victory according to His decree. Their infantry charged from all sides; the center came on like one man, uttering a mighty cry; God filled the hearts of the infidels with terror (for He has said), '*Due from Us it was to help the believers*' (*Qu'ran* xxx. 47). The count (Raymond of Tripoli), the most intelligent man of that race, and famous for his keenness of perception, seeing signs of the catastrophe impending over his brothers in religion, was not prevented by thoughts of honor from taking measures for his personal safety. He fled in the beginning of the action, before the fighting had become serious, and set out in the direction of Tyre. Several Muslims started in pursuit of him, but he succeeded in evading them; true believers had nothing thereafter to fear from his cunning. The upholders of Islam surrounded the upholders of infidelity and impiety on every side, overwhelming them with arrows and harassing them with their swords. One group of the enemy took to flight, but they were pursued by our Muslim heroes, and not one of the fugitives escaped. Another group climbed Hattin hill, so called from the name of a village, near which is the tomb of the holy patriarch Shu'aib (Jethro). The Muslims hemmed them in, and lit fires all round them, so that, tortured by thirst and reduced to the last extremity, they gave themselves up to escape death. Their leaders were taken captive, and the rest were killed or made prisoners. Among the leaders who surrendered were King Guy, the King's brother, Prince Reynald (Renaud de Chatillon), Lord of el-Kerak, and of esh-Shawbak, the son of el-Honferi (Humfrey de Toron), the son of the Lord of Tiberias (Raymond of Tripoli), the master of the Templars, the Lord of Jubayl, and the master of the Hospitallers.[2] The others who were missing had met their death; and as to the common people, some were killed and others taken captive. Of their whole army none remained alive, except the prisoners. More than one of their chief leaders accepted captivity to save his life. A man, whom I believe to be reliable, told me that he saw one soldier in the Hawran leading more than thirty prisoners, tied together with a tent cord. He had taken them all himself, so great had been the panic caused by their defeat.

Questions for Discussion:

1. Compare the two accounts of the battle at Hattin. What is the primary difference between them?
2. How does Otto describe the fate of the Frankish leaders? Does Ibn Shaddad give the same details? How might you explain the differences?

---

[2]The Hospitallers were another monastic military order formed following the First Crusade.

9.15   A Letter of Clement III Concerning the Third Crusade

In response to the news of the capture of Jerusalem, that "grievous and horrible calamity of persecution," Pope Clement III (r. 1187–1191) issued the following letter in which he urged the bishops to raise men and money for another crusade. His message insisted upon rapid action on the part of the Europeans to combat the growing strength of the Muslims.

(From *Giraldus: On the Instruction of Princes,* in *Church Historian of England,* vol. v, pt. 1, trans. by Joseph Stevenson [London: Seeleys, 1858], pp. 186–189.)

Letter of Pope Clement (1188)

"CLEMENT, a bishop, servant of the servants of God, to the venerable brethren, the archbishop of Canterbury, and his suffragans, health and apostolical benediction.

"We think that your whole body cannot be ignorant of the grievous and horrible calamity of persecution which has lately fallen upon the parts of the Holy Land around Jerusalem, at the instigation of a multitude of open sinners, both from the atrocity of the deed itself, which common report has made everywhere known, and also from our letters which have been sent upon this subject into different areas. But it is of consequence to the Christian state, that the greater as well as the lesser prelates of the churches faithfully fulfill their part with diligent solicitude to succor those portions of the world, lest, if succor is not quickly sent to that land, this slavish and accursed progeny of Ishmael, which has already begun in a hostile manner to pull down the peculiar inheritance of the Lord in these parts, should, in the meantime, assume an increase of strength, and, growing powerful in his own vanity, should more insolently raise his heel against the Christian, the son of the free woman, (which God forbid!) and should more fiercely persecute him. Since, therefore, the loss and calamities of the land of Jerusalem itself generally affect all Christians, as being that land in which Christ, by his death, redeemed the human race, we have thought fit, with the advice of our brethren, to direct our letters for the subsidies destined for that land, to yourselves in the first instance, as being placed to watch over the church, and afterwards to others. We entreat you therefore, and exhort you in the Lord, and by this our apostolical rescript[3] we enjoin you, that you yourselves transmit to us suitable assistance, both by sending men and money for the aid of this same province, that others, when they see you doing this, may more readily be excited to imitate your example, Also, we will that you effectually induce those who are subject to your authority to join in this work, that since you and they have been partakers together in suffering, you may be, as the apostle says, partakers of the consolation, and of that remission which has generally been granted in former time by our predecessor pope Gregory, of blessed memory, and a short time since by ourselves, to all who themselves go there in person, or send suitable assistance. But we will, that, by our authority and your own, you compel the clergy who are under your jurisdiction forthwith to assist that land out of the worldly goods which they possess; also that you appoint, each one of you throughout his diocese, discreet, faithful, and provident clerks, who may zealously collect the money of the subsidy, and may faithfully dispense the same, with your advice, and that of other prudent persons if it shall be necessary. Moreover, whoever, being truly penitent, shall go there in his own person, shall have remission of all his sins. But those who shall send a competent subsidy out of their worldly goods to those parts, or shall send anyone who may remain there in their stead, for the defense of the Christian people, to them we stand pledged to remit their sins by your authority; it being granted with due consideration both to the quality and quantity of their assistance, and that they themselves are truly penitent. Moreover, if there are any of those who are going there, who may be held bound by a solemn engagement to pay interest for money borrowed, that,

---

[3]An apostolical rescript was a letter from the pope.

without the delay of an appeal to us, you compel their creditors, by canonical censure, that they altogether desist from the exaction of the fulfillment of their solemn promise. But if there are any who, perhaps, are held bound for debts due, and which they are unable for the present to discharge, we will that, sufficient security being received of their possessions and their other goods, the time of payment be put off until their return; or if they shall die there, until certain information be received of their death, lest on an occasion of this kind the advantage of so necessary a journey at this moment in the meanwhile may be retarded; but so that when they return, or a certain report of their death shall have become publicly known, each creditor shall be competently satisfied accordingly. But since, 'unless the Lord keep the city, the watchman waketh but in vain;' nor does human wisdom profit, but fail, if it be destitute of divine help: above all things, invoke the mercy of God by your prayers, and order it to be invoked continually throughout the churches, that He would not regard the sins of the people; but that from heaven, for his mercy alone, He would look upon and defend his sanctuary, his holy city Jerusalem, and would not suffer it to be defiled by the wicked hands of the infidels. Moreover, whomsoever you

shall discover to be at enmity between themselves, you shall earnestly strive to recall to peace and goodwill, by exhortation, or even by the censures of the church; so that, every ground of animosity and jealousy being removed, they may be rendered more courageous and more united to break down that haughty nation, and with the help of God to drive them utterly out of those parts. All those also who go there in their own persons, and send their families, we take under the protection of the blessed Peter, and under our own, until they shall have returned; and we will that they enjoy all their possessions in as great security as they can desire.

"Given at the Lateran, on the fourth of the ides of February [10th Feb.] and in the first year of our pontificate." [A.D. 1188]

Questions for Discussion:

1. Compare Clement's letter with Urban's speech in the previous century (Documents 7.8 through 7.11). How does Clement expand upon the promises made to the crusaders by Pope Urban?
2. Which is more appealing from a rhetorical point of view: the speech or the letter? Why?

9.16 The Death of Frederick Barbarossa: From the *Chronicle* of Otto of St. Blasien

The relationships between the three kings who led their forces in the Third Crusade were not peaceful. During the course of the war, Philip Augustus of France, feigning ill health, returned to his homeland. One of the great tragedies of the twelfth century was the death of Frederick Barbarossa, which occurred during this crusade. Hence, Richard the Lion Heart was the one remaining leader of the three who began the campaign. The following excerpt from the Chronicle of Otto St. Blasien *describes the circumstances of Frederick's demise.*

(From *A Source Book for Medieval History*, by Oliver J. Thatcher and Edgar H. McNeal [New York: Charles Scribner's Sons, 1905], pp. 533–535.)

Now the Greek emperor, not being able to withstand the power of Frederick, made amends for what he had done, and entered into a treaty with him. He appeased the army by supplying them with provisions. Thus, having been reconciled with Frederick, he set him and his army across the Propontis [Sea of Marmara] [March 22–28, 1190, from Gallipolis]. Frederick now entered Asia with his army. He marched for some time, meeting everywhere with success, and all the people in Romania [western Asia Minor] submitted to him. As the emperor approached Iconium [in present-day

Turkey], the sultan broke his treaty, caused all the provisions to be carried into the fortresses, and, like a barbarian and Scythian, refused to sell the army provisions. The army suffered from hunger and were compelled to eat the flesh of mules, donkeys, and horses. Besides, the pagans attacked the rear and those who went out foraging, and killed some of them. In this way they hindered the army. Our troops wished to meet the Saracens in open battle and often drew themselves up in battle array, but the Saracens always withdrew and refused to join in a general engagement. Now although the army was annoyed in this way and was suffering from hunger and want, the emperor, out of regard for the treaty with the sultan, kept his army from devastating and plundering the country, because he thought the people were attacking him without the permission of the sultan. But when he learned from couriers that the sultan had perfidiously ordered the people to attack him, he was angry, and, declaring the sultan an enemy, he permitted the army to take vengeance. They devastated Cilicia, Pamphilia, and Phrygia [all in present-day Turkey] with slaughter, rapine, fire, and sword, while the pagan army constantly withdrew before them. The army now turned toward Iconium, which is the capital of Cilicia, and the chief residence of the sultan, and quickly took it [May 18, 1190]. It was a very populous city, well fortified with strong walls and high towers, and had in its midst an impregnable citadel. It was well supplied with victuals against a siege, while all the surrounding country was stripped of provisions, in order that when the emperor came he would not be able to support an army there for very long. But God overruled their efforts so that the outcome was just the opposite of what they sought. For the emperor suddenly attacked the city with great violence before the third hour of the day [9 o'clock], killed a great many of the inhabitants and took the city by storm before the ninth hour [3 o'clock P.M.]. Many people, of both sexes and of all ages, were put to the sword. The sultan with many of his nobles fled into the citadel, which the emperor began to besiege the same day. Now the sultan saw that nothing could resist the force of the Germans and that, supported by some divine power, they despised death and without hesitation attacked everything that resisted them. So, taught by dangerous experience, and thinking it necessary to demand peace from the emperor, he asked to speak with him. The emperor granted his request. The sultan then marched out of the citadel and surrendered at the discretion of the emperor, and gave hostages. After peace was made the city of Iconium and his kingdom were restored to him.

The army was thus made rich with spoil and the emperor left Iconium in triumph. The Armenian princes from all sides began to come to him, among them Leo, the noblest Christian prince of all that country. They all welcomed Frederick with joy and thanked him heartily for coming and attacking the Saracens. They were all well disposed toward him, so he set out for Tarsus, famous as the birthplace of St. Paul. But God who is terrible in his doing toward the children of men [Ps. 66:5], showing that the time had not yet come for showing mercy on Zion [Ps. 102:13], cut the anchor of the little boat of St. Peter and permitted it to be tossed about and beaten by the storms of this world. For the great emperor, Frederick, while on the road to Tarsus, after a part of the army had crossed a certain river, went into the water to refresh himself, for it was very hot and he was a good swimmer. But the cold water overcame him and he sank. So the emperor, powerful by land and sea, met with an unfortunate death. Some say that this happened in the Cydnus River, in which Alexander the Great almost met the same fate. For the Cydnus is near Tarsus. He died in the 38th year of his reign, the 35th of his rule as emperor [June 10, 1190]. If he had lived he would have been a terror to all the orient, but by his death the army lost all its courage, and was overwhelmed with grief. His intestines and flesh were buried in Tarsus, but his bones were carried to Antioch and buried with royal ceremony.

Questions for Discussion:

1. How does Otto explain Frederick's death?
2. Is Otto's view of the emperor's character generally positive? Discuss your opinion.

Chapter 10

❧❦❧

Social and Cultural Revival in the Twelfth Century

The twelfth century has been regarded by generations of scholars as a time of rejuvenation and renewal, although in many ways it represented a further development of earlier cultural traditions. Nonetheless, the important accomplishments of this period of "Renaissance" warrant careful attention, and should be viewed as substantial achievements rather than simply precursors of its more famous counterpart in the fifteenth and sixteenth centuries.

Many of the architectural, philosophical, and literary innovations of this era occurred as a result of population growth and relative political stability; they took place in large urban centers that provided the milieu for the artistic and intellectual developments of the era. The description of London by William FitzStephen included in this chapter (Document 10.1) offers an example typical of great cities that offered an environment in which new ideas could take root.

The economic life of urban areas was organized by the system of guilds and confraternities that had many functions. They controlled wages and prices, supervised the training of apprentices, and provided social benefits and spiritual solace for the guild members. Document 10.2 presents two examples of guild activity as stipulated by the statutes of the Spur-Makers and Leather-Tanners.

The era also witnessed the birth of the architectural style known as "Gothic." Although modern scholars have pointed out that the new manner developed alongside the late Romanesque tradition (see Chapter 8), Abbot Suger of St. Denis (1081–1151) has generally been given credit for the innovations. The rebuilding of his abbey church, which was a result of his planning and patronage, embodies many of the novel stylistic features. An excerpt from his account, De Consecratione, is included in this chapter, accompanied by a photograph of the ambulatory of the church at St. Denis (Document 10.3).

This chapter introduces several other individuals who made unique contributions to the history and culture of the twelfth century. The author Chrétien de Troyes (1135–1183) built upon the legends surrounding King Arthur and his knights to create romantic tales of compelling interest. These stories have been studied and enjoyed by scholars as well as the general public for hundreds of years. Furthermore, the plots have furnished material for artists as well as writers, as may be seen in the "Interpreting the Evidence" feature that accompanies Chrétien's Lancelot (Document 10.4).

Marie de France (fl. c. 1160–1215) was another important author of the twelfth century. She wrote short narrative poems known as lays (lais), in addition to animal fables and stories based on the legends of King Arthur. The "Lay of the Nightingale" (Document 10.5) recounts an amusing tale of an extramarital romance.

Like Chrétien de Troyes, the twelfth-century author Andreas Capellanus (Andreas the Chaplain) was active at the court of Marie, Countess of Champagne, who requested that he write a treatise on courtly love. His work, The Art of Courtly Love (Document 10.6), was probably based upon the fanciful writings of the Roman poet Ovid. The excerpt included in this chapter offers an analysis of gender relationships in the medieval aristocracy.

The tradition of courtly love is perhaps best exemplified in the songs of troubadours, trouvères, and trobairitz. These lyrics, primarily expressions of love and longing, were composed by men and women of the nobility. Several examples are included in this chapter, demonstrating the intense emotional atmosphere cultivated in the courts of France (Document 10.7).

This section continues with an account of a real-life "romance." In the realm of ideas, the charismatic Peter Abelard provided a new philosophical methodology, based upon careful organizational principles, as we will see later in this chapter. However, his fame does not rest solely upon his intellectual accomplishment. In his autobiography, Abelard recounted details of his personal life and his romance with his pupil, Heloise (1098–1164), which became a "cause célèbre" of the era. This chapter also includes a letter from Heloise to Abelard, which offers her perspective on their relationship (Document 10.9).

The urban environment proved to be fertile ground for the emergence of sophisticated theological and philosophical discourse. One of the most innovative of the philosophers was Peter Abelard (1079–1142), whose work Sic et Non ("Yes and No") was fundamental to the development of Scholasticism in the High Middle Ages. He described his methodology in the Prologue to this work (Document 10.10).

Equally important twelfth-century thinkers were two prominent scholars, the Muslim writer Averroes (1126–1198) and the Jewish philosopher Maimonides (1135–1204), both of whom were educated in Muslim Spain. In differing ways, they both worked to combine Greek philosophy with Christian, Hebrew, and Muslim *religious thought to create a universal intellectual system. Their works are represented in this chapter (Documents 10.11 and 10.12).*

Rational thought, which characterized the search for religious knowledge by Abelard, Averroes, and Maimonides, was not the only path to God sanctioned by medieval people. Mysticism was also recognized as a valid form of religious cognition. One of the first mystics to record her visions was Hildegard of Bingen (1098–1179); she was also a

composer and a well-known abbess who advised important ecclesiastical dignitaries as well as monarchs. Excerpts from her writings describe her revelations, which are among the earliest accounts of mystical experiences written down by medieval women (Document 10.13).

By studying the rich mixture of art and architecture, literature and philosophy, and the charismatic individuals of this vibrant era, it is possible to see why scholars continue to speak of a "twelfth-century Renaissance."

The Urban World: Cities and Guilds

10.1   A Description of Twelfth-Century London by William Fitzstephen

As a result of economic growth, several sizeable cities developed in England and western Europe by the twelfth century, including Paris, Cologne, Venice, and London. These urban centers were fueled by the use of cash and credit, as well as burgeoning long-distance trade. One of the most vivid portraits of twelfth-century urban life may be found in the works of the historian William FitzStephen (d. 1190), who was one of the close associates of Archbishop Thomas Becket (see Documents 9.3 through 9.5). FitzStephen wrote a biography of the Canterbury martyr that began with a description of London. His account of the city shows that it was thriving with intellectual advantages, as well as trade and commercial activity. This excerpt offers information about education, markets, commerce, and sports and recreation.

(From *Documents Illustrating the History of Civilization in Medieval England (1066–1500),* by R. Trevor Davies. New York: E.P. Dutton & Co, 1926, pp. 115–122. Translation modernized. Reprinted by permission of Taylor & Francis Books UK.)

Among the noble and celebrated cities of the world that of London, the capital of the kingdom of the English, is one which extends its glory farther than all the others and sends its wealth and merchandise more widely into distant lands. Higher than the rest does it lift its head. It is happy in the healthiness of its air; in its observance of Christian practice; in the

strength of its fortifications; in its natural situation; in the honor of its citizens; and in the modesty of its matrons. It is cheerful in its sports, and the fruitful mother of noble men. Let us look into these things in turn. . . .

[London] has on the east the Palatine Castle [the Tower of London], very great and strong, of which the ground plan and the walls rise from a very deep foundation, fixed with a mortar tempered by the blood of animals. On the west are two towers very strongly fortified, with the high and great wall of the city having seven double gates, and towered to the north at intervals. London was walled and towered in like manner on the south, but the great fish-bearing Thames River which glides there, with ebb and flow from the sea, by course of time has washed against, loosened, and thrown down those walls. Also upwards to the west the royal palace is conspicuous above the same river, an incomparable building with ramparts and bulwarks, two miles from the city, joined to it by a populous suburb.

Markets and Trade:

Those engaged in the several kinds of business, sellers of several things, contractors for several kinds of work, are distributed every morning into their several localities and shops. Besides, there is in London on the river bank, among the wines in ships and cellars sold by the vintners, a public cook shop; there eatables are to be found every day, according to the season, dishes of meat, roast, fried and boiled, great and small fish, coarser meats for the poor, more delicate for the rich, of game, fowls, and small birds.

Sports and Recreation:

Let us now come to the sports and pastimes, seeing it is fit that a city should not only be commodious and serious, but also merry and sportful. But London, for the shows in theatres, and comical pastimes, has holy plays, representations of miracles, which holy confessors have wrought, or representations of torments in which the constancy of martyrs appeared. Every year also at Shrove Tuesday, that we may begin with children's sports, seeing we all have been children, the schoolboys bring cocks of the game to their master, and all morning they delight themselves in cock-fighting: after dinner, all the youths go into the fields to play the ball.

The scholars of every school have their ball, or baton, in their hands; the ancient and wealthy men of the city come forth on horseback to see the sport of the young men, and to take pleasure in looking at their agility. Every Friday in Lent a fresh company of young men comes into the field on horseback and the best horseman leads the rest. Then the citizens' sons march forth, and other young men, with disarmed lances and shields, and there they practice feats of war. Likewise, many courtiers, when the king is near, and attendants of noblemen, come to these exercises; and while the hope of victory inflames their minds, they show good proof of how serviceable they would be in martial affairs.

In Easter holidays they fight battles on the water; a shield is hung upon a pole, fixed in the midst of the stream, a boat is prepared without oars, to be carried by violence of the water, and in the front stands a young man, ready to give charge upon the shield with his lance; if so be he breaks his lance against the shield, and does not fall, he is thought to have performed a worthy deed; if it happens that, without breaking his lance, he runs strongly against the shield, down he falls into the water, for the boat is violently forced with the tide; but on each side of the shield ride two boats, furnished with young men, which recover the one that falls as soon as they may. Upon the bridge, wharfs, and houses, by the river's side, stand great numbers to see and laugh thereat.

In the holidays all the summer the youths are exercised in leaping, dancing, shooting, wrestling, casting the stone, and practicing their shields; the maidens trip in their timbrels, and dance as long as they can well see. In winter, every holiday before dinner, the boars prepared for brawn are set to fight, or else bulls and bears are baited.

When the great fen, or moor, which is next to the walls of the city on the north side, is frozen, many young men play upon the ice; some, striding as wide as they may, slide swiftly; others make themselves seats of ice, as great as millstones; one sits down, many draw him hand in hand, and if one slips suddenly, all fall together. Some tie bones to their feet and under their heels; and shoving themselves by a little picked staff, slide as swiftly as a bird flies in the air, or an arrow out of a cross-bow. Sometimes two run together with poles, and hitting one the other, either one or both fall, not without hurt; some break their arms, some their legs, but youth, desiring glory in this sort of activity, exercises itself against the time of war. Many of the citizens delight themselves in hawks and hounds; for they have liberty of hunting in Middlesex, Hertfordshire, all Chiltern, and in Kent to the water of Cray.

Questions for Discussion:

1. Describe the various commodities that were available to the residents and travelers in London.
2. According to FitzStephen, does this seem to have been a friendly environment?
3. What sports and recreational activities were available to the citizens?

10.2 Guild Statutes: Spur-Makers and Leather-Tanners

An important feature of urban life was the existence of guilds. These were organizations of merchants and crafts-people that joined together in order to establish regulations for the wages and products of the guild, and to provide aid to the members in times of hardship. Similar organizations that were devoted mostly to religious activities were known as confraternities. Whereas the guilds were primarily interested in regulating the material pursuits of their members, the goal of the confraternities was spiritual salvation. However, since both guilds and confraternities were involved in religious and charitable concerns, the distinction between the two is not clear-cut.

As may be seen in the "Articles of the Spur-Makers of London," the statutes of the guild attempted to regulate the behavior of the tradesmen, establish and define the period of apprenticeship, and restrict membership in the trade to individuals of British origin, unless they obtained permission from the city authorities. Although these articles date from the fourteenth century, they document procedures and traditions dating from an earlier period.

(From *Translations and Reprints from the Original Sources of European History,* vol. ii, ed. by Edward P. Cheyney [Philadelphia: University of Pennsylvania Press, n.d.], pp. 21–23.)

Articles of the Spurriers (Spur-Makers) of London, A.D. 1345

In the first place,—no one of the trade of spurriers shall work longer than from the beginning of the day until curfew rings out at the Church of St. Sepulchre, because no man can work so neatly by night as by day. And many persons of the said trade, who know how to practice deception in their work, desire to work by night rather by day; and then they introduce false iron, or substitute tin for iron that has been cracked; also they put gilt on false copper. And further,—many of the said trade are wandering about all day, without working at all at their trade; and then, when they have become drunk and frantic, they take to their work, to the annoyance of the sick, and all their neighborhood, as well by reason of the brawls that

arise between them and the strange folks who are dwelling among them. And then they blow up their fires so vigorously, that their forges begin all at once to blaze, causing great peril to themselves and all the neighborhood around. And then, too, all the neighbors are much in dread of the sparks, which so vigorously issue forth in all directions from the mouths of the chimneys in their forges. For these reasons, it seems to them that working by night should be put an end to, in order to avoid such false work and such perils . . . Henceforth such time for working, and such false work made in the trade, shall be forbidden. And if any person shall be found in the said trade to do the contrary, let him be fined, the first time in 40d., one-half to go to the use of the Chamber of the Guildhall of London, and the other half to the use of the said trade; the second time, in half a mark, and the third time in 10s., to the use of the same Chamber and trade; and the fourth time, let him forswear the trade forever.

Also, that no one of the said trade shall take an apprentice for a less term than seven years,[1] and such apprentice shall be enrolled according to the usages of the said city.

Also, that if anyone of the said trade, who is not a freeman, shall take an apprentice for a term of years, he shall be fined as stipulated before.

Also, that no one of the said trade shall receive the apprentice, serving-man or journeyman of another in the same trade, during the term agreed upon between his master and him; on the fine stipulated before.

Also, that no alien of another country, or foreigner of this country, shall follow or use the said trade, unless he is enfranchised before the mayor, alderman and chamberlain; and that by witness and

---

[1]Seven years was a typical term for an apprenticeship. See Chaucer's "The Cook's Tale" for an amusing view of an apprentice (Document 14.16).

surety of the good folks of the said trade, who will undertake for him as to his loyalty and his good behavior.

Also, that no one of the said trade shall work on Saturdays, after None has been rung out in the City; and not from that hour until the Monday morning following.

Questions for Discussion:

1. What reasons are given in the articles for restricting the practice of the spur-makers' trade to the daylight hours? Do you know of regulations such as this in the contemporary world?
2. Why was membership in the guild restricted to citizens of England?

The leather-tanners' guild (the "white-tawyers") stipulated certain religious activities, in addition to making certain that the organization would provide for any member who was too old or ill to work, for the widows of guild members, and for burial expenses. There were also rules about wages, prices, and proper behavior.

(From *Translations and Reprints from the Original Sources of European History,* vol. ii, ed. by Edward P. Cheyney [Philadelphia: University of Pennsylvania Press, n.d.], pp. 23–25. Translation modernized.)

Ordinances of the White-Tawyers

In the first place, they have ordained that they will find a wax candle, to burn before our Lady in the church of Allhallows, near London wall. Also, that each person of the said trade shall put in the box such sum as he shall think fit, in aid of maintaining the said candle.

Also, if by chance anyone of the said trade shall fall into poverty, whether through old age or because he cannot labor or work, and have nothing with which to keep himself, he shall have every week from the said box 7 d. for his support, if he be a man of good repute. And after his decease, if he have a wife, a woman of good repute, she shall have weekly for her support 7 d. from the said box, so long as she shall behave herself well and keep single.

And that no stranger shall work in the said trade, or keep house for the same in the city, if he be not an apprentice, or a man admitted to the franchise of the said city.

And that no one shall take the serving-man of another to work with him, during his term, unless it is with the permission of his master.

And if anyone of the said trade shall have work in his house that he cannot complete, or if for want of assistance such work shall be in danger of being lost, those of the said trade shall aid him, that so the said work be not lost.

And if anyone of the said trade shall depart this life, and have not the means to be buried, he shall be buried at the expense of their common box. And when anyone of the said trade shall die, all those of the said trade shall go to the vigil, and make offering on the next morning.

And if any serving-man shall conduct himself in any other manner than properly towards his master, and act rebelliously toward him, no one of the said trade shall give him work, until he shall have made amends before the mayor and aldermen; and before them such misbehavior shall be redressed.

Also,—that the good folks of the same trade shall once in the year be assembled in a certain place, convenient for them, in order to choose two men of the most loyal and reliable of the said trade, to be overseers of work and all other things touching the trade for that year . . . to inquire and make search, and loyally to present to the said mayor and aldermen such defaults as they shall find touching the said trade without sparing anyone for friendship or for hatred, or in any other manner. And if anyone of the said trade shall be found rebellious against the said overseers, so as not to let them properly make their search and inspection, as they ought to do, or if he shall absent himself from the meeting aforesaid, without reasonable cause, after due warning by the said overseers, he shall pay to the Chamber, upon the first default, 40d.; and on the second like default, half a mark; and on the third one mark; and on the fourth, 20s., and shall forswear the trade forever.

Also, that if the overseers shall be found lax and negligent about their duty, or partial to any person for gift or for friendship, maintaining him or voluntarily permitting him to continue in his default, and shall not present him to the mayor and aldermen, as before stated, they are to incur the penalty aforesaid.

Also, that all skins falsely and deceitfully wrought in their trade which the said overseers shall find on sale in the hands of any person, citizen or foreigner, within the franchise shall be forfeited to the said chamber, and the worker thereof fined in the manner aforesaid.

Also, that no one who has not been an apprentice, and has not finished his term of apprenticeship in the said trade, shall be made free of the same trade; unless it be attested by the overseers for the time being, or by four persons of the said trade, that such person is able and sufficiently skilled to be made free of the same.

Also, that no one of the said trade shall induce the servant of another to work with him in the said trade, until he has made a proper fine with his first master, at the discretion of the said overseers, or of four reputable men of the said trade. And if anyone shall do to the contrary thereof, or receive the serving workman of another to work with him during his term, without leave of the trade, he is to incur the said penalty.

Also, that no one shall take for working in the said trade more than they were accustomed to receive before now, or be fined; that is to say, for the dyker[2] of Scotch stags, half a mark; the dyker of Irish stags, half a mark; the dyker of Spanish stags, 10s.; for the hundred of goat skins, 20s.; the hundred of roe leather, 16s.; for the hundred skins of young deer, 8s.; and for the hundred of kid skins, 8s.

Questions for Discussion:

1. What measures offered a degree of security to the guild member?
2. Why do you think the rules concerning behavior were stipulated?
3. How was the association protected financially?

---

[2]A dyker was ten hides or skins.

Architecture: Birth of the Gothic Style

INTERPRETING THE EVIDENCE

10.3 *De Consecratione* by Abbot Suger and the Ambulatory of Saint Denis

One of the most important men of the twelfth century was Suger (1081–1151), Abbot of St. Denis, a monastery in the environs of Paris. Suger, as we have seen, functioned as adviser and biographer to King Louis VI (see Chapter 9), and to his son, Louis VII. In addition to his activities as a statesman, his ideas concerning the construction and expansion of his abbey church were of great importance in the history of architecture. Although current scholars believe that his influence was not as crucial as previously assumed, the innovations undertaken under his direction contributed significantly to the emergence of Gothic style. Suger

described his motivation for the new design in his work De Consecratione.

(From Panofsky, Erwin; *Abbot Suger on the Abbey Church of St. Denis and Its Art Treasures.* © 1946 Princeton University Press, 1974 renewed PUP. Reprinted by permission of Princeton University Press.)

Through a fortunate circumstance attending this singular smallness [of the basilica of St. Denis]— the number of the faithful growing and frequently gathering to seek the intercession of the Saints— the aforesaid basilica had come to suffer grave inconveniences. Often on feast days, completely

(continued)

filled, it disgorged through all its doors the excess of the crowds as they moved in opposite directions, and the outward pressure of the foremost ones not only prevented those attempting to enter from entering but also expelled those who had already entered. At times you could see, a marvel to behold, that the crowded multitude offered so much resistance to those who strove to flock in to worship and kiss the holy relics, the Nail and Crown of the Lord, that no one among the countless thousands of people because of their very density could move a foot; that no one, because of their very congestion, could [do] anything but stand like a marble statue, stay benumbed or, as a last resort, scream. The distress of the women, however, was so great and so intolerable that you could see with horror how they, squeezed in by the mass of strong men as in a winepress, exhibited bloodless faces as in imagined death; how they cried out horribly as

though in labor; how several of them, miserably trodden underfoot {but then} lifted by the pious assistance of men above the heads of the crowd, marched forward as though upon a pavement; and how many others, gasping with their last breath, panted in the cloisters of the brethren to the despair of everyone. Moreover the brethren who were showing the tokens of the Passion of Our Lord to the visitors had to yield to their anger and rioting and many a time, having no place to turn, escaped with the relics through the windows. When I was instructed by the brethren as a schoolboy I used to hear of this; in my youth I deplored it from without; in my mature years I zealously strove to have it corrected. *But when it pleased Him who separated me from my mother's womb, and called me by His grace,* to place insignificant me, although my merits were against it, at the head of the so important administration of this sacred church; then, impelled to a correction of the aforesaid inconvenience only by the ineffable mercy of Almighty God and by the aid of the Holy Martyrs our Patron Saints, we resolved to hasten, with all our soul and all the affection of our mind, to the enlargement of the aforesaid place—we who would never have presumed to set our hand to it, nor even to think of it, had not so great, so necessary, so useful and honorable an occasion demanded it.

Since in the front part, toward the north, at the main entrance with the main doors, the narrow hall was squeezed in on either side by twin towers neither high nor very sturdy but threatening ruin, we began, with the help of God, strenuously to work on this part, having laid very strong material foundations for a straight nave and twin towers, and most strong spiritual ones of which it is said: *For other foundation can no man lay than that is laid, which is Jesus Christ.* Leaning upon God's inestimable counsel and irrefragable aid, we proceeded with this

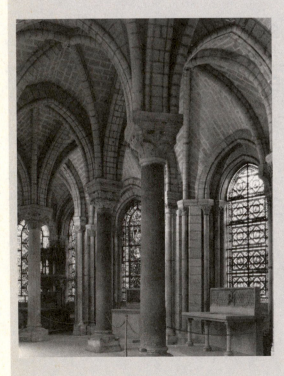

The Ambulatory of Saint Denis, Paris. 1140–1144.
(Caisse Nationale des Monuments Historique et des Sites.)

so great and so sumptuous work such an extent that, while at first, expending little, we lacked much, afterwards, expending much, we lacked nothing at all and even confessed in our abundance: *Our sufficiency is of God.* Through a gift of God a new quarry, yielding very strong stone, was discovered such as in quality and quantity had never been found in these regions. There arrived a skillful crowd of masons, stonecutters, sculptors and other workmen, so that—thus and otherwise—Divinity relieved us of our fears and favored us with Its goodwill by comforting us and by providing us with unexpected {resources}. I used to compare the least to the greatest: Solomon's riches could not have sufficed for his Temple any more than did ours for this work had not the same Author of the same work abundantly supplied His attendants. The identity of the author and the work provides a sufficiency for the worker.

The ambulatory[3] at St. Denis shown on page 282 was a harbinger of Gothic style, featuring pointed arches, *ribbed vaults, and large stained-glass windows. Abbot Suger believed that the colored light resulting from these magnificent expanses of glass encapsulated the presence of God, and that, when observing them, worshippers would be drawn to intense religious experience.*

Questions for Discussion:

1. Compare the photograph of the ambulatory at Saint Denis with the image of the nave at Vezelay (Document 8.2). What are the differences? Are there any similarities?
2. Based upon your analysis in Question 1, what are the hallmarks of Gothic style?
3. What "miraculous" circumstances enabled Abbot Suger to complete his project?

---

[3]The ambulatory was a walkway around the apse of a cathedral. This passageway allowed access to the apsidal chapels during services. See the groundplan of Chartres Cathedral in Document 13.10 for another example.

Secular Literature

INTERPRETING THE EVIDENCE

10.4   Images of *Lancelot*, by Chrétien De Troyes

During the twelfth century a new genre of historical romance emerged that, like the Song of Roland, *combined historical incident with tales of heroism and love. Many of these stories were based upon the actions of the legendary King Arthur and his knights. Among the most popular were the writings of Chrétien de Troyes (1135–1183), who was active in the court of Marie, Countess of Champagne, the daughter of Eleanor of Aquitaine. Indeed, Chré-* *tien's romance known as* The Knight of the Cart, *or* Lancelot, *was written at the request of the countess. The plot tells of the love of the hero for Queen Guinevere, the wife of his liege lord, King Arthur. In order to win the affection of the queen, Lancelot was forced to undergo various trials.*

Despite Lancelot's fame as a lover of the queen, he is rarely pictured on medieval objects, except for manuscript illuminations. This fourteenth-century ivory casket made in

(continued)

Ivory Box with an image of Lancelot Crossing the Swordbridge. (© The Trustees of the British Museum.)

(Lancelot Crossing the Swordbridge and Guinevere in the Tower. (From *Le Roman de Lancelot du Lac*. Northeastern France, early 14th cent. M. 805, fol. 166. The Pierpont Morgan Library, New York, NY, U.S.A.)

Paris is one of the rare depictions. It shows the hero attempting to cross a sword bridge that spans a raging stream below, while being threatened by spears from above. Lancelot is attempting to reach the castle where the Queen is imprisoned.

The accompanying manuscript illumination, "Lancelot Crossing the Swordbridge and Guinevere in the Tower," which decorates a fourteenth-century version of The Romance of Lancelot, *provides another interpretation of Lancelot's adventure on the sword bridge.*

(From *Medieval Decorative Art*, by John Cherry [London: British Museum Press, 1991], p. 60. The box is in the collection of the British Museum, 1856.6-23.166.)

Questions for Discussion:

1. Study the two interpretations of Lancelot's adventure on the sword bridge. What artistic variations may be seen in the two designs? How might these be explained?
2. As you read the following excerpt, keep these images in mind.

Lancelot

(From *Arthurian Romances by Chrétien de Troyes*, trans. by
W. Wistar Comfort [London: J.M. Dent, n.d.], pp. 326–329.)

When each was seated on his horse, they all asked
for leave to depart from their host who had served
them so honorably. Then they ride along the road
until the day draws to a close, and late in the afternoon they reach the sword-bridge.

   At the end of this very difficult bridge they dismount from their steeds and gaze at the wicked-look-
ing stream, which is as swift and raging, as black and
turgid, as fierce and terrible as if it were the devil's
stream; and it is so dangerous and bottomless that
anything falling into it would be as completely lost as
if it fell into the salt sea. And the bridge, which spans
it, is different from any other bridge; for there never
was such a one as this. If anyone asks of me the truth,
there never was such a bad bridge, nor one whose
flooring was so bad. The bridge across the cold stream
consisted of a polished, gleaming sword; but the
sword was stout and stiff, and was as long as two
lances. At each end there was a tree trunk in which the
sword was firmly fixed. No one need fear to fall because of its breaking or bending, for its excellence was
such that it could support a great weight. But the two
knights who were with the third were much discour-
aged; for they surmised that two lions or two leopards
would be found tied to a great rock at the other end
of the bridge. The water and the bridge and the lions
combine so to terrify them that they both tremble
with fear, and say: "Fair sire, consider well what con-
fronts you; for it is necessary and needful to do so. This
bridge is badly made and built, and the construction
of it is bad. If you do not change your mind in time,
it will be too late to repent. You must consider which
of several alternatives you will choose. Suppose that
you once get across (but that cannot possibly come to
pass, any more than one could hold in the winds and
forbid them to blow, or keep the birds from singing,
or re-enter one's mother's womb and be born again—
all of which is as impossible as to empty the sea of its
water); but even supposing that you got across, can
you think and suppose that those two fierce lions that
are chained on the other side will not kill you, and

suck the blood from your veins, and eat your flesh and
then gnaw your bones? For my part, I am bold
enough, when I even dare to look and gaze at them. If
you do not take care, they will certainly devour you.
Your body will soon be torn and rent apart, for they
will show you no mercy. So take pity on us now, and
stay here in our company! It would be wrong for you
to expose yourself intentionally to such mortal peril."
And he, laughing, replies to them: "Gentlemen, receive my thanks and gratitude for the concern you feel
for me: it comes from your love and kind hearts. I
know full well that you would not like to see any
mishap come to me; but I have faith and confidence
in God, that He will protect me to the end. I fear the
bridge and stream no more than I fear this dry land;
so I intend to prepare and make the dangerous attempt to cross. I would rather die than turn back
now." The others have nothing more to say; but each
weeps with pity and heaves a sigh. Meanwhile he pre-
pares, as best he may, to cross the stream, and he does
a very marvelous thing in removing the armor from
his feet and hands. He will be in a sorry state when he
reaches the other side. He is going to support himself
with his bare hands and feet upon the sword, which
was sharper than a scythe, for he had not kept on his
feet either sole or upper or hose. But he felt no fear of
wounds upon his hands or feet; he preferred to maim
himself rather than to fall from the bridge and be
plunged in the water from which he could never escape. In accordance with this determination, he passes
over with great pain and agony, being wounded in the
hands, knees, and feet. But even this suffering is sweet
to him: for Love, who conducts and leads him on, as-
suages and relieves the pain. Creeping on his hands,
feet, and knees, he proceeds until he reaches the other
side. Then he recalls and recollects the two lions
which he thought he had seen from the other side;
but, on looking about, he does not see so much as a
lizard or anything else to do him harm. He raises his
hand before his face and looks at his ring, and by this
test he proves that neither of the lions is there which
he thought he had seen, and that he had been
enchanted and deceived; for there was not a living
creature there. When those who had remained behind
upon the bank saw that he had safely crossed, their joy

(continued)

was natural; but they do not know of his injuries. He, however, considers himself fortunate not to have suffered anything worse. The blood from his wounds drips on his shirt on all sides. Then he sees before him a tower, which was so strong that never had he seen such a strong one before: indeed, it could not have been a better tower. At the window there sat King Bademagu, who was very scrupulous and precise about matters of honor and what was right, and who was careful to observe and practice loyalty above all else; and beside him stood his son, who always did precisely the opposite so far as possible, for he found his pleasure in disloyalty, and never wearied of villainy, treason, and felony. From their point of vantage they had seen the knight cross the bridge with trouble and pain. Meleagant's[4] color changed with the rage and displeasure he felt; for he knows now that he will be challenged for the Queen; but his character was such that he feared no man, however strong or formidable. If he were not base and

disloyal, there could no better knight be found; but he had a heart of wood, without gentleness and pity. What enraged his son and roused his ire, made the king happy and glad. The king knew of a truth that he who had crossed the bridge was much better than anyone else. For no one would dare to pass over it in whom there dwelt any of that evil nature which brings more shame upon those who possess it than prowess brings of honor to the virtuous. For prowess cannot accomplish so much as wickedness and sloth can do: it is true beyond a doubt that it is possible to do more evil than good.

Questions for Discussion:

1. Which of the images more clearly portrays the text of the trial of the swordbridge—the ivory box or the manuscript illumination? Describe the distinctive features of each.
2. What characteristics of vassalage are evident in this account of Lancelot's ordeal?

---

[4]Meleagant is the wicked knight who has abducted Queen Guinevere.

10.5   Marie de France: *The Lay of the Nightingale*

Another popular author of romantic tales was Marie de France. Although her identity remains unclear, it is believed that she was a French noblewoman, who may have lived in England at the court of Henry II. She wrote short narrative poems known as lais, *in addition to animal fables and stories based on the legends of King Arthur. Her works form one of the first extensive collections of vernacular writings by a woman, dating from between 1160 and 1215. The following tale again demonstrates the nature of courtly love, in which the hero is enamoured with an unattainable woman. In this story the object of his adoration is married to his close friend and fellow knight.*

(From *The Lays of Marie de France*, trans. By Eugene Mason [London: J.M. Dent & Sons, 1911], pp. 57–60.)

In the realm of Brittany stands a certain rich and mighty city, called Saint Malo. There were citizens of this township two knights, so well spoken and reputed of all, that the city drew from them great profit and fame. The houses of these lords were very near to one another. One of the two knights had for a wife a fair lady, very gracious of manner and sweet of tongue. This lady found great pleasure in dressing richly, according to the style and fashion of her time. The other knight was still a bachelor. He was well regarded by his fellows as a hardy knight and an honorable man. He gave hospitality gladly. Largely he gained, largely he spent, and willingly bestowed gifts of all that he had.

This bachelor set his love upon his neighbor's wife. By reason of his urgent prayers, his long suit and service, and by reason that all men spoke nothing of him but praise—perchance, also, for reason that he was never far from her eye—presently this lady came to set her heart on him as well. Though these two friends loved very tenderly, yet they were so private and careful in their loves that none perceived what was in their hearts. No man spied on them, or disturbed their goings and comings. These were the more easy to devise since the bachelor and the lady were such near neighbors. Their two houses stood side by side, hall and cellar and combles [attic]. Only between the gardens was built a high and ancient wall, of worn gray stone. When the lady sat within her bower, by leaning from the casement she and her friend might speak together, he to her, and she to him. They could also throw messages in writing, and diverse pretty gifts, the one to the other. They had little to displease them, and were very much at their ease, except that they might not take their pleasure together so often as their hearts had wished. For the dame was guarded very carefully when her husband was away. Yet not so strictly but that they might have word and speech, now by night and now by day. At least, however close the watch and ward, none might prevent that at times these fair lovers stood within their casements, and looked fondly on the other's face.

Now after these friends had loved for a long while the season became warm and sweet. It was the time when meadow and copse are green; when orchards grow white with bloom, and birds break into song as thickly as the bush to flower. It is the season when he who loves would win to his desire. Truly I tell you that the knight would have done all in his power to attain his wish, and the lady, for her part, yearned for sight and speech of her friend. At night, when the moon shone clearly in the sky, and her lord lay sleeping at her side, often the dame slipped softly from her bed and hastening to the casement, leaned forth to have sight of him who watched. The greater part of the dark they kept vigil together, for very pleasant it is to look upon your friend, when sweeter things are denied. This happened so often, and the lady rose so frequently from her bed, that her lord was altogether wrathful, and many a time inquired the reason of her unrest.

"Husband," replied the dame, "there is no dearer joy in this world, than to hear the nightingale sing. It is to listen to the song that rises so sweetly on the night, that I lean forth from the casement. What tune of harp or viol is half so lovely! Because of my delight in his song, and of my desire to hear, I may not shut my eyes until it is dawn."

When the husband heard the lady's words he laughed in himself for wrath and malice. He decided that very soon the nightingale should sing within a net. So he bade the servants of his house to devise fillets and snares, and to set their cunning traps about the orchard. All the chestnut and hazel trees within the garth [yard] were limed and netted for the caging of this bird. It was not long before the nightingale was taken, and the servants hurried to give him to the pleasure of their lord. Wondrous merry was the knight when he held him living in his hand. He went straightway to the chamber of his dame, and entering, said,

"Wife, are you within? Come near, for I must speak with you. Here is the nightingale, all limed and taken, who made vigil of your sleeping hours. Take now your rest in peace, for he will never disturb you more."

When the lady understood these words she was dreadfully sorrowful and unhappy. She prayed to her lord to grant her the nightingale for a gift. But for an answer he wrung his neck with both hands so fiercely that the head was torn from the body. Then, quite foully, he flung the bird upon the knees of the dame, in such fashion that her breast was sprinkled with the blood. So he departed from the chamber in a rage.

The lady took the little body in her hands, and wept over his evil fate. She railed on those who with nets and snares had betrayed the nightingale to his death; for anger and hate beyond measure had gained hold on her heart.

"Alas," cried she, "evil has come upon me. Never again may I rise from my bed in the night, and watch from the casement, so that I may see my friend. One thing I know full well, that he will think I no longer love him. Woe to her who has none to advise her. This I will do. I will bestow the nightingale upon him, and tell him what had happened."

So this doleful lady took a beautiful piece of white samite,[5] embroidered with gold, and wrought

---

[5]Samite was a heavy silk fabric.

thereon the whole story of this adventure. In this silken cloth she wrapped the body of the little bird, and calling to her a trusty servant of her house, charged him with the message and told him to take it to her friend. The varlet went his way to the knight, and having saluted him on the part of the lady, he told him the story, and bestowed the nightingale upon him. When all had been rehearsed and shown to him, and he had well considered the matter, the knight was very sorrowful; yet in no way would he avenge himself wrongfully. So he had a small container made, not of iron or steel, but of fine gold and rich and precious stones, strongly clasped and bound. In this little chest he set the body of the nightingale, and having sealed the shrine, carried it with him wherever he went.

This adventure could not long be hidden. Very swiftly it was noised about the country, and the Breton folk made a Lay thereon, which they called the Lay of the Laustic [Nightingale], in their own tongue.

Questions for Discussion:

1. What qualities did the bachelor possess that embody the virtues of a courtly gentleman?
2. There are religious overtones in the story, as there were in the tale of Lancelot and Queen Guinevere. Identify them. Why do you think that twelfth-century secular literature reflected these values?

10.6   *The Art of Courtly Love* by Andreas Capellanus

Very little is known about the twelfth-century author Andreas Capellanus (Andreas the Chaplain). Like Chrétien de Troyes, he was active at the court of Marie, Countess of Champagne, and it is clear that he also wrote his treatise on love at the request of the countess. Andreas's work, written between 1184–1186, was probably based upon the amorous ideas of the Roman poet Ovid. It provides a vivid picture of life in a medieval court, and offers a source for understanding the manners of that society and their tradition now known as "courtly love."

(From *The Art of Courtly Love, by Andreas Capellanus,* trans. by John Jay Parry. Copyright © 1941 Columbia University Press. Reprinted with permission of the publisher.)

Chapter VI: In What Manner Love May Be Acquired, and in How Many Ways

It remains next to be seen in what ways love may be acquired. The teaching of some people is said to be that there are five means by which it may be acquired: a beautiful figure, excellence of character, extreme readiness of speech, great wealth, and the readiness with which one grants that which is sought. But we hold that love may be acquired only by the first three, and we think that the last two ought to be banished completely from Love's court, as I shall show you when I come to the proper place in my system.

A beautiful figure wins love with very little effort, especially when the lover who is sought is simple, for a simple lover thinks that there is nothing to look for in one's beloved besides a beautiful figure and face and a body well cared for. I do not particularly blame the love of such people, but neither do I have much approval for it, because love between uncautious and unskilled lovers cannot long be concealed, and so from the first it fails to increase. For when love is revealed, it does not help the lover's worth, but brands his reputation with evil rumors and often causes him grief. Love between such lovers seldom lasts; but if sometimes it should endure it cannot indulge in its former solaces, because when the girl's chaperone hears the rumors, she becomes suspicious and watches her more carefully and gives her no opportunities to talk, and it makes the man's relatives more careful and watchful, and so serious unfriendliness arises. In such cases, when love cannot have its solaces, it increases beyond all measure and drives the lovers to lamenting their terrible torments, because "we strive for what is forbidden and always want what is denied us."

A wise woman will therefore seek as a lover a man of praiseworthy character—not one who anoints himself all over like a woman or makes a rite of the care of the body, for it does not go with a masculine figure to adorn oneself in womanly fashion or to be devoted to the care of the body. It was people like this the admirable Ovid meant when he said,

Let young men who are decked out like women stay
far away from me,
A manly form wants to be cared for within moderate
limits.

Likewise, if you see a woman too heavily rouged you will not be taken in by her beauty unless you have already discovered that she is good company besides, since a woman who puts all her reliance on her rouge usually doesn't have any particular gifts of character. As I said about men, so with women—I believe you should not seek for beauty so much as for excellence of character. Be careful therefore, Walter, not to be taken in by the empty beauty of women, because a woman is apt to be so clever and such a ready talker that after you have begun to enjoy the gifts you get from her you will not find it easy to escape loving her. A person of good character draws the love of another person of the same kind, for a well-instructed lover, man or woman, does not reject an ugly lover if the character within is good. A man who proves to be honorable and prudent cannot easily go astray in love's path or cause distress to his beloved. If a wise woman selects as her lover a wise man, she can very easily keep her love hidden forever; she can teach a wise lover to be even wiser, and if he isn't so wise she can restrain him and make him careful. A woman, like a man, should not seek for beauty or care of the person or high birth, for "beauty never pleases if it lacks goodness," and it is excellence of character alone which blesses a man with true nobility and makes him flourish in ruddy beauty. For since all of us human beings are derived originally from the same stock and all naturally claim the same ancestor, it was not beauty or care of the body or even abundance of possessions, but excellence of character alone which first made a distinction of nobility among men and led to the difference of class. Many there are, however, who trace their descent from these same first nobles, but have degenerated and gone in the other direction. The converse of this proposition is likewise true.

Character alone, then, is worthy of the crown of love. Many times fluency of speech will incline to love the hearts of those who do not love, for an elaborate line of talk on the part of the lover usually sets love's arrows a-flying and creates a presumption in favor of the excellent character of the speaker. How this may be I shall try to show you as briefly as I can. . . .

Questions for Discussion:

1. Andreas Capellanus offers an analysis of the means necessary to attract love. Are these similar to the qualities attributed to the bachelor in the "Lay of the Nightingale"? (See the previous selection.) Discuss.
2. According to Capellanus, what quality is worthy of "the crown of love"? What reason does the author give for this belief?
3. Would the advice offered in this selection be applicable today? Why or why not?

10.7 Songs by Troubadours, Trouvères, and Trobairitz

The tradition of courtly love exemplified in the works of Chrétien de Troyes and Marie de France became popular throughout the courts of Europe during the twelfth century. In addition to the lais and longer tales, brief love lyrics were written to be sung at the courts. The practice was developed by aristocratic men and women in France, who were influenced by Arabic poetry (see Document 3.15), which the knights may have heard while on crusade. These men were known as troubadours *in the south and* trouvères *in the north, and the women were often called* trobairitz.

The German counterparts of these poets/musicians were known as minnesinger.

Many of the troubadours were patronized by Eleanor of Aquitaine (1122–1204) and her daughter, Marie, who often arranged contests between the knights. Eleanor's son, Richard the Lion Heart (1157–1199), was one notable practitioner of the art. Once again, many of the songs deal with love for an unapproachable woman.

(From *Readings in European History*, vol. 1, by James Harvey Robinson [Boston: Ginn and Co., 1904], pp. 435–438.)

Lyrics by Troubadours and Trouvères:

By Arnault de Maruelh (1170–1200)

Fair to me is April, bearing
Winds that o'er me softly blow,—
Nightingales their music airing
While the stars serenely glow;
All the birds as they have power,
While the dews of morning wait,
Sing of joy in sky or bower,
Each consorting with his mate.

And as all the world is wearing
New delight while new leaves grow,
'Twould be vain to try forswearing
Love which makes my joys o'erflow;
Both by habit and by dower
Gladness is my rightful state,
And when clouds no longer lower
Quick my heart throws off its weight.

Helen were not worth comparing,
Gardens no such beauty show;
Teeth of pearl,—the truth declaring,
Blooming cheeks, a neck of snow,
Tresses like a golden shower,
Courtly charms, for baseness, hate,—
God who made her thus o'ertower
All the rest, her way make straight!

Kindness may she do me, sparing
Courtship long and favor slow,
Give a kiss to cheer my daring—
More, if more I earn, bestow;
Then the path where pleasures flower
We shall tread nor slow nor late,—
Ah, such hopes my heart o'erpower
When her charms I contemplate.

By Peire Vidal (1175–1205)

Oh, 'tis good and fair
When the trees all wear
Fresh green leaves,—the air
Sweet with flowers new,
Song birds, here and there,

Chanting full in view,
While gay lovers sue,
Amorous and true;
Loved and lover I would be,
Yet such answers to my plea
It hath been my lot to find
That I've nearly lost my mind.

Strength and heart and mind,
Lovingly inclined,
I have all resigned
To my lady fair;
Glad new life I find
Like the boughs that wear
Fruit again,—birds air
All their music there;
Springing leaves and blossoms new
In my heart I ever view,
And this joy will ever be
Mine, for she hath heard my plea.

By Bernard de Ventadorn (c. 1130–c.1200)

Whene 'er the lark's glad wings I see
Beat sunward 'gainst the radiant sky
Till, lost in joy so sweet and free,
She drops, forgetful how to fly,—
Ah, when I view such happiness
My bosom feels so deep an ache,
Me seems for pain and sore distress
My longing heart will straightway break.

Alas, I thought I held the key
To love! How ignorant am I!
For her that ne'er will pity me
I am not able to defy;
My loving heart, my faithfulness,
Myself, my world, she deigns to take,
Then leaves me bare and comfortless
To longing thoughts that ever wake.

By the minnesinger, Walther von der Vogelweide (1170–1230)

When from the sod the flow'rets spring,
And smile to meet the sun's bright ray,
When birds their sweetest carols sing
In all the morning pride of May,

What lovelier than the prospect there?
Can earth boast anything more fair?
To me it seems an almost heaven,
So beauteous to my eyes that vision bright is given.

But when a lady, chaste and fair,
Noble and clad in rich attire,
Walks through the throng with gracious air,
As sun that bids the stars retire,—
Then, where are all thy boastings, May?
What hast thou beautiful and gay
Compared with that supreme delight?
We leave thy loveliest flowers, and watch
    that lady bright.

Wouldst thou believe me,—come and place
Before thee all this pride of May;
Then look but on my lady's face,
And, which is best and brightest? say:
For me, how soon (if choice were mine)
This would I take, and that resign!
And say, "Though sweet thy beauties, May,
I'd rather forfeit all than lose my lady gay."

*The imagery employed by trobairitz (women troubadours)
often resembled the poetic expression of their male counterparts. The following lyric by Azalais de Porcairagues, a
"noble and educated lady" from the region of Montpellier,
begins by equating her own lovelorn state to winter. In
Stanza 2 she mentions the city of Orange, and the strife
there may refer to a love relationship. Stanzas 3–5 are the
core of the love lyric, and Stanza 6 is a lament upon departure. The lady she addresses in Stanza 7 is the countess Ermengarda of Narbonne (1143–1192). Andreas
Capellanus, in the* Art of Courtly Love, *attributes three
judgments of love to her (see Document 10.6).*

By Azalais de Porcairagues
(late twelfth century)

Here we've come to the frigid weather
with ice and snow and mud,
and the little birds are mute

for not a single one yearns to sing.
Dry are the branches of the hedgerows,
bereft of flower and leaf.
No nightingale cries there—
whose song once wakened me in the
    May time of the year.

So unruly is my heart
that I'm estranged from everyone,
and I know that my losses
are greater than my gains.
And if my true words falter
the strife from Orange torments me.
That is why I stand distraught—
I've lost my share of serenity.

A lady loves unwisely
if she tries to plead with a powerful man
who ranks higher than a vassal.
If she does so, she's a fool.
They say in Velay
that money doesn't help things along,
and the lady who is chosen by a man
    of wealth
will in time be gossiped about.

I have a friend of great mettle—
he is superior to any man.
He doesn't treat me with a treacherous heart
for he grants me his love.
And I say to you that I love him in return.
And anyone who says I don't—
may God send him misfortune!
I feel safeguarded from that!

Dear friend, most willingly
I'm bound to you
with courtesy and mannerliness
so long as you demand no scandal of me.
Soon we'll come to the test of battle,
and I'll place myself at your mercy.
You've solemnly vowed
you wouldn't ask me to go astray.

To God's care I entrust Beauregard Castle
and the city of Orange besides—
and Glorieta Palace and the old fortress,

and the lord of Provence,
and all those who wish me well,
and the triumphal arch that bears
    the marks of battle.
I have lost the one for whom all my life
I must forever mourn.

Messenger joyful of heart—
over there in Narbonne, carry
my song, with its ending,
to the Lady who is guided by joy and youth.

*As may be seen in the following lyric, women often recipro-
cated the love of the amorous knight, sometimes in words even
more explicit than those of the men. One of the most famous of
the female poets was the Comtessa de Dia (c. 1150–1200),
who was married to Guillaume de Poitiers. She was not restrained in her adulterous love for Rambard d'Orange.*

(From *Songs of the Women Troubadors* by Matilda Tomaryn
Bruckner, Laurie Shepard, and Sarah White. Copyright © 1995 by
TAYLOR & FRANCIS GROUP LLC - BOOKS. Reproduced with
permission of TAYLOR & FRANCIS GROUP LLC - BOOKS in
the format Textbook via Copyright Clearance Center.)

By La Comtessa de Dia

I. I have been sorely troubled
about a knight I had;
I want it known for all time
how exceedingly I loved him.
Now I see myself betrayed
because I didn't grant my love
to him; I've suffered much distress
from it, in bed and fully clothed.

II. I'd like to hold my knight
in my arms one evening, naked,

for he'd be overjoyed
were I only serving as his pillow,
and he makes me more radiant
than Floris his Blanchaflor.
To him I grant my heart, my love,
my mind, my eyes, my life.

III. Fair, agreeable, good friend,
when will I have you in my power,
lie beside you for an evening,
and kiss you amorously?
Be sure I'd feel a strong desire
to have you in my husband's place
provided you had promised me
to do everything I wished.

Questions for Discussion:

1. Troubadours, trouvères, and trobairitz all used
   images from nature in their lyrics. Describe
   these, and discuss their metaphorical meaning.
   Notice particularly the reference to the
   nightingale, which is a frequent image in *lais*
   (see Document 10.5).
2. Does the poetry of the troubadours seem
   more chaste than that of the Countess de
   Dia? Discuss the differences.
3. Feminist scholarship of the twentieth century
   has pointed out the "objectification" of the
   woman in the courtly love tradition.
   Comment on this view, pointing to specific
   aspects of the poetry that support this
   contention.

A Medieval Romance: Abelard and Heloise

*Peter Abelard (1079–1142) was one of the most impor-
tant philosophers of the twelfth century; his career and
intellectual contributions will be discussed in the next section of the book. He was also famous, or rather, infamous,
as a result of his relationship with Heloise, the niece of
Fulbert, a canon at the cathedral of Notre Dame in
Paris. When he was asked by Fulbert to become the tutor
of Heloise, a woman twenty-two years his junior, unfore-*
seen consequences resulted. In his autobiography, Historia Calamitatum *("The Story of My Sufferings"),
Abelard tells of his love for Heloise and the unfortunate
ending to the romance.*

(From *Historia Calamitatum: An Autobiography* by Peter Abelard,
translated by Henry Adams [Bellows, St. Paul: Thomas A. Boyd,
1922], pp. 16–22, 25–26, 28–30.)

10.8   *Historia Calamitatum* by Peter Abelard

Of How, Brought Low by his Love for Heloise, he was Wounded in Body and Soul

Now there dwelt in that same city of Paris a certain young girl named Heloise, the niece of a canon who was called Fulbert. Her uncle's love for her was equaled only by his desire that she should have the best education which he could possibly procure for her. Of no mean beauty, she stood out above all by reason of her abundant knowledge of letters. Now this virtue is rare among women, and for that very reason it doubly graced the maiden, and made her the most worthy of renown in the entire kingdom. It was this young girl whom I, after carefully considering all those qualities which usually attract lovers, determined to unite with myself in the bonds of love, and indeed the thing seemed to me very easy to be done. So distinguished was my name, and I possessed such advantages of youth and comeliness, that no matter what woman I might favor with my love, I dreaded rejection of none. Then, too, I believed that I could win the maiden's consent all the more easily by reason of her knowledge of letters and her zeal for them; so, even if we were parted, we might yet be together in thought with the aid of written messages. Perhaps, too, we might be able to write more boldly than we could speak, and thus at all times could we live in joyous intimacy.

Thus, utterly aflame with my passion for this maiden, I sought to discover means whereby I might have daily and familiar speech with her, in order to more easily win her consent. For this purpose I persuaded the girl's uncle, with the aid of some of his friends, to take me into his household—for he lived close to my school—in return for the payment of a small sum. My pretext for this was that the care of my own household was a serious handicap to my studies, and likewise burdened me with an expense far greater than I could afford. Now, he was a man keen in avarice, and likewise he was most desirous for his niece that her study of letters should always go forward, so, for these two reasons, I easily won his consent to the fulfillment of my wish, for he was fairly agape for my money, and at the same time believed that his niece would vastly benefit by my teaching. More even than this, by his own earnest entreaties he fell in with my desires beyond anything I had dared to hope, opening the way for my love; for he entrusted her wholly to my guidance, begging me to give her instruction whenever I might be free from the duties of my school, no matter whether by day or by night, and to punish her sternly if ever I should find her negligent of her tasks. In all this the man's simplicity was nothing short of astounding to me; I should not have been more smitten with wonder if he had entrusted a tender lamb to the care of a ravenous wolf. When he had thus given her into my charge, not alone to be taught but even to be disciplined, what had he done save to give free scope to my desires, and to offer me every opportunity, even if I had not sought it, to bend her to my will with threats and blows if I failed to do so with caresses? There were, however, two things which particularly served to allay any foul suspicion: his own love for his niece, and my former reputation for continence.

Why should I say more? We were united first in the dwelling that sheltered our love, and then in the hearts that burned with it. Under the pretext of study we spent our hours in the happiness of love, and learning held out to us the secret opportunities that our passion craved. Our speech was more of love than of the books which lay open before us; our kisses far outnumbered our reasoned words. Our hands sought less the book than each other's bosoms; love drew our eyes together far more than the lesson drew them to the pages of our text. In order that there might be no suspicion, there were, indeed, sometimes blows, but love gave them, not anger; they were the marks, not of wrath, but of a tenderness surpassing the most fragrant balm in sweetness. What followed? No degree in love's progress was left untried by our passion, and if love itself could imagine any wonder as yet unknown, we discovered it. And our inexperience of such delights made us all the more ardent in our pursuit of them, so that our thirst for one another was still unquenched.

In measure as this passionate rapture absorbed me more and more, I devoted ever less time to philosophy and to the work of the school. Indeed it became loathsome to me to go to the school or to linger there; the labor, moreover, was very burdensome, since my nights were vigils of love and my days of study. My lecturing became utterly careless and lukewarm; I did nothing because of inspiration, but everything merely as a matter of habit. I had become nothing more than a reciter of my former discoveries, and though I still wrote poems, they dealt with love, not with the secrets of philosophy. Of these songs you yourself well know how some have become widely known and have been sung in many lands, chiefly, I think, by those who delighted in the things of this world. As for the sorrow, the groans, the lamentations of my students when they perceived the preoccupation, nay, rather the chaos, of my mind, it is hard even to imagine them.

A thing so manifest could deceive only a few, no one, I think, save him whose shame it chiefly bespoke, the girl's uncle, Fulbert. The truth was often enough hinted to him, and by many persons, but he could not believe it, partly, as I have said, by reason of his boundless love for his niece, and partly because of the well-known continence of my previous life. Indeed we do not easily suspect shame in those whom we most cherish, nor can there be the blot of foul suspicion on devoted love. Of this St. Jerome in his epistle to Sabinianus (Epist. 48) says: "We are wont to be the last to know the evils of our own households, and to be ignorant of the sins of our children and our wives, though our neighbors sing them aloud." But no matter how slow a matter may be in disclosing itself, it is sure to come forth at last, nor is it easy to hide from one what is known to all. So, after the lapse of several months, did it happen with us. Oh, how great was the uncle's grief when he learned the truth, and how bitter was the sorrow of the lovers when we were forced to part! With what shame was I overwhelmed, with what contrition smitten because of the blow which had fallen on her I loved, and what a tempest of misery burst over her by reason of my disgrace! Each grieved most, not for himself, but for the other. Each sought to allay, not his own sufferings, but those of the one he loved. The very sundering of our bodies served but to link our souls closer together; the plentitude of the love which was denied to us inflamed us more than ever. Once the first wildness of shame had passed, it left us more shameless than before, and as shame died

within us the cause of it seemed to us ever more desirable. And so it chanced with us as, in the stories that the poets tell, it once happened with Mars and Venus when they were caught together.

It was not long after this that Heloise found that she was pregnant, and of this she wrote to me in the utmost exultation, at the same time asking me to consider what had best be done. Accordingly, on a night when her uncle was absent, we carried out the plan we had determined on, and I stole her secretly away from her uncle's house, sending her without delay to my own country. She remained there with my sister until she gave birth to a son, whom she named Astrolabe. Meanwhile her uncle, after his return, was almost mad with grief; only one who had then seen him could rightly guess the burning agony of his sorrow and the bitterness of his shame. What steps to take against me, or what snares to set for me, he did not know. If he should kill me or do me some bodily hurt, he feared greatly lest his dear-loved niece should be made to suffer for it among my kinsfolk. He had no power to seize me and imprison me somewhere against my will, though I make no doubt he would have done so quickly enough had he been able or dared, for I had taken measures to guard against any such attempt.

At length, however, in pity for his boundless grief, and bitterly blaming myself for the suffering which my love had brought upon him through the baseness of the deception I had practiced, I went to him to entreat his forgiveness, promising to make any amends that he himself might decree. I pointed out that what had happened could not seem incredible to anyone who had ever felt the power of love, or who remembered how, from the very beginning of the human race, women had cast down even the noblest men to utter ruin. And in order to make amends even beyond his most extreme hope, I offered to marry her whom I had seduced, provided only the thing could be kept secret, so that I might suffer no loss of reputation thereby. To this he gladly assented, pledging his own faith and that of his kindred, and sealing with kisses the pact which I had sought of him—and all this that he might the more easily betray me.

Although Fulbert agreed to the marriage, Heloise objected, arguing that marriage would hinder Abelard's career, and that his scholarship and philosophical writings would suffer.

Then, turning from the consideration of such hindrances to the study of philosophy, Heloise told me to observe what were the conditions of honorable wedlock. What possible concord could there be between scholars and domestics, between authors and cradles, between books or tablets and distaffs, between the stylus or the pen and the spindle? What man, intent on his religious or philosophical meditations, can possibly endure the whining of children, the lullabies of the nurse seeking to quiet them, or the noisy confusion of family life? Who can endure the continual untidiness of children? The rich, you may reply, can do this, because they have palaces or houses containing many rooms, and because their wealth takes no thought of expense and protects them from daily worries. But to this the answer is that the condition of philosophers is by no means that of the wealthy, nor can those whose minds are occupied with riches and worldly cares find time for religious or philosophical study. For this reason the renowned philosophers of old utterly despised the world, fleeing from its perils rather than reluctantly giving them up, and denied themselves all its delights in order that they might repose in the embraces of philosophy alone. One of them, and the greatest of all, Seneca,[6] in his advice to Lucilius, says; "Philosophy is not a thing to be studied only in hours of leisure; we must give up everything else to devote ourselves to it, for no amount of time is really sufficient thereto" (Epist. 73).

It matters little, she pointed out, whether one abandons the study of philosophy completely or merely interrupts it, for it can never remain at the point where it was thus interrupted. All other occupations must be resisted; it is vain to seek to adjust life to include them, and they must simply be eliminated. This view is maintained, for example, in the love of God by those among us who are truly called monastics, and in the love of wisdom by all those who have stood out among men as sincere philosophers. For in every race, gentiles or Jews or Christians, there have always been a few who excelled their fellows in faith or in the purity of their lives, and who were set apart from the multitude by their continence or by their abstinence from worldly pleasures.

Now, she added, if laymen and gentiles, bound by no profession of religion, lived after this fashion, what ought you, a cleric and a canon, to do in order not to prefer base voluptuousness to your sacred duties, to prevent this Charybdis[7] from sucking you down headlong, and to save yourself from being plunged shamelessly and irrevocably into such filth as this? If you care nothing for your privileges as a cleric, at least uphold your dignity as a philosopher. If you scorn the reverence due to God, let regard for your reputation temper your shamelessness. Remember that Socrates was chained to a wife, and by what a filthy accident he himself paid for this blot on philosophy, in order that others thereafter might be made more cautious by his example. Jerome thus mentions this affair, writing about Socrates in his first book against Jovinianus: "Once when he was withstanding a storm of reproaches which Xantippe was hurling at him from an upper story, he was suddenly drenched with foul slops; wiping his head, he said only, 'I knew there would be a shower after all that thunder.'"

Her final argument was that it would be dangerous for me to take her back to Paris, and that it would be far sweeter for her to be called my mistress than to be known as my wife; nay, too, that this would be more honorable for me as well. In such case, she said, love alone would hold me to her, and the strength of the marriage chain would not constrain us. Even if we should by chance be parted from time to time, the joy of our meetings would be all the sweeter by reason of its rarity. But when she found that she could not convince me or dissuade me from my folly by these and like arguments, and because she could not bear to offend me, with grievous sighs and tears she made an end of her resistance, saying: "Then there is no more left but this, that in our doom the sorrow yet to come shall be no less than the love we two have already known." Nor in this, as now the whole world knows, did she lack the spirit of prophecy.

So, after our little son was born, we left him in my sister's care, and secretly returned to Paris. A few

---

[6]Seneca (c. 4 B.C.E.–65 C.E.) was a Roman philosopher.

---

[7]Charybdis was a sea monster whose gigantic whirlpool in the Straits of Messina sucked sailors to their doom. She was mentioned by Homer in the *Odyssey* as one of the terrors to be avoided by Odysseus.

days later, in the early morning, having kept our nocturnal vigil of prayer unknown to all in a certain church, we were united there in the benediction of wedlock, her uncle and a few friends of his and mine being present. We departed forthwith stealthily and by separate ways, nor thereafter did we see each other save rarely and in private, thus striving our utmost to conceal what we had done. But her uncle and those of his household, seeking solace for their disgrace, began to divulge the story of our marriage, and thereby to violate the pledge they had given me on this point. Heloise, on the contrary, denounced her own kin and swore that they were speaking the most absolute lies. Her uncle, aroused to fury thereby, visited her repeatedly with punishments. No sooner had I learned this than I sent her to a convent of nuns at Argenteuil, not far from Paris, where she herself had been brought up and educated as a young girl. I had them make ready for her all the garments of a nun, suitable for the life of a convent, excepting only the veil, and these I bade her put on.

When her uncle and his kinsmen heard of this, they were convinced that now I had completely played them false and had rid myself forever of Heloise by forcing her to become a nun. Violently incensed, they laid a plot against me, and one night, while I, all unsuspecting, was asleep in a secret room in my lodgings, they broke in with the help of one of my servants, whom they had bribed. There they had vengeance on me with a most cruel and most shameful punishment, such as astounded the whole world, for they cut off those parts of my body with which I had done that which was the cause of their sorrow. This done, straightway they fled, but two of them were captured, and suffered the loss of their eyes and their genital organs. One of these two was the aforesaid servant, who, even while he was still in my service, had been led by his avarice to betray me.

Questions for Discussion:

1. How do you interpret the relationship between Abelard and Heloise in contemporary terms? That is, which partner has the "power" in the relationship? Do you think Abelard's motives derived from love or lust?
2. Was the punishment inflicted by Fulbert justified? (Keep in mind that castration was a common penalty for theft and other transgressions in the Middle Ages.)
3. What would happen to a teacher who behaved in this manner in the twenty-first century?
4. Comment on the reasons given by Heloise for resisting marriage.
5. Why do you think the "romance" of Abelard and Heloise remains one of the most famous relationships in history?

10.9   Letter to Abelard from Heloise

Heloise became prioress at the convent of Argenteuil, where Abelard had sent her. She remained a nun for the rest of her life, and eventually became abbess of the Paraclete, a convent founded by Abelard. Her sadness and frustration may be observed in the following letter, where she pours out her longing and pleads with Abelard to write to her.

(From *The Letters of Abelard and Heloise* by Peter Abelard & Heloise, translated by C. K. Moncrieff, translation copyright 1926, copyright renewed 1954 by Alfred A. Knopf, a division of Random House, Inc. Used by permission of Alfred A. Knopf, a division of Random House, Inc.)

For who among kings or philosophers could equal you in fame? What kingdom or city or village did not burn to see you? Who, I ask, did not hasten to gaze upon you when you appeared in public, nor on your departure with straining neck and fixed eye follow you? What wife, what maiden did not yearn for you in your absence, nor burn in your presence? What queen or powerful lady did not envy me my joys and my bed? There were two things, I confess, in you especially, with which you could at once captivate the heart of any woman; namely the arts of making songs and of singing them. Which we know that other philosophers have seldom followed. Wherewith as with a game, refreshing the labor of philosophic exercise, you have left many songs composed in amatory measure or rhythm, which for the suavity both of words and of tune being often repeated, have kept your name without ceasing on the lips of all; since the sweetness of your melodies did not allow even illiterates to forget you. It was on this account chiefly that women sighed for love of you. And as the greater part of your songs descanted of our love, they spread my fame in a short time through many lands, and inflamed the jealousy of many women against me. For what excellence of mind or body did not adorn your youth? What woman who envied me then does not my calamity now compel to pity one deprived of such delights? What man or women, albeit an enemy at first, is not now softened by the compassion due to me?

And, though exceedingly guilty, I am, as you know, exceedingly innocent. For it is not the deed but the intention that makes the crime. It is not what is done but the spirit in which it is done that equity considers. And in what state of mind I have ever been towards you, only you, who has knowledge of it, can judge. To your consideration I commit all, I yield in all things to your testimony. Tell me one thing only, if you can, why, after our conversion, which you alone did decree, I have fallen into such neglect and oblivion with you that I am neither refreshed by your speech and presence nor comforted by a letter in your absence. Tell me, one thing only, if you can, or let me tell you what I feel, nay what all suspect. Concupiscence [lust] joined you to me rather than affection, the ardor of desire rather than love. When therefore what you desired ceased, all that you had exhibited at the same time failed. This, most beloved, is not mine only but the conjecture of all, not peculiar but common, not private but public. Would that it seemed thus to me only, and your love found others to excuse it, by whom my grief might be a little quieted. Would that I could invent reasons by which in excusing you I might cover in some measure my own vileness.

Give your attention, I beseech you, to what I demand; and you will see this to be a small matter and most easy for you. While I am cheated of your presence, at least by written words, whereof you have an abundance, present to me the sweetness of your image. In vain may I expect you to be liberal in things if I must endure you niggardly in words. Until now I believed that I deserved more from you when I had done all things for you, persevering still in obedience to you. Who indeed as a girl was allured to the asperity of monastic conversation not by religious devotion but by your command alone. Wherein if I deserve nothing from you, you may judge my labor to have been vain. No reward for this may I expect from God, for the love of Whom it is well known that I did not do anything. When thou hastened to God, I followed you in the habit, or rather, preceded you. For as though mindful of the wife of Lot, who looked back from behind him, you delivered me first to the sacred garments and monastic profession before you gave yourself to God. And for that in this one thing you should have had little trust in me I vehemently grieved and was ashamed. For I (God knows) would without hesitation precede or follow you to the Vulcanian fires according to your word. For not with me was my heart, but with you. But now, more than ever, if it be not with you, it is nowhere. For without you it cannot anywhere exist. But so act that it may be well with you, I beseech you. And it will be well with you if it find you propitious, if you give love for love, little for much, words for deeds. Would that thy love, beloved, had less trust in me, that it might be more anxious! But the more confident I have made you in the past, the more neglectful now I find you. Remember, I beseech you, what I have done, and pay heed to what you owe me. While with you I enjoyed carnal pleasures, many were uncertain whether I did so from love or from desire. But now the end shows in what spirit I began. I have forbidden myself all pleasures that I might obey your will. I have reserved nothing for myself, save this, to be now entirely yours. Consider therefore how great is your injustice, if to me who deserve more you pay less, nay nothing at all, especially when it is a small thing that is demanded of you, and very easy for you to perform. And so in His Name to whom you have offered yourself, before God I beseech you that in whatsoever way you can you restore to me your presence, to wit by writing me some word of comfort. To this end alone that, thus refreshed, I may give myself with more alacrity to the service of God. When in time past you sought me out for temporal pleasures, you visited me with endless letters, and by frequent songs did set thy Heloise on the lips of all men. With me every public place, each house resounded. How more rightly should you excite me now towards God, whom you excited then to desire. Consider, I beseech thee, what you owe me, pay heed to what I demand; and my long letter with a brief ending I conclude. Farewell, my all.

Questions for Discussion:

1. In relation to Abelard's account in the previous selection, how does Heloise characterize their relationship as she looks back?
2. What arguments does she offer as she begs Abelard for a letter?
3. Heloise signs the letter, "Farewell, my all." Comment.

Religious and Philosophical Literature

10.10 *Sic et Non* by Peter Abelard

Abelard, as we have seen, was a charismatic person, and his fame as a lecturer, based upon the practice of disputatio *(disputation), spread throughout France. His philosophical writings were also based upon this style of argumentation, which was an essential component of the curriculum in the cathedral schools where he had been trained. His treatise* Sic et Non *("Yes and No"), written in 1120, was a precursor to the work of Thomas Aquinas and other philosophers of the thirteenth century (see Documents 13.4 and 13.6).*

Abelard realized that the vast trove of biblical, theological, and philosophical sources from the late antique world and the early Middle Ages contained numerous statements that were contradictory. His method, described in Sic ed Non, *organized these writings into categories, either "for" or "against" a given proposition. The Prologue explains his reasons for his innovative approach to philosophical discourse. Notice that Ablelard refers to the works of Augustine (Document 1.10).*

(From *Medieval Literary Theory,* pp. 87, 94, 99–100. Translated from "Peter Abailard: Sic et non", ed. B. Boyer & R. McKeon. University of Chicago Press.)

Prologue to *Yes and No*

In the vast amount of writings which exist, some statements, even those of the holy Fathers, appear not only to differ from each other, but even to be contradictory. Consequently, one should not make a rash judgment on those by whom the world itself is to be judged, according as it is written: 'the saints shall judge nations' [Book of Wisdom 3:8], and again: 'You shall sit judging' [Matthew 19:28]. We must not presume to accuse of lying, or despise as erroneous, those to whom our Lord said: 'He that heareth you, heareth me, and he who despiseth you despiseth me' [Luke 10:16]. So we must have regard to our own inadequacy, and believe that it is we who lack God's grace to understand, rather than they who lacked it in their writings. For the Truth Himself said to them: 'It is not you who speak, but the spirit of our Father that speaks in you' [Matthew 10:20]. So it is little wonder that if we lack that Spirit, by whose agency these writings were written and dictated, and communicated directly by it [i.e., that Spirit] to the writers, we may fail to understand their actual writings. . . .

The careful reader will attempt to resolve controversial points in the writings of the holy Fathers in all the ways I have mentioned. But if the dispute is so obvious that it cannot be resolved by having recourse to reasoning [i.e., rational argument], then authorities must be compared, and that authority retained which has more value as evidence and greater weight. Hence the words of Isidore,[8] writing to Bishop Massius: 'I thought that this ought to be added at the end of the letter, so that whenever contradictory opinions are found in the *acta* of councils, one should retain the opinion which is based on the older or better authority.' . . .

---

[8]Isidore of Seville (c. 560–636). See an example of his work in Document 2.5.

This having been said by way of preliminary, it is my purpose, according to my original intention, to gather together various sayings of the holy Fathers which have occurred to me as being surrounded by some degree of uncertainty because of their seeming incompatibility. These may encourage inexperienced readers to engage in that most important exercise, enquiry into truth, and as a result of that enquiry give an edge to their critical faculty. For consistent or frequent questioning is defined as the first key to wisdom. Aristotle, the most clear-sighted of all philosophers, urges us to grasp this wholeheartedly. For he exhorts the studious in the prologue *Ad aliquid,* in the words: 'Perhaps it is difficult to make a confident pronouncement on matters of this sort unless they have been thoroughly gone over many times. Likewise, it will not be amiss to have doubts about individual points.' For by doubting we come to enquiry, and by enquiry we perceive the truth. As the Truth Himself says: 'Seek and you shall find, knock and it shall be opened to you' [Matthew 7:7]. Christ gave us spiritual instruction by his own example when, at the age of about twelve, he sat and asked questions, and wanted to be found in the midst of the teachers, showing us the example of a pupil, by his asking questions, before he showed us that of a teacher by his preaching, even though God's wisdom is full and perfect. . . .

When writings are quoted they arouse and encourage the reader to enquire into truth all the more, in proportion to the level of regard in which a given piece of writing is held. That is why I decided to prefix to this work of mine, which I have compiled from the statements of the holy Fathers gathered into one volume, the well-known decree of Pope Gelasius on the subject of authentic books. In this way it may be clearly understood that I have not introduced anything from the apocryphal writings. I have also added excerpts from the *Retractions* of St Augustine, from which it may be clearly seen that none of the views which he later retracted has been inserted here. . . .

Questions for Discussion:

1. How does Abelard's objective differ from that of Justinian in compiling his *Codex*? (See Document 2.13.)
2. Using a method common for philosophers and theologians in the Middle Ages, Abelard cites authorities in this Prologue. Identify these.

10.11 Averroes: *On the Harmony of Religion and Philosophy*

During the twelfth century the intellectual life of southern Spain was characterized by a rich combination of Islamic and Greek philosophy, mathematics, and literature. Two of the most famous scholars of the era were educated in this environment: Ibn Rushd, known in the west as Averroes (1126–1198), and Maimonides (1135–1204), also known as Rabbi Moses ben Maimon. The works of both of these men show the significant influence of the philosophy of Aristotle, as did the works of Abelard (see the previous selection).

Averroes was most famous for his commentaries on the works of "the Philosopher," as Aristotle was known in the Middle Ages. In the preface to his commentary on Aristotle's Physics *he demonstrated his reverence for the Greek philosopher—an attitude that contributed to the general intellectual milieu of the following century, in which Aristotle was held in virtually superstitious regard (see,* for example, the works of Aquinas and Bonaventure, Documents 13.4 through 13.6). Averroes's writings on Aristotle were considered to be the most authoritative commentaries available in the twelfth century, and when they were translated from Arabic into Latin, he became known among scholars as "the Commentator."*

(From *Readings in European History*, vol. 1, ed. by James Harvey Robinson [Boston: Ginn and Co., 1904], p. 456.)

Preface to Aristotle's *Physics*

Aristotle was the wisest of the Greeks and constituted and completed logic, physics, and metaphysics. I say that he constituted these sciences, because all the works on these subjects previous to him do not deserve to be mentioned and were completely eclipsed by his writings. I say that he put the finishing touches

on these sciences, because none of those who have succeeded him up to our time, to wit, during nearly fifteen hundred years, have been able to add anything to
his writings or find in them any error of any importance. Now that all this should be found in one man
is a strange and miraculous thing, and this privileged
being deserves to be called divine rather than human.

In the following excerpt from The Future Life, *Averroes
discusses a philosophical and religious problem debated by
all religions. He provides a clear analysis of the Muslim
view of the problem, and describes his attitude toward corporeal symbolism.*

(Derived from *Averroes on the Harmony of Religion and Philosophy,*
translation by G. F. Hourani. This work is published by the
Trustees of the E. J. W. Gibb Memorial Trust, who have granted
their consent.)

From *The Future Life*

[Corporeal symbols are more effective than spiritual
ones in instructing the masses about the life beyond,
and are used in the *Qu'ran*, which is primarily concerned with the majority.]

All religions, as we have said, agree on the fact
that souls experience states of happiness or misery after death, but they disagree in the manner of symbol-
izing these states and explaining their existence to
men. And it seems that the [kind of] symbolization
which is found in this religion of ours is the most perfect means of explanation to the majority of men, and
provides the greatest stimulus to their souls to [pursue
the goals of] the life beyond; and the primary concern
of religions is with the majority. Spiritual symbolization, on the other hand, seems to provide less stimulus
to the souls of the masses towards [the goals of] the life
beyond, and the masses have less desire and fear of it
than they do of corporeal symbolization. Therefore it
seems that corporeal symbolization provides a stronger
stimulus to [the goals of] the life beyond than spiritual; the spiritual [kind] is more acceptable to the class
of debating theologians, but they are the minority.

[There are three interpretations of the symbols by
Muslims. (1) The life beyond is the same in kind as this
one, but it is permanent, not limited in duration. (2)
It differs in kind: (a) The life beyond is spiritual, and
is only symbolized by sensible images for the purpose

of exposition. (b) It is corporeal, but the bodies are
other, immortal ones not these perishable ones. This
opinion is suitable for the elite. It avoids the absurdity
of (1), arising from the fact that our bodies here provide material for other earthly bodies and so cannot at
the same time exist in the other world. But every opinion is permissible except total rejection of another life.]

For this reason we find the people of Islam divided into three sects with regard to the understanding of the symbolization which is used in [the texts
of] our religion referring to the states of the future
life. One sect holds that that existence is identical
with this existence here with respect to bliss and
pleasure, i.e. they hold that it is of the same sort and
that the two existences differ only in respect of per-
manence and limit of duration, i.e. the former is permanent and the latter of limited duration. Another
group holds that there is a difference in the kind of
existence. This [group] is divided into two subdivi-
sions. One [sub-] group holds that the existence symbolized by these sensible images is spiritual; and that
it has been symbolized thus only for the purpose of
exposition; these people are supported by many well-
known arguments from Scripture, but there would be
no point in enumerating them. Another [sub-] group
thinks that it is corporeal, but believes that that corporeality existing in the life beyond differs from the
corporeality of this life in that the latter is perishable
while the former is immortal. They too are supported
by arguments from Scripture, and it seems that Ibn
'Abbas was one of those who held this opinion, for he
is reported to have said, 'There is nothing in this
lower world like the next world except the names.'

It seems that this opinion is more suitable for the
elite; for the admissibility of this opinion is founded on
facts which are not discussed in front of everyone. One
is that the soul is immortal. The second is that the return of the soul to other bodies does not involve the
same absurdity as (its) return (to) those same [earthly]
bodies. This is because it is apparent that the materials
of the bodies that exist here are successively transferred
from one body to another: i.e. one and the same material exists in many persons at different times. Bodies
like these cannot possibly all exist actually [at the same
time], because their material is one: for instance, a man
dies, his body is transformed into dust, that dust is
transformed into a plant, another man feeds on that

plant; then semen proceeds from him, from which another man is born. But if other bodies are supposed, this state of affairs does not follow as a consequence.

The truth in this question is that every man's duty is [to believe] whatever his study of it leads him to [conclude], provided that it is not such a study as would cause him to reject the principle altogether by denying the existence [of the future life] altogether; for this manner of belief obliges us to call its holder an unbeliever, because the existence of this [future] state for man is made known to people through their Scriptures and their intellects.

[The basic assumption of all the permissible views is the immortality of the soul. It can be proved from the *Qu'ran,* which equates death with sleep; now since we know that the soul is not dissolved in sleep, the same applies to death. In both cases the organ, not the soul itself ceases.]

The whole of this [argument] is founded on the immortality of the soul. If it is asked 'Does Scripture contain an indication of the immortality of the soul or [at least] a hint of it?', we reply: This is found in the precious Book in the words of the Exalted, 'God receives the souls at the time of their death, and those which have not died He receives in their sleep', [and so on to the end of] the verse. The significant aspect of this verse is that in it He has equated sleep and death with respect to the annihilation of the soul's activity.

Thus if the cessation of the soul's activity in death were due to the soul's dissolution, not to a change in the soul's organ, the cessation of its activity in sleep [too] would have to be due to the dissolution of its essential being; but if that were the case, it would not return on waking to its normal condition. So since it does return to it, we know that this cessation does not happen to it through anything which attaches to it in its substantial nature, but is only something which attaches to it owing to a cessation of its organ; and [we know] that it does not follow that if the organ ceases the soul must cease. Death is a cessation; it must therefore be of the organ, as is the case in sleep. As the philosopher says, 'If the old man were to find an eye like the young man's eye, he would see as the young man sees.'

This is as much as we see fit to affirm in our investigation of the beliefs of this religion of ours, the religion of Islam.

Questions for Discussion:

1. Discuss the concepts of Averroes regarding the afterlife. What are the basic points he draws from Muslim teachings?
2. Compare and contrast this excerpt by Averroes with that of Peter Abelard in the previous selection. Do you see any similarities? Were their goals similar?

10.12   Maimonides: *Guide for the Perplexed*

Maimonides (1138–1204) was educated in Spain, but eventually moved to Egypt. He worked as the court physician to the local ruler, and served as chief rabbi for the Jewish community. Like Averroes, he viewed the writings of Aristotle as the apex of philosophy, and his intellectual goal was to synthesize Aristotelian thought with the Old Testament and the Jewish intellectual tradition. His treatise, Guide for the Perplexed, *achieved this assimilation. In the introduction to this work, Maimonides set forth his objectives and methodology.*

My primary object in this work is to explain certain words occurring in the prophetic books [of the Old Testament]. Of these some are homonyms,[9] and of their several meanings the ignorant choose the wrong ones; other terms which are employed in a figurative sense are erroneously taken by such persons in their primary signification. There are also hybrid terms, denoting things which are of the same class from one point of view and of a different class from another. It is not here intended to explain all

(From *The Guide for the Perplexed,* by Moses Maimonides, trans. by M. Friedländer. New York: Dover Publications, 1956, p. 2. Reprinted by permission of the publisher.)

[9]Two words are homonyms if they are spelled or pronounced the same way, but have different meanings.

these expressions to the unlettered or to mere tyros [novices], a previous knowledge of Logic and Natural Philosophy being indispensable, or to those who confine their attention to the study of our holy Law, I mean the study of the canonical law alone; for the true knowledge of the Torah is the special aim of this and similar works.

The object of this treatise is to enlighten a religious man who has been trained to believe in the truth of our holy Law, who conscientiously fulfils his moral and religious duties, and at the same time has been successful in his philosophical studies. Human reason has attracted him to abide within its sphere; and he finds it difficult to accept as correct the teaching based on the literal interpretation of the Law, and especially that which he himself or others derived from those homonymous, metaphorical, or hybrid expressions. Hence he is lost in perplexity and anxiety. If he be guided solely by reason, and renounce his previous views which are based on those expressions, he would consider that he had rejected the fundamental principles of the Law; and even if he retains the opinions which were derived from those expressions, and if, instead of following his reason, he abandon its guidance altogether, it would still appear that his religious convictions had suffered loss and injury. For he would then be left with those errors which give rise to fear and anxiety, constant grief and great perplexity.

This work has also a second object in view. It seeks to explain certain obscure figures which occur in the Prophets, and are not distinctly characterized as being figures. Ignorant and superficial readers take them in a literal, not in a figurative sense. Even well informed persons are bewildered if they understand these passages in their literal signification, but they are entirely relieved of their perplexity when we explain the figure, or merely suggest that the terms are figurative. For this reason I have called this book *Guide for the Perplexed*.

Questions for Discussion:

1. In his *Guide for the Perplexed,* Maimonides indicates that he will solve the intellectual problems encountered by "bewildered" persons. What are these?
2. Discuss the methodology advanced by Maimonides; what is the primary focus of his remarks in the Introduction?

INTERPRETING THE EVIDENCE

10.13 "Cry Out Therefore, and Write Thus!": The Visions of Hildegard of Bingen

The previous selections have presented medieval religious knowledge as a result of rational thought. Abelard and Averroes, in particular, were important philosophers of the twelfth century who made significant contributions to the development of this tradition, which would reach its apogee in the works of Thomas Aquinas (to be discussed in Chapter 13). There was, however, another path to religious enlightenment that was accepted by medieval people. This was the journey of mysticism, an emotional and non-rational experience that led to direct apprehension of the presence of God. Many earlier selections in this volume have discussed this phenomenon, such as the account of the martyrdom of Perpetua and Felicity, the belief in various miracles, and the pilgrimage journey. But the direct revelation
of God through visions, experienced primarily by women, began to be written down in the twelfth century. One of the first to document her revelations was Hildegard of Bingen (1098–1179), who received the command "Write!" from God. In the following chapters we will meet other mystics, including Mechtild of Magdeburg (1212–1282) and Margery Kempe (c. 1373–c. 1440).

Hildegard of Bingen was one of the most exceptional women of the era. Her accomplishments comprise a number of disciplines, including theology, medicine, and music. She was given as an oblate to the Church at age eight by her aristocratic parents, who offered her, their tenth child, as a "tithe," just as they donated a tenth of their income. She was placed in the care of an anchoress, Jutta of Spanheim, who educated her in the basic skills of literacy and music along with several other girls. Although Hildegard wrote that she had visions from early childhood, her mystical revelations were not recorded until she was almost forty years old. By this time she had been elected Abbess of Disibodenberg. In 1141 she was given permission by the abbot to write down her visions. The following passage from her work, Scivias, *describes her revelations from God.*

The illumination pictures Hildegard in her abbey receiving the word of God as if her head is on fire, as she described. A companion, perhaps her scribe Volmar, watches from the side. The image shows Hildegard seated within an elaborate frame, following a long tradition in which the apostles, Matthew, Mark, Luke, and John, are presented in this way. She is writing on a slate, in a manner quite similar to portrayals of these men from the Carolingian era.

These are True Visions Flowing from God

And behold! In the forty-third year of my earthly course, as I was gazing with great fear and trembling attention at a heavenly vision, I saw a great splendor in which resounded a voice from Heaven, saying to me,

"O fragile human, ashes of ashes, and filth of filth! Say and write what you see and hear. But since you are timid in speaking, and simple in expounding, and untaught in writing, speak and write these things not by a human mouth, and not by the understanding of human invention, and not by the requirements of human composition, but as you see and hear them on high in the heavenly places in the wonders of God. Explain these things in such a way that the hearer, receiving the words of his instructor, may expound them in those words, according to that will, vision and instruction. Thus therefore, O

A Vision of Hildegard of Bingen. "The Seeress." *(Hildegard of Bingen receiving the Light from Heaven, c. 1151 [vellum] (later colouration) by German School (12th century). Private Collection/The Bridgeman Art Library.)*

human, speak these things that you see and hear. And write them not by yourself or any other human being, but by the will of Him Who knows, sees and disposes all things in the secrets of His mysteries."

And again I heard the voice from Heaven saying to me, "Speak therefore of these wonders, and, being so taught, write them and speak."

It happened that, in the eleven hundred and forty-first year of the Incarnation of the Son of God, Jesus Christ, when I was forty-two years and seven months old, Heaven was opened and a fiery light of exceeding brilliance came and permeated my whole

(continued)

brain, and inflamed my whole heart and my whole breast, not like a burning but like a warming flame, as the sun warms anything its rays touch. And immediately I knew the meaning of the exposition of the Scriptures, namely the Psalter, the Gospel and the other catholic volumes of both the Old and the New Testaments, though I did not have the interpretation of the words of their texts or the division of the syllables or the knowledge of cases or tenses. But I had sensed in myself wonderfully the power and mystery of secret and admirable visions from my childhood—that is, from the age of five—up to that time, as I do now. This, however, I showed to no one except a few religious persons who were living in the same manner as I; but meanwhile, until the time when God by His grace wished it to be manifested, I concealed it in quiet silence. But the visions I saw I did not perceive in dreams, or sleep, or delirium, or by the eyes of the body, or by the ears of the outer self, or in hidden places; but I received them while awake and seeing with a pure mind and the eyes and ears of the inner self, in open places, as God willed it. How this might be is hard for mortal flesh to understand.

But when I had passed out of childhood and had reached the age of full maturity mentioned above, I heard a voice from Heaven saying, "I am the Living Light, Who illuminates the darkness. The person [Hildegard] whom I have chosen and whom I have miraculously stricken as I willed, I have placed among great wonders, beyond the measure of the ancient people who saw in Me many secrets; but I have laid her low on the earth, that she might not set herself up in arrogance of mind. The world has had in her no joy or lewdness or use in worldly things, for I have withdrawn her from impudent boldness, and she feels fear and is timid in her works. For she suffers in her inmost being and in the veins of her flesh; she is distressed in mind and sense and endures great pain of body, because no security has dwelt in her, but in all her undertakings she has judged herself guilty. For I have closed up the cracks in her heart that her mind may not exalt itself in pride or vainglory, but may feel fear and grief rather than joy and wantonness. Hence in My love she searched in her mind as to where she could find someone who would run in the path of salvation. And she found such a one and loved him [the monk Volmar of Disibodenberg], knowing that he was a faithful man, working like herself on another part of the work that leads to Me. And, holding fast to him, she worked with him in great zeal so that My hidden miracles might be revealed. And she did not seek to exalt herself above herself but with many sighs bowed to him whom she found in the ascent of humility and the intention of good will.

"O human, who receives these things meant to manifest what is not in the disquiet of deception but in the purity of simplicity, write, therefore, the things you see and hear."

But I, though I saw and heard these things, refused to write for a long time through doubt and bad opinion and the diversity of human words, not with stubbornness but in the exercise of humility, until, laid low by the scourge of God, I fell upon a bed of sickness; then, compelled at last by many illnesses, and by the witness of a certain noble maiden of good conduct [the nun Richardis of Stade] and of that man whom I had secretly sought and found, as mentioned above, I set my hand to the writing, While I was doing it I sensed, as I mentioned before, the deep profundity of scriptural exposition; and, raising myself from illness by the strength I received, I brought this work to a close—though just barely—in ten years.

These visions took place and these words were written in the days of Henry, Archbishop of Mainz, and of Conrad, King of the Romans, and of Cuno, Abbot of Disibodenberg, under Pope Eugenius.

And I spoke and wrote these things not by the invention of my heart or that of any other person, but as by the secret mysteries of God I heard and received them in the heavenly places.

And again I heard a voice from Heaven saying to me, "Cry out therefore, and write thus!"

Questions for Discussion:

1. How does Hildegard explain her visions?
2. Hildegard claims in the excerpt from *Scivias* (*"Ways of Knowing"*) that she was not equipped intellectually to record her experiences, and that they came directly from God. Do you regard this as valid, or is she merely denigrating herself? If so, why?

Chapter 11

❧❧❧❧

Political and Economic Developments in the Thirteenth Century

During the thirteenth century, the leaders of the fledgling kingdoms of the earlier era moved to consolidate their power and control. In order to maintain and strengthen their authority, the kings of England, France, Spain, and the Holy Roman Empire took measures to institute legislative bodies of various kinds. In France, King Louis IX (Saint Louis) was a pious and benevolent ruler who believed in dispensing justice personally. His successors were able to expand the holdings of the Crown and to maintain relative peace in the realm. His grandson, Philip IV ("the Fair"), called the first Estates General, which became the legislative body of France.

Philip IV was involved in several wars, and he was desperate to generate funds by any means. In order to augment his treasury, he moved to seize the assets of the Templars, whose great wealth constituted a significant resource. He accused them of moral corruption, embezzlement, and robbery, and used violent and cruel measures to obtain confessions in order to confiscate their property and money (Document 11.3). Philip also decided to levy a tax on Church lands, and his actions brought him into conflict with Pope Boniface VIII, leading to yet another confrontation between the monarchy and the papacy (Document 11.4).

In England, King John compromised with the barons in a famous document, Magna Carta, which has long been viewed as a step toward representative government and democratic freedom. In reality, it was a feudal agreement that reinforced the rights of the nobility and limited the power of the king. Nonetheless, by establishing the Council of Barons, the measure was a step toward the creation of the Parliament, which developed gradually toward the summoning of the "Model Parliament" by Edward I in 1295.

Frederick II was the Holy Roman Emperor during the first half of the century. He spent most of his life in Sicily and southern Italy, thus neglecting his German holdings. As a result, the German princes were able to continue building their own structures of power (Document 11.6). Frederick's actions in Italy were resented by Pope Adrian IV, and he became involved in another protracted struggle with the papacy. Adrian was suspicious of Frederick's association with Muslims, and excommunicated him with accusations of blasphemy. The pope's decree and the imperial reaction are described in Document 11.7. The Iberian Peninsula was also blessed with effective rulers, and one of the most important was Alfonso X ("the Wise") (r. 1252–1284). Alfonso strengthened the

legislative system and brought stability to his kingdom. One of the most important of the medieval law codes, the Siete Partidas ("Seven Part Code"), was compiled under his direction, although it was implemented by his successor. An excerpt from this work describes the qualities of the ideal king, and many scholars believe that the characterization pertains to Alfonso X. Among his other contributions, he patronized learning and the arts, and reputedly composed several of the songs in a series known as The Cantigas de Santa Maria; two of them are included in Document 11.9.

Thirteenth-century Spain contained a population that was religiously and culturally diverse, including substantial numbers of Muslims and Jews in addition to Christians. There were various governmental restrictions placed upon the actions, and even the clothing, of the non-Christian inhabitants. Document 11.10 presents letters from Pope Gregory IX to the archbishop of Compostela and the king of Navarre, which give examples of these prohibitions.

During the Fourth Crusade, as a response political maneuvering, the knights of western Europe attacked and sacked the city of Constantinople, which had long been coveted as a rich prize. A selection from the Chronicle by Villehardouin describes the slaughter and destruction from the point of view of the Crusaders (Document 11.11). Two contrasting sources by the Byzantine writers Nicholas Mesarites and Nicetas Choniates provide evidence of the angry and sorrowful reactions of the residents of the capital (Documents 11.12 and 11.13).

The thirteenth century also witnessed a continuation of the growth of commerce and mercantilism that had begun in the preceding two centuries. Two large and important areas of maritime trade developed—one in the region of the Baltic and North seas, known as the Hanseatic League, and the other in Italy and the Mediterranean Sea. Documents 11.14 through 11.16 demonstrate the mutual protection agreements between the cities of the north, and the cartel issues of trade in the Mediterranean area are presented in Documents 11.17 and 11.18.

Eastern Europe and Russia were threatened in the thirteenth century by the emergence of a new empire created primarily through the efforts of one man, Genghis Khan, who was able to weld the nomadic tribes of Central Asia into a vicious fighting force. The Mongols, as they are known, were able to conquer China, subjugating the Chinese population. The army then turned to the west, as may be seen in Document 11.19.

France and England

INTERPRETING THE EVIDENCE

11.1 A Paragon of Kingly Virtue: Joinville's *Chronicles of the Crusades,* the *Life of Saint Louis,* and a Manuscript Illumination from the *Bible abrégée*

Louis IX, or Saint Louis (1226–1270), is commonly regarded as the greatest French king of the Middle Ages. He believed that his destiny was to serve as a Christian king, and as a result he was pious, serious, and generous; in addition, he was intent upon providing justice for his subjects. As part of his Christian mission he participated in two crusades, proving himself to be a valiant warrior. In the following excerpt from the Chronicles of the Crusades, *probably begun by his biographer Joinville (1224–1317) around 1270, the king's piety is evident in his attention to the liturgical requirements of his religion even while involved in warfare.*

(From *Chronicles of the Crusades* [London: Bell and Daldy, 1870], pp. 362–364.)

The king's mode of living was such, that every day he heard prayers chanted, and a mass of requiem, and then the service of the day, according to what saint it was dedicated to, was sung. It was his custom to repose himself daily on his bed after dinner, when he repeated privately, with one of his chaplains, prayers for the dead, and every evening he heard complines [the last of the canonical hours].

One day a good Cordelier friar [a Franciscan] came to the king, at the castle of Hieres, where we had disembarked, and addressed him, saying, that he had read in the Bible, and other good books which spoke of unbelieving princes; but that he never found a kingdom of believers or unbelievers was ruined but from want of justice being duly administered. "Now," continued the Cordelier, "let the king, who I perceive is going to France, take care that he administer strict and legal justice to his people, in order that our Lord may suffer him to enjoy his kingdom, and that it may remain in peace and tranquility all the days of his life.

It is said that this discreet Cordelier, who thus advised the king, is buried at Marseilles, where our Lord, through him, does many fair miracles.

This Cordelier would not remain longer with the king than one day, in spite of all the entreaties that were made him. The good king was not forgetful of what the friar had told him, to govern his realm loyally according to the laws of God, but was anxious that justice should be done to all, according to the manner you shall hear.

It was customary after the lord de Neeles, the good lord de Soissons, myself, and others that were about the king's person had heard mass, for us to go and hear the pleadings at the gateway, which is now called the Court of Requests, in the palace at Paris. When the good king was in the morning returned from the church, he sent for us, and inquired how things had passed, and if there were any matters that required his decision. And when we told him that there were some, he sent for the parties, and asked them why they would not be contented with the sentence of his officers, and then instantly made their differences up to their satisfaction, according to the custom of this godly king.

(continued)

A Manuscript Illumination from *Bible abrégée* (Moralized Bible) 14 3/4 × 101/4 inches. *(Blanche of Castile and King Louis IX of France; Monk Dictating to a Scribe. Moralized Bible, France, c.1230. M.240, F.8. The Pierpont Morgan Library, New York, U.S.A./Art Resource, New York.)*

Another instance of the dispensation of justice by King Louis is recounted in the following excerpt from Joinville's Life of Saint Louis, *(c. 1270).*

(From *Readings in European History,* vol. 1, by James Harvey Robinson [Boston: Ginn and Co., 1904], pp. 217–218.)

When it was summer King Louis went and sat down in the forest of Vincennes after mass, taking his place under an oak tree, and making us sit down by him. Then those who had anything to say to him might come without the interposition of any usher or other attendant. Then he would ask of them, "Is there anyone here who has any case to be decided?" and those who had a case would rise; then he would say, "All must keep silence, for we must take up one matter after another." And then he called M. de Fontaines and M. Geoffrey de Villette, and said to one of them, "Hand the brief to me"; and when he saw anything to better in the words of those who spoke for another, he corrected them with his own mouth.

Sometimes in summer I have seen him, in order to dispose of his people's affairs, come into the garden in Paris dressed in a coat of camelot,[1] with a sleeveless garment of linsey-woolsey, a cloak of black taffeta about his shoulders, his hair carefully dressed, but with no headdress save a hat of white peacock feathers. He would have carpets spread down so that we might sit about him, and all the people who had business to bring before him stood round about. And then he would attend to them in the manner I have described above in the forest of Vincennes.

Questions for Discussion:

1. Describe the method of dispensing justice practiced by Louis IX. How does it compare with the feudal custom of "Suit to Court"? (Refer to Documents 5.13 and 5.14).

2. What are the advantages of such a judicial "system"? The disadvantages?

The illumination from the thirteenth-century Bible abrégée (Moralized Bible) *on page 308 shows the young King Louis IX enthroned with orb and scepter. His mother, Blanche of Castile, who was the regent of France during her son's minority, seems to be offering advice to the king. Blanche had been a strong and powerful ruler, who personally led her armies into the field to quell the potential revolts of her vassals—powerful potentates who were tempted to weaken the power of the Crown during a female regency. She was able to maintain a strong centralized monarchy to pass on to Louis. His expression in this illumination seems to demonstrate his willingness to take direction from his experienced mother.*

In the lower part of the image, the monk on the left is offering instruction to the scribe, who is preparing the vellum for text and illumination. There is an interesting parallel between the experienced Queen Mother and the knowledgeable monk on the left side, and the neophyte king and scribe on the right. The didactic message is clear: Trust your seasoned advisers.

Questions for Discusssion:

1. Look closely at the activities of the young scribe on the right. What is he doing?
2. Compare the image of Louis IX with that of Otto III (Document 6.10) and the accompanying documents describing Otto's clothing. What common features do you observe? How does the regal raiment establish royal authority?
3. Study the clothing of the Queen Mother. How does it differ from that of her son?

---

[1]Camelot was a woven fabric made of camel or goat's hair.

11.2   Philip IV Calls the First Estates General

Saint Louis was succeeded by his son Philip III (1270–1285), who continued the consolidation of the French monarchy. He was able to expand the realm through marriage, and managed to maintain peace. His successor, Philip IV ("the Fair," 1268–1314), is considered by scholars to have been one of the most important kings of the late Middle Ages. He followed the policies of his father and grandfather, continuing to curb the power of his vassals and strengthening the bureaucratic aspects of his rule. One of his most enduring actions was the summoning of the first legislative body in France, known as the Estates General. It was comprised of delegates from the nobility, the clergy, and representatives of towns.

The following document is representative of the letters sent by the king to summon the "prominent and learned" members of the community.

(From *Readings in European History*, ed. by Leon Bernard and Theodore B. Hodges [New York: The MacMillan Co., 1958], p. 132.)

Philip, by the grace of God King of the French, to the seneschal of Beaucaire, or his lieutenant, greeting. We wish to deliberate with the prelates, barons and other our loyal subjects on many serious matters closely touching ourselves, our estate and liberty, and that of our kingdom, as well as of the churches, ecclesiastics, nobles and secular persons, and all the inhabitants of the said kingdom. We bid you on our behalf to order and command the consuls and communities of the cities of Nîmes, Uzès, le Puy, Mende and Viviers, and the towns of Montpellier and Beaucaire . . . to be present at Paris on the coming Sunday before Palm Sunday, in the persons of two or three of the more prominent and learned of their several communities. These last are to have full and express powers from the said consuls and communities, without making any excuse about the need for reporting back (to their principals), to hear, receive, do and consent to everything that shall be ordained by us in this matter. . . .

Questions for Discussion:

1. How does the governance style of Philip IV differ from that of Saint Louis in the previous selection? Do you see this change as an advance toward just government, or not?
2. Why was Philip's convening of the Estates General a significant event in the history of France?

11.3   "An Execrable Evil": Philip IV and the Templars

The Templars, founded as a monastic military order, were originally sworn to the oaths of poverty, chastity and obedience, as were other monks. As discussed in Documents 7.15 and 7.16, their primary responsibility was to protect pilgrims and merchants on the roads of the Holy Land. Over time the Templars amassed great wealth and extensive property. In addition, they became, in a sense, the caretakers of finance, especially in France, where they conducted an annual audit of the royal revenues. By 1300 the accounts of the French kingdom had grown so complicated that the Templars were unable to deal with them efficiently. Philip IV, who was eager to raise money by any means, used the pretext of their administrative deficiencies to seize their vast holdings. Among other things, as the following document shows, he accused the order of moral corruption, embezzlement, and outright thievery. The methods used by Philip were cruel and ruthless, including torture to extract confessions and burning of the men who retracted their statements. Modern scholarship has shown that the Templars were, for the most part, not guilty of the charges lodged against them.

(From *The Templars*, translated by Malcolm Barber and Keith Bate. Manchester, UK: Manchester University Press, 2002, pp. 244–248. Reprinted by permission.)

Order for the Arrests
(14 September 1307)

Philip, by the grace of God King of the Franks, to our beloved and faithful lord of Onival and John of Tourville, knight and *bailli* of Rouen, greetings and love.

There has recently echoed in our ears, to our not inconsiderable astonishment and vehement horror, vouched for by many people worthy to be believed, a bitter thing, a lamentable thing, a thing horrible to contemplate, terrible to hear, a heinous crime, an execrable evil, an abominable deed, a hateful disgrace, a completely inhuman thing, indeed remote from all humanity. Having weighed up its seriousness we felt the immensity of our grief increase in us the more bitterly as it became evident that crimes of this nature and importance were so great as to constitute an offence against the divine majesty, a loss for the orthodox faith and for all Christianity, a disgrace for humanity, a pernicious example of evil and a universal scandal. Indeed, a spirit that is rational feels pity for someone who goes beyond the bounds of nature and in its pity is troubled by a people that does not understand why it once had a position of honor, because it has forgotten its origins, is unaware of its own condition, ignorant of its worth, wasteful of itself and given to reprehensible sentiments. It is comparable to stupid beasts, or rather in its stupendous bestiality it transcends the very stupidity of those beasts and exposes itself to the most nefarious of crimes which the sensuality of those very beasts themselves abhors and rejects. It has forsaken God its maker, it has departed from God its savior, it has forsaken God who brought it to life, forgotten its creator, made offerings to devils and not to God; it is a people lacking foresight and care. If only it had sensed and understood and foreseen these most recent events!

Some time ago indeed, we received insistent reports from very reliable people that brothers of the Order of the knights of the Temple, wolves in sheep's clothing, in the habit of a religious order vilely insulting our religious faith, are again crucifying our Lord Jesus Christ in these days, He who was crucified for the redemption of the human race. But they are causing Him greater injuries than those he received on the Cross. When they enter the Order and make their profession, they are confronted with His image, and their miserable or rather pitiful blindness makes them deny Him three times and spit in His face three times. Afterwards, they remove the clothes they wore in the secular world, and naked in the presence of the Visitor or his deputy, who receives their profession, they are kissed by him first on the lower part of the dorsal spine, secondly on the navel and finally on the mouth, in accordance with the profane rite of their Order but to the disgrace of the dignity of the human race. When they have offended divine law by such criminal activities and hateful acts, they do not fear to offend human law. By the vow of their profession they are unequivocably bound to accept the request of another to perform the vice of that horrible, dreadful intercourse, and this is why the wrath of God has fallen on these sons of infidelity. This unclean tribe has abandoned the source of living water, has exchanged its glory for the likeness of the Calf and made offerings to idols.

These and other acts this perfidious people, this mad people dedicated to the cult of idols, does not shrink from committing. It is not only their activities and acts that are detestable, for their hasty words also defile the earth with their filth, remove the benefits of the dew, poison the purity of the air and bring confusion to our faith.

At first we found it difficult to listen to these informers and purveyors of such ominous news, because we suspected they were acting more from malice and envy, moved by hatred and greed than from any religious fervor, desire for justice or charitable feelings. However, with an increase in the number of the informers and the said denunciators and as the bad reputation grew worse, the presumptions, the legitimate, well-founded arguments and conjectures became probabilities. Because of the strength of these presumptions and suspicions we decided on a full investigation to determine the truth in these matters. After having a far-reaching discussion in a meeting with Clement, the most holy father in the Lord, by divine providence the highest bishop in the holy Roman and universal Church, and deliberated in a plenary meeting with our prelates and barons, we have begun to set up the most effective means of enquiry and positive channels of procedure to bring out into the light the truth in this matter. The deeper and fuller the investigation has become, the greater are the abominations that are uncovered, as when one knocks down a wall.

Wherefore, we, who have been placed by the Lord on the watchtower of regal eminence to defend the liberty of the faith of the Church, and who place the extension of the Catholic faith before all desires of our mind, set up an enquiry made by our beloved brother in Christ G. of Paris, inquisitor of heretical depravity under the authority of the pope, into these affairs, based on adverse public opinion, but informed by careful investigation of the facts. In view of the very strong suspicions raised by the enquiry, the other various presumptions, legitimate arguments and probable conjectures, we have agreed to the justifiable requests of the said inquisitor who has invoked the help of our arm in this matter against the aforementioned enemies of God, religion and nature, those opponents of human society. Despite the fact that some may be guilty and others innocent, because of the extreme seriousness of this affair in which the truth cannot be fully brought out into the light in any other way, and that vehement suspicion has fallen on all, it is fitting that if there are any innocent ones among them these should be tested in the furnace like gold and cleared by the due process of judicial examination. Hence, after a plenary session on the matter with the prelates, barons of our kingdom, and our other advisers, as stated above, we have decreed that all individuals of the Order without exception within our kingdom shall be arrested, held prisoner and reserved for an ecclesiastical court; their movable and immovable goods shall be seized, and these seizures kept in all good faith in our possession.

Wherefore we entrust to you and strictly order you personally or two of your agents to proceed to the *bailliage* of Rouen and arrest all the brothers of that Order without exception; you will hold them captive to appear before an ecclesiastical court; you will seize their movable and immovable goods and hold the seizures under strict supervision in our name without any diminution or damage of any sort, according to our orders and instructions transmitted to you under our counterseal, until you receive further instructions from us on this matter. Further, we give instructions by the terms of the present document to those who are faithful to us, judges and sub-

jects, effectively to obey you and to observe the aforementioned totally and individually, and all things relative to them.

Done in the royal abbey of St Mary, near Pontoise, on the Feast of the Exaltation of the Holy Cross in the year of our Lord 1307.

Also included in the records are specific instructions as to how the commissioners should proceed in the arrests of the Templars:

Firstly, when they arrive and have informed the seneschals and *baillis* of the matter, they will investigate in secret all their houses, and as a precaution, should there be need to, they can investigate houses of other religious orders, on the pretence that it is in connection with tithes or on some other pretext.

After this, the person sent with the seneschal or the *bailli* early on the appointed day will choose powerful *prud'hommes* [skilled workmen] of the region who are above suspicion, knights, *echevins* [members of the administration], and councillors, in relation to the number of houses and granges; he will inform them of the task under oath of secrecy and of the fact that the king has been informed of it by the pope and the Church. Without delay these people will be sent to each place to arrest the persons there, seize the property and arrange its guard. They will ensure that the vines and estates are cultivated and planted properly, and will entrust them to good, rich men of the region, together with the servants found in the houses, and in their presence this same day they will make inventories of all movable assets in each place, will append their seal, and will go with sufficient forces to obviate any resistance from the brothers or their servants, and they will be accompanied by sergeants to make them obey.

Afterwards they will place the persons individually under separate and secure guard, and will investigate them first before calling the commissioners of the enquiry, and will determine the truth carefully, with the aid of torture if necessary; and if these persons confess the truth, they will put their depositions in writing to be witnessed.

Procedure for the enquiry:

The articles of the faith will be impressed upon them and they will be told that the king and the pope have been informed by several trustworthy witnesses in the Order of the errors and the buggery (*bougrerie*) they commit particularly on their entry and their profession. They will be promised a pardon if they confess the truth and return to the faith of the holy Church; otherwise they will be condemned to death.

They will be asked carefully and intelligently to say under oath how they were received, what vow or promise they made, and they will be asked in general terms until the truth has been elicited from them and they persevere in this truth.

Articles of the errors provided by several witnesses:

Those who are received first ask for the bread and water of the Order, and then the commander or master who receives each of them takes him behind the altar out of sight or to the sacristy or to another place where they cannot be seen, and shows him the Cross and the image of our Lord Jesus Christ, and makes him deny the prophet three times, that is to say our Lord Jesus Christ whose image it is, and makes him spit on the Cross three times. The one who receives him then has him stripped, kisses him on the base of his spine beneath the waist, then on his navel and then on his mouth; he tells him that if any brother of the Order wishes to lie with him carnally he shall accept this because it is a duty he is constrained to put up with under the statutes of the Order, and that many of them lie with each other carnally in the manner of sodomites because of

this. Each brother ties a small cord around his waist over his chemise and has to wear it as long as he lives. It is said that these small cords have been touched and put around an idol in the form of a man's head with a large beard, which head they kiss and worship in their provincial chapters; however not all the brothers are aware of this, only the Grand Master and the elders. Moreover, the priests of their Order do not consecrate the body of Our Lord; thus the priests of the Order will be interrogated specially about this.

The commissioners shall send to the king under their own seal and those of the commissioners of the enquiry as soon as possible the copy of the deposition of those who confess the said errors or in particular the denial of Our Lord Jesus Christ.

Questions for Discussion:

1. What were the specific accusations lodged against the Templars?
2. Do the accusations seem plausible to you? Why or why not?
3. Discuss the motives of the king in relation to the Templars.
4. The Templars fascinated people in the late Middle Ages, and this interest has continued to the present time. What reasons can you give for their popular appeal?

11.4   *Unam Sanctam*: Pope Boniface VIII and Philip IV

Philip IV was involved in several wars, and he was desperate to generate funds. His advisers suggested that since the military circumstances were "unusual," he might levy a tax on Church lands, which comprised about one-fourth of the area of France. This attempt to raise funds brought the king into a confrontation with Pope Boniface VIII, who claimed that only he had the right to tax the clergy. He thundered forth in a papal bull known as "Clericis Laicos" that any clergyman who paid taxes to the kings would suffer excommunication.

Philip's next move was to arrest a bishop in southern France on the pretext of treason. This action precipitated another papal bull, "Unam Sanctam," in which the pope asserted that the papacy held supreme authority over secular

rulers. This bull clearly states the papal position concerning universal sovereignty; according to Boniface, the "two swords"—temporal as well as spiritual authority—were held by the pope.

Following the promulgation of the bull, Philip ordered his agents to travel to the pope's residence at Agnani, south of Rome, to capture Boniface and bring him to France to answer charges of heresy. The pope probably suffered physical abuse by Philip's henchmen, and though the royal agents were driven out the papal residence, Boniface, who was eighty-two years old, died the next month.

The next pope, Benedict XI, pardoned Philip and his agents during his reign of only one year. Significantly, the next conclave elected a Frenchman, and the papacy was soon to move to Avignon in southern France. This so-called "Babylonian Captivity of the Church" will be discussed in Chapter 14.

(From *A Source Book for Mediaeval History*, by Oliver J. Thatcher and Edgar H. McNeal [New York: Charles Scribner's Sons, 1905], pp. 314–317.)

The Bull "Unam Sanctam" of Boniface VIII, 1302

The true faith compels us to believe that there is one holy catholic apostolic church, and this we firmly believe and plainly confess. And outside of her there is no salvation or remission of sins, as the Bridegroom says in the Song of Solomon: "My dove, my undefiled is but one; she is the only one of her mother, she is the choice one of her that bare her" [Song of Sol. 6:9]; which represents the one mystical body, whose head is Christ, but the head of Christ is God [1 Cor. 11.3]. In this church there is "one Lord, one faith, one baptism" [Eph. 4:5]. For in the time of the flood there was only one ark, that of Noah, prefiguring the one church, and it was "finished above in one cubit" [Gen. 6:16], and had but one helmsman and master, namely, Noah. And we read that all things on the earth outside of this ark were destroyed. This church we venerate as the only one, since the Lord said by the prophet: "Deliver my soul from the sword; my darling from the power of the dog" [Ps. 22:20]. He prayed for his soul, that is, for himself, the head; and at the same time for the body; and he named his body, that is, the one church, because there is but one Bridegroom [cf. John 3:29], and because of the unity of the faith, of the sacraments, and of his love for the church. This is the seamless robe of the Lord which was not rent but parted by lot [John 19:23]. Therefore there is one body of the one and only church, and one head, not two heads, as if the church were a monster. And this head is Christ and his vicar, Peter and his successor; for the Lord himself said to Peter: "Feed my sheep" [John 21:16]. And he said "my sheep," in general, not these or those sheep in particular; from which it is clear that all were committed to him. If therefore Greeks or anyone else say that they are not subject to Peter and his successors, they thereby necessarily confess that they are not of the sheep of Christ. For the Lord says in the Gospel of John, that there is one fold and only one shepherd [John 10:16]. By the words of the gospel we are taught that the two swords, namely, the spiritual authority and the temporal are in the power of the church. For when the apostles said "Here are two swords" [Luke 22:38]—that is, in the church, since it was the apostles who were speaking—the Lord did not answer, "It is too much," but "It is enough." Whoever denies that the temporal sword is in the power of Peter does not properly understand the word of the Lord when he said: "Put up thy sword into the sheath" [John 18:11]. Both swords, therefore, the spiritual and the temporal, are in the power of the church. The former is to be used by the church, the latter for the church; the one by the hand of the priest, the other by the hand of kings and knights, but at the command and permission of the priest. Moreover, it is necessary for one sword to be under the other, and the temporal authority to be subjected to the spiritual; for the apostle says, "For there is no power but of God: and the powers that are ordained of God" [Rom. 13:1]; but they would not be ordained [i.e., arranged or set in order; note the play on the words] unless one were subjected to the other, and, as it were, the lower made the higher by the other. For, according to St. Dionysius, it is a law of divinity that the lowest is made the highest through the intermediate. According to the law of the universe all things are not equally and directly reduced to order, but the lowest are fitted into their order through the intermediate, and the lower through the higher. And we must necessarily admit that the spiritual power surpasses any earthly power in dignity and honor, because spiritual things surpass temporal things. We clearly see that this is true from the paying of tithes, from the benediction, from the sanctification, from the receiving of the power, and from the governing of these things. For the truth itself declares that the spiritual power must establish the temporal power and pass judgment on it if it is not good. Thus the prophecy of Jeremiah concerning the church and the ecclesiastical power is fulfilled: "See, I have this day set thee over the nations and over the kingdoms, to root out, and to pull down, and to destroy, and to throw down, to build, and to plant" [Jer. 1:10]. Therefore if the temporal power errs, it will be judged by the spiritual power, and if the lower spiritual power errs, it will be judged by its superior. But if the highest spiritual power errs, it can not be judged by men, but by God alone. For the apostle says: "But he that is spiritual judgeth all things, yet he himself is judged of no man" [1 Cor. 2:15]. Now this authority, although it is given to man and exercised through man, is not human, but divine. For it was given by the word of the Lord to Peter, and the rock was made firm to him and his successors, in Christ himself, whom he had confessed. For the Lord said to Peter:

"Whatsoever thou shalt bind on earth shall be bound in heaven: and whatsoever thou shalt loose on earth shall be loosed in heaven" [Matt. 16:19]. Therefore whosoever resisteth this power thus ordained of God, resisteth the ordinance of God [Rom. 13:2], unless there are two principles (beginnings), as Manichaeus pretends there are. But this we judge to be false and heretical. For Moses says that, not in the beginnings, but in the beginning [note the play on words], God created the heaven and the earth [Gen. 1:1]. We therefore declare, say, and affirm that submission on the part of every man to the bishop of Rome is altogether necessary for his salvation.

Questions for Discussion:

1. The conflict between Philip IV and Boniface VIII is yet another struggle between secular and religious power. Compare this confrontation with the Investiture Controversy (Documents 6.14 through 6.18). Are the same issues at stake?
2. How does Boniface substantiate his claim to universal sovereignty? Does he use the same arguments as Gregory VII (Document 6.14)?

11.5   *Magna Carta (1215)*

Magna Carta ("the Great Charter") is one of the most famous documents in the history of England. Although the charter was viewed by generations of scholars as a first step toward representative government, the agreement between King John (1167–1284) and his barons was essentially a reaffirmation of feudal practices, rather than a grant of freedom to the commoners. The king had been charging greater fees than were customary for his feudal rights, delaying the granting of inheritance rights, and keeping bishops' offices vacant so that he might collect the revenues from their dioceses. The barons rebelled in an effort to correct these abuses, and the king met with them to address their grievances; Magna Carta was an outgrowth of this encounter. Hence, the charter deals with such aspects of governance as the relationship of the Crown to the Church, rights of wardship and inheritance, and the use of common measures to be observed in the trading of commodities. The charter also established a council of twenty-five barons to oversee the government.

(From *Select Historical Documents of the Middle Ages*, trans. by Ernest F. Henderson [London: G. Bell & Sons, 1925], pp. 135–142, 146–147.)

John, by the grace of God king of England, lord of Ireland, duke of Normandy and Aquitaine, count of Anjou: to the archbishops, bishops, abbots, earls, barons, justices, foresters, sheriffs, prevosts, serving men, and to all his bailiffs and faithful subjects, greeting.

1. First of all have granted to God, and, for us and for our heirs forever, have confirmed, by this our present charter, that the English church shall be free and shall have its rights intact and its liberties uninfringed upon. And thus we will that it be observed. As is apparent from the fact that we, spontaneously and of our own free will, before discord broke out between ourselves and our barons, did grant and by our charter confirm— and did cause the lord pope Innocent III. to confirm—freedom of elections, which is considered most important and most necessary to the church of England. Which charter both we ourselves shall observe, and we will that it be observed with good faith by our heirs forever. We have also granted to all free men of our realm, on the part of ourselves and our heirs forever, all the subjoined liberties, to have and to hold, to them and to their heirs, from us and from our heirs:

2. If any one of our earls or barons, or of others holding from us in chief through military service, shall die; and if, at the time of his death, his heir be of full age and owe a relief: he shall have his inheritance by paying the old relief;—the heir, namely, or the heirs of an earl, by paying one hundred pounds for the whole barony of an earl; the heir or heirs of a baron, by paying one hundred pounds for the whole barony; the heir or heirs of a knight, by paying one hundred shillings at most for a whole knight's fee; and he who shall owe less shall give less, according to the ancient custom of fees.

3. But if the heir of any of the above persons shall be under age and in wardship,—when he comes of age he shall have his inheritance without relief and without fine.

4. The administrator of the land of such heir who shall be under age shall take none but reasonable issues from the land of the heir, and reasonable customs and services; and this without destruction and waste of men or goods. And if we shall have committed the custody of any such land to the sheriff or to any other man who ought to be responsible to us for the issues of it, and he cause destruction or waste to what is in his charge: we will fine him, and the land shall be handed over to two lawful and discreet men of that fee who shall answer to us, or to him to whom we shall have referred them, regarding those issues. And if we shall have given or sold to anyone the custody of any such land, and he shall have caused destruction or waste to it,—he shall lose that custody, and it shall be given to two lawful and discreet men of that fee, who likewise shall answer to us, as has been explained.

5. The administrator, moreover, so long as he may have the custody of the land, shall keep in order, from the issues of that land, the houses, parks, warrens, lakes, mills, and other things pertaining to it. And he shall restore to the heir when he comes to full age, his whole land stocked with ploughs and wainnages,[2] according as the time

of the wainnage requires and the issues of the land will reasonably permit.

6. Heirs may marry without disparagement; so, nevertheless, that, before the marriage is contracted, it shall be announced to the relations by blood of the heir himself.

7. A widow, after the death of her husband, shall straightway, and without difficulty, have her marriage portion and her inheritance, nor shall she give any thing in return for her dowry, her marriage portion, or the inheritance which belonged to her, and which she and her husband held on the day of the death of that husband. And she may remain in the house of her husband, after his death, for forty days; within which her dowry shall be paid over to her.

8. No widow shall be forced to marry when she prefers to live without a husband; so, however, that she gives security not to marry without our consent, if she hold from us, or the consent of the lord from whom she holds, if she hold from another.

9. Neither we nor our bailiffs shall seize any revenue for any debt, so long as the chattels of the debtor suffice to pay the debt; nor shall the sponsors of that debtor be distrained[3] so long as that chief debtor has enough to pay the debt. But if the chief debtor fail in paying the debt, not having the wherewithal to pay it, the sponsors shall answer for the debt. And, if they shall wish, they may have the lands and revenues of the debtor until satisfaction shall have been given them for the debt previously paid for him; unless the chief debtor shall show that he is quit in that respect towards those same sponsors.

10. If anyone shall have taken any sum, great or small, as a loan from the Jews, and shall die before that debt is paid,—that debt shall not bear interest so long as the heir, from whomever he may hold, shall be under age. And if the debt fall into our hands, we shall take nothing save the chattel contained in the deed.

---

[2] Wainnage refers to the means to carry on agriculture and the raising of animals.

[3] To distrain is to confiscate property in payment of a debt.

11. And if anyone dies owing a debt to the Jews, his wife shall have her dowry, and shall restore nothing of that debt. But if there shall remain children of that dead man, and they shall be under age, the necessaries shall be provided for them according to the nature of the dead man's holding; and, from the residue, the debt shall be paid, saving the service due to the lords. In like manner shall be done concerning debts that are due to others besides Jews.

12. No scutage[4] or aid shall be imposed in our realm unless by the common counsel of our realm; except for redeeming our body, and knighting our eldest son, and marrying once our eldest daughter. And for these purposes there shall only be given a reasonable aid. In like manner shall be done concerning the aids of the city of London.

13. And the city of London shall have all its old liberties and free customs as well by land as by water. Moreover we will and grant that all other cities and boroughs, and towns and ports, shall have all their liberties and free customs.

. . .

35. There shall be one measure of- wine throughout our whole realm, and one measure of ale and one measure of corn—namely, the London quart; — and one width of dyed and russet and hauberk cloths—namely, two ells below the selvage. And with weights, moreover, it shall be as with measures.

. . .

41. All merchants may safely and securely go out of England, and come into England, and delay and pass through England, as well by land as by water, for the purpose of buying and selling, free from all evil taxes, subject to the ancient and right customs—save in time of war, and if they are of the land at war against us. And if such be found in our land at the beginning of the war, they shall be held, without harm to their bodies and goods, until it shall be known to us or our chief justice how the merchants of

our land are to be treated who shall, at that time, be found in the land at war against us. And if ours shall be safe there, the others shall be safe in our land.

. . .

61. Inasmuch as, for the sake of God, and for the bettering of our realm, and for the more ready healing of the discord which has arisen between us and our barons, we have made all these aforesaid concessions,—wishing them to enjoy for ever entire and firm stability, we make and grant to them the following security: that the barons, namely, may elect at their pleasure twenty five barons from the realm, who ought, with all their strength, to observe, maintain and cause to be observed, the peace and privileges which we have granted to them and confirmed by this our present charter. In such wise, namely, that if we, or our justice, or our bailiffs, or anyone of our servants shall have transgressed against anyone in any respect, or shall have broken some one of the articles of peace or security, and our transgression shall have been shown to four barons of the aforesaid twenty five: those four barons shall come to us, or, if we are abroad, to our justice, showing to us our error; and they shall ask us to cause that error to be amended without delay. And if we do not amend that error, or, we being abroad, if our justice do not amend it within a term of forty days from the time when it was shown to us or, we being abroad, to our justice: the aforesaid four barons shall refer the matter to the remainder of the twenty five barons, and those twenty five barons, with the whole land in common, shall distrain and oppress us in every way in their power, —namely, by taking our castles, lands and possessions, and in every other way that they can, until amends shall have been made according to their judgment. Saving the persons of ourselves, our queen and our children. And when amends shall have been made they shall be in accord with us as they had been. previously. And whoever of the land wishes to do so, shall swear that in carrying out all the aforesaid measures he will obey the mandates of the aforesaid twenty five

[4]Scutage was money paid in lieu of military service.

barons, and that, with them, he will oppress us to the extent of his power. And, to anyone who wishes to do so, we publicly and freely give permission to swear; and we will never prevent anyone from swearing. Moreover, all those in the land who shall be unwilling, themselves and of their own accord, to swear to the twenty five barons as to distraining and oppressing us with them: such ones we shall make to swear by our mandate, as has been said. And if any-one of the twenty five barons shall die, or leave the country, or in any other way be prevented from carrying out the aforesaid measures,—the remainder of the aforesaid twenty five barons shall choose another in his place, according to their judgment, who shall be sworn in the same way as the others. Moreover, in all things en-trusted to those twenty five barons to be car-ried out, if those twenty five shall be present and chance to disagree among themselves with regard to some matter, or if some of them, hav-ing been summoned, shall be unwilling or un-able to be present: that which the majority of those present shall decide or decree shall be considered binding and valid, just as if all the twenty five had consented to it. And the aforesaid twenty five shall swear that they will faithfully observe all the foregoing, and will cause them to be observed to the extent of their power. And we shall obtain nothing from

anyone, either through ourselves or through another, by which any of those concessions and liberties may be revoked or diminished. And if any such thing shall have been obtained, it shall be vain and invalid, and we shall never make use of it either through ourselves or through another.

Questions for Discussion:

1. Analyze the first nine provisions of the docu-ment. Do they extend or merely codify the privileges that were customary features of feudal contracts as described in Documents 5.1 through 5.6 How were they modified?

2. *Magna Carta* stipulates that a council of twenty-five barons be formed. What were the rights and responsibilities of these men? Do you see this as a step toward representative government? Why or why not?

3. What provisions would allow the growth of trade in England? What restrictions were placed on the merchants?

4. What stipulations are made in the document concerning the monetary dealings of the Jews? Why do you think these provisions were included?

5. Compare the council of barons with the Es-tates General (Document 11.2). Do you see any common features? How do they differ?

The Holy Roman Empire

11.6   Frederick II and Germany

Frederick II (r. 1215–1250) inherited the crown of the Holy Roman Empire as an infant in 1197. He was placed under the guardianship of Pope Innocent III, and was given a brilliant education. Frederick could speak several languages and was a great patron of the arts; because of his abilities and accomplishments, his contemporaries called him "Stupor Mundi" ("Wonder of the World").

The emperor spent his childhood in Sicily and, perhaps as a result, he was more interested in securing

the imperial position in Italy than he was in his hold-ings in Germany. The following document demon-strates the degree to which he abandoned the Empire to the princes.

(From *A Source Book for Mediaeval History*, ed. by Oliver J. Thatc her and Edgar H. McNeal [New York: Charles Scribner's Sons, 1905], pp. 238–240.)

Statute In Favor of the Princes [1231]

In the name of the holy and undivided Trinity. Frederick II, by divine mercy emperor of the Romans, Augustus, king of Jerusalem, king of Sicily.

1. No new castles or cities shall be erected by us or by anyone else to the prejudice of the princes.
2. New markets shall not be allowed to interfere with the interests of former ones.
3. No one shall be compelled to attend any market against his will.
4. Travelers shall not be compelled to leave the old highways, unless they desire to do so.
5. We will not exercise jurisdiction within the ban-mile of our cities.
6. Each prince shall possess and exercise in peace according to the customs of the land the liberties, jurisdiction, and authority over counties and hundreds which are in his own possession or are held as fiefs from him.
7. Centgrafs[5] shall receive their office from the prince or from the person who holds the land as a fief.
8. The location of the hundred court shall not be changed without the consent of the lord.
9. No nobleman shall be amenable to the hundred court.
10. The citizens who are known as *phalburgii* [i.e., persons or corporations existing outside the city, but possessing political rights within it] shall be expelled from the cities.
11. Payments of wine, money, grain, and other rents, which free peasants have formerly agreed to pay [to the emperor], are hereby remitted, and shall not be collected henceforth.
12. The serfs of princes, nobles, ministerials, and churches shall not be admitted to our cities.
13. Lands and fiefs of princes, nobles, ministerials, and churches, which have been seized by our cities, shall be restored and shall never again be taken.

14. The right of the princes to furnish safe-conduct within the lands which they hold as fiefs from us shall not be infringed by us or by anyone else.
15. Inhabitants of our cities shall not be compelled by our judges to restore any possessions which they may have received from others before they moved there.
16. Notorious, condemned, and proscribed persons shall not be admitted to our cities; if they have been, they shall be driven out.
17. We will never cause any money to be coined in the land of any of the princes which shall be injurious to his coinage.
18. The jurisdiction of our cities shall not extend beyond their boundaries, unless we possess special jurisdiction in the region.
19. In our cities the plaintiff shall bring suit in the court of the accused.
20. Lands or property which are held as fiefs shall not be pawned without the consent of the lord from whom they are held.
21. No one shall be compelled to aid in the fortifying of cities unless he is legally bound to render that service.
22. Inhabitants of our cities who hold lands outside shall pay to their lords or advocates the regular dues and services, and they shall not be burdened with unjust exactions.
23. If serfs, freemen subject to advocates, or vassals of any lord, shall dwell within any of our cities, they shall not be prevented by our officials from going to their lords.

Question for Discussion:

1. In this document Frederick II cedes a great deal of control to the German princes. Discuss specific provisions, explaining how they would affect the authority of the emperor.

---

[5]Centgrafs were presiding officials of the hundreds courts.

11.7   Frederick II and Pope Innocent IV

Yet another chapter in the ongoing conflict between the papacy and the imperial power concerns the policies of the emperor in his Italian holdings. The actions of Frederick II resulted in an extended conflict with Pope Innocent IV, who ultimately excommunicated and deposed him. The papal bull issued by Innocent, which was proclaimed at the Council of Lyons, describes the pope's attitude toward the emperor's exploits.

(From Brian Tierney, *The Middle Ages: Sources of Medieval History*, vol. 1, 5th Ed. New York: McGraw-Hill, 1991, pp. 272–273.)

Innocent's Proclamation at the Council of Lyons [1245]

Bishop Innocent, servant of the servants of God, to the present holy Council for the eternal record of the matter.

Having been exalted to the summit of the Apostolic dignity, although unworthy of such a favor from the Divine Majesty, we have to take care of all Christians with a vigilant and diligent solicitude, discern their merits through the eye of intimate consideration and weigh them carefully on the scales of our deliberation; so that we elevate with adequate favors those whom the strength of a just examination shows worthy and afflict with due penalties the guilty ones, weighing always the merits and rewards impartially and recompensing each one for the quality of his deeds with a just amount of punishment or grace. . . .

[Frederick] has committed four very grave offences, which can not be covered up by any subterfuge (we say nothing for the moment about his other crimes); he has abjured God on many occasions; he has wantonly broken the peace which had been re-established between the Church and the Empire; he has also committed sacrilege by causing to be imprisoned the Cardinals of the holy Roman Church and the prelates and clerics, regular and secular,[6] of other churches, coming to the Council which our predecessor had summoned; he is also accused of heresy not by doubtful and flimsy but by formidable and clear proofs.

. . . Also after he had joined himself in a detestable friendship to the Saracens, he sent messengers and presents to them on several occasions and received them from the Saracens in return with honor and joy; he embraced their customs, observing them notoriously in his daily life, for he did not even blush to appoint as guardians for his wives (descendants from royal stock) eunuchs. What is more abominable still is that once, when he was in the countries beyond the sea, he made a treaty or rather a conspiracy with the Sultan and allowed the name of Mahomet to be publicly proclaimed day and night in the Temple of the Lord. And lately, as it is said, he caused the messengers of the Sultan of Babylon (after the same Sultan had inflicted personally and through his subordinates very grave and inestimable injuries upon the Holy inhabitants) to be honorably received and magnificently entertained in the kingdom of Sicily, with praises for the prestige of the same Sultan.

We therefore, who are the vicar, though unworthy, of Jesus Christ on earth and to whom it was said in the person of blessed Peter the Apostle: "Whatsoever thou shalt bind on earth," etc., show and declare an account of the above-mentioned shameful crimes and of many others, having held careful consultation with our brethren and the holy Council, that the aforesaid prince—who has rendered himself so unworthy of all the honor and dignity of the Empire and the kingdom and who, because of his wickedness, has been rejected by God from acting as king or Emperor—is bound by his sins and cast out and deprived of all honor and dignity by God, to which we add our sentence of deprivation also. We absolve for ever all who owe him allegiance in virtue of an oath of fealty from any oath of this kind; and we strictly forbid by Apostolic authority that anyone should obey him or look upon him henceforth as king or Emperor, and we decree that whoever shall in the future afford him advice, help or goodwill as if he were Emperor or king, shall fall "ipso facto" under the binding force of excommunication. But let those in the same Empire whose duty it is to look to

---

[6]Regular clergy were monks living according to a *Rule*; secular clergy served in ecclesiastical positions in the world.

the election of an Emperor, elect a successor freely. We shall make it our business to provide for the aforesaid kingdom of Sicily as seems best to us with the advice of our brethren.

Question for Discussion:

1. What is the primary accusation lodged by the pope against Frederick?

Frederick's Reply to the Deposition: a Letter Addressed to the Princes of Europe

What is implied by our maltreatment is made plain by the presumption of Pope Innocent IV for, having summoned a council—a general council he calls it—he has dared to pronounce a sentence of deposition against us who were neither summoned nor proved guilty of any deceit or wickedness, which sentence he could not enact without grievous prejudice to all kings. You and all kings of particular regions have everything to fear from the effrontery of such a prince of priests when he sets out to depose us who have been divinely honored by the imperial diadem and solemnly elected by the princes with the approval of the whole church at a time when faith and religion were flourishing among the clergy, us who also govern in splendor other noble kingdoms; and this when it is no concern of his to inflict any punishment on us for temporal injuries even if the cases were proved according to law. In truth we are not the first nor shall we be the last that this abuse of priestly power harasses and strives to cast down from the heights; but this indeed you also do when you obey these men who feign holiness, whose ambition hopes that "the whole Jordan will flow into their mouth" (*cf.* Job 40:18) O if your simple credulity would care to turn itself "from the leaven of the Scribes and Pharisees which is hypocrisy" (Luke 12:1) according to the words of the Savior, how many foul deeds of that court you would be able to execrate, which honor and shame forbid us to relate. The copious revenues with which they are enriched by the impoverishment of many kingdoms, as you yourself know, make them rage like madmen.

Christians and pilgrims beg in your land so that Patarene[7] heretics may eat in ours. You are closing up your houses there to build the towns of your enemies here. These poor followers of Christ are supported and enriched by your tithes and alms, but by what compensating benefit, or what expression of gratitude even do they show themselves beholden to you? The more generously you stretch out a hand to these needy ones the more greedily they snatch not only the hand but the arm, trapping you in their snare like a little bird that is the more firmly entangled the more it struggles to escape.

We have concerned ourselves to write these things to you for the present, though not adequately expressing our intentions. We have decided to omit other matters and to convey them to you more secretly; namely the purpose for which the lavishness of these greedy men expends the riches of the poor; what we have found out concerning the election of an emperor if peace is not established at least superficially between us and the church, which peace we intend to establish through eminent mediators; what dispositions we intend to make concerning all the kingdoms in general and each in particular; what has been arranged concerning the islands of the ocean; how that court is plotting against all princes with words and deeds which could not be concealed from us who have friends and subjects there, although clandestinely; with what stratagems and armies trained for war we hope in this coming spring to oppress all those who now oppress us, even though the whole world should set itself against us.

But whatever our faithful subjects, the bearers of this letter, relate to you you may believe with certainty and hold as firmly as if St. Peter had sworn to it. Do not suppose on account of what we ask of you that the magnanimity of our majesty has been in any way bowed down by the sentence of deposition launched against us, for we have a clean conscience and so God is with us. We call him to witness that it was always our intention to persuade the clergy of every degree that they should continue to the end as they were in the early days of the church living an

---

[7]Patarenes formed an eleventh-century religious movement intent upon reforming the clergy and ecclesiastical government in Milan.

apostolic life and imitating the Lord's humility, and that it was our intention especially to reduce those of highest rank to this condition. Those clergy [of former days] used to see angels and were resplendent with miracles: they used to heal the sick, raise the dead and subject kings and princes to themselves by holiness, not by arms. But these, drunk with the pleasures of the world and devoted to them, set aside God, and all true religion is choked by their surfeit of riches and power. Hence, to deprive such men of the baneful wealth that burdens them to their own damnation is a work of charity. You and all princes, united with us, ought to be as diligent as you can in achieving this end so that, laying aside all superfluities and content with modest possessions, they may serve the God whom all things serve.

Questions for Discussion:

1. What cautionary message does Frederick send to the kings of Europe?
2. What criticisms of the clergy are contained in the emperor's letter?
3. Compare the struggle of Frederick II and Innocent IV with the Investiture Controversy (Documents 6.14 through 6.18) and the quarrel of his father, Frederick I, with Eugene III and Adrian IV (Documents 9.6 through 9.10). What common themes emerge?
4. How does Frederick's quarrel with Innocent IV compare with the confrontation between Philip IV and Boniface VIII (Document 11.4)? Discuss.

The Iberian Peninsula

11.8   The Proper Virtues of a King: From the *Siete Partidas*

The Siete Partidas *("Seven-Part Code") was one of the most important law codes of the Middle Ages. Although it was not implemented until the early fourteenth century, the compilation was supervised by Alfonso X, King of Leon and Castile (1252–1284), who was known as "El Sabio" ("the Learned" or "the Wise"). In many ways the code incorporated provisions from the Visigothic Code of the seventh century (Document 2.6). The following excerpt describes the virtues of the ideal king, and may refer to Alfonso himself, especially since he was an avid patron of art, science, and education.*

(From *Medieval Iberia*, edited by Olivia Remie Constable. Philadelphia: University of Pennsylvania Press, 1997, pp. 255–258. Reprinted with permission of the University of Pennsylvania Press.)

A. A King Should Perform His Actions with a Good Demeanor

Not only should the king observe caution in the two kinds of action which relate to the interior of his body, as we have shown in the preceding laws, but he should also be careful in regard to the other two, which are exterior, and relate to daily intercourse with men. The first of what we desire to speak now, is his demeanor: for, in this the king should be very correct, while walking, as well as standing; also while sitting, and riding on horseback; as well as when he eats or drinks, and when he lies down, or even when he gives a reason for anything; and as to his gait, it should not be too rapid, nor should it be loitering. He should not stand long, except in church while hearing the service, or on account of something else which he cannot avoid. Moreover, it does not become him to remain for a long time in one position, or to change his seat frequently, sitting down in one place, and then in another. When he rises up, he should not appear very straight nor very bent, this also should be the case while he is on horseback; and he should not ride too fast through a town, or linger too long on the way.

In eating and drinking he should be careful to do so in a well-bred manner, because this is something in which men cannot readily restrain themselves, on account of their great eagerness; and, for this reason, the king should be very circumspect, in order that he may not eat and drink too fast, or, on the other hand, too slowly: and he should be careful not to sleep too much, nor, when he retires, should he lie drawn up, nor across the bed, like some do who do not know where to keep their heads or their feet. Moreover, he should take care to assume a good mien when he speaks, especially as regards his mouth, his head, and his hands, which are members that are constantly employed by men in conversation. He should also be careful rather to explain by words, than by gestures, what he desires to say. The ancient sages, who considered everything minutely, showed that kings should observe all this which we have mentioned, in order that they may act with propriety; and this is the case because they are more accustomed to it, and more noble, for it is something which is especially suitable for them, as men imitate their example in what they see them do. With regard to this, the ancient sages said of them, that they resemble a mirror, in which men view their images, whether they display elegance, or its opposite. And, for another similar reason, they should be solicitous not to act improperly in these matters which we have mentioned; and this is because it appears worse in them than it does in other men, and they will be the more readily censured on that account. Moreover, God will not fail to punish them in the next world as being persons who should be polite and noble, because of the surpassing elegance and nobleness of their master whose place they occupy; while, on the other hand, they make themselves vile, and afford an example to others to be so.

B. A King Should Dress with Great Elegance

Dress has much to do with causing men to be recognized either as noble, or servile. The ancient sages established the rule that kings should wear garments of silk, adorned with gold and jewels, in order that men might know them as soon as they saw them, without inquiring for them; and the bridles and saddles with which they ride, should be ornamented with gold, silver, and precious stones. Moreover, on grand holidays, when they assemble their Cortes, they should wear crowns of gold, richly decorated with magnificent jewels. There are two reasons for this; first, in order to indicate the splendor of Our

Lord God, whose position they occupy on earth; second, that men may recognize them, as we have stated above, so as to approach them to serve and honor them, and ask favors of them, when it is necessary. All these honorable decorations, which we have mentioned above, should be worn by them at proper times and used by them in an elegant manner; and no one else should attempt to make use of them, or wear them; and he who does this in order to compare himself with the king, and occupy his position, should lose his life and all his property; as being a person who dares to usurp the honor and place of his master, without having the right to do so. Where a king consents that anyone may do this—leaving out of consideration the great degradation he would be guilty of on account of his bad behavior in this world—God will require an account of him for it in the next; as being a vassal who did not value the honor which his lord conferred upon him, or make use of it as he should have done. Where anyone, however, through presumption or want of understanding, acts contrary to what is stated in this law, the king should inflict such punishment upon him as he thinks he deserves.

C. A King Should Be Gentle, and What Distinctions Exist Between Habits and Manners

A king should have very good habits and manners. For, although he may be well-bred in his demeanor and his dress, if his habits and manners are not good, he will display much incongruity in his actions, for the reason that he will be greatly deficient in nobility and elegance. And because men hold that habits and manners are one and the same thing, since they originate from the same source, so far as they refer to the actions of men; we desire to show that there is a distinction between them, as the ancient sages have declared. For habits are excellent qualities which man has in himself, and obtains through long practice: manners are things which man performs by his own exertions through natural knowledge. These two virtues are very becoming to a king and much more so than to another man—in order that he may know how to live properly and honorably; and also in order to govern his people well, by pointing out to them excellent examples, and showing them ways by means of which they may do good: for he cannot know God, or how to fear or love Him; or how to keep a watch upon his heart, or his words, or his actions, as we have stated above in other laws; or how to govern his people well; if his own habits and manners are not good.

D. A King Should Be Eager to Learn to Read and to Know What He Can of the Sciences

A king should be eager to learn the sciences, for, by means of them, he will understand the affairs of sovereigns and will better know how to act with regard to them. Moreover, by knowing how to read, he will be better able to keep his secrets, and be master of them, which, under other circumstances, he could not well do. For, by want of familiarity with these things, he would necessarily have to admit someone else into his confidence, in order that he might know them, and there might happen to him what King Solomon said, namely: "He who places his secret in the power of another, becomes his slave; and he who knows how to keep it, is the master of his own heart, which is very becoming to a king." And, even without this, by means of the Scriptures he will the better understand the Faith, and will know more perfectly how to pray to God. By reading, he can become acquainted with the remarkable events that

transpire, from which he will learn many good habits and examples. Not only did the wise men of the ancients deem it proper that a king should know how to read, but also that he should study all the sciences in order to be able to profit by them. On this subject King David, while giving advice to kings, said, that they should be learned and wise, since they had to judge the earth. King Solomon, his son, also said that kings should learn the sciences and should not forget them, for by means of them they would have to judge and protect their people. . . .

Questions for Discussion:

1. Section B advises the king on how he should dress. How does this advice correlate with the illumination of Otto III (Document 6.10) and the image of Saint Louis (Document 11.1)? What reasons are given for wearing such elaborate clothing?
2. According to Section C, the king is an example for his people. In this context, what specific aspects of behavior are considered to be important?
3. The king's proper education is described in Section D. How does this compare with Charlemagne's devotion to the liberal arts (Documents 4.11, 4.12, and 4.13)?
4. How would you compare Alfonso X with Louis IX (Document 11.1) in terms of kingly virtue?

11.9   *The Cantigas de Santa Maria* by Alfonso X, "The Wise"

One of Alfonso's most significant cultural accomplishments was a collection of songs, The Cantigas de Santa Maria, *which was compiled at his court and contained several songs by the king himself. Most of the songs deal with miracles performed by the Virgin Mary; the collection was an important manifestation of the cult of the Virgin Mary that was growing in popularity during the thirteenth century. Two of the lyrics are printed here.*

(From *Songs of Holy Mary of Alfonso X, the Wise*, trans. by Kathleen Kulp-Hill. Tempe, AZ, Arizona Center for Medieval and Renaissance Studies, 2000, pp. 12–14. Copyright Arizona Board of Regents for Arizona State University. Reprinted with permission.)

1. This is how Holy Mary saved the pregnant abbess who had gone to sleep weeping before Her altar.

    We should love Holy Mary and pray that She shed Her grace on us, so that the shameless devil will not cause us to err or sin.

    Concerning this, I shall tell you a miracle I found which the Mother of the Great King performed for an abbess who, as I learned, was very devoted to Her. The devil ensnared her, and she became pregnant by a man from Bologna who served her as steward.

The nuns, when they found out about this, were very gleeful. Because the abbess would not allow them to misbehave, they had ill will for her. They accused her to the bishop in charge of the place, and he came from Cologne. He had her called before him, and she came without delay, cheerful and smiling.

The bishop spoke to her thus: "Lady, according to what I have learned, you have managed your affairs very badly. I came here for this reason, that you make amends for your misdeeds before me." The lady at once prayed to the Mother of God, and as though in a dream, Holy Mary had the child removed and sent it to be reared in Soissons.

When the lady awoke and found herself delivered, she appeared before the bishop. He looked at her carefully and bade her to undress. When he saw her belly, he began to praise God and to berate the nuns of the Order of Ona, saying: "May God save me, I declare this woman innocent, for I know of none who could impugn her."

2. This is how in Rocamadour Holy Mary caused a candle to descend to the fiddle of a minstrel who sang before Her.

We who hope for the blessings of Holy Mary should all praise Her with songs and joyfulness.

Concerning this, I shall tell you a miracle performed by the Holy Virgin Mary, Mother of Our Lord, in Rocamadour, which will please you when you hear it. Listen now to the story, and we shall relate it to you.

There was a minstrel whose name was Pedro of Sieglar who could sing very well and play the fiddle even better. In all the churches of the Peerless Virgin he always sang a lay of hers, according to what I learned.

The lay which he sang before Her statue, with tears in his eyes, was about the Mother of God. Then he said: "Oh, Glorious One, if you are pleased by these songs of mine, give us a candle so that we may dine."

Holy Mary was pleased at how the minstrel sang and made a candle descend onto his fiddle. However, the monk who was treasurer snatched it out of his hand, saying: "You are an enchanter and we shall not let you have it."

But the minstrel, whose heart was dedicated to the Virgin, would not stop singing, and the candle once more came to rest on his fiddle. The irate friar snatched it away again, quicker than it takes to tell it.

When that monk had taken the candle away from the fiddle of the minstrel, he put it right back where it was before and fastened it down tight. He said: "Sir minstrel, if you take it from there, we shall consider you a sorcerer."

The minstrel paid no attention to all this, but played his fiddle as before, and the candle again came to rest on it. The monk tried to snatch it, but the people said: "We shall not permit you to do this."

When the obstinate monk saw this miracle, he realized that he had greatly erred and repented at once. He prostrated himself on the ground before the minstrel and asked his pardon in the name of Holy Mary, in whom we one and all believe.

After the Glorious Virgin performed this miracle which rewarded the minstrel and converted the unenlightened monk, each year the minstrel of whom we have spoken brought to Her church a long wax candle.

Questions for Discussion:

1. How do the two lyrics portray the clergy? Comment.
2. What is the didactic message of these songs?

11.10 The Church and the Jews in Thirteenth-Century Spain

The kings of thirteenth-century Spain ruled over a population that was religiously and culturally diverse, including substantial numbers of Muslims and Jews in addition to Christians; all three groups colonized Muslim areas in southern Spain which had been taken during the Reconquista. There were various restrictions placed upon the actions, and even the clothing of the non-Christian inhabitants. Both the Muslims and the Jews were forbidden by law to have intercourse with Christians, and it was illegal for them to own Christian slaves. The following letters from the pope to the archbishop of Compostela and the king of Navarre, provide examples of these prohibitions.

(*Letters* of Gregory IX translated by Kay Slocum.)

Letter from Gregory IX to the Archbishop of Compostela and to his suffragans

May 18, 1233

Because their own sin delivered them to perpetual servitude when they nailed Him to the cross (the one whom their prophets had predicted would come to redeem Israel), the Jews ought to recognize the misery of their circumstances, and ought to live without annoying those who accept and support them because of kindness alone. But they, ungrateful for the compassion shown to them, heinously repay kindness with insults and friendship with scorn.

For example, it has come secretly to our ears that the Jews living in Spain have become so insolent that they are not afraid to perpetrate excesses which would be not only improper, but even brutal for the faithful of Christ to bear. For although it was mandated after careful deliberation that such people of either sex should, in all the Christian provinces and at all times, be publicly distinguished from other people by the nature of their attire, nevertheless it is reported that this is not observed in Spanish areas. Because of this it is to be feared that they will wickedly associate with one another's women. And although it has been stipulated in the Council of Toledo and reconfirmed in the General Council that Jews are not to be placed in public offices, because in such a public position they are very threatening to Christians, and since it is very illogical that one

who blasphemes against Christ should wield the power of public authority over Christians, nonetheless secular authority and public offices are entrusted to them, by which they are brutal to the Christians; on occasion they force some to observe their rites. For this purpose, the previously mentioned Jews make Christian women nurses for their children and they keep both male and female Christian servants, and Christian slaves. They also extort unreasonable usury from Christians in violation of the statute of the General Council, and they perpetrate abominable and unheard of deeds against the Catholic faith. Because of this the faithful must be afraid lest they incur divine wrath when they force them to perpetrate things that bring dishonor on our faith. Therefore, so that it may be evident that these insults to his creator touch our most esteemed son in Christ, the illustrious king of Castile and Leon, we have urged him, asking and admonishing repeatedly, and adding a remission of his sins, that he should suppress and punish the aforementioned deviations of the Jews in the kingdoms of Castile and Leon, causing those Jews and Christians to remain completely separate, so that they shall not dare to straighten their necks, bent under the yoke of everlasting servitude, against the honor of the Christian faith. Therefore, we declare that you shall attempt in our name to warn and persuade the aforementioned king thus, that the treacherous Jews shall never in the future become insolent, but in servile fear they shall always suffer the disgrace of their sin publicly. But if they do not desist from this sort of presumption, you shall, each one of you in his district and diocese, restrain them through denial of intercourse with the faithful on all occasions without exception.

Given at the Lateran, on the fifteenth of the Kalends of June, in the seventh year.

Gregory IX to the King of Navarre

June 7, 1233

Even though it was mandated by the General Council, following careful deliberation, that Jews throughout the land be marked off from Christians by a distinction in their clothing, lest there be a damnable joining together of Jews and Christian women, yet we have been told that the Jews of your kingdom do not comply with this order; as a result the crime of abominable intercourse may be presumed under the veil of deception. Thus we plead and fervently warn your serene highness to compel the Jews, by the power bestowed upon you by God, and by denying to them any relations with the faithful, to wear clothing by which they may be distinguished from the Christians.

Given at the Lateran, on the seventh before the Ides of June, in the seventh year.

Questions for Discussion:

1. According to Gregory's letter to the archbishop of Compostela, why were Jews restricted from holding public office?
2. What reasons did Gregory give for the clothing restrictions pertaining to the Jews?

The Byzantine Empire

11.11 Villehardouin's *Chronicle*: The Conquest of Constantinople

Constantinople had long been considered a rich prize by western Europeans as well as groups of Arabs, Turks, Syrians, Armenians, and Kurds, all of whom assaulted the Byzantine Empire during the twelfth century. In 1201 there was a rebellion in the empire, and the Byzantine prince Alexius (eventually Emperor Alexius IV—r. 1203–1204) was deposed. He appealed to the western powers, promising to aid crusaders with money, supplies, and soldiers for their Holy War once he had regained his throne. Alexius was ultimately unable to fulfill his part of the bargain, and the crusaders, along with Venetian soldiers, attacked the city. When they had cut through the walls they set fire to many parts of the city, and most of the population, including Emperor Alexius, fled.

The emperor had become unpopular with the Byzantine citizens, who accused him of consorting with the Crusaders. He was deposed (and strangled) in January 1204 by the leader of the anti-western faction, Alexius Murtzoupholos, who became the next emperor. The following account of the sack of Constantinople is from the Chronicle *of Geoffrey de Villhardouin (c. 1150–1213), a crusader and eyewitness to the events.*

(From *Memoirs of the Crusades by Villehardouin & De Joinville*, tran slated by Frank Marzials [London: E.P. Dutton & Co., 1908], pp. 31–32, 64–65.)

Arrival at St. Stephen

All started from the port of Abydos together. Then might you have seen the Straits of St. George (as it

were) in flower with ships and galleys sailing upwards, and the beauty thereof was a great marvel to behold. Thus they sailed up the Straits of St. George till they came, on St. John the Baptist's Eve, in June [23rd June 1203] to St. Stephen, an abbey that lay three leagues from Constantinople. There had those on board the ships and galleys and transports full sight of Constantinople; and they took port and anchored their vessels.

Now you may know that those who had never before seen Constantinople looked upon it very earnestly, for they never thought there could be in all the world so rich a city; and they marked the high walls and strong towers that enclosed it round about, and the rich palaces, and mighty churches— of which there were so many that no one would have believed it who had not seen it with his eyes—and the height and the length of that city which above all others was sovereign. And be it known to you, that no man there was of such hardihood but his flesh trembled; and it was no wonder, for never was so great an enterprise undertaken by any people since the creation of the world. . . .

The Crusaders Occupy the City

The Marquis Boniface of Montferrat rode all along the shore to the palace of Bucoleon, and when he arrived there it surrendered, on condition that the lives of all therein should be spared. At Bucoleon were found the larger number of the great ladies who had fled to the castle, for there were found the sister of the King of France, who had been empress, and the sister of the King of Hungary, who had also been empress, and many other ladies. Of the treasure that was found in that palace I cannot describe well, for there was so much that it was beyond end or counting.

At the same time that this palace was surrendered to the Marquis Boniface of Montferrat, the palace of Blachernae surrendered to Henry, the brother of Count Baldwin of Flanders, on condition that no harm should be done to the bodies of those who were there. There too was found much treasure, not less than in the palace of Bucoleon. Each garrisoned with his own people the castle that had been surrendered to him, and set a guard over the treasure. And the other people, spread around throughout the city, also gained much booty. The booty gained was so great that none could tell you the end of it: gold and silver, and vessels and precious stones, and samite,[8] and cloth of silk, and robes vair[9] and grey, and ermine,

and every choicest thing found upon the earth. And well does Geoffry of Villehardouin, the Marshal of Champagne, bear witness, that never, since the world was created, had so much booty been won in any city.

Every one took quarters where he pleased, and of lodgings there was no stint. So the host of the pilgrims [Crusaders] and of the Venetians found quarters, and greatly did they rejoice and give thanks because of the victory God had vouchsafed to them—for those who before had been poor were now in wealth and luxury. Thus they celebrated Palm Sunday and the Easter Day following [25th April 1204] in the joy and honor that God had bestowed upon them. And well might they praise our Lord, since in all the host there were no more than twenty thousand armed men, one with another, and with the help of God they had conquered four hundred thousand men, or more, and in the strongest city in all the world—yea, a great city—and very well fortified.

Questions for Discussion:

1. Describe the impressions of the Crusaders as they entered Constantinople.
2. How does Villehardouin explain the victory and justify the opportunity for plunder?

---

[8]Samite was heavy silk fabric, often embroidered with gold and silver.
[9]Vair was a fur, probably squirrel, used for trim.

11.12   Nicolas Mesarites: A Byzantine Lament

The description of the plunder by the Crusaders in the writings of the theologian and chronicler Nicholas Mesarites (1163–1224) portrayed the events of the sack of Constantinople from the Byzantine point of view. The author used vivid literary imagery in his account of the desecration of the beloved Byzantine capital, which is virtually a lament for the city.

(From *Byzantium: Church, Society, and Civilization Seen through Contemporary Eyes*, by Deno John Geanakoplos. © 1984 by The University of Chicago Press. All rights reserved.)

And so the streets, squares, houses of two and three stories, sacred places, nunneries, houses for

nuns and monks, sacred churches, even the Great Church of God and the imperial palace, were filled with men of the enemy, all of them maddened by war and murderous in spirit, all clad in armor and bearing spears, swords and lances, archers and horsemen boasting terribly, barking like Cerberus[10] and exhaling like Charon,[11] as they sacked the

---

[10]In Greek mythology, Cerberus was the three-headed dog who guarded the entrance to the underworld.
[11]In Greek mythology, Charon was the ferryman who transported the souls of the dead across the River Styx.

sacred places and trampled on the divine things [and] ran riot over the holy vessels. . . . Moreover, they tore children from their mothers and mothers from their children, and they defiled the virgins in the holy chapels, fearing neither God's anger nor man's vengeance. They searched breasts of women to find out whether some womanly ornament or gold was attached or hidden in the body; hair was loosened and head-coverings removed, and those without homes or money were struck down.

Question for Discussion:

1. Compare the accounts of the sack of Constantinople by Nicholas Mesarites and Villehardouin. Are either of the authors reporting objectively?

11.13 Nicetus Choniates: *On the Statues*

The city of Constantinople contained many treasures preserved from the early Greek world, many of which had been collected by the Emperor Constantine in the fourth century. Especially precious were a number of sculptures, which the Byzantines viewed as linking them to their ancestors. In this section of his Historia, *often referred to as "On the Statues," the courtier Nicetus Choniates (c. 1150–c. 1215) describes the wanton destruction of these and other works of classical art by the Crusaders.*

(From *Byzantium: Church, Society, and Civilization Seen through Contemporary Eyes*, by Deno John Geanakoplos. © 1984 by The University of Chicago Press. All rights reserved.)

From the very beginning they [the Latins] revealed their race to be lovers of gold; they conceived of a new method of plundering, which had completely escaped the notice of all who had [just] sacked the imperial city. Having opened the graves of those emperors which were in the burial ground situated in the area of the church of Christ's Holy Apostles, they stripped all of them during the night and, if any golden ornament, pearl, or precious stone still lay inviolate in these [tombs], they sacrilegiously seized it. When they found the corpse of the Emperor Justinian, which had remained undisturbed for so many years, they marveled at it, but they did not refrain from [looting] the funeral adornments. We may say that these Westerners spared neither the living nor the dead. They manifested [toward all], beginning with God and his servants [i.e., the clergy], complete indifference and impiety: quickly enough they tore down the curtain in the Great Church [Hagia Sophia], the value of which was reckoned in millions of purest silver pieces, since it was entirely interwoven with gold.

Even now they were still desirous of money (for nothing can satiate the avarice of the barbarians). They eyed the bronze statues and threw them into the fire. And so the bronze statue of Hera, standing in the agora [marketplace] of Constantine, was broken into pieces and consigned to the flames. The head of this statue, which could hardly be drawn by four oxen yoked together, was brought to the great palace. . . .

These barbarians—who do not appreciate beauty—did not neglect to overturn the statues standing in the Hippodrome [Stadium], or any other marvelous works. Rather, these too they turned into coinage, exchanging great things [i.e., art] for small [i.e., money], thus acquiring petty coins at the expense of those things created at enormous cost.

Questions for Discussion:

1. What were the character flaws of the Crusaders, according to Choniates? How were these evident in the actions of the invaders?

2. Compare the description of the Crusaders by Choniates with the analysis of the Franks by Anna Comnena (Document 7.13). How are their perceptions similar? Do you see any significant differences?

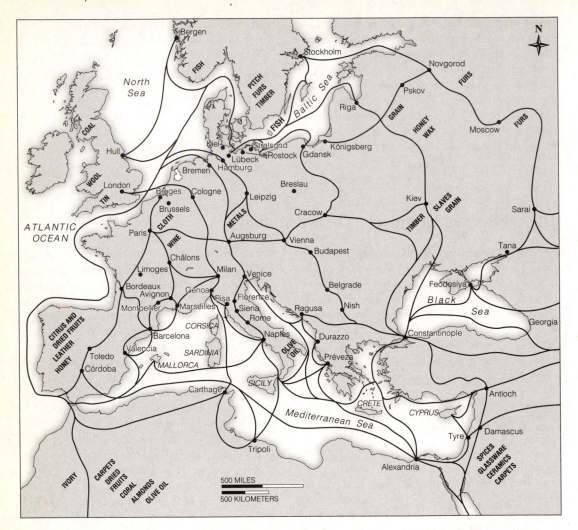

Medieval Trade Routes (From Kagan et al., *The Western Heritage*, 10th ed., p. 237)

Commerce and Trade

The Growth of Trade in Northern and Southern Europe

11.14 Lübeck and Hamburg Seek Mutual Protection (1241)

During the course of the eleventh, twelfth, and thirteenth centuries, significant trading networks developed in northern and southern Europe. As shown in the first of the

documents in this section, cities such as Lübeck and Hamburg in northern Germany enacted a mutual protection agreement (1241). Their purpose was to provide a safe atmosphere for commerce, and the success of covenants such as this soon led to the formation of the Hanseatic League.

(From *A Source Book for Mediaeval History*, ed. by Oliver J. Thatcher and Edgar H. McNeal [New York: Charles Scribner's Sons, 1905], p. 610.)

The advocate, council and commune of Lübeck . . . .

We have made the following agreement with our dear friends, the citizens of Hamburg.

1. If robbers or other depredators attack citizens of either city anywhere from the mouth of the Trave River to Hamburg, or anywhere on the Elbe River, the two cities shall bear the expenses equally in destroying and extirpating them.
2. If anyone who lives outside the city, kills, wounds, beats, or mishandles, without cause, a

citizen of either city, the two cities shall bear the expenses equally in punishing the offender. We furthermore agree to share the expenses equally in punishing those who injure their citizens in the neighborhood of their city and those who injure our citizens in the neighborhood of our city.

3. If any of their citizens are injured near our city [Lübeck], they shall ask our officials to punish the offender, and if any of our citizens are injured near their city [Hamburg], they shall ask their officials to punish the offender.

Question for Discussion:

1. What does this pact demonstrate about the conditions for trade in the thirteenth century?

11.15 The Hanseatic League (1253)

The agreement between Lübeck and Hamburg provided the pattern for the formation of merchant protective organizations, and during the thirteenth century many cities joined such alliances. In the north a coalition known as the Hanseatic League was formed; it functioned primarily in the areas of the Baltic and North seas. The cities of Münster, Dortmund, Soeast, and Lippstadt joined forces to protect their merchants, stipulating the measures set forth in the following document (1253).

(From *Readings in European History*, vol. I, ed. by James Harvey Robinson [Boston: Ginn & Co., 1904], pp. 413–415.)

In the name of the holy and indivisible Trinity, Amen. The magistrates, consuls, and the whole community of burghers and citizens in Münster, Dortmund, Soest, and Lippstadt, to all who may read this document, greeting:

We hereby make known to all men, now and in the future, that because of the manifold dangers to which we are constantly exposed, of capture, robbery, and many other injuries, we have, by common counsel and consent, decided to unite in a perpetual

confederation under the following terms, and we have mutually given and received word and oath:

First, that if any man shall take captive one of our citizens or seize his goods without just cause, we will altogether deny to him opportunity to trade in all our cities aforesaid. And if the castellan of any lord shall be the author of an injury that has been done, the afore-mentioned privileges shall be altogether withheld from the lord of that castellan, and from all his soldiers and servants, and all others dwelling with him in his castle. . . .

If any robber has taken goods from one of our citizens . . . and the injured man shall go to anyone of our [federated] cities seeking counsel and aid, in order that justice may be done upon the malefactor, the citizens of that city shall act as they would be obliged to act if executing justice for a similar crime committed against one of their own fellow-citizens.

And if any of our burgesses shall chance to go to any of our cities and fear to go forth because of peril to life and property, the burgesses of that city shall conduct him to a place whence his fellow-citizens can receive him in safety.

If a knight shall be denounced to us on reasonable grounds as a violator of faith and honor, we will denounce him in all our cities, and will by mutual consent withhold from him all privileges in our cities until he shall pay the whole debt for which he broke his word.

If anyone of us shall buy goods taken from any of our confederates by theft or robbery, . . . he shall not offer the goods at retail anywhere and shall be held guilty with the thief and robber.

Questions for Discussion:

1. What activities does this agreement attempt to curtail?
2. How do you explain the motivation for the pact?

11.16   London and the *Hansa* Negotiate

The following document illustrates the way in which the towns of the Hanseatic League negotiated with the mayor and citizens of London (1282). The subject is a dispute over the responsibility of repairing Bishopsgate, one of the central portals of the city, which had fallen into disrepair.

(From *Readings in European History*, vol 1, ed. by James Harvey Robinson [Boston: Ginn and Co., 1904], pp. 413–415.)

In the tenth year of the reign of King Edward I [r. 1272–1307], son of Henry [III], Henry de Maleys being mayor of London, a contention arose between the mayor and citizens of London and the merchants of the German Hansa, concerning the gate called Bishopsgate, which was falling into ruin. For the mayor and citizens of London claimed that the merchants of the German Hansa were bound to repair this gate in return for the liberties granted to them; but the merchants said that they were not so bound.

Then the lord king of England, at the suggestion of the aforesaid mayor and citizens, wrote to his treasurer and the barons of the treasury, and commanded them to call together the contending parties and inquire into the facts of the matter; and if they should find that the said merchants were bound to keep this gate in repair, they should compel the Germans to rebuild it.

When the two parties came before the treasurer and barons, the merchants could show no cause wherefore they should not make the repairs in question, especially since it is clearly prescribed in the liberty which they have from the aforesaid city that they should make them. Therefore the treasurer and barons did enjoin the mayor and council aforesaid that they compel the merchants to repair the gate in question.

The merchants, Gerard Merbade, alderman of the Hansa, Ludolph of Cusfeld, burgher of Cologne, Bertram, burgher of Hamburg, John of Erest, burgher of Tremoine, John of Dalen, burgher of Münster, did, for themselves and all their associates of the Hansa then dwelling in the city, promise to pay to the mayor and citizens of London for the present repairs of the gate 240 marks sterling. Further they agreed that they and their successors, merchants of the Hansa, would at all times repair the aforesaid gate whenever it should be necessary; and that when need should arise to defend the gate, they would furnish a third part of the guard, to hold it above, while the mayor and citizens furnished two thirds, to guard it below.

The mayor and citizens confirmed to the merchants . . . the liberties which they had possessed before this time, to be enjoyed by themselves and their successors forever. And, moreover, in consideration of the repairs and defense of the gate aforesaid, the citizens shall, so far as in them lies, hold their peace forever concerning the duty of watch and ward. . . .

The mayor and citizens agreed that the merchants should have their own alderman as in former times, so that the alderman be free of the city aforesaid; provided that, after his election by the merchants, he be presented to the mayor and aldermen of the city, and swear to do right and justice to every man, according to the law and custom of the city.

Questions for Discussion:

1. Why did the king become involved in the controversy?

2. What were the provisions of the agreement?
3. Which group benefited more from the contract—the Londoners or the Germans? Why?
4. Compare this account with provision 41 in the *Magna Carta* (Document 11.5) and comment on the context of the negotiation.

Italy

11.17 Trade in the Mediterranean Sea: Venice

Trade in southern Europe was more complex, as the major powers—primarily Venice, Genoa, and the Byzantine Empire—vied for control. The following documents from Venice in the late thirteenth century show that the city was determined to protect its citizens. If cartels were of benefit to Venetian merchants, the government was in favor. If the merchant societies were not in the interest of the Commune, the dignitaries were opposed.

(From *Medieval Trade in the Mediterranean World: Illustrative Documents*, trans. by Robert S. Lopez and Irving W. Raymond. New York: Columbia University Press, 1955, pp. 129–130. Copyright © 1955 Columbia University Press. Reprinted by permission of the publisher.)

[Venice, July 22, 1283]

Item, a motion was passed in the Great Council [the governing body of Venice] to the effect that the following instructions should be added to the commission of the bailiff of Ayas, or should be sent to him and be binding upon him under oath:

That in the Great Council which he shall hold at Ayas he shall move that our merchants present there shall form a *societas* for the [purchase of] cotton, buckrams,[12] and pepper. And if two thirds of that Great Council pass [the motion] regarding the formation of that *societas,* he may and shall order under such penalties as shall seem proper to him that [the merchants] form that *societas* and that nobody may purchase [the

aforesaid wares] except those [representatives of the *societas*} appointed for this purpose. And those who will go there later are to be [received] into that *societas* and have such share [of the merchandise] as is due to them pro rata after their arrival. And in regard to the formation of this *societas* it should be understood [that it applies only] to the [merchants] who have [taken along] with them 200 bezants or more.

Venice, April 28, [1358]

On April 28 [motion was] passed [in the Senate as follows]:

Whereas our [fellow citizens] frequenting Cyprus have of late engaged in the formation of rings and conspiracies (*conyenticulas et conspirationes*) in the business of transporting cotton to Venice, entering upon mutual obligations and pacts to prevent the transport of more than a certain amount [of cotton].

And whereas this is against the interest of the Commune, which loses its customs duties upon what would be imported and used to be imported beyond the said amount; and it is also against the welfare of the city because cotton needed in the West is transported to Ancona and elsewhere while it ought to be transported to Venice, and [thus the conspirators] are building up foreign countries while ruining ours; and it is also against the good of the community and of individual persons because such profit as used to be distributed among the whole community is turned over to three or four [persons].

---

[12]Buckram was a coarse cotton fabric stiffened with glue; it was used for bookbinding and stiffening clothing.

And [whereas] it is useful in view of all above considerations to provide a remedy to this [situation]:

Let a motion be put to vote that three wisemen shall be elected within the assembly of the Senate, who shall make an inquiry in regard to these rings [of dealers] in cotton as well as to [others dealing] in powdered sugar, salt, and other merchandise, and also in regard to those in shipping and to all conspiracies that may be formed in Venice, in Cyprus, and in any other place. And they shall draft provisions and give us their advice in writing. We shall meet here with this [advice at hand], and we shall act as shall seem proper, and any one [of us] shall be entitled to put a motion to vote. And [the wisemen] may be chosen from any post, but each is to accept only one office.

And the first vote is to be for the said proposal and [its individual] articles, and the second for the election [of the wisemen].

And [the wisemen] are to have as a deadline [for the completion of the inquiry] the end of the coming month of May.

Questions for Discussion:

1. What measures were proposed by the Venetians to protect their interests in the cloth and spice trades?
2. Compare the Venetian documents with those of the Hanseatic League (Documents 11.15 and 11.16). Are the objectives of the agreements similar? What differences are evident?

11.18 Padua: The State Promotes Commerce

Commercial enterprise was an important concern of the administration of the Italian communes, as may be seen in the following document from Padua. As noted in the provisions, there was concern about trading venues as well as foreign competition.

(From *The Towns of Italy in the Later Middle Ages*, translated by Trevor Dean. Manchester, UK: Manchester University Press, 2000, pp. 136–137. Reprinted by permission.)

[May 1301] This order is issued for the honor of the commune of Padua and for the splendor and embellishment of the palace of the magnificent commune of Padua. Its purposes are that the palace, in its lower part towards the north, be inhabited by merchants, and resume its reputation, which was spreading through many parts of Italy a long time ago, for these workshops were a finer place for selling cloth than in any city of Italy; furthermore, that between foreign and citizen cloth-merchants there be no discord. Therefore we establish and ordain that foreigners, whose trading in cloth and sendal[13] in the stalls described below at present seems to be beneficial in the view of the stewards of the merchants' guild of Padua, may without penalty for five years sell at retail cloths and sendals, under the said palace and not elsewhere in Padua or its suburbs. This period may be extended if this satisfies a majority of the Paduan-born citizen merchants who have shops under the main palace of the commune towards the north . . . And if at the end of five years the majority of traders born in the city of Padua who then have stalls under the main palace on the north side wish that the foreigners . . . leave those stalls . . . then they must leave them within fifteen days of being notified by the stewards of the merchants' guild . . . and must fully empty and vacate the stalls . . . and no longer there or in any other place in the city or suburbs of Padua sell cloth or sendal, themselves or through another person. . . .

And that henceforth no person or college or community may sell . . . at retail cloth or sendal in the city of Padua or the suburbs, except under the main palace in the stalls placed towards the north and south, and in the stalls under the communal chancery, and under the palace of the Greater Council, where it is customary for cloth to be sold. Saving only that citizens of Padua may in the said stalls . . . sell all cloth except French and Florentine and sendal. . . .

---

[13]Sendal was light, thin silk cloth.

Questions for Discussion:

1. Why do you think the sale of cloth is confined to such a restricted area?
2. Notice the reference to the opinion of the merchants' guild and compare this clause to the guild regulations in Document 10.2. Although this excerpt refers to a merchant guild rather than a craft guild, do you see similarities?
3. Do you think the regulations concerning foreign merchants are fair? How might these rules benefit the commune of Padua?

The Mongol Threat

11.19   *The History of the World-Conqueror* by Juvaini

During the thirteenth century another powerful empire emerged in Central Asia, known as the Tatar or Tartar Empire. It was the result of the actions of one man, Genghis (also spelled Jenghis or Chingiz) Khan (1167–1227), who united the nomadic tribes of Central Asia into a ferocious fighting force. The Mongols were able to conquer China, breaking through the Great Wall, and forcing the Chinese population to submit to their rule. The forces then turned toward Russia, subduing everything in their path with their superior military tactics and almost sadistic terror measures. The biography of Genghis Kahn, The History of the World-Conqueror, *written by the thirteenth-century Persian historian Ata-Malik Juvaini, contains much information about the methods used to subjugate vast areas. His semi-chronological account was based on research, observation, and participation.*

(Reprinted by permission of the publisher from Ata-Malik Juvaini's *The History of the World Conqueror,* translated by Andrew Boyle, pp. 95–107, Cambridge, Mass.: Harvard University Press. Copyright © 1958 by Manchester University Press.)

A Short Account of the Conquest of Transoxiana

Chingiz-Khan came to these countries in person. The tide of calamity was surging up from the Tartar army, but he had not yet soothed his breast with vengeance nor caused a river of blood to flow, as had been inscribed by the pen of Destiny in the roll of Fate. When, therefore, he took Bokhara and Samarqand, he contented himself with slaughtering and looting once only, and did not go to the extreme of a general massacre. As for the adjoining territories that were subject to these towns or bordered on them, since for the most part they tendered submission, the hand of molestation was to some extent withheld from them. And afterwards, the Mongols pacified the survivors and proceeded with work of reconstruction, so that at the present time [i.e. in 658/1259–60], the prosperity and well-being of these districts have in some cases attained their original level and in others have closely approached it. It is otherwise with Khorasan and Iraq, which countries are afflicted with a hectic fever and a chronic ague: every town and every village has been several times subjected to pillage and massacre and has suffered this confusion for years, so that even though there be generation and increase until the Resurrection the population will not attain to a tenth part of what it was before. The history thereof may be ascertained from the records of ruins and midden-heaps declaring how Fate has painted her deeds upon palace walls.

Of the Capture of Bokhara

And from thence Chingiz-Khan proceeded to Bokhara, and in the beginning of Muharram, 617 [March, 1220], he encamped before the gates of the citadel.

And then they pitched the king's pavilion on the plain in front of the stronghold.

And his troops were more numerous than ants or lo-custs, being in their multitude beyond estimation or computation. Detachment after detachment ar-rived, each like a billowing sea, and encamped round about the town. At sunrise twenty thousand men from the Sultan's auxiliary (biruni) army issued forth from the citadel together with most of the in-habitants; being commanded by Kok-Khan and other officers such as Khamid-Bur, Sevinch-Khan and Keshli-Khan. Kok-Khan was said to be a Mon-gol and to have fled from Chingiz-Khan and joined the Sultan (the proof of which statements must rest with their author); as a consequence of which his affairs had greatly prospered. When these forces reached the banks of the Oxus [River], the patrols and ad-vance parties of the Mongol army fell upon them and left no trace of them.

When it is impossible to flee from destruction in any man-ner, then patience is the best and wisest course.

On the following day when from the reflection of the sun the plain seemed to be a tray filled with blood, the people of Bokhara opened their gates and closed the door of strife and battle. The imams and notables came on a deputation to Chingiz-Khan, who entered to inspect the town and the citadel. He rode into the Friday mosque and pulled up before the maqsura, whereupon his son Toli dismounted and ascended the pulpit. Chingiz-Khan asked those present whether this was the palace of the Sultan; they replied that it was the house of God. Then he too got down from his horse, and mounting two or three steps of the pulpit he exclaimed: 'The countryside is empty of fodder; fill our horses' bellies.' Whereupon they opened all the magazines in the town and be-gan carrying off the grain. And they brought the cases in which the Korans were kept out into the courtyard of the mosque, where they cast the Korans right and left and turned the cases into mangers for their horses. After which they circulated cups of wine and sent for the singing-girls of the town to sing and dance for them; while the Mongols raised their voices to the tunes of their own songs. Mean-while, the imams, shaikhs, sayyids, doctors and schol-ars of the age kept watch over their horses in the stable under the supervision of the equerries, and executed their commands. After an hour or two Chingiz-Khan arose to return to his camp, and as the multitude that had been gathered there moved away the leaves of the Koran were trampled in the dirt beneath their own feet and their horses' hoofs. In that moment, the Emir Imam Jalal-ad-Din 'Ali b. al-Hasan Zaidi, who was the chief and leader of the sayyids of Transoxiana and was famous for his piety and asceticism, turned to the learned imam Rukn-ad-Din Imarnzada, who was one of the most excellent savants in the world—may God render pleasant the resting-places of them both—and said: 'Maulana, what state is this?

That which I see do I see it in wakefulness or in sleep, O Lord?'

Maulana Imamzada answered: 'Be silent: it is the wind of God's omnipotence that bloweth, and we have no power to speak.'

When Chingiz-Khan left the town he went to the festival musalla[14] and mounted the pulpit; and, the people having been assembled, he asked which were the wealthy amongst them. Two hundred and eighty persons were designated (a hundred and ninety of them being natives of the town and the rest strangers, viz. ninety merchants from various places) and were led before him. He then began a speech, in which, after describing the resistance and treachery of the Sultan (of which more than enough has been said already) he addressed them as follows: 'O peo-ple, know that you have committed great sins, and that the great ones among you have committed these sins. If you ask me what proof I have for these words, I say it is because I am the punishment of God. If you had not committed great sins, God would not have sent a punishment like me upon you.' When he had finished speaking in this strain, he continued his discourse with words of admonition, saying, 'There is no need to declare your property that is on the face of the earth; tell me of that which is in the belly of the earth.' Then he asked them who were their men of authority; and each man indicated his own people. To each of them he assigned a Mongol or Turk as

---

[14]A musalla is a temporary sacred place where worshippers congregate for prayer.

basqaq[15] in order that the soldiers might not molest them, and, although not subjecting them to disgrace or humiliation, they began to exact money from these men; and when they delivered it up they did not torment them by excessive punishment or demanding what was beyond their power to pay. And every day, at the rising of the greater luminary, the guards would bring a party of notables to the audience-hall of the World-Emperor.

Chingiz-Khan had given orders for the Sultan's troops to be driven out of the interior of the town and the citadel. As it was impossible to accomplish this purpose by employing the townspeople and as these troops, being in fear of their lives, were fighting, and doing battle, and making night attacks as much as was possible, he now gave orders for all the quarters of the town to be set on fire; and since the houses were built entirely of wood, within several days the greater part of the town had been consumed, with the exception of the Friday mosque and some of the palaces, which were built with baked bricks. Then the people of Bokhara were driven against the citadel. And on either side the furnace of battle was heated. On the outside, mangonels [catapults] were erected, bows bent and stones and arrows discharged; and on the inside, ballistas [catapults in the form of crossbows] and pots of naphtha were set in motion. It was like a red-hot furnace fed from without by hard sticks thrust into the recesses, while from the belly of the furnace sparks shoot into the air. For days they fought in this manner; the garrison made sallies against the besiegers, and Kok-Khan in particular, who in bravery would have borne the palm from male lions, engaged in many battles: in each attack he overthrew several persons and alone repelled a great army. But finally they were reduced to the last extremity; resistance was no longer in their power; and they stood excused before God and man. The moat had been filled with animate and inanimate and raised up with levies and Bokharians; the outworks (*fasil*) had been captured and fire

hurled into the citadel; and their khans, leaders and notables, who were the chief men of the age and the favorites of the Sultan and who in their glory would set their feet on the head of Heaven, now became the captives of abasement and were drowned in the sea of annihilation.

Fate playeth with mankind the game of the sticks with the ball,
Or the game of the wind blowing (know thou!) a handful of millet.
Fate is a hunter, and man is naught but a lark.

Of the Qanqli no male was spared who stood higher than the butt of a whip and more than thirty thousand were counted amongst the slain; whilst their small children, the children of their nobles and their womenfolk, slender as the cypress, were reduced to slavery.

When the town and the citadel had been purged of rebels and the walls and outworks leveled with the dust, all the inhabitants of the town, men and women, ugly and beautiful, were driven out on to the field of the *musalla*. Chingiz-Khan spared their lives; but the youths and full-grown men that were fit for such service were pressed into a levy (*bashar*) for the attack on Samarqand and Dabusiya. Chingiz-Khan then proceeded against Samarqand; and the people of Bokhara, because of the desolation, were scattered like the constellation of the Bear and departed into the villages, while the site of the town became like '*a level plain.*'

Questions for Discussion:

1. Analyze the writing style of Juvaini. How does it compare to the works of twenty-first-century historians?
2. Discuss Genghis Kahn's characterization of himself as "God's punishment."

---

[15]A basqaq was an official in charge of taxes and administration.

Chapter 12

Religious Ferment and Social Change

Europen life was dramatically altered during the twelfth through fourteenth centuries, as urban growth and development created a new lifestyle that differed significantly from the predominately rural pattern of earlier medieval experience. The spiritual landscape was changing, and all levels of society were affected. In particular, the established Church was unable or unwilling to deal with the problems of the urban poor, and new religious movements emerged that attempted to address their needs. The earliest of these, known as the Waldensians and the Cathars, were regarded as heresies, and were severely punished by the ecclesiastical authorities, who hoped to eradicate those who criticized their practices and morals. The selections in this chapter describe the emergence and mission of the Waldensians (Documents 12.1 and 12.2), and provide details concerning the beliefs and practices of the Cathars, or Albigensians, as given by Eckbert, Abbot of Schönau (Document 12.3). The response of the Church eventually led to sporadic, localized inquisitions; a letter from Pope Gregory IX (r. 1227–1241) describes the difficulty of dealing with the increasing number of heretics (Document 12.4). An excerpt from the Inquisitor's Guide of Bernard Gui shows the technique of questioning employed by the ecclesiastical representatives in attempting to control the Albigensian heresy (Document 12.5).

Ultimately the Church came to recognize the importance of the new approach to human experience exemplified by the Waldensians, and the pope granted the foundation of two new religious orders with similar teachings, the Franciscans and the Dominicans. Saint Francis was the founder of the first of these; his spiritual experience and avowed mission were similar to those of Peter Waldo, several decades earlier. Like Waldo, his principles were based upon a return to the apostolic life; the Rule he established for his followers stipulated a life of poverty and required them to subsist through the collecting of alms; in other words, they were mendicants. As we shall see, his doctrine came to be accepted by the Church, which was less threatened because of his conformity to ecclesiastical dictates (Document 12.6).

The teachings of Saint Francis held great appeal to women as well as men. One of the women with whom he came into contact was Clare of Assisi, who determined to create a Rule for women based on the tenets of the Franciscans. Her statute provides for a similar mission, although women were not allowed to live by begging (Document 12.7).

The Dominican order (The Order of Preachers) was begun by Saint Dominic, a Spanish nobleman whose early mission was to preach to the Cathars. The order gradually became allied with the Holy See, and was often called "The Watchdog of the Papacy" because of the order's activities undertaken to control heresy. Document 12.8 contains a portion of the Dominican Constitutions. Dominic was committed to the continual practice of personal devotion, as may be seen in the excerpt from his "Nine Ways of Prayer," which indicates that he approached a mystical state during his reverential worship (Document 12.9).

Another aspect of religious and spiritual change was evident as groups of laymen and laywomen established communities devoted to the pursuit of the apostolic life; they were less threatening to the established Church. Most of these people lived in the Germany and the Low Countries. The communities of women, known as Beguines, are represented in this chapter by a description of the Beguinage at Ghent (Document 12.10), and the ecstatic visions of one of their members in Germany, Mechthild of Magdeburg (Document 12.11). Both men and women participated in a movement known as the Devotio Moderna. The mission and goals of these people will be studied in the work of the founder, Gerard Groote (Document 12.12), and a female member of the movement, Salome Stricken (Document 12.13).

The mystical tradition that had begun centuries before continued to grow in the thirteenth and fourteenth centuries. In the late Middle Ages, the visionary experience was centered on a personal relationship with a humanized Christ, and the desire for an emotionally heightened devotional practice led to the popular Cult of the Virgin Mary. Many individuals claimed to experience visions of direct contact with God, Christ, and the virgin, which they recounted in autobiographical writings. Included in this chapter is an excerpt from the work of the fourteenth-century English mystic, Margery Kempe, which demonstrates the intense emotional focus of mystical devotion (Document 12.14).

In 1215 Pope Innocent III summoned prelates from all over Europe to the Fourth Lateran Council. In addition to confirming vital aspects of the reform of the Church begun in the previous century, the assembly dealt with issues concerning heresy (Document 12.15) and promulgated rules that restricted the Jews (Document 12.16). These included measures that were designed to prevent untoward social and legal interactions with Christians. The Provisions of the Council are reflected in a sculpture of Blind Synagoga, as may be observed in Document 12.16. This artwork may be viewed within the context of widespread anti-Semitism that had developed in Europe following the First Crusade.

New Directions in Spirituality: Waldensians and Cathars

12.1   Peter Waldo: From an Anonymous Chronicle (c. 1218)

Peter Waldo (c. 1140–1217), a man who had become wealthy by lending money, underwent a spiritual conversion when hearing the legend of St. Alexis, the son of a prosperous Roman who gave away his possessions and lived by begging and seeking alms. Waldo, desiring to emulate the saint by returning to the apostolic way of life, divested himself of his property and adopted a mendicant lifestyle. He did not join a monastic order, since he was committed to the idea that the Christian gospel could and should be preached by laymen and laywomen.

Waldo became the leader of a group of like-minded people who were known as "The Poor of Lyons." They often gathered to pray, read the Bible, and recite psalms, developing their own devotional tradition. The Church viewed them as unsophisticated and illiterate, and ecclesiastical dignitaries were offended by their teachings. In 1181 their preaching was forbidden by the pope because they did not have a canonical mission. Since Waldo and his followers viewed the Church and sacraments as totally unnecessary, the reaction of the church authorities is not surprising.

(From *Readings in European History*, vol. 1, by James Harvey Robinson [Boston: Ginn & Co., 1904], pp. 380–381.)

And during the same year, that is the 1173rd since Lord's Incarnation, there was at Lyons in France a certain citizen, Waldo by name, who had made himself much money by wicked usury. One Sunday, when he had joined a crowd which he saw gathered around a troubadour, he was smitten by his words and, taking him to his house, he took care to hear him at length. The passage he was reciting was how the holy Alexis died a blessed death in his father's house. When morning had come the prudent citizen hurried to the schools of theology to seek counsel for his soul, and when he was taught many ways of going to God, he asked the master what way was more certain and more perfect than all others. The master answered him with this text: "If thou wilt be perfect, go and sell all that thou hast," etc.

Then Waldo went to his wife and gave her the choice of keeping his personal property or his real estate, namely, what he had in ponds, groves and fields, houses, rents, vineyards, mills, and fishing rights. She was much displeased at having to make this choice, but she kept the real estate. From his personal property he made restitution to those whom he had treated unjustly; a large part of it he gave to his two little daughters, who, without their mother's knowledge, he placed in the convent of Font Evrard; but the greatest part of his money he spent for the poor. A very great famine was then oppressing France and Germany. The prudent citizen, Waldo, gave bread, with vegetables and meat to everyone who came to him for three days in every week from Pentecost to the feast of St. Peter's bonds.

At the [feast of the] Assumption of the blessed Virgin, casting some money among the village poor, he cried, "No man can serve two masters, God and mammon." Then his fellow-citizens ran up, thinking he had lost his mind. But going on to a higher place, he said: "My fellow-citizens and friends, I am not insane, as you think, but I am avenging myself on my enemies, who made me a slave, so that I was always more careful of money than of God, and served the creature rather than the Creator. I know that many will blame me that I act thus openly. But I do it both on my own account and on yours; on my own, so that those who see me henceforth possessing any money may say that I am mad, and on yours, that you may learn to place hope in God and not in riches."

On the next day, coming from the church, he asked a certain citizen, once his comrade, to give him something to eat, for God's sake. His friend, leading him to his house, said, "I will give you whatever you need as long as I live." When this came to the ears of his wife, she was quite troubled, and as though she had lost her mind, she ran to the archbishop of the city and implored him not to let her husband beg bread from anyone but her. This moved all present to tears.

[Waldo was accordingly conducted into the presence of the bishop.] And the woman, seizing her husband by the coat said, "Is it not better, husband, that I should redeem my sins by giving you alms than that strangers should do so?" And from that time he was not allowed to take food from anyone in that city except from his wife.

Questions for Discussion:

1. How did Peter Waldo affirm his belief in a return to the apostolic life?

2. What was his justification for changing his life circumstances?

3. Compare Peter Waldo's mission with that of Saint Bernard (Document 7.2). How are they similar? What differences may be observed between the two?

4. How does Waldo's movement differ from the general monastic reform movement of the tenth and eleventh centuries? Are there similarities of motivation?

12.2 Walter Map: On the Waldensians (1179)

The ministry of Peter Waldo and his followers, known as the Waldensians, was focused on the concept of returning to the apostolic life, and they were intent on preaching their beliefs publicly. In the following excerpt their mission and activities are described by Walter Map (1140–1210), a court dignitary appointed by King Henry II to represent him at the Third Lateran Council (1179), where he debated with the Waldensians concerning their activities.

(From *Heresy and Authority in Medieval Europe,* edited by Edward Peters, Philadelphia: University of Pennsylvania Press, 1980, pp. 144–146. Reprinted with permission of the University of Pennsylvania Press.)

I saw in the council at Rome under the celebrated Alexander, third pope of the name, Waldenses, illiterate laymen, called from their founder Waldes (Waldo), a citizen of Lyons on the Rhone. These men presented to His Holiness a book written in the French tongue, containing the text and gloss of the Psalter and of many books of both Old and New Testaments. They beseeched him with great insistence to confirm the license of their preaching, because they thought that they were experts, although they were mere dabblers. For it usually happened that birds which do not see the subtle snares or nets believe that there is free passage everywhere. Do not those persons who are occupied all their days with sophistries—men who can ensnare and yet can hardly be snared, and who are ever delvers in the deep abyss—do not those men, in fear of disfavor, profess with reverence to bring forth all things from God, whose dignity is so lofty that no praises or no merits of preaching can attain to that height, unless sovereign mercy has borne them aloft? On every dot of the divine page, noble thoughts are wafted on so many wings, and such wealth of wisdom is amassed that he alone to whom God hath given something [to draw with] may drink from the full [well]. Shall, therefore, in any way pearls be cast before swine, and the word given to laymen who, as we know, receive it foolishly, to say nothing of their giving what they have received? No more of this, and let it be rooted out! "Let the precious ointment run down from the head upon the beard and thence upon the clothing"; "let clean waters be drawn from the fountain, not muddy from the marketplace." I, the least of the many thousand who were called to the council, derided them, because their petition produced so much arguing and hesitation, and when I was summoned by a certain great bishop, to whom that mightiest of popes had entrusted the charge of confessions, I sat down, "a mark for their arrows." After many masters of the law and men of learning had been admitted, two Waldenses who seemed the chief of their sect were brought before me, eager to argue with me about the faith, not for the love of seeking the truth, but because, by convicting me of error, they might stop my mouth as of "one speaking lies." I sat full of fear—I confess—lest under pressure of my sins the power of speech in so great a council should be denied me. The bishop ordered me, as I was preparing to reply, to try my eloquence against them. At the outset I suggested the easiest questions, which anybody should be able to answer, for I knew that when an ass is eating thistles, its lips disdain lettuce: "Do you believe in God the Father?" They answered, "We believe." "And in the Son?" They replied, "We believe." "And in the Holy Spirit?" Their reply still was, "We believe." I kept on, "In the Mother of Christ?" And they again, "We believe." Amid the derisive shouts of all, they withdrew with anxiety, which was richly deserved, because they were ruled by none, and sought to be made rulers, like Phaethon[1] who "did not know the names of his horses."

These have nowhere a fixed abode, but wander about by two and two, barefooted, clad in sheepskins, possessing nothing, "having all things in common" like the apostles, naked following the naked Christ. Now their beginnings are lowly because they can find no entrance anywhere, for, should we let them in, we should be driven out. Let him who does not believe hear what has already been said of like sort. In these times of ours which we condemn and deride, there are doubtless those who wish to keep faith, and should they be put to the test, they would, as in times gone by, lay down their lives for their shepherd, Lord Jesus, but because we have been led astray or lured away by a strange sort of zeal, our times have grown as base as though of iron. Ancient days pleased as though they shone with gold.

Questions for Discussion:

1. What do you regard as the primary complaint the ecclesiastical authorities presented against the Waldensians?
2. Why were the Waldensians such a threat to the Church?
3. The Waldensians presented the pope with several books of scripture translated into French. How do you suppose this gift was received?

12.3   The Cathar Movement According to Eckbert, Abbot of Schönau

Another lay religious movement was the Cathar, or Albigensian, heresy, which developed primarily in the cities of southern France, especially among the skilled craftsmen. Much the same as the Manicheans of the third century, Cathars were dualists, meaning that they believed there were two sources of divine power in the universe, one good and the other evil. According to their teachings, all physical matter was the product of the Evil God, whereas the God of Good was the source of light, spirit, and Christ. They believed that the established Church was a product of evil, and that it was a false church. As may be seen in the following letter from the Abbot of Schönau to the rector of Cologne Cathedral, the Cathars had entered Germany, offering a potent threat to religious orthodoxy.

(From *Facts and Documents Illustrative of the History, Doctrine, and Rites, of the Ancient Albigenses & Waldenses*, trans. by S. R. Maitland [London: C.J.G. and F. Rivington, 1832], pp. 350–359. Translation modernized.)

From Eckbert, Abbot of Schönau to Reginald, rector of Cologne Cathedral (1160).

It often happens in your Diocese, that certain heretics are apprehended of those who are most notorious for their errors in these days. These are those who are most commonly called Cathari; a race most pernicious to the Catholic faith, which, going about with great subtlety, they destroy like moths. They are furnished with words of Holy Scripture which seem in a certain way to countenance their sect, and by means of these they know how to defend their own errors, and abuse the Catholic faith. They are extremely ignorant, however, of the right sense which is contained in the words, and which ought not to be

---

[1]Phaethon was a character in Greek mythology who insisted on driving his father's chariot of the sun, even though he lacked experience. The chariot veered out of control and set the earth on fire, infuriating Zeus, who stopped him by throwing a thunderbolt.

interpreted without great discretion. I have therefore thought it worthwhile to describe their errors, and to set down the authorities of Scripture by which they defend themselves, and to show their real meaning. At the same time, I will state those parts of our faith which they oppose, and by the help of God show by what authorities of Scripture, and by what arguments, they may be defended. I do this so that those who read these things, and take pains to remember them, may be somewhat better prepared to dispute with these persons, if, as frequently happens, they shall be detected among the people. For they are very talkative, and are always prepared with what they have to say against us, and it is no small disgrace to us who are learned, that we should be mute and have nothing to say in reply to them. . . . For, behold, many persons affecting concealment, seduced and seducers, who for a long time have been hidden, and have secretly corrupted the Christian faith in many persons of foolish simplicity, are so multiplied in all lands, that the church of God suffers great danger from the most wicked poison which they pour forth against her on every side. For their discourse eats as does a canker, and flies far and wide, like an infectious leprosy, contaminating the precious members of Christ. These are called with us in Germany *Cathari,* in Flanders *Piphles,* in France *Texerant,* because they are weavers. As our Lord predicted concerning them, they say that Christ is in the secret chambers; because they say that the true faith of Christ, and true worship of Christ, exist no where except in their conventicles [secret meetings], which they hold in cellars, in workshops, and such like under-ground places. They say that they lead the life of the Apostles, but they are contrary to the holy faith, and sound doctrine, which has been delivered to us by the holy Apostles, and by the Lord the Savior himself. For they are the persons of whom St. Paul thus speaks, in his Epistle to Timothy, 'Now the Spirit speaketh expressly, that in the latter times some shall depart from the faith, giving heed to seducing spirits, and doctrines of devils, speaking lies in hypocrisy, having their conscience seared with a hot iron, forbidding to marry, and commanding to abstain from meats, which God hath created to be received with thanksgiving.' And truly these [Cathars] are the ones to whom this discourse refers, since they reprobate and condemn marriage, so

that they assign to those who remain until death in a state of marriage, nothing less than eternal damnation. Some of them, indeed, say that they approve of the marriage of those who are both virgins; but they say that even these cannot be saved unless they are separated before death, and by this also they forbid such marriage. They who have become *perfect* members of the sect avoid all flesh; not abstaining from the same reason as monks, and other persons living a religious life do, but they say that the eating of flesh is to be avoided on account of the means by which it is produced, and on account of which they consider it unclean; and this is the reason which they publicly give: but in secret they say what is worse—namely, that all flesh is made by the devil, and therefore they never taste it even in the greatest extremities. Concerning baptism they speak variously. They say that baptism profits nothing to children who are baptized, for they cannot seek baptism by themselves, because they can make no profession of faith. There is also another thing which they say more generally but more privately—namely, that no water baptism is profitable to salvation; for which reason they rebaptize those who enter their sect, in a certain secret manner of their own; which baptism they say is done in the Holy Ghost and fire.

Concerning the souls of the dead they hold, that at the time of their death they pass either to everlasting blessedness, or to eternal damnation, for they do not receive what the universal Church believes—namely that there are certain purgatorial punishments, in which the souls of some of the elect are for a time tried for their sins, from which they are not fully purified in this life by due satisfaction. On this account therefore they think it vain, and superfluous, to pray for the dead, to give alms, to say masses—and they ridicule the tolling of bells which we make, which is nevertheless done by our Church from pious motives, namely that the living may be admonished to pray for the dead, and be led to consider their own mortality.

They altogether despise, and consider as of no value, the masses which are celebrated in the Churches; for if it happens that they go with the rest of their neighbors to hear masses, or even to receive the eucharist, they do this in mere dissimulation lest their infidelity should be discovered. For they say that the order of the Priesthood is altogether lost in the Church of Rome, and in all the Churches of the Catholic faith, and the true Priests are not to be found except in their Sect. They believe that the body and blood of Christ can be by no means made by our consecration, or received by us in our communion; but they say that they alone make the body of Christ at their tables; but in those words there is this deceit—for they do not mean that true body of Christ which we believe to have been born of the Virgin, and to have suffered on the cross, but they call their own flesh the body of the Lord; and forasmuch as they nourish their bodies by the food on their tables, they say that they make the body of the Lord.

Nor will I pass over what I heard from a certain faithful man, who, having discovered their infidelity, and some secret wickednesses, left their Society; for he affirmed that they so erred respecting the Lord the Savior as to say, that he was not truly born of the Virgin, nor had true human flesh, but only an appearance of flesh, and that he did not rise from the dead, but only pretended his death and resurrection. On which account, if they are among Christians who are celebrating Easter, they either conform in a negligent manner, or they seek occasions of being absent from their own home, lest they should be compelled to keep the feast with their neighbors. Instead of this however they celebrate another festival, in which their Heresiarch Manichaeus[2] was slain, whose heresy without doubt they follow which St. Augustine, writing against the Manichaeans says was called *Beina.* My informant, however, says that among those with whom he was connected, it was called *Malilosa,* and was celebrated in the autumn.

Beside these things, we have discovered a new, and hitherto unheard of, madness of theirs, which some of them when they were examined by the clergy in the city of Cologne (where by the people full of fervent zeal they were burned) openly confessed—for they said that human souls were no other than those apostate spirits who in the beginning of the world were cast out of the Kingdom of Heaven, and that they might obtain salvation in human bodies, by means of good works; but this only among those who belonged to their sect.

"Such things as these they have for a long while privately whispered, going about everywhere to the houses of such persons as were liable to be seduced; and we have heard that these most wicked whisperers do in these times lead captive many unhappy souls in their bonds. They compass, if I may so speak, sea and land that they may make one Catharus, and defame every other mode of religion by impious detraction, and affirm that no one can be saved unless he joins their sect. It is therefore necessary that all who have zeal for God and their senses exercised by the holy scriptures should watch with all diligence in order to take these most wicked little foxes which destroy the vineyard. Their errors indeed are so many that no one can number them; but I have distinguished and set in order those which appeared to me the most dangerous, because I intend by God's help to write against them in particular.

I am not ignorant however that you hold as great a heresy concerning the baptism of adults as that which has now been discussed concerning infant-baptism; for you say, that a man is indeed to be baptized when he comes to years of discretion, not however in water, but in fire; and that the baptism of water is of no use to any body. You defend this error by the words which John spoke with reference to the Lord the Savior; 'He shall baptize you in the Holy Ghost and fire.' Hence it is that those whom you receive into your Catharist Society (as I have heard from one who had been initiated into your mysteries) you re-baptize in the following manner—assembling yourselves in some obscure chamber, your first care is, lest there should be any window, or door, through which those who are without might see or hear what is going on within. Since it is written he that does evil hates the light, lamps are placed in great numbers in all the walls. The company stand arranged in a circle, with great reverence, for they are engaged in a holy service, though certainly one more pleasing to the devil than to God. The unhappy person who is to be baptized, or Catharized, is placed in the middle, and the Archicatharus [leader] stands by him, holding in his hand a book appointed for this purpose. Placing it upon his head, he utters benedictions (which might more

---

[2]Manichaeus was a third-century philosopher whose works were based on the concept of dualism (a god of good and a god of evil). His teachings were explored by Augustine prior to his conversion to Christianity (see Document 1.10).

properly be called maledictions) while the rest of the company pray; and they make a child of hell, and not of the kingdom of God, and thus this baptism is performed. It is said moreover to be made in fire, on account of the fire of the lights which burn all around.

Questions for Discussion:

1. According to the abbot, what were the central beliefs of the Cathars?

2. Compare the Cathars with the Waldensians. Do they have similar practices? What are the differences you can ascertain from a study of the documents?

3. Although there is no direct correlation between the beliefs and practices of the Waldensians, the Cathars, and the Anabaptists of the Reformation Era, there are some similarities. Discuss these.

12.4 Pope Gregory IX: *Vox in Rama*

The decretal letter Vox in Rama *was written by Pope Gregory (1227–41) to the archbishop of Mainz, the bishop of Hildesheim, and to Conrad of Marburg, a priest whom the archbishop had instructed to find heretics in his diocese. The beginning of the letter describes the difficulties faced by the Church in dealing with the growing number of heretics. It is evident that the pope had been influenced by various accounts of heretical practices, and that he equated heresy with the use of black magic.*

(From *Witchcraft in Europe, 400–1700: A Documentary History*, edited by Alan Charles Kors and Edward Peters, 2001, pp. 114–116. Reprinted with permission of the University of Pennsylvania Press.)

THE FOLLOWING RITES of this pestilence are carried out: when any novice is to be received among them and enters the sect of the damned for the first time, the shape of a certain frog appears to him, which some are accustomed to call a toad. Some kiss this creature on the hind-quarters and some on the mouth; they receive the tongue and saliva of the beast inside their mouths. Sometimes it appears unduly large, and sometimes equivalent to a goose or a duck, and sometimes it even assumes the size of an oven. At length, when the novice has come forward, he is met by a man of marvelous pallor, who has very black eyes and is so emaciated and thin that, since his flesh has been wasted, seems to have remaining only skin drawn over the bone. The novice kisses him and feels cold, like ice, and after the kiss the memory of the catholic faith totally disappears from

his heart. Afterwards they sit down to a meal and when they have arisen from it, from a certain statue, which is usual in a sect of this kind, a black cat about the size of an average dog, descends backwards, with its tail erect. First the novice, next the master, then each one of the order who are worthy and perfect, kiss the cat on its hindquarters; the imperfect, who do not estimate themselves worthy, receive grace from the master. Then each returns to his place and, speaking certain responses, they incline their heads toward the cat. "Forgive us," says the master, and the one next to him repeats this, a third responding and saying, "We know master"; a fourth says, "And we must obey."

When this has been done, they put out the candles, and turn to the practice of the most disgusting lechery, making no distinction between those who are strangers and those who are kin. Moreover, if by chance those of the male sex exceed the number of women, surrendering to their ignominious passions, burning mutually in their desires, men engage in depravity with men. Similarly, women change their natural function, which is against nature, making this itself worthy of blame among themselves. When these most abominable sins have been completed, and the candles have been lit again and each has resumed his place, from a dark corner of the assembly, which is not lacking in the most damned of men, a certain man emerges, from the loins upward gleaming more brightly than the sun, so they say, whose lower part is shaggy like a cat and whose light illuminates the whole place. Then the master, picking out something from the clothing of the novice, says to the shining figure, "This which has been given to me, I give to you," and the shining figure replies, "You have served me well and will serve more and better. I commit what you have given into your custody," and having said that at once disappears. They even receive the body of the Lord every year at Easter from the hand of a priest, and carrying it in their mouths to their homes, they throw it into the latrine in contempt of the savior.

Furthermore, these most unhappy of wretches, blaspheming the Lord in Heaven with polluted lips, assert in their madness that the Lord violently and deceitfully against justice threw Lucifer down into the lower world. These wretches also believe in him

and affirm that he is the creator of heaven, and will return there in his glory when the Lord has fallen, through which with him and not before him they hope that they will have eternal happiness. They acknowledge all acts which are not pleasing to the Lord, and instead do what he hates.

Questions for Discussion:

1. Why do you think the pope equated heresy with the practices of so-called black magic?
2. How does this description of heresy correlate with the account of Cathar practices in the letter of the Abbot of Schönau (Document 12.3)?

12.5   Albigensians: From the *Inquisitor's Guide* of Bernard Gui

By the early thirteenth century, the Cathar, or Albigensian, heresy had spread throughout southern France and into Germany and Christian Spain, as the previous letters indicate. After his legate, Peter of Castelnau, was brutally murdered by a group of Cathars in 1207, Pope Innocent III proclaimed a crusade and then an Inquisition in an attempt to quell the heresy. Technically an "official inquiry," a heretic could be reported to the authorities by a clergyman or a layperson. He (or she) was then questioned, and given the opportunity to abjure the belief, in which case he received various penalties and requirements to attend Mass. If he held fast to his heretical doctrine, he would be released to the secular authorities, and often sentenced to be burned at the stake. In the following document Bernard Gui (1261–1331), an experienced inquisitor, describes the Cathars, or Albigensians. It is important to remember that the inquisitors were not unbiased observers, and their writings should be viewed within that context.

(From *Readings in European History*, ed. by James Harvey Robinson [Boston: Ginn & Co., 1904], pp. 381–383.)

It would take too long to describe in detail the manner in which these same Manichaean heretics preach and teach their followers, but it must be briefly considered here.

In the first place, they usually say of themselves that they are good Christians, who do not swear, or lie, or speak evil of others; that they do not kill any

man or animal, nor anything having the breath of life, and that they hold the faith of the Lord Jesus Christ and his gospel as Christ and his apostles taught. They assert that they occupy the place of the apostles, and that, on account of the above-mentioned things, they of the Roman Church, namely the prelates, clerks, and monks, and especially the inquisitors of heresy, persecute them and call them heretics, although they are good men and good Christians, and that they are persecuted just as Christ and his apostles were by the Pharisees.

Moreover they talk to the laity of the evil lives of the clerks and prelates of the Roman Church, pointing out and setting forth their pride, cupidity, avarice, and uncleanness of life, and such other evils as they know: They invoke, with their own interpretation and according to their abilities, the authority of the Gospels and the Epistles against the condition of the prelates, churchmen, and monks, whom they call Pharisees and false prophets, who say, but do not.

Then they attack and vituperate, in turn, all the sacraments of the Church, especially the sacrament of the eucharist, saying that it cannot contain the body of Christ, for had this been as great as the largest mountain Christians would have entirely consumed it before this. They assert that the host comes from straw, that it passes through the tails of horses, to wit, when the flour is cleaned by a sieve (of horse hair); that, moreover, it passes through the body and comes to a vile end, which, they say, could not happen if God were in it.

Of baptism, they assert that water is material and corruptible, and is therefore the creation of the evil power and cannot sanctify the soul, but that the churchmen sell this water out of avarice, just as they sell earth for the burial of the dead, and oil to the sick when they anoint them, and as they sell the confession of sins as made to the priests.

Hence they claim that confession made to the priest of the Roman Church is useless, and that, since the priests may be sinners, they cannot loose nor bind, and, being unclean themselves, cannot make others clean. They assert, moreover, that the cross of Christ should not be adored or venerated, because, as they urge, no one would venerate or adore the gallows upon which a father, relative, or friend had been hung. They urge, further, that they who adore the cross ought, for similar reasons, to worship all thorns and lances, because as Christ's body was on the cross during the passion, so was the crown of thorns on his head and the soldier's lance in his side. They proclaim many other scandalous things in regard to the sacraments.

Moreover they read from the Gospels and the Epistles in the vulgar tongue, applying and expounding them in their favor and against the condition of the Roman Church in a manner which it would take too long to describe in detail; but all that relates to this subject may be read more fully in the books they have written and infected, and may be learned from the confessions of such of their followers as have been converted.

Questions for Discussion:

1. Discuss the various aspects of Gui's charge of anti-clericalism in the teachings of the Cathars.
2. What were the points of defense cited by the Cathars when accused?

New Religious Orders

The Franciscans

12.6   The *Rule* of St Francis of Assisi

The impulses that caused Peter Waldo and the Waldensians, among others, to search for a return to the apostolic way of life resulted in the creation of a new monastic order, the Franciscans. These men were mendicants; because they called each other by the name "brother," they were known as friars, which is an Anglicization of frère, *or* fra *(brother). They owned no property and supported themselves by working at menial tasks or accepting alms. Thus, they differed from earlier monastic orders, such as the Benedictines and Cistercians, because they lived among the laypeople, rather than secluding themselves in isolated monasteries.*

The new order was founded by Francis of Assisi (1181–1226), the son of a nobleman. Much as Peter Waldo had done some fifty years earlier, he broke all ties with his family and sought to practice the apostolic way of life. In 1209 he decided that he should begin to preach, but he could not do so without a license; this was, of course, the same problem faced by Peter Waldo. Rather than beginning his mission without authorization, Francis decided to go to Rome to approach Innocent III. The pope, recognizing that Francis possessed an unusual spiritual quality, granted the license to preach and instructed him to create a Rule for his new order.

In the Rule, Francis stipulated that his followers own no possessions, and that they practice chastity and obedience. He revised the document several times; the commonly accepted version is the document that follows (1223). It should be observed that rather than presenting a challenge to ecclesiastical authority, Francis insisted on obedience to the pope and the Church.

(From *Select Historical Documents of the Middle Ages*, trans. and ed. by Ernest F. Henderson [London: G. Bell and Sons, 1925], pp. 344–349.)

1. This is the rule and way of living of the minorite brothers [friars minor, or Franciscans]: namely to observe the holy Gospel of our Lord Jesus Christ, living in obedience, without personal possessions, and in chastity. Brother Francis promises obedience and reverence to our lord pope Honorius [III, r. 1216–1227] and to his successors who canonically enter upon their office, and to the Roman Church. And the other brothers shall be bound to obey brother Francis and his successors.

2. If any persons shall wish to adopt this form of living, and shall come to our brothers, they shall send them to their provincial ministers; to whom alone, and to no others, permission is given to receive brothers. But the ministers shall diligently examine them in the matter of the catholic faith and the ecclesiastical sacraments. And if they believe all these, and are willing to faithfully confess them and observe them steadfastly to the end; and if they have no wives, or if they have them and the wives have already entered a monastery, or if they shall have given them permission to do so—they themselves having already taken a vow of continence by the authority of the bishop of the diocese, and their wives being of such age that no suspicion can arise in connection with them:—the ministers shall say unto them the word of the holy Gospel, to the effect that they shall go and sell all that they have and strive to give it to the poor. But if they shall not be able to do this, their good will is enough. And the brothers and their ministers shall be on their guard and not concern themselves for their temporal goods; so that they may freely do with those goods exactly as God inspires them. But if advice is required, the ministers shall have permission to send them to some God-fearing men by whose counsel they shall dispense their goods to the poor. Afterwards there shall be granted to them the garments of probation: namely two gowns without cowls and a belt, and hose and a cape down to the belt; unless to these same ministers something else may at some time seem to be preferable in the sight of God. But, when the year of probation is over, they shall be received into obedience; promising always to observe that manner of living, and this Rule. And, according to the mandate of the lord pope, they shall never be allowed to break these bonds. For according to the holy Gospel, no one

putting his hand to the plough and looking back is fit for the kingdom of God. And those who have now promised obedience shall have one gown with a cowl, and another, if they wish it, without a cowl. And those who are compelled by necessity, may wear shoes. And all the brothers shall wear humble garments, and may repair them with sack cloth and other remnants, with the benediction of God. And I warn and exhort them lest they despise or judge men whom they shall see clad in soft garments and in colors, using delicate food and drink; but each one shall the rather judge and despise himself.

3. The clerical brothers shall perform the divine service according to the order of the holy Roman Church; excepting the psalter, of which they may have extracts. But the lay brothers shall say twenty four Paternosters at matins, five at the service of praise, seven each at the first, third, sixth and ninth hour, twelve at vespers, seven at the completorium; and they shall pray for the dead. And they shall fast from the feast of All Saints to the Nativity of the Lord; but as to the holy season of Lent, which begins from the Epiphany of the Lord and continues forty days, which the Lord consecrated with his holy fast—those who fast during it shall be blessed of the Lord, and those who do not wish to fast shall not be bound to do so; but otherwise they shall fast until the Resurrection of the Lord. But at other times the brothers shall not be bound to fast save on the sixth day (Friday); but in time of manifest necessity the brothers shall not be bound to fast with their bodies. But I advise, warn and exhort my brothers in the Lord Jesus Christ, that, when they go into the world, they shall not quarrel, nor contend with words, nor judge others. But they shall be gentle, peaceable and modest, merciful and humble, honestly speaking with all, as is becoming. And they ought not to ride unless they are compelled by manifest necessity or by infirmity. Into whatever house they enter they shall first say: peace be to this house. And according to the holy Gospel it is lawful for them to eat of all the dishes which are placed before them.

4. I firmly command all the brothers by no means to receive coin or money, of themselves or through an intervening person. But for the needs of the sick and for clothing the other brothers, the ministers alone and the guardians shall provide through spiritual friends, as it may seem to them that necessity

demands, according to time, place and cold temperature. This one thing being always regarded, that, as has been said, they receive neither coin nor money.

5. Those brothers to whom God has given the ability to labor, shall labor faithfully and devoutly; in such way that idleness, the enemy of the soul, being excluded, they may not extinguish the spirit of holy prayer and devotion; to which other temporal things should be subservient. As a reward, moreover, for their labor, they may receive for themselves and their brothers the necessaries of life, but not coin or money; and this humbly, as becomes the servants of God and the followers of most holy poverty.

6. The brothers shall appropriate nothing to themselves, neither a house, nor a place, nor anything; but as pilgrims and strangers in this world, in poverty and humility serving God, they shall confidently go seeking for alms. Nor need they be ashamed, for the Lord made Himself poor for us in this world. This is that height of most lofty poverty, which has constituted you my most beloved brothers, heirs and kings of the kingdom of Heaven, has made you poor in possessions, has exalted you in virtues. This is your portion, which leads on to the land of the living. Adhering to it absolutely, most beloved brothers, you will wish to have for ever in Heaven nothing else than the name of our Lord Jesus Christ. And wherever the brothers are and shall meet, they shall show themselves as of one household; and the one shall safely tell the other what he needs. For if a mother loves and nourishes her son in flesh, how much more zealously should one love and nourish one's spiritual brother? And if any of them fall into sickness, the other brothers ought to serve him, as they would wish themselves to be served.

7. But if any of the brothers at the instigation of the enemy shall mortally sin: for those sins concerning which it has been ordained among the brothers that recourse must be had to the provincial ministers, the aforesaid brothers shall be bound to have recourse to them, as quickly as they can, without delay. But those ministers, if they are priests, shall with mercy enjoin penance upon them. But if they are not priests, they shall cause it to be enjoined upon them through others, priests of the order; according as it seems to them to be most expedient in the sight of God. And they ought to be on their guard lest they grow angry and be disturbed on account of the sin of any one; for wrath and indignation impede love in themselves and in others.

8. All the brothers shall be bound always to have one of the brothers of that order as general minister and servant of the whole fraternity, and shall be firmly bound to obey him. When he dies, the election of a successor shall be made by the provincial ministers and guardians, in the chapter held at Pentecost; in which the provincial ministers are bound always to come together in whatever place shall be designated by the general minister. And this, once in three years; or at another greater or lesser interval, according as shall be ordained by the aforesaid minister. And if, at any time, it shall be apparent to the whole body of the provincial ministers and guardians that the aforesaid minister does not suffice for the service and common utility of the brothers: the aforesaid brothers to whom the right of election has been given shall be bound, in the name of God, to elect another as their guardian. But after the chapter held at Pentecost the ministers and the guardians can, if they wish it and it seems expedient for them, in that same year call together, once, their brothers, in their districts, to a chapter.

9. The brothers may not preach in the bishopric of any bishop if they have been forbidden to by him. And no one of the brothers shall dare to preach at all to the people, unless he have been examined and approved by the general minister of this fraternity, and the office of preacher have been conceded to him. I also exhort those same brothers that, in the preaching which they do, their expressions shall be chaste and chosen, to the utility and edification of the people; announcing to them vices and virtues, punishment and glory, with briefness of discourse; for the words were brief which the Lord spoke upon earth.

10. The brothers who are the ministers and servants of the other brothers shall visit and admonish their brothers and humbly and lovingly correct them; not teaching them anything which is against their soul and against our Rule. But the brothers who are subjected to them shall remember that, before God, they have discarded their own wills. Wherefore I firmly command them that they obey their ministers in all things which they have promised God to observe, and which are not contrary to their souls and to our Rule. And wherever there are brothers who know

and recognize that they can not spiritually observe the Rule, they may and should have recourse to their ministers. But the ministers shall receive them lovingly and kindly, and shall exercise such familiarity towards them, that they may speak and act towards them as masters to their servants; for so it ought to be, that the ministers should be the servants of all the brothers. I warn and exhort, moreover, in Christ Jesus the Lord, that the brothers be on their guard against all pride, vainglory, envy, avarice, care and anxiety for this world, detraction and murmuring. And they shall not take trouble to teach those ignorant of letters, but shall pay heed to this that they desire to have the spirit of God and its holy workings; that they pray always to God with a pure heart; that they have humility, patience, in persecution and infirmity; and that they love those who persecute, revile and attack us. For the Lord said: "Love your enemies, and pray for those that persecute you and speak evil against you; Blessed are they that suffer persecution for righteousness' sake, for of such is the kingdom of Heaven; He that is steadfast unto the end shall be saved."

11. I firmly command all the brothers not to have suspicious intercourse or to take counsel with women. And, with the exception of those to whom special permission has been given by the Apostolic Chair, let them not enter nunneries. Neither may they become fellow god-parents with men or women, lest from this cause a scandal may arise among the brothers or concerning brothers.

12. Whoever of the brothers by divine inspiration may wish to go among the Saracens and other infidels, shall seek permission to do so from their provincial ministers. But to none shall the ministers give permission to go, save to those whom they shall see to be fit for the mission.

Furthermore, through their obedience I enjoin on the ministers that they demand from the lord pope one of the cardinals of the holy Roman Church, who shall be the governor, corrector and protector of that fraternity, so that, always subjected and lying at the feet of that same holy Church, steadfast in the catholic faith, we may observe poverty and humility, and the holy Gospel of our Lord Jesus Christ; as we have firmly promised.

Questions for Discussion:

1. What were the requirements for entrance into the order?
2. Compare the Franciscan *Rule* with the *Rule* of Saint Benedict (Document 1.15). What aspects are common to both documents? What are the essential differences?
3. What governance structure did this document establish for the Franciscans?
4. Why was Saint Francis successful in creating a new religious order when the Waldensians were not?

12.7   "Little Flower of the Blessed Francis": The *Rule* of Saint Clare

The teachings of Saint Francis appealed to women as well as men. One of the most prominent was Clare of Assisi (1194–1253), a noblewoman who desired to follow the precepts of the Franciscans. Clare gathered a number of women who were also inspired by the message of the apostolic life, and they worked along with the monks in helping the poor and the sick. Francis encouraged their participation, but did not advocate their being allowed to beg for alms. In 1219, Cardinal Hugolino[3] (c. 1145–1241), a patron and protector of the Franciscans, provided a rule for the women based upon enclosure and strict adherence to the Rule *of St. Benedict; his stipulations reflected the views of the medieval church hierarchy that women religious should be enclosed. Clare was not satisfied with these provisions, and eventually composed her own rule, included here.*

(From *The Life of Saint Clare*, trans. by Paschal Robinson [Philadelphia: The Dolphin Press, 1910], pp. 99–102.)

---

[3]Cardinal Hugolino became Pope Gregory IX in 1227. See Document 12.4 for his decretal letter *Vox in Rama*.

The Rule and Life of the Poor Sisters

I. Of the Evangelical Rule and of Catholic and Seraphic Obedience

The form of life of the Order of the Poor Sisters, which the Blessed Francis founded is this: to observe the holy Gospel of our Lord Jesus Christ by living in obedience, with poverty and in chastity. Clare, unworthy handmaid of Christ and little flower of the most blessed Father Francis, promises obedience and reverence to the Lord Pope Innocent and his successors canonically elected and to the Roman Church. And as, in the beginning of her conversion, she with her Sisters promised obedience to the Blessed Francis, so does she promise to observe the same inviolably to his successors. And the other Sisters are bound always to obey the successors of the Blessed Francis and of Sister Clare and the other Abbesses canonically elected who shall succeed her.

II. Of Sisters About to Enter the Monastery

If any one, moved by Divine inspiration, should come to us wishing to embrace this life, the Abbess is bound to ask the consent of all the Sisters, and if the majority give their consent, she may receive her, having obtained leave of our Lord Cardinal Protector. And if it shall seem fitting to receive her, let the Abbess examine her carefully or have her examined as to the Catholic faith and the Sacraments of the Church; and if she believes all these things and is willing to confess them faithfully and to observe them steadfastly to the end, and if she has no husband or, having one, if he has already entered Religion [a monastic order] with the authority of the Bishop of the diocese and has made a vow of continence, and if there is no impediment to the observance of this life by reason of her advanced age or ill-health or foolishness, let the tenor of our life be clearly explained to her. If she is found worthy, let the words of the holy Gospel be said to her that she should go and sell all that she has and endeavor to distribute it to the poor, but if she cannot do this her good will is sufficient. Let the Abbess and her Sisters take care not to be anxious about her worldly goods, so that she may freely do with her goods whatsoever the Lord may inspire her. If, however, there be need of advice, let them send her to some prudent and God-fearing men by whose counsel let her goods be distributed to the poor.

Afterward, her hair having been cut off round and her secular dress laid aside, let them allow her three tunics and a mantle. After that, it shall not be permitted for her to go outside the monastery except for some useful, reasonable, manifest and probable cause. When the year of probation is over, she shall be received to obedience, promising to observe perpetually our life and form of poverty. No one shall be veiled during the time of probation. The Sisters may also have little mantles for the convenience and propriety of their service and labor. But let the Abbess provide them discreetly with garments according to the qualities of persons and places and times and cold climates as necessity may seem to require. The young girls who are received into the monastery before they have reached the proper age, shall have their hair cut off round and, their secular dress being laid aside, they shall be clothed in religious garb of such sort as may seem befitting to the Abbess. But when they have reached the proper age they shall make their profession clothed after the manner of the others. And both for these and for the other novices the Abbess shall be careful to provide a mistress from among all those who are the more prudent who shall diligently instruct them in holy living and becoming behavior according to the form of our profession. The same form shall be followed in the examination and reception of the Sisters who serve outside the monastery; these Sisters may wear shoes. No one may live with us in the monastery unless she is received according to the form of our profession. And for the love of the most holy and most sweet Child Jesus wrapped in poor little swaddling clothes and laid in a manger and of His most holy Mother, I admonish, beseech and entreat my Sisters that they be always clothed in poor garments.

Questions for Discussion:

1. Compare the *Rule* of Clare with that of Francis. Are there different requirements for women and men? Which aspects apply to both documents?
2. What gender issues arise from your analysis of Clare's *Rule*?

The Dominicans

12.8   Concerning Reading: From the Dominican *Constitutions*

Another of the new monastic orders formed in the thirteenth century was founded by a Spanish priest named Dominic de Guzman (1170–1221). From the beginning, the Dominican order (officially known as the Order of Preachers) was dedicated to scholarship and learning, as well as pastoral responsibility. The movement originated as a response to the challenge of the heretics in southern France (see Document 12.3). Dominic had requested that he be sent as a missionary to the Mongols in western Asia, but Pope Innocent III assigned him to preach to the Cathars instead. Hoping to engage the Cathar perfecti in public debates, he began itinerant sermonizing, visiting southern French towns on foot. Dominic eventually established a central headquarters in Toulouse, where he trained a number of assistants. In 1215, he traveled to Rome to ask for authorization for a new monastic order. After some resistance, papal confirmation was granted by Pope Honorius III (r. 1216–1227) in 1216. Although the pope recognized the existence of Dominic's order, he did not approve a new rule, and the Order of Preachers followed the Rule of Saint Augustine.

Dominic began to draw up written guidelines for his order as early as 1216, and continued work on the legislation in the next decade. The constitutions for the order stipulated strict rules and customs with regard to food and clothing in addition to the customary regulations concerning prayer and the liturgy. The following excerpt from the Constitutions of 1228 provides regulations for the behavior of the monks during the prescribed reading hours.

(Excerpts from *Early Dominicans: Selected Writings* (CWS), edited by Simon Tugwell, OP. Copyright © 1982 by the Missionary Society of St. Paul the Apostle in the State of New York. Paulist Press, Inc., New York/Mahwah, NJ. Reprinted by permission of Paulist Press, Inc. www.paulistpress.com)

How the Brethren Are to Behave During the Time for Reading

All the brethren are to settle down to read, except those who are too busy with their official jobs to have time to read. They too, when they have finished, are to go back to their reading. While the Work of God is being celebrated in church, they are not to read, except for those who do not know the psalms by heart, and those who need to look something up in connection with the particular Office, or who have to read or sing something during it. When they are sitting in the cloister, they should behave as good religious, each one reading his own book, except for those who are singing something from the antiphonars, graduals or hymnbooks, and those who are preparing readings. The person who has been deputed for this task is to fix and listen to the readings. They are not to disturb each other by asking questions. If anyone has his hood up when he is in the cloister or in choir, he must hold himself in such a way that it can be gauged whether he has gone to sleep. If anyone needs to go out, he should put his book back in the cupboard, or, if he prefers to leave it in his place, he is to signal to the brother who is sitting next to him to keep an eye on it. If anyone wants to take a book which someone else is reading or singing from, because he needs to consult something in it, he is to give him another book in its place, and the other brother is to surrender his book peacefully. But if the brother refuses to let him have his book, the one who wanted it is to accept this peacefully until he can accuse him of it in Chapter.

Question for Discussion:

1. How did Saint Dominic expand upon the guidelines for reading contained in the *Rule of Saint Benedict* (Document 1.15)?

INTERPRETING THE EVIDENCE

12.9 *De Modo Orandi*: From the *Nine Ways of Prayer* of Saint Dominic

Saint Dominic was exceptionally committed to devotional practices, advocating nine modes of prayer in his teachings. The work De modo orandi *("Concerning the Way of Praying"), written between 1260 and 1288 by an anonymous witness, emphasized Dominic's individualistic responses to images of Christ. In "The Second Way of Prayer," Dominic prostrates himself before the cross, and in "The Fourth Way" he stands before the crucifix.*

(From *The Nine Ways of Prayer of Saint Dominic,* ed. and trans. by Simon Tugwell, Dublin: Dominican Publications, 1978, pp. 26–28. Reprinted by permission of Dominican Publications, Dublin, Ireland, www.dominicanpublications.com)

The Second Way of Prayer *(After The Nine Ways of Prayer of Saint Dominic. ed. and trans. by Simon Tugwell, O.P. with drawings by Sheelagh Wilsden O.P. after the Miniatures in Codex Rossianus 3 in the Vatican Library [Dublin: Dominican Publications, 1978], p. 19.)*

SAINT DOMINIC used also often to pray, throwing himself down flat on his face on the ground, and then his heart would be pricked with compunction, and he would chide himself and say, sometimes loudly enough to be heard: "God, be merciful to me a sinner." And with great love and reverence he would recite the word of David: "it is I who have sinned and done unjustly." He would weep and groan passionately, and then say, "I am not worthy to look upon the heights of heaven, because of the greatness of my sin; I have provoked your anger and done evil in your sight." He would also say, emphatically and devoutly, that verse from Psalm 43: "my soul is laid low in the dust, my heart is stuck to the earth." And again: "my soul sticks to the floor; make me alive according to your promise."

Sometimes, when he wanted to teach the brethren with what reverence they ought to pray, he would say to them: "the Magi, those holy kings, fell down and worshipped when they entered the house and found the child with Mary his mother. Now we know for certain that we have found him too, man and God, with Mary his handmaid; so come, let us worship and fall down before God, let us weep before the God who made us."

(continued)

The young men he also exhorted, saying, "if you cannot weep for your own sins, because you have none, still there are many sinners to be directed to God's mercy and love, and the prophets and apostles prayed for them with great groanings, and for their sake too Jesus wept when he saw them, and similarly the holy David, saying, 'I saw the half-hearted and I pined away'."

AFTER THIS, Saint Dominic, standing before the altar or in the Chapter Room, would fix his gaze on the crucifix, looking intently at Christ on the Cross and kneeling down over and over again. Sometimes he would spend the whole time from the end of Compline until midnight kneeling down and standing up again, like the apostle James, and the leper in the gospel who knelt down and said, "Lord, if you will, you can make me clean"; and like Stephen, who knelt down and cried out with a loud voice, "Do not reckon up to them this sin." While he prayed, our holy father Dominic would become more and more assured of the mercy of God, both for himself and for all sinners, and for the protection of the novices whom he used to send all over the place to preach and win souls. Sometimes he could not contain his voice, and the brethren would hear him saying, "To you, Lord, will I cry, do not turn away from me in silence . . ." and other such words from sacred scripture.

But also, at times, he spoke in his heart and his voice was not heard at all, and he would remain on his knees, his mind caught up in wonder, and this sometimes lasted a long time. Sometimes, when he was praying like this, his gaze seemed to have penetrated into the spiritual heavens, and he would suddenly be radiant with joy, wiping away the abundant tears running down his face. At such times he would be in an intensity of desire, like a thirsty man coming to a spring of water, or a traveler at last approaching his homeland. His prayer became stronger and more insistent, his movements rapid yet always sure and orderly, as he stood up and knelt down.

He came to be so used to this prayer of kneeling, that when he was on a journey, both in the guesthouse, after the toils of the road, and on the road itself, when the others were sleeping and

The Fourth Way of Prayer *(After The Nine Ways of Prayer of Saint Dominic. ed. and trans. by Simon Tugwell, O.P. with drawings by Sheelagh Wilsden O.P. after the Miniatures in Codex Rossianus 3 in the Vatican Library [Dublin: Dominican Publications, 1978], p. 26.)*

resting, he would turn to his genuflections as to his own special practice, his own personal service. This way of prayer he taught the brethren more by his example than by anything he said.

Question for Discussion:

1. In the Fourth Way of Prayer, the writer describes Dominic's mystical experience. Compare this with the account by Hildegard of Bingen regarding her visions (Document 10.13).

New Communities: The Beguines and the *Devotio Moderna*

12.10   *Cartulaire du Beguinage de Sainte-Elizabeth a Gand*: Concerning the Beguines

During the twelfth century a group of women in the Low Countries (now Belgium, Luxembourg, and the Netherlands) desired, like the Waldensians, to imitate the apostolic life. Known as Beguines, these women renounced their possessions and earned their living through manual labor, mostly spinning and weaving, and by providing elementary education. They were also committed to service and charitable activities. By the thirteenth century the movement had spread, partly as a result of the formal approval of Pope Gregory IX, and communities of these women were established in France and Germany as well as the Low Countries. The following fourteenth-century document explains the motivation behind the foundation of the Beguine movement, and describes their way of life.

Why the Beguinage Was Founded

Those ladies of good memory, Joanna and her sister Margaret, successive countesses of Flanders and Hainault, noticed that the region was greatly abounding in women for whom, because of their own position or that of their friends, suitable marriages were not possible, and they saw that the daughters of respectable men, both nobles and commoners, wished to live chastely, but could not easily enter a monastery because of the great number of these girls and the poverty of their parents, and that respectable and noble but impoverished damsels had to go begging or shamefully support themselves or seek support from their friends, unless some solution could be found. Then by divine inspiration, as it is piously believed, having first obtained the advice and consent of respectable men of the diocese and elsewhere, in various parts of Flanders they set up certain spacious places which are called Beguinages, in which the aforesaid women, girls and damsels were

received, so that living in common therein, they might preserve their chastity, with or without taking vows, and where they might support and clothe themselves by suitable work, without shaming themselves or their friends.

The Beguinage of Saint Elizabeth

Among these Beguinages, they founded one in Ghent, which is called the Beguinage of Saint Elizabeth, which is encircled by ditches and walls. In the middle of it is a church, and next to the church a cemetery and a hospital, which the aforesaid ladies endowed for the weak and infirm of that same Beguinage. Many houses were also built there for the habitation of the said women, each of whom has her own garden, separated from the next by ditches or hedges; and two chaplains were established in this place by the same ladies.

The Manual Work Which They Do

In these houses, indeed, many dwell together communally and are very poor, having nothing but their clothing, a bed and a chest, nor are they a burden to anyone, but by manual work, washing the wool and cleaning the pieces of cloth sent to them from the town, they earn enough money daily that, making thereby a simple living, they also pay their dues to the church and give a modest amount in alms. And in each convent there is one who is called the mistress of work, whose duty is to supervise the work and the workers, so that all things are faithfully carried through according to God's will.

Their Way of Working and Praying

On work days they hold to the practice of rising early in the morning and coming together in the church, each going to her own place, which she has specially assigned to her, so that the absence of anyone may thereby be more easily noticed. After they have heard the Mass and said their prayers there, they return to their houses, working all day in silence, in which thing they are considered very useful to the whole country. And while working thus, they do not cease from prayer, for in each convent the two women who are best suited for this recite clearly the psalm "Miserere" and other psalms which they know, and the "Ave Maria," one singing one verse, the other the next, and the rest recite silently with them, or diligently listen to those who are reciting. Late at night, after Vespers, they go into the church, devoting themselves to prayers and meditations, until the signal is given and they go to bed. On Sundays and holy days, with masses and sermons, prayers and meditations, they devote themselves to the Lord's service in all things; nor may anyone leave the Beguinage on these days without special permission from the principal mistress.

The Severity of Their Life

We shall not say much of their abstinence from food and drink but this: that many of them are satisfied for the whole day with the coarse bread and pottage which they have in common in each convent, and with a drink of cold water they lessen their thirst rather than increase their appetite. And many among them are accustomed to fast frequently on bread and water, and many of them do not wear linen on their bodies, and they use straw pallets instead of beds.

Their Training in Manners

And in all these things, they have such respectable manners and are so learned in domestic affairs that great and respectable persons often send them their daughters to be raised, hoping that, to whatever estate they may later be called, whether in the religious life or in marriage, they may be found better trained than others. Their way of living, in fear of God and in obedience to the holy Mother Church, has been such that nothing unusual or suspect has ever been heard concerning their congregation.

Their Prayers for the Dead

When anyone of them dies, each member of the convent visits the corpse individually, with devout prayers and intercessions, and each, according to her obligation, devoutly performs fasts, vigils, psalms and prayers for the one who has died.

The Color and Form of Their Clothing

All wear the same color and style of clothing, so that they may thereby very strictly avoid anything that might distinguish them from the others or be suspect. For they wear a habit which is grey in color, humble, and of a coarse shape, and none may have anything which is unusual or suspect in its shape, sewing, or belting, or in the way of nightcaps, hoods, gloves, mitts, straps, purses and knives.

Government and Correction

One woman, nominated by the conventual mistresses, rules the previously mentioned hospital. She is called the principal mistress of the Beguinage, or the great mistress, and each year, after the accounts are rendered, it is customary for her to be retained in or removed from this office according to the will of the aforementioned conventual mistresses. And she appoints the mistresses in the individual convents, with the advice and consent of the convents and of respectable men; and only with the permission and at the will of the said principal mistresses is anyone permitted to build or to tear down in that place, or to give or assign a place in the convent. To her also falls the correction of those who transgress against the praiseworthy rules of the said place, so that she may combat vices through restraint within the Beguinage, or by the transfer of a person from one convent to another, or by other similar penalties, or she may, through the complete expulsion of the rotten member from the Beguinage, preserve the body of the rest from shame and decay. And no one may be away from the Beguinage for long or spend the night in the town without her permission. Nor may anyone leave the Beguinage for an hour, without the special permission of the conventual mistress; and she who has that permission may not go alone but must have one or more companions, taken only from her own convent. Those who go out are required to avoid anything suspect in all their movements, and in the places they go, and in the persons they meet; those who do otherwise are warned about these matters, and unless they immediately desist they are deprived of the consolation of the Beguinage.

The Fame of the Place

That benevolent confessor, the most pious king Saint Louis, personally visited this place in devotion, and, pleased with the zeal of these women, arranged with the venerable father, the lord bishop of Tournai, that a church should be consecrated for them, and acquired and conferred on them many privileges and liberties for their devotion, and he established and endowed a Beguinage like this one at Paris, and others in various places. There is also another Beguinage in Ghent, which is called "Oya," and many houses throughout the town where women dwell in a similar situation.

Questions for Discussion:

1. Describe the reasons given for the foundation of Beguinages.
2. How did these communities differ from Benedictine or Franciscan convents? What similarities do you see?
3. What does the author of this document describe as the virtues of these communities?

12.11   Mechthild of Magdeburg: *The Flowing Light of the Godhead*

Mysticism continued to flourish during the thirteenth century, and was often experienced by women visionaries who expressed their religious piety in erotic imagery of divine love. Their work drew upon the tradition of the troubadours and minnesinger (see Chapter 10), as well as the biblical "Song of Songs." One of these ecstatic authors was Mechthild of Magdeburg (c. 1212–c. 1282), a noble woman who became a Beguine when she was twenty-three. Although the description of the Beguinage in the previous selection does not reflect the erotic content of Mechthild's work, these religious communities of women were characterized in the following way by the Bishop of Acre, Jacques de Vitry (d. 1240): "They melted altogether in wondrous love for God until it seemed that they bowed under the burden of desire and for many years they did not leave their beds except on rare occasions. . . ."

In the following selection Mechthild draws from the tradition of the minnesinger, the German troubadours. "Minne" in German means "Love," and thus Lady Minne, God's messenger in this dialogue, is the personification of Love. (A similar personification is the character Lady Philosophy in the Consolation of Philosophy *by Boethius in Document 2.4). Medieval romances often theorized about the question "What is Minne?" and the absorption of the concept by Mechthild is not unusual; however, the erotic imagery of her vision is quite daring.*

From *Writings of Medieval Women: An Anthology* by Marcelle Thiebaux. Copyright © 1994 by Taylor & Francis Group LLC - Books. Reproduced with permission of Taylor & Francis Group LLC - Books in the format Textbook via Copyright Clearance Center.)

1. Minne's Greeting to the Queen, Mechthild's Soul, and the Hunt of Love

How Minne and the Soul spoke together:

Mechthild's Soul came to Minne and greeted her with deep meaning, saying, "God greet you Lady Minne."
Minne: God reward you, dear lady Queen.
Soul: Lady Minne, you are very welcome to me.
Minne: Lady Queen, I'm honored by your greeting.
Soul: Lady Minne, you struggled a long time with the high holy ghost, and you conquered him so that he gushed all at once into Mary's humble maidenhead.
Minne: Lady Queen, it was for your honor and delight.
Soul: Lady Minne, you have taken from me everything I ever won on earth.
Minne: Lady Queen, you've made a blissful exchange.

Soul: Lady Minne, you've taken my childhood from me.
Minne: Lady Queen, I've given you heavenly freedom for it.
Soul: Lady Minne, you've taken my whole youth.
Minne: Lady Queen, I've given you many holy virtues for it.
Soul: Lady Minne, you've taken my friends and kin.
Minne: Ah, Lady Queen, that's a worthless lament!
Soul: Lady Minne, you've taken the world from me, worldly honor, and all worldly riches.
Minne: Lady Queen, in an hour I'll recompense you on earth with all you desire of the Holy Ghost.
Soul: Lady Minne, you have so harassed me that my body is seized by sundry ills.
Minne: Lady Queen, I've given you much high wisdom.
Soul: Lady Minne, you have squandered my flesh and my blood.
Minne: Lady Queen, by that you've been enlightened and raised up with God.
Soul: Lady Minne, you are a robber woman. Pay me back for that!
Minne: Lady Queen, then take my very self!
Soul: Lady Minne, now you have repaid me a hundredfold here on earth.
Minne: Lady Queen, now have you claimed God and his whole kingdom!

The Soul's handmaids and Minne's beatings:
The holy Christian virtues are the Soul's handmaids.
The Soul in sweet sorrow cries out her anguish to Minne.

Mechthild's Soul speaks:
Ah, dearest Lady,
you've been my lady-in-waiting, lurking so long,
now tell me what's to become of me?
You have hunted, seized, and tied me so fast
and wounded me so deeply
that I shall never be healed.
You have beaten me with a club.
Tell me whether I shall ever finally recover!
Shall I not be slain by your hand?
It would have been better for me if I had never known you.

Lady Minne's reply:
I hunted you for my delight;
I seized you for my desire;
I bound you tightly for my joy;
When I wounded you, you became one with me.
When I beat you with a club, I became your strong ravisher.
It was I who drove out the Almighty from heaven's kingdom and deprived him of his human life,
then gave him gloriously back to his father.
How could you, vile worm, think you could recover from me?

Mechthild's Soul:
Tell me, my Queen, I thought a small medicine
from heaven that God had often given me
might help me to escape you.

Lady Minne:
If a captive wants to escape death,
let her reach for water and bread.
The medicines that God has given you
are nothing more than days of grace in this life.
But when your Easter Day dawns
and your body then meets its death blow,
I shall be there, encircling you, piercing you,
and I shall steal your body
and give it to Love.

Mechthild's Soul:
Ah, Lady Minne,
I have written this letter dictated from your lips.
Now give me your great seal to affix to it.

Lady Minne:
She whom God has captured for himself
knows where the seal must be pressed.
It lies between the two of us.

Mechthild's Soul:
Be quiet, Minne, give me no more advice; I and all earthly creatures bow to you.
Oh my dearest lady,
tell my friend his couch is ready,
and I am lovesick for him.

If this letter is too long, I have plucked a few
blossoms from its meadow.
This is its sweet lament:
Whoever dies of love shall be entombed in God.

Questions for Discussion:

1. Mechthild frames the account of her vision as
   a dialogue. Compare her mode of expression
   and her literary purpose with that of
   Roswitha of Gandersheim (Document 8.9).
   Are they similar in any way?

2. What imagery has Mechthild drawn from
   troubadour and trobaritz lyrics (Document
   10.7)?

3. The vision of Mechthild has overtones that
   twenty-first-century readers would recognize
   as masochistic. Discuss.

12.12 *The Following of Christ:* The Spiritual Diary of Gerard Groote

The Devotio Moderna ("Modern Devotion") *was
begun in Holland in the late fourteenth century. The
founder of the movement, eventually known as the
"Brethren of the Common Life," was Gerhard Groote, also
spelled Geert Grote (1340–1384). There were four primary aspects to the movement: (1) His followers, both men
and women, were pious persons who lived together (the men
separate from the women) and supported their community
with the labor of their own hands. (2) They had no intention of founding another religious order, but rather worshipped devoutly in their parish churches. (3) They were
obedient to their prelates and the Roman Church, although
they did extensive devotional reading in the vernacular
languages. (4) Their primary objective was to live together
in humility and love.*

*Groote was motivated by his belief that each indi-
vidual must discover for himself a way of life compatible
with his own religious needs, and his conviction that manual work was an essential aspect of a religious existence.
In order to provide his followers with a marketable craft,
Groote entered the printing industry. The brethren were
among the first to provide accurate texts of devotional and
liturgical works.*

The following excerpt from Groote's Spiritual
Diary, *written between 1375 and 1378, shows his
expectations for a peaceful and cooperative attitude among
his brothers.*

(From *The Following of Christ: The Spiritual Diary of Gerard Groote*,
trans. by Joseph Malaise. New York: America Press, 1937,
pp. 83–85. Reprinted by permission of America Press, Inc.)

Chapter III

Of a Good Peaceful Man

1. First be contented yourself; and then you will
   be able to make others contented.

2. A peace-loving man is of greater service to others than a learned man.

3. A peace disturber turns good into evil; and
   readily believes what is evil.

4. But a peaceful man draws good from everything.

5. He who is truly in peace thinks no evil of anyone; but he who is discontented and wrathful is
   tormented with diverse suspicions; he has no
   rest nor suffers others to have rest.

6. He often says what he ought not to say, and
   omits important things he ought to do.

7. He calls attention to what others ought to do,
   and neglects what he himself is obliged to do.

8. Therefore, have an earnest zeal for your own self
   first; and then you may rightly also exercise
   your zeal on your neighbor.

9. You can readily find excuses for your own actions,
   but you will not accept the excuses of others.

10. It would be much more just to blame yourself,
    and to excuse your brother.

11. If you wish others to bear with you, then bear with others.

12. And see how far you still are from that true charity and humility which never takes offense, nor is displeased with anyone except with itself.

13. It is nothing great to associate with the good and gentle, for that is naturally agreeable to all men; every man gladly lives in peace and prefers those who are of the same mind with him.

14. But to be able to live in peace with hard, obstinate and undisciplined persons, or with those who stand always in opposition to us, that is a wonderful grace and a most praiseworthy and manly accomplishment.

15. There are some who are at peace with themselves and also with others.

16. And there are some who neither have peace nor leave others in peace; they are a burden to others, but always a greater burden to themselves.

17. And there are some who keep themselves always in peace, and also endeavor to bring others to a peaceful mind.

18. But all our peace in this miserable life is to be placed rather in humble forbearance than in being free from opposition.

19. He who is best resigned to suffer enjoys the greatest peace.

20. Such a one is a conqueror of self, a lord of the world, a friend of God and an heir of the kingdom of Heaven.

Questions for Discussion:

1. According to Groote, what are the characteristics of a "good peaceful man"?
2. Which of the religious orders we have studied might emphasize the same qualities?

12.13 Salome Stricken: A Way of Life for Sisters

Women had been participants in the Devotio Moderna *from the beginning. Indeed, soon after Gerhard Groote determined the path for his spiritual life, he turned his home into a hospice for poor women, retaining only a small space for himself. As the movement grew, women gathered together and established residences for their communities. A record exists that gives information about the customs practiced in the sisters' houses. It was written by Salome Stricken (1369–1449), who joined Groote's household when she was twenty. Her sincere religiosity marked her as a leader, and she became rectress of Groote's house. In the following document she presents a summary of her views on the devout way of life, which she offered to sisters founding a new house. One of the most important aspects of her formula was the emphasis on work as an essential component of the virtuous life.*

(From *Devotio Moderna: Basic Writings (CWS), translated* by John Van Engen. Copyright © by John Van Engen. Paulist Press, Inc., New York/Mahwah, NJ. Reprinted by permission of Paulist Press, Inc. www.paulistpress.com)

If you wish to achieve a truly spiritual life, you must refrain from too much talking, especially during manual labor, because work is a kind of medicinal plaster for the wound of our sins. If we are concerned to salve our wounds and apply medicine, we must be very careful lest through much talking we instead add wound to wound, which comes when we act unfaithfully and seek our own comfort in labor. It is said of the brothers of St. Bernard that when they were all engaged in serious work they proceeded in such silence that only the sound of the picks, axes, and other tools could be heard. May it be common among you to pray devoutly and lift your hearts up to the Lord God during your labor, because the Lord God is to be sought and found not only in churches, through the prayers poured out there, but in every place and as present to everyone, at least to everyone who by grace desires him. Indeed a greater measure of grace is to be found in humble, vile, and abject labors done in love with a desire to please him. And to express for your edification what work did for me, let me tell you that in all my life I never felt so affected toward the Lord as what I sensed when, still strong in body, I went out to the common labor with the convent, there to knead, to brew, to card, pick, or wash the wool, and all the other heavy or vile things that must be done in our house. It seems to me that if I could still do it as I once could I would find the Lord Jesus nowhere more delightfully and lovingly than in such labor, even though entering the church is also very precious to me.

In all good congregations the custom is that from morning to evening on ordinary days the sisters work in a lively and faithful way, except when they go to hear mass. The exceptions are those sisters whom this does not suit because of business they cannot put off, ministry in the kitchen, or the like. They remain in their places without murmuring, seeking and calling upon the most loving and sweet Lord Jesus in their heart since they cannot go to church. It is also the custom in our house that after prime each sister goes vigorously to work, be it to card the wool, to weave, to sew, or the like, except during the time when they go to hear mass or when they read and sing the hours in choir. The rest who do not visit choir, however, work continuously from prime to vespers, except during the time of mass. Our sisters think they suffer a great loss in divine love if they do not persist faithfully and alertly in manual labor. I know too that in the early days of our house's founding even some of the novices who had just come carried out hard labor from morning to evening, carrying rocks, filling carts with earth, providing lime, and preparing the foundations for the supports and beams. In this hard and continuous labor they were suffused with such a grace from the Lord that they paid almost no attention to externals. And when, for instance, they carried rocks with some companion they were so filled with grace that they walked inwardly absorbed, knowing not where they were going but simply following the file of carriers. Our regulations put first that we concentrate vigorously for God's sake on manual labor. Whoever therefore thinks that the grace of God and inner sweetness is to be found only in leisure and contemplation errs badly. As Bernard says, work of the hands frequently expresses remorse of the heart and makes devotion purer. For this and many other reasons, the holy fathers in Egypt were constant in labor, and therefore magnificently lauded by the holy fathers.

Dearest sisters, I ask as well that you wear humble and plain garb and that its cloth be crude and plain, as it is among our sisters in the house of Master Geert Grote, for external shapelessness and ugliness covers the Lord Jesus within. I specially desire, beloved sisters in Christ, that you submit yourselves in all humility to your confessor, and that you receive whatever he says or counsels as if it came from the Lord God.

Most beloved sisters, to sense and to taste the sweetness of the Lord God is highly delightful, but the foundation of all sanctity lies rather in complete self-denial, mortification of the evil affections in our corrupt natures, and the conversion of our will to the Lord in an effort to conform it totally to his will. Master Geert Grote, our venerable father, wrote in a certain place that "I am abandoned inwardly by the Lord, outwardly I am of no consequence and looked down upon by all men, and to bear this patiently exceeds in merit all contemplation." Because, when the Lord gives us sweetness and solace, he is ministering to us, but when we cling to him faithfully through temptation and trouble, then we are serving him, which is of greater merit. I do not say these things to make you lukewarm and lazy in your prayers or to have you spend the time set aside for prayer uselessly, for we and all mankind must seek the grace of God with great diligence and with vigilant souls. If consolation and internal sweetness is proffered us from the Lord, we should receive it with an expression of great gratitude. But if he sometimes withdraws that which he gives, we should strive to cling to the Lord nonetheless with devout desire and pious affection just as in previous times and places.

Dearest sisters, I write these simple and crude things to you as if you did not know them. I hope however, that you know many more and greater things than I am able to write.

Questions for Discussion:

1. What are the specific instructions of Salome regarding work?
2. Compare this document with the *Rule* of Saint Claire (Document 12.7). What are the differences between the two ways of religious life? Do you see any similarities?

A Female Visionary: Margery Kempe and the Vicar

12.14   *The Book of Margery Kempe*

As we have seen, mysticism was not a new phenomenon in the thirteenth century. The mystical tradition extended as far back as biblical times, and some medieval mystics, such as Hildegard von Bingen (Document 10.13), were well known. Accounts of mystical experience became much more widespread in the thirteenth and fourteenth centuries; one example is the visionary account by the Beguine Mechthild of Magdeburg included in this chapter (Document 12.11). Ordinary laypeople also reported receiving messages directly from God, Christ, or the Virgin Mary. Their visions were usually accompanied by hypnotic trances, fainting, tears, and passionate outbursts. Most of these mystics were women, and one of the most famous of these was Margery Kempe (c. 1373–1440), who lived in England. She was criticized by her contemporaries as fraudulent and heretical, and she remains a controversial figure among current scholars. Nonetheless, her autobiography, The Book of Margery Kempe, *is important as one of the earliest known biographies in English. The work describes her life, her pilgrimages to Jerusalem and Rome, and her mystical experiences. In the following chapter, Margery tells of the instructions she received from Christ that led her to visit a vicar in Norwich.*

(From *The Book of Margery Kempe*, ed by W. Butler-Bowdon. London: Jonathan Cape, 1936, pp. 67–70. Translation modified. Reprinted by permission of the Estate of William Butler-Bowdon.)

Chapter 17

On a day, long before this time, while this creature [Margery] was bearing children and she was newly delivered of a child, Our Lord Jesus Christ said to her that she should bear no more children, and therefore He bade her to go to Norwich.

And she said:—'Ah! dear Lord, how shall I go? I am both faint and feeble.'

'Do not dread the journey. I shall make you strong enough. I bid you go to the Vicar of Saint Stephen's and say that I greet him well, and that he is a highly chosen soul of Mine, and tell him he pleases Me much with his preaching and show him your secrets, and My counsels such as I show you.'

Then she made her way toward Norwich, and came into his church on a Thursday a little before noon. And the Vicar went up and down with another priest, who was his ghostly [spiritual] father, who lived when this book was made. And this creature was clad in black clothing at that time.

She saluted the Vicar, praying him that she might speak with him an hour or two in the afternoon, when he had eaten, in the love of God.

He, lifting up his hands and blessing her, said:—'Benedicite. How could a woman occupy an hour or two in the love of Our Lord? I shall never eat meat till I learn what you can say of Our Lord God in the time of an hour.'

Then he sat down in the church. She, sitting a little aside, showed him all the words that God had revealed to her in her soul. Afterwards she showed him all her manner of life from her childhood, as soon as it would come to her mind; how unkind she had been against Our Lord Jesus Christ, how proud and vain she had been in her behavior, how obstinate against the laws of God, and how envious against her fellow Christians. Later, when it pleased Our Lord Christ Jesus, [she told] how she was chastised with many tribulations and horrible temptations and afterwards how she was fed and comforted with holy meditations and especially in the memory of Our Lord's Passion.

And, while she conversed on the Passion of Our Lord Jesus Christ, she heard so hideous a melody that she could not bear it. Then this creature fell down, as if she had lost her bodily strength, and lay still a great while, desiring to put it away, and she might not. Then she knew well, by her faith, that there was great joy in Heaven where the least point of bliss, without any comparison, passes all the joy that ever might be thought or felt this life.

She was greatly strengthened in her faith and more bold to tell the Vicar her feelings, which she had by revelation both of the quick and the dead, and of his own self.

She told him how sometimes the Father of Heaven spoke to her soul as plainly and as truly as one friend speaks to another by bodily speech. Sometimes the Second Person in Trinity, sometimes all Three Persons in Trinity; and one substance in Godhead spoke to her soul, and informed her in her faith and in His love, how she should love Him, worship Him and dread Him, so excellently that she never heard of any book, either Hylton's[4] book or Bride's book, or Stimulus Amoris [Torment of Love], or Incendium Amoris [Fire of Love], or any other that she ever heard read, that spoke so highly of the love of God. But she felt that, as highly working in her soul, as if she could have shown what she felt.

Sometimes Our Lady spoke to her mind; sometimes St. Peter, sometimes St. Paul, sometimes St. Katherine, or whatever Saint in Heaven she had devotion to, appeared in her soul and taught her how she should love Our Lord, and how she should please Him. Her dalliance was so sweet, so holy and so devout, that this creature might not oftentimes bear it, but fell down and wrested with her body, and made wondrous faces and gestures with boisterous sobbings, and great plenty of tears, sometimes saying 'Jesus, Mercy', sometimes, 'I die'.

And therefore many people slandered her, not believing that it was the work of God, but that some evil spirit vexed her in her body or else that she had some bodily sickness.

Notwithstanding the rumors and the grutching [complaining] of the people against her, this holy man, the Vicar of Saint Stephen's Church of Norwich, whom God had exalted, and through marvelous works shown and proved to be holy, ever held with her and supported her against her enemies, unto his power, after the time that she, by the bid-

ding of God, had shown him her manner of governance and living, for he trustfully believed that she was well learned in the law of God, and imbued with the grace of he Holy Ghost, to Whom it belonged to inspire where He will. And though His voice is heard, it is not known in the world from where it comes or where it goes.

This holy Vicar, after this time, was confessor to this creature always when she came to Norwich, and houselled [administered the Eucharist to] her with his own hands.

And when she was at one time admonished to appear before certain officers of the Bishop, to answer to certain articles which would be put against her by the stirring of envious people, the good Vicar, preferring the love of God before any shame of the world, went with her to hear her examination, and delivered her from the malice of her enemies. And then it was revealed to this creature that the good Vicar would live seven years after, and then should pass hence with great grace, and he did as she foretold.

Questions for Discussion:

1. Compare the mystical experiences of Hildegard von Bingen (Document 10.13) and Mechthild of Mageburg (Document 12.11) with those described by Margery. What similarities do you see? What differences?

2. Hildegard was an abbess, Mechthild was a Beguine, and Margery was a layperson. How did these different life circumstances affect their visions?

3. Hildegard lived in the twelfth century, Mechthild in the thirteenth, and Margery in the late fourteenth and early fifteenth centuries. Do you think the variety in their visionary experiences derived from the change of circumstance and environment over time? Discuss.

---

[4]Walter Hilton (Hylton) (d. 1396) was an Augustinian mystic whose most famous work was the *Ladder of Perfection*. Margery was probably referring to this book.

The Fourth Lateran Council: Heretics and Jews

12.15   Raymond of Toulouse and the Cathar Heresy

In 1215, Innocent III summoned a general council to Rome to finalize and codify the reform measures of the Church. It was the largest gathering of church prelates since the Council of Nicaea in 325 (Document 1.6). Much of the work, based on earlier calls for reform (see the discussions in Chapters 6 and 7), had been completed before the meeting; the actions of the assembly formalized the ecclesiastical legislation. Among other matters, the group organized the papal bureaucracy, established the seven sacraments of the Church, and enacted rules concerning clerical celibacy and obedience.

The Council also dealt with matters regarding heresy, as, for example, the charges against Raymond VI, count of Toulouse from 1194 to 1222. During his rule the suppression of the Cathars was begun, and the count was accused of heresy. This report from an eyewitness provides an account of the proceedings.

(From *Readings in Western Civilization, Vol. 4: Medieval Europe*, ed. by Julius Kirshner and Karl F. Morrison. © 1986 The University of Chicago Press. All rights reserved.)

For several days afterwards the count of Toulouse was dealt with. Because heretics had at one time stayed on his land, he had been accused of heresy. As a result he lost his castles and a great part of his land through the efforts of the king of France, and was indeed thoroughly ruined by yet other crusaders who had been sent against him. But because at one time the count was present at the council with his wife . . . took up the cross, and is going to remain overseas forever, the lord pope allotted forty marks for his support to him from all the income God had conferred upon him. To the countess he awarded whatever land beyond the Jordan the count had held from the king of France. It is said that he intended to use a sentence of excommunication to force the King of France to leave her in peace. The count of Montfort, however, will hold the rest of the land from the hands of the lord pope and St. Peter. . . . Here I must pass over many other matters whose truth I could not ascertain because I only heard rumors about them, which usually add falsehoods to the truth, thrive on their changeability, and gain in strength as they make the rounds.

Question for Discussion:

1. How do you explain the compromise made by the Council regarding the accusations of heresy directed at the count?

INTERPRETING THE EVIDENCE

12.16 *Blind Synagoga* and the Provisions of the Council

The Fourth Lateran Council also enacted measures regarding Jews. These concerned, among other things, the practice of lending money at high rates of interest, interactions between Jews and Christians, and the behavior of Jewish converts.

(From *Decrees of Ecumenical Councils* by Norman P. Tanner. Copyright 1990 by Continuum Publishing Company. Reproduced with permission of Continuum Publishing Company in the format Textbook via Copyright Clearance Center.)

The more the Christian religion is restrained from usurious practices, so much the more does the perfidy of the Jews grow in these matters, so that within a short time they are exhausting the resources of Christians. Wishing therefore to see that Christians are not savagely oppressed by Jews in this matter, we ordain by this synodal decree that if Jews in future, on any pretext, extort oppressive and *excessive* interest from Christians, then they are to be removed from contact with Christians until they have made adequate satisfaction for the immoderate burden. Christians too, if need be, shall be compelled by ecclesiastical censure, without the possibility of an appeal, to abstain from commerce with them. We enjoin upon princes not to be hostile to Christians on this account, but rather to be zealous in restraining Jews from so great oppression. We decree, under the same penalty, that Jews shall be compelled to make satisfaction to churches for tithes and offerings due to the churches, which the churches were accustomed to receive from Christians for houses and other possessions, before they passed by whatever title to the Jews, so that the churches may thus be preserved from loss.

68. Jews appearing in public

A difference of dress distinguishes Jews or Saracens from Christians in some provinces, but in others a certain confusion has developed so that they are indistinguishable. Whence it sometimes happens that by mistake Christians join with Jewish or Saracen women, and Jews or Saracens with Christian women. In order that the offence of such a damnable mixing may not spread further, under the excuse of a mistake of this kind, we decree that such persons of either sex, in every Christian province and at all times, are to be distinguished in public from other people by the character of their dress—seeing moreover that this was enjoined upon them by Moses himself, as we read. They shall not appear in public at all on the days of lamentation and on passion Sunday; because some of them on such days, as we have heard, do not blush to parade in very ornate dress and are not afraid to mock Christians who are presenting a memorial of the most sacred passion and are displaying signs of grief. What we most strictly forbid however, is that they dare in any way to break out in derision of the Redeemer. We order secular princes to restrain with condign punishment those who do so presume, lest they dare to blaspheme in any way him who was crucified for us, since we ought not to ignore insults against him who blotted out our wrongdoings.

69. Jews not to hold public offices

It would be too absurd for a blasphemer of Christ to exercise power over Christians. We therefore renew in this canon, on account of the boldness of the offenders, what the council of Toledo providently decreed in this matter: we forbid Jews to be appointed to public offices, since under cover of them they are very hostile to Christians. If, however, anyone does commit such an office to them let him, after an admonition, be curbed by the provincial council, which we order to be held annually, by means of an appropriate sanction. Any official so appointed shall be denied commerce with Christians in business and in other matters until he has converted to the use of poor Christians, in accordance with the directions of the diocesan bishop, whatever he has obtained from Christians by reason of his office so acquired, and he shall surrender with shame the office which he irreverently assumed. We extend the same thing to pagans.

70. Jewish converts may not retain their old rite

Certain people who have come voluntarily to the waters of sacred baptism, as we learnt, do not wholly cast off the old person in order to put on the new more perfectly. For, in keeping remnants of their former rite, they upset the decorum of the Christian religion by such a mixing. Since it is written, cursed is he who enters the land by two paths, and a garment that is woven from linen and wool together should not be put on, we therefore decree that such people shall be wholly prevented by the prelates of churches from observing their old rite, so that those who freely offered themselves to the Christian religion may be kept to its observance by a salutary and necessary coercion. For it is a lesser evil not to know the Lord's way than to go back on it after having known it.

(continued)

The image below is a sculpture of Blind Synagoga, *a female figure representing the Jewish faith. She wears a blindfold, indicating moral or spiritual blindness, and in her hand she holds the Laws of Moses. Statues such as this one from Strasbourg Cathedral in France were often paired with figures of "Ecclesia" that personified the Christian religion.*

Blind Synagoga (Hirmer Fotoarchiv, Munich, Germany.)

Questions for Discussion:

1. Why were the Jews ordered by the Lateran Council to wear distinctive clothing?
2. Jews were prohibited from holding public office. What were the reasons given for this restriction?
3. How did the rules of the council restrict the lending of the Jews? Why do you think these measures were included?
4. How does the image of *Blind Synagoga* serve as a reminder to Christians of their faith?
5. Compare the style of the sculpture of *Blind Synagoga* with the figures in the tympanum of Autun Cathedral (Document 8.3). What differences do you see?
6. *Magna Carta* (Document 11.5) contains provisions that concern the monetary activities of the Jews. How do the rulings of the Lateran Council correlate with these stipulations?

Chapter 13

❧❀❧

Intellectual and Artistic Development in the High Middle Ages

Most scholars believe that the high point of medieval intellectual and cultural expression occurred in the thirteenth century. By this time the population of Europe had grown significantly, and urban centers had developed that provided the dynamic energy necessary for the creation of sophisticated institutions of higher education and the great monuments of Gothic architecture.

Universities emerged in response to the needs of the urban environment. The increasingly bureaucratic governments of the cities and the complex structure of the religious establishments required men trained in both civil and canon law. The study of medicine became an important part of the curriculum of some universities, and scientific advancement was fostered at other institutions, particularly in England. The documents in this chapter (13.1, 13.2, and 13.3) provide evidence of the lives of students at the University of Paris. As you will see, medieval students faced many of the same problems as their twenty-first-century counterparts.

The most famous philosophers of the era were teachers at the University of Paris, which was the preeminent theological institution of the Middle Ages. Two of the most important were Saint Thomas Aquinas, a Dominican, and Saint Bonaventure, a Franciscan. The excerpts from their works included in this chapter (Documents 13.4–13.6) demonstrate that although they were concerned with the same philosophical questions, their methods and solutions were quite different.

Roger Bacon (c. 1214–1292) was a scholar at the University of Paris who was interested in languages and scientific experiment. In an excerpt from his work (Document 13.7), Bacon offered reasons why, in his view, experimentation is the vital component of knowledge.

Literature also flourished in the thirteenth century, when poets and writers of romances fully incorporated the ideals of chivalry and courtly love. The Romance of the Rose, written by Guillaume de Lorris and Jean de Meun (Document 13.8), reflects the imagery and traditions evident in the works of twelfth-century writers such as Chrétien de Troyes and Marie de France (Documents 10.4 and 10.5), as well as the system of vassalage discussed in Chapter 5.

Another thirteenth-century literary work, the poem The Owl and the Nightingale, makes use of the technique of disputation so characteristic of philosophical discourse in the High Middle Ages (Document 13.9). The verses portray a debate between two birds that represent contrasting value systems—the nightingale presenting the ideas of courtly love poetry and the owl arguing for the traditional moral views expressed by the Church.

The spectacular cathedrals of the Gothic era, such as those in Paris, London, Cologne, and eastern European cities, have often been compared structurally to the great philosophical systems, embodied most clearly in the works of Thomas Aquinas. They had great symbolic value for people in the medieval era, who saw them as representations of heaven on earth. A comparison of the analysis presented in The Symbolism of Churches and Church Ornaments by William Durandus with the groundplan of Chartres Cathedral (Document 13.10) offers an illustration of the medieval aesthetic view.

The techniques of medieval architects remain somewhat mysterious, since extant documentation is practically nonexistent. A clue may be found in the Portfolio of Villard de Honnecourt (Document 13.11), which contains geometrical sketches probably indicating their methods.

The practical problems encountered by medieval builders, who did not have the advantage of electricity or modern tools, were daunting, as may be seen in the writings of the monk Gervase of Canterbury (Document 13.12). His description of the rebuilding of Canterbury Cathedral following a fire in 1174 recounted the problems and successes of the new construction. The document concludes by comparing the new choir with the old structure; his analysis provides a succinct contrast between the earlier style and the new Gothic features.

Virtually all Gothic cathedrals contained at least one elaborate circular window known as a "Rose" window. One of the most beautiful is in Notre Dame Cathedral in Paris. In Document 13.13, the cathedral and its Rose windows are described in glowing terms by the philosopher Jean de Jandun.

The documents in this chapter demonstrate the vitality and beauty of thirteenth-century intellectual and artistic expression. Moreover, these philosophical, literary, and architectural monuments remain a source of wonder and inspiration in the twenty-first-century world.

The Medieval University

The modern university was born during the later part of the Middle Ages. Most scholars believe that earliest evidence of what we would recognize as university structure appeared in the town of Salerno, in southern Italy.[1] The faculty of medicine of this institution had become famous, and the school of liberal arts was an important center for the translation and dissemination of Jewish, Greek, and Arabic philosophy and science. Whereas the university at Salerno remained primarily dedicated to the study of medicine, the emerging institutions at Bologna, Paris, Oxford, and Cambridge developed a full curriculum; however, Bologna was most famous as a law school, and Paris was best known for theology.

The following documents from early statutes of the Sorbonne, a college of the University of Paris for students of theology that was founded about 1257 by Robert de Sorbonne (1201–1274), stipulate the rules for resident students. These excerpts deal with such issues as whether the students could eat in their rooms, whether they might have guests, and what fines they must pay for female visitors. There are also admonitions about collegial behavior and restrictions as to proper clothing. As you read the statutes, compare the experiences of medieval students with your own and those of your friends.

(From *University Records and Life in the Middle Ages*, by Lynn Thorndike. Copyright © 1944 Columbia University Press. Reprinted by permission of the publisher.)

13.1   Early Statutes of the College of the Sorbonne

Rules Concerning Dining:

. . . no one shall eat in his room except for cause. If anyone has a guest, he shall eat in hall [in the main dining room]. If, moreover, it does not seem expedient to the fellow to bring that guest to hall, let him eat in his room and he shall have the usual portion for himself, not for the guest. If, moreover, he wants more for himself or his guest, he should pay for it himself. But if in the judgment of the fellow who introduces him, the guest is a person of consequence or one through whom the house might be aided or the fellow promoted, then the said fellow may invite one or two others to entertain the guest and do him honor. These shall similarly have the portions due them from the community but always without loss to the community.

Also, no one resident in town shall eat in the house except in hall, and if he eats in a private room for cause, he shall scrupulously give his excuse before the bearer of the roll [attendance record].

Also, when fellows eat in private rooms, the fragments are collected lest they be lost and are returned to the dispenser who puts them in the common repository for poor clerks.

Also, the fellows should be warned by the bearer of the roll that those eating in private rooms must conduct themselves quietly and abstain from too much noise, lest those passing through the court and street be scandalized and lest the fellows in rooms adjoining be hindered in their studies.

Also, those eating in private rooms shall provide themselves with what they need in season as best they can, so that the service of the community may be disturbed as little as possible. But if there are any infringers of this statute who are accustomed to eat in private rooms without cause, they shall be warned by the bearer of the roll to desist, which if they will not do, he shall report it to the master. If, moreover, other reasons arise for which anyone can eat in a private room, it shall be left to the discretion of the roll-bearer and proctors [residence officials] until otherwise ordered.

Also, no outsider shall be placed on pension without permission of the master, nor shall he eat or sleep in the house as a guest more than three or four days without his permission.

Also, no women of any sort shall eat in the private rooms. If anyone violates this rule, he shall pay the assessed penalty, namely, sixpence.

---

[1]Some scholars believe that the first recognizable university was at Bologna.

Also, the rule does not apply to the sick. If anyone eats in a private room because of sickness, he may have a fellow with him, if he wishes, to entertain and wait on him, who also shall have his due portion. What shall be the portion of a fellow, shall be left to the discretion of the dispenser. If a fellow shall come late to lunch, if he comes from classes or a sermon or business of the community, he shall have his full portion, but if from his own affairs, he shall have bread only.

Rules Concerning Clothing and Books:

Also, all shall wear closed outer garments, nor shall they have trimmings of vair[2] or gris[3] or of red or green silk on the outer garment or hood.

Also, no one shall have loud shoes or clothing by which scandal might be generated in any way.

Also, no one shall be received in the house unless he shall be willing to leave off such and to observe the aforesaid rules.

Also, no one shall be received in the house unless he pledges faith that, if he happens to receive books from the common store, he will treat them carefully as if they were his own and on no condition remove or lend them out of the house, and return them in good condition whenever required or whenever he leaves town.

Also, let every fellow have his own mark on his clothes and one only and different from the others. And let all the marks be written on a schedule and over each mark the name of whose it is. And let that schedule be given to the servant so that he may learn to recognize the mark of each one. And the servant shall not receive clothes from any fellow unless he sees the mark. And then the servant can return his clothes to each fellow.

Rules Concerning Behavior:

Also, if anyone has spoken opprobrious or shameful words to a fellow, provided it is established by two fellows of the house, he shall pay a purse which ought to belong to the society.

Also, if one of the fellows shall have insulted, jostled or severely beaten one of the servants, he shall pay a sextarium of wine to the fellows, and this wine ought to be *vin superieur* [wine of a superior quality] to boot.

Also, no one shall presume to take a dish or tray either at lunch or dinner except as it is passed to him by the provost and his helpers or the servants. Moreover, he who has done otherwise shall be penalized two quarts of wine. And therefore each provost should be diligent in serving the fellows well.

Also, no one shall form the habit of talking too loudly at table. Whoever after he has been warned about this by the prior shall have offended by speaking too loudly, provided this is established afterwards by testimony of several fellows to the prior, shall be held to the usual house penalty, namely, two quarts of wine.

Questions for Discussion:

1. Compare the dormitory and dining rules of the University of Paris with those of a contemporary institution. Do you see any similarities? How are they different?
2. Do you know of any preparatory schools or universities that enforce a dress code? Why do you think these restrictions were imposed in the Middle Ages? Do modern dress codes have the same purpose? Discuss.

13.2   Rules of the University of Paris (1215)

The statutes of the University of Paris from 1215 established specific rules concerning the course of study and the qualifications for teaching. These included stipulations concerning the age and the amount of training required to be a lecturer at the university, as well as rules about the proper curriculum. Notice that the trivium *and the* quadrivium *are part of the course of study; this requirement followed a tradition that began in the classical world of ancient Rome and extended through the Middle Ages. (See Document 2.3 for the continuation of the Greco-Roman educational program by Cassiodorus, and Documents 4.11*

---

[2]Vair was one of the furs used in heraldry; it was composed of skins of small squirrels, joined head to tail.

[3]Grise refers to a quality of luminous intensity. It would probably be called psychedelic in the twenty-first century.

and 4.13 for the curriculum and intellectual expectations during the reign of Charlemagne).

(From *University Records and Life in the Middle Ages*, by Lynn Thorndike. Copyright © 1944 Columbia University Press. Reprinted by permission of the publisher.)

Robert [de Courcon], . . . legate [representative] of the apostolic see [the pope], to all the masters and scholars of Paris eternal greeting in the Lord. Let all know that, since we have had a special mandate from the pope to take effective measures to reform the state of the Parisian scholars for the better, wishing with the counsel of good men to provide for the tranquility of the scholars in the future, we have decreed and ordained in this way:

No one shall lecture in the arts at Paris before he is twenty-one years of age, and he shall have heard lectures for at least six years before he begins to lecture, and he shall promise to lecture for at least two years, unless a reasonable cause prevents, which he ought to prove publicly or before examiners. He shall not be stained by any infamy, and when he is ready to lecture, he shall be examined according to the form which is contained in the writing of the lord bishop of Paris. . . . And they shall lecture on the books of Aristotle on dialectic old and new in the schools ordinarily and not *ad cursum.*[4] They shall also lecture on both Priscians[5] ordinarily, or at least on one. They shall not lecture on feast days except on philosophers and rhetoric and the quadrivium and *Barbarismus* [the third book of the *Ars major* by Donatus] and ethics, if it please them, and the fourth book of the *Topics.*[6] They shall not lecture on the books of Aristotle on metaphysics and natural philosophy or on summaries of them or concerning the doctrine of master David of Dinant or the heretic Amaury or Mauritius of Spain.

In the meetings of the masters and in the responses [to the lessons] or arguments of the boys and youths there shall be no drinking. They may summon some friends or associates, but only a few. We urge that the customary donations of clothing or other things, or even more, should be made, especially to the poor. None of the masters lecturing in arts shall have a cope except one round, black and reaching to the ankles, at least while it is new. Use of the pallium is permitted. No one shall wear with the round cope shoes that are ornamented or with elongated pointed toes. . . .

Each master shall have jurisdiction over his scholar. No one shall occupy a classroom or house without asking the consent of the tenant, provided one has a chance to ask it. No one shall receive the licentiate from the chancellor or another for money given or promise made or other condition agreed upon. Also, the masters and scholars can make, both between themselves and with other persons, obligations and constitutions supported by faith or penalty or oath in these cases: namely, the murder or mutilation of a scholar or atrocious injury done a scholar, if justice should not be forthcoming, arranging the prices of lodgings, costume, burial, lectures and disputations, so, however, that the university be not thereby dissolved or destroyed.

As to the status of the theologians, we decree that no one shall lecture at Paris before his thirty-fifth year and unless he has studied for eight years at least, and has heard the books faithfully and in classrooms, and has attended lectures in theology for five years before he gives lectures himself publicly. And none of these shall lecture before the third hour on days when masters lecture. . . . No one shall be a scholar at Paris who has no definite master.

Moreover, that these decrees may be observed inviolate, we by virtue of our legatine[7] authority have bound by the knot of excommunication all who shall contumaciously presume to go against these our statutes, unless within fifteen days after the offense they have taken care to emend their presumption before the university of masters and scholars or other persons constituted by the university. Done in the year of Grace 1215, the month of August.

---

[4]*Ad cursum* refers to supplementary lectures.
[5]Priscian (491–518) was a Latin grammarian whose books on the Latin language were widely studied throughout the Middle Ages.

[6]The *Topics* was one of the approved works of Aristotle. Note that the end of the paragraph, his works on metaphysics and natural philosophy are forbidden.
[7]Robert de Courcon was a legate, or representative of the pope—hence, he had "legantine authority."

Questions for Discussion:

1. Do the requirements for lecturing in theology seem extremely demanding? How do these compare with the usual time frame for obtaining the degree of Doctor of Philosophy in contemporary American universities?

2. The statutes specify aspects of the relationships between masters and students at Paris. Do you see any reflections of these rules in the modern educational system? Discuss.

13.3 "Please Send Money": The *Balade* of a Student at Orleans

The following letter from a student at the University of Orleans makes clear that the financial difficulties of scholars in the Middle Ages were not any different from the problems of students in the twenty-first century.

(From *A Medieval Garner*, by G. G. Coulton [London: Constable & Co., 1910], pp. 559–560. Translation modernized.)

THUS runs the Orleans Scholar's Letter: "Well-beloved father, I have not a penny, nor can I get any except through you, for all things at the University are so expensive: nor can I study in my Code or my Digest,[8] for they are all tattered. Moreover, I owe ten crowns in dues to the Provost, and can find no man to lend them to me. Wherefore, I send you word of greetings and of money.

The Student needs many things if he is to be successful here; his father and his kin must supply him freely, so that he is not compelled to pawn his books, but has ready money in his purse, with gowns and furs and decent clothing, or he will be damned for a beggar. Wherefore, so that men may not take me for a beast, I send you word of greetings and of money.

Wines are expensive, and hostels, and other good things; I owe in every street, and am unable to free myself from such snares. Dear father, please help me! I fear that I will be excommunicated; already have I been cited, and there is not even a dry bone in my larder. If I do not find the money before this feast of Easter, the church door will be shut in my face; wherefore grant my supplication, for I send you word of greetings and of money."

Question for Discussion:

1. Even without credit cards, this student is in debt. Compare his pleas with those of your friends.

Philosophy and Science in the Thirteenth Century

13.4 The Scholastic Method: From the *Summa Theologica* by Thomas Aquinas

Although the Dominican Order was devoted to scholarship and learning from its foundation by St. Dominic (see Document 12.8) and the Franciscans saw their calling as a pastoral mission, eventually members of both orders became involved in university teaching and scholarship. During the thirteenth century they were practitioners of the "Scholastic Method"—a way of structuring philosophical argument that had its roots in the systematic approach of

Peter Abelard (see Document 10. 10). As you recall, in his work Sic et Non *("Yes and No"), Abelard gathered various scriptural references as well as philosophical and theological writings in order to compare them; this enabled him to evaluate their controversial points relative to specific questions. He did not make an attempt to synthesize these statements; in other words, there was no resolution to the questions, only an ordered presentation.*

In the thirteenth century, Thomas Aquinas, a famous philosopher and professor at the University of Paris, built upon this system, developing a systematic approach that was

---

[8]The student is referring to the *Code* and *Digest* from Justinian's *Corpus Iuris Civilis* (Document 2.13).

more highly structured. The most famous of his writings is the Summa Theologica, *written between 1265 and 1274, which makes use of his technique of synthesizing the writings of the Greek and Roman philosophers, as well as biblical sources and the works of early medieval philosophers. The system of the* Summa *reflects the popular practice of oral* disputatio *(disputation), in which scholars would debate a question. This style of debate was a common feature at the universities, and participants often gained much attention and notoriety from charismatic argument. Further on in this chapter we will read a poem based on this kind of debate:* The Owl and the Nightingale.

In this Article from the Summa, *Aquinas deals with the question: Whether the Intellectual Habit* Art *Is a Virtue? One of his points concerns the difference between the liberal arts (i.e., the* trivium *and the* quadrivium) *and the mechanical arts as produced by craftsmen, such as goldsmiths, ivory carvers, and workers in stained glass. Notice that Aquinas relies upon the authorities of the past, citing Augustine (see Document 1.10) and Aristotle, who was called "The Philosopher" by writers in the Middle Ages. The format of the highly structured argument, which exemplifies the "Scholastic Method," is: (1) Question; (2) Objections 1, 2, 3; (3) On the contrary, . . . ; (4) I answer that . . . ; (5) Reply Objections 1, 2, 3. Each objection is countered by a reply.*

(From *Basic Writings of Saint Thomas Aquinas*, vol. ii, edited by Anton C. Pegis. New York: Random House, 1945, pp. 433–434. Reprinted by permission of Hackett Publishing Company, Inc. All rights reserved.)

The Intellectual Virtues

Third Article

Whether the Intellectual habit Art Is a Virtue?

We proceed thus to the Third Article:

Objection 1. It would seem that art is not an intellectual virtue. For Augustine[9] says that *no one makes bad use of virtue.* But one may make bad use of art, for a craftsman can work badly according to the science of his art. Therefore art is not a virtue.

Obj. 2. Further, there is no virtue of a virtue. But *there is a virtue of art,* according to the Philosopher [Aristotle]. Therefore art is not a virtue.

---

[9]See Chapter 1 for a discussion of Augustine's work.

Obj. 3. Further, the liberal arts excel the mechanical arts. But just as the mechanical arts are practical, so the liberal arts are speculative. Therefore, if art were an intellectual virtue, it would have to be reckoned among the speculative virtues.

On the contrary, The Philosopher says that art is a virtue. However, he does not reckon it among the speculative virtues, which, according to him, reside in the scientific part of the soul.

I answer that, Art is nothing else but *the right reason about certain works to be made.* And yet the good of these things depends, not on the disposition of man's appetite, but on the goodness of the work done. For a craftsman as such is commendable, not for the will with which he does a work, but for the quality of the work. Art, therefore, properly speaking, is an operative habit. And yet it has something in common with the speculative habits, since the disposition of the things considered by them is a matter of concern to the speculative habits also, although they are not concerned with the disposition of the appetite towards their objects. For as long as the geometrician demonstrates the truth, it matters not how his appetite is disposed, whether he be joyful or angry; even as neither does this matter in a craftsman, as we have observed. And so art has the nature of a virtue in the same way as the speculative habits, in so far, namely, as neither art nor a speculative habit makes a good work as regards the use of the habit, which is distinctive of a virtue that perfects the appetite, but only as regards the ability to work well.

Reply Obj. 1. When anyone endowed with an art produces bad workmanship, this is not the work of that art; in fact, it is contrary to the art. In the same way, when a man lies, while knowing the truth, his words are not in accord with what he knows, but contrary thereto. Therefore, just as science has always a relation to good, as was stated above, so it is with art; and it is for this reason that it is called a virtue. And yet it falls short of being a perfect virtue, because it does not make its possessor to use it well; for which purpose something further is requisite, even though there cannot be a good use without the art.

Reply Obj. 2. In order that a man may make good use of the art he has, he needs a good will, which is perfected by moral virtue; and for this reason the Philosopher says that there is a virtue of art, namely, a moral virtue, in so far as the good use of art requires a moral virtue. For it is evident that a craftsman is inclined by justice, which rectifies his will, to do his work faithfully.

Reply Obj. 3. Even in speculative matters there is something by way of work: *e.g.,* the making of a syllogism[10] or of a fitting speech, or the work of counting or measuring. Hence whatever habits are ordained to such works of the speculative reason are, by a kind of comparison, called arts indeed, but *liberal* arts, in order to distinguish them from those arts that are ordained to works done by the body; for these arts are, in a fashion, servile, inasmuch as the body is in servile subjection to the soul, and man, as regards his soul, is free *{liber}*. On the other hand,

those sciences which are not ordained to any such work are called sciences absolutely, and not arts. Nor, if the liberal arts be more excellent, does it follow that the notion of art is more applicable to them.

Questions for Discussion:

1. How does Aquinas distinguish liberal arts from works of art?
2. Several scholars have compared the systematic method of Aquinas with the structure of the Gothic cathedral. Keep this parallel in mind when you study Documents 13.10 through 13.13 in this chapter.

13.5   *The Journey of the Soul unto God* by Saint Bonaventure

Aquinas, one of the most important of the Scholastic philosophers, was a Dominican. As we have seen, his vast works were carefully structured, and were characterized by a highly rational approach. The intellectual tradition of the Franciscans, by contrast, tended to be more mystical. One of the most famous scholars from this order was St. Bonaventure (Giovanni di Fidanza, c. 1221–1274), who also taught at the University of Paris. His philosophical works were primarily concerned with two problems: the ability of human beings to understand the mystery of God, and the progress of the soul toward eventual union with God. One of his treatises, The Journey of the Soul unto God, *demonstrates Bonaventure's belief in the power of mystical vision in attaining true knowledge of God. In the following excerpt, he discusses the power of numbers in encouraging mystical experience. His dependence on classical theologians such as Augustine is evident in his work, as in the writings of all Scholastic philosophers.*

(From *Itinerarium Mentis in Deum* by Saint Bonaventure, trans. by Philotheus Boehner. Saint Bonaventure, NY: The Franciscan Institute, 1956, pp. 59–61. Reprinted by permission of the publisher.)

10. This speculation is extended by considering the seven differences of numbers by which, as by seven steps, we ascend to God, as St. Augustine makes

clear in his books, *De Vera Religione* and *De Musica,* Book Six. In these passages he points out the differences of numbers, which ascend step by step from these visible creatures to the artificer of all, so that God may be seen in all of them.

He declares that there are numbers in bodies and especially in sounds and voices, and these he calls "sounding numbers." Secondly, there are numbers which are drawn from these and which are received into the sense faculty, and these he calls "occurring numbers." Thirdly, there are numbers that proceed from the soul into the body, as is clear in gesturing and in dancing, and these he calls "forthcoming numbers." Fourthly, there are numbers in the pleasures of the senses, which result when the attention turns towards the likenesses they have perceived, and these he calls "sensuous numbers." Fifthly, there are numbers retained in the memory, and these he calls "memorial numbers." Sixthly, there are numbers by which we judge all the foregoing numbers, and these he calls "judicial," which, as has been said, are necessarily above the mind, since they are infallible and beyond any judgment on our part. These last are the ones that impress on our minds the "artistic numbers," which, however, St. Augustine does not enumerate in the classification because they are bound up with the "judicial numbers." And from these "judicial numbers" also flow the "forthcoming numbers" from which are created the numerous forms of artifacts. Thus from the highest numbers, through the

---

[10]A syllogism is a logical construction that, put in simplistic terms, has the following form: *If a* = b, and b = c, then a = c.

intermediate, to the lowest, there is a gradated descent. And to the highest numbers in turn, we ascend step by step from the "sounding numbers," by means of the "occurring," the "sensuous," and the "memorial numbers."

Therefore, since all things are beautiful and in some way delightful, and since beauty and delight do not exist without proportion, and since proportion exists primarily in numbers, all things are subject to number. Hence *number is the principal exemplar in the mind of the Creator,* and in things, the principal vestige leading to Wisdom. And since number is most evident to all and very close to God, it leads us, by its sevenfold distinction, very close to Him; it makes Him known in all bodily and visible things when we apprehend numerical things, when we delight in numerical proportions, and when we judge irrefutably by the laws of numerical proportions.

11. From these first two steps by which we are led to behold God in vestiges, like the two wings drooping about the feet of the Seraph, we can gather that all creatures in this visible world lead the spirit of the contemplative and wise man to the eternal God. For creatures are shadows, echoes, and pictures of that first, most powerful, most wise, and most perfect Principle, of that eternal Source, Light, Fullness, of that efficient, exemplary and ordering Art. They are the vestiges, images, and displays presented to us for the contuition of God, and the divinely given signs wherein we can see God. These creatures are exemplars, or rather illustrations offered to souls as yet untrained and immersed in the senses, so that through these sensible things that they see they may be transported to the intelligible which they do not see, as through signs to that which is signified.

12. For creatures of this visible world signify the invisible things of God: partly, because God is the origin, exemplar, and end of every creature and the effect is the sign of the cause; the thing exemplified, of the exemplar; and the way, of the end to which it leads. This they do also partly by their own proper representation; partly because of their prophetic prefiguration; partly. by reason of angelic operation; partly also by reason of superadded institution. For every creature is by its very nature some kind of image and likeness of the eternal Wisdom, but especially one who, according to the Book of Scriptures, has been raised by the Spirit of Prophecy to prefigure spiritual things; and more especially those creatures in whose likeness it pleased God to appear through the ministry of the angels; and, finally, most especially, that one which He willed to institute for signifying, and which not only has the character of sign in the ordinary sense of the term, but also the character of sacrament as well.

13. From all this, one can gather that *since the creation of the world his invisible attributes are clearly seen, being understood through the things that are made. And so they are without excuse* who are unwilling to take notice of these things, or to know, bless, and love God in them, since they are unwilling to be transported *out of darkness into* the *marvelous light* of God. *But thanks be to God through our Lord, Jesus Christ,* who has transported us *out of darkness into his marvelous light,* since by the light externally given, we are disposed to re-enter the mirror of our mind, wherein shine forth divine things.

Question for Discussion follows Document 13.6.

13.6   *Summa Contra Gentiles* by Saint Thomas Aquinas

The following excerpt from Summa Contra Gentiles *(begun in 1258), another, less obviously structured work by Aquinas, also deals with the question posed by Bonaventure in the preceding selection: How is the mind of the human being directed to God? By comparing the two statements it is possible to see the differences between the philosophical styles of the two theologians.*

(From *The Summa Contra Gentiles* of Thomas Aquinas, trans. by The English Dominican Fathers [London: Burns Oates & Washbourne, Ltd., 1928], pp. 101–103.)

That the Divine Law Binds Men to the True Faith

That our Mind is Directed to God by Certain Sensible Things

SINCE it is connatural to man to acquire knowledge through the senses, and since it is most difficult to arise above sensible things, divine providence has appointed sensible things as a reminder to man of things divine, so that thus man's intention might the more readily be recalled to divine things, not excluding the man whose mind is not equal to the contemplation of divine things in themselves.

For this reason sensible sacrifices were instituted; since man offers these to God, not because God needs them, but that man might be reminded that he must refer both himself and all that is his to God as his end, and as the Creator, Governor and Lord of all.

Again, sensible things are employed for man's sanctification, in the shape of washings, anointings, meat and drink, and the uttering of sensible words, as signifying to man that he receives intelligible gifts from an external source, and from God whose name is expressed by sensible words.

Moreover man performs certain sensible actions, not to arouse God, but to arouse himself to things divine: such as prostrations, genuflexions, raising of the voice and singing. Such things are not done as though God needed them, for He knows all things, and His will is unchangeable, and He looks at the affection of the heart, and not the mere movement of the body: but we do them for our own sake, that by them our intention may be fixed on God, and our hearts inflamed. At the same time we thereby confess that God is the author of our soul and body, since we employ both soul and body in the worship we give Him.

Hence we must not wonder that heretics who deny that God is the author of our body, decry the offering of this bodily worship to God. Wherein it is clear that they forget that they are men, inasmuch as they deem the presentation of sensible objects to be unnecessary for interior knowledge and affection. For experience shows that by acts of the body the soul is aroused to a certain knowledge or affection. Wherefore it is evidently reasonable that we should employ bodies in order to raise our minds to God.

The offering of these bodily things to God is called the worship (*cultus*) of God. For we speak of *cultivating* those things to which we give our thought in the shape of deeds. Now, we give our thought to God in our actions, not indeed that we may be of advantage to Him, as when we cultivate other things by our actions: but because by such actions we advance towards God. And since by internal acts we tend to God directly, therefore properly speaking we worship God by internal acts. Nevertheless external acts also belong to the divine worship, forasmuch as by these acts the mind is raised to God, as we have said.

This divine worship is also called *religion:* because by these acts man tethers (*ligat*) himself, as it were, lest he stray from God. Also, because by a kind of natural instinct he feels himself *obliged* in his own way to show reverence to God, from whom flows His being and every good.

Wherefore religion is called *piety.* Because by piety we give due honor to those who begot us. Hence it would seem reasonably to belong to piety to honor God the Father of all. For this reason those who are averse to the *worship* of God are said to be *impious.*

And since not only is God the cause and source of our being, but also our whole being is in His power, and all that we have we owe to Him, and because of this He is truly our master, that which we do to honor Him is called *service.* Now, God is Lord not accidentally, as man of his fellow-man, but by nature. Hence we owe service to God otherwise than to a fellow-man, to whom we are subject accidentally, and who wields over things a restricted dominion, that he receives from God. Wherefore the service due to God is called by the special name of *latria* by the Greeks.

Question for Discussion:

1. Compare the writings of Bonventure and Aquinas. What essential differences do you see? Are there any commonalities?

13.7 Roger Bacon and the Beginning of Modern Experimental Science

Roger Bacon (c. 1214–1292) was a scholar at the University of Paris who was among the first to witness the acceptance of the works of Aristotle into the curriculum of the university. His own special interest lay in the fields of languages and scientific experiment. He was able to create a model of experimental science based upon his study of optics. In the following excerpt from On Experimental Science, *Bacon emphasized the value of empirical knowledge.*

(From *The Library of Original Sources*, vol. v, ed. by Oliver J. Thatcher [New York University Research Extension, 1907], pp. 369, 374–375.)

. . . I wish now to review the principles of wisdom from the point of view of experimental science, because without experiment it is impossible to know anything thoroughly.

There are two ways of acquiring knowledge, one through reason, the other by experiment. Argument reaches a conclusion and compels us to admit it, but it neither makes us certain nor so annihilates doubt that the mind rests calm in the intuition of truth, unless it finds this certitude by way of experience. Thus many have arguments toward attainable facts, but because they have not experienced them, they overlook them and neither avoid a harmful nor follow a beneficial course. Even if a man that has never seen fire, proves by good reasoning that fire burns, and devours and destroys things, nevertheless the mind of one hearing his arguments would never be convinced, nor would he avoid fire until he puts his hand or some combustible thing into it in order to prove by experiment what the argument taught. But after the fact of combustion is experienced, the mind is satisfied and lies calm in the certainty of truth. Hence argument is not enough, but experience is. . . .

Experimental science is also that which alone, as the mistress of the speculative sciences, can discover magnificent truths in the fields of the other sciences, to which these other sciences can in no way attain. And these truths are not of the nature of former truths, but they may be even outside of them, in the fields of things where there are neither as yet conclusions or principles, and good examples may be given of this, but in everything which follows it is not necessary for the inexperienced to see a reason in order to understand at the beginning, but rather he will never have a reason before he has tried the experiment. Whence in the first place there should be credulity until experiment follows, in order that the reason may be found. If one who has never seen that a magnet draws iron nor heard from others that it attracts, seeks the reason before experimenting, he will never find it. Indeed, in the first place, he ought to believe those who have experimented or who have it from investigators, nor ought he to doubt the truth of it because he himself is ignorant of it and because he has no reason for it.

Question for Discussion:

1. Discuss the reasons Bacon gives to prove that experiment is the true road to knowledge.

Literature in the Thirteenth Century

13.8 *The Romance of the Rose*

One of the most important vernacular literary works of the thirteenth century was The Romance of the Rose. *Its popularity among medieval readers is demonstrated by the large number of manuscripts that exist, many of which are beautifully illustrated. The poem was probably composed between 1268 and 1285; it contains two sections, written by two different authors, Guillaume de Lorris and Jean de Meun.*

Medieval readers were familiar with the subject of the work, which focuses on courtly love—a tradition well-established by the works of Chrétien de Troyes and Marie de France (see Chapter 10). In the following brief excerpt we see the Lover attacked by the God of Love, who forces the hero to become his vassal.

(From Guillaume de Lorris: *The Romance of the Rose.* © 1971 Princeton University Press, 1999 renewed PUP. Reprinted by permission of Princeton University Press.)

The God of Love and the Affair of the Heart

The God of Love, who had maintained his constant watch over me and had followed me with drawn bow, stopped near a fig tree and when he saw that I had singled out the bud that pleased me more than did any of the others, he immediately took an arrow and, when the string was in the nock, drew the bow—a wondrously strong one—up to his ear and shot at me in such a way that with great force he sent the point through the eye and into my heart. Then a chill seized me, one from which I have, since that time, felt many a shiver, even beneath a warm fur-lined tunic. Pierced thus by the arrow, I fell straightway to the earth. My heart failed; it played me false. For a long time I lay there in swoon, and when I came out of it and had my senses and reason, I was very weak and thought that I had shed a great quantity of blood. But the point that pierced me drew no blood whatever; the wound was quite dry. I took the arrow in my two hands and began to pull hard at it, sighing as I pulled. I pulled so hard that I drew out the feathered shaft, but the barbed point called Beauty was so fixed inside my heart that it could not be withdrawn. It remains within; I still feel it, and yet no blood has ever come from there.

I was in great pain and anguish because of my doubled danger: I didn't know what to do, what to say, or where to find a physician for my wound, since I expected no remedy for it, either of herbs or roots. But my heart drew me toward the rosebud, for it longed for no other place. If I had had it in my power, it would have restored my life. Even the sight and scent alone were very soothing for my sorrows.

I began then to draw toward the bud with its sweet exhalations. Love selected another arrow, worked in gold. It was the second arrow and its name was Simplicity. It has caused many a man and woman all over the world to fall in love. When Love saw me approach, he did not threaten me, but shot me with the arrow that was made of neither iron nor steel so that the point entered my heart through my eye. No man born, I believe, will ever dislodge it from there, for I tried, without any great joy, to pull the shaft from me, but the point remained within. Now know for a truth that if I had been full of desire for the rosebud before, my wish was greater now. As my woes gave me greater distress, I had an increased desire to go always toward the little rose that smelled sweeter than violets. I would have done better to go farther away, but I could not refuse what my heart commanded. I had to go perforce, always where it aspired to be. But the bowman, who strove mightily and with great diligence to wound me, did not let me move without hurt in that direction. To madden me further, he caused the third arrow, called Courtesy, to fly to my heart. The wound was deep and wide, and I had to fall in a swoon beneath a branching olive tree. I lay there a long time without moving. When I was able to stir, I took the arrow and straightway removed the shaft from my side, but, no matter what I might do, I could not draw out the point.

There I sat, in deep distress and thought. My wound tormented me very much and urged me to approach the rosebud that pleased me. But the bowman frightened me away, as indeed he should, for he who has been scalded must fear all water. However, necessity is a powerful force; even if I had seen it raining stones and crossbow bolts as thick as hail, I would still have had to go toward the rosebud, for Love, who excels all other things, gave me the strength and heart to perform his commandment. I rose then to my feet, as feeble and weak as a wounded man, and made a great effort to move forward, nothing daunted by the archer, toward the rosebush where my heart longed to be. But there were so many thorns, thistles, and brambles, that I hadn't the power to pass through the thicket of thorns and reach the rosebud. I had to remain near the hedge, which was next to the rosebushes and made of very sharp thorns. But it was a delight for me to be so near that I smelled the sweet perfume that came from the rosebud, and I was very pleased with what I could see freely. My reward at this sight was so great that I forgot my woes in my delight and joy. I was greatly healed and comforted; nothing ever pleased me as much as to rest in that place. I would never have sought to leave it. But after I had been there a long time, the God of Love, who had shattered my heart in making it his target, made a new assault upon me. To my discomfort he shot another arrow and made a new wound in my heart, under my breast. This arrow's name was Company, and there is none that subdues a lady or young man more quickly. Immediately the great anguish of my wounds began again. I swooned three times in a row.

When I revived, I wailed and sighed, for my anguish was growing so much worse that I had no hope, either of cure or of relief. I would rather have been dead than alive, for, in my opinion, Love would make a martyr of me in the end. I could not part from him by any other means. Meanwhile he had taken another arrow, one that I value highly and consider very powerful. This arrow is Fair Seeming; it does not allow any lover to repent of serving Love, no matter what woes he may suffer. It has a point for piercing and an edge as keen as a steel razor. But Love had anointed it very well with a precious unguent so that it might not hurt too greatly. He did not want me to die but to be relieved by the power of the unguent, one which was full of healing comfort. Love had made it with his own hands to comfort pure lovers and to help them support their troubles. When he shot the arrow at me he made a great wound in my heart, but the ointment, spreading throughout the wound, gave me back the heart which I had lost. Without the sweet ointment I would have been dead and in an evil plight.

Then I drew the shaft from me, but the head, newly polished, remained inside. Thus five of them were so well embedded that they would never be removed. Although the ointment was worth a great deal to me, nevertheless my wound hurt so much that the pain made me change color. This arrow has an unusual property; it brings both sweetness and bitterness. Indeed I felt and understood that it helped me at the same time that it harmed; while the point gave me anguish, the ointment gave relief. One part heals, the other pains, and thus it helps and harms.

Then straightway Love came toward me with quick steps, and as he came he cried out: "Vassal, you are taken. There is no chance for escape or struggle. Surrender without making any resistance. The more willingly you surrender the sooner will you receive mercy. He is a fool who resists the one whom he should flatter and before whom he would do better to beg. You cannot struggle against me, and I want to teach you that you can gain nothing through folly or pride. Rather submit yourself as a prisoner, as I wish in peace and with a good will."

I replied simply: "Sir, I surrender willingly, and I shall never defend myself against you. May it never please God for me even to think of ever resisting you, for to do so is neither right nor reasonable. You may do with me what you wish, hang me or kill me. I know very well that I cannot change things, for my life is in your hand. Only through your will can I live until tomorrow, and, since I shall never have joy and health from any other, I await them from you. If your hand, which has wounded me, does give me a remedy, if you wish to make me your prisoner or if you do not deign to do so, I shall not count myself deceived. Know too that I feel no anger whatever. I have heard so much good spoken about you that I want to give my heart and body over to your service, to be used entirely at your discretion, for if I do your will I cannot complain of anything. I still believe that at some time I shall receive the mercy that I await, and under such conditions I submit myself prostrate before you."

With these words, I wanted to kiss his foot, but he took me by the hand and said, "I love you very much and hold you in esteem for the way that you have replied here. Such a reply never came from a lowborn fellow with poor training. Moreover, you have won so much that, for your benefit, I want you to do homage to me from now on: You will kiss me on my mouth, which no base fellow touches. I do not allow any common man, any butcher, to touch it; anyone whom I take thus as my man must be courteous and open. Serving me is, without fail, painful and burdensome; but I do you a great honor, and you should be very glad—since Love carries the standard and banner of courtesy—that you have so good a master and a lord of such high renown. His bearing is so good, so sweet, open, and gentle, that no villainy, no wrong or evil training can dwell in anyone who is bent on serving and honoring him."

Immediately, with joined hands, I became his man. And you may understand that I grew very proud when his mouth kissed mine; this gift gave me great joy. Then he required sureties from me: "Friend," he said, "I have received many homages from one and another person by whom I was later deceived. These criminals, full of falsity, have tricked me many times. I have heard many a complaint about them, and they know how much they burden me. If I can get them into my power, I shall sell them dearly. Now, because I love you, I wish to be very certain of you and to bind you to me so that you may not repudiate your promise or covenant with me nor do anything you ought not to do. Since you seem loyal to me, it would be a sin if you were to play me false."

"Sir," I said, "hear me. I don't know why you ask pledges or surety of me. Already you know for a truth that you have so ravished and captured my heart that without your permission it could do nothing for me even if it wished to do so. This heart is yours, not mine, for it is bound, for good or ill, to do your pleasure, and no man can dispossess you of it. You have placed within it a garrison that will guard and rule it well. Beyond all that, if you fear anything, make a key for it and carry it with you. The key will serve in place of a pledge."

"By my head," said Love, "that idea is not a wild one, and I agree to it. He who has command over the heart is sufficiently lord of the body; and he who asks more is unreasonable." Then from his purse he drew a small, well-made key made of pure, refined gold. "With this," he said, "I shall lock your heart, and I require no other guarantee. My jewels are under this key; it is smaller than your little finger, yet it is the mistress of my jewelbox, and as such its power is great." Then he touched my side and locked my heart so softly that I hardly felt the key.

Thus I did all his will, and when I had put him out of doubt, I said:

"Sir, I have a great capacity for doing what you wish. But, by the faith that you owe me, receive my service with thanks. I do not say so out of weakness, for I do not fear your service in any way, but because a sergeant exerts himself in vain to perform worthy service if it does not please the lord for whom he does it."

Love replied, "Now do not be distressed. Since you are installed in my household, I shall take your service with thanks and raise you to high station if some wickedness does not steal it from you. Perhaps, however, such elevation will not come immediately. Great fortunes do not come in a few hours; pain and delay are necessary for them. Wait and endure the distress that now pains and wounds you, for I know very well by what potion you will be brought to your cure. If you maintain your loyalty I shall give you a marsh mallow unguent that will heal your wounds. By my head, it will certainly appear if you serve with a good heart, and it will depend on how you fulfill, night and day, the commandments that I prescribe for pure lovers."

"Sir," I said, "for the grace of God, before you move from here charge me with your commandments. I am in good heart to perform them, but perhaps if I didn't know them I could go astray immediately. Therefore, since I don't want to be mistaken in anything, I desire very much to learn them."

Love replied: "What you say is very good. Now listen and remember them. A master wastes his effort when the disciple does not turn his heart toward retaining what he hears so that he might remember it." The God of Love then charged me, word by word, with his commandments; this romance portrays them well. Let him who wishes to love give his attention to it, for the romance improves from this point on. From now on one will do well to listen to it, if he is one who knows how to recount it, for the end of the dream is very beautiful, and its matter is new. I tell you that he who will hear the end of the dream can learn a great deal about the games of Love, provided that he wishes to wait while I tell the tale in French and explain the dream's significance. The truth, which is hidden, will be quite open to you when you hear me explain the dream, for it doesn't contain a lying word.

Questions for Discussion:

1. Discuss the use of literary symbolism in *The Romance of the Rose*.
2. Compare *The Romance of the Rose* with the excerpt from *Lancelot* by Chrétien de Troyes (Document 10.4). How are the two romances similar? How do they differ?
3. What specific actions from the traditional homage ceremony take place as the God of Love secures his vassal? (Refer to Documents 5.1 and 5.2.)

4. How does the vision of Mechthild of Magdeburg (Document 12.11) utilize the love imagery also present in *The Romance of the Rose*?

Discuss her ecstatic religious experience in
these terms.

13.9   A Poetic Disputation: *The Owl and the Nightingale*

*The Owl and the Nightingale is an early thirteenth-
century poem, written by an anonymous author. It is a debate between two birds; each represents allegorically a value
system traditionally associated with that bird in earlier literature and popular medieval bestiaries.[11] The debate takes
place during one night, beginning in early evening and lasting until the early morning. In the course of the poem each
bird defends her own position and attacks her rival vehemently. Almost all of the speeches end in an amusing way,
in which the bird is overcome by anger and confusion. At the
end, the birds agree to submit their cases to a judge.*

*The intention of the poet appears to have been to pres-
ent conflicting contemporary ideas within the standard format of the scholarly debate, or* disputatio. *(See the
introduction to Document 10.10). The nightingale represents the ideas of courtly love poetry, and the owl stands for
the traditional moral views expressed by the Church. Scholars have identified the birds with various historical persons: in one interpretation, the Nightingale is King Henry
II, standing for the values espoused by the courtly love tradition, and the Owl is Thomas Becket, representing the
Church. (See Documents 9.3 and 9.4 for a discussion of
their conflict). Various verses in the poem support this view.*

*In one part of the poem the two birds argue about the
role of the Nightingale in the tale that Marie de France
used in the "Lay of the Nightingale" (Document 10.5). It
is interesting to compare the defense by the Nightingale
with Marie's version of the story.*

(From *The Owl and the Nightingale/; Cleanness; St Erkenwald*, translated and introduced by Brian Stone (Penguin Classics 1971,
Second Edition 1988). Copyright © Brian Stone, 1971, 1988.)

The Owl and the Nightingale

It happened in the summery heart
Of a secret vale's most hidden part,

I heard an Owl and Nightingale
Disputing on a mighty scale;
Most keen and strenuous the debate,
Now gentle, now in furious spate.
And each against the other swelled,
Each her spleen and ire expelled,
Saying the worst of every feature
That she could mock in the other creature;
Contention was especially strong
When each abused the other's song.

The first to speak, the Nightingale,
In a corner of the vale
Was perched upon a pretty twig
Where blossom showed on every sprig
And, fast entwined with reeds and sedge,
There grew a thick and lovely hedge.
She sang her varying tuneful lay,
Delighting in that flowering spray.
It seemed the melody she made
Was on a pipe or harpstring played,
That pipe or harp, not living throat,
Was shooting forth each pleasant note.
Nearby there stood a stump alone,
Decayed, with ivy overgrown.
And here the Owl had made her den,
And here sang out her 'hours'[12] to men.

The Nightingale surveyed the Owl,
And reckoned her opponent foul;
Indeed all men declare with right
That she's a hideous, loathsome sight.
'Monster!' she cried, 'Away! Fly off!'
Simply to see you's quite enough
To make me lose the urge to sing.
You're such an ugly, evil thing.
When you thrust out before my eyes,

---

[11]Bestiaries were treatises, usually illustrated, that contained alle-
gorical descriptions of birds and animals, both real and imaginary.

[12]The canonical hours of prayer as observed in monasteries. See
the *Rule* of Saint Benedict in Document 1.15.

My tongue is tied, my spirit dies,
Because your filthy clamoring
Makes me rather spit than sing.'
    The Owl held back till evening fell:
Then, as her heart began to swell,
Her breath to catch, her rage to grate,
She felt she could no longer wait,
And straight away exploded, 'How
Does this my singing strike you now?
D'you think I have no singing skill
Merely because I cannot trill?
You're always loading me with blame,
Girding at me with mock and shame.
If you were off that twig of yours,
And I could get you in my claws
(And would I could is all my boon),
You'd sing a different kind of tune.'
    To this the Nightingale replied,
'So long as I can safely hide
And shield myself against the cold
In quiet within this hedge's fold,
I neither attend to what you say,
Nor hear your threatenings with dismay.
I know how cruelly you attack
Small birds who cannot fight you back;
At every opportunity
You peck and tear them wantonly
And that is why all birds detest you,
Why when they find you they molest you,
Screeching and crying as they chase
And mob you till you leave the place.
Even the tiniest of the tits
Would gladly tear you into bits!
For you are loathsome through and through
And wholly hateful to the view:
Your neck is thin, your body squat,
Your head much bigger than the lot.
Your eyes are black as coal, and broad,
As if they had been daubed with woad.[13]
You glare as if you'd gorge on such
As come within your talons' clutch.
Your beak is hooked and sharp and strong.
A buckled awl, its shape gone wrong.
With it you gabble loud and long,
And that is what you call your song.

The Owl had grown distinctly vexed
While listening, and protested next:
'I know that Nightingale's your name
But "Chatterbox" would suit your fame
Because you have too much to say:
Tie down your tongue for a holiday!
You think all day belongs to you.
But I must have my own time, too,
So hold your peace and let me speak;
To take revenge is what I seek.
Observe how in my own defense
I speak with point and truth and sense.
You swear I hide myself by day,
And that I never shall gainsay,
So listen to me while I try
To tell the wherefore and the why.
I have a beak that's big and strong,
And splendid claws both sharp and long,
Which for the race of hawks is right.
It is my custom and delight
To lead the life to which I'm born;
At this no man can gibe in scorn.
In me it can be dearly seen
That Nature made me fierce and keen,
And loathed by little birds who fly
Low down and in the thickets ply.
They make a screaming, twittering sound
And flock in force to mob me round;
But I prefer to stay at rest.
Sitting quietly in my nest.
What profit should I then produce
By routing them with loud abuse,
Reviling them with shout and curse
As foul-mouthed shepherds do, or worse?
Upbraiding shrews affords few joys,
So I keep dear of all their noise.
There is a proverb wise in word;
On sages' lips it's often heard:
"To rail at fools brings only scorn,
Like trying to match an oven's yawn."
Another time I heard one quote
A maxim that King Alfred[14] wrote:
"As for scolding, brawls and strife,
A void the place where they are rife.
Let fools contend. and go your way."

---

[13]Woad was blue dye.

[14]King Alfred "the Great" of England (r. 871–899).

These words of wisdom I obey.
And Alfred said, still yet again,
A maxim widely known to men:
"He who meddles with what is mean
Never escapes entirely dean."
What harm do crows do to the hawk,
When in the marsh they cry and squawk,
Approaching him with rasping caw
As if they wished to start a war?
The hawk removes himself, being wise.
And leaves them with their grating cries.

    "Besides, another lie you tell
Is that I cannot sing too well,
But have a doleful voice and drear,
The sound of which is harsh to hear.
You lie: my voice in very truth
Is blithe, melodious and smooth.
You think that every voice is foul
Which differs from your squeaky howl.
My voice is masterful and strong,
And like a mighty horn in song,
While yours is like a tiny pipe
Fashioned from a reed unripe.
My voice is greatest, yours is least;
You chatter like an Irish priest.
I sing at eve, when song is due,
Give utterance at bed-time too,
And then at midnight once again,
And lastly lift my glad refrain
When I see rising from afar
In light of dawn, the morning star.
And so my song brings benefit,
Forewarning men with message fit,
But you sing all the livelong night
From evening time till morning light.
No matter that the night is long,
You always sing the selfsame song.
You never rest your wretched voice,
But fill the night and day with noise,
And constantly assault the ear,
So that people living near
Become so hostile to the din
They reckon it not worth a pin.
Thus pleasure can be overdone
And last so long it gladdens none.
For harp's, or pipe's, or bird's sweet song
Displeases if kept up too long;

However glad the song may be,
It brings delight in no degree
To him who hears against his will.
So I suggest your tongue be still.
For it is time, as Alfred said,
And in a book it may be read,
"The virtue of a thing grows less
By overdoing and excess."
Satiety corrupts all pleasure:
Disgust attends on lack of measure.
There's no delight that I can name
Which will survive if kept the same
Except the Kingdom of God above,
Unchanging in its endless love.
That basket, when you've seized your fill,
Is full to overflowing still;
God's kingdom, wonderful in fame,
Gives ceaselessly, yet stays the same.

    'You mock me with another slur,
To my defective eyes refer,
Because, you say, I fly by night
And cannot see when it is light.
But there you lie, for it is clear
In seeing I can have no peer,
Because however dark the night,
I penetrate it with my sight.
You think because it is my way
To fly by night, I'm blind by day.
But then by day the hare lies low,
Whose vision is faultless, even so.
If he is hounded by the pack,
He winds his way by narrow track,
Escaping by a motion quick,
Exploiting every clever trick,
Hopping and leaping from the chase
Until he finds his hiding place.
He could not so effect his flight
Unless his eyes possessed good sight.
And I can see, just like the hare,
And stay in daytime in my lair.
When valiant men prepare for war,
Then go campaigning near and far,
And overrun the folk they fight,
They often operate by night,
And then I follow such bold thanes,
Accompanying their battle trains.

    By now the Nightingale was cross.

Ashamed and rather at a loss,
Because the Owl in her harangue
Had mocked the place in which she sang—
Behind the house among the weed
Where men relieve their bodies' need.
But yet she sat and thought it through,
For in her heart of hearts she knew
That rage destroys wise counseling,
As Alfred says, that learned king:
'The hated man can't intercede;
The angry man's not fit to plead.'
For wrath stirs up the spirit's blood
With raging surges like a flood,
And overpowers the beating mind
Until with passion it is blind.
The spirit thus loses all its light,
Perceiving neither truth nor right.
All this, the bird well understood,
And waited for a calmer mood.
She'd speak much better, feeling quiet,
Than wrangling in a mood of riot.
      'Now listen to me, Owl,' said she,
'You'll trip: your path is slippery.
I flee behind the house, you say?
Of course, it's ours. What better way?
Where lord and lady lie in love,
I sit and sing, close by, above.
Do you suppose wise men forsake
The high road for the muddy brake!
Or that the sun will shine no more
Because your nest has a filthy floor?
So why should I my true place quit
For a board with hole cut out of it,
And sing no longer near the bed
Where lord and lady lay the head?
It is my duty and my law
To follow the highest evermore.
And if you vaunt aloud your song,
And boast of yelling fierce and strong,
And say that's how you tell mankind
To weep and leave their sins behind,
My answer is, if all lamented,
Screaming out as if tormented,
And screeching like an Owl, at least
They'd terrify the parish priest.
Man should be calm and not cry out,

Though tears for error are devout.
But when he honors Christ in song,
Man's praises should be loud and long:
Too loud and long can never be
For psalm and hymn sung fittingly.
You scream and wail; I sing with measure.
Your voice is tearful; mine gives pleasure.
Ever may you waste your breath
And squall as if you longed for death!
And may you howl your song accursed
Till both your eyes pop out and burst!
Of two, which is the better way,
That humans should be glum, or gay?
May you and I be ever so fated,
That you be glum, and I elated!
You ask me why I do not travel
To sing to strangers. What a cavil!
What should I do with folk to whom
Content and pleasure never come?
The land is poor, a barren place,
A wilderness devoid of grace,
Where crags and rocks pierce heaven's air,
And snow and hail are everywhere—
A grisly and uncanny part
Where men are wild and grim of heart.
Security and peace are rare,
And how they live they do not care.
The flesh and fish they eat are raw;
Like wolves, they tear it with the paw.
They take both milk and whey for drink;
Of other things they cannot think,
Possessing neither wine nor beer.
They live like wild beasts all the year
And wander clad in shaggy fell
As if they'd just come out of hell.
If some good man to them would come
—As once one came from holy Rome
To teach them virtue's better way
And help them shake off evil's sway—
He'd wish he'd stayed at home, I swear:
He'd only waste his time up there;
For he could get a bear to wield
A spear and hold a warrior's shield
More easily than men so wild
To hear my song and be beguiled.
What use would be my singing there?

However long-drawn-out or fair,
It would be wasted, wholly idle.
Since not the halter, not the bridle,
Nor tool of iron or weapon of steel
Could bring such maddened dogs to heel.
But in a land of pleasant charm
Where folk are gentle, kind and calm,
I exercise my tuneful throat
And render services of note.
Glad tidings to such folk I bring;
The Church's hymns are what I sing.
It stated in the law of old
—That wisdom yet assures the fold—
The harvest that a man should mow
Is where he went to plough and sow,
For he is mad who sows his seed
Where grass and blossom cannot speed.'
　　These words filled Owl with conflict dire;
Her eyes grew huge and rolled with ire.
'You say you guard man's homely bower
Adorned with leaf and fairest flower,
Where lovers lie in close embrace,
One bed their sheltered hiding place.
Once you sang—and I know where—[15]
Outside a certain house, and there,
By singing high and singing low
You taught the lady how to know
And do the lustful deed of shame—
Foul passion to her body's blame.
The lord, observing how things were,
Set bird-lime, traps and many a snare
To catch you at your little game,
And when to the lattice then you came,
A trap soon gripped you by the shins
And paid you out for all your sins.
Your doom was to be torn in bits
By raging horses: and it fits.
So if you try to soil the life
Again of virgin or of wife,
Expect your song to bring despair
And hopeless fluttering in a snare.'

The Nightingale, enraged to hear
These words, with sword and point of spear
As human warrior would have fought,
But being unable, next she sought
The weapon of her prudent tongue.
'Who talks well fights well' once was sung.
And to her tongue she turned instead:
('Who talks well fights well' Alfred said.)
'You say all this to give me shame.
The husband got the final blame.
He was so jealous of his wife
He could not bear, to save his life,
To see her with a man converse,
For that would break his heart, or worse.
He therefore locked her in a room
—A harsh and savage kind of doom.
And this aroused my pity so
That I was sorry for her woe,
And often pleasured her with song,
Singing early, singing long.
And this enraged the jealous knight;
He hated me with purest spite.
He tried to put on me the blame,
But it redounded to his shame.
King Henry came to know of this—
May Christ preserve his soul in bliss!
And outlawed that suspicious knight,
Who out of evil wrath and spite
In such a worthy king's domain
Had made his wicked purpose plain
By seizing one so small and thin
And robbing her of life and limb.
So honor came to all our kind.
The knight lost all, and he was fined
A hundred pounds, which came to me.
Since then in blithe security
My birds have lived, as well they might,
In utmost joy and high delight.
With such revenge so well consoled,
Since then my speech has been more bold.
The precedent of that one case
Gives me my ever-happy face,
For I can lift my voice at will,
And none can do me any ill.
But you, you starveling! Stinking spook!
You cannot find a single nook

---

[15]In the next exchange, the Owl and the Nightingale comment on the well-known tale of courtly love that existed in many versions, including "The Lay of the Nightingale" by Marie de France (Document 10.5).

Or hollow log to cower in
Secure from foes who'll pinch your skin.
For boy and girl, master and groom,
Conspire to bring about your doom.
When you sit still, they pouch up stones
And clods to pelt your ugly bones,
And then let fly until you're battered
Off your perch, your body shattered.
And if you're toppled off or shot,
The first good use can then be got
From you, for, hoist upon a rod,
Your bag-shaped body, foul and odd,
Your ghastly neck, most surely scare
From cornfields birds who wander there.
You're useless, full of life and blood,
But as a scarecrow, pretty good.
For sparrow, goldfinch, rook and crow
Will never venture where they know
The seed's new-sown if on that land
Your carcass dangles close at hand.
When trees put forth their blooms in spring,
And young seeds come to burgeoning,
No bird will dare to pluck them if
You're hanging overhead all stiff.
Alive, you fill mankind with dread;
It's just the same when you are dead.
So surely now you realize
How your appearance terrifies
When you're alive and drawing breath,
Since dangling upside down in death
You still inspire the utmost awe
In those who screamed at you before.
And men are right to loathe you, for
You sing of troubles evermore.
All that you sing of, soon or late,
Is men's misfortunes, which they hate.
When they have heard you screech at night
Most men are filled with dread and fright.
You sing when death is due to strike,

Or any woe that men dislike.
The loss of goods your song portends,
Or ruin and disgrace of friends.
Forays of warriors you foretell,
Thief-hunts and houses burnt as well.
Of farmers' coming woes you cry,
And hoot when stock is going to die.
Of husband's death you warn the wife,
And also herald legal strife.
You sing of man's disasters, so
Through you he comes to ruin and woe.
You never sing except when some
Adversity is bound to come,
And that is why men always shun you,
Why they pelt and beat and stun you
With sticks and stones and turf and clods—
Then your escape's against all odds.
Cursed be the beadle with his shout
Who spreads such wretched truths about!
Who always brings unpleasant news,
And burdens men with loathsome views!
May all who wear good linen cloth,
And God as well, split you with wrath!'

{*At the end of the poem the Owl and the Nightingale fly off together to submit their case to an impartial judge.*}

Questions for Discussion:

1. Discuss the various insults the birds trade in order to prove their preeminence.
2. How does the explanation of the Nightingale concerning the wife in "The Lay of the Nightingale" differ from that of Marie de France?
3. How does the author use the Owl as a symbol of serious moral purpose, as opposed to the frivolity of the Nightingale? Cite specific verses in your discussion.

Gothic Architecture

INTERPRETING THE EVIDENCE

13.10   The Cathedral as Symbol: From *The Symbolism of Churches and Church Ornaments* by William Durandus

An important facet of medieval thought is the concept of the symbol. Just as Bonaventure and Aquinas devoted much thought to the question of the relationship between human beings and God, the architects of churches and cathedrals designed their buildings to reflect the hidden, God-given meaning that, according to scholastic thought, existed in the objects of the physical world. In the following excerpt from The Symbolism of Churches and Church Ornaments, *William Durandus (1230–1296), a French churchman and professor of canon law, provides a key for understanding the theological essence hidden within the structural pattern.*

(From *The Symbolism of Churches and Church Ornaments*, by William Durandus, trans. by John Mason Neale and Benjamin Webb [London: J.G.F. & J. Rivington, 1843], pp. 24–35.)

14. The arrangement of a material church resembles that of the human body: the Chancel, or place where the Altar is, represents the head: the Transepts, the hands and arms, and the remainder, —towards the west,—the rest of the body. The sacrifice of the Altar denotes the vows of the heart. Furthermore, according to Richard of Saint Victor, the arrangement of a church typifies the three states in the Church: of virgins, of the continent, of the married. The Sanctuary is smaller than the Chancel, and this than the Nave: because the virgins are fewer in number than the continent, and these than the married. And the Sanctuary is more holy than the Chancel; and the Chancel than the Nave: because the order of virgins is more worthy than that of the continent, and the continent more worthy than the married.

15. Furthermore, the church consists of four walls, that is, is built on the doctrine of the Four Evangelists; and has length, breadth, and height: the height represents courage,—the length fortitude, which patiently endures till it attains its heavenly Home; the breadth is charity, which, with long suffering, loves its friends in God, and its foes for God; and again, its height is the hope of future retribution, which despises prosperity and adversity, hoping to see the goodness of the Lord in the land of the living.

16. Again, in the Temple of God, the foundation is Faith, which is conversant with unseen things: the roof, Charity, which covers a multitude of sins. The door, Obedience, of which the Lord says, "If you will enter into life, keep the commandments." The pavement, humility, of which the Psalmist said, my soul cleaves to the pavement.

17. The four side walls, the four cardinal virtues, justice, fortitude, temperance, prudence. Hence the Apocalypse says, "The city lies four square." The windows are hospitality with cheerfulness, and tenderness with charity. Concerning this house says the Lord, "We will come unto him, and make our abode with him." But some churches are built in the shape of a Cross, to signify, that we are crucified to the world. . . . Some also are built in the form of a circle: to signify that the Church has been extended throughout the circle of the world. . . .

18. The Choir is so called from the harmony of the clergy in their chanting, or from the multitude collected at the divine offices. The word *chorus* is derived from *chorea,* or from *corona.* For in early times they stood like a crown round the Altar, and thus sung the Psalms in one body: but Flavianus[16]

---

[16]Flavianus and Theodorus (fl. mid 4th century) were laymen who introduced antiphonal singing in the services. They later became bishops, Flavianus at Antioch, and Theodorus at Tarsus.

(continued)

and Theodorus taught the antiphonal method of chanting, having received a vision from St. Ignatius, who learned it himself by inspiration. The two choirs then typify the angels, and the spirits of just men, while they cheerfully and mutually excite each other in this holy exercise. Others derive *chorus* from *concord,* which consists of charity; because he who has not charity, cannot sing with the spirit. But what this Choir signifies, and why the greatest in it sit last, shall be explained in the fourth book. And observe, that when one sings, it is called in Greek a *monody,* in Latin *tycinium.* When two sing, it is called *bicinium*; when many, a *chorus.*

19. The Exedra is an apsis, separated a little from a temple or palace; so called because it projects a little from the wall, and signifies the lay portion of the Faithful joined to Christ and the Church. The Crypts, or subterranean caves, which we find in some churches, are hermits who are devoted to a solitary life.

20. The open court signifies Christ, by Whom an entrance is administered into the heavenly Jerusalem: this is also called porch, from *porta,* a gate, or because it is *aperta,* open.

21. The towers are the preachers and Prelates of the Church, which are Her bulwark and defense. Whence the Bridegroom in the Canticles said to the Bride, "Thy neck is like the tower of David built for an armory." The pinnacles of the towers signify the life or the mind of a Prelate which aspires heavenwards. . . .

24. The glass windows in a church are Holy Scriptures, which expel the wind and the rain, that is all things hurtful, but transmit the light of the True Sun, that is, God, into the hearts of the Faithful. These are wider within than without, because the mystical sense is the more ample, and precedes the literal meaning. Also, by the windows the senses of the body are signified: which ought to be shut to the vanities of this world, and open to receive with all freedom spiritual gifts.

25. By the lattice work of the windows, we understand the prophets or other obscure teachers of the Church Militant: in which windows there

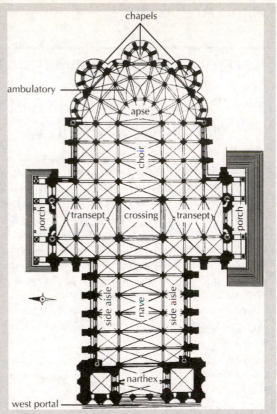

The Cathedral as Symbol: Groundplan of Chartres Cathedral (© 1996 Harry N. Abrams, Inc.)

are often two shafts, signifying the two precepts of charity, or because the Apostles were sent out to preach two and two.

26. The door of the church is Christ: according to that saying in the Gospel, "I am the door."...

Chartres Cathedral is often cited as the best example of Gothic style. Some scholars have studied its measurements in order to demonstrate that medieval architects were striving to replicate the "Divine Numbers" and proportions of the Christian-Platonic conception of the universe in this building. It is also possible to see in the cruciform groundplan various features of architectural symbolism discussed by William Durandus.

Questions for Discussion:

1. Do you think Aquinas and Bonaventure would agree with the symbolic analysis of Durandus? How would each philosopher interpret the descriptions?
2. Using the groundplan of Chartres Cathedral, point out the various symbols, according to Durandus.
3. Several scholars have compared the systematic method of Thomas Aquinas with the Gothic cathedral. Do you agree that they have common features? What are these?

INTERPRETING THE EVIDENCE

13.11   Architecture and Geometry: From the *Portfolio* of Villard de Honnecourt

The practical techniques of medieval architects remain shrouded in mystery, with only a few clues available to historians of architecture. One source that indicates the importance of geometry in the training of the architect and the practice of masonry is the Portfolio *of the thirteenth-century Frenchman Villard de Honnecourt. In his preface, Villard tells us: ". . . in this book may be found good help to the knowledge of the great powers of masonry, and of devices in carpentry. It also shows the power of the art of delineation, the outlines being regulated and taught in accordance with geometry." His portfolio contains sketches of sacred and secular people, symbolic and moral figures, studies of antique objects and natural phenomena, and animals of all kinds. There are several plates of churches and other buildings, including the tower of Laon Cathedral, and the chapels of Rheims Cathedral. The following chart of drawings, which was added to the* Portfolio *by an anonymous successor of Villard, indicates the importance of geometry in the training and practice of medieval builders, providing exercises for apprentices to follow. The various drawings have somewhat nebulous captions, but many can be thought of as problems in practical measurement. It is clear from later writings that the chart provided, among other things, the*

directions for the elevation of pinnacles through the use of geometrical methodology.

(From *Facsimile of the Sketch-Book of Wilars de Honecort,* trans. and ed. by Robert Willis [London: John Henry and James Parker, 1859], PL. XXXIII, pp. 118–133.)

1. "Par cu prenum la grosse done conlonbe que on ne voit mie tote." ["How to take the diameter of a column of which only half is visible."]
2. "Ar chu trovom le point en mi on canpe a conpas." ["How to find the point in the centre of a circular area."]
3. "Ar chu tail om le mole don grant arc dedens. III. Pies de tere." ["How to cut the mold of a great arch in a space of three feet."]
4. "Ar chu vosom une arc le cintreel de vers le ciel." ["This shows an arch, the centering of which is on the outer side."]
5. "Ar chu fait om on cavece a XII verrieres." ["How to make an apse with twelve windows."]
6. "Ar chu tail om erracenmens." ["Thus are shaped the first, or springing stones of a vault, or arch."]
7. "Ar chu fait om cheir deus pires a un point si lons ne seront." ["By this means two stones

(continued)

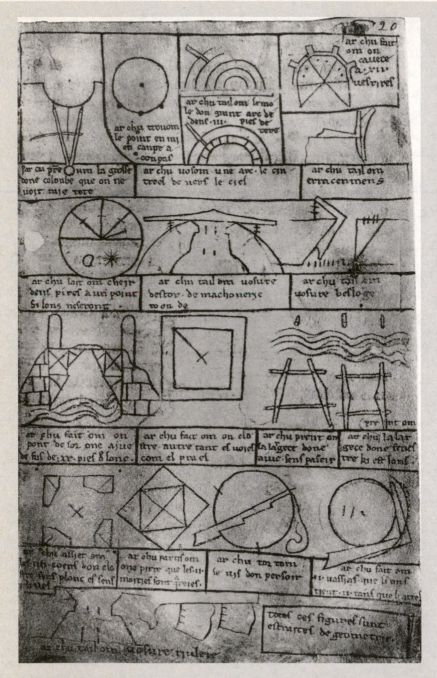

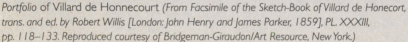

Portfolio of Villard de Honnecourt (From Facsimile of the Sketch-Book of Villard de Honecort, trans. and ed. by Robert Willis [London: John Henry and James Parker, 1859], PL. XXXIII, pp. 118–133. Reproduced courtesy of Bridgeman-Giraudon/Art Resource, New York.)

can be brought to the same point, if they are not far distant."]

8. "Ar chu tail om vosure destor de machonerie roonde." ["Thus is cut the voussoir (of a window) in a building of circular masonry."]

9. "Ar chu tail om vosure besloge." ["In this way is cut a skew voussoir."]

10. "Par chu fait om on pont de sor one aive de fus de XX pies de lonc." ["This is the way to make a bridge over a river of wood of twenty feet in length."]

11. "Ar chu fait om on clostre, autretant es voies com el prael." ["Thus a cloister may be laid out, both with regard to the passages and to the garden."]

12. "Ar chu prent on la largece done aive. sens paseir." ["Thus is measured the breadth of a stream without crossing it."]

13. "Ar chu prent om la largece done fenestre ki est lons." ["Thus is measured the breadth of a distant window, or other opening."]

14. "Ar chu assiet am les .IIII. coens don clostre sens plonc es sens linel." ["Thus may be set the four corner-stones of a cloister without plummet or level."]

15. "Ar chu partis om one pirre que les .II. moities sont a queres." ["How to divide a stone so that both halves are quadratic."]

16. "Ar chu tor tom le vis don persoir." ["Thus is turned (or carved) the screw of a press."]

17. "Ar chu fait om .II. vassias. que li ons tient .II. tans que li atres." ["How to make two vessels so that one shall hold twice as much as the other."]

18. "Ar chu tail on vosure riuleie." ["How to cut a voussoir according to rule."]

Of particular interest are Figures 11 and 15, which foreshadow the process by which medieval masons were able to design and build the architectural details of their structures. This method was confirmed more clearly in the notebooks of the fifteenth-century architect of Regensburg Cathedral, Mathes Roriczer. Squares were inscribed and rotated within the initial square, which enabled the architect to produce plans of the vertical components such as gables and pinnacles. By taking selected lengths from the initial square with a compass and multiplying them, the heights of each stage of the elevation were determined. Using this technique, the masons were able to elevate their buildings so that all parts of the structure were in proportion to each other and to the whole. The geometrical basis for the process probably held symbolic, as well as practical, importance, as medieval architects strived to replicate the divine ratios that God was believed to have used in creating the universe. (See Document 13.5 for a discussion of divine numbers by Saint Bonaventure.)

Question for Discussion:

1. Compare the groundplan of Chartres Cathedral (Document 13.10) with the figures in Villard's *Portfolio*. Are there specific areas where such directions might have been used in constructing the building?

INTERPRETING THE EVIDENCE

13.12 Trinity Chapel in Canterbury Cathedral and Gervase of Canterbury

In addition to drawings such as those of Villard, architectural historians also use written descriptions in an attempt to understand the methodology of medieval architects. One valuable account was written by Gervase of Canterbury (c. 1141–c. 1210), a monk in Canterbury who lived through the struggle between King Henry II and Thomas Becket and the murder of the archbishop. He was a keen observer of the political situation, which he recounted in his many chronicles. Of particular interest is his description of the fire and the rebuilding of

(continued)

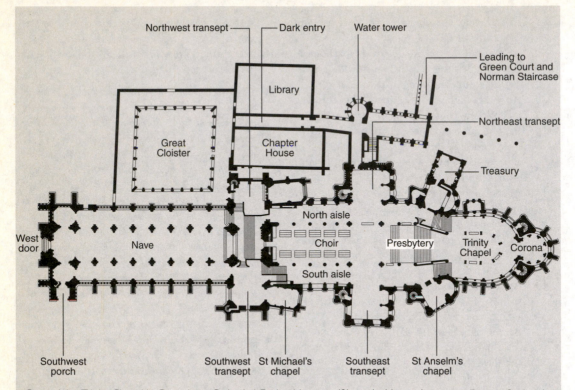

Groundplan, Trinity Chapel in Canterbury Cathedral, England. Late twelfth–early thirteenth century. *(Drawn after Jonathan Keates and Angelo Hornak, Canterbury Cathedral [London: Summerfield Press Ltd. and Philip Wilson Publishers, 1980], p. 95.)*

Canterbury Cathedral. The fire occurred in 1174, and the construction of the new choir began shortly thereafter. Gervase reports that many architects from England and France were summoned to present proposals for the project, and William of Sens was chosen "because of the liveliness of his spirit and his good reputation." The following portion of Gervase's work tells of the problems and triumphs of the new construction. The document concludes with a comparison between the new choir and the old cathedral, providing a succinct contrast between the earlier style and the new Gothic features.

(From Paul Frankl, *The Gothic*. © 1960 by Princeton University Press. Reprinted by permission of Princeton University Press.

In that summer [1178] he [William of Sens] erected ten piers, starting from the transept *(crux)*, five on a side. The first two of these he decorated with marble engaged columns and constituted

piers of the crossing like the two other {western} ones. Above these he set ten arches and the vaults. But after the two triforia and the upper windows on both sides were completed and he had prepared the machines *(machinas)* for vaulting the great vault in the beginning of the fifth year [September 1178], he suddenly plunged to the ground, as beams gave way under his feet, stones and timbers falling with him, from the height of the capitals of the upper vault, namely, fifty feet. Painfully injured by the impact of the stones and timbers, he had become of no use to himself or the work, but no one else was in any way hurt. Against the master alone raged the vengeance of God or the malice of the devil.

The master, thus injured, although he lay long in bed under care of doctors in the hope of recovering his health, was disappointed in his expectation and could not recover. Since, however, the winter

Trinity Chapel in Canterbury Cathedral *(Erich Lessing/Art Resource, New York.)*

[1178] was approaching and it was necessary that the upper vault be completed, he delegated the finishing of the work to an industrious and gifted monk, who had supervised the masons; from this much envy and intrigue resulted, because the monk, though younger, seemed wiser than others, richer and more powerful. The master, however, gave orders from his bed as to what should be done first and what later. Thus the vault between the four main piers was completed; in the keystone of this quadripartite ribbed vault *(ciborii)* the choir and the arms of the transept seem, as it were, to convene *(convenire)*. Two quadripartite ribbed vaults were also constructed on each side before winter [1178]. Heavy continuous rains did not permit of more work. With that the fourth year was concluded and the fifth begun [September 5, 1178]. In the same year, the fourth [1178], there occurred an eclipse of the sun [September 13, 1178] at the sixth hour before the master's fall. Since the master knew that no art or diligence of the physicians could enable him to recover, he gave

up the work and returned home across the sea to France. He was followed, however, in the charge of the work by another of the name of William, of English descent, small in stature, but very wise and skilled in various kinds of work. In the summer of the fifth year [1179] he completed both arms of the transept, the southern and the northern, and constructed the vault over the great altar, the completion of which had been prevented by the heavy rains of the preceding year in spite of all the preparations. Beside this, he laid the foundation for the extension of the church to the east, since there the chapel of St. Thomas [Becket] was to be built. This place, then, was destined for him, namely, the chapel of the Holy Trinity, where he had celebrated his first mass, where he was wont to prostrate himself with tears and prayers, under whose crypt he had lain buried for so many years, where God through his merits performed so many miracles, where rich and poor, kings and princes had revered him, from whence the sound of his praise had gone forth to all the lands of the earth.

It was said above, that after the fire practically all the old parts of the choir were torn down and transformed into a new edifice of noble form. But now it must be stated in what the difference of the two works consists. The form of the old and new piers is the same and also their thickness is the same, but their length is different. That is to say, the new piers were increased in their length by about twelve feet. In the old capitals the work was plane; in the new ones the chisel work is subtle. There, twenty-two piers stood in the passage around the choir; here, on the other hand, are twenty-eight. There, the arches and everything else had been made flat [in relief], as though done with an axe and not with a chisel; here, there is suitable chisel work on almost all things. No marble columns were to be found there, but here there are innumerable ones. There, in the passage around the choir, there were quadripartite groined vaults *(fornices planae);* here, they are provided with ribs *(arcuatae)* and keystones *(clavatae).* There, a wall, built above the piers, divided the arms of the transept from the choir, but here, not separated

(continued)

from the crossing, they seem to meet in the one keystone in the middle of the great vault that rests on the four main piers. There was a wooden ceiling there, adorned with excellent painting; here, there is a vault, gracefully wrought of stone and light tufa. There is only one triforium; here, there are two in the nave of the choir and a third in the aisle. All this, if one wishes to understand it, will be revealed more clearly by the sight of the church than by words. In any case, this must be known, that the new work is as much higher than the old as the upper windows, both those of the nave *(corporis chori)* and those of the aisles of the choir, are raised by the marble intermediate story. But lest anyone in future times be doubtful as to why the great width of the choir next to the tower should be so much contracted at its head at the end of the church, I did not consider it superfluous to give the reason.

Questions for Discussion:

1. According to Gervase, what were the differences between the cathedral as it stood before the fire of 1174 and the new construction?
2. Compare the images of Canterbury Cathedral with the groundplan and photograph of the basilica of St. Madeleine at Vézelay (Document 8.2). What differences are evident in the two buildings? What are the common features?
3. How does Canterbury Cathedral embody the vision of Abbot Suger as described in his work, *De Consecratione* (Document 10.3)?

INTERPRETING THE EVIDENCE

13.13   Rose Window of Notre Dame and Jean de Jandun's Description

Jean de Jandun (c. 1286–c. 1328) was a philosopher who taught at the University of Paris. He is best known for his commentaries on the works of Averroes (see Document 10.11). He obviously found Paris to be an extraordinary city, and his affection resulted in his Treatise on the Praises of Paris *(1323). The following excerpt describes the cathedral of Notre Dame, which remains one of the extraordinary buildings of the world.*

(From *Medieval Cathedrals,* by William W. Clark. Westport, CT: Greenwood Press, 2006, pp. 248–249. Copyright © 2006 by Greenwood Press. Reprinted by permission of ABC-CLIO, LLC.)

In Paris, the privileged sanctuary of the Christian religion, beautiful buildings consecrated to God have been founded in such great numbers that there are probably not many cities, even among the most powerful cities of Christianity that can count so many houses of God. Among these houses, the imposing church of the most glorious Virgin Mary, Mother of God, shines brilliantly at the first rank, like the sun among the stars. And if certain people, by the freedom of their appreciation can only see a few things easily, testify to the beauty of other churches before her, I think, if they examine the whole [church] and the details, will quickly abandon that opinion. Where can you find, I ask you, two towers of such magnificence, so perfect, so high, so large, so strong, enriched with such a variety and multiplicity of

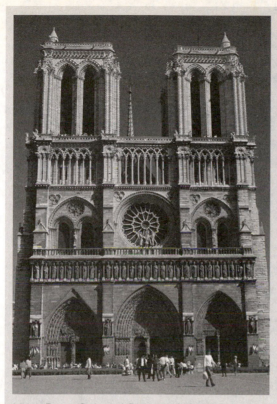

Notre Dame Cathedral, Paris, ca. 1200–1250
(Corbis RF)

Notre Dame Cathedral: South Rose Window
(Giraudon/Art Resource, New York.)

decoration. Where can you encounter, I beg you, so complex a series of lateral vaults both below and above. When do you find, I repeat, the splendid light from such a ring of chapels. That's not all: tell me in what other church will I see a transept of comparable grandeur where this arm separates the choir from the nave. Finally, it gives me pleasure to say, where could I see two similar rose windows opposite one another in a straight line, roses the resemblance to which gives them the name of the fourth vowel [O]. Below, smaller roses, rosettes arranged with marvelous art, some in circles, others in lozenges [diamond shapes], surrounding the glittering windows embellished in precious colors

and with figures painted with the most exquisite delicacy. In truth, I think that this church offers to those who look attentively such a subject for admiration that the soul never tires of contemplating it.

Questions for Discussion:

1. What specific features of Notre Dame are singled out by Jean de Jandun as exceptional?
2. This description is realistic, rather than symbolic. What aspects of the church could be understood symbolically, as in the excerpt by Durandus (Document 13.10).?

Chapter 14

※

The Fourteenth Century: Disorder and Vitality

The fourteenth century was an era that presented great challenges, ultimately producing new social, religious, and artistic attitudes. It began with a period of climate change, during which the temperatures of most of Europe became approximately twenty degrees cooler. This meant that the growing season was considerably shorter, and the grain harvests significantly smaller. There was not enough food for the population, which had been increasing rapidly during the previous three hundred years, and, according to various Chronicles, including that of Jean de Venette, serious famines occurred in many areas (Document 14.1). Weakened by lack of nutrition, the people were susceptible to disease, and in mid-century, the bubonic plague, or Black Death, claimed as much as one-third to one-half of the European population. Moreover, the pestilence, which took several forms, was not an exclusively European phenomenon. This chapter offers an account of the origins of the plague by Nicephorus Gregoras, followed by descriptions of the disease in Constantinople by John VI Kantakouzenos and in Palestine by Abu Hafs Umar Ibn al-Wardi. Further documents by the European writers Boccaccio, Jean de Venette, and Henry Knighton demonstrate the vast extent of the epidemic (Documents 14.2–14.7).

The people who did survive the plague found themselves in a very different world. The "feudal contract" that had provided stability since the eleventh century disintegrated, as inheritance procedures were impossible to implement. Furthermore, the manorial system dissolved, as serfs were able to bargain for better situations. A rising level of expectation in the next generation led to revolt when the nobles attempted to resurrect the old seigniorial dues. One example of this type of regulation is the Statute of Laborers enacted in England in 1349 (Document 14.8). An analysis of this law gives an indication of some of the reasons for peasant uprisings. These rebellions occurred in several areas of western Europe, as the peasants resisted noble dominance. They were joined in these uprisings by the unskilled and oppressed urban workers. (See Document 14.9)

War provided yet another catastrophe, as England and France engaged in the longest conflict in western history—the so-called Hundred Years War. The details of this conflict are complicated, as the excerpt from Froissart's Chronicles indicates. In the early decades the English, by virtue of their superior technology, won many significant and decisive battles. However, the French were eventually victorious, and in the mid-fifteenth century, England lost all of its French possessions, with the exception of the port of Calais. (See Document 14.10)

The Church also suffered a crisis, brought on partially by the new religious currents that began during the twelfth century (see Chapter 12) and partly because of the inability of ecclesiastical leaders to address questions pertaining to the reasons for famine, plague, war, and revolt. As a result of political difficulties within the hierarchy of the Church, as well as influence by the French king Philip IV, the papacy moved to Avignon, in southern France, where it remained from 1304 to 1377—a period known as the "Avignon Papacy." During this time the Church developed an extraordinarily efficient bureaucracy, although there was criticism of clerical immorality. Two letters in this chapter, one by Petrarch and another by Catherine of Siena (Documents 14.11 and 14.12), describe the atmosphere of the papal court, but it must be remembered that they were writing as religious zealots with their own political agendas.

Taken together, these crises caused a change in every aspect of life, including artistic and literary expression. The response of artists and writers brought about new styles and new preoccupations, as they began to examine the natural world and human emotions in a more realistic way. Although they did not depart entirely from a religiously centered approach, their works were infused with new values of realism; art was no longer simply a vehicle for religious instruction, and literature began to portray actual human experience, rather than idealized behavior.

One of the finest poets of the late Middle Ages was Dante, whose Divine Comedy is often considered to be the apogee of medieval literature. As may be seen in the Canto from Paradiso, the third part of his vast work, he combined religious motivation and imagery with human love to create a new synthesis (Document 14.13). Love is also the subject of the Sonnets of Petrarch (Document 14.14), whose poems reflect the courtly tradition evident in the lyrics of the troubadours, trouvères, and trobairitz (Document 10.7).

As will be seen in the works of Giovanni Boccaccio (1313–1375) and Geoffrey Chaucer (1342–1400), literature became entertaining, rather than didactic (Documents 14.15 and 14.16). It is important to remember that the works of these men, as well as Dante and Petrarch, were written in the vernacular languages—Italian or, in the case of Chaucer, English. This meant that a much wider audience had access to their writings. In addition, women's literary voices were in evidence in the fourteenth century, as shown by the excerpt from the works of Christine de Pizan

(1364–1430), whose diatribe against The Romance of the Rose *is included here (Document 14.17).*

The works of the artist Giotto also began to portray the physical aspects and emotions of actual human beings, rather than maintaining the stiff, stylized approach of artistic expression in the Middle Ages. The "Interpreting the Evidence" feature, Document 14.18, presents one of his

frescoes, Lamentation, *along with comments by his fellow artist, Ghiberti, as well as Boccaccio.*

This chapter will explore various facets of this transitional era, demonstrating that the chaotic circumstances of famine, plague, rebellion, and war fostered a vital new approach to life that would ultimately lead to the early modern world.

Famine and Plague

14.1   Famine: The *Chronicle of Jean De Venette*

Jean de Venette (c. 1308-1369), a Carmelite monk, was head of the order's French province from 1342 to 1366. He was a keen observer of the contemporary world, and, as his Chronicle *demonstrates, his sympathies lay with the peasants who were the victims of famine, pestilence, war, and plunder. His work, a valuable eyewitness document, begins with his account of a prophecy.*

(From *The Chronicle of Jean de Venette*, translated by Jean Birdsall. Copyright © 1953 Columbia University Press. Reprinted with permission of the publisher. Translation modified.)

1340

In the year of the Lord 1315, on the fifteenth day of the month of March, shall begin so great a famine on earth that the people of low degree shall strive and struggle against the mighty and rich of this world. Also the wreath of the mightiest boxer shall fall to the ground very quickly afterwards. Also its flowers and its branches shall be broken and crushed. Also a noble and free city shall be seized and taken by slaves. Also [the population of] strangers shall increase there. Also the Church shall totter and the line of Saint Peter shall

be execrated. Also the blood of many shall be poured out on the ground. Also a red cross shall appear and shall be lifted up. Therefore, good Christians, watch.

These are the words of this vision, but what they mean is not known.

Yet you must know that I, at the age of seven or eight, saw this great and mighty famine begin in the very year foretold, 1315. It was so severe in France that most of the population died of hunger and want. And this famine lasted two years and more, for it began in 1315 and ceased in 1318.

Questions for Discussion:

1. What are the specific catastrophes prophesied in the vision? As you read this chapter, keep these prognostications in mind.
2. "The people of low degree shall strive and struggle against the mighty and rich of this world." Discuss this statement within the context of the information in the previous chapters concerning serfdom.

The Black Death: Pestilence from East to West

14.2   The Origins of the Plague: *Historia Byzantina*

Most scholars agree that the plague began in Asia. By the spring of 1347 the pestilence had arrived at Constantinople, which was the central port for Italian shipping from the Black Sea. From this point the disease was rapidly transferred to the ports along the Mediterranean Sea, especially Italy, southern France, and Spain. The first selection concerning the plague as written by the historian Nicephorus Gregoras

(c. 1295–c. 1359), who documented the arrival of the disease in the Greek world in his work Historia Byzantina.

(Originally titled "Nicephorus Gregoras, Byzantine History, 1347-1349.' From Christos S. Bartsocas, "Two Fourteenth Century Greek Descriptions of the 'Black Death'" in *Journal of the History of Medicine and Allied Sciences* 21 (1966). Reprinted by permission of Oxford University Press.)

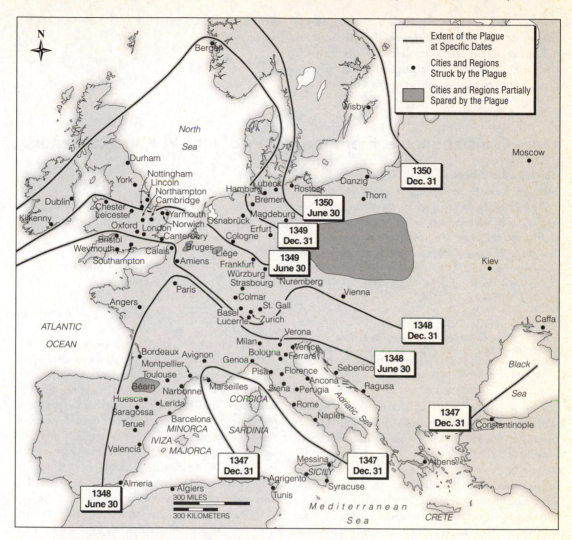

Spread of the Black Death (From Kagan et al., *The Western Heritage*, 10th ed., p. 259.)

During that time [1347], a serious and pestilential disease invaded humanity. Starting from Scythia [southern Russia] and Maeotis and the mouth of the Tanais [Don River], just as spring began, it lasted for that whole year, passing through and destroying, to be exact, only the continental coast, towns as well as country areas, ours and those that are adjacent to ours, up to Gadera and the columns of Hercules [Straits of Gibraltar].

During the second year [1348] it invaded the Aegean Islands. Then it affected the Rhodians, as well as the Cypriots and those colonizing the other islands. The calamity attacked men as well as women, rich and poor, old and young. To put matters simply, it did not spare those of any age or fortune. Several homes were emptied of all their inhabitants in one day or sometimes in two. No one could help anyone else, not even the neighbors, or the family, or blood relations.

The calamity did not destroy men only, but many animals living with and domesticated by men. I speak of dogs and horses and all the species of birds, even the rats that happened to live within the walls of the houses. The prominent signs of this disease, signs indicating early death, were tumorous outgrowths at the roots of thighs and arms and simultaneously bleeding ulcerations, which, sometimes the same day, carried the infected rapidly out of this present life, sitting or walking.

Questions for this section follow Document 14.7.

14.3   Constantinople: From the *History* of John VI Kantakouzenos

The following description of the plague was written by John VI Kantakouzenos, emperor of Byzantium from 1341 to 1354. In the latter year he was forced to abdicate, and he retired to a monastery, where he wrote a History of the Byzantine Empire. *His account of the symptoms of the Black Death, taken from this work, was based on first-hand experience, since his youngest son, Andronkos, died of the pestilence shortly after the plague struck Constantinople. John VI lived until 1383.*

(Originally titled "John VI Kantakouzenos, History, 1347–1348." From Christos S. Bartsocas, "Two Fourteenth Century Greek Descriptions of the 'Black Death'" in *Journal of the History of Medicine and Allied Sciences* 21 (1966). Reprinted by permission of Oxford University Press.)

So incurable was the evil, that neither any regularity of life, nor any bodily strength could resist it. Strong and weak bodies were all similarly carried away, and those best cared for died in the same manner as the poor. No other disease of any kind presented itself that year. If someone had a previous illness he always succumbed to this disease and no physician's art was sufficient; neither did the disease take the same course in all persons, but the others, unable to resist, died the same day, a few even within the hour. Those who could resist for two or three days had a very violent fever at first, the disease in such cases attacking the head; they suffered from speechlessness and insensibility to all happenings and then appeared as if sunken into a deep sleep. Then, if from time to time they came to themselves, they wanted to speak but the tongue was hard to move and they uttered inarticulate sounds because the nerves around the occiput [back of the head] were dead; and they died suddenly. In others, the evil attacked not the head, but the lung, and forthwith there was inflammation inside which produced very sharp pains in the chest.

Sputum suffused with blood was brought up and disgusting and stinking breath from within. The throat and tongue, parched from the heat, were black and congested with blood. It made no difference if they drank much or little. Sleeplessness and weakness were established forever.

Abscesses formed on the upper and lower arms, in a few also in the maxillae [jaw], and in others on other parts of the body. In some they were large and in others small. Black blisters appeared. Some people broke out with black spots all over their bodies; in some they were few and very manifest; in others they were obscure and dense. Everyone died the same death from these symptoms. In some people all the symptoms appeared, in others more or fewer of them, and in no small number even one of these was sufficient to provoke death. Those few who were able to escape from among the many who died were no longer possessed by the same evil, but were safe. The disease did not attack twice in order to kill them.

Great abscesses were formed on the legs or the arms, from which, when cut, a large quantity of foul-smelling pus flowed and the disease was differentiated as that which discharged much annoying matter. Even many who were seized by all the symptoms unexpectedly recovered. There was no help from anywhere; if someone brought to another a remedy useful to himself, this became poison to the other patient. Some, by treating others, became infected with the disease. . . . Most terrible was the discouragement. Whenever people felt sick there was no hope left for recovery, but by turning to despair, adding to their prostration and severely aggravating their sickness, they died at once. No words could express the nature of the disease.

14.4 Palestine: Al-Wardi's "Essay on the Report of the Pestilence" (c. 1348)

Abu Hafs Umar al-Wardi (c. 1290–1349) was a religious judge in the town of Aleppo whose writings cover a range of topics, including grammar, history, law, and mysticism. His "Essay on the Report of the Pestilence" was written at the height of the epidemic in Palestine.

("Palestine." Originally titled "Abū Hafs 'Umar Ibn al-Wardï." From Michal W. Dols, "Ibn al-Wardï's 'Risalah al-naba' 'an al-waba,' A Translation of a Major Source for the History for the Black Death in the Middle East," in *Near Eastern Numismatics, Iconography, Epigraphy and History,* ed. Dickran Kouymjian (Beirut: American University of Beirut Press, 1974), pp. 443–55. Reprinted by permission of the American University of Beirut Press.)

God is my security in every adversity. My sufficiency is in God alone. Is not God sufficient protection for His servant? Oh God, pray for our master, Muhammad, and give him peace. Save us for his sake from the attacks of the plague and give us shelter.

The plague frightened and killed. It began in the land of darkness. Oh, what a visitor! It has been current for fifteen years. China was not preserved from it nor could the strongest fortress hinder it. The plague afflicted the Indians in India. It weighed upon the Sind.[1] It seized with its hand and ensnared even the lands of the Uzbeks. How many backs did it break in what is Transoxiana! The plague increased and spread further. It attacked the Persians, extended its steps toward the land of the Khitai,[2] and gnawed away at the Crimea. It pelted Rum[3] with live coals and led the outrage to Cyprus and the islands. The plague destroyed mankind in Cairo. Its eye was cast upon Egypt, and behold, the people were wide-awake. It stilled all movement in Alexandria. The plague did its work like a silkworm. It took from the tiraz factory its beauty and did to its workers what fate decreed.

---

[1] This was the region of the lower Indus River, along the present-day border between northwest India and Pakistan.
[2] Khitai is Cathay, the medieval term for China.
[3] Anatolia, or modern-day Turkey.

14.5 Florence: From *The Decameron* by Giovanni Boccaccio

In 1347 a ship carrying grain from the area of the Black Sea docked in Messina. In addition to the cargo, the ship brought hundreds of black rats, infested with fleas, which carried the plague. Before the ship could be turned away from port, the rats ran down the ropes and into the city. As the rat population died, the fleas sought the closest host, and attached themselves to humans. Since the level of hygiene in the walled and crowded medieval cities was primitive, with raw sewage flowing in the streets, the disease spread rapidly. During the next three years various strains of the Black Death (pneumonic and bubonic) extended northward through Europe, killing one-third to one-half of the population. The following description from the prologue to The Decameron *by Giovanni Boccaccio (1313–1375) provides vivid detail about the reaction to the catastrophe in Florence.*

(From *The Decameron of Giovanni Boccaccio,* trans. by Richard Aldington. New York: Doubleday & Co., 1930, pp. 344–347. © The Estate of Richard Aldington. Extracts from Richard Aldington's translation of *The Decameron* reproduced by kind permission of the Estate of Richard Aldington c/o Rosica Colin Limited, London.)

In the year 1348 after the fruitful incarnation of the Son of God, that most beautiful of Italian cities, noble Florence, was attacked by deadly plague. It started in the East either through the influence of the heavenly bodies or because God's just anger with our wicked deeds sent it as a punishment to mortal men; and in a few years killed an innumerable quantity of people. Ceaselessly passing from place to place, it extended its miserable length over the West. Against this plague all human wisdom and foresight were vain. Orders had been given to cleanse the city of filth, the entry of any sick person was forbidden, much advice was given for keeping healthy; at the same time humble supplications were made to God by pious persons in processions and otherwise. And yet, in the beginning of the spring of the year mentioned, its horrible results began to appear, and in a miraculous manner. The symptoms were not the same as in the East, where a gush of blood from the nose was the plain sign of inevitable death; but it began both in men and women with certain swellings in the groin or under the armpit. They grew to the size of a small apple or an egg, more or less, and were vulgarly called tumors. In a short space of time these tumors spread from the two parts named all over the body. Soon after this the symptoms changed and black or purple spots appeared on the arms or thighs or any other part of the body, sometimes a few large ones, sometimes many little ones. These spots were a certain sign of death, just as the original tumor had been and still remained.

No doctor's advice, no medicine could overcome or alleviate this disease. An enormous number of ignorant men and women set up as doctors in addition to those who were trained. Either the disease was such that no treatment was possible or the doctors were so ignorant that they did not know what caused it, and consequently could not administer the proper remedy. In any case very few recovered; most people died within about three days of the appearance of the tumors described above, most of them without any fever or other symptoms.

The violence of this disease was such that the sick communicated it to the healthy who came near them, just as a fire catches anything dry or oily near it. And it even went further. To speak to or go near the sick brought infection and a common death to the living; and moreover, to touch the clothes or anything else the sick had touched or worn gave the disease to the person touching. . . .

Some thought that moderate living and the avoidance of all superfluity would preserve them from the epidemic. They formed small communities, living entirely separate from everybody else. They shut themselves up in houses where there were no sick, eating the finest food and drinking the best wine very temperately, avoiding all excess, allowing no news or discussion of death and sickness, and passing the time in music and suchlike pleasures. Others thought just the opposite. They thought the sure cure for the plague was to drink and be merry, to go about singing and amusing themselves, satisfying every appetite they could, laughing and jesting at what happened. They put their words into practice, spent day and night going from tavern to tavern, drinking immoderately, or went into other people's houses, doing only those things which pleased them. This they could easily do because everyone felt doomed and had abandoned his property, so that most houses became common property and any stranger who went in made use of them as if he had owned them. And with all this bestial behavior, they avoided the sick as much as possible.

In this suffering and misery of our city, the authority of human and divine laws almost disappeared, for, like other men, the ministers and the executors of the laws were all dead or sick or shut up with their families, so that no duties were carried out. Every man was therefore able to do as he pleased.

Many others adopted a course of life midway between the two just described. They did not restrict their victuals so much as the former, nor allow themselves to be drunken and dissolute like the latter, but satisfied their appetites moderately. They did not shut themselves up, but went about, carrying flowers or scented herbs or perfumes in their hands, in the belief that it was an excellent thing to comfort the brain with such odors; for the whole air was infected with the smell of dead bodies, of sick persons and medicines.

Others again held a still more cruel opinion, which they thought would keep them safe. They said that the only medicine against the plague-stricken was to go right away from them. Men and women, convinced of this and caring about nothing but themselves, abandoned their own city, their own houses, their dwellings, their relatives, their property, and went abroad or at least to the country round Florence, as if God's wrath in punishing men's wickedness with this plague would not follow them but strike only those who remained within the walls of the city, or as if they thought nobody in the city would remain alive and that its last hour had come.

Not everyone who adopted any of these various opinions died, nor did all escape. Some when they were still healthy had set the example of avoiding the sick, and, falling ill themselves, died untended.

One citizen avoided another, hardly any neighbor troubled about others, relatives never or hardly ever visited each other. Moreover, such terror was struck into the hearts of men and women by this calamity, that brother abandoned brother, and the uncle his nephew, and the sister her brother, and very often the wife her husband. What is even worse and nearly incredible is that fathers and mothers refused to see and tend their children, as if they had not been theirs.

Thus, a multitude of sick men and women were left without any care except from the charity of friends (but these were few), or the greed of servants, though not many of these could be had even for high wages. Moreover, most of them were coarse-minded men and women, who did little more than bring the sick what they asked for or watch over them when they were dying. And very often these servants lost their lives and their earnings. Since the sick were thus abandoned by neighbors, relatives and friends, while servants were scarce, a habit sprang up which had never been heard of before. Beautiful and noble women, when they fell sick, did not scruple to take a young or old manservant, whoever he might be, and with no sort of shame, expose every part of their bodies to these men as if they had been women, for they were compelled by the necessity of their sickness to do so. This, perhaps, was a cause of looser morals in those women who survived.

In this way many people died who might have been saved if they had been looked after. Owing to the lack of attendants for the sick and the violence of the plague, such a multitude of people in the city died day and night that it was stupefying to hear of, let alone to see. From sheer necessity, then, several ancient customs were quite altered among the survivors.

The custom had been (as we still see it today), that women relatives and neighbors should gather at the house of the deceased, and there lament with the family. At the same time the men would gather at the door with the male neighbors and other citizens. Then came the clergy, few or many according to the dead person's rank; the coffin was placed on the shoulder' of his friends and carried with funeral pomp of lighted candles and dirges to the church which the deceased had chosen before dying. But as the fury of the plague increased, this custom wholly or nearly disappeared, and new customs arose. Thus, people died, not only without having a number of women near them, but without a single witness. Very few indeed were honored with the piteous laments and bitter tears of their relatives, who, on the contrary, spent their time in mirth, feasting and jesting. Even the women abandoned womanly pity and adopted this custom for their own safety. Few were they whose bodies were accompanied to church

by more than ten or a dozen neighbors. Nor were these grave and honorable citizens but grave-diggers from the lowest of the people who got themselves called sextons, and performed the task for money. They took up the bier and hurried it off, not to the church chosen by the deceased but to the church nearest, preceded by four or six of the clergy with few candles and often none at all. With the aid of the grave-diggers, the clergy huddled the bodies away in any grave they could find, without giving themselves the trouble of a long or solemn burial service.

The plight of the lower and most of the middle classes was even more pitiful to behold. Most of them remained in their houses, either through poverty or in hopes of safety, and fell sick by thousands. Since they received no care and attention, almost all of them died. Many ended their lives in the streets both at night and during the day; and many others who died in their houses were only known to be dead because the neighbors smelled their decaying bodies. Dead bodies filled every corner. Most of them were treated in the same manner by the survivors, who were more concerned to get rid of their rotting bodies than moved by charity towards the dead. With the aid of porters, if they could get them, they carried the bodies out of the houses and laid them at the doors, where every morning quantities of the dead might be seen. They then were laid on biers, or, as these were often lacking, on tables.

Often a single bier carried two or three bodies, and it happened frequently that a husband and wife, two or three brothers, or father and son were taken off on the same bier. It frequently happened that two priests, each carrying a cross, would go out followed by three or four biers carried by porters; and where the priests thought there was one person to bury, there would be six or eight, and often, even more. Nor were these dead honored by tears and lighted candles and mourners, for things had reached such a pass that people cared no more for dead men than we care for dead goats. Thus it plainly appeared that what the wise had not learned to endure with patience through the few calamities of ordinary life, became a matter of indifference even to the most ignorant people through the greatness of this misfortune.

Such was the multitude of corpses brought to the churches every day and almost every hour that there was not enough consecrated ground to give them burial, especially since they wanted to bury each person in the family grave, according to the old custom. Although the cemeteries were full they were forced to dig huge trenches, where they buried the bodies by hundreds. Here they stowed them away like bales in the hold of a ship and covered them with a little earth, until the whole trench was full.

14.6   France: From the *Chronicle of Jean de Venette*

The suffering was not isolated, as the plague spread rapidly to Spain, France, Germany, England, and the Scandinavian countries. In France the situation was described in the Chronicle *of Jean de Venette (c. 1308–1369). For information about the author and the* Chronicle *see Document 14.1).*

(From *The Chronicle of Jean de Venette*, trans. by Jean Birdsall. Copyright © 1953 Columbia University Press. Reprinted with permission of the publisher.)

In A.D. 1348, the people of France and of almost the whole world were struck by a blow other than war. For in addition to the famine which I described in the beginning and to the wars which I described in the course of this narrative, pestilence and its attendant tribulations appeared again in various parts of the world. In the month of August, 1348, after Vespers when the sun was beginning to set, a big and very bright star appeared above Paris, toward the west. It did not seem, as stars usually do, to be very high above our hemisphere but rather very near. As the sun set and night came on, this star did not seem to me or to many other friars who were watching it to move from one place. At length, when night had come, this big star, to the amazement of all of us who were watching, broke into many different rays and, as it shed these rays over Paris toward the east, totally disappeared and was completely annihilated. Whether it was a comet or not, whether it was composed of airy exhalations and was finally resolved into vapor, I leave to the decision of astronomers. It is, however, possible that it was a presage of the amazing pestilence to come, which, in fact, followed very shortly in Paris and throughout France and elsewhere, as I shall tell. All this year and the next, the mortality of men and women, of the young even more than of the old, in Paris and in the kingdom of France, and also, it is said, in other parts of the world, was so great that it was almost impossible to bury the dead. People lay ill little more than two or three days and died suddenly, as it were in full health. He who was well one day was dead the next and being carried to his grave. Swellings appeared suddenly in the armpit or in the groin—in many cases both—and they were infallible signs of death. The sickness or pestilence was called an epidemic by the doctors. Nothing like the great numbers who died in the years 1348 and 1349 has been heard of or seen or read of in times past. This plague and disease came from *ymaginatione* or association and contagion, for if a well man visited the sick he only rarely evaded the risk of death. Wherefore in many towns timid priests withdrew, leaving the exercise of their ministry to such of the religious as were more daring. In many places not two out of twenty remained alive. So high was the mortality at the Hotel-Dieu in Paris that for a long time, more than five hundred dead were carried daily with great devotion in carts to the cemetery of the Holy Innocents in Paris for burial. A very great number of the saintly sisters of the Hotel-Dieu who, not fearing to die, nursed the sick in all sweetness and humility, with no thought of honor, a number too often renewed by death, rest in peace with Christ, as we may piously believe.

This plague, it is said, began among the unbelievers, came to Italy, and then crossing the Alps reached Avignon, where it attacked several cardinals and took from them their whole household. Then it spread, unforeseen, to France, through Gascony and Spain, little by little, from town to town, from village to village, from house to house, and finally from person to person. It even crossed over to Germany, though it was not so bad there as with us. During the epidemic, God of His accustomed goodness deigned to grant this grace, that however suddenly men died, almost all awaited death joyfully. Nor was there anyone who died without confessing his sins and receiving the holy viaticum. To the even greater benefit of the dying, Pope Clement VI through their confessors mercifully gave and granted absolution from penalty to the dying in many cities and fortified towns. Men died the more willingly for this and left many inheritances and temporal goods to churches and monastic orders, for in many cases they had seen their close heirs and children die before them.

Some said that this pestilence was caused by infection of the air and waters, since there was at this time no famine nor lack of food supplies, but on the contrary great abundance. As a result of this theory of infected water and air as the source of the plague the Jews were suddenly and violently charged with infecting wells and water and corrupting the air. The whole world rose up against them cruelly on this account. In Germany and other parts of the world where Jews lived, they were massacred and slaughtered by Christians, and many thousands were burned everywhere, indiscriminately. The unshaken, if fatuous, constancy of the men and their wives was remarkable. For mothers hurled their children first into the fire that they might not be baptized and then leaped in after them to burn with their husbands and children. It is said that many bad Christians were found who in a like manner put poison into wells. But in truth, such poisonings, granted that they actually were perpetrated, could not have caused so great a plague nor have infected so many people. There were other causes; for example, the will of God and the corrupt humors and evil inherent in air and earth. Perhaps the poisonings, if they actually took place in some localities, reinforced these causes. The plague lasted in France for the greater part of the years 1348 and 1349 and then ceased. Many country villages and many houses in good towns remained empty and deserted. Many houses, including some splendid dwellings, very soon fell into ruins. Even in Paris several houses were thus ruined, though fewer here than elsewhere.

After the cessation of the epidemic, pestilence, or plague, the men and women who survived married each other. There was no sterility among the women, but on the contrary fertility beyond the ordinary. Pregnant women were seen on every side. Many twins were born and even three children at once. But the most surprising fact is that children born after the plague, when they became of an age for teeth, had only twenty or twenty-two teeth, though before that time men commonly had thirty-two in their upper and lower jaws together. What this diminution in the number of teeth signified I wonder greatly, unless it be a new era resulting from the destruction of one human generation by the plague and its replacement by another. But woe is me! the world was not changed for the better but for the worse by this renewal of population. For men were more avaricious and grasping than before, even though they had far greater possessions. They were more covetous and disturbed each other more frequently with suits, brawls, disputes, and pleas. Nor by the mortality resulting from this terrible plague inflicted by God was peace between kings and lords established. On the contrary, the enemies of the king of France and of the Church were stronger and wickeder than before and stirred up wars on sea and on land. Greater evils than before pullulated everywhere in the world. And this fact was very remarkable. Although there was an abundance of all goods, yet everything was twice as dear, whether it were utensils, victuals, or merchandise, hired helpers or peasants and serfs, except for some hereditary domains which remained abundantly stocked with everything. Charity began to cool, and iniquity with ignorance and sin to abound, for few could be found in the good towns and castles who knew how or were willing to instruct children in the rudiments of grammar . . .

In the year 1349, while the plague was still active and spreading from town to town, men in Germany, Flanders, Hainaut, and Lorraine rose up and began a new sect on their own authority. Stripped to the waist, they gathered in large groups and bands and marched in procession through the crossroads and squares of cities and good towns. There they formed circles and beat upon their backs with weighted scourges, rejoicing as they did so in loud voices and singing hymns suitable to their rite and newly composed for it. Thus for thirty-three days they marched through many towns doing their penance and affording a great spectacle to the wondering people. They flogged their shoulders and arms with scourges tipped with iron points so zealously as to draw blood. But they did not come to Paris nor to any part of France, for they were forbidden to do so by the king of France, who did not want them. He acted on the advice of the masters of theology of the University of Paris, who said that this new sect had been formed contrary to the will of God, to the rites of Holy Mother Church, and to the salvation of all their souls. That indeed this was and is true appeared shortly. For Pope Clement VI was fully informed concerning this fatuous new rite by the masters of Paris through emissaries reverently sent to him and, on the grounds that it had been damnably formed, contrary to law, he forbade the Flagellants under threat of anathema to practice in the future the public penance which they had so presumptuously undertaken. His prohibition was just, for the Flagellants, supported by certain fatuous priests and monks, were enunciating doctrines and opinions which were beyond measure evil, erroneous, and fallacious. For example, they said that their blood thus drawn by the scourge and poured out was mingled with the blood of Christ. Their many errors showed how little they knew of the Catholic faith. Wherefore, as they had begun fatuously of themselves and not of God, so in a short time they were reduced to nothing. On being warned, they desisted and humbly received absolution and penance at the hands of their prelates as the pope's representatives. Many honorable women and devout matrons, it must be added, had done this penance with scourges, marching and singing through towns and churches like the men, but after a little like the others they desisted.

14.7   England: From the *Chronicle* of Henry Knighton (1349)

Henry Knighton was a fourteenth-century English chronicler (d. 1396), who was an Augustinian monk at St. Mary's of the Meadows, Leicestershire. His account of the plague is helpful in understanding the impact of the plague on the manorial system, and how the loss of manpower affected the standard feudal arrangements.

(From *Knighton's Chronicle* [1337–1396], translated by G. H. Martin. Oxford: Clarendon Press, 1995, pp. 95–107. Translation modified. Reprinted by permission of Oxford University Press.)

1348. *A universal mortality.* In this year and the next there was a general plague upon mankind throughout the world. It began in India, then spread to Tartary, and then to the Saracens, and finally to the Christians and the Jews, so that in the space of a single year, from one Easter to the next, as the report ran in the papal court, some 8,000 legions of people died suddenly in those distant parts, besides Christians. . . .

Then a lamentable plague traveled by sea to Southampton and on to Bristol, where almost the whole population of the town perished, snatched away, as it were, by sudden death, for there were few who kept their beds for more than two or three days, or even half a day. And thence cruel death spread everywhere with the passage of the sun. There died in Leicester, in the little parish of St Leonard's, more than nineteen score [380], 400 in the parish of Holy Cross [St Martin's] and in St Margaret's parish 700, and so on in every parish, in great numbers. . . .

In the same year there was a great plague of sheep everywhere in the realm, so that in one place 5000 died in one pasture, and they so rotted that neither beast nor bird would touch them. . . . Sheep and cattle went wandering over fields and through crops, and there was no one to go and drive or round them up, and they perished in out-of-the-way places among the furrows and under hedges, for want of a keeper, in numbers beyond reckoning throughout the land, for there was such a shortage of hands and servants that no one knew what ought to be done. . . . In the following autumn no one could get a reaper for less than 8d. with his food. . . .

At that time there was such a shortage of priests everywhere that many churches were without a pastor, and lacked the divine offices, masses, matins, vespers, sacraments, and other rites . . . but within a short time a great multitude of those whose wives had died in the plague flocked into orders, of whom many were illiterate and little more than laymen, who if they were able to read at all were unable to understand what they read.

In the mean time the king sent word into every shire that mowers and other workmen should take no more than they had before, under the penalties laid down in the order, and thereupon made a statute. Nevertheless the workmen were so puffed up and contrary-minded that they did not heed the king's decree, and if anyone wanted to hire them he had to pay what they asked: either his fruit and crops rotted, or he had to give in to the workmen's arrogant and greedy demands.

When it came to the king's notice that they had not obeyed his order, and had given their employees higher wages, he inflicted heavy fines upon abbots and priors, and upon greater and lesser knights, and upon the others, great and small, of the land: from some 100s., from some 20s., from every ploughland in the kingdom, and received not less than a fifteenth would yield.

Then the king caused many laborers to be arrested, and put them in prison. Many ran away, and took to the woods and forests for a time, but those who were caught were grievously fined. And most were sworn that they would not take more than the old established daily rate, and so were freed from prison. And artisans in the boroughs and townships were treated in the same way. . . .

After the plague, many buildings, large and small, fell into ruins in every city, borough, and village for lack of occupants, and similarly many small villages and hamlets were deserted, with not a house left in them, for all who had lived there were dead, and it was likely that many of those villages would never be inhabited again. In the following winter there was such a want of servants in work of all kinds, that people believed that the like shortage had never been known at any time in the past, for cattle and such livestock as a man might have wandered about without a keeper, and there was no one to look after people's possessions. And thus the necessities of life became so dear, that what in previous times was worth 1d. now cost 4d. or 5d.

Magnates and lesser lords of the realm who had tenants made adjustments in the rent in order that the tenants should not go away on account of the lack of servants and the general high cost of living: some half the rent, some more, some less, some for two years, some for three, some for one year, according as they could agree.

Similarly those who had tenants with day-work throughout the year, such as bondmen, had to relax and remit such works, and either give them up altogether, or manage them in a looser way, at a low rent, lest their tenements should fall into utter and irredeemable decay, and the land everywhere lie wholly unworked. And foodstuffs and necessities of all kinds became very expensive.

Questions for Discussion:

1. Compare the accounts of the plague as experienced in Constantinople, Palestine, Italy, France, and England. What similarities are there? Which account is the most helpful in understanding the effects of the plague?
2. What reasons are given by the authors concerning the reasons for the pestilence?
3. Describe the various ways survivors responded to the plague.
4. Describe and discuss the adjustments that were made in the feudal relationship between manor lords and their serfs as a result of the plague.
5. Jean de Venette describes the activities of a sect of people known as Flagellants. How do you explain this phenomenon? Why did the king of France forbid them to come into the kingdom?

Peasant Revolt

14.8   Statute of Laborers (1349)

In 1349, as a result of conditions such as those described by Henry Knighton in the previous selection, the government of England passed a law known as the Statute of Laborers. *It was designed to stabilize prices and to guarantee a workforce. As we shall see in the next document, the measure had unexpected results.*

(From *Source Problems in English History*, edited by Albert Beebe White and Wallace Notestein [New York: Harper & Brothers, 1915], pp. 141–142. Translation modernized.)

The king to the sheriff of Kent, greeting. A great portion of the people, especially workmen and servants, recently died of the plague. Those who survived see that masters need servants, which are scarce, and they will not serve unless they receive excessive wages. Some are willing to beg, rather than to earn their living by labor. We, considering the great inconvenience, especially the lack of ploughmen and such laborers, have decided after consulting with the prelates and nobles and learned men who assist us, the following:

That every man and woman of our realm of England, whether he is free or bound, able in body, and within the age of threescore years, not living in merchandise, nor exercising any craft, nor having of his own property or income by which he may live, nor proper land, about whose tillage he may himself occupy, and not serving any other; if he is required to serve in suitable service, his estate considered, he shall be bound to serve him which shall so require him; and take only the wages, livery, meed [reward], or salary, which were accustomed to be given in the places where he owes service, during the twentieth year of our reign of England, or five or six other common years next before. Provided always, that the lords should be preferred before others in their bondmen or their land tenants, so they will be retained in their service; nevertheless, the said lords shall retain no more than be necessary for them; and if any such man or woman, being so required to serve, will not do the same, that proved by two true men before the sheriff or the constables of the town where the same shall happen to be done, he shall immediately be taken by them or any of them, and committed to the next gaol [prison], there to remain under strait keeping, until he finds surety to serve in the form specified before.

Item, if any reaper, mower, or other workman or servant, of whatever estate or condition that he be, retained in any man's service, departs from the said service without reasonable cause or license, before the term agreed, he shall have the penalty of imprisonment. And no one, under the same penalty, shall presume to receive or to retain any such person in his service.

Item, that no man pay, or promise to pay, any servant any more wages, liveries, meed, or salary than was accustomed, as said before; nor that anyone shall demand or receive them, upon pain of doubling of that which shall be paid, promised, required, or received, to him who shall feel himself aggrieved by this, suing for the same; and if he will not sue, then the same will be applied to any of the people that will sue; and such suit shall be in the court of the lord of the place where such case shall happen.

Questions for Discussion:

1. The document states that the ordinances were laid forth "as the present necessity requires." What was this necessity, and how did the Statute of Laborers attempt to deal with it?
2. Do you think the penalties were unnecessarily harsh? Were there any alternatives?
3. Compare the Statute of Laborers with the Edict on Prices issued by Diocletian (Document 1.3). What similarities do you see? Were the two rulers attempting to solve the same problems?

INTERPRETING THE EVIDENCE

14.9 Peasant Revolts from the *Chronicles* of Froissart and an Illumination Depicting Wat Tyler and John Ball

Laws such as the Statute of Laborers caused peasant rebellions, another of the calamitous events of the fourteenth century. These violent uprisings occurred initially in France and England, and similar revolts spread throughout Europe. As noted in the Chronicle of Henry Knighton, *the famines and the plague had reduced the available manpower, and peasants and urban laborers were able to bargain for higher wages and better working conditions. When the aristocracy attempted to return to the old rules of serf-dom, the lower classes erupted in bloody revolt.*

In England the common people rebelled when there was an attempt to bind peasants to the land, to freeze wages and prices, and to impose new taxes (see the previous selection). The immediate cause of the rebellion of 1381 ("The Wat Tyler Rebellion") was an attempt to impose a poll tax. This account of the revolt is from the Chronicles of Jean Froissart (c. 1337–c. 1405), a man who traveled widely throughout Europe and England; his writings provide a lively impression of fourteenth-century events. In this excerpt describing the English rebellion of 1381, Froissart claimed that the lower classes were incited by a crazy priest named John Ball. They were then led into revolt by a man named Wat Tyler. The details are presented in the following document.

(From *The Chronicles of England, France, Spain, etc.*, by Sir John Froissart [London: J.M. Dent & Sons Ltd., 1906], pp. 207–209, 213–214, 216, 221, 222–223. Translation modernized.)

While these conferences were going forward there occurred great commotions among the lower orders in England, by which that country was nearly ruined. In order that this disastrous rebellion may serve as an example to mankind, I will speak of all that was done from the information I had at the time. It is customary in England, as well as in several other countries, for the nobility to have great privileges over the commonalty; that is to say, the lower orders are bound by law to plough the lands of the gentry, to harvest their grain, to carry it home to the barn, to thrash and winnow it; they are also bound to harvest and carry home the hay. All these services the prelates and gentlemen exact of their inferiors; and in the counties of Kent, Essex, Sussex, and Bedford, these services are more oppressive than in other parts of the kingdom. As a consequence of this, the evil men in these districts began to murmur, saying that in the beginning of the world there were no slaves, and that no one ought to be treated as such, unless he had committed treason against his lord, as Lucifer had done against God; but they had done no such thing, for they were neither angels nor spirits, but men formed after the same likeness as these lords who treated them as beasts. This they would bear no longer; they were determined to be free, and if they labored or did any work, they would be paid for it. A crazy priest in the county of Kent, called John Ball, who for his absurd preaching had been confined in prison three times by the Archbishop of Canterbury, was greatly instrumental in exciting these rebellious ideas. Every Sunday after mass, as the people were coming out of church, this John Ball was accustomed to assemble a crowd around him in the marketplace and preach to them. On such occasions he would say, "My good friends, matters cannot go on well in England until all things shall be in common; when there shall be neither vassals nor lords; when the lords shall be no more masters than ourselves. How ill they behave to us! For what reason do they thus hold us in bondage? Are we not all descended from the same parents, Adam and Eve? And what can they show, or what reason can they give, why they should be more masters than ourselves? They are clothed in velvet and rich stuffs, ornamented with ermine and other furs, while we are forced to wear poor clothing. They have wines, spices, and fine bread, while we have only rye and the refuse of the straw; and when we drink, it must be water. They have handsome seats and manors, while we must brave the wind and rain in our labors in the field; and it is by our labor they have wherewith to support their pomp. We are called slaves, and if we do not perform our service we are beaten, and we have no sovereign to whom we can complain or who would be willing to hear us. Let us go to the king [Richard II (r.1367–1399)] and remonstrate with him; he is young, and from him we may obtain a favorable answer, and if not we must ourselves seek to amend our condition." With such language as this John Ball harangued the people of his village every Sunday after mass. The archbishop, on being informed of it, had him arrested and imprisoned for two or three months by way of punishment; but the moment he was out of prison, he returned to his former course. Many in the city of London envious of the rich and noble, having heard of John Ball's

(continued)

preaching, said among themselves that the country was badly governed, and that the nobility had seized upon all the gold and silver. These wicked Londoners, therefore, began to assemble in parties, and to show signs of rebellion; they also invited all those who held like opinions in the adjoining counties to come to London; telling them that they would find the town open to them and the commonalty of the same way of thinking as themselves, and that they would so press the king, that there should no longer be a slave in England.

By this means the men of Kent, Essex, Sussex, Bedford, and the adjoining counties, in number about 60,000, were brought to London, under the command of Wat Tyler, Jack Straw, and John Ball. This Wat Tyler, who was chief of the three, had been a tiler of houses, a bad man and a great enemy to the nobility. When these wicked people first began their disturbances, all London, with the exception of those who favored them, was much alarmed. The mayor and rich citizens assembled in council and debated whether they should shut the gate and refuse to admit them; however, upon mature reflection they determined not to do so, as they might run the risk of having the suburbs burnt. The gates of the city were therefore thrown open, and the rabble entered and lodged as they pleased. True it is that full two-thirds of these people knew neither what they wanted, nor for what purpose they had come together; they followed one another like sheep. In this manner did many of these poor fellows walk to London from distances of one hundred, or sixty leagues, but the greater part came from the counties I have mentioned, and all on their arrival demanded to see the king. The country gentlemen, the knights and squires, began to be much alarmed when they saw the people thus assembling, and indeed they had sufficient reason to be so, for far less causes have excited fear. . . . When the king and his lords saw this crowd of people, and the wildness of their manner, the boldest of the party felt alarm, and the king was advised not to land, but to have his barge rowed up and down the river. "What do you wish for?" he demanded of the multitude; I have come here to listen to what you have to say. Those near him cried

out, "We wish you to land, and then we will tell you what our wants are." Upon this the Earl of Salisbury cried out, "Gentlemen, you are not properly dressed, nor are you in a fit condition for a king to talk with." Nothing more was said on either side, for the king was prevailed upon at once to return to the Tower. . . . Their leaders, John Ball, Jack Straw, and Wat Tyler, then marched through London, attended by more than 20,000 men, to the palace of the Savoy, which is a handsome building belonging to the Duke of Lancaster, situated on the banks of the Thames on the road to Westminster. Here they immediately killed the porters, pushed into the house, and set it on fire. . . . After this they paraded the streets [pillaging and murdering].

The king was frightened into making the following statement:

"My good people, I am your king and your lord, what is it you want? What do you wish to say to me?" Those who heard him made answer, "We wish you to make us free for ever. We wish to be no longer called slaves, nor held in bondage." The king replied, "I grant your wish; now therefore return to your homes, and let two or three from each village be left behind, to whom I will order letters to be given with my seal, fully granting every demand you have made. . . ."

The king's words did not pacify the leaders of the rebellion, who continued to incite their followers. Several days later Wat Tyler, Jack Straw, and John Ball confronted the king once again. At this encounter Tyler was killed by one of the king's squires.

When the rebels found that their leader was dead, they drew up in a sort of battle array . . . the king, . . . riding up to the rebels . . . said, "Gentlemen, what are you about: you shall have me for your captain: I am your king, remain peaceable." The greater part, on hearing these words, were quite ashamed, and those among them who were inclined for peace began to slip away. . . . When the rabble had dispersed, the king and his lords, to their great joy, returned to London. . . . John Ball and Jack Straw were found hidden in an old ruin, where they had secreted themselves, thinking to steal away when

An Illumination Depicting Wat Tyler and John Ball. (HIP/Art Resource, New York)

things were quiet; but this they were prevented doing, for their own men betrayed them. With this capture, the king and his barons were much pleased and had their heads cut off, as was that of Tyler, and fixed on London-bridge, in the room of those whom these wretches themselves had placed there.

This illumination from a manuscript in the British Library (Royal MS 18 E. I, fol. 165v.) shows the "Crazy Priest" John Ball on horseback speaking to crowds of people; he may be identified by the name on his cloak. His ideas, as seen in the accompanying document, advocated the redistribution of wealth and the leveling of social classes. These radical concepts contributed to the rebellion of 1381. The leader of the revolt, Wat Tyler, stands at the left.

Questions for Discussion:

1. What were the reasons given by John Ball for peasant resistance to their control by the aristocracy?
2. Discuss the response of Richard II to the demands of the peasants and urban workers of the lower classes.

The Hundred Years War

14.10 The Battle of Crécy (1346): Description from the *Chronicles* of Froissart

The Hundred Years War, fought by England and France between 1337 and 1453, was the longest war in western history. Although the fighting was not continuous, the havoc caused by the conflict had serious effects on the French countryside. England won the early battles of the war, mostly due to the superior military technology of the longbow. The crossbow was even more powerful, because it shot metal bolts called quarrels, which were able to penetrate the thickest armor and shatter the bones beneath. However, as another excerpt from Froissart's Chronicle *recounts, the weapon was not effective at the important Battle of Crécy (1346), in which the English longbowmen triumphed over the French.*

(From *The Chronicles of England, France, Spain, etc.*, by Sir John Froissart [London: J.M. Dent & Sons, Ltd., 1906], pp. 42–46. Translation modernized.)

That night the King of France [Philip VI (1293–1350)] entertained at supper, in Abbeville, all the princes and chief lords of his army. There was much conversation relative to the war; and after supper the king entreated them always to remain in friendship with each other; " to be friends without jealousy, and courteous without pride." All the French forces had not yet arrived, for the king was still expecting the Earl of Savoy, who ought to have been there with a thousand lances, as he had paid well for them at Troyes in Champaign, three months in advance. That same evening the King of England [Edward III (1312–1377)] also gave a supper to his earls and barons, and when it was over he withdrew into his oratory, where falling on his knees before the altar, he prayed to God that if he should combat his enemies on the morrow, he might come off with honor. About midnight he retired to rest, and rising early the next day, he and the Prince of Wales heard mass and took communion. The greater part of his army did the same. After mass the king ordered his men to arm themselves and assemble at the place he had chosen.

There was a large park near a wood, behind the army, which King Edward enclosed, and in it placed all his baggage, wagons and horses; for his men-at-arms and archers were to fight on foot. He afterwards ordered, through his constable and his two marshals, that the army should be divided into three battalions. In the first, he placed the young Prince of Wales . . . and many other knights and squires whom I cannot name. There might be, in this first division, about 800 men-at-arms, 2,000 archers, and 1,000 Welshmen; all of whom advanced in regular order to their ground, each lord under his banner and pennon [small banner], and in the center of his men. In the second battalion were the Earl of Northampton . . . and many others, amounting in the whole to about 800 men-at-arms, and 1,200 archers. The third bat-

talion was commanded by the king in person, and was composed of about 700 men-at-arms, and 2,000 archers. The king was mounted on a small palfrey [horse], having a white wand in his hand, and attended by his two marshals. In this manner he rode at a foot's pace through all the ranks, encouraging the army and entreating that they would guard his honor and defend his right; so sweetly and with such a cheerful countenance did he speak, that all who had been depressed before, were directly comforted by hearing him. By the time he had thus visited all the battalions it was nearly ten o'clock: he then retired to his own division, having ordered the men to regale [feed] themselves, after which all returned to their own battalions, according to the marshal's orders, and seated themselves on the ground, placing their helmets and bows before them, in order that they might be the fresher when their enemies should arrive.

That same Saturday the King of France also rose early, heard mass in the monastery of St. Peter's in Abbeville, where he lodged; and having ordered his army to do the same, left that town after sunrise. When he had marched about two leagues from Abbeville and was approaching the enemy, he was advised to form his army in order of battle, and to let those on foot march forward that they might not be trampled on by the horses. This being done, he sent off four knights, the Lord Moyne, of Bastleberg, the Lord of Noyers, the Lord of Beaujeu, and the Lord of Aubigny, who rode so near to the English, that they could clearly distinguish their position. The English plainly perceived that these knights came to reconnoitre; however, they took no notice of it, but allowed them to return unmolested.

When the King of France saw them coming back, he halted his army, and the knights pushing through the crowds came near to the king, who said to them, "My lords, what news?" Neither chose to speak first— at last the king addressed himself personally—to the Lord Moyne, who said, "Sir, I will speak since it pleases you to order me, but under correction of my companions. We have advanced far enough to reconnoitre your enemies. Know, then, that they are drawn up in three battalions, and are waiting for you. I would advise for my part (submitting, however, to your better counsel) that you halt your army here and quarter them for the night; for before the rear shall come up, and the army be properly drawn up, it will be very late, and your men will be tired and in disorder, while they will find your enemies fresh and properly arrayed. Tomorrow you may draw up your army more at your ease, and may at leisure reconnoitre on what part it will be most advantageous to begin the attack, for be assured they will wait far you." The king commanded that it should be so done and the two marshals rode, one to the front and the other to the rear, crying out, "Halt banners, in the name of God and St. Denis." Those that were in front, halted; but those that were behind, said, they would not halt until they were as forward as the front. When the front perceived the rear pressing on, they pushed forward; and as neither the king nor the marshals could stop them, they marched on without any order until they came in sight of their enemies. As soon as the foremost rank saw the English they fell back at once in great disorder, which alarmed those in the rear, who thought they had been fighting. All the roads between Abbeville and Crécy, were covered with common people, who, when they were came within three leagues of their enemies, drew their swords, bawling out, "Kill, kill;" and with them were many lords eager to make a show of their courage.

There is no man, unless he had been present, that can imagine or describe truly the confusion of that day, especially the bad management and disorder of the French, whose troops were out of number. What I know, and shall relate in this book, I have learned chiefly from the English, and from those attached to Sir John of Hainault, who was always near the person of the King of France. The English, who, as I have said, were drawn up in three divisions, and seated on the ground, on seeing their enemies advance, rose up undauntedly and fell into their ranks. The prince's battalion, whose archers were formed in the manner of a portcullis [a protective gate], and the men-at-arms in the rear, was the first to do so. The Earls of Northampton and Arundel, who commanded the second division, posted themselves in good order on the prince's wing to assist him if necessary.

You must know that the French troops did not advance in any regular order, and that as soon as their king came in sight of the English his blood began to boil, and he cried out to his marshals, "Order the Genoese [mercenaries] forward and begin the battle in the name of God and St. Denis." There were about 15,000 Genoese crossbow men" but they were quite fatigued, having marched on foot that day six leagues, completely armed and carrying their crossbows, and accordingly they told the constable they were not in a condition to do any great thing in battle. The Earl of Alencon hearing this, said, "This is what one gets by employing such scoundrels, who fall off when there is any need for them." During this time a heavy rain fell, accompanied by thunder and a very terrible eclipse of the sun; and, before this rain, a great flight of crows hovered in the air over all the battalions, making a loud noise; shortly afterwards it cleared up, and the sun shone very bright; but the French had it in their faces, and the English on their backs. When the Genoese were somewhat in order they approached the English and shouted loudly, in order to frighten them; but the English remained quite quiet and did not seem to notice it. They then sent up a second shout, and advanced a little forward; the English never moved. Still they hooted a third time, advancing with their crossbows presented, and began to shoot. The English archers then advanced one step forward, and shot their arrows with such force and quickness, that it seemed as if it snowed. When the Genoese felt these arrows, which pierced through their armor, some of them cut the strings of their crossbows, others flung them to the ground, and all turned about and retreated quite discomfited.

The French had a large body of men-at-arms and horseback to support the Genoese, and the king, seeing them thus fall back, cried out, "Kill those scoundrels for me, for they stop up our road without any reason." The English continued shooting, and some of their arrows fell among the horsemen, driving them back upon the Genoese; they were in such confusion, they could never rally again.

In the English army there were some Cornish and Welsh men on foot, who had armed themselves with large knives. They advanced through the ranks of the men-at-arms and archers, who made way for them, and came upon the French when they were in this danger. Falling upon earls, barons, knights, and squires, slew many, at which the King of England was exasperated. The valiant King of Bohemia was slain there; he was called Charles of Luxembourg, for he was the son of the gallant king and emperor, Henry of Luxembourg. Having heard the order for the battle, he inquired where his son the Lord Charles was; his attendants answered that they did not know, but believed he was fighting. Upon hearing this, he said to them, "Gentlemen, you are all my people, my friends, and brethren at arms this day; therefore, as I am blind, I request of you to lead me so far into the engagement that I may strike one stroke with my sword." The knights consented, and in order that they might not lose him in the crowd, fastened all the reins of their horses together, placing the king at their head so that he might gratify his wish, and in this manner advanced towards the enemy. The Lord Charles of Bohemia, who already signed his name as King of Germany, and bore the arms, had come at the proper time to the engagement; but when he

perceived that it was likely to turn out against the French he departed. The king, his father, rode in among the enemy, and he and his companions fought most valiantly; however, they advanced so far that they were all killed, and on the next day they were found on the ground with all their horses tied together.

Questions for Discussion:

1. How does Froissart explain the English victory?
2. Compare the account of the battle of Crécy with the descriptions of the Battle of Lechfeld by Liudprand of Cremona (Document 6.8) and the battles of the Third Crusade (Documents 9.13 and 9.14). What similarities do you observe? Is there evidence of the advance of military technology?

The Avignon Papacy: Crisis in the Church

In addition to the traumas of plague, war, and revolt, the people of the fourteenth century witnessed a crisis in the Church. When Pope Benedict XI died in 1304, Frenchman Clement V (r. 1305–1314) was elected to the papacy, and it was rumored that the French king, Philip IV ("the Fair"), might have manipulated the election. Following a series of violent protests against the new pope, he and his cardinals were granted land by the French king at Avignon in southern France. The pope's move to France began the "Avignon Papacy" of the Church, which lasted for seventy years.

Although the papal court at Avignon is noted for its efficient bureaucracy, it was severely criticized because it was viewed as a mere extension of French power. In

addition, the papal establishment was chastised on moral grounds. Furthermore, there was a crisis of belief because the Church was unable to solve the problems arising from the plague, the Hundred Years War, and the various popular revolts. A negative view of the papacy during this period is reflected in the following selections. The first is a letter by the poet Petrarch (1304–1374), who had spent his childhood in Avignon, where his father was a notary, and the second is a letter to the pope from Catherine of Siena.

(From *Readings in European History*, by James Harvey Robinson [Boston: Ginn and Co., 1905], pp. 502–504.)

14.11 Letter of Petrarch Concerning the Avignon Papacy

. . . Now I am living in France, in the Babylon of the West. The sun in its travels sees nothing more hideous than this place on the shores of the wild Rhone, which suggests the hellish streams of Cocytus and Acheron. Here reign the successors of the poor fishermen of Galilee; they have strangely forgotten their origin. I am astounded, as I recall their predecessors, to see these men loaded with gold and

clad in purple, boasting of the spoils of princes and nations; to see luxurious palaces and heights crowned with fortifications, instead of a boat turned downwards for shelter.

We no longer find the simple nets which were once used to gain a frugal sustenance from the lake of Galilee, and with which, having labored all night and caught nothing, they took, at daybreak, a multitude of fishes, in the name of Jesus. One is stupefied nowadays to hear the lying tongues, and to see worthless parchments turned by a leaden seal into nets which are used, in Christ's name, but by the arts of Belial, to catch hordes of unwary Christians. These fish, too, are dressed and laid on the burning coals of anxiety before they fill the insatiable maw of their captors.

Instead of holy solitude we find a criminal host and crowds of the most infamous satellites; instead of soberness, licentious banquets; instead of pious pilgrimages, preternatural and foul sloth; instead of the bare feet of the apostles, the snowy coursers of brigands fly past us, the horses decked in gold and fed on gold, soon to be shod with gold, if the Lord does not check this slavish luxury. In short, we seem to be among the kings of the Persians or Parthians, before whom we must fall down and worship, and who cannot be approached unless presents are offered. O ye unkempt and emaciated old men, is it for this you labored? Is it for this that you have sown the field of the Lord and watered it with your holy blood? But let us leave the subject.

Commiserate the cruel fate which holds your friend here. He may merit punishment, but certainly not one like this. Here I am, at a more advanced age, back in the haunts of my childhood, dragged again by fate among the disagreeable surroundings of my early days, when I thought I was freed from them. I have been so depressed and overcome that the heaviness of my soul has passed into bodily afflictions, so that I am really ill and can only give voice to sighs and groans. Although many things offer themselves which I wanted to communicate to you, as both my stomachs are troubling me you need look for nothing agreeable from me today. Sweet water cannot come from a bitter source. Nature has ordered that the sighs of an oppressed heart shall be distasteful, and the words of an injured soul harsh.

Question for Discussion:

1. What are the abuses Petrarch attributes to the papacy at Avignon?

14.12   A Letter of Catherine of Siena to Pope Gregory XI

Catherine of Siena (1347–1380) was a female mystic akin to Hildegard of Bingen (see Document 10.13). She experienced visions beginning in early childhood, and joined the Dominican Tertiaries[4] when she was sixteen; she then isolated herself in a small room in her father's house where she believed she could effectively seek Christ. In 1370 she received a vision in which she was directed by God to enter the public life of the world. From this time on, like Hildegard, she corresponded with important officials in the Church and state. Hoping to heal the rift in the Church, she wrote several letters imploring Pope Gregory XI to leave Avignon and return to Rome, where he could effectively reform the clergy and ecclesiastical administration. Notice that she identifies herself as "your poor unworthy daughter

Caterina," denigrating herself in the same manner as Roswitha, Hildegard, and Heloise.

(Excerpt from *Letters of Catherine of Siena*, Volume II, translated by Suzanne Noffke. MRTS Volume 203. Tempe, AZ 2000. Copyright Arizona Board of Regents for Arizona State University. Reprinted with permission.)

To Pope Gregory XI, in Avignon Mid-August 1376
In the name of Jesus Christ crucified and of gentle Mary.

Most holy father in Christ gentle Jesus,
Your poor unworthy daughter Caterina sends you greetings in the precious blood of the Lamb of God. I long to see you strong and firm as a rock in the good holy resolution you have already taken up, so that all the contrary winds beating against you won't hurt you. They come from human enemies, rising up out of malice through the devil's ministry and satanic furies, who want to prevent all the good that will follow from your going [to Rome].

I understood from the note you sent me that you are being harassed by the enemies of all good,

---

[4]This teritiary order was a third order attached to the Dominicans. By a vow that indicated a commitment to pious living, men and women could remain in the secular world rather than living in a monastic community.

who never stop tempting you. And to persuade you the more convincingly of the evil they want, they are claiming that Pope Clement IV, whenever he had to do anything, never wanted to act without the advice of his brother cardinals. True, he usually preferred their intentions and pronouncements to his own, even when he saw that his own were materially better, just as you yourself see what is right. Oimé! Most holy father, what malice and how much evil are arising because of the devil! These men cite Clement IV, plenty concerned about themselves and what is theirs, but much less concerned about the universal good to which everything else ought to be subordinate. Why don't these pious men also cite Pope Urban [V], who sought the cardinals' advice when he was in doubt as to whether or not to act, but who, when the matter was clear and obvious to him—as is your going [to Rome] to you, of which you are certain—didn't feel bound by their opinion even though they might all be against him. Let your enemies direct your attention to *him*—but they can't, because they are your enemies.

What sane person doesn't see that the holiest thing is for the lord of all the world to be seated on his proper throne? Surely, unless they are blind, they will admit this easily. And this is what the counsel of the good will always tell you. It seems to me the advice of good people is concerned only with God's honor, the salvation of souls, and the reform of holy Church, and not with their own selfish love for themselves. The advice of such people should be followed, I'm saying, but not the advice of those who love only their own life, honor, status, and pleasure—for their advice goes where their love is.

I beg you in the name of Christ crucified: let it please your holiness to hurry! Make use of a holy trick. I mean, let it look as if you are going to take a few more days, and then all of a sudden go! For the sooner you act, the sooner you will escape these tormenting anxieties. In fact, it seems to me their malice is becoming much more astute. Now they want to instruct you by giving you the example of the wild animals who, once they escape from a trap, never go back to it! But I am begging you to follow with complete commitment [my] sound advice. The blessed God freed you once from their wicked counsel when they interrupted your journey last year. The devil had in fact laid a trap on their tongues. You were caught, and holy counsel was taken captive. Evil and harm followed because of it—indeed the worst evil and harm we have suffered until now! So now that you're the wiser, with the Holy Spirit's guidance you *won't* fall back into it.

Let's go quickly, my dear *babbo,* and fearlessly! If God is for you, no one will be against you. God himself will move you; God himself will be your guide, your helmsman, and your sailor. So God *is* with you. Go quickly to your bride, who is all pale, and is waiting for you to bring back her color. And the moment you arrive she will be more beautiful than any other. I don't want to burden you with more words, for I would have much to say.

Keep living in God's holy and tender love. I am presumptuous: forgive me. I humbly ask your blessing. . . .

Gentle Jesus! Jesus love!

Question for Discussion:

1. What points does Catherine make in her urgent request for the pope to return to Rome?

Fourteenth-Century Literature and Art

14.13 "Heavenly Love": From *The Divine Comedy* by Dante

Dante Alighieri (1265–1321), one of the greatest poets of all time, is often viewed as a pivotal figure whose works embody both the apogee of medieval literary expression and the origins of Renaissance literary style. His most important work, The Divine Comedy, *reflects the theological preoccupation of medieval writers and philosophers, while investing the subject matter with the emotional content of the courtly love tradition. Much of the poem deals with the redeeming power of human love, personified in Beatrice, who is his guide through Paradise.*

The Comedy *also makes use of the numerological structures that were so important to the architects and philosophers of the Middle Ages (see, for example the Portfolio of Villard de Honnecourt, Document 13.11). Dante's masterpiece is divided into three parts (Inferno, Purgatorio, and Paradiso), each of which has thirty-three sections (cantos). The following excerpt, Canto XXXI from Paradiso, recounts Dante's meeting with Saint Bernard and Beatrice, and his vision of the Virgin Mary in Paradise.*

(Dante Alighieri, *Paradiso*, translated by Robert and Jean Hollander. New York: Doubleday, 2007, pp. 763–771.)

Canto XXXI

In form, then, of a luminous white rose
I saw the saintly soldiery that Christ,
with His own blood, took as His bride.

But the others—who, even as they fly, behold
and sing the glory of the One who stirs their love,
and sing His goodness that raised them up so high,

as a swarm of bees that in one instant plunge
deep into blossoms and, the very next, go back
to where their toil is turned to sweetness—

these descended to the splendid flower,
adorned with its many petals, and then flew up
to where their love forever dwells.

Their faces were of living flame,
their wings were gold, the rest
was of a whiteness never matched by snow.

When they descended to the flower, they bestowed
the peace and love acquired with their beating wings
upon the petals, row on row.

Nor did so vast a flying throng,
coming between the flower and the light above,
obstruct the looking up or shining down,

for the light of God so penetrates the universe,
according to the fitness of its parts to take it in,
that there is nothing can withstand its beam.

This sure and joyful kingdom,
thronged with souls from both the old times and
   the new,
aimed sight and love upon a single goal.

O threefold Light, which, in a single star
sparkling in their sight, contents them so!
Look down upon our tempest here below.

If the barbarians, coming from that region
which Helice covers every day,
wheeling with her son, in whom she takes delight,

were dumbstruck at the sight of Rome
and her majestic monuments,
when the Lateran surpassed all other works of man,

I, who had come to things divine from man's estate,
to eternity from time,
from Florence to a people just and sane,

with what amazement must I have been filled!
Indeed, between the wonder and my joy, I was content
neither to hear nor speak a word.

And, as a pilgrim, in the temple of his vow,
content within himself, looks lovingly about
and expects to tell his tale when he gets home,

so, through the living light I let my eyes
range freely through the ranks, now up, now down,
now circling freely all around again.

I saw visages informed by heavenly love, resplendent
with Another's light and their own smiles,
their every movement graced with dignity.

My gaze by now had taken in
the general form of Paradise
but not yet fixed on any single part of it,

and I turned, with newly kindled eagerness
to ask my lady many things
that kept my mind yet in suspense.

I expected one thing but found another:
instead of Beatrice, an old man, adorned
as were the rest of those in glory, met my eyes.

His eyes and cheeks were quite suffused
with kindly joy, and from his whole appearance
   shone
a loving father's tenderness.

Then 'Where is she?' I asked at once
and he replied: 'To lead your longing to its goal
Beatrice called me from my place.

'If you raise your eyes to the third circle
below the highest tier, you shall see her again,
now on the throne her merits have assigned.'

Without a word, I lifted up my eyes
and saw that she, reflecting the eternal rays,
appeared to be encircled by a crown.

From the highest region where the thunder breaks
down to the bottom of the deepest sea,
no mortal eye is ever quite so far

as was my sight removed from Beatrice.
Yet to me that mattered not, because her image
came down undimmed by anything between.

'O lady who give strength to all my hope
and who allowed yourself, for my salvation,
to leave your footprints there in Hell,

'of all the many things that I have seen,
I know the grace and virtue I've been shown
come from your goodness and your power.

'It is you who, on no matter what the path,
have drawn me forth from servitude to freedom
by every means that you had in your power.

'Keep your munificence alive in me, so that
my soul, which you have healed,
may please you when it leaves its mortal frame.'

This was my prayer. And she, however far away
she seemed, smiled and looked down at me,
then turned again to the eternal fountain.

And the holy ancient spoke: 'So that you may achieve
your journey's consummation now,
both sacred love and prayer have sent me here:

'Let your sight fly through this garden,
for seeing it will help prepare your eyes
to rise, along the beam of holy light.

'And Heaven's queen, for whom I burn
with love, will grant us every grace,
since I am her own, her faithful Bernard.'

As the man who, perhaps from Croatia, has come
to set his gaze on our Veronica,
his ancient craving still not satisfied,

and who thinks to himself while it is shown:
'My Lord Jesus Christ, God Himself,
was this then how you really looked?',

just so was I, gazing on the living love
of him who, still within the confines of this world,
in contemplation tasted of that peace.

'Child of grace,' he said, 'you will not know
this joyful state if you maintain your gaze,
instead of upward, fixed down here.

'Rather to the highest circles raise your eyes
so that you may behold the queen enthroned,
her to whom this realm is subject and devout.'

I raised my eyes. As, at break of day,
the eastern part of the horizon shines
with a brighter glow than where the sun goes down,

so, as though my eyes were moving from a valley
up a mountain, I saw that one far crest
surpassed in brightness all the others.

Where we await the shaft of Phaeton's
poorly guided car, there, where it is most aflame,
while on this side and on that the light shades off,

just so that peaceful oriflamme showed brightest
in the middle, while on either side
the flame was dimmed in equal measure.

Around that point I saw more than a thousand angels,
their wings outspread, in joyful festival,
each distinct in brightness and in movement.

I saw there, smiling at their games and songs,
beauty that brought pleasure to the gaze
of all the other gathered saints.

Were I as rich with words as in my store of images,
I still would never dare attempt to tell
the least of these delights that came from her.

Bernard, who saw my eyes were fixed, intent
upon the very fire that made him warm,
turned his own on her with such affection
that he made mine more ardent in their gaze.

Questions for Discussion:

1. The poems of the troubadours studied in Document 10.7 reflect the tradition of "courtly love." What common aspects are evident in the earlier works and this canto of *The Divine Comedy*?
2. Compare this canto of *The Divine Comedy* with the description of heaven by Roswitha of Gandersheim in Scene II of *Abraham* (Document 8.9). What similarities do you observe?
3. What aspects of Dante's work are clearly situated in the aesthetic and religious environment of the Middle Ages?

14.14   "Earthly Love": Sonnets by Petrarch

Francesco Petrarch (1304–1374) grew up in Avignon, where his father was a notary (see Document 14.11). Although he studied law as a young man, he did not find training for the legal profession to be fulfilling, and he decided to enter a monastic order; this provided him with an adequate amount of time for study. He was able to devote much of his life to the recovery and editing of ancient manuscripts, and traveled to monasteries throughout Europe in his quest.

Petrarch wrote many essays in both Latin and Italian, but he is most famous for his sonnets. Many of these fourteen-line poems were dedicated to Laura, a married Florentine woman; as you will see, they also reflect the tradition of courtly love.

(From *The Sonnets and Stanzas of Petrarch*, trans. by C. B. Cayley [London: Longmans, Green & Co., 1879], pp. 47, 122.)

Sonnet XXVIII: A Lover's Walk

Alone, engrossed, the least frequented strands
I traverse with my footsteps faint and slow,
And often wary glances round me throw
To flee, should human trace imprint the sands.

I find no other shelter that withstands
The people's view obtrusive, for I know
That each one by my cheerless outward show
Reads easily my passion's inward brands.

Wherefore I am convinced each bank and hill
And wood and river hath now learnt the tone
Of this life in which no others pry.

But path so difficult or steep I still
Have never found, that there I must not own
Love with me walks and talks, and with him I.

Sonnet LXIX: A Reappearance

Her golden tresses to the breeze were spread,
Which wrought of them a thousand winsome ties;
And the fine splendor lit her fairest eyes
Sans measure—beams on me so seldom shed!

Across her face, too, pity's tinges fled,
As I beheld, in true or seeming guise;
And, since my breast love's fuel must comprise,
If straightway I was fired, needs scarce be said.

Her moving was not mortal nature's play,
But very angel; and her utterance one,
That had no fellowship with human tone.

A heavenly spirit and a breathing sun
Was that I saw; look henceforth how she may,
Wound healed by bow's relapse was never known.

Questions for Discussion:

1. Compare Petrarch's Sonnets with the poems of the troubadours in Document 10.7. What similarities do you observe? How are they different?
2. Dante and Petrarch are both writing about love. Compare and contrast their works presented in this chapter.

14.15   "Earthly Pleasure": A Tale from *The Decameron* by Boccaccio

The Decameron *by the Italian author Giovanni Boccaccio (1313–1375) consists of a series of stories set within a "frame," or specific context. A group of young people have left Florence in an attempt to avoid the plague (see Boccaccio's description of the Black Death in Document 14.5). In order to entertain themselves, the men and women take turns telling amusing and amorous tales. Written in the vernacular (Italian), Boccaccio's work became extremely popular. Many of the stories are bawdy and highly irreverent, often satirizing members of the clergy and monastic*

orders. Another common theme is that of adulterous love; the following tale provides one comic example.

(From *The Decameron of Giovanni Boccaccio*, trans. by Richard Aldington. New York: Doubleday & Co., 1930, pp. 344–347. © The Estate of Richard Aldington. Extracts from Richard Aldington's translation of *The Decameron* reproduced by kind permission of the Estate of Richard Aldington c/o Rosica Colin Limited, London.)

Dearest ladies, men, and especially husbands, play so many tricks upon you that whenever a woman plays one on her husband you should not only be glad that it has occurred and that you are hearing it talked of, but you should go about repeating it to everyone, so that men may know that women know as much about such things as they do. This cannot but be useful to you, for when any person knows that another is aware of such things he does not lightly attempt to deceive him. Who then can doubt that, when what we say on this topic today is know to men, it can fail to restrain them from such deceits, since they will discover that you too can play tricks when you wish? So I intend to tell you what a young woman—although of base extraction—did to her husband almost in a twinkling, to save herself from his anger.

Not long ago in Naples a poor man married a pretty and charming girl named Peronella. He was a bricklayer and she a wool-comber, and together they earned enough to live moderately well. One day a handsome young man saw this Peronella, and liked her so much that he fell in love with her; and he made up to her so successfully in one way and another that he became familiar with her. They agreed upon the following arrangement for meeting: that when her husband got up each morning to go to work or to find work the lover should hide somewhere to see him depart, and when he had gone the lover was to come into the house, since Avorio, the place where they lived, was very little frequented. And this they often did.

But one day when the husband had gone out for the whole day and Giannello Strignario (this was the young man's name) had gone into the house and was with Peronella, the husband unexpectedly returned, and finding the house barred from within, knocked; and, as he knocked, said to himself:

"O Lord, praise be to Thee for ever, for although Thou hast made me a poor man, Thou hast consoled me with a good and chaste young wife who bars the door from inside while I am away, so that nobody can enter and do her harm." Peronella knew it was her husband from his way of knocking, and said: "Alas, Giannello, I am as good as dead! Here is my husband—bad luck to him—and I don't know what his coming back means, for he never returns at this hour. Perhaps he saw you when you came in. But in any case, for the love of God get into this butt [barrel] and be silent, and I will go and open the door, and will find out what brings him back home so early today."

Giannello quickly got into the butt, and Peronella went down and opened the door to her husband, and said sharply:

"What new idea of yours is this to come home so early today? From what I can see, you don't intend to do any work today, since you've brought back your tools. If you go on like this, how are we to live? How shall we get our bread? Do you think I'll let you pawn my petticoat and other clothes? I do nothing but spin day and night and work my fingers to the bone to earn at least enough oil to keep our lamp burning. Husband, husband, every woman in the place is amazed and mocks at me for all my labor, and you come back here with your hands dangling when you ought to be at work."

Then she began to weep, and went off again:

"Alas, poor me, unhappy me, what an unlucky hour I was born in! I could have married such a good young man and I wouldn't have him for the sake of a man who thinks nothing of the woman he has brought into his house. Other women enjoy themselves with their lovers, and there's not one of them but has two or three, and has a good time, and makes her husband think the moon is the sun. But poor me! Because I'm good and pay no heed to such things, life goes wrong and I have bad luck. I don't know why I don't have lovers like other women. Understand me, husband. If I wanted to do wrong I could easily find someone to do it with, for there are plenty of gay young men in love with me, and they've offered me money or dresses or jewels if I preferred, but I'd never take anything of the kind, for I'm not the daughter of a woman of that sort; and here you come back home when you ought to be at work."

"Wife," said the husband, "don't be angry, for the love of God. You must believe that I know your value, and indeed only this morning I partly realized it. I did indeed start out to work this morning, but all this shows that you did not know, any more than I did, that today is the festival of Santo Caleone, and as there's no work to be done I've come home at this early hour. And yet I've found a way to provide us with bread for more than a month, for the man you see here with me has bought the butt, which, as you know, has been littering up the house, and he's giving me five florins for it."

"And all that's the more woe to me," said Peronella, "you're a man, and go about the world and should know things, and you've sold the butt for five florins, while a little woman like me who hardly ever goes out of the door and knew what a nuisance the butt was in the place, has sold it for seven florins to a man who, when you returned, had just got inside to see if it were sound."

The husband was more than delighted when he heard this, and said to the man who had come for the butt:

"God be with you, good man. You hear how my wife has got seven florins for the butt which you would only pay five for."

"Very well," said the man, and went away.

Then Peronella said to her husband:

"Come along, since you are here, and attend to our affairs."

Giannello had kept his ears pricked up to know if he had to fear or invent anything, and since he had heard what Peronella said he jumped quickly out of the butt, and pretending to know nothing about the husband's return said:

"Where are you, good woman?"

The husband came up to him, and said:

"Here I am, what do you want?"

"Who are you?" said Giannello. "I want the lady with whom I made the bargain for this butt."

"You can do what you want with me," said the good man, "I'm her husband."

Then Giannello said:

"The butt seems quite sound to me, but I think you must have kept wine lees in it, for it's all encrusted with some dry matter which I can't scrape off with my nails. But I won't take it unless I first see it cleaned."

"The bargain shan't be called off for that," said Peronella. "My husband will clean it all."

"Yes, indeed," said the husband.

He put down his tools, tripped himself to his shirt-sleeves, got a light and a scraper and, getting into the butt, began to scrape it. Peronella, as if she wanted to see what he was doing, put her head and shoulder and one arm into the large opening of the butt, and kept saying:

"Scrape here, scrape there, and there too. A little bit's left there."

As she stood there pointing things out to her husband, Giannello, who had scarcely satisfied his appetite that morning when the husband returned, saw that he could not do so, as he wanted, and determined to do it as he could. He went up behind her as she stood over the mouth of the butt, and, even as the unbridled and love-heated stallions of Parthia assail the mares, so did he satisfy his young desire, which was brought to its summit and himself removed precisely at the moment when the scraping of the butt was ended, and Peronella drew her head out, and the husband climbed out.

So Peronella said to Giannello:

"Take the light, good man, and see if it's cleaned as you want."

Giannello looked in, said it was all right, and that he was content. He paid the seven florins, and had the butt taken to his house.

Questions for Discussion:

1. Does this tale by Boccaccio represent a complete break from the literature of the Middle Ages? Why or why not?
2. What issues concerning gender roles are brought out in this comic story?
3. Compare the love described by Petrarch in his *Sonnets* with the relationships in this tale.

14.16 "The Cook's Tale" by Geoffrey Chaucer

Geoffrey Chaucer (c. 1343–1400) was one of the greatest English writers. He possessed exceptional linguistic skills, and was frequently sent on diplomatic missions by King Edward III. He was interested in science, especially astronomy, physics, and alchemy. He was familiar with The Romance of the Rose, *which he began to translate, and knew the works of Boccaccio. Chaucer's writings also reflect the naturalism in literature and art that emerged following the Black Death.*

His most famous work is The Canterbury Tales, *a collection of stories recounted by a group of pilgrims on the*

way to visit the shrine of St. Thomas Becket in Canterbury.
Thus, like The Decameron, *the action takes place within*
a "frame." The characters in Chaucer's tales represent a
wide spectrum of individuals, taken from all social levels,
all professions, and both genders. The stories are entertain-
ing, and although many of them have an underlying moral
point, the primary focus is on human experience, rather
than theological discourse.

(From *The Canterbury Tales*, by Geoffrey Chaucer, trans. by Frank Ernest Hill [London: Longmans, Green and Co., 1935], pp. 110–112.)

The Prologue of the Cook's Tale

While the Reeve[5] spoke, the Cook of London
   clawed him
For very glee upon the back he pawed him.
"Ha! Ha!" he cried, "I tell you, by Christ's passion,
This miller got it in a lively fashion
In that affair of lodging for the night!
Solomon had the tongue to put it right:
'Bring ye not every man,' his words run thus,
'Into thine house.' Such things are dangerous.
It pays a man to study carefully
Whom he shall welcome to his privacy.
I pray God that he give me grief and care
If ever, since my name was Hodge of Ware,
I heard of miller tricked a neater way.
They fooled him badly in the dark, I say.
But God forbid that we should stop with this.
And therefore, if ye take it not amiss
That I should speak, who am a plain, rude man,
I will relate as fairly as I can
A jest that happened in our town," said he.
   Our host replied, and said: "I grant it thee.
Now tell on, Roger—look that it be good.
For many a pasty hast thou drawn the blood,
And many a Jack o'Dover hast thou sold
That hath been two times hot and two times cold.
From many a pilgrim hast thou had Christ's curse,
That after eating knew he fared the worse
For parsley on a fat goose of thy warming;
For in thy shop the flies are fairly swarming.
Tell on now, by thy name, for I am done;
And be not angry for a little fun;

A man may say true things in play and jest."
"Thou say'st right, by my troth," the Cook
   confessed;
But, "True play, bad play," as the Fleming saith,
And therefore, Harry Bailly, by thy faith,
Be thou not wroth if something I relate
About a Host, before we separate.
I will not tell it now, and yet I say
Before I leave thee, thou shalt have thy pay."
With this he laughed, and all in jollity
He told his tale, as follows presently.

Thus ends the Prologue of the Cook's Tale

Here begins the Cook's Tale

Once an apprentice[6] dwelt within our town,
By guild a victualer. And he was brown
As is a berry, of figure short and good,
As gay as any goldfinch in the wood,
With black locks always combed with elegance.
He moved so well and merry in a dance
That he was known as Perkin Reveller.
Lucky the wench that had this lad with her!
He was as full of love-making and love
As any hive is with its honey-trove.
At every wedding he would sing and hop;
He loved the tavern better than the shop!
   For if through Cheapside some procession passed,
Out of the shop this Perkin leapt full fast;
Tell he had seen the sighs in full, and then
Jigged for a spell, he would not come again.
And he had gathered up a following
Of such as he, that loved to dance and sing,
And by appointment they would plan to meet
And play at dice upon a certain street.
For there was no apprentice anywhere
Could cast a pair of dice with better air
Than Perkin could; and he was generous, too,
In spending, in some places that he knew.
Of that his master came to be aware,
For many a time he found his cash-box bare;
For an apprentice busied constantly
At dice, and making love, and revelry,
Will always make his master suffer by it,
Though he, poor man, have no part in the riot.

---

[5]A reeve was an administrative officer of a town or district.

[6]See the guild provisions concerning apprentices in Document 10.2

For theft and riot—of a kind they are,
Though the thief play the rebec or guitar.
　　This gay apprentice with his master stayed
Till he had almost served his time of trade,
Though he was reprimanded early and late,
And sometimes piped by minstrels to Newgate.[7]
But in the end his master called to mind,
When once he asked to have his quittance[8] signed,
A proverb that this word of warning bore:
"Better take one bad apple from the store
Than let it rot the rest." And this is true
Of a bad servant and his fellows, too;
It is the lesser harm to let him fare
Thank ruin all the other servants there.
Therefore his master gave him his discharge,
And with a curse he bade him go at large;
Thus jolly Perkin came by his release.
Now let him revel all the night—or cease.

---

[7]Newgate was a prison.
[8]A quittance was a release from his obligation.

And since there is no thief without a crony
To help him eat or drink or waste the money
That he can get by borrowing or theft,
He sent his bed and clothing when he left
Unto a friend who loved, like him, a life
Of revel, dice, and pleasure, and whose wife
For mere appearance feigned to keep a store,
But really got her living as a whore.
Of this Cook's Tale Chaucer wrote no more

Questions for Discussion:

1. Chaucer's words make it possible to envision the physical appearance of Perkin, the apprentice. Describe him.
2. What happened to Perkin as a result of his behavior?
3. Do you see a didactic purpose, or moral, in the story? What is it?

14.17　A Feminine Voice: The Debate on *The Romance of the Rose* by Christine de Pizan

Christine de Pizan (c. 1364–1430) was born in Italy, but moved with her family to France as a young child. She was raised at the court of the French king Charles V, where she received an excellent education. In 1379 she married a royal secretary, with whom she had three children. Ten years after the marriage, her husband died in an epidemic and she was faced with earning a living for herself and her children. Instead of following the conventional path by entering a convent, Christine decided to support herself and her family by writing. She wrote many poems in the courtly style, and composed a number of lyrics that expressed the sorrows of widowhood, an innovative poetic topic.

*　　Christine composed many essays expressing her perceptions of contemporary misogyny. She was especially vocal in a debate about* The Romance of the Rose, *a popular thirteenth-century poem (see Document 13.8). Notice that she denigrates herself as "a little grasshopper" in the same fashion as the medieval women writers we have studied, including Roswitha of Gandersheim* (Document 8.9), Hildegard von Bingen (10.13), *and* Heloise (10.9).

(From *The Selected Writings of Christine de Pizan*, A Norton Critical Edition, translated and edited by Renate Blumenfeld-Kosinski and Kevin Brownlee. Copyright © 1997 by W. W. Norton & Company, Inc. Used by permission of W. W. Norton & Company, Inc.)

I do not know why we debate these questions so much, for I do not believe that either you or I intend to change our minds: you say he is good; I say he is bad. You will convince me that he is good when you and your accomplices will have debated—with all your subtle reasoning—and will have found that bad is good: then I will believe that the *Romance of the Rose* is good! But I know well that this opinion is characteristic of those who want to lead an evil life and who want to be on their guard against other people rather than have other people be on their guard against them. But for those who want to live well and simply, without being too much wrapped up in worldly licentiousness, and who do not wish to deceive anyone or be deceived themselves, this book has no use. And truly I would much rather belong to the party of its opponents than to that of its supporters, for I am of the opinion that the wolf profits less; and as the good gentleman said who composed the above plaidoyer[9]: "May it please God that such a Rose will never be planted in the garden of Christendom." And I don't care whether you call yourself one of its disciples. If you want to be one, be one; as for me, I reject its lessons, for I am concerned with others that I believe to be more profitable and which I find more agreeable. And I am not alone in holding this opinion and I don't know why you disciples attack me so much more than others: it is hardly honorable to attack the weakest party. There are so many wise learned men worthy of being believed and filled with knowledge, and truly there are so many great princes of this kingdom, knights, nobles, and so many others, who are of the same opinion as I and who think that this is useless and dishonorable reading. Why do you not then break the thick stem of the tree, from which issue forth the sap and juices, until it is dried and torn up instead of taking on the little branches above which have no strength? In order to eradicate everything you attack me who is nothing but the voice of a little grasshopper who beats his wings and makes a lot of noise, and who is nevertheless nothing compared to the grand chanting of the gracious birds.

But you say that you "cannot be surprised enough how someone can blame not only him but also those who appreciate and love his book on the *Rose.*" Answer: I can only be surprised how someone dares to praise this book in which there are so many things that horrify the human heart and lead it to damnation.

You say that as far as you are concerned you "prefer to be blamed for appreciating and loving a book rather than be one of those subtle blamers." You resemble Heloise of the Paraclete who said that she would rather be called *meretrix* by Master Abelard than be a crowned queen. [See Document 10.9.] This shows very well that those wishes that please most are not always the most reasonable.

You say that everyone knows "that there are still seven thousand people ... who are more than ready to defend it." Answer: it is a general rule that bad sects

grow easily, just like weeds, but there are cases where greater numbers do not mean that their cause is better. And may it please God that there will never be such a group assembled; it is not an article of faith: may everyone have his own opinion.

[*Christine states that the great theologian Gerson, attacked by Col, has no desire for this book.*]

As far as I am concerned, despite my ignorance, I assure you I have no desire for it either. And why would I? It makes me neither hot nor cold, it gives me or takes from me neither anything good nor anything bad; I have no cause to be indignant, for it does not speak about my way of life, since I am not married or hope to be, nor am I a nun, nor does he say anything that touches me personally: I am not Fair Welcome nor do I fear the Old Woman, nor do I have any buds to guard. And I assure you that I love beautiful and subtle books and treatises, and I seek them out and look for them and read them gladly, though I can understand them only on a simple level. And if I do not love this book of the *Rose* the reason is simply and absolutely because it gives very bad advice and is dishonest reading and fills people's hearts with more bad than good things. In my judgment it can be the cause of damnation and of leading a worse life: I swear on my soul and my faith that this is my only motivation. And what you say later, namely that perhaps we blame the book so that people will have a greater desire to see it, and thus our opinion would be positive, you can be certain that this is not our motivation.

[*Christine now responds to some of Col's rather rude accusations of presumption.*]

I do not consider my deeds or my knowledge to be a great thing. The only fact is—and I can say this honestly—that I love learning and a solitary life. It is possible that in pursuing that life I picked the lower flowers of the delicious garden and did not climb the high trees in order to gather their beautiful perfumed and savory fruits (not that I did not have the desire and the will, but my weak understanding did not permit it). And as far as the fragrance of the little flowers is concerned of which I fashioned dainty garlands, those who wanted them—that is, those to whom I did not dare or could not deny them—marveled at my labor, not for its greatness but for the novelty to which they were not accustomed.

---

[9]A plaidoyer is a defense of an idea.

And I ask of you and of those who hold your opinions: do not resent me for writing in this current debate on the *Romance of the Rose*. For its beginning was accidental and not at all a conscious proposition, whatever opinion I may have uttered, as you can see in a little treatise where I spoke of the first and last issues of our debate. And I would suffer too much to be constrained in such servitude that I could not answer someone with the truth according to my conscience in a matter that one cannot hold against me.

* * *

And it means nothing when you say that the Holy Church, where there are so many worthy men, from its beginning tolerated it for so long without reproach (it waited for me and the others to come and accuse it!): for you know that everything comes to a head at a certain point, and nothing is long across the expanse of years; and it often happens that a little pointed instrument cures a big boil. How could the Church tolerate for so long the opinion on the conception of Our Lady—something worthier of note—without accusing anyone? And sometimes things which were not debated for a long time come to the forefront through a great uprising; and this is not an article of faith, and neither is our matter: may everyone believe whatever he wants and what pleases him most. As for me, I will write nothing further on this subject, whoever may write to me, for I have not undertaken to drink the entire Seine [River]: what I have written is written. I will not be silent because I doubt my opinions—however much my lack of ingenuity and knowledge prevent me from having a beautiful style—but I prefer to devote myself to other matters that please me more.

I beg all those who will see my little writings, that they may overlook the defects of my learning in view of my person and take everything with a good end in mind and a pure intention—without which it would not be worth to present anything. Thus I end my writing about the debate which was never spiteful but was begun, pursued, and ended as a pastime and not to reproach anyone. I pray to the Holy Trinity, perfect and complete wisdom, that It may illuminate you and especially all those who love knowledge and the nobility of good conduct, with true light so that they can be led to heavenly joy. Amen.

Written and completed by me, Christine de Pizan, the second day of October in the year 1402.

Your well-wishing friend of learning,
Christine de Pizan

Questions for Discussion:

1. What criticisms does Christine advance concerning *The Romance of the Rose*?
2. What feminist issues are evident in Christine's statements?

INTERPRETING THE EVIDENCE

14.18 *Lamentation*: A Fresco by Giotto and Remarks by Boccaccio and Ghiberti

Authors such as Petrarch, Boccaccio, and Chaucer created a new style in literature, as we have seen. Although they did not completely eschew didactic religious topics, all three emphasized the human characteristics of their subjects. Similarly, the artists of the fourteenth century were concerned with portraying nature as it actually appeared and people with realistic emotion. One of the first painters to explore this new approach was the Italian painter Giotto de Bondone (c. 1266–1337). Most of his works dealt with traditional religious subjects, but rather than portraying rigid, iconic figures, as in eleventh- and twelfth-century sculpture and painting, he enlivened the images with emotional depth.

(continued)

Lamentation: A Fresco of Giotto, 7 ft. 7 in. × 7 ft. 9 in., 1305–1306. Arena Chapel (Cappella Scrovegni), Padua. (Giotto de Bondone, *The Lamentation* c. 1305 fresco. Chapel of the Scrovegni, Padua. Arena Chapel/SuperStock, Inc.)

(See an example of the medieval artisitic spirit in the images of the tympanum at Autun (Document 8.3), and the manuscript illumination of Lancelot on the Sword-Bridge (Document 10.4). As may be seen in Lamentation, *the fresco pictured here, Giotto emphasized the human and emotional aspects of the people gathered around as Christ was taken down from the cross. It is possible to see the forms of arms and bodies underneath the clothing, as opposed to earlier styles, in which the covering of the figure was stiff and unyielding, giving no evidence of the human anatomy. Further, in addition to body language, there are intense emotional expressions on the faces of the mourners, as well as those of the angels flying above.*

Giotto's contemporaries, including authors such as Boccaccio, realized the importance of his artistic goals and abilities. This is made clear in the following tale from The Decameron.

(From *The Decameron of Giovanni Boccaccio,* trans. by Richard Aldington. New York: Doubleday & Co., Inc., 1930, pp. 319–320. © The Estate of Richard Aldington. Extracts from Richard Aldington's translation of *The Decameron* reproduced by kind permission of the Estate of Richard Aldington c/o Rosica Colin Limited, London.)

"The Shining Light of Florentine Glory": Boccaccio on Giotto

Messer Forese da Rabatta and Master Giotto, the painter, returning from Mugello, laugh at each other's mean appearance

THE ladies were delighted by Chichibio's reply, and when Neifile had finished, Pamfilo then spoke by the queen's command.

Most dear ladies, it often happens, as Fortune hides great treasures of virtue under base occupations, as Pampinea just now showed us, that the marvelous minds of Nature are to be found in very ugly men. This will appear from two of our citizens, of whom I mean to tell you a short tale.

One of these was Messer Forese da Rabatta, small and deformed in his person, with a flat ugly face, as if he were worse than one of the nasty Baronci family; and yet he was so skilled in the laws that many worthy men considered him a repository of Civil Law. The other was Giotto, whose genius was of such excellence that with his art and brush or crayon he painted anything in Nature, the mother and mover of all things under the perpetual turning of the heavens, and painted them so like that they seemed not so much likenesses as the things themselves; whereby it often happened that men's visual sense was deceived, and they thought that to be real which was only painted.

Now he who brought back to light that art which for many centuries had lain buried under errors (and thus was more fitted to please the eyes of the ignorant than the minds of the wise), may rightly be called one of the shining lights of Florentine glory. And the more so since he performed it with the greatest humility, and, although the master of all painters living, always refused to be called master. This title he refused shone the brighter in him, in that it was eagerly usurped by his disciples or by those who were less skilled than he. But although he was a very great artist, he was no more handsome in his person or aspect than Messer Forese. But let us come to the tale.

Messer Forese and Giotto had estates in Mugello [in the rural area outside of Florence]. Messer Forese had gone to visit his in the summer time when the law courts have their vacation; and as he rode along on a poor hack of a horse he fell in with Giotto who was also returning to Florence, after visiting his own estate. He was no better dressed or horsed than the other. And the two old men rode along gently together.

As often happens in the summer, a sudden shower of rain came on. As quickly as possible they took shelter in the cottage of a workman, who was a friend to them both. But, as the rain showed no signs of abating and they wanted to reach Florence that day, they borrowed two old serge cloaks from the laborer and two hats all rusty with age, because he had no better, and set out on their way again. They had gone a long way, were wet through, and splashed with mud from their plodding horses (which is not likely to improve anyone's appearance), when the weather cleared up a little, and they began to talk after having been silent for a long time.

As Messer Forese rode along listening to Giotto, who was an admirable talker, he began to look at him from head to foot and, noticing how shabby and unkempt he was, he began to laugh, without remembering his own appearance, and said:

"Giotto, suppose we met a stranger who had never seen you before; do you think he would believe you are the greatest painter in the world, as you are?"

But Giotto immediately replied:

"Messer, I think he would believe if, when he looked at you, he could believe that you know your A B C."

Messer Forese at once recognized his error, and found himself paid back in the same coin for which he had sold the goods.

Questions for Discussion:

1. What does Boccaccio consider to be Giotto's artistic merits?
2. How does the fresco with the image of the deposition from the cross reflect Boccaccio's assessment of the artist's skills?

"Art According to Nature and Genteleness": Ghiberti on Boccaccio

Lorenzo Ghiberti (1378–1455) was an Italian sculptor, goldsmith, architect, and writer who is most famous for his creation of the gilt-bronze doors of the Baptistry in Florence, often called the "Gates of Paradise." His appreciation for Giotto's innovative work is reflected in this exurpt.

The art of painting began to rise in Tuscany in a village near the city of Florence called Vespignano. There was born a child of marvelous talent who drew a sheep from nature. Cimabue,[10] the painter, passing

---

[10]Cimabue (c. 1240–c. 1302) was the outstanding painter of the generation before Giotto.

(continued)

(continued)

along the road to Bologna saw the boy sitting on the ground, drawing a sheep on a flat stone. He was seized with great wonder that the child, being of such a tender age, could do so well, seeming to have the gift from nature, and he asked the boy what he was called. He replied and said, "I am called Giotto, and my father is named Bondoni and lives in that house which is close by." Cimabue went with Giotto to the father; he had a very fine appearance, and he asked the father for the boy. And the father was very poor. He gave the boy to Cimabue who took Giotto with him, and Giotto became the pupil of Cimabue.

He [Cimabue] followed the "Greek manner"; in this style he had won very great fame in Tuscany. Giotto made himself great in the art of painting. He brought in the new art, abandoned the stiffness of the Greeks, rose to fame most excellently in Tuscany. And he made the most notable works, especially in the city of Florence, and in many other places, and about him there were a number of disciples, all learned like the ancient Greeks. Giotto saw in art what the others did not add to it; he brought into being art according to nature and gentleness with it, not exceeding measure. He was most expert in all aspects of art; he was an inventor and a discoverer of much knowledge which had been buried about the year 600. When nature wishes to grant anything, she grants it in truth without any stint. Giotto was prolific in everything; he worked in murals, he worked in oil, he worked on wood. He made in mosaic the Navicella of St. Peter in Rome and with his own hand painted the chapel and the altarpiece of St. Peter. He painted most nobly the hall of King Robert [of Sicily] with pictures of famous men. In Naples he painted in the Castello dell' Uovo. He painted, that is, all by his own hand, in the church of the Arena of Padua, and by his own hand a Last Judgment. And in the Palazzo della Parte [Guelph] he did a story of the Christian faith, and many other things in the said palace. He painted in the church at Assisi [San Francesco] of the order of Friars Minor almost all the lower part. He also painted in Santa Maria degli Angeli in Assisi and in Santa Maria della Minerva in Rome a crucifix and a panel.

The works painted by him in Florence were the following. In the Badia of Florence, in an arch above the portal, our Lady, half-length, with two figures at the sides, very exquisitely, and also the great chapel and the panel. In the church of the Friars Minor [Santa Croce] four chapels and four panels. Very excellently he painted in Padua in the Friars Minor. Most skillfully in the church of the Humiliati [Ognissanti] in Florence, a chapel and a large crucifix, and four panels made very excellently; in one was shown the death of our Lady with angels and with the twelve apostles and our Lord round about, made most perfectly. And there a very large panel with our Lady sitting on a throne with many angels round about. And there over the door leading into the cloister, our Lady, half-length, with the Child in her arms. And in St. Giorgio a panel and a crucifix. In the Friars Preachers [Santa Maria Novella] there is a crucifix and a most perfect panel by his hand; also many other things there. . . .

He painted for many lords. He painted in the palace of the podesta[11] in Florence; within he represented the commune, showing how it was robbed, and the chapel of Santa Maria Maddalena.

Giotto deserved the highest praise. He was most worthy in all branches of art, even in the art of sculpture. The first compositions in the edifice which was built by him, of the bell tower of Santa Reparata [Santa Maria del Fiore—Florence Cathedral], were sculptured and designed by his hand. In my time I have seen the models of these reliefs in his hand, most nobly designed. He was skilled in the one kind of art and in the other. Since from him came and developed such great knowledge, he is the one to whom the highest praise should be given, because nature is seen to produce in him every skill. He led art to its greatest perfection. He had very many disciples of the greatest fame. . . .

Questions for Discussion:

1. Ghiberti praises Giotto for superlative skill in a variety of artistic media. Describe these.
2. Giotto "saw in art what the others did not add to it." Discuss.

---

[11] A podesta was a ruler (usually temporary) who was called in to settle strife in an Italian city-state.